DATE DUE

			PRINTED IN U.S.A.

A COMMON DESTINY

BLACKS AND AMERICAN SOCIETY

Gerald David Jaynes and
Robin M. Williams, Jr.
Editors

Committee on the Status of Black Americans

Commission on Behavioral and
Social Sciences and Education

National Research Council

NATIONAL ACADEMY PRESS
Washington, D.C.   1989

...tion Avenue, NW • Washington, DC 20418

...this report was approved by the Governing Board
...nbers are drawn from the councils of the National
... of Engineering, and the Institute of Medicine.
The members of the committee responsible for the report were chosen for their special competences and with regard for appropriate balance.

This report has been reviewed by a group other than the authors according to procedures approved by a Report Review Committee consisting of members of the National Academy of Sciences, the National Academy of Engineering, and the Institute of Medicine.

The work that provided the basis for this volume was supported by grants from the Carnegie Corporation of New York, the Ford Foundation, the Robert Wood Johnson Foundation, the Andrew W. Mellon Foundation, the Pew Charitable Trusts, the Rockefeller Foundation, and the Alfred P. Sloan Foundation. Additional support came from the National Research Council Fund, a pool of private, discretionary, nonfederal funds that is used to support a program of Academy-initiated studies of national issues in which science and technology figure significantly. The NRC Fund consists of contributions from a consortium of private foundations including Carnegie Corporation of New York, Charles E. Culpeper Foundation, William and Flora Hewlett Foundation, John D. and Catherine T. MacArthur Foundation, Andrew W. Mellon Foundation, Rockefeller Foundation, and Alfred P. Sloan Foundation; and from the Academy Industry Program, which seeks annual contributions from companies that are concerned with the health of U.S. science and technology and with public policy issues with technological content.

Library of Congress Cataloging-in-Publication Data

A common destiny: Blacks and American society/Gerald D. Jaynes and
  Robin M. Williams, Jr., editors: Committee on the Status of Black
  Americans, Commission on Behavioral and Social Sciences and
  Education, National Research Council.
    p. cm.
  Papers and studies resulting from a four-year study conducted
under the aegis of the Committee on the Status of Black Americans.
  Bibliography: p.
  Includes index.
  1. Afro-Americans—Social conditions—1975–   2. Afro-Americans—
Economic conditions. 3. Afro-Americans—Politics and government.
  4. United States—Race relations. I. Jaynes, Gerald David.
  II. Williams, Robin M. III. National Research Council. Committee
of the Status of Black Americans.

E185.86.C582   1989   89-12253
305.8′96073—dc20   CIP

ISBN 0–309–03998–3

Art research by Richard Powell, Director of Programs, Washington Project for the Arts.

Cover: Romare Bearden, *The Family* (1948), watercolor and gouache on paper. Evans-Tibbs Collection, Washington, DC.

COMMITTEE ON THE STATUS OF BLACK AMERICANS

---

*Did not participate in committee activities after June 1987.

PANEL ON EDUCATION

ROBERT M. HAUSER (*Chair*), Department of Sociology, University of Wisconsin
HUBERT M. BLALOCK, JR., Department of Sociology, University of Washington
BERNARD R. GIFFORD, Apple Computer, Inc.
NATHAN GLAZER, Graduate School of Education, Harvard University
JENNIFER HOCHSCHILD, Woodrow Wilson School, Princeton University
LYLE V. JONES, L. L. Thurstone Psychometric Laboratory, University of North Carolina, Chapel Hill
JOHN U. OGBU, Department of Anthropology, University of California, Berkeley

PANEL ON EMPLOYMENT, INCOME, AND OCCUPATIONS

JAMES TOBIN (*Chair*), Department of Economics, Yale University
SHELDON H. DANZIGER, Department of Economics and Population Studies Center, University of Michigan
DAVID T. ELLWOOD, John F. Kennedy School of Government, Harvard University
JAMES J. HECKMAN, Department of Economics, Yale University
NORMAN HILL, A. Philip Randolph Institute, New York, New York
FRANK LEVY, School of Public Affairs, University of Maryland
GLENN C. LOURY, John F. Kennedy School of Government, Harvard University
ELEANOR HOLMES NORTON, Georgetown University Law Center
PHYLLIS A. WALLACE, Sloan School of Management, Massachusetts Institute of Technology
WILLIAM JULIUS WILSON, Department of Sociology, University of Chicago

PANEL ON HEALTH AND DEMOGRAPHY

BEATRIX A. HAMBURG (*Chair*), Division of Child and Adolescent Psychiatry, Mt. Sinai School of Medicine
KAREN P. DAVIS, School of Hygiene and Public Health, Johns Hopkins University
M. ALFRED HAYNES, Charles R. Drew Postgraduate Medical School
JAMES S. JACKSON, Institute for Social Research, University of Michigan
STANLEY LIEBERSON, Department of Sociology, Harvard University
HARRIETTE PIPES MCADOO, School of Social Work, Howard University
DELORES L. PARRON, National Institute of Mental Health, U.S. Department of Health and Human Services
DOROTHY P. RICE, Department of Social and Behavioral Sciences, University of California, San Francisco
LEE NELKENS ROBINS, School of Medicine, Washington University

PANEL ON POLITICAL PARTICIPATION AND ADMINISTRATION OF JUSTICE

JOEL F. HANDLER (*Chair*), School of Law, University of California, Los Angeles

LEE P. BROWN, Police Department, Houston, Texas

CHARLES V. HAMILTON, Department of Political Science, Columbia University

JAMES JENNINGS, College of Public and Community Services, University of Massachusetts, Cambridge

MICHAEL LIPSKY, Department of Political Science, Massachusetts Institute of Technology

LESLIE BURL MCLEMORE, Department of Political Science and Dean, Graduate School, Jackson State University

STEVEN J. ROSENSTONE,* Department of Political Science, University of Michigan

ELSIE L. SCOTT, National Organization of Black Law Enforcement Executives, Landover, Maryland

RAYMOND E. WOLFINGER, Department of Political Science, University of California, Berkeley

PANEL ON SOCIAL AND CULTURAL CHANGE AND CONTINUITY

JOHN HOPE FRANKLIN (*Chair*), Department of History, Duke University

JAMES LOWELL GIBBS, JR., Department of Anthropology, Stanford University

THOMAS F. PETTIGREW, Psychology Board of Studies, University of California, Santa Cruz

NANCY J. WEISS, Department of History, Princeton University

ROBIN M. WILLIAMS, JR., Department of Sociology, Cornell University

---

*Did not participate in panel activities after July 1986.

The National Academy of Sciences is a private, nonprofit, self-perpetuating society of distinguished scholars engaged in scientific and engineering research, dedicated to the furtherance of science and technology and to their use for the general welfare. Upon the authority of the charter granted to it by the Congress in 1863, the Academy has a mandate that requires it to advise the federal government on scientific and technical matters. Dr. Frank Press is president of the National Academy of Sciences.

The National Academy of Engineering was established in 1964, under the charter of the National Academy of Sciences, as a parallel organization of outstanding engineers. It is autonomous in its administration and in the selection of its members, sharing with the National Academy of Sciences the responsibility for advising the federal government. The National Academy of Engineering also sponsors engineering programs aimed at meeting national needs, encourages education and research, and recognizes the superior achievements of engineers. Dr. Robert M. White is president of the National Academy of Engineering.

The Institute of Medicine was established in 1970 by the National Academy of Sciences to secure the services of eminent members of appropriate professions in the examination of policy matters pertaining to the health of the public. The Institute acts under the responsibility given to the National Academy of Sciences by its congressional charter to be an adviser to the federal government and, upon its own initiative, to identify issues of medical care, research, and education. Dr. Samuel O. Thier is president of the Institute of Medicine.

The National Research Council was organized by the National Academy of Sciences in 1916 to associate the broad community of science and technology with the Academy's purposes of furthering knowledge and advising the federal government. Functioning in accordance with general policies determined by the Academy, the Council has become the principal operating agency of both the National Academy of Sciences and the National Academy of Engineering in providing services to the government, the public, and the scientific and engineering communities. The Council is administered jointly by both Academies and the Institute of Medicine. Dr. Frank Press and Dr. Robert M. White are chairman and vice chairman, respectively, of the National Research Council.

CONTENTS

PREFACE

This report documents the unfinished agenda of a nation still struggling to come to terms with the consequences of its history of relations between black and white Americans. In many ways this history has left a legacy of pain, and the report would be remiss if it did not acknowledge and emphasize that fact. In the pages that follow, we describe many improvements in the economic, political, and social position of black Americans. We also describe the continuance of conditions of poverty, segregation, discrimination, and social fragmentation of the most serious proportions.

The study was initiated early in 1985 after more than 3 years of preliminary investigation, planning, and organization. That preliminary work included consideration of the status of other racial and ethnic minorities in America. After much discussion, it was decided to restrict the study to black Americans. The decision arose from limited resources and time and from recognition of the great variations in the experience of different racial and ethnic groups in the United States. And the case of black Americans is unique—in its history of slavery and of extreme segregation, exclusion, and discrimination.

We recognize the potential value of comparative studies and hope that they will be carried out in the future. Each minority has its unique history, and the reasons for variations in current status vary widely. At this time, however, a crucial factor is the availability of data: information on blacks is far more extensive and of better quality than that for other major racial and ethnic minorities. Most important, however, the historical significance of blacks to the nation and the importance of black-white relations in U.S. society today are surely more than adequate grounds for the focus of this study.

The original charge to the Committee on the Status of Black Americans from the National Research Council and its Commission on Behavioral and Social Sciences and Education (CBASSE) reads as follows:

> . . . marshall descriptive data on the changing position of blacks in American society since 1940; draw from the wealth of existing research to describe the cultural context, including an increasingly complex framework of laws, policies, and institutions within which the observed changes have occurred; and explore the consequences, anticipated and unanticipated, of public and private initiatives to ameliorate the position of blacks in America.

The historical dimension of this task has reinforced our awareness of the distinctive history of black Americans. Due in part to that special history, blacks are the most studied racial or ethnic population group in the nation. This report will undoubtedly be compared to earlier studies of American race relations, especially to two reports that, like it, were collaborative efforts: *An American Dilemma* (1944) and the *Report of the National Advisory Commission on Civil Disorders* (1968). [An earlier, rarely noted effort of this type was Charles S. Johnson, editor, *The Negro in American Civilization* (1930), which has not been given its just due as a treatise on black-white relations in the United States.] Readers of this report might profit from a brief reminder of the legacy of those well-known studies.

In the midst of World War II, Gunnar Myrdal's monumental survey of race relations, *An American Dilemma,* predicted slow improvement in the educational, political, and social status of blacks; a worsening economic situation; rising self-confidence and assertiveness among blacks; and an impending breakdown among whites of formerly accepted beliefs and attitudes of white race dominance.

An American Dilemma correctly anticipated increasing black solidarity and activism, increasing dissension over racial practices among whites, heightened conflict, and a national movement toward "equalitarian reforms." It correctly saw that the impending domestic changes would be strongly affected by World War II and by the international status of the nation that claimed to represent democracy in a race-conscious world. The accuracy of many of these forecasts is documented in the present report.

What Myrdal did not correctly forecast was the strong resistance to full equality for blacks that would remain after the old system of legalized segregation had been eliminated. In hindsight, *An American Dilemma* appears overly confident that change "in the hearts and minds" of men and women would eliminate racial separation and discrimination.

A quarter century later, the urban uprisings of blacks during the 1960s prompted another major inquiry—this time through the appointment of a presidential commission. The *Report of the National Advisory Commission on Civil Disorders*, "the Kerner report" (1968), is a forthright and vivid report whose basic conclusion stressed a condition, also emphasized in *An American Dilemma,* of a nation continuing to move toward "two societies, one black, one white—separate and unequal" (p. 1). The Kerner report emphasized how the legacy of past discrimination in the forms of segregation and poverty had created a black ghetto whose environment was destructive to many of its inhabitants—a ghetto "largely maintained by white institutions and condoned by white society" (pp. 1–2). After this diagnosis, the report called for prompt national action and presented a set of recommendations aimed at reducing segregation and discrimination, safeguarding civil and political rights, and increasing educational and economic opportunities.

Two decades after that landmark report, we now find that—despite important changes—there are striking resemblances between the description of 1968 and the position of black Americans reflected in our findings. To the extent that such continuity of black status exists, it derives from persisting basic conditions not yet removed by either private initiatives or the national actions that have been taken, much less by those repeatedly proposed but never fully undertaken.

Contemporary views of the status of black-white relations in America vary widely. Perspectives range from optimism that the main problems have been solved, to the view that black progress is largely an illusion, to assessments that the nation is retrogressing and moving toward increased racial disparities. To some observers, the present situation is only another episode in a long history of recurring cycles of apparent improvement that are followed by new forms of dominance in changed contexts: the level of black status changes, it is said, but the one constant is blacks' continuing subordinate social position. To other observers, the opposite conception is correct: long-run progress is the dominant trend. Listening to these discordant views, reasonable men and women may well wonder what, indeed, is the case. To this serious question the present report has sought to bring to bear a large compilation of facts and analyses. It would be unrealistic to expect all readers to agree with all the emphases and nuances of the report. We hope, however, that it is clear that we have tried to search out and critically assess objective evidence wherever available. Our interpretations are those that have survived a lengthy and intensive process of criticism and refinement.

To the extent possible, existing data and published and unpublished research were used, but we also developed new data and analyses. A great many studies over the years since World War II have dealt with specific aspects of the position of black people in the United States. But there remained a need for a synthesis of existing research that could serve as a point of departure for future analyses and for the informed development of policies by business, voluntary associations, and local, state, and federal governments. The availability of an unprecedented resource of data and research findings from diverse sources makes such a synthesis possible; controversies over the facts of the case, as well as over past and current policies, make the study especially timely.

This report concentrates on description and analysis of the position of black Americans—now some 30 million people—in our complex society. During the nearly 50 years covered in our survey, significant changes occurred in almost every aspect of the national society, from family life to international relations, from manufacturing technologies to styles of life, from employment patterns to civil rights. All Americans were affected, but as the body of the report makes clear, in many ways black people were uniquely involved.

The large inventory of data and research analyses used by the committee and its panels and consultants made it feasible to complete a difficult assignment. At the same time, we found that many important questions simply could not be answered because crucial data were missing. Some of these serious gaps in the nation's resources of information are noted in Appendix A. Considerable uncertainty must attend any attempt to develop effective social policies unless vital statistical series are maintained and more adequate support provided for research on the economic and social changes that are now transforming the lives of the American people.

While the study proceeded, the dynamic nature of black-white relations was being repeatedly demonstrated through changes occurring in American society. Thus, U.S. Representative William Gray became chair of the House Budget Committee in 1985, and, 4 years later, chair of the House Democratic Caucus, a major leadership position; also in 1989, Ronald Brown became national chair of the Democratic Party, Bill White became president of professional baseball's National League, and Barbara C. Harris became the first female bishop in the Episcopal Church. Other significant events also occurred, and as participants suggested that we were compelled to comment on this or another event, it became clear that the report could not be completed and keep apace of American society. Consequently, we chose 1985–1986 as a rough terminal point for the report's analyses. In some instances data or easily interpreted events that occurred after 1986 are reported, but they are relatively infrequent.

The committee's 22 members were selected from most of the major disciplines in the social and behavioral sciences. The committee was subdivided into five working panels, dealing, respectively, with economic status, education, health and demography, political participation and criminal justice, and social and cultural continuity and change. These panels also included 22 additional members having relevant special knowledge. Biographical sketches of committee, panel, and staff members appear in Appendix B. The work of the committee, its panels, and its staff was aided by still other scholars and research specialists who prepared more than 30 commissioned papers; a list of papers is in Appendix C, along with a list of committee and panel meetings. Altogether, nearly 100 people thus brought their professional skills to the task of analyzing the status of black Americans during nearly five eventful decades of American history. We also note with thanks all those people who communicated with us in person, by mail and telephone, and by published commentaries. We thereby received many useful suggestions, and the report gained from the criticisms freely offered at all stages of its development.

The interdisciplinary character of the committee and its panels allowed our deliberations to draw on a wide range of knowledge and differing perspectives. The members also held strong convictions, of course, on many of the problems and issues that we considered. Consequently, our frequent meetings were marked by lively discussions, some surprising discoveries, and a lengthy process of debate and mutual education. By the end of 4 years of immersion in the subject matter, an impressive convergence of views had developed, greatly facilitated by repeated confrontations with the accumulated evidence. Individual differences of view among the participants remain, of course, especially concerning questions of social policy. Still, the level and quality of agreement reached are noteworthy, and we appreciate the patience, objectivity, and vision of the participants in the study.

The committee notes its very special debt to David A. Goslin, then executive director of CBASSE, and Alexandra Wigdor, staff officer, whose indispensable initiatives conceived and developed the launching of the project within CBASSE. Crucial at many important points of the study were the advice and support of CBASSE executive director Robert Caplan, associate executive director Brett Hammond, and the two people who served as CBASSE chairs during the life of the study, Ira Hirsh and Robert McC. Adams.

We acknowledge with deep appreciation the generous financial support that made possible the completion of this enterprise. Accordingly, our special thanks go to the Carnegie Corporation of New York, the Ford Foundation, the Robert Wood Johnson Foundation, the Andrew W. Mellon Foundation, the Pew Charitable Trusts, the Rockefeller Foundation, the Alfred P. Sloan Foundation, and the National Research Council Fund. The understanding and patience of foundation staffs have been of special importance.

Without the staff there would, of course, have been no report. The work of the senior staff, Lawrence Bobo, Thomas Cavanagh, John Brown Childs, Darnell Hawkins, and Mary Beth Moore, was crucial in preparing memoranda and other background materials covering the variety of topics discussed in the report. Reynolds Farley, as senior research consultant, was a major contributor to essential background materials and research analyses used in writing the report. Eugenia Grohman, associate director for reports of CBASSE, played an instrumental intellectual role in aiding the editors during the writing of the final draft of the report.

The background materials produced during the committee's work were rewritten, supplemented with additional material, and often reinterpreted by the committee, its chair, and its study director. The synthesis that forms the report is thus the sole responsibility of those individuals.

We hope that the evidence and analysis presented is compelling. Our touchstone has been credible evidence; our mandate, to describe and analyze. At the same time, the report necessarily deals directly with value-laden issues—discrimination, prejudice, equality of opportunity, inequality of condition. We have not avoided or minimized the deep contradictions and conflicts that surround these issues, and our diagnosis certainly leaves no ground for complacency. It is our hope that the report will provide a solid base for fruitful debate and reasonable policy initiatives in the years ahead.

We believe that the present critical synthesis deals with matters of central importance for the future of our society. We believe that research data and thoughtful analysis can help to tell us where we have come from and where we may be going in terms of the welfare of Americans. The differences in the status of whites and blacks herein described do not overshadow the many crucial ways in which all our people are interdependent; we share a common destiny. The nation's future depends critically on the health, skill, and commitment of all of its people. Because of a unique past and distinctive present, the analysis of the special situation of black Americans is an essential part of any careful appraisal of American society.

GERALD DAVID JAYNES, *Study Director*
ROBIN M. WILLIAMS, JR., *Chair*
Committee on the Status of Black Americans

A COMMON DESTINY

BLACKS AND
AMERICAN SOCIETY

SUMMARY AND CONCLUSIONS

Romare Bearden
The Family (1948)
Watercolor and gouache on paper
The Evans-Tibbs Collection, Washington, D.C.

J ust five decades ago, most black Americans could not work, live, shop, eat, seek entertainment, or travel where they chose. Even a quarter century ago—100 years after the Emancipation Proclamation of 1863—most blacks were effectively denied the right to vote. A large majority of blacks lived in poverty, and very few black children had the opportunity to receive a basic education; indeed, black children were still forced to attend inferior and separate schools in jurisdictions that had not accepted the 1954 decision of the Supreme Court declaring segregated schools unconstitutional.

Today the situation is very different. In education, many blacks have received college degrees from universities that formerly excluded them. In the workplace, blacks frequently hold professional and managerial jobs in desegregated settings. In politics, most blacks now participate in elections, and blacks have been elected to all but the highest political offices. Overall, many blacks have achieved middle-class status.

Yet the great gulf that existed between black and white Americans in 1939 has only been narrowed; it has not closed. One of three blacks still live in households with incomes below the poverty line. Even more blacks live in areas where ineffective schools, high rates of dependence on public assistance, severe problems of crime and drug use, and low and declining employment prevail. Race relations, as they affect the lives of inhabitants of these areas, differ considerably from black-white relations involving middle-class blacks. Lower status blacks have less access to desegregated schools, neighborhoods, and other institutions and public facilities. Their interactions with whites frequently emphasize their subordinate status—as low-skilled employees, public agency clients, and marginally performing pupils.

The status of black Americans today can be characterized as a glass that is half full—if measured by progress since 1939—or as a glass that is half empty—if measured by the persisting disparities between black and white Americans since the early 1970s. Any assessment of the quality of life for blacks is also complicated by the contrast between blacks who have achieved middle-class status and those who have not.

The progress occurred because sustained struggles by blacks and their allies changed American law and politics, moving all governments and most private institutions from support of principles of racial inequality to support of principles of racial equality. Gradually, and often with much resistance, the behaviors and attitudes of individual whites moved in the same direction. Over the 50-year span covered by this study, the social status of American blacks has *on average* improved dramatically, both in absolute terms and relative to whites. The growth of the economy and public policies promoting racial equality led to an erosion of segregation and discrimination, making it possible for a substantial fraction of blacks to enter the mainstream of American life.

The reasons for the continuing distress of large numbers of black Americans are complex. Racial discrimination continues despite the victories of the civil rights movement. Yet, the problems faced today by blacks who are isolated from economic and social progress are less directly open to political amelioration than were the problems of legal segregation and the widely practiced overt discrimination of a few decades past. Slow overall growth of the economy during the 1970s and 1980s has been an important impediment to black progress; in the three previous decades economic prosperity and rapid growth had been a great help to most blacks. Educational institutions and government policies have not successfully responded to underlying changes in the society. Opportunities for upward mobility have been reduced for all lower status Americans, but especially for those who are black. If all racial discrimination were abolished today, the life prospects facing many poor blacks would still constitute major challenges for public policy.

SUMMARY OF MAJOR FINDINGS

This report summarizes and interprets a large body of data and research analyses concerning the position of blacks in American society since the eve of World War II. We write at a time 20 years after the Kerner Commission, following the summer riots of 1967, warned that ours was becoming a racially divided and unequal nation. We write 45 years after Gunnar Myrdal in *An American Dilemma* challenged Americans to bring their racial practices into line with their ideals. Despite clear evidence of progress against each problem, Americans face an unfinished agenda: many black Americans remain separated from the mainstream of national life under conditions of great inequality. The American dilemma has not been resolved.

The new "American dilemma" that has emerged after the civil rights era of the 1960s results from two aspirations of black Americans: equal opportunity—the removal of barriers to employment, housing, education, and political activities—and the actual attainment of equality in participation in these sectors of life.

Central to the realization of these aspirations are national policies promoting equality of opportunity for the most disadvantaged blacks (especially in areas such as employment and education) and the preservation among black people of attitudes and behaviors toward self-help and individual sacrifice that have enabled them to benefit from such opportunities. Black-white relations are important in determining the degree to which equal opportunity exists for black Americans. Whites desire equality of treatment in social institutions and in governmental policy; however, many whites are less likely to espouse or practice equality of treatment for blacks in their personal behavior. Thus, at the core of black-white relations is a dynamic tension between many whites' expectations of American institutions and their expectations of themselves. This state of relations is a significant improvement from 45 years ago when majorities of white people supported discrimination against blacks in many areas of life. But the divergence between social principle and individual practice frequently leads to white avoidance of blacks in those institutions in which equal treatment is most needed. The result is that American institutions do not provide the full equality of opportunity that Americans desire.

Foremost among the reasons for the present state of black-white relations are two continuing consequences of the nation's long and recent history of racial inequality. One is the negative attitudes held toward blacks and the other is the actual disadvantaged conditions under which many black Americans live. These two consequences reinforce each other. Thus, a legacy of discrimination and segregation continues to affect black-white relations.

In the context of American history, this continuing legacy is not surprising. Racial and ethnic differences have had crucial effects on the course of American history. In particular, black Americans' central role in several constitutional crises—their past status as slaves and the debates over slavery during the Constitutional Convention of 1787; the fighting of the Civil War; the denial of blacks' basic citizenship until the civil rights movement of the 1950s and 1960s—has frequently focused international attention on black-white relations in the United States. In view of this history, race is likely to retain much of its saliency as a feature of American society for some time.

Indeed, as the twenty-first century nears, demographic conditions will increase Americans' awareness that theirs is a multiracial society. The Bureau of the Census projects that the black population will increase from 11.7 percent of the U.S. total in 1980 to 15 percent in 2020; blacks will be nearly 1 of 5 children of school age and 1 of 6 adults of prime working age (25–54). Rising numbers of blacks will be represented both in influential occupations and positions, and among the poor, the least educated, and the jobless. At the same time, immigration trends are also increasing the numbers and proportions of Asian-Americans and Hispanics in the U.S. population. Thus, the importance of racial and ethnic minorities in general to the nation's well-being is growing.

We can summarize our main findings on the status of blacks in America in the late 1980s succinctly:

- By almost all aggregate statistical measures—incomes and living standards; health and life expectancy; educational, occupational, and residential opportunities; political and social participation—the well-being of both blacks and whites has advanced greatly over the past five decades.
- By almost all the same indicators, blacks remain substantially behind whites.

Beyond this brief picture lies a more complex set of changes that affect the *relative* status of black Americans:

- The greatest economic gains for blacks occurred in the 1940s and 1960s. Since the early 1970s, the economic status of blacks relative to whites has, on average, stagnated or deteriorated.
- The political, educational, health, and cultural statuses of blacks showed important gains from the 1940s through the 1960s. In addition, some important indicators continued to improve after the early 1970s.
- Among blacks, the experiences of various groups have differed, and status differences among those groups have increased. Some blacks have attained high-status occupations, income, education, and political positions, but a substantial minority remain in disadvantaged circumstances.

These patterns of change have been largely determined by three factors:

- Political and social activism among black Americans and their white allies led to changes in governmental policies; particularly important were sweeping improvements in the legal status of blacks.
- Resistance to social change in race relations continues in American society.
- Broad changes in overall economic conditions, especially the post-1973 slowdown in the nation's economic growth, have significantly affected social and economic opportunities for all Americans.

The rest of this section explicates these main findings and their causes. The next section presents a summary of the committee's detailed findings for the various areas we studied. The final section presents the committee's conclusions and some projections for the future.

BLACKS AND WHITES IN A CHANGING SOCIETY

Two general developments in the status of black Americans stand out; each is reflective of a near-identical development in the population at large.

First, for the period 1940–1973, real earnings of Americans improved steadily, but they stagnated and declined after 1973. Similarly, over these same periods, there was a clear record of improving average material status of blacks relative to whites followed by stagnation and decline. Second, during the post-1973 period, inequality increased among Americans as the lowest income and least skilled people were hurt most by changes in the overall economy. Similarly, there were increasing differences in material well-being and opportunities among blacks, and they have been extremely pronounced.

These developments may be understood as consequences of four interdependent events that have altered the status of blacks, relative black-white status, and race relations in the United States. These events were the urbanization and northern movement of the black population from 1940 to 1970; the civil rights movement that forced the nation to open its major institutions to black participation during the same three decades; the unprecedented high and sustained rate of national economic growth for roughly the same period; and the significant slowdown in the U.S. economy since the early 1970s.

The civil rights movement, blacks' more proximate location near centers of industrial activity, and high economic growth enabled those blacks best prepared to take advantage of new opportunities to respond with initiative and success. Increases in educational opportunities were seized by many blacks who were then able to translate better educations into higher status occupations than most blacks had ever enjoyed. Black incomes and earnings rose generally, with many individuals and families reaching middle-class and even upper middle income status (Chapter 6). The new black middle class moved into better housing, frequently in the suburbs, and sometimes in desegregated neighborhoods. Despite much confrontation between whites and blacks as blacks abandoned traditional approaches to black-white relations, race relations eventually advanced closer to equal treatment.

At the same time, many blacks were not able to take advantage of the new conditions that developed: some were still located in areas relatively untouched by the changes; some lacked the family support networks to provide assistance; for some, better opportunities simply did not arise. Those who were left behind during the 1960s and 1970s faced and still face very different situations than poor blacks immediately before that period.

A major reason is the performance of the economy. Real weekly earnings (in constant 1984 dollars) of all American men, on average, fell from $488 in 1969 to $414 in 1984; real weekly earnings of women fell from $266 in 1969 to $230 in 1984. For the first time since the Great Depression of the 1930s, American men born in one year (e.g., 1960) may face lower lifetime real earnings than men born 10 years earlier (Chapter 1). Among the myriad and complex responses to these economic conditions have been rising employment rates among women, but falling rates among men, while the unemployment rates of both men and women have been on an upward trend for three decades (Chapter 6).

A generation ago, a low-skilled man had relatively abundant opportunity to obtain a blue-collar job with a wage adequate to support a family at a lower middle class level or better. Today the jobs available to such men—and women—are often below or just barely above the official poverty line for a family of four. For example, black males aged 25–34, with some high school but no diploma, earned on average $268 weekly in 1986; in 1969, black male dropouts of that age had averaged $334 weekly (in constant 1984 dollars). For white men of the same age and education, work conditions have been better, but changes over time cannot be said to have been good: in the years 1969 and 1986, mean weekly earnings were $447 and $381. Thus, among men who did not complete high school, blacks and whites had lower real earnings in 1986 than in 1969.

Obtaining a well-paying job increasingly requires a good education or a specific skill. Many young blacks and whites do not obtain such training, and the educational system in many locations is apparently not equipped to provide them. Recent reports on the state of American education sound great alarm about the future status of today's students. One in six youths dropped out of high school in 1985, and levels of scholastic achievement are disturbingly low by many measures. Young men with poor credentials, finding themselves facing low-wage job offers and high unemployment rates, frequently abandon the labor force intermittently or completely. Some choose criminal activity as an alternative to the labor market.

Greater numbers of people are today susceptible to poverty than in the recent past. With some year-to-year variation, the percentage of Americans living in poverty has been on an upward trend: from 11.2 percent in 1974 to 13.5 percent in 1986. In addition, the poor may be getting poorer in the 1980s: the average poor family has persistently had a yearly income further below the poverty line than any year since 1963.

More and more of the poor are working family heads, men and women who are employed or seeking employment but who cannot find a job that pays enough to prevent their families from sliding into or near poverty. For the more fortunate, reasonably secure from the fear of poverty, such middle-class advantages as a home in the suburbs and the ability to send their children to the best college for which they qualify are goals that were reached by their parents but may be unattainable for many of them.

Perhaps the most important consequences of the stagnating U.S. economy have been the effects on the status of children. Many members of the next generation of young adults live in conditions ill suited to prepare them to contribute to the nation's future. In 1987, 1 of 5 (20 percent) American children under age 18—white, black, Hispanic, Native American, and Asian-American—were being raised in families with incomes below official poverty standards. Among minorities the conditions were worse: for example, 45 percent of black children and 39 percent of Hispanic children were living in poverty. During the 1970s, approximately 2 of every 3 black children could expect to live in poverty for at least 1 of the first 10 years of their childhood, while an astounding 1 of 3 could expect at least 7 of those 10 years to be lived in poverty.

We cannot emphasize too much the gravity of the fact that in any given year more than two-fifths of all black children live under conditions of poverty as the 1980s draw to a close. As fertility rates decrease, the total youth population of the United States will contain a larger proportion of comparatively disadvantaged youths from minority ethnic and racial groups. This change may in turn lead to major changes in labor markets, childbearing, the armed forces, and education.

Under conditions of increasing economic hardship for the least prosperous members of society, blacks, because of their special legacy of poverty and discrimination, are afflicted sooner, more deeply, and longer. But the signs of distress that are most visible in parts of the black population are becoming more discernible within the entire population. This distress should be viewed in the context of the underlying changes within American society that affect not only black-white differences, but all disadvantaged blacks and whites who face the difficult economic conditions of the late 1980s.

DETERMINANTS OF BLACK STATUS

One major determinant of black status has been noted in the previous sections: the stagnation of the U.S. economy since 1973, which has particularly hurt lower class blacks. In this section we note two other determinants: organizational and individual resistance to change, intended and otherwise, that has erected and maintained barriers to black opportunities; and the policies of governments and private organizations aimed at improving blacks' position, which have resulted in large measure from black activism, initiative, and self-identity.

Barriers and disadvantages persist in blocking black advancement. Three such barriers to full opportunity for black Americans are residential segregation, continuance of diffuse and often indirect discrimination, and exclusion from social networks essential for full access to economic and educational opportunities (Chapters 2–7). These barriers also existed for blacks who overcame them in earlier decades, but those successes were achieved in an economy that was growing rapidly and providing good wage opportunities even to low-skilled and less educated job seekers. In the 1960s, blacks seeking to help themselves also were benefited by a society more willing to expend energy and resources toward improving opportunities for the poor and minorities.

The past five decades have shown that purposeful actions and policies by governments and private institutions make a large difference in the opportunities and conditions of black Americans. Such purposeful actions and policies have been essential for past progress, and further progress is unlikely without them. Many blacks attained middle-class status because government and private programs enabled them to achieve better educations and jobs, through employment and education programs and government enforcement of equal employment opportunity (Chapters 5–8).

Black initiative and identity have increasingly played primary roles in bringing about changes in government and private institutions and improvements in blacks' economic, social, and political status. This is of course evident in blacks' leadership of the civil rights movement and in their response to industrial opportunity during the great rural-to-urban migration of 1940–1970. But it is also evident in the strivings of individuals to finish high school or attain higher education; to enter a predominantly white factory, secretarial pool, or corporate law office; or to desegregate an entire institution, such as a professional sport, military combat corps, or legislative body (Chapters 2 and 4).

Many blacks who have not succeeded live in environments in which social conditions and individual behavioral patterns are often detrimental to self-improvement. Such behaviors may be natural responses to group conditions and social forces perceived as beyond personal control. One-half of black families with children must manage their affairs with only one parent—almost always a mother. These families are overwhelmingly poor (59 percent were below the poverty line in 1987), have high rates of dependence on family assistance benefits, and live in areas with a high percentage of families in similar circumstances (Chapters 6 and 10).

Why do such behaviors and conditions persist? There are no simple answers to this crucial question and no answers that can be validated as scientific findings. We can say, however, that the evidence does not support some popular hypotheses that purport to explain female-headed households, high birth rates to unmarried women, low labor force participation by males, or poor academic performance solely on the basis of government support programs or, more generally, on the existence of a "culture of poverty" among the black poor. Black-white cultural differences have narrowed since 1960, not widened (Chapters 2–4 and 10).

Our analysis of the problem does identify a number of important contributory factors. Discrimination plays an important role in the lives of many blacks, and even in the absence of discrimination the opportunities of many blacks are limited. Black youths in poor environments probably anticipate little payoff from working for academic achievement and may underestimate their opportunities. Those in poorly staffed, dilapidated schools populated with underachieving students can easily fall into the trap of perceiving the pursuit of academic excellence as a poor investment (Chapter 7). Inequalities in economic status to a large extent cause and interact with other status features to maintain overall black-white differences in status. Consequently, status gaps between blacks and whites will remain as long as blacks' economic status lags behind that of whites. For example, differences in black-white voting patterns result from persistent economic and social inequalities that impede electoral participation regardless of race; individual blacks now participate as much or more than whites of comparable socioeconomic status (Chapter 5). Similarly, differences in socioeconomic status account for the entire black-white difference in high school dropout rates (Chapter 7). In health, differences in black and white infant mortality are similarly linked to differences in economic status (Chapter 8). In the criminal justice system, much of the differential sentencing of blacks and whites can be attributed to differences between sentences for defendants of higher and lower economic status (Chapter 9).

Yet the status of blacks is determined by the presence of both racial stratification and class (position within the socioeconomic structure of society). Changes in black-white relations and social opportunities do not affect blacks of different status in similar ways. For example, because of higher geographic concentrations of poor households among blacks, segregated residential areas affect the quality of schools and medical care available to low-income blacks more than they affect the availability of these resources to higher income blacks or low-income whites. And we have already noted that changes in the national economy have had particularly negative effects on lower status Americans, white and black. But changes have been most detrimental to the fortunes of blacks, and opportunities were curtailed most for blacks of lowest status (Chapter 6).

A RECORD OF THE STATUS OF
BLACK AMERICANS

This section presents the committee's detailed findings on the status of black Americans. The presentation follows the topical approach of the material in Chapters 2–10 of the report.

ATTITUDES, PARTICIPATION, IDENTITY, AND INSTITUTIONS

Large majorities of blacks and whites accept the principles of equal access to public institutions and equal treatment in race relations. For whites this is the result of a long upward trend from a low base in the 1940s; blacks have favored equality since survey data have been collected. Yet there remain important signs of continuing resistance to full equality of black Americans. Principles of equality are endorsed less when they would result in close, frequent, or prolonged social contact, and whites are much less prone to endorse policies meant to implement equal participation of blacks in important social institutions. In practice, many whites refuse or are reluctant to participate in social settings (e.g., neighborhoods and schools) in which significant numbers of blacks are present; see Figures S-1, S-2, and S-3.

Whether one considers arts and entertainment, religious institutions, public schools, or a number of other major institutions, black participation has increased significantly since 1940 and since 1960. Yet increased black participation has not produced substantial integration. An exception is the U.S. Army, where a true modicum of integration—significant numerical participation on terms of equal treatment—has been accomplished. The other three military services, although generally ahead of the civilian sector, have not attained the level of equality found in the Army. Although large-scale desegregation of public schools occurred in the South during the late 1960s and early 1970s—and has been substantial in many small and medium-sized cities

FIGURE S-1 Whites with *no* objection to sending their children to a school in which a few or more than half of the children are black.

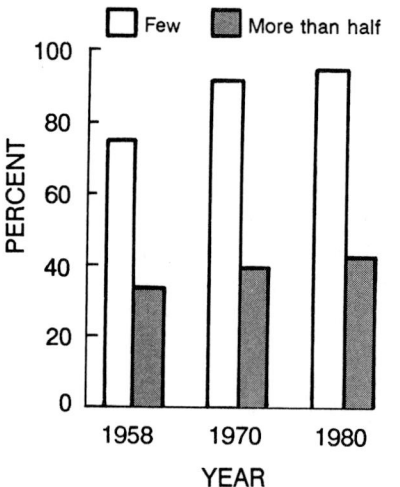

FIGURE S-2 Whites who would *not* move if black people came to live next door or in great numbers in the neighborhood.

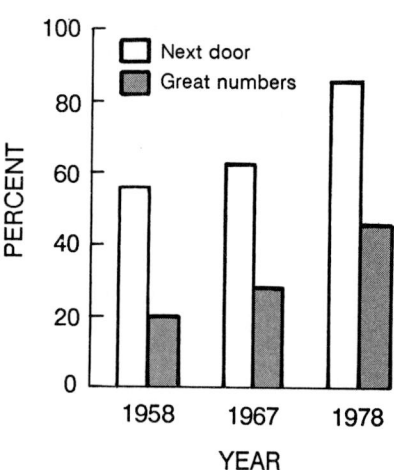

FIGURE S-3 Median residential segregation in 29 metropolitan areas with the largest black populations.

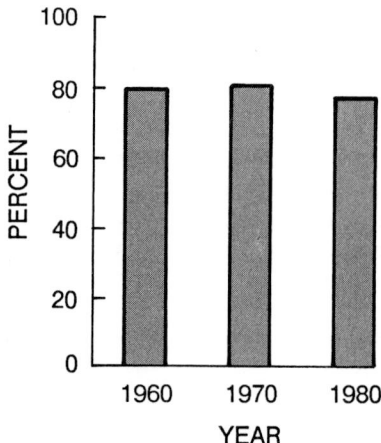

Note: 100 = total segregation;
0 = no segregation.

elsewhere—the pace of school desegregation has slowed, and racial separation in education is significant, especially outside the South. And residential separation of whites and blacks in large metropolitan areas remains nearly as high in the 1980s as it was in the 1960s.

These findings suggest that a considerable amount of remaining black-white inequality is due to continuing discriminatory treatment of blacks. The clearest evidence is in housing. Discrimination against blacks seeking housing has been conclusively demonstrated. In employment and public accommodations, discrimination, although greatly reduced, is still a problem (Chapter 3).

The long history of discrimination and segregation produced among blacks a heightened sense of group consciousness and a stronger orientation toward collective values and behavior than exists generally among Americans, and group consciousness remains strong among blacks today (Chapters 3–5). Contemporary conditions in the United States reinforce a recognition of group identity and position among blacks, who continue to be conspicuously separated from the white majority. This separation is manifested in a range of specific findings: two findings of special importance are separation of blacks and whites in residential areas and public schools. The residential separation of blacks and whites is nearly twice the rate of white and Asian-Americans, and it is often much greater than residential separation between Hispanic Americans and whites in many cities (Chapters 2–3).

These past experiences and current conditions have important consequences for the status of blacks and the manner in which they attempt to improve their status. Blacks overwhelmingly believe in values such as individual responsibility and free competition, but they are more likely to disapprove of the ubiquity of individualism and market autonomy throughout American society than are whites. This disapproval has appeared primarily in black support, at levels higher than whites, of such federal policies as guaranteed full employment, guaranteed income floors, and national health care (Chapter 5).

Given blacks' history, the sources of this desire for change are not difficult to identify. Data show that blacks generally believe that basic social institutions are biased in favor of whites and against blacks (Chapters 3–5). Many blacks believe that their relative position in society cannot be improved without government policies to intervene with social institutions on behalf of minorities and the disadvantaged. In contrast with whites, blacks have highly favorable views of the high activity years of government policy intervention of the 1960s.

As a consequence of their heightened group consciousness, their belief that racial discrimination remains a major deterrent to black progress, and their history of collective social expression, black Americans vote at the same or higher rates than whites of comparable socioeconomic status, support redistributive policies more often than do whites, and participate in a wider variety of political activity.

This political participation has had some important effects on American politics. After the legislative and judicial successes of the civil rights movement during the 1960s, there have been continuous struggles to enforce laws and administrative measures aimed at eliminating discrimination and improving opportunities. As a result, blacks' right of access to public facilities and accommodations is now widely accepted. Arbitrary harassment and intimidation of blacks by legal authorities, by organized antiblack organizations, and by unorganized individuals have greatly diminished, although there are regular reports of such incidents.

The changes since 1940—and particularly since the 1960s—have had important effects on the nature of black communities. The organizations and institutions created by blacks, as well as changing concepts of black identity, were two crucial foundations on which the achievement of sweeping improvements in blacks' legal and political status were attained. Changes in black social structure have resulted from the rising incomes, occupations, and educations of many blacks. The exit of higher status blacks from inner cities has accentuated problems of increasing social stratification among blacks. The service needs of poorer blacks have placed strains on many black institutions, including schools, churches, and voluntary service organizations. These strains have resulted in a proliferation of activities devoted to the material needs of poor blacks by black organizations (Chapter 4).

Other effects on black institutions and organizations have been produced by the civil rights movement. Greater access to majority white institutions by higher status blacks' has led to alterations in black leadership structure, problems of recruitment and retention of black talent by black organizations, and reduced participation in many spheres of black life by those blacks. As a result, the often well-knit, if poor and underserviced, black communities of the past have lost some of their cultural cohesion and distinct identity. However, most blacks retain a high degree of racial pride and a conscious need to retain aspects of black culture as a significant component of their American identity. Because of these desires and needs, black institutions continue to play important roles in the lives of most blacks.

POLITICAL PARTICIPATION

Until the 1960s, black political activity was primarily directed toward the attainment of basic democratic rights. Exclusion of black Americans from voting and office holding meant that blacks had to seek political and civil rights through protest and litigation. The civil rights movement arose out of long-standing grievances and aspirations. It was based on strong networks of local organizations and given a clear focus and direction by articulate leadership. Because most blacks were unable to vote, move freely, or buy and sell property as they wished, their efforts were directed to the objective of attaining these basic rights of citizenship. During the civil rights movement, civic equality and political liberty came to be viewed by increasing percentages of Americans as basic human rights that blacks should enjoy. By the

FIGURE S-4 Reported voter participation as a percentage of the voting-age population, by race.

FIGURE S-5 Black elected officials.

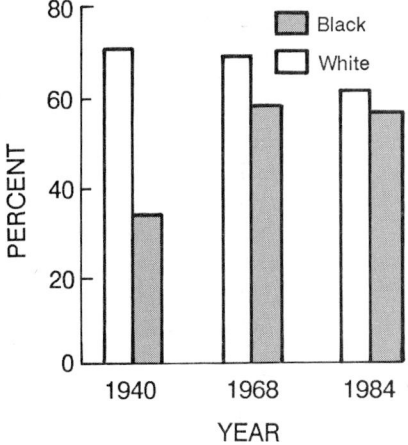

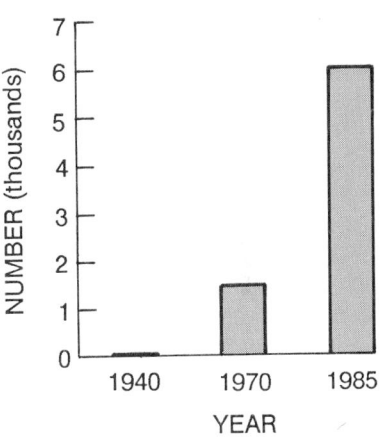

FIGURE S-6 Black national convention delegates, by party.

FIGURE S-7 Black officials and administrators, by level of government.

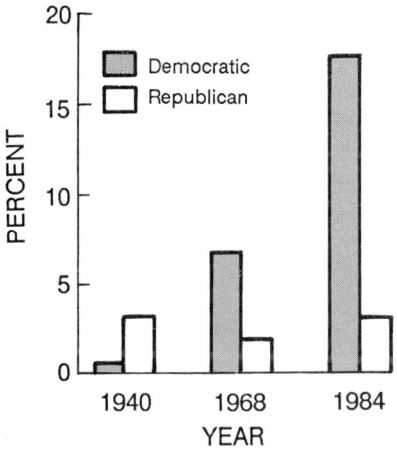

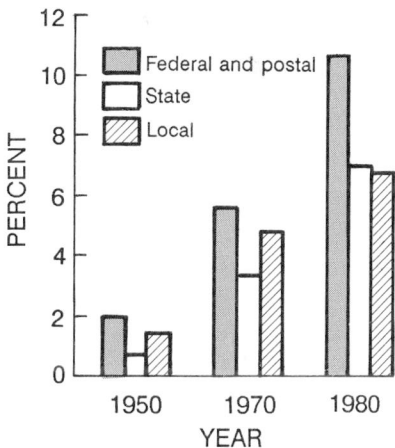

1960s, the federal executive branch and a congressional coalition backed by a sufficient public opinion was finally able to legislate black civil equality.

Active participation by blacks in American political life has had a major impact on their role in the society. Figures S-4 to S-7 highlight some of the effects. The number of black elected officials has risen from a few dozen in 1940 to over 6,800 in 1988. However, blacks comprise only about 1.5 percent of all elected officials. The election of black officials does result in additional hiring and higher salaries for blacks in public-sector jobs and more senior positions for blacks in appointive public office. The black proportion of federal, state, and local public administrators rose from less than 1 percent in 1940 to 8 percent in 1980; even so, it was less than blacks' 13 percent proportion of the U.S. population. As measured by the proportion of delegates to the national party conventions, black participation in the political party organizations has increased dramatically among Democrats since 1940, while black participation in Republican party affairs, after declining during the 1960s and 1970s, has returned to be about the same level as in 1940.

Blacks' desires for political rights were not merely based on abstract principles of equality, but also on the practical fruits of political participation. Blacks sought democratic rights because they believed that direct access to political institutions through voting, lobbying, and office holding would lead to greater material equality between themselves and the rest of society. However, changes in blacks' socioeconomic status, although complex, have not attained levels commensurate to black-white equality with respect to civil rights. But black influence in the political sector has been an important factor in determining many of the important gains that have occurred. In particular, the extensive development of equal opportunity law has improved the status of blacks (as well as that of women and other minorities) in the areas of education, occupations, health care, criminal justice, and business enterprise. Blacks have also benefited from increased public-sector provision of job training, health care, Social Security, and other cash and in-kind benefit programs.

Although political participation has not been the only important determinant of changes in black opportunities, resulting alterations in American politics have had influence in many areas of life. A review of blacks' status shows that increased civil rights have been important in all areas of society.

ECONOMIC STATUS

Changes in labor market conditions and social policies of governments have had many beneficial effects on the economic status of black Americans. Yet the current economic prospects are not good for many blacks. Adverse changes in labor market opportunities and family conditions—falling real wages and employment, increases in one-parent families with one or no working adults—have made conditions especially difficult for those blacks from the most disadvantaged backgrounds. However, among blacks, changes in family structure per se have not been a major cause of continuing high poverty rates since the early 1970s.

Black-white differences are large despite significant improvements in the absolute and relative positions of blacks over the past 50 years. After initial decades of rising relative black economic status, black gains stagnated on many measures after the early 1970s. Lack of progress in important indicators of economic status during the past two decades is largely a consequence of two conflicting trends: while blacks' weekly and hourly wages have risen

FIGURE S-8 Persons below the poverty level, by race.

FIGURE S-9 Per capita income, by race.

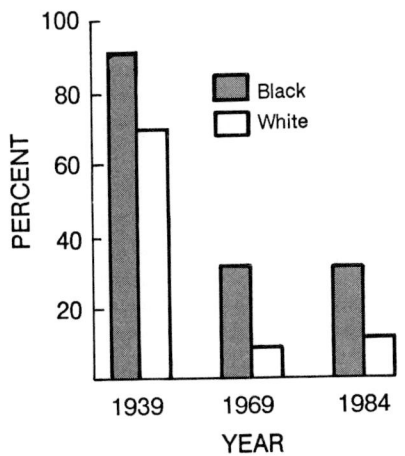

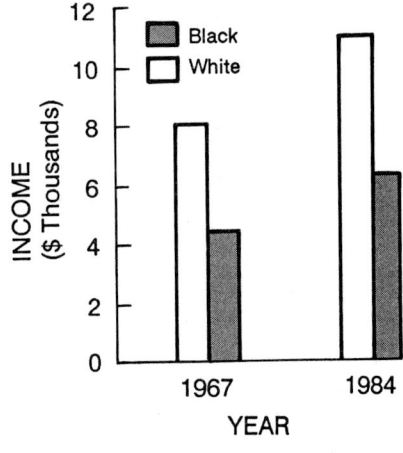

Note: Per capita income is calculated in 1984 constant dollars.

relative to whites, blacks' relative employment rates have deteriorated significantly. Figures S-8 to S-11 present some key data.

In terms of per capita incomes, family incomes, and male workers' earnings, blacks gained relative to whites fairly steadily from 1939 to 1969; measures of relative status peaked in the early to mid-1970s and since have remained stagnant or declined. Women earn much less than men, but the gap between black and white women decreased steadily throughout the period until, by 1984, black women had earnings very close to those of white women. Employment rates of adult black men and women have been falling relative to those of white men and women throughout the period; black unemployment rates remain approximately twice those of white rates. The proportion of working black men and women in white-collar occupations and in managerial and professional positions increased throughout the period, but these gains show signs of slowing in the 1980s.

Uneven change in the average economic position of blacks has been accompanied, especially during the past 25 years, by accentuated differences in status among blacks. An important aspect of the polarization in the incomes of black families has been the growth of female-headed black families since 1960. It is among such families that the incidence of poverty is highest. It is no exaggeration to say that the two most numerically important components of the black class structure have become a lower class dominated by female-headed families and a middle class largely composed of two-parent families. The percentage of both blacks and whites living in households with incomes below the poverty line declined during the 1939–1975 period. But poverty

FIGURE S-10 Employment to population ratios, by race.

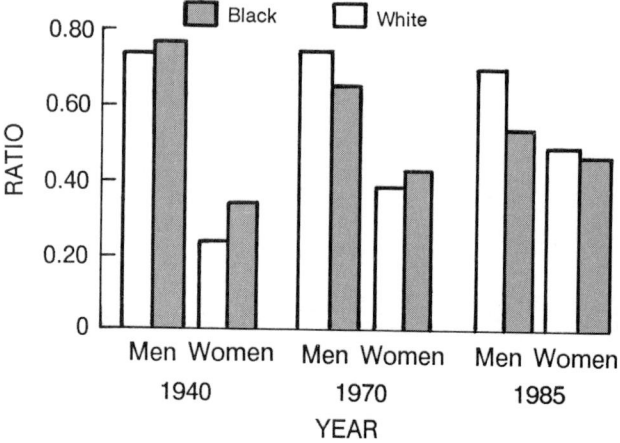

FIGURE S-11 Employed workers holding professional or managerial jobs, by race.

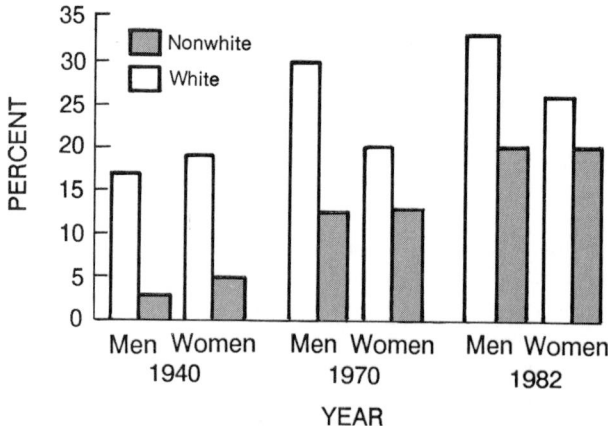

rates have risen in the past decade, and black poverty rates have been 2 to 3 times higher than white rates at all times.

The major developments accounting for black gains in earnings and occupation status from 1939 to 1969 were South-to-North migration and concurrent movement from agricultural to nonagricultural employment, job creation, and national economic growth. After 1965, major factors responsible for improvements in blacks' status have been government policies against discrimination, government incentives for the equal employment opportunity of minorities, general changes in race relations, and higher educational attainment.

SCHOOLING

Substantial progress has been made toward the provision of educational resources to blacks. Yet black and white educational opportunities are not generally equal. Standards of academic performance for teachers and students are not equivalent in schools that serve predominantly black students and those that serve predominantly white students. Nor are equal encouragement and support provided for the educational achievement and attainment of black and white students. Figures S-12, S-13, and S-14 highlight some of the effects of the progress that has been made and the gaps that remain.

Measures of educational outcomes—attainment and achievement—reveal substantial gaps between blacks and whites. Blacks, on average, enter the schools with substantial disadvantages in socioeconomic backgrounds and tested achievement. American schools do not compensate for these disadvantages in background: on average, students leave the schools with black-white gaps not having been appreciably diminished.

There remain persistent and large gaps in the schooling quality and achievement outcomes of education for blacks and whites. At the pinnacle of the educational process, blacks' life opportunities relative to whites' are demonstrated by the fact that the odds that a black high school graduate will enter college within a year of graduation are less than one-half the odds that a white high school graduate will do so. College enrollment rates of high school graduates, after rising sharply since the late 1960s, declined in the mid-1970s; while white enrollment rates have recovered, black rates in the 1980s remain well below those of the 1970s. The proportion of advanced degrees awarded to blacks has also decreased. While we cannot conclude with certainty that the cause has been the decline in (real) financial aid grants to students, other reasonable hypotheses can explain only a negligible component of this change.

Segregation and differential treatment of blacks continue to be widespread in the elementary and secondary schools. We find that school desegregation does not substantially affect the academic performance of white students, but it does modestly improve black performance (in particular, reading). When several key conditions are met, intergroup attitudes and relations improve after schools are desegregated. And desegregation is most likely to reduce racial isolation as well as improve academic and social outcomes for blacks when it is part of a comprehensive and rapid desegregation plan.

Differences in the schooling experienced by black and white students contribute to black-white differences in achievement. These differences are closely tied to teacher behavior; school climate; and the content, quality, and organization of instruction. Early intervention compensatory education programs, such as Head Start, have had positive effects on blacks' educational performance. Among the most recent cohorts to complete their education—people born in the late 1950s and early 1960s—blacks have a median education close to that of whites, 12.6 years, compared with 12.9 years for whites. But a remaining substantial gap in overall

FIGURE S-12 High school graduates aged 25–29, by race.

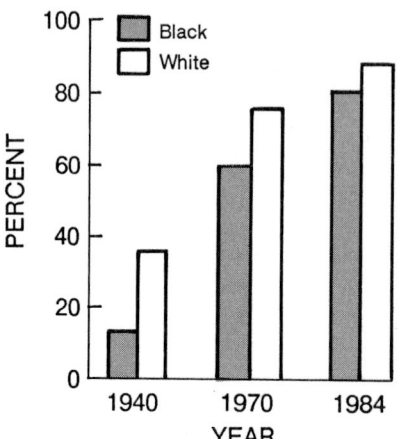

FIGURE S-13 High school graduates enrolled in college, by race.

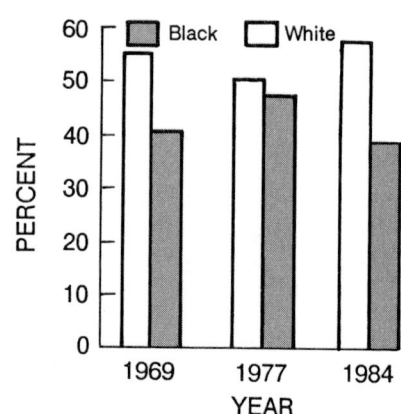

Note: Percentages are smoothed 3-year averages.

FIGURE S-14 College graduates aged 25–29, by race.

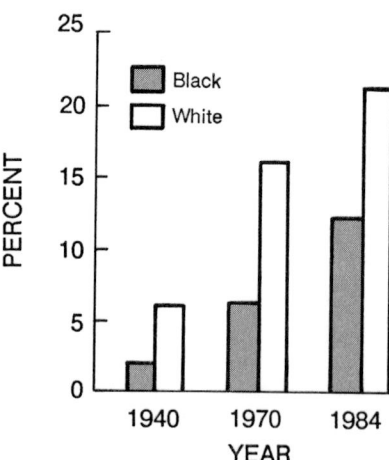

educational attainment is noncompletion: high school dropout rates for blacks are double those for whites.

Changes in academic achievement test scores show that, while black students' average scores remain well below white students' average scores, black performance has improved faster, and black-white differences have become somewhat smaller.

HEALTH

There have been substantial improvements in life expectancy and health status for Americans since 1940. However, overall gains have not been evenly shared. Poor blacks, people on Medicaid, and uninsured groups have unmet needs despite expanded health services. Since 1982, access to health care may be worsening for these groups: 22 percent of blacks and 14 percent of whites under age 65 are not covered by private health insurance or Medicaid.

Persisting wide gaps in the mortality and morbidity of blacks compared to whites remain at all ages except among the oldest old (people 85 and older). Figures S-15, S-16, and S-17 highlight a few aspects of the health status of black Americans. Infant mortality rates have dropped steadily since 1940, for both whites and blacks, but the odds of dying shortly after birth are consistently twice as high for blacks as for whites.

Blacks are underrepresented in the health professions (as compared to their population percentage); this is important since access to care by minorities and the poor increases with the availability of minority providers.

Preventive or remedial interventions could reduce black-white health gaps at each period of the life cycle. Access to early and appropriate prenatal care prevents low birthweight, infant mortality, and infant neurological damage and other morbidity and reduces maternal mortality. Prenatal care for black mothers lags behind that for whites.

Significant improvement in the health status of blacks will also depend on reducing health-damaging personal behaviors such as substance abuse, injuries (accidental and nonaccidental), homicide, and sexual activities that can

FIGURE S-15 Life expectancy at birth, by race.

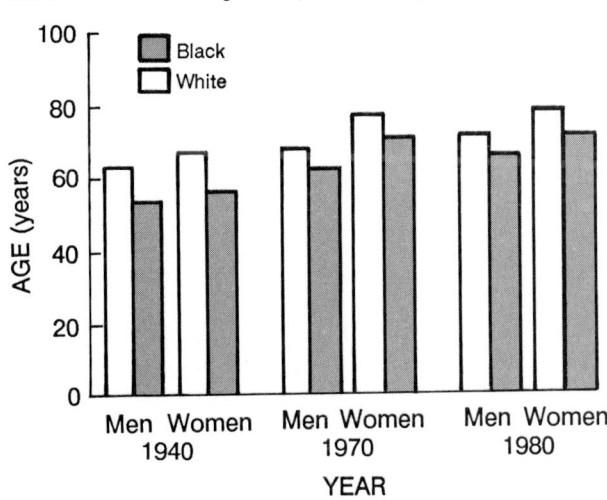

FIGURE S-16 Annual number of physician visits per capita, by race.

FIGURE S-17 Black physicians.

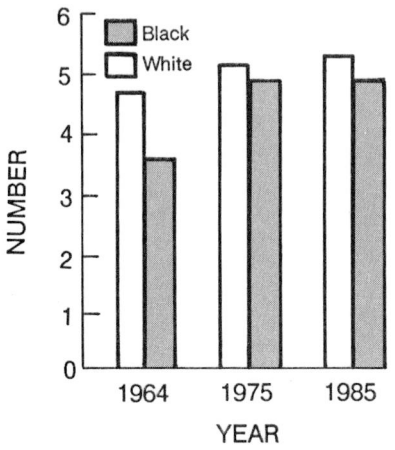

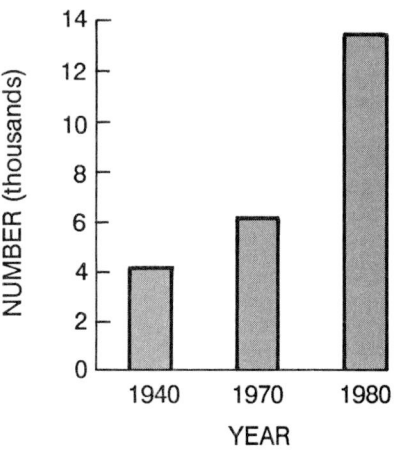

cause ill-timed pregnancy or risk infection with sexually transmitted diseases. Slowing the transmission rate of the acquired immune deficiency syndrome (AIDS) in the black community is critical. This will require preventive strategies tailored to the special needs of intravenous drug users and other groups at high risk for human immunodeficiency virus (HIV) infection. Risky behavior is an increasing health problem among young blacks: for example, the homicide rate is more than 6 times higher for black men than for white men.

In adulthood, the cumulative effects of health disadvantages and delaying medical visits until conditions are serious predispose black adults to higher incidences of chronic illness and disability. Preventive health services as well as assured continuity in management of chronic health conditions would reduce deaths and disability. Poverty and limited bed capacity in care centers, combined with discrimination, pose special problems of access to long-term health care for elderly blacks.

CRIME AND CRIMINAL JUSTICE

Among black Americans, distrust of the criminal justice system is widespread. Historically, discrimination against blacks in arrests and sentencing was ubiquitous. Prior to the 1970s, very few blacks were employed as law enforcement officials, but in the 1980s, the percentage of blacks in police forces has increased to substantial levels. Black representation among attorneys and judges has also increased, although it is not as high as that in the police.

Blacks are arrested, convicted, and imprisoned for criminal offenses at rates much higher than are whites. Currently, blacks account for nearly one-half of all prison inmates in the United States; thus, blacks' representation in prisons is about 4 times their representation in the general population. Compared with the total population, black Americans are disproportionately victims of crime: they are twice as likely to be victims of robbery, vehicle theft, and aggravated assault, and 6 to 7 times as likely to be victims of homicide, the leading cause of death among young black males. Blacks also suffer disproportionately from injuries and economic losses due to criminal actions.

Most black offenders victimize other blacks. But offenders and victims are often in different socioeconomic strata: most offenders are poor; many victims are not. Consequently, middle-income and near-poor blacks have greater economic losses due to criminal acts than the black poor or than whites at any income level.

The role of discrimination in criminal justice has apparently varied substantially from place to place and over time. Some part of the unexplained differences in black-white arrest rates may be due to racial bias and the resulting differential treatment. Current black-white differences in sentencing appear to be due less to overt racial bias than to socioeconomic differences between blacks and whites: people of lower socioeconomic status—regardless of race—receive more severe sentences than people of higher status. An important exception may be bias in sentencing that is related to the race of the victim: criminals whose victims are white are on average punished more severely than those whose victims are black.

As long as there are great disparities in the socioeconomic status of blacks and whites, blacks will continue to be overrepresented in the criminal justice system as victims and offenders. And because of these disparities, the precise degree to which the overrepresentation reflects racial bias cannot be determined.

CHILDREN AND FAMILIES

Changes since the mid-1960s among both blacks and whites have brought higher rates of marital breakup, decreased rates of marriage, rapidly rising proportions of female-headed households, and increasing proportions of children being reared in single-parent families. The changes have been much greater among blacks than among whites. Some characteristics of families are shown in Figures S-18, S-19, and S-20.

Birthrates for both the white and black populations have fallen since the baby boom of the 1950s, and fertility rates have declined for women of all ages. By the mid-1980s, the lifetime fertility rates were similar for black and white women. Contrary to popular myth, birthrates among black teenagers—although still an important problem—have declined significantly during the past two decades.

In 1970, about 18 percent of black families had incomes over $35,000 (1987 constant dollars); by 1986 this proportion had grown to 22 percent. The increase in well-to-do families was matched by an increase in low-income

FIGURE S-18 Children in poverty, by race.

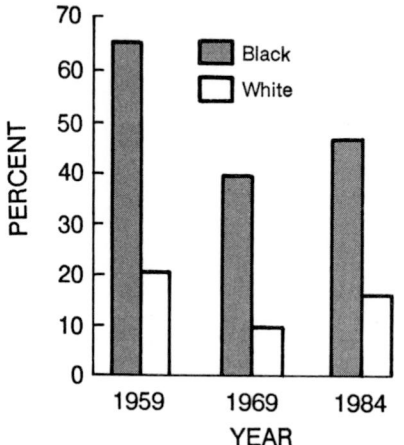

FIGURE S-19 Median family income, by race.

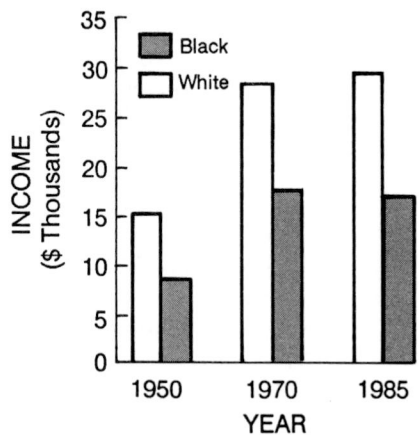

Note: Median family income is calculated in 1985 constant dollars.

FIGURE S-20 Childless women aged 20–24, by race.

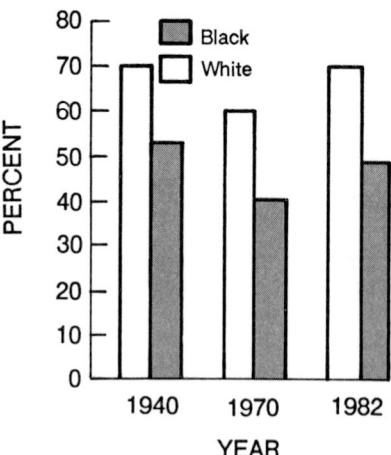

families. During the same 1970–1980 period, the proportion of black families with incomes of less than $10,000 grew from about 26 to 30 percent. After declining during earlier decades, the percentage of black and white children in poverty began to increase in the 1970s. In 1986, 43 percent of black children and 16 percent of white children under age 18 lived in households below the poverty line.

Black and white children are increasingly different with regard to their living arrangements. As we noted above, a majority of black children under age 18 live in families that include their mothers but not their fathers; in contrast, four of every five white children live with both parents. (Although some fathers who are not counted as household members may actually aid in child rearing, there are no data to estimate the number, and it is believed to be small.) In the course of their childhood, 86 percent of black children and 42 percent of white children are likely to spend some time in a single-parent household.

The greater inequality between family types among blacks has important consequences for the welfare of future generations. Black female-headed families were 50 percent of all black families with children in 1985, but had 25 percent of total black family income, while 70 percent of black family income was received by black husband-wife families.

The data and analyses we have examined throw doubt on the validity of the thesis that a culture of poverty is a major cause of long-term poverty. Although cultural factors are important in social behavior, arguments for the existence of unalterable behaviors among the poor are not supported by empirical research. The behaviors that are detrimental to success are often responses to existing social barriers to opportunity. The primary correlates of poverty are macroeconomic conditions of prosperity or recession and changes in family composition. However, increases in female-headed families have had only negligible effects on increasing black poverty rates since the mid-1970s. Importantly, attitudes toward work and the desire to succeed are not very different among the poor and the nonpoor.

Black-white differences in family structures result from a complex set of interrelated factors. The most salient are black-white differences in income and employment, greater (relative) economic independence of black women, and a more limited pool of black men who are good marriage prospects.

THE FUTURE:
ALTERNATIVES AND POLICY IMPLICATIONS

BLACKS' STATUS IN THE NEAR FUTURE

In assessing the status of black Americans, we have asked what roles blacks play in the nation today and what role they are likely to play in the near future. Our conclusion is largely positive, but it is mixed. The great majority of black Americans contribute to the political, economic, and social health of the nation. The typical black adult—like the typical white adult—is a full-time employee or homemaker who pays taxes, votes in public elections, and sends children to school. Blacks make important contributions to all forms of American life, from the sciences and health care, to politics and education, to arts and entertainment.

However, this role is not available to a sizable minority of black—and of a small but growing group of white—Americans. The evidence for this assessment is clear. High school dropout rates among young black adults have risen, and attaining high standards of academic competence seems unavailable to millions of poor black youths attending school systems that are not able to teach them. During the 1980s, thousands of young black men who were not enrolled in school have also not been active participants in the labor market. Many of these men are incarcerated or have dropped out of society into the escape offered by alcohol and drug addiction. And, on the basis of the fertility rates of 1986, 170 of 1,000 black females become mothers before the age of 20, often disrupting or discontinuing their secondary educations. These young mothers are likely to be poor as they establish households, and they will frequently have to receive family assistance benefits. These alarming developments are mirrored by similar, if more modest, trends among whites.

Barring unforeseen events or changes in present conditions—that is, no changes in educational policies and opportunities, no increased income and employment opportunities, and no major national programs to deal directly with the problems of economic dependency—our findings imply several negative developments for blacks in the near future, developments that in turn do not bode well for American society:

• A substantial majority of black Americans will remain contributors to the nation, but improvements in their status relative to whites are likely to slow even more as the rate of increase of the black middle class is likely to decline.

• Approximately one-third of the black population will continue to be poor, and the relative employment and earnings status of black men is likely to deteriorate further.

• Drugs and crime, teenage parenthood, poor educational opportunities, and joblessness will maintain their grip on large numbers of poor and near-poor blacks.

• High rates of residential segregation between blacks and whites will continue.

• The United States is faced with the prospect of continued great inequality between whites and blacks and a continuing division of social status within the black population.

• A growing population of poor and undereducated citizens, disproportionately black and minority, will pose challenges to the nation's abilities to solve the emerging economic and social problems of the twenty-first century.

These short-term projections emerge as important implications of our assessment of the status of black Americans and of black-white relations since 1940. They are especially crucial to the future well-being of the United States, as a common destiny continues to connect black and other Americans. Throughout the five decades covered by this report, all Americans have been affected by the same general social processes: technological change, national and international economic developments, and large population movements. Generally, when conditions have been improving for blacks, they have been improving for the entire population. Yet while the same general factors affect all Americans in similar ways, blacks—who as a group still carry many of the effects of systematic discrimination and segregation—are especially sensitive both to changes in the national economy and to changes in public policies.

RESIDENTIAL SEGREGATION

Time alone does not resolve America's racial problems. When the status of blacks has improved, it has not been simply because time has passed. Two reasons for the continuing exclusion of many blacks from the economic mainstream are persisting discriminatory barriers and the residential concentration of poor blacks. It is therefore appropriate to consider the future prospects for reducing current levels of black residential separation.

Black-white residential segregation declined more in the 1970s than in previous decades. Despite these changes, however, levels of black-white segregation remain very high. Considering the 16 metropolitan areas that had the largest black populations in 1980 and using an index for which 100 means all blacks and all whites live in distinct racially homogeneous neighborhoods and zero if all people are randomly distributed, the average index value for black-white residential segregation was about 80. This reflects a drop of about 6 points, on average, from the segregation level of 1970. In contrast, one can compare the indices for Hispanic and Asian-Americans, who entered many metropolitan areas in large numbers during the 1970s. One might expect them to be highly segregated from whites, but their segregation indices average about 45 points. If the historically high 1970s pace of reduction in black-white segregation were to persist, it would take about 60 years for the black-white index to fall to the values currently observed for Hispanic and Asian-Americans.

INCOME AND POVERTY

Between 1940 and 1974, poverty as officially measured by cash income declined sharply. The percentage of blacks living in poor households fell from 92 percent in 1939 to 30 percent in 1974; among whites, the change was from 65 to 9 percent. If that trend had continued, the percentage of poor people in the year 2000 would be about 1 percent among whites and

9 percent among blacks. However, the trends toward lower poverty rates came to an end in the early 1970s; since 1974 rates have stagnated or even increased. If the post-1974 trend is extrapolated to the year 2000, the poverty rate among blacks will be about 32 percent and the rate among whites about 15 percent. These are approximately the rates of the late 1960s. Of course such predictions are tentative, since economic conditions or government policies could change.

A similar picture results from the projection of current trends in the incomes of black families vis-à-vis those of white families. When the Bureau of the Census first measured family incomes in 1947, blacks' median incomes were 51 percent of whites'. During the years of economic expansion and civil rights legislation, the status of blacks improved: by 1974, the median income of black families was 62 percent that of white families. A projection of 1947–1974 trends to the year 2000 shows black families with median income about 70 percent of whites. But in fact the median income of black families has not gone up quite as rapidly as that of whites in the past 15 years. Projection of the 1974–1986 trend implies that in the year 2000, the median income of black families would be 54 percent of those of white families—the same as that in 1960.

During the decades from the 1940s through the 1970s, the hourly wage rates and annual earnings of employed black men rose more rapidly than those of white men. Between 1960 and 1980, the relative annual earnings of black men increased from 49 percent of those of white men to 64 percent.

With respect to the relative annual earnings of men aged 25–64, the trend of improvement ended in the 1980s. Between 1960 and 1980, the black/white ratio rose from 49 to 64 percent, but it then fell back to 62 percent by 1987. This reversal arose from an increasing black-white difference in hours of employment. In 1960, black men averaged annually about 8 fewer hours of work per week than white men; this difference declined to about 5 hours per week in 1980, but it then moved up to 7 hours in 1987. If these trends continue to the year 2000, the decrease in black men's employment will offset their gains in hourly wage rates, and the average annual earnings of black men will be 58 percent those of white men, the level observed in the early 1970s.

POLICY ALTERNATIVES

It was not part of the mandate of this committee to make specific recommendations for public policy. It is, however, an implication of our analyses that such rapid progress as that attained by black Americans in the 1960s will not be attainable in the immediate future without both public and private programs to increase opportunities and to reduce race-connected constraints and disadvantages. On the basis of the findings and analyses of this study, we have identified four areas of national life in which there are major options for constructive social policies to improve opportunities for disadvantaged Americans and especially to reduce impediments to black advancement:

- Provision of education, health care, and other services to enhance people's skills and productive capabilities;
    - Facilitation of national economic growth and full employment;
    - Reduction of discrimination and involuntary segregation; and
- Development and reform of income-maintenance and other family assistance social welfare programs to avoid long-term poverty.

Each type of policy contains many complex possibilities. Feasible alternatives necessarily must be developed through the political processes by which collective decisions are made. Here we wish only to note some salient options.

Several specific policy interventions have been effective in promoting black advancement and greater opportunities for all Americans. Most successful have been employment and training programs such as the Job Corps; early intervention and other compensatory education programs such as Head Start; governmental financial aid for postsecondary education; increased access to health care, particularly for pre- and postnatal clinical service for low-income women; and greater health insurance coverage for all poor and near-poor people. These specific policy interventions have been shown to work and to be beneficial to the nation. Improvements in program design are surely possible and should be given the highest priority by policy makers and practitioners.

The one issue that stands out above all others in this study is that of bringing the black population into gainful full employment. This is a major task for public policy. Economic opportunity alone will not solve all problems, of course, but it is the essential ground for other constructive developments. All the evidence reviewed in this report points to the central importance of jobs for men and women at pay levels that permit families to live above the poverty line.

Macroeconomic growth and reduced joblessness create favorable conditions, but they do not remove some crucial barriers that exist for blacks. Improvement depends also on active promotion and vigorous enforcement of antidiscrimination laws and administrative measures to reduce discrimination in employment, education, and housing. Carefully designed programs intended to increase black participation in social institutions can be useful in counteracting the persisting effects of past exclusion, discrimination, and segregation. Both the removal of barriers and compensatory programs are needed for full equality of opportunity. Persistent segregation in neighborhoods and schools, for example, are barriers to equal opportunity, and they cannot be ameliorated without large-scale efforts—national, state, and local.

Economic growth and removal of barriers create many opportunities. To take advantage of such opportunities, however, black Americans must further develop their education, skills, health, and other "human capital." The efforts of individuals and of voluntary associations and groups are likely to increase in the near term. But these efforts can be fully effective only when public programs provide access to job training and education for children and youths from low-income families. The decreases in black college enrollment in the late 1970s and 1980s that followed reductions in federal financial aid to students attest to the importance of such support.

This brings us to the fourth type of social policy on our list: policies to reduce extreme and long-term poverty. Income-maintenance and family assistance programs have developed to meet residual problems not solved by general economic growth and equal opportunity measures. For example, although better education and job training programs have a potential for helping to place workers into available jobs, they will not overcome all the barriers that keep many single mothers and men out of the labor force.

Furthermore, the provision of employment is not enough, by itself, to raise all families out of poverty. Three-fourths of recipients of family assistance and other benefits are unable to find work at wages sufficient to produce incomes above the poverty level even if they worked yearlong at full-time jobs. To reduce the extreme poverty of such families—primarily mothers and children in female-headed households—thus requires supplementary programs and changes in tax policies and child support programs.[1]

Programs specifically aimed at the reduction of poverty may take two contrasting approaches: a single comprehensive program such as the negative income tax or a set of programs directed to different categories of individuals and families, such as child allowances, Social Security for the aged, special aid for the ill and disabled, and so on. The latter approach characterizes the present situation in the United States. Although this diversity is often criticized, plausible arguments can be advanced that the more differentiated approach can be made both more efficient and politically feasible.

BLACK PERSPECTIVES

The historical record of black people in America shows a persisting tension between the goals of social separation from whites and inclusion within the broader society. This tension differs from—although it has some similarities to—the tension between cultural assimilation and pluralism among groups of different national origins. Black Americans have long debated the merits of integrated participation with whites as opposed to the development of autonomous organizations and communities.

In the past, segregation and discrimination helped to create strong currents of so-called "black nationalism," illustrated in separatist politics as well as in cultural autonomy movements (Chapters 3–5). But blacks' political and economic interdependence with white Americans is very great and is growing. Our data show that black separatism is not a dominant orientation. The likelihood appears low that separatism will be important in the near future,

---

1. The Family Support Act of 1988 was passed by Congress late in the year, and we were not able to assess its likely effects.

with the exception of some use of separatist ideology in political debate. Yet there is much evidence that racial identities and interests are likely to remain significant in political affairs, and in public life generally, for the foreseeable future. We do not find convincing evidence that such identities and interests are diminishing in importance.

Full assimilation of blacks in a "color-blind" society is unlikely in any foreseeable future. Existing social and economic separation, very low rates of intermarriage, and group preferences and images ensure the continued existence of distinct racial groups. It does not mean a continuation of discrimination in public life, but it does mean that black Americans will claim acceptance and equality on their own terms. Although a "color-blind" society is not foreseen, integrated participation in public affairs is becoming more acceptable. Indeed, political and civic coalitions and joint collective activities are now common. As shown in Chapters 4 and 5, a high degree of cooperation and coalition between blacks and whites has been and is now important on selective issues of legislative and administrative politics. Coalitions with other racial and ethnic minorities will likely grow in importance as such minorities become an increasing proportion of the total citizenry.

We cannot exclude the possibility of confrontation and violence. The urban revolts and civil disorders of the 1960s and later are still vividly present in memory; the 1980s had barely begun when blacks in Miami exploded in anger and dissatisfaction. The ingredients are there: large populations of jobless youths, an extensive sense of relative deprivation and injustice, distrust of the legal system, frequently abrasive police-community relations, highly visible inequalities, extreme concentrations of poverty, and great racial awareness. Such conditions sometimes produce apathy when disadvantaged persons feel that their situation is hopeless. But the surface calm can disappear very quickly. A specific source of possible social turbulence is widespread dissatisfaction with the operation of the criminal justice system, which is evident among black Americans. The allegations of bias are two sided: that law enforcement officials, judicial proceedings, and the correctional system treat blacks with undue harshness, and that the system is too lenient with whites who commit criminal offenses against blacks. Given the high likelihood that young urban males, blacks and whites, will continue on occasion to find themselves in confrontational situations, and given the continuing high incidence of street crime, it is realistic to expect future episodes of racial violence, followed by concentrated pressures on legal and correctional institutions to deal with alleged racial bias.

CONCLUSION

After our intensive review, the committee has a concluding reflection on the wider implications of the findings. We believe it is consistent with the research data and the best available historical understandings of how American society functions.

Every society to survive has to adapt to its environment and maintain its resources over time. It must cope with the basic economic problem—the efficient allocation of scarce resources—as well as with its external relations to other societies. Every society must also develop practical arrangements for the internal distribution of power, economic goods, and social prestige and respect. Finally, societies over the long term must safeguard their own legitimacy and historical meaning. These latter tasks of social integration and cultural maintenance tend to be discounted and neglected in a task-oriented society that focuses attention on short-run payoffs. In the United States of the coming decades, any agenda for these basic needs will have to give high priority to dealing with the fissures that have been created by the history of relations among black and white Americans. Our review leads us to believe that now is an appropriate time for a serious national effort to grasp the means at hand to accomplish this vital assignment.

1

OVERVIEW:

THEN AND NOW

Ellis Wilson
Field Workers (no date)
Oil on masonite
National Museum of American Art, Smithsonian Institution,
Gift of the Harmon Foundation

In 1940, one-tenth of the U.S. population, 13 million black Americans, were almost completely excluded from the political system, confined to the least prosperous sectors of the economy, and geographically and socially segregated. One-half of all blacks lived in the rural South, and another one-fourth lived elsewhere in the South. Among blacks of voting age in the South, fewer than 1 in 20 were registered to vote. Blacks of working age were overwhelmingly concentrated in agriculture and domestic service. For all blacks, their expected life span of 54 years was very short by modern standards.

By 1985, the nation's 30 million blacks constituted one-eighth of the U.S. population, and enormous changes had occurred in their geographic, economic, political, and health status. Blacks were geographically dispersed regionally, although many were concentrated in inner cities under conditions of high unemployment and poverty. Agriculture was an insignificant employer of blacks; although disproportionately concentrated in lower paying jobs, blacks were generally dispersed throughout American industry, some in prestigious occupations. Only a little more than 1 percent of all elected officials were black, but 63 percent of the nation's 6,000 black officials had been elected in the South. The life expectancy of blacks was 70 years.

During the span of these four and one-half decades, five major events transformed race relations in America. First and most fundamental, three decades of South-North and rural-urban migration by the black population produced conditions leading to profound changes in blacks' social status. Second, concurrent with this migration, the civil rights revolution moved blacks toward full citizenship rights; perhaps more than any single event, this revolution produced important changes in the nation's political and educational institutions. Third, during World War II and for 25 years afterward, the U.S. economy grew at an unprecedented high and sustained rate; this sustained economic growth facilitated efforts to improve blacks' status throughout society. Fourth, during the early 1970s, the rate of economic growth slowed, just as 30 years of black migration came to a halt. Subsequently, improvement in the status of blacks was significantly slowed. The fifth event, like the first, was demographic. Rapid changes in the family living arrangements of children, beginning in the 1960s, have split most of the black population into two groups: those living in families with one adult head—overwhelmingly poor—and those living in families with two adult heads—largely middle income.

The above major events dramatically altered American society. The social changes that have most affected the lives of blacks have invariably been directly or indirectly due to underlying conditions that have had important effects for all Americans. Thus, a great urbanization and suburbanization of the entire American population accompanied black migration; the civil rights movement revolutionized American institutions, not just black ones; changing economic conditions have affected the well-being of all Americans; and while changes in family composition have not been nearly as significant among whites as among blacks, general changes in family structure have been consequential and in similar directions.

To an extent not always fully appreciated, social and material changes for black Americans have usually followed from conditions that have had important effects on all Americans. Gains for blacks often lag behind gains for other groups when social conditions improve, and blacks frequently suffer losses first when conditions worsen. Thus, while blacks may be gaining or losing relative to whites during any particular period, the absolute status of both groups has usually been moving in a similar direction. Improvements in the health and educational status of white Americans during the 1940s and 1950s were followed by improvements among blacks. Now that increasing poverty rates in the United States may indicate greater material stratification among Americans, it is not surprising that greater inequality among blacks is occurring and that many blacks appear to be stuck in a cycle of poverty. In these senses, blacks and all Americans living in this vast society face a common destiny.

CHANGE AND CONTINUITY IN
BLACK-WHITE STATUS SINCE 1940

It is difficult for Americans who are too young to recall World War II to imagine the status of black Americans in 1940—the baseline year for this report—or to visualize the state of black-white relations as the decade of the Great Depression had just ended. In 1940, when it was about to engage in a great war against nations advocating racism, the United States was itself a society in which racial inequalities were enormous, and black people were essentially excluded from political power and from full participation in public facilities and community life. The black population of the United States, even after large migrations to the North, was still concentrated in the South: some 77 percent lived in 13 southern states. The majority of black people, 51 percent nationally, were in rural areas. Although their education had been increasing, blacks on average received far less schooling than whites, and black pupils attended segregated schools in all southern states and in most northern ones. The incomes of blacks in 1939 were just 39 percent of those of whites. Racial discrimination and segregation were pervasive, rigid, and institutionalized in law and practice. In the South, blacks were almost totally without political voice.

These conditions and changes over time can be described by comparing the status of all blacks born in a given year (a birth cohort) to the status of black cohorts born at successive 10-year intervals. Using a few general measures—expected life span, electoral participation, educational attainment, and lifetime earnings—we describe the comparative status of several cohorts at age 25.

In general, significant improvements have occurred for all cohorts born in 1914 through 1959. For both blacks and whites, the quality of life, as measured by those indices, has improved appreciably. This improvement is true both in absolute terms—blacks born 30 years ago fare much better than did blacks born 75 years ago—and in relative terms—blacks born 30 years ago also compare more favorably with whites of their age than blacks born 75 years ago compare with whites of their age.

In addition to overall comparisons, comparing 10-year birth cohorts allows us to examine how uniform or disparate improvement has been over time. Here the picture presented is less favorable than that suggested by a simple comparison of the first (1914) and last (1959) birth cohorts. Improvement has been much more impressive for cohorts born in the early to middle part of the period than for those born most recently. And in one important measure of status, expected lifetime earnings of men, the earlier trend of increasing status across cohorts has recently been reversed.

THE BASELINE COHORT

Black Americans who were 25 years old in 1939 were born into a society very different from the nation we know in the 1980s. Blacks born in 1914 were in many cases no more than two or three generations removed from slavery. The consequences of this fact still loomed large in their lives and the lives of their future children. American slaves had been overwhelmingly a southern agricultural people, and in 1914 almost 9 of every 10 black Americans lived in a southern state, and more than 6 of them were in rural areas; among white Americans, the corresponding numbers were 1 of 4 and 4 of 10.

This highly rural society had significant implications for life prospects. The

..FIGURE 1-1   High school graduates aged 25, by race.

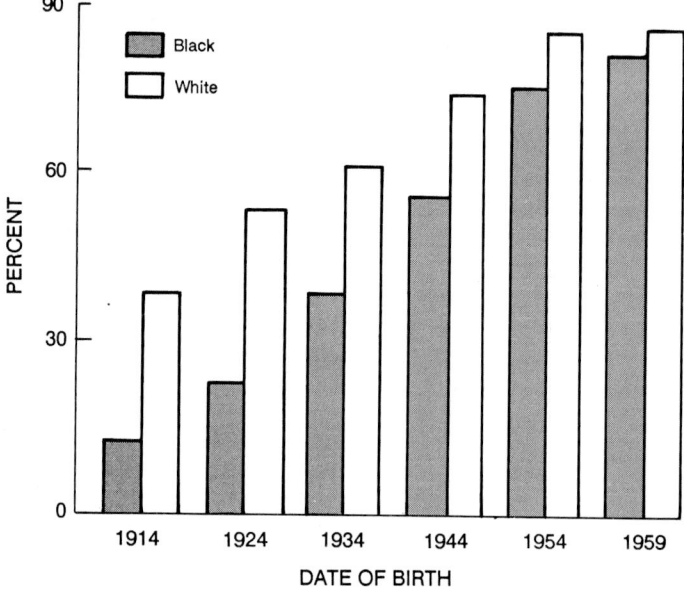

Source: Data from decennial censuses and Current Population Surveys.

FIGURE 1-2   College graduates aged 25, by race.

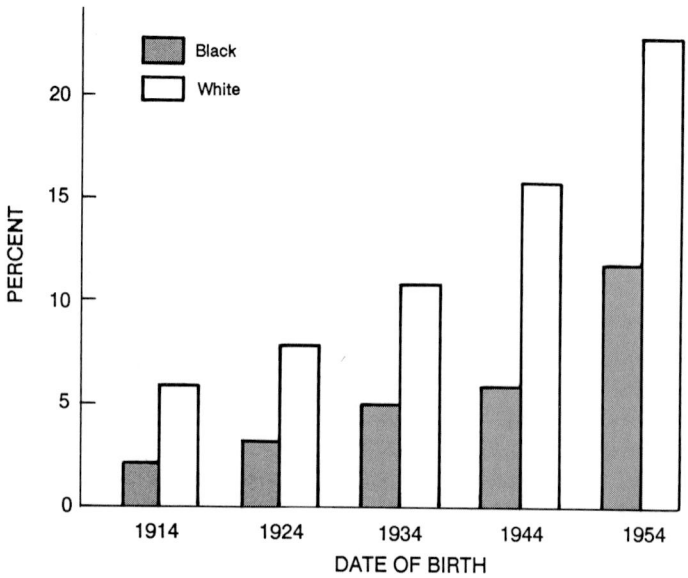

Source: Data from decennial censuses and Current Population Surveys.

FIGURE 1-3   Median lifetime earnings of men after age 25, by race.

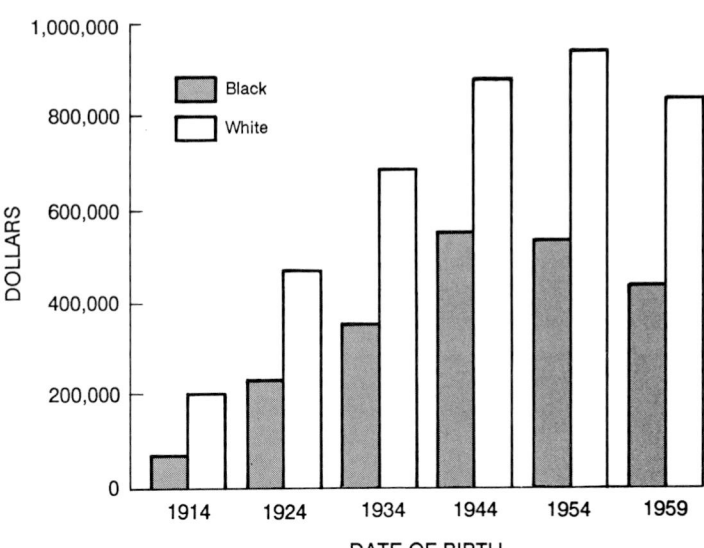

Notes: Earnings are calculated in 1984 constant dollars. The median is the midpoint of the distribution; one-half of all earnings are above the median, and one-half are below it. See Note at the end of this chapter for details of the calculation.

educational opportunities for southerners in particular, and black southerners more especially, were driven by the minimal educational requirements of the cotton, sugar, and tobacco industries. During the 1920s, when this birth cohort was schooled, a black in the South could expect to attend school about two-thirds as many days a year as a white (Welch, 1973:900). He or she could also expect to be a student for a significantly shorter number of years. A black born in 1914 had, at 25 years of age, a 12 percent chance of having completed high school and a 2 percent chance of being a college graduate; in comparison, 25-year-old whites in 1939 had a 38 percent chance of having completed high school and a 6 percent chance of being a college graduate (see Figures 1-1 and 1-2).

At age 25, black males born in 1914 had expected future median lifetime earnings equal to $71,000 (calculated in 1984 constant dollars); this amounted to 36 percent of the expected lifetime median earnings of a white male of the same cohort (see Figure 1-3; see Note at the end of this chaper for details of the calculation). Because the majority of both black and white women had no reported labor market earnings during a given year, it would be meaningless to estimate lifetime median earnings for females.

The political and civil environment in which this cohort of whites and blacks lived is succinctly described by the fact that in 1940, less than 1 of 20 blacks of voting age were registered to vote in the South. Nationwide, just

FIGURE 1-4 Self-reported voter turnout, by race, 1940–1984.

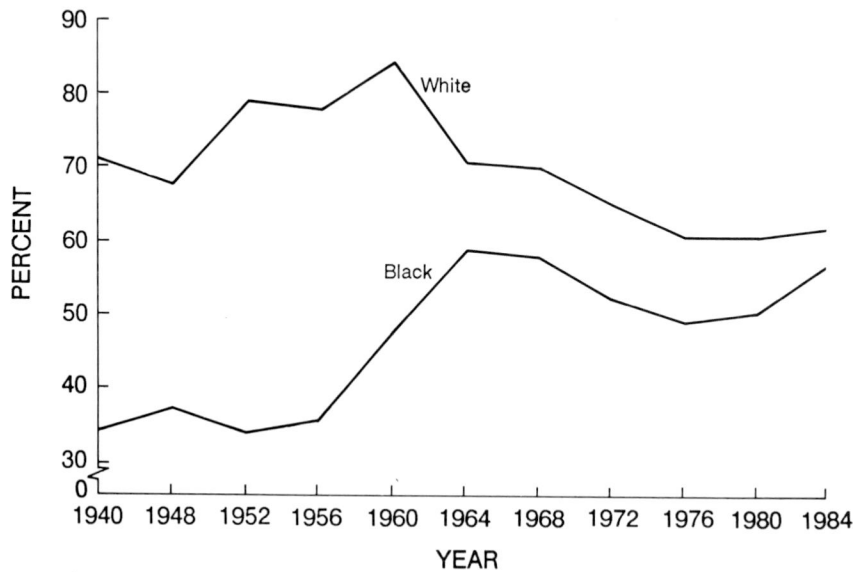

Source: Data from decennial censuses and Current Population Surveys.

1 of 3 blacks of eligible age reported voting in the 1940 presidential election; this compared with a reported voter turnout rate of 7 of 10 among whites (see Figure 1-4).

Living under these circumstances, with minimal education and very poor earnings, health conditions were often hazardous. Black men of the 1914 cohort who reached age 25 could expect to live to age 61, and black women could expect to reach age 63; white men of that cohort who were alive in 1939 could expect to live until age 68 and white women to age 72 (see Figure 1-5).

Under any measuring rod, the socioeconomic status of the black population born in 1914 was very low in 1939. Social relationships with whites in the South emphasized blacks' subordinate position. A little more than 10 years later, conditions were little improved. Earl Warren, chief justice of the Supreme Court, described the situation of blacks in the South during the early 1950s in the following terms (Warren, 1973:20–21):

> They could not live where they desired; they could not work where white people worked, except in menial positions. . . . They could not use the same restrooms, drinking fountains, or telephone booths. They could not eat in the same restaurants, sleep in the same hotels, be treated in the same hospitals. . . .
> They could not attend the same public schools. . . . They were bused for hours each day to inferior and crowded schools where there were unoccu-

FIGURE 1-5 Total life expectancy for (a) males and (b) females aged 25, by race.

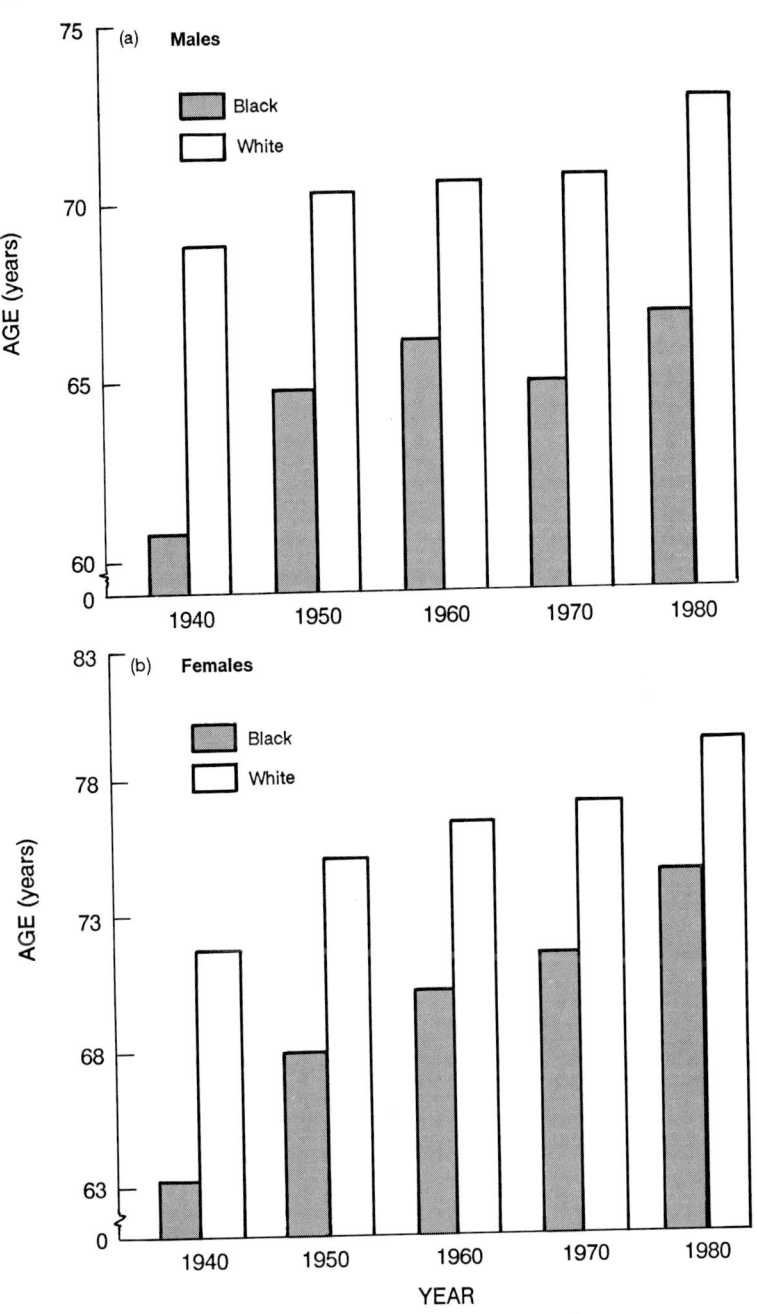

Source: Data from decennial censuses and Current Population Surveys.

pied white school rooms in proximity to where they lived. They were denied admission to any university or college attended by whites, whether public or private.

They were denied the right to sit on juries even when their own lives, freedom, or property rights were involved. . . .

They were segregated on buses, street cars, trains, ships, and airplanes and at terminals of all kinds. They were not allowed to vote.

This institutionalized segregation and discrimination appeared to many Americans to be an entrenched system immune to change.

THE MOST RECENT COHORT

Change did occur, although it was slow and uneven. Change also occurred against great resistance (see Chapters 2–5). By the mid-1970s, the old system of legally enforced segregation had been dismantled; black voting and office holding had increased; average black incomes had grown both absolutely and relative to white incomes; and educational levels had risen. In addition, white Americans had come to accept the principle of equal treatment in law, politics, education, public accommodations, and, to a lesser extent, in housing. However, whites were less prepared to affirm policies intended to implement that principle (see Chapter 3).

Change has not been complete. Many whites continue to resist equal treatment of blacks; evidence of widespread discrimination is still found in the 1980s; and negative stereotyping, although much diminished, has not disappeared. The data show that even though black and white Americans share many important beliefs and values, there remain crucial differences in their respective perceptions of the history and present state of black-white relations. Intense public debate continues about the actual status of black Americans and about public policies aimed at affecting that status.

These changes were reflected in the comparative social status of the last cohort at age 25 (born in 1959) in our study. A black born in 1959 became a member of a rapidly relocating population. Blacks residing in the South were 60 percent of all blacks, and 27 percent of blacks lived in rural areas; for white Americans, 27 and 30 percent were the comparable numbers. These regional and rural-urban origins, when compared with the 1914 cohorts, signify the great urbanization of the American population during the past 75 years. Corresponding changes in life chances are evident.

The likelihood that a black American born in 1959 had completed high school by age 25 (1984) was 81 percent. This was nearly 7 times the likelihood that a black born in 1914 had completed high school by age 25. The difference between black and white high school graduation rates had fallen 21 percentage points so that black-white rates were much closer for the 1959 cohort than for the 1914 cohort (see Figure 1-1). Chances for college graduation had also improved significantly. The college graduation rate of the 1959 black cohort was also 7 times that of blacks born 45 years earlier (see

Figure 1-2). However, the black-white difference in college graduation had not decreased comparably.

Changes in the labor market opportunities available to blacks are illustrated by the fact that the median earnings of $71,000 that black men born in 1914 could expect to earn over their lifetimes after age 25 had grown by a factor of 6 to $427,000 for black men born in 1959. Yet, while the relative expected lifetime earnings of black men had risen 15 percentage points, black mens' expected median lifetime earnings were one-half that of white men of the same age cohort, a small improvement over 45 years (see Figure 1-3). Black political freedoms had been greatly altered. By 1984, 56 percent of eligible blacks reported voting in the presidential election.

The expected life spans of 25-year-old black women and men in 1980 were much greater than the expected life spans of 25-year-old blacks in 1939. For this general measure of overall life conditions, blacks born in 1959 compared much more favorably with corresponding whites (see Figure 1-5).

UNEVEN CHANGES

With the important exception of men's lifetime earnings, comparisons between the first and last cohorts show a tremendous amount of improvement in the status of black Americans over the 45-year period. However, change has been very uneven, across age cohorts as well as across measures of status. This conclusion is clearly illustrated by examining changes in educational and earnings status. As shown in Figure 1-3, expected lifetime earnings is one measure for which change in the status of cohorts has not been one of continuing improvement. For both black and white males, cohorts born in 1959 have lower expected lifetime earnings than an earlier cohort.

Among blacks, increases in lifetime expected earnings were much greater for the earliest cohorts—those whose expected earnings were calculated on the basis of the economic situation existing in the decades of the 1940s, 1950s, and 1960s. Black men born in 1924 had expected lifetime earnings 3.28 times higher than those of black men born 10 years earlier. Blacks born in 1934 and 1944 could expect lifetime earnings 1.49 and 1.54 times higher, respectively, than the earnings of the black cohort born 10 years earlier. On the basis of the economic situation in 1979, however, the cohort born in 1954 has a lower expectation of lifetime earnings than the previous cohort: 0.97 times that of the cohort born in 1944. Prospects for the 1959 cohort appear to be even worse.

The earnings data tell a similar story for the status of black men relative to white men. The ratio of black-to-white expected lifetime median earnings rose 14 percentage points between the 1914 and 1924 birth cohorts, rose 1 point between the 1924 and 1934 cohorts, increased 11 points between the 1934 and 1944 cohorts, and fell 6 points between the 1944 and 1954 cohorts. Again, this deterioration in cohort status is continuing with the 1959 group, as the black/white ratio of expected lifetime earnings of the

1959 cohort is the same as that of the 1934 cohort. Thus, although the economic environment has deteriorated for whites and blacks, the status of black men has been more affected. This deterioration in the earnings position of black men is primarily due to the weak performance of the economy during the 1970s (see Chapter 6).

Changes in the educational status of cohorts do not follow a pattern similar to that in earnings. The educational attainment of blacks follows a path of consistent improvement across successive cohorts. However, black-white differences in the likelihood of high school and college graduation do not follow a consistent pattern of improvement (see Figures 1-1 and 1-2).

Every cohort of blacks had greater rates of graduation from high school and college than those of any previous cohort. In addition, with the exception of the 1944 cohort's likelihood of graduating from college, the increase in the likelihood of graduation was greater than that of any previous cohort. However, because the educational attainment of whites also increased, sometimes at faster rates than that of blacks, the differences in educational attainment probabilities did not always narrow between cohorts.

Interestingly, the changes in educational differences between whites and blacks within cohorts do not match changes in earnings. For example, the 1924 cohort of black men had the greatest gain in relative expected lifetime earnings, but this was the only cohort that lost ground to whites in the likelihood of graduating from high school. Black-white differences in the likelihood of graduating from college actually increased with each successive cohort except for the men born in 1959, yet this group has suffered most in terms of its relative earnings.

In general, changes in earnings status are quite different from the overall steady increase in black status indicated by measures such as political participation and life expectancy. The 1939–1984 period, during which each of the birth cohorts in our study reached maturity, has seen steady increases in the regional dispersion of blacks, their educational attainment, and their life expectancy. That the earnings status of males has not been consonant is a finding of particular concern (see Chapter 6). This brief descriptive survey of changes in selected measures of blacks' status does not do justice to the broad and varied findings discussed in this report. However, even this short discussion points out some important issues that emerge in the more detailed analyses.

The patterns of change displayed in the demographic data reflect two basic sets of conditions in American life. The changes in life expectancy, education, real earnings, and political participation were based on macrolevel changes in economic productivity, scientific and technical advances, and increased provision of public opportunities and services. These things affected all Americans. The uneven changes across black cohorts reflect both these general conditions and the special legacy of segregation and discrimination as it was altered during the decades after 1939.

The general conclusion that thus emerges from our survey is that the status of black Americans is especially sensitive both to changes in the national economy and to changes in public policies. This condition is characteristic of a minority population that still carries the effects of long-term discrimination and segregation.

This report may come at an opportune time in the nation's history. The great social, economic, and legal changes of the 1960s—the civil rights movement, sustained economic growth, and new legal and political policies—are two decades in the past. Since the mid-1970s, many signs of stagnation or even retrogression have appeared in some important measures of income, health, education, and conditions of black community and family life: increased poverty, a decrease in college enrollment of blacks, an increased proportion of households headed by poor single women, and continuing high unemployment of both men and women. After a decade and a half of devoting great attention but little pragmatic action to these conditions, they have reached a critical stage. Our review leads us to think that now is an appropriate time for a serious national effort to find the practical means to change those conditions.

DATA, FINDINGS, AND INTERPRETATIONS: CONCEPTS AND METHODS

What are the positions of black people with respect to various measures of status in American society? What is the current status of black-white relations? How do blacks and whites perceive their relative social positions? What changes have occurred in economic position, health, education, political participation, residence, civil rights, community associations, self-conceptions, and attitudes? The subsequent chapters report detailed findings and conclusions as they pertain to these deceptively simple questions. Almost all social indicators lead us to conclude that contemporary relations between blacks and whites involve more subtle and complicated behavior than did such relations in the past. As a result, an assessment of black status is more difficult than in earlier decades.

We aim to avoid oversimplification of complex findings and to be even-handed in presenting differing interpretations of data. These objectives may lead to a text that disappoints readers who want simple answers and conclusions, but no other approach will do justice to the realities of American society. Nonetheless, the report is not restricted to a purely descriptive presentation of the evidence. We attempt, whenever the data are sufficient, to give an analysis of causes and of likely implications for social policy.

We had the task of sorting out and evaluating a large set of diverse measures and indicators of conditions and their changes. The report documents numerous scientific challenges confronted by this task. First, at the most elementary level, there is the sheer absence of vital pieces of information. The data necessary for thorough analysis of what is happening to the nation often are not collected. We have had to cope with gaps and other inadequacies in the data, even for elementary descriptive tasks.

Even when data do exist, many of the most interesting questions involve quite difficult problems of scientific inference. For example, how does one estimate the outcomes of political participation? Conclusions about changes in the economic status of blacks are strongly influenced by choices of definitions and measures. What factors should be considered in an evaluation of the fairness of the nation's criminal justice system? Hundreds of such choices underlie the text that follows.

For understanding the why of changes such as those we discuss, it is often important to have longitudinal information—measurements in the same units over time—because correlations based on cross-sectional data are tricky to analyze and often misleading. There is also the challenge of measurement and modeling in order to draw conclusions. A great deal has been learned about these methods in the past decade, but there is a long way to go.

This study involves many important dilemmas with regard to values, ethics, and relationships between scientific analysis and social policy. The facts never speak for themselves in any field. There is no way of avoiding value-laden choices. Our conclusions concerning a number of questions will matter to many people. For example:

• Have the educational opportunities available to black people improved? Have public policies had important effects?
• Has discrimination in the workplace decreased? Can equal employment opportunity be left to market forces?
• Has segregation in housing and residential areas decreased?
• What has happened to marriage and family institutions among black Americans? What are the causes of change?

Each of these questions is marked by active debate, many different views, high political interest, and strong feelings. This report aims to provide factually based clarification of certain important national public concerns.

STUDY METHODS

As we examined one substantive area after another, we found that apparently contradictory or anomalous findings often simply reflect differences in indicators, definitions, data samples, or statistical models. Detecting such variations should make it possible to at least reduce disagreements over "the facts of the case" in analyses of public policies.

Our tasks involved four principal approaches:

• verification: checking of facts and analyses;
• extension: widening of scope and elaboration of analyses;
• discovery: finding new knowledge; and
• assessment: evaluation of significance and implications.

Verification involves ascertaining the validity of evidence. It also entails updating, that is, bringing forward historical series of data into the present to ascertain their continuing validity.

Extension of prior studies means that we have found it essential to bring into a single report a wide range of complex evidence, linking together economic and political changes with changes in family structure, residence, health, and organizational and community life. We found that many widely accepted global generalizations are misleading, and we often had to disaggregate national data to see important differences, among regions of the country, among individuals and families, and among people grouped by other demographic factors such as age, sex, and education.

Discovery of new knowledge has been sought primarily by reanalysis of existing information, as in our study of the changing income distributions of black men and women in comparison with whites (Chapter 6). In some cases we collected new information that led to a discovery, such as the large amount of organized self-help activity in black communities (Chapter 4).

Assessment of the significance and of the implications of data and findings cannot be a simple extension of analysis, but represents an integration of empirical findings with knowledge of the broader sociocultural setting and with an interpretation of choices, values, and potential policy options.

The basic conception that lies beneath our analysis is that of a human society as a dynamic collection of subsystems. ''Race relations'' is an abstraction from the criss-crossing of social processes that make up a living society. In the case of the United States, that society is deeply pluralistic, loosely articulated, highly energetic, and full of possible futures.

DETERMINANTS OF BLACK STATUS

Black status results from American social institutions and the race relations that have developed within that institutional structure. Statistical indices of blacks' social positions are concrete indicators of that status. As such, status indices are the primary objects of our analysis, and their study encompasses most of the material presented throughout the report. However, beliefs and attitudes—perceptions—are also important in a study of group status. People's attitudes and beliefs about one another are important consequences of the structure of society and its race relations, as well as major determinants of race relations.

The report focuses on the relationships between three fundamental determinants: social institutions, black-white relations, and underlying social conditions (demographic change and economic growth, for example). Effects on blacks' social positions are generally inferred from changes in statistical indices of social status and black and white attitudes. But it is important to note that changes in indices of status and attitudes are both consequences and causes of change in the three more fundamental determinants of blacks' social positions.

To understand the status of blacks, it is necessary to consider black-white relations. Blacks' status both influences and is influenced by the existing pattern of black-white relations. For example, opportunities for the status of blacks to advance in terms of their employment, education, and general health were quite different under pre-1960s de jure segregation than after-ward. Changes in black status can begin a dynamic process that results in alterations in black-white relations: for example, when blacks gained the right to vote, serve on juries, and become officers of the courts, black-white relations in the civil and criminal justice systems changed.

In the United States, the structure of social institutions has always played an important role in determining blacks' status and black-white relations. Thus, black-white relations and blacks' status changed after southern public schools were desegregated in the late 1960s and the 1970s. Furthermore, changes in more fundamental social conditions can effect change in black status and in black-white relations by acting on either or both. One such force is change in the underlying structure of the economy. For example, between 1940 and 1970, large losses of black jobs due to the mechanization of southern agriculture and the expansion of industrial employment oppor-tunities for blacks outside the South accelerated the urbanization of the black population. These changes set the stage for at least two important alterations in black status and in black-white relations: urbanized blacks, especially outside the South, gained the elective franchise and greater access to political office, and industrial employment raised black incomes so that blacks' power as consumers affected a variety of black-white relations (Chap-ter 5). Less spectacularly, what laws are passed and how they are enforced continue to be affected by and to affect race relations and the status of blacks (Chapters 3–5).

In sum, there is a large, complex system of mutually dependent phenom-ena. Sources of change, for better or worse, exist at nearly every position of the system. However, some kinds of changes can be expected to have larger effects of longer duration than others. In theory, one can trace out the likely effects of a change in any of the variables upon the entire system, but it is a very complicated process.

INTERPRETING DATA

Throughout this report we make assessments of the consequences of some of the conditions described: these are inferences about causes and effects. Any such cause-effect judgments concerning the dynamics of complex social systems require great care. Yet such appraisals are vitally necessary—for oth-erwise little that is sensible could be said about crucial issues of public and private policies for the years ahead. Because appraisals of interrelated causal sequences are highly dependent on particular social contexts, our inferences are embedded at widely separated points in the analysis. When thus dis-persed, these judgments may not stand out in their full import. Hence, we wish to call special attention to them here.

There are systematic patterns evident in the data we analyzed. A central example is the reciprocal effects of economic changes and political actions. Thus, we regard the evidence as compelling that long-term changes in the economic status of black Americans have been powerfully shaped by the interaction of large-scale changes in the economy with reductions in racial discrimination. In turn, reductions in discrimination, and in enforced segregation, have been possible only because of political mobilization of black people and their white allies. We conclude that increased political participation has been enhanced by improvements in economic status and in education.

Most policy proposals are based either on assumptions about individual behavior and decisions or about the constraints the social environment places on people's choices. Thus, much of the policy debate concerning the status of black Americans is over whether policy needs to change people's behavior directly or whether it should change their opportunities and range of choices. Changes in the opportunity structure available to blacks and their responses to those changes have been substantial during the past few decades. Many of the findings discussed in the following chapters have been consequences of these patterns of social opportunity and individual responses.

Explaining Black-White Differences

The U.S. Commission on Civil Rights, investigating Miami, Florida, in the aftermath of the violent racial disorders there in May 1980, reported that one of the most frustrating conditions perceived by blacks was lack of job opportunities. There were two major explanations for the lack of jobs. The commission found that "young black job seekers" faced discrimination from employers—many of whom held very negative stereotypic perceptions of blacks. The commission also found that large numbers of unemployed black youths lacked the "basic entry level skills" required to compete effectively for jobs (U.S. Commission on Civil Rights, 1982:147–148).

Both race and lower status backgrounds limit the opportunities of many blacks. The two reinforce each other, and each has some independent influence. The importance of race is clear from examining a large inventory of research and statistical data. Those data show nationwide discrimination against blacks—although diminished since the mid-1960s—throughout the decades since World War II. In the 1980s, differential treatment of blacks infrequently takes the form of blatant hostility and overt discrimination. Differential treatment is most likely to occur when it allows someone to avoid close interracial contact; it prevents the establishment of interracial relations of equal status or black dominance, especially in employment and housing; and it is possible to find a nonracial explanation for differential treatment. For example, blacks who find little difficulty gaining entry- and even middle-level employment positions frequently encounter barriers to upper-level positions that would involve significant authority over whites or the need to interact with them in social settings like private clubs.

Residential Segregation and Its Effects

The clearest evidence of discrimination comes from audits of practices in the rental and sale of residential properties. Black and white people of equal economic means, education, and credit worthiness have very different experiences in the housing market. Blacks are more likely to be excluded from renting or buying in certain residential areas, to be given quotations of higher prices and rents, and to be "steered" to areas already primarily populated by blacks. Estimates of the frequency of these practices vary, but it appears that in many metropolitan areas one-quarter to one-half of all inquiries by blacks are met by clearly discriminatory responses (Chapter 3).

Urban residential segregation of blacks is far greater than that of any other large racial or ethnic group, and there is extensive documentation of the purposeful development and maintenance of involuntary residential exclusion and segregation. Residential segregation has not been an unplanned, spontaneous process, nor has it disappeared along with legal segregation. Black suburbanization rates remain low, and objective indicators of socioeconomic status that predict suburbanization for Hispanics and Asian-Americans do not do so for blacks. The social changes of the 1960s and 1970s that affected black status had only slight effects on the residential segregation of blacks in large cities. Blacks are not free to live where they wish, whatever their economic status. Thus, black-white residential separation continues to be a fundamental cleavage in American society.

Discrimination in housing markets forces blacks into separate residential areas. Because of the large incidence of poverty and relatively low education levels among blacks, many are then concentrated into areas with high percentages of economically poor and poorly educated families. The resulting social patterns generate persisting disadvantages. For example, residential separation greatly restricts educational and employment opportunities and thereby directly limits the economic and social status of the next generation.

In a report of this kind, much of the description and analysis relies on aggregate statistics. But population aggregates and averages frequently conceal important differences among various groups. Thus, while we report a 1987 national poverty rate among blacks of 30 percent, the rate was 45 percent among blacks living in Houston, Texas, but 19 percent among blacks in Los Angeles. Similarly, national high school dropout rates among blacks are about 25 percent, but many large city school districts such as New York and Chicago report black and Hispanic dropout rates twice as high, about 50 percent. Recent concern has focused on the fact that national black infant mortality rates are twice the white rate, but in the District of Columbia, Chicago, and Detroit, black infant mortality rates in 1985 were almost 3 times higher than the national white rate.

These disparities are not arbitrarily chosen examples. Inner-city areas contain densely populated neighborhoods of very poor families and individuals. Poverty has severely detrimental effects on the life chances of children. Children from low-income households have, on average, lower educational attainment and achievement, poorer health, and inferior job prospects. During the mid-1980s, the rate of poverty among black children has been about 3 times the rate among white children. Furthermore, one-half of all black children were poor for at least 4 of their first 10 years of life during the

1970s; only one-twelfth of white children experienced poverty so severe. About 33 percent of black children were poor for at least 7 of 10 years in the 1970s, compared with 3 percent of white children (Chapter 6).

Poor blacks are much more likely than poor whites to live in residential areas of concentrated poverty (Chapter 6). A consequence is that poor blacks are far less likely than poor whites to have social contacts with higher income individuals—in neighborhoods, churches, recreation areas, school-related activities, and so on. They are less likely to have access to information or contacts useful in locating educational and economic opportunities. Children and youths in areas of concentrated poverty have fewer models of successful attainment and are less likely to receive adult support, guidance, and discipline conducive to educational and occupational attainment (Chapters 6 and 7).

Black youths living in poor areas face daily challenges that jeopardize their chances of reaching adulthood prepared for a satisfying and materially prosperous life. The destructive pressures of peer groups and the dangers of ghetto streets abound. Crime rates and violent behavior among young black males have become epidemic. The unemployment rates for blacks aged 15–24 are very high: in March 1985 they were 28 percent for females and 32 percent for males. Young adult blacks have higher rates of addiction and arrest for drug use and sale of drugs than whites. Among the black population, the deadly acquired immune deficiency syndrome (AIDS) is reaching alarming rates, primarily because of needle sharing among drug users. Illiteracy rates among black youth are very high in many areas. Violence and absenteeism are reported to be prohibitive obstacles to effective teaching and learning in many schools located in high-poverty areas.

DESCRIPTION OF THE REPORT

The following nine chapters of this report present detailed findings and conclusions on a wide range of measures of black status. In the next chapter, we assess change and continuity since 1940 in black-white relations and in the extent and nature of black participation in predominantly white social institutions. A primary distinction is made between black numerical access (desegregation) to such institutions and equality of treatment between races (integration).

Chapter 3 continues our assessment of intergroup relations and black participation in the wider society. It also looks forward to Chapter 4, which analyzes changing attitudes and social structure within black communities. Chapter 3 thus provides a general analysis of black and white attitudes and behaviors toward one another and toward many of the important issues treated in Chapters 2 and 4 (e.g., desegregation of schools and housing, equal versus discriminatory treatment in black-white relations, and black identity).

Chapter 4 reverses direction. It is concerned with the status of black communities themselves. Thus, while much of the discussion treats many of the same kinds of organizations and institutions discussed in Chapter 2, the focus is on change and continuity in concepts of black self-identity and in black-controlled institutions and organizations. Black-white relations are not of primary concern in Chapter 4.

Chapters 5–9 report findings with respect to blacks' status in political participation, the economy, education, health, and criminal justice. Finally, in Chapter 10, we report on the conditions of families and the status of children. Throughout these last six chapters, the conceptual focus is on both a comparative analysis of blacks' absolute social status at different times and on their status relative to white status across time. As a consequence, a rather broad picture of the status of the white population is also presented.

Chapters 2–4 thus provide a discussion of changes in black-white relations, attitudes toward racial issues, and effects of these changes on aspects of social structure in black and white communities. These chapters provide one side of the factors determining blacks' status, black-white relations within social institutions. The last six chapters report on various dimensions of blacks' status that (as we argued above) also determine blacks' general social position.

We close this overview with two observations. One is that the unique historical experience of black Americans is a strong living force in the present, encouraging pride in achievement against great odds and in unique cultural contributions to national life. A strong sense of common destiny and group identity is widespread and is important to a degree not fully appreciated by white Americans. Our second observation is that the changing status of blacks affects the lives of all Americans. The social position of black people is an indicator of the functioning of American institutions.

REFERENCES

U.S. Commission on Civil Rights
  1982 *Confronting Racial Isolation in Miami*. Washington, D.C.: U.S. Government Printing Office.
Warren, Earl
  1973 Equal opportunity: the Constitution and the law. Pp. 16–27 in Robert C. Rooney, ed., *Equal Opportunity in the United States: A Symposium on Civil Rights*. Austin: University of Texas Press.
Welch, Finis
  1973 Black-white differences in returns to schooling. *American Economic Review* LXIII(5):893–907.

NOTE

Figure 1–3 summarizes calculations of the hypothetical earnings of black and white men over their working lives, ages 20 to 64. They are hypothetical because they assume that the distributions of annual earnings by age for a given date will continue over the 45 years of a career of a man aged 20 at that date. For each date, and for blacks and whites separately, an age-earnings profile was computed for a man with median earnings at every age.

Using five age brackets and ten earnings brackets (in 1984 constant dollars), median earnings figures for each age were estimated by linear interpolations across the earnings brackets. Rather than assuming that a man at the median received the same earnings for every year he was in one of the five age brackets, a year-by-year profile was estimated by linear interpolation. When this interpolation gave negative estimates for initial or terminal years, zeros were substituted.

The lifetime sums of profile earnings are converted to an annual figure simply by dividing the sums by 45. "Discounted" or "corrected" figures allow for mortality, growth of earnings, and time discounting. For example, the discounted figure for 1984 uses the 1983 mortality table (*Statistical Abstract of the United States*, 1987:Table 108) for white men and black men; a rate of growth of per-worker earnings of 1.5 percent; and a real rate of interest discounting future earnings by 3 percent per year. These values are meant to approximate recent trends while adjusting them optimistically. The discounted figure for 1970 uses the 1971 mortality table (*Statistical Abstract of the United States*, 1974:Table 82) for white males and Negro and other males; the growth and time rates are 2.5 percent and 1.5 percent, respectively, reflecting the different macroclimate of those times.

Black men have significantly higher death rates than white men, especially among the young. The probability that a 20-year-old man will survive to age 65 was 67 percent for whites and 50 percent for blacks by the 1971 table and 76 percent for whites and 58 percent for blacks by the 1983 table. This implies that later earnings mean less for blacks than for whites and also that the joint result of expected growth and of time discount, positive for 1970 and negative for 1985, means less for blacks than for whites. Although it is probable that survival rates are correlated with earnings, it was not possible to allow for this relationship in our calculation.

Likewise, it could be argued that the time discount for blacks should be higher than for whites, and in general that the time discount should be higher for lower income men. It is harder for blacks, especially low-income blacks, to convert future earnings prospects into current spending through borrowing.

2

BLACK PARTICIPATION IN

AMERICAN SOCIETY

Kenneth Hayes Miller
Bargain Hunters (1940)
Oil on canvas
National Museum of American Art, Smithsonian Institution,
Gift of the Sara Roby Foundation

Black-white relations in the United States have historically involved black subordination and exclusion from the major social institutions of society. In this chapter, we assess change over time in blacks' participation in American institutions and in black-white relations. Thus, we address the questions of how much "desegregation" and "integration" have occurred in the United States since World War II. Throughout the discussion, desegregation refers only to the absence of segregation—the complete numerical exclusion of a group, in this case, blacks. Integration refers to the nature of intergroup relations, to the quality of group treatment or interaction that exists.

Complete integration exists in a multiracial institution if: (1) there is significant numerical representation for each group; (2) each group is distributed throughout the institutional structure; and (3) each group enjoys equality, authority, and power within the institution. These conditions will not develop, according to Williams (1947) and Allport (1954), unless equal status of the races is achieved, common superordinate goals exist for all, and the process has authoritative sanction and support. In the 1980s, nearly all institutions in the United States are desegregated; few, if any, are completely integrated in this sense of the term.

The first section notes conditions affecting the lives of blacks during the 10-year period before and during World War II. That period marked the end of an era in American race relations and is a good baseline against which subsequent social conditions can be appraised. However, as noted in Chapter 1, comparisons of social positions in the 1940s with those of the 1980s invariably lead to assessments of large improvement. Intermediate time points are therefore considered to assess whether change has been sporadic or continuous. Our descriptions of black participation in areas such as housing, schools, the military, and sports also pay attention to social developments during the past 20 years, thus using the 1960s as a secondary baseline period. This strategy of comparison is used throughout the report.

This chapter focuses on black participation in three major areas: social institutions, the military, public schools, and public accommodations and workplaces; residential neighborhoods; and social life, religious organizations, sports, and arts and entertainment. Black participation varies considerably across these areas. General policies toward desegregation were instituted earliest, and perhaps most successfully, in the military, where governmental authority is greatest. The desegregation of public schools was also the focus of considerable governmental authority, with less clear-cut results. The role of governmental authority and equality of treatment and black participation in housing and other sectors of social life vary greatly. In organized sports and arts and entertainment, in the absence of much governmental pressure, levels of black participation and equal treatment have been higher than those in most other areas of social life. In contrast, black participation in predominantly white residential neighborhoods has shown little change since 1960 despite some governmental pressure. Evidently, understanding patterns of black participation involves complicated issues of governmental authority, attitudes toward black-white relations, and other social conditions. These issues are discussed in detail in Chapter 3.

THE BASELINE PERIOD: 1935–1945

SOCIAL RELATIONS UNDER JIM CROW

The basic demographic character of the black population during the 1930s was rural and southern. Segregation was the rule in public accommodations, health care, housing, schooling, work, the legal system, and interpersonal relations. This segregation was not "separate but equal"; virtually all facilities and services for blacks were fewer in number, much lower in quality, or more inaccessible than those for whites (Bell, 1986b:1, 5; Johnson, 1943). For example, in public education, states operating under legislated segregated school systems spent far more on the education of white pupils than on that for black pupils. In the southern states for which data are available, per-pupil expenditures for whites averaged more than 3 times those for blacks (see Table 2-1). In Mississippi, the rate of expenditure for whites was 7 times greater than that for blacks. Another example was health care, which was negligible for most rural black people, and in urban areas all-white hospitals and hospitals with less-than-equal, segregated black wings were common. Differential access to health care for blacks was reflected in great disparities in black and white mortality and morbidity rates (see Chapter 8).

In many parts of the South, Jim Crow laws segregated blacks in public

TABLE 2-1 Per-Pupil Expenditures and Value of School Property in Selected Southern States, 1939–1940 School Year

State	Value of School Property per Negro Pupil	Expense per Pupil		Percent that $ per White Pupil Exceeds $ per Black Pupil
		White	Negro	
Alabama	$ 29	$47.59	$14.63	225.3%
Arkansas	40	36.87	13.73	168.5
Florida	57	69.76	26.95	158.8
Georgia	45	55.56	16.95	227.8
Louisiana	—	77.11	20.49	276.3
Maryland	186	—	—	—
Mississippi	14	52.01	7.36	606.6
North Carolina	54	46.02	28.30	62.6
South Carolina	44	57.33	15.42	271.8
Texas	80	72.72	28.49	155.2
Virginia	77			
Average	—	$58.69	$18.82	211.8%

Note: Data are based on average daily attendance.

Source: Unpublished data from U.S. Department of Education.

transportation by restricting waiting room, restroom, and transportation vehicle areas. Marriage between blacks and whites was illegal in all the southern states and in some other states as well. In the Deep South especially, blacks were expected to ''know their place'' by exhibiting deferential behavior in all relations with whites. Infringements of the norms of segregation or any open resistance to white domination were often met by violence. By official estimates, 46 black people were lynched in the South during the 1930s. Lynching did not always involve just hanging but sometimes included burning, mutilation, other forms of torture, and physical degradation (McAdam, 1982). Such atrocities seldom resulted in the arrest of those involved. Local authorities often colluded in lynchings or stood by while they occurred.

Segregation was more than simple black-white separation. With its potential violence and basic inequality, segregation was a potent system of white control over the black population. While most black people did not have to confront lynch mobs, the potential for such violence loomed before them, and they could not depend on the legal system for protection (Franklin, 1969; Raper, 1933).

Segregation of whites and blacks was widely supported by whites throughout the nation. Data reported by Horowitz (1944) and surveys by the National Opinion Research Center (NORC) during the 1940s provide key information on preferences for segregation and the extent of racist beliefs. Although there were North-South differences, the data reported by Horowitz (1944) show that most white Americans in 1939 thought blacks were less intelligent than whites (69 percent), and unambiguously endorsed segregated restaurants, neighborhoods, and schools (99, 97, and 98 percent of southerners and 62, 82, and 58 percent of northerners, respectively). In 1944, the NORC found 80 and 47 percent of southerners and northerners, respectively, condoned labor market discrimination, agreeing with the statement that whites "should have the first chance at any kind of job," and thought that black-white inequality was essentially fair and mainly the fault of the shortcomings of blacks themselves. These beliefs were overwhelmingly accepted in the South, where it is fair to say that Jim Crow and the ideology of white supremacy were clearly dominant (Bobo, 1987).

Black-white segregation was pervasive throughout the United States, not just in the legally segregated South. Exclusion of black people was common in government, business, community associations, and in most unions. Moreover, the media generally promulgated the subordinate position of black people through widespread racist caricatures (see Norford, 1976:877–878). The images and understandings of black Americans held by whites were distinctly shaped by existing prejudices, and the gulf between these two groups was immense. Yet North-South differences and pressures toward change during World War II suggested both that the future would bring change in black-white relations and that many people, especially in the South, would resist.

MIGRATION AND URBANIZATION

Students of black-white relations in the United States have observed that World War II was a major catalyst to change. The war led to increased black migration to urban and northern areas, provided greater economic opportunities for blacks, brought many blacks and whites into close social contact for the first time, broadened the social and political horizons of many blacks, and led increasingly to the views that racist ideology and practice were evils inconsistent with basic democratic principles.

During World War II and for 25 years afterward, the nation's economy grew at a rapid rate. Facing labor shortages, many industries, especially durable goods manufacture, drew from a sector of the American economy that had a large labor surplus: agriculture, particularly the labor-intensive farms of the South. As a result, some of the northeastern and midwestern states and California gained large black populations between 1940 and 1970.

During each of the three decades beginning in 1940, there was a net outmigration from the South of about 1.5 million blacks (see Figure 2-1). This was about 15 percent of the South's black population at the middle of each decade. Thus, while 77 percent of blacks lived in the South in 1940, this figure had decreased to 53 percent by 1970.

Many aspects of this migration have been clearly documented: migrants were younger and more extensively educated than those who remained, although their attainments were below those of comparably aged northern-born blacks; migration to the North frequently took place in steps, from a

FIGURE 2-1 Regional distribution of black population, 1939–1979.

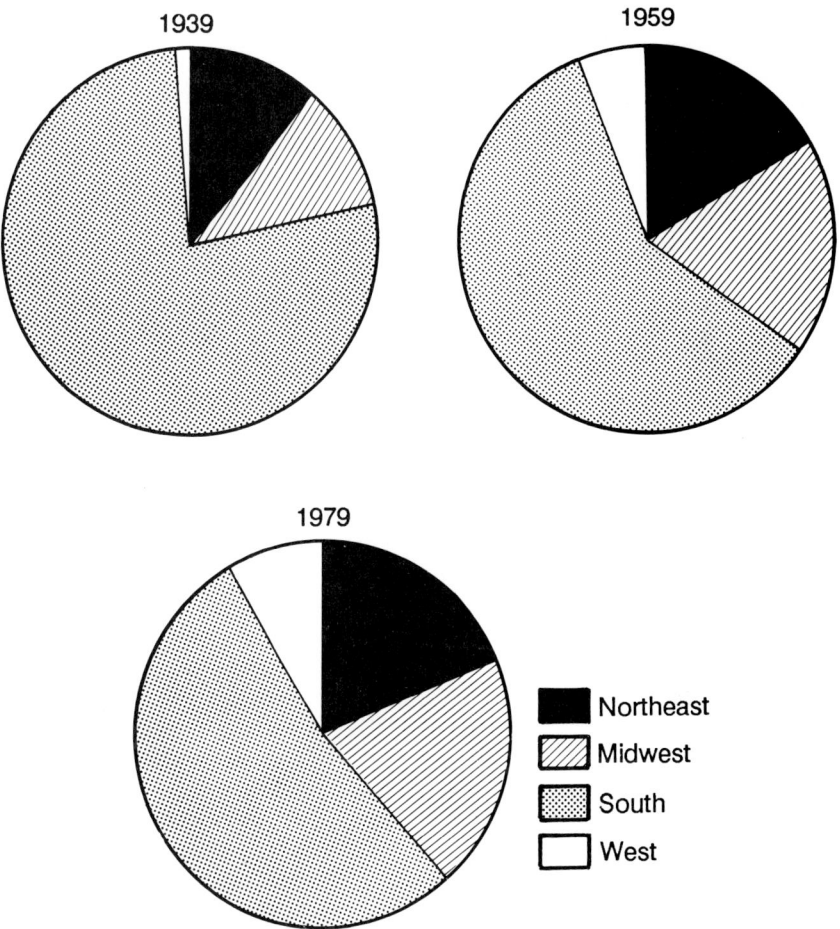

Source: Data from decennial censuses.

rural farm area to a southern city, and then a second move to a northern city. Blacks most frequently went to large cities, such as Chicago, St. Louis, Philadelphia, and New York, as those cities were easily accessible by the rail lines linking the South and North. Later, there was movement into other northern areas, but many cities in the North—Minneapolis, Akron, and the manufacturing centers of upstate New York—attracted few black migrants and still have small black populations (see reviews in Farley, 1987; Letwin, 1986).

Blacks who moved to the North were relatively successful. In the 1960s, many commentators speculated—quite incorrectly, it is now known—that

TABLE 2-2 Black Percentage of Population of the 20 Largest U.S. Cities, 1940–1980

City[a]	1940	1960	1980
New York	6	14	25
Chicago	8	23	40
Philadelphia	13	26	38
Detroit	9	29	63
Los Angeles	4	14	17
Cleveland	10	29	44
Baltimore	19	35	55
St. Louis	13	29	45
Boston	3	9	22
Pittsburgh	9	17	24
Washington, D.C.	28	54	70
San Francisco	<1	10	13
Milwaukee	2	9	23
Buffalo	3	13	27
New Orleans	30	37	55
Minneapolis	1	2	8
Cincinnati	12	21	34
Newark	21	34	58
Kansas City	5	17	27
Indianapolis	3	21	22

[a]Cities are listed by rank in total population in 1940.

the problems of declining northern cities were caused by the arrival of a poorly educated rural black population. They suggested that the southern blacks were culturally and intellectually unsuited for the complex life of the modern city. Given these deficiencies, it was argued that migrants withdrew from the search for regular employment and either depended on welfare or became criminals. A variety of studies since then have shown the error of many of these assertions. Compared with northern-born blacks, those born in the South who moved North were not extensively educated, but they worked longer hours, were less likely to be unemployed, and were somewhat more effective than northern-born blacks in translating their educational attainments into earnings. In addition, southern-born blacks were less likely to use welfare than those born in the North (Farley, 1987; Letwin, 1986).

One of the most dramatic consequences of the post-1940 migration was the change in the racial composition of the nation's cities. The 20 largest cities in 1940 are listed in Table 2-2 along with the percentage of their populations that were black in 1940, 1960, and 1980. In 1940, the populations of just two of these cities, Washington and New Orleans, were one-quarter or more black; only five major northern cities had a black population equal to or exceeding the national average of 10 percent. In 1960, as a result of black migration, along with the suburbanization of whites, eight of those large cities were at least one-quarter black. This trend persisted in the following decades, and by 1980 five cities had black majorities and another seven were more than one-quarter black. Only one city—Minneapolis—had a black population smaller than the national average of 11.7 percent.

Black urbanization in turn had several consequences. As black voters became more influential in local and national affairs, articulate spokesmen for civil rights, such as Congressmen William L. Dawson of Chicago, Adam Clayton Powell of Harlem (New York), and Charles C. Diggs of Detroit, were elected in the 1940s and 1950s. The development of a somewhat larger black middle class resulted in personnel and financial support for the civil rights struggle of the 1950s and 1960s.

RISING BLACK PROTEST

Many black Americans recognized the opportunity for change made possible by World War II. Painfully aware of the disparity between democratic ideals and practice in the United States, blacks organized to use the international crisis to further their demands for equality at home. As the *Pittsburgh Courier*, a black-owned newspaper, stated (Dalfiume, 1968:96–97): "What an opportunity the crisis has been . . . to persuade, embarrass, compel and shame our government and our nation . . . into a more enlightened attitude toward a tenth of its people."

In the face of almost universal discrimination against blacks in the armed forces and defense industries, organizations like the National Association for the Advancement of Colored People (NAACP) increased their protest activities. A. Philip Randolph, a veteran black activist and founder of a major black union, the Brotherhood of Sleeping Car Porters, consolidated the protest sentiment and focused it on the seat of government. Arguing that only the power of the organized masses could effect change, he suggested that 10,000 blacks march on Washington, D.C., on July 1, 1941, under the banner: "We loyal Negro-American citizens demand the right to work and fight for our country." In response to Randolph's call, President Roosevelt issued *Executive Order 8802*, which forbade discrimination in defense industries and established the President's Committee on Fair Employment Practices to monitor the private sector. With this victory in hand, Randolph cancelled the proposed march (Franklin, 1966:78).

Some important increases in black participation occurred in war industries, especially in shipbuilding and steel. In general, these increases came as pressures from the wartime economy and from civil rights groups grew more intense, forcing industry to hire more black workers (Weaver, 1946). There were also major increases during the war in black participation in the military forces and civilian government service. These increases in the number of black workers were accompanied by opposition and conflict from management and white workers.

Evidence that black protest during the war was likely to continue came from the worldwide surveys of American soldiers conducted by the War Department from 1941 to 1946 (Stouffer et al., 1949, Vol. I:Ch. 10). These studies showed that black soldiers defined their circumstances in racial terms, rejected discrimination and segregation, and emphasized equal rights. White soldiers, in contrast, did not think that blacks were dissatisfied and said that blacks were being treated fairly. Stouffer and colleagues (1949:507) concluded: "This underlying theme of Negro protest against and white complacency toward the racial status quo [could], in broad and somewhat oversimplified fashion, be perceived in almost every aspect of Negro-white relationships."

The studies also showed large North-South differences among black soldiers, with northern black men more likely to reject racial separation and to express willingness to enter combat (Stouffer et al., 1949:526–530). The authors of *The American Soldier* summarized their interpretation of the broader implications of the research findings in words that foreshadowed much of the national debates in subsequent decades (Stouffer et al., 1949:599):

> The problem, then, was one of justice within our existing institutional framework. Defenders of segregation and of other aspects of a system based upon racial categorization were in the difficult position of having no defense on the level of accepted principle against the claims of the Negroes. . . . That no more generally satisfactory solution to these conflicts emerged within the Army only reflects the inability of a single segment like the Army to accomplish what the larger society has yet to achieve.

The war years saw an increase in black community activism, which formed a base for major changes in black-white relations in the 1950s and 1960s. Indeed, the issues of concern to blacks during the war years prefigured those that would become central to the civil rights movement and to the general issue of equal opportunity. Conflicts over public accommodations, occupational mobility, housing, and media images were important both in the civilian and military domains. For many blacks, all of these were crucial issues. Whether it was outright violence or restrictive regulations aimed against black use of an officers club or black seating on a train, segregation and discrimination were viewed as barriers that black activism could and should change.

BLACK PARTICIPATION IN SOCIAL INSTITUTIONS SINCE 1945

As the civil rights movement grew and black community organizations accelerated their campaigns, an increasing number of judicial, presidential, and congressional decisions, orders, and legislation aimed at dismantling barriers to black participation appeared. The first 20 years after World War II were an era of challenge to discriminatory barriers to black participation. We note a few important dates:

1948 President Truman in *Executive Order 9981* directs the Armed Forces to institute equal opportunity and treatment among the races.

1954 The Supreme Court in *Brown v. Board of Education of Topeka* rules against segregation of blacks and whites in public schools.

1955 President Eisenhower in *Executive Order 1059* establishes the President's Committee on Government Employment Policy to fight discrimination in employment (replacing the Fair Employment Practices Committee established by President Truman in 1948).

1955 The 1955 Interstate Commerce Commission issues an order banning segregation of passengers on trains and buses used in interstate travel.

1957 The 1957 Civil Rights Act creates a six-member presidential commission to investigate allegations of the denial of citizen's voting rights.

1960 The 1960 Civil Rights Act strengthens the investigatory powers of the 1957 civil rights commission.

1961 President Kennedy establishes the Committee on Equal Employment Opportunity aimed against discrimination in employment.

1961 The Justice Department moves against discrimination in airport facilities under the provisions of the Federal Airport Act and against discrimination in bus terminals under the Interstate Commerce Commission Act.

1962 President Kennedy in *Executive Order 11063* bars discrimination in federally assisted housing.

1964 The Civil Rights Act prohibits discrimination in public accommodations and employment.

1965 The Voting Rights Act suspends literacy tests and sends federal examiners into many localities to protect rights of black voters.

1968 Fair housing legislation outlaws discrimination in the sale or rental of housing.

Few of these laws led to immediate implementation of their stated objectives. When practical gains did occur, they came after great efforts by many people to see that laws were enforced (Chapter 5). There was intense congressional resistance to proposed changes, and many proposed laws were not enacted: anti-poll tax and anti-lynching legislation were defeated in Congress in 1949; a transportation bill prohibiting segregation or discrimination in interstate transportation was not cleared by the House Rules Committee in 1954; civil rights legislation in 1956 was held up by the Judiciary Committee. And the 1960 Civil Rights Act was substantively altered to suit southern congressional opposition.

There were widespread attempts to intimidate black people who attempted to vote and engage in other political and social activities. Between 1955 and 1970, dozens of blacks and some white supporters were killed; private homes, places of business, and churches were bombed and fired on. Much of the violence, and especially the bombings and attacks on demonstrators, was planned and often supported—or at least judiciously ignored—by local white authorities. The Ku Klux Klan, White Citizens' Councils, and other local organizations attempted to intimidate black people in order to halt the struggle for civil rights.

But the movement continued. As it did so, the entry of one or a few blacks into areas of previous exclusion became symbolic of possible future progress. The period of 1940–1965 produced a plethora of firsts: black generals, black athletes, black actors in mainstream films, and so on. These pioneer blacks were experiments and symbols of what might change in black-white relations. For example, in 1945 Woody Strode and Kenny Washington joined the Los Angeles Rams and became the first blacks to play in the National Football League (NFL). In 1947 Jackie Robinson became the first black during the modern era to play in what black people had always called baseball's "white leagues." In 1949 Congressman William L. Dawson became the first black to head a congressional committee (the House Committee on Government Operations). In the same year Wesley Brown became the first black to graduate from the U.S. Naval Academy. In 1950 Gwendolyn Brooks was awarded the Pulitzer Prize for poetry, and the acquisition of Chuck Cooper made the Boston Celtics the first team in the National Basketball Association (NBA) to sign a black player. (See list of firsts herein.)

As black participation increased, the significance of a few black people in a social domain diminished, but there were increasing questions about how many more black people would enter and what positions they would hold. With this shift of emphasis, if further change did not follow soon, appointment of the first black or the first few blacks in an institution became increasingly seen as tokens instead of signs of real change.

THE MILITARY

Blacks have fought in every war in the nation's history, often acquitting themselves with great distinction and valor. Yet second-class status and inferior treatment of black personnel was official military policy, and this discrimination continued during World War II. With a few small and highly "experimental" exceptions, blacks and whites served in segregated units, and most black soldiers were kept in the United States, usually in the South (Moskos and Butler, 1987:2). One notable exception to this pattern of segregation took place during the final months of World War II against the German Army. Needing all the troops it could get into the field, the army sent black platoons, all of whom were volunteers, to fight alongside whites (Davis, 1966:645–647). Army research subsequently found that whites who fought with blacks displayed reduced levels of prejudice (Stouffer et al., 1949, Vol. I:586–595).

There was one major exception to the pattern of segregation, the nationalized Merchant Marine. Black merchant marines served in a full variety of occupations during the war. Four Merchant Marine ships had black captains and officers in command of black and white crews. Fourteen ships were named after famous black people, including Frederick Douglass and Harriet Tubman; four ships were named after a black seaman who had died in active service (Franklin, 1976:588).

Discrimination in the military involved more than separation and unequal assignments. Attacks on black soldiers by military and civilian police and by white civilians and soldiers were common, especially in the South. In general, the norms and cultural codes of the wider society were reflected in the military (MacGregor, 1981:45). The military leadership tended to take a "local-culture" approach to its black-white relations: for example, some bases in the North were more or less desegregated, while all bases in the South were segregated. The Army consciously analyzed base locations in terms of anticipated white resistance (Childs, 1987). Therefore, Chanute Field in Illinois was partially desegregated while the Tuskegee Army air base in Alabama was segregated, and black airmen and pilots were at times confined to the base in order to avoid difficulties with local whites.

These policies of segregation and differential treatment of black military personnel led to many nonviolent and violent confrontations between blacks and whites, both at home and in European and Asian theaters of war (Childs, 1987). The policies and the incidents repeatedly demonstrated the second-class status of black Americans. "In places, Negro service men do not have as many civil rights as prisoners of war. In at least one Army camp down South, for a time there was one drinking fountain for white guards and German prisoners, and a segregated fountain for Negro soldiers" (Houston, 1944).

Desegregation of the Armed Forces

Desegregation began in a very limited way during World War II, met with much resistance in the late 1940s, and quickened thereafter. Faced with the Korean War, black community action, political pressure, and genuine desire on the part of some for desegregation, the military moved from 1948 on toward desegregation. Formal segregation was essentially dismantled by the end of the 1950s, before any extensive desegregation in civilian institutions. By 1965, the last vestiges of separation had been laid to rest.

The changes arose from a convergence of several major conditions. The large pool of increasingly better educated blacks was a military resource that could not be ignored. Segregation increasingly was seen by military officials as an ineffective use of personnel, and the argument for efficient use of resources was extensively used to support policies of desegregation (MacGregor, 1981). Pressures from black organizations and shifts in the political climate also played major roles in bringing about military desegregation. As noted above, these pressures and shifts led to various official steps, such as the issuance by President Truman of *Executive Order 9981* (July 16, 1948) calling for equality of treatment and opportunity in the armed forces. After the subsequent appointment by Truman of the President's Committee on Equality of Treatment and Opportunity in the Armed Services (the Fahy Committee), the Army began to desegregate training and to assign some blacks to formerly all-white units (Davis, 1966:652–656); the Air Force took similar actions (Stillman, 1976:899).

The accelerating importance of civil rights issues was crucial to military

Selected Black Firsts in American Society: 1945–1982

1945   Colonel **B. O. Davis, Jr.,** becomes the first black to command an Army Air Corps base in the United States.

1945   **Kenny Washington** and **Woody Strode** of the Los Angeles Rams become the first blacks to play in the National Football League (NFL).

1947   **Jackie Robinson** breaks the racial barrier in modern major league baseball when he joins the Brooklyn Dodgers.

1949   **Wesley Brown** becomes the first black to graduate from the U.S. Naval Academy.

1949   U.S. Congressman **William L. Dawson** becomes chair of the House Committee on Government Operations.

1950   **Althea Gibson** becomes the first black to play in the National Tennis Tournament at Forest Hills, Long Island.

1950   **Gwendolyn Brooks** is awarded the Pulitzer Prize for poetry.

1950   **Chuck Cooper** becomes the first black drafted and signed to play in the National Basketball Association (NBA). However, because of a quirk in the schedule, **Earl Lloyd** becomes the first black to play in the NBA by 1 day.

1950   **Ralph J. Bunche** is the first black American to receive the Nobel Peace Prize.

1954   **B. O. Davis, Jr.,** becomes the first black general in the Air Force.

1959   **Althea Gibson** becomes the first black golfer to play on the Woman's Professional Golf Association tour.

1961   **Charlie Sifford** becomes the first black golfer to play on the Men's Professional Golf Association tour.

1963   **Arthur Ashe** becomes the first black named to the American Davis Cup team.

1964   **Sidney Poitier** becomes the first black to win an Oscar for best actor in a leading role (for 1963).

1965   **David H. Blackwell** becomes the first black elected to the National Academy of Sciences.

1966   **Edward W. Brooke** (R.—Mass.) elected first black U.S. Senator in the twentieth century.

1966   **Robert C. Weaver** is appointed the first black member of a president's cabinet, as secretary of the U.S. Department of Housing and Urban Development.

1966 **Andrew F. Brimmer** becomes the first black member of the Federal Reserve Board.

1967 **Richard G. Hatcher,** Gary, Indiana, and **Carl B. Stokes,** Cleveland, Ohio, become first elected black mayors of major U.S. cities.

1967 **Thurgood Marshall** is appointed the first black justice of the U.S. Supreme Court.

1968 **Henry Lewis** becomes first black to head a symphony orchestra in the United States (New Jersey Symphony).

1969 **Clifton R. Wharton, Jr.,** becomes first black president of a major, predominantly white university (Michigan State University).

1970 **John M. Burgess** becomes a bishop and the first black to head an Episcopal diocese in the United States (Boston).

1970 **Joseph L. Searles** becomes first black member of the New York Stock Exchange.

1971 **Dance Theatre of Harlem,** the first all-black classical ballet company in the United States, makes its debut at the Guggenheim Museum of Art in New York City.

1971 **Samuel L. Gravely, Jr.,** becomes the first black admiral in the U.S. Navy.

1972 Major General **Frederick E. Davidson** becomes the first black commander of an Army division.

1972 **Benjamin Hooks** is appointed the first black member of the Federal Communications Commission.

1972 **Barbara Jordan** (D.—Texas) and **Andrew Young** (D.—Georgia) are the first blacks elected to the House of Representatives from the South in the twentieth century.

1975 **Daniel James, Jr.,** becomes the first black four-star general in the Air Force.

1977 **Clifford Alexander, Jr.,** becomes the first black secretary of the Army.

1979 **Marcus Alexis** becomes the first black chair of the Interstate Commerce Commission.

1982 **Thomas Bradley** becomes the first black nominated to run for governor of a state by a major party (Democratic party).

1982 **Roscoe Robinson, Jr.,** becomes the first four-star general in the Army.

desegregation. Linked to these developments were changing white attitudes that were increasingly favorable to some movement toward desegregation (see Chapter 3). President Truman's order to the military to institute equal treatment was issued in response to pressures from black leaders and civil rights organizations. In particular, A. Philip Randolph had threatened to organize a massive black civil disobedience campaign against the draft if segregation continued in the military. In the context of the increasingly intense Cold War and the 1948 election, the threat of major domestic upheaval played an important role in President Truman's action (Brisbane, 1976:562).

By 1953 the logistical and tactical difficulties of fielding all-black units in the Korean War zone (Bogart, 1969; Stillman, 1976:900–901), combined with willingness on the part of some members of the military establishment to push for desegregation and with external pressures from the black community, led to a desegregation of the armed forces in the Far East. Segregation continued briefly to be the norm in much of the European command areas and in the United States, but the Korean War proved to be a watershed (MacGregor, 1981:430–434). From that point on, albeit with varied degrees of speed and scope, desegregation proceeded in the military.

Overall, blacks in 1955 were about 9 percent of enlisted men and 2 percent of officers (Moskos and Butler, 1987); 10 years later, in 1965, blacks were 10 percent of enlisted personnel and still 2 percent of officers. In addition, black enlisted men were disproportionately in lower grades and nontechnical jobs. Nevertheless, there was greater participation by blacks in the armed forces and a measure of increasing equality of opportunity (Moskos and Butler, 1987).

As bases became more desegregated, the issue of segregation in surrounding civilian communities became salient. Well into the early 1960s, military desegregation reforms were widely viewed by top military officials as applying only on-base. However, pressures from black organizations and sympathetic white political figures led to some changes in local situations. In 1953, President Eisenhower ordered that any schools receiving federal funds would have to be desegregated. The order did not extend to dependents of federal employees in local public schools, but the U.S. Department of Defense did begin a campaign against segregated schools on federal property. By November 1955, hundreds of on-base classrooms had been desegregated. However, many schools not on federal property, but heavily used by military personnel, remained segregated as military officials invoked the rationale of conformity to local custom (Childs, 1987).

By the beginning of the Kennedy administration in 1961, the main focus in the military had shifted to issues of public accommodations, schools, and housing for military personnel, on- and off-base. Desegregation also led to increasing concern with equitable placement of black personnel in various job positions and ranks. It was the very success of general desegregation of all-black and all-white units that laid the groundwork for a second tier of issues about black-white stratification within the military.

The military by 1965 was in front of the private sector in many of the changes it had made. Indeed, in its desegregation of on-base facilities, including schools, the military prefigured later changes being fought for on the civilian front. In this sense, the older image of the military as a reflection of the wider society's norms had been transformed into the reality of the military as a leading institution in changes in the nation's social patterns.

In 1945, Col. B. O. Davis, Jr., had become the first black to command a military base—of the Army Air Corps—in the United States; 9 years later, Davis became the first black general in the Air Force; and 11 years later he became the first black lieutenant general. These 20 years cover the time of massive change in the U.S. military. The presence of some black officers in mixed units commanding white troops could hardly have been envisioned, let alone accepted, by most officers and men during World War II. In 1977, the secretary of the Army was black (Clifford Alexander, Jr.), and in 1987 full general Bernard P. Randolph became commander of the U.S. Air Force Systems Command. Against the historical background, the changes in the officer corps are striking. Against the criterion of equality, blacks are still underrepresented in the officer corps and, within the corps, in the assignments most likely to lead to the highest ranks. Nevertheless, promotion of blacks to flag rank is no longer rare or even a cause for comment in the black community (Moskos, 1985:21).

The Modern Military

Recent rates of military service differ considerably from earlier decades. For the cohort of males born between 1957 and 1962 and who passed the physical and aptitude tests, a much larger proportion of black males (42 percent) than white males (18 percent) served in the military (Moskos and Butler, 1987:12, Table 19). At the same time, data from a 1973 national survey, "Occupational Changes in a Generation," show that among men aged 25–65, blacks were less likely than whites, on average, to have served in the military forces in each of four periods: World War II, the Korean War, 1955–1965, and the Vietnam War. Although blacks were more likely to be drafted, they were less likely to meet the requirements for service (Fligstein, 1980:303–304). Fligstein's study concluded that neither blacks nor men from low socioeconomic origins served more frequently than others (although college attendance made an individual less likely to serve).

The Army represents a special case. No other branch of the services compares with it. For example, as of 1982, the black percentage of commissioned officers in the Army was more than 3 times the percentage in the Navy and more than 2 times that in the Marine Corps (see Table 2-3). These two branches of the military service have continually had low rates of black participation in their officer corps. In 1986, 30 percent of the Army was black; the percentages for the other services were Marines, 20; Air Force, 17; and Navy, 14. Among female enlistees in the Army in 1986, 32 percent were black. In the military officer corps, the proportion of blacks has risen

TABLE 2-3 Black Officers in U.S. Armed Services, by Rank (as percentage of officers), June 1982

Rank	Army	Navy	Marine Corps	Air Force	All Services
Commissioned officers	8.6	2.8	3.8	5.0	5.6
General	0.0	0.0	0.0	0.0	0.0
Lt. General	4.5	0.0	0.0	0.0	1.7
Maj. General	5.3	1.2	0.0	1.6	2.8
Brig. General	7.8	1.6	2.9	4.7	5.0
Colonel	4.6	0.8	0.3	1.9	2.4
Lt. Colonel	4.8	0.7	0.7	2.4	2.7
Major	4.8	1.8	1.9	2.3	2.9
Captain	9.3	3.7	5.0	5.5	6.4
1st Lieutenant	15.0	3.7	5.1	8.3	9.0
2nd Lieutenant	9.7	3.6	4.4	7.2	6.7
Warrant officers	6.1	5.1	7.3	—	6.0
All officers	8.2	2.9	4.1	5.0	5.6

Source: Moskos and Butler (1987).

from less than 1 percent in 1949 to 6.5 percent in 1986. In the Army the increase has been larger: in 1986, 10 percent of all officers and 7 percent of the generals were black (Moskos and Butler, 1987:Tables 2–4).

Major trends in black participation in the Army from 1962 to 1986 are shown in Table 2-4. Several features of the data warrant comment. First, black participation in both enlisted grades and officer ranks has increased, with the greatest increases in the lowest levels. Second, although blacks are still underrepresented relative to their total numbers in the higher enlisted grades, there have been large increases in the proportions of senior noncommissioned officers (sergeant major, master sergeant, and sergeant 1st class). The U.S. Army has become one of the few sectors of American life in which large numbers of blacks are in positions of authority over whites.

In military occupations, blacks are concentrated in support roles, slightly underrepresented in combat arms, and greatly underrepresented in technical fields. This places many of them in the position of being "bereft of skills and competencies which are readily transferable to the civilian marketplace" (Schexnider, 1983:249, 253).

Average black combat casualties have not been disproportionate to the black military population; over the period 1945–1985, the percentage of total black personnel assigned to combat arms varied greatly, from 12 in 1945 to a peak of 33 in 1962, followed by relative stability at about 20–25 percent thereafter, except for a short period during the Vietnam War. Disproportionately high casualties in 1965–1966 among blacks serving in Vietnam aroused dissent in the civilian sector. The Pentagon's sensitivity to this criticism resulted in a U.S. Department of Defense order to reduce the proportion of blacks on the front lines during the later period of the war, and the casualty rates for blacks decreased (Schexnider, 1983:249). Over the entire course of the war in Vietnam, casualties among blacks were proportionate to the percentage of blacks in the Army in Vietnam as well as in the total Army (Moskos and Butler, 1987:12).

Black and white rates of attrition, promotion, and retention in the military exhibit some anomalies. These anomalies reflect a complicated pattern of differences in relative opportunities between civilian and military life, as well as possible differential treatment in both areas. Blacks are more likely than whites to complete their first 3-year term of enlistment (with education held constant). Overall, 37 percent of whites as compared with 26 percent of blacks fail to complete their initial enlistment. In general, blacks and whites differ only very slightly in rates of honorable discharges, and black reenlistment rates average about 1.5 times those of whites.

Military personnel who have low scores on standardized tests generally account for a disproportionate amount of first-term attrition and are overrepresented in disciplinary infractions, absenteeism, and unauthorized absence (Sabrosky, 1980:603). Black enlistees, especially in the Army, have higher educational levels than whites, and black enlistees have higher aptitude scores than the general black population. Among white males and females, the lower the score on the Armed Forces Qualification Test (AFQT), the higher the attrition. But among black females there is no relationship, and among

TABLE 2-4 Black Participation in the U.S. Army (as percentage of officers and enlisted personnel), 1962–1986

Rank	1962	1972	1980	1986
Officers				
General	—	0.7	5.4	7.0
Colonel	0.1	1.6	4.5	5.0
Lt. Colonel	0.9	5.1	4.9	4.4
Major	2.5	5.1	4.4	6.8
Captain	5.2	3.7	7.5	12.7
1st Lieutenant	4.3	2.9	10.2	14.4
2nd Lieutenant	2.3	2.5	10.4	11.4
Total	3.2	3.9	7.2	10.4
Enlisted				
Sergeant Major	2.9	7.0	20.5	30.9
Master Sergeant	5.5	14.0	25.3	24.4
Sergeant 1st Class	7.8	19.6	24.7	25.5
Staff Sergeant	12.7	23.9	23.9	35.7
Sergeant	15.7	16.6	31.2	36.0
Specialist 4	13.0	13.5	37.2	29.9
Private 1st Class	10.8	15.9	39.0	23.6
Private	13.3	17.9	37.0	22.2
Recruit	11.4	18.3	27.0	22.8
Total	12.3	17.0	32.5	29.6

Source: Moskos and Butler (1987:27).

black males the relationship is reversed: the higher the AFQT score, the higher the attrition. Consistent with this striking finding, blacks with high AFQT scores are promoted much more slowly than high-scoring whites and much more slowly than low-scoring blacks (Moskos and Butler, 1987:Tables 21, 23). The puzzling pattern would be understandable if high-scoring blacks are perceived by superior officers as insufficiently deferential or conformist in the military hierarchy, but no systematic data are available on this point. It is possible that blacks with higher aptitude scores are less willing to accept what they perceive as institutional discrimination, while blacks with lower scores who see less opportunity in the civilian sector may be more willing to tolerate such conditions (Moskos and Butler, 1987:17–18).

Although blacks are promoted more slowly than whites with similar AFQT scores, enlisted blacks are less likely to be dissatisfied with military services: when recent veterans compare military and civilian life, blacks are more likely than whites to evaluate service life favorably. Yet blacks more often than whites believe that they receive worse treatment in the Army and believe that race influences the likelihood of fair treatment.

Military forces are rarely "representative" of their societies; this is true across societies and historically within the United States (Enloe, 1980). Under a volunteer system, unless quotas are used, it is not possible to ensure a representative mix of socioeconomic or ethnic and racial backgrounds. Relatively poor employment opportunities in civilian life inevitably result in relatively high military enlistments from economically disadvantaged populations. Without a system of national conscription, blacks will continue to constitute a relatively large proportion of enlisted military personnel.

In 1964, just before the Vietnam War, 12 percent of enlisted Army personnel were black; in 1972, the last year of the draft, 18 percent were black; and by 1979, 33 percent. The increase began before the inauguration of a volunteer system; it reflected blacks' rising educational levels, their high unemployment in the civilian economy, and the relative lack of discrimination in the Army. The increasing proportion of black enlistees also reflects the low rate of participation of the much larger white population. In absolute numbers, the period 1964–1977 saw a decrease in new enlistments of whites, from 228,000 to 153,000 (Butler, 1980:595).

Considerable concern has been noted in the scholarly literature over the possibility that the relatively low rates of white enlistment and retention would result in "resegregation" of the military forces. Clearly, however, a high overall proportion of black personnel does not necessarily entail either segregated occupations or segregated units. If concerted efforts and policies are pursued to ensure that assignments are nondiscriminatory and sufficient numbers of well-qualified persons are recruited, blacks and whites can be spread across the full range of ranks, occupational specialties, branches of service, and types of units.

PUBLIC SCHOOLS

In *Brown* v. *Board of Education of Topeka* (May 17, 1954), the Supreme Court held that segregation of public schools violated the constitutional rights of black children. With that decision and the implementing decree of May 1955 instructing lower courts to order a prompt and reasonable beginning of desegregation to be accomplished "with all deliberate speed," the Court removed the state-enforced basis for exclusion and separation in the schools. As the effects of the decision took place, the processes of civic inclusion of racial minorities extended into a major institution and weakened the racial caste-class system of stratification.

The Supreme Court's 1954 and 1955 *Brown* rulings upheld the principle of school integration, but initially few districts dismantled their dual systems. The early processes of desegregation were extremely slow, as southern legislatures, officials, and school districts engaged in protracted resistance and evasion. Private groups such as the White Citizens' Councils engaged in widespread threats and intimidation of people favoring desegregation. Many school administrators openly resisted the law and, in some southern districts, public schools were closed rather than desegregated (Kluger, 1976:451–464; Wolters, 1984:Part 2).

In 1954, the proportion of black pupils attending schools with whites in 11 southern states was less than one-tenth of 1 percent; 10 years later it had only increased to about 2 percent. Legal change, persuasion, and national public opinion had not produced any significant level of desegregation. The decade of resistance did not even end with the passage of the 1964 Civil Rights Act, but only when, on the basis of that act, the U.S. Department of Health, Education, and Welfare (HEW) linked federal aid for local education to compliance with federal desegregation requirements. Finally, with strong federal financial sanctions and some important court orders, large-scale desegregation did occur—in the South. The proportion of black pupils in desegregated schools in the South rose from 2 percent in 1964 to 15 percent in 1966, to 18 percent in 1968, and reached 46 percent in 1973. The proportions in the North and West, where the financial sanctions were not invoked, were constant at 28–29 percent (Williams, 1977:17).

By 1972 a series of authoritative Supreme Court decisions had spurred a substantial reduction in school segregation. In 1967, the Supreme Court declared that freedom-of-choice plans were not acceptable remedies if they left blacks and whites in separate schools (*Green* v. *New Kent Co.,* 391 U.S. 430 [1968]); in 1969, the Court overturned the principle that school desegregation should proceed with "all deliberate speed" and ordered the immediate desegregation of southern schools (*Alexander* v. *Holmes,* 1969); and in 1971, the Court called for the use of busing and proportionate pupil assignments (*Swann* v. *Charlotte-Mecklenburg,* 1971).

After a 1973 ruling found that de facto segregation outside the South was as unconstitutional as de jure segregation in the South (*Keyes* v. *Denver School District No. 1,* 1973), federal courts in the North and West issued similar desegregation orders; however, the pace of litigation and of desegregation has been much slower outside the South.

Trends in School Desegregation

Since the late 1960s, the Office for Civil Rights (then in HEW, now in the U.S. Department of Education) has gathered data about the race of students and faculty at individual schools in a sample of school districts. There are difficulties in measuring segregation because the survey refers to entire schools, not classrooms or programs within schools, and because the sample is one of school districts rather than students. Nevertheless, these data provide a picture of racial change and allow us to pinpoint the timing of desegregation.

Figure 2-2a shows the percentage of black students who attended public schools in which 90 percent or more of the students were minorities, that is, blacks, Hispanics, Asians, or Native Americans. Since the history of both school segregation and litigation varies by area, data are shown for five groups of states. In 1968 approximately 4 of every 5 black students in the South went to schools whose enrollments were at least 90 percent minority. Four years later, this had fallen to 1 black student in 4—largely because of the encompassing federal court orders. There were declines in extreme school segregation (as measured in this manner) in the border states, the Midwest, and the West, although much smaller than those occurring in the South.

For more than a decade, public schools in the South have been less segregated than those in the North or West. Nevertheless, racial concentration is very evident. Black children in 1980 made up about one-fifth of the nation's public elementary and secondary enrollment, but almost two-thirds of them went to schools in which more than one-half the students were minorities (see Figure 2-2b).

The major achievements in school desegregation occurred between 1966 and 1973. Court decisions and demographic trends since that time have limited or halted the further desegregation of schools. In the South, many school districts are organized on a countywide basis that includes both a central city and much of its suburban ring. Hence, within-district desegregation orders effectively mixed black and white students. However, in the North and in several major southern locations (including Atlanta), the central city and suburban schools are in separate districts. Consequently, migration to the suburbs has drastically reduced white enrollment in the public schools of the nation's largest cities. By 1980, whites made up only 4 percent of the public school enrollment in Washington, 8 percent in Atlanta, 9 percent in Newark, and 12 percent in Detroit (Orfield, 1983).

Residential segregation was high in the 29 metropolitan areas that contained one-half of the country's black population in 1980 (see Table 2-5). The central city school districts of just two of these areas had a majority white enrollment in 1980: the countywide districts that included Jacksonville and Greensboro. Major reductions in school segregation would require

FIGURE 2-2   Black students attending public schools in which (a) 90 percent or (b) 50 percent or more of the students were minorities (blacks, Hispanics, Asian-Americans, and Native Americans), 1968–1980.

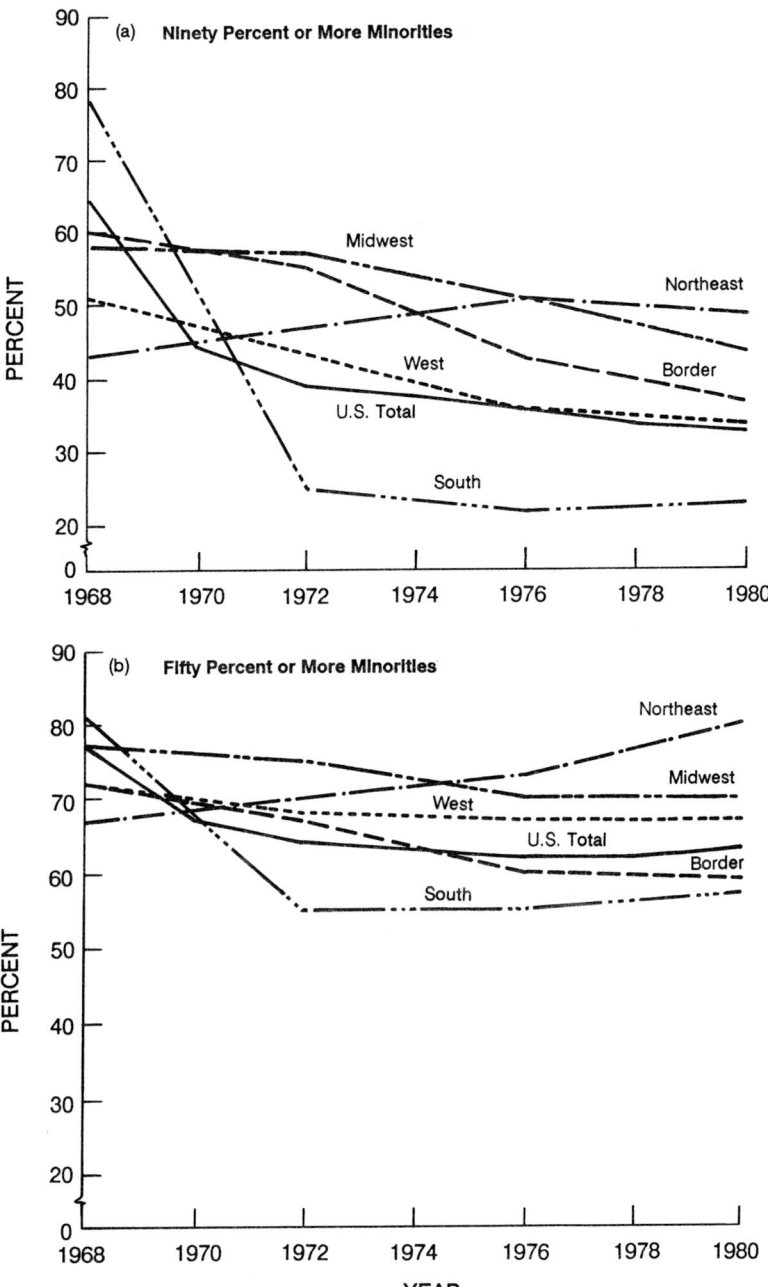

Source: Orfield (1983). Reprinted with permission.

TABLE 2-5 Measures of Residential Segregation for Metropolitan Areas with the Largest Black Populations in 1980

Metropolitan Area	Population in 1980 (in thousands)		Indices of Black-White Residential Segregation[a]			Interracial Contact Measures[b]			
	Total	Black	1980	1970	1960	% Black for Whites	% White for Blacks	% White for Whites	% Black for Blacks
New York	9,120	1,941	78	74	74	9	28	84	64
Chicago	7,104	1,428	88	91	91	4	15	90	84
Los Angeles	7,478	944	79	89	89	6	30	79	61
Detroit	4,353	890	88	89	87	5	20	93	80
Philadelphia	4,717	884	78	78	77	7	28	92	70
Washington, D.C.	3,061	853	71	81	78	12	30	84	69
Baltimore	2,174	557	75	81	87	9	26	89	73
Houston	2,905	529	74	78	81	8	31	85	66
Atlanta	2,030	499	78	82	77	9	26	90	73
Dallas	2,975	419	78	87	81	5	30	90	67
Newark	1,966	418	80	79	73	8	27	89	70
St. Louis	2,356	408	83	87	86	5	24	94	75
San Francisco	3,251	391	71	77	79	7	42	81	51
New Orleans	1,187	387	73	74	65	14	27	85	72
Memphis	913	364	71	79	73	16	24	83	76

Cleveland	1,899	88	90	90	4	18	94	81
Miami	1,626	79	86	90	7	30	89	68
Birmingham	847	75	68	64	10	26	89	74
Norfolk	807	63	77	77	14	36	83	63
Pittsburgh	2,264	73	75	74	4	44	96	55
Richmond	632	66	77	75	13	34	86	66
Cincinnati	1,401	79	82	83	5	36	94	59
Kansas City	1,327	79	87	83	5	30	93	69
Nassau-Suffolk	2,606	77	—	—	3	49	95	49
Greensboro	827	69	75	67	9	37	90	63
Boston	2,763	77	79	81	3	40	95	55
Jacksonville	737	68	82	78	10	35	89	65
Indianapolis	1,167	80	84	79	5	33	94	67
Milwaukee	1,397	84	90	90	4	29	95	70
Average	2,617	77	81	80	8	31	89	68

Notes: These measures are calculated from data for census tracts. No adjustments have been made for changes over time in the boundaries of metropolitan areas.

[a]These are indices of dissimilarity comparing the distributions of the white and black populations across census tracts. If individuals were randomly distributed, the index would approach its minimum value of zero. In a situation of total separation, the index would equal 100. The 1970 and 1980 indices compare blacks and whites; the 1960 indices compare whites and nonwhites.

[b]These measures of potential interracial contact for 1980 show the percentage of blacks in the census tract of the typical white, the percentage of whites for blacks, the percentage of whites for whites, and the percentage of blacks for blacks.

Source: Data from 1960, 1970, and 1980 decennial censuses.

the pooling of central city and suburban students, but Supreme Court decisions disallowing metropolitan desegregation plans in Detroit and Richmond have made this unlikely (*Millikin* v. *Bradley,* 1974).

Effects of School Desegregation

School desegregation has had varied effects. The *Brown* decision stated that psychological damage was done to black children by segregated schooling and held that the "separate but equal" doctrine was unconstitutional because segregated schooling was inherently unequal. Thus, tight connections were assumed to exist between segregation and the quality of education received. Many social scientists argued that under certain conditions school desegregation would raise the self-esteem and educational aspirations of black children, increase their academic achievement, and improve black-white relations (Cook, 1979:420). The discussion in this section is primarily devoted to questions surrounding the last types of issues: Does desegregation produce better black-white relations? Questions concerning the effect of desegregated school environments on pupils' self-esteem, educational aspirations, and academic achievement are considered in Chapter 7.

Our analysis of relevant studies leads to the conclusion that when several key conditions are met, intergroup attitudes and relations improve after schools are desegregated. Furthermore, desegregation is most likely to reduce racial isolation as well as to improve academic and social outcomes for blacks when it is part of a comprehensive and rapid program of change in the schools; conversely, partial and slow implementation may worsen educational outcomes and black-white relations. We note also that school desegregation does not substantially affect the academic performance of white students, while it modestly improves black performance, in particular, reading (see Chapter 7). These findings are interrelated in important ways. Two features—the timing and scale of the desegregation process—influence the potential gains of minority children. Minimal conflict and disruption occur when all schools in a community are desegregated simultaneously and when faculty and other staff as well as the pupils are racially mixed.

Black pupils who begin to attend schools with whites in the first or second grade differ systematically from their randomly selected age-mates who attend segregated schools. An extensive longitudinal study in Hartford, Connecticut (begun in 1966), found that students who had the interracial experience, in comparison with those who remained in segregated schools, have higher test scores and high school graduation rates, are more likely to attend predominantly white colleges, and are more likely to graduate from college. Also, as adults, they were less likely to be involved in police incidents, less likely to perceive discrimination, more likely to live in nonsegregated residential areas, and more likely to have frequent social contacts with whites (Crain et al., 1986).

Patchen's (1982) study of Indianapolis high schools found extremely complex effects of opportunities for black-white contacts. Friendliness was greatest when pupils experienced friendly interracial contacts prior to high school, when seating arrangements encouraged interaction, when there was opportunity for joint participation in extracurricular activities, and in general when the proportion of black schoolmates in classes increased. But there was a curvilinear relationship between friendliness and the proportion of the other race: as the proportion of black students increased to a large minority, avoidance and unfriendly contact increased; but when blacks were a majority, attitudes of both whites and blacks were more positive, and negative interracial interaction was less. These results suggest that positive relations are most likely when neither blacks nor whites feel threatened by anticipated dominance of a hostile majority or large minority. A relevant finding is that it is the black pupils with relatively high academic aspirations and achievements who are most likely to have friendly relationships with white pupils (Patchen, 1982:335).

When intensive efforts have arranged cooperative learning groups, some studies show marked increases in friendly interracial relationships (Schofield, 1986:36–40; Slavin, 1978, 1980). Because of uncontrolled contextual factors, there are some divergent findings, but several studies have reported that when black and white students work together in small groups on cooperative tasks, helping behavior occurs and the sense of threat can diminish, while performance on subsequent achievement tests improves (Longshore and Prager, 1985:80; Schofield, 1986; Slavin, 1978, 1980). Thus, interdependence in task performance in classroom learning groups appears to be consistently associated with cross-racial friendships and to support norms of equal-status interaction (see references cited in Longshore and Prager, 1985). Unfortunately, however, the conditions required for positive outcomes in race relations infrequently exist. In general, studies carried out in the 1960s and 1970s show only limited integration within desegregated schools, both in classroom behavior and in extracurricular activities (Hawley, 1981; Patchen, 1982; Rist, 1979).

Resegregation Within Desegregated Schools

A primary distinction exists between formal desegregation and actual integration of schools. Desegregation refers to the removal of both legal and social practices that separate white and black pupils and to the physical presence of both in the same schools. There are many degrees of desegregation. Black and white students may attend the same schools but be separated in classrooms, or they may be fully included in all school activities. Integration is a further step. As Williams (1977:95) notes:

> Mere proximity is not integration; integration occurs only if there then develops joint participation and mutual acceptance in all activities normally associated with school attendance, from classroom to extracurricular activities. . . . Between sheer mechanical desegregation and the most highly developed integration are many intermediate gradations.

The actual processes of desegregation vary so greatly from one community to another and across time that "desegregation" cannot be regarded as a unitary event or process. In some cities, desegregation has been limited to freedom-of-choice plans involving very small numbers of pupils. In others, racial balance has been sought by redistricting, school pairings, busing, and magnet schools. Great variations exist also in staff desegregation, teacher training, curricula, parental involvement, testing and pupil assignment policies, and many other conditions likely to affect outcomes (see Chapter 7).

Cohen's (1975) review of the literature on desegregation and intergroup relations showed that only one-fifth of the studies done between 1968 and 1974 reported whether there was actual interracial contact in the schools studied. It is clear, however, that resegregation—separation of pupils by race or ethnicity within a desegregated school—frequently occurs. Sometimes it is quite extreme. For example, interviews with students in a previously all-white southern high school that was desegregated as the result of a court order found the students saying that "all the segregation in the city was put in one building." The resegregation was so pronounced that the authors of the study spoke of "two schools within a school" (Schofield, 1986:10).

The most common sources of resegregation are ability grouping and tracking of students into separate academic programs, compensatory educational services and special education, and discipline practices. To the extent that race is correlated with the criteria used to sort students, ability grouping or tracking results in racial imbalance of classes. Similarly, categorical aid programs that separate disadvantaged students for compensatory services may lead to resegregation. Discipline practices can lead to racial imbalances in classrooms if there is discrimination or inept management of cultural differences in the enforcement of school rules.

Interviews of professionals in 10 school districts undergoing court-ordered desegregation led the investigators to conclude that resegregation had occurred within most desegregated schools. Tracking is generally noted as the major cause, and its use increases as the proportion of black students in the school rises. The greatest amount of resegregation occurs in schools that are racially balanced (Epstein, 1980; Eyler et al., 1983:130–131).

Blacks in desegregated schools are overrepresented on virtually every measure of disciplinary or remedial action (e.g., suspension rates, remedial classes), and they are underrepresented on positive educational outcomes (e.g., assignment to enrichment classes, attending college or vocational schools). These observations have led many researchers to use the term second-generation discrimination.

Although many studies have documented great black-white disparities, there is little hard evidence that ability grouping and differential punishment of black students are generally adopted in desegregated schools in order to resegregate students (Eyler et al., 1983). However, there are indications that decisions about tracking and ability grouping are influenced by racial considerations. For example, analysis of data from 94 elementary schools concludes that ability grouping is used most frequently by teachers in southern schools and by those with negative attitudes toward integrated education. Also, Gerard and Miller (1975) found that low measures of teacher prejudice are associated with the use of teaching techniques that encourage interracial contact (see Schofield, 1986:10–11).

In this connection, black participation at decision-making levels has been shown to have an impact on the treatment of black students in desegregated schools. The fact that the prevalence of disciplinary actions varies widely across districts and among schools within districts suggests that administrative actions by personnel in specific schools, rather than district policy, may explain some of the variation. Thus, it is not surprising that the presence of black teachers appears to reduce the prevalence of disciplinary actions and that the presence of black school board members predicts the presence of black teachers (Meier, 1984; Meier and England, 1984).

In general, finding black-white disparities on either positive (enrichment classes) or negative (disciplinary actions) measures cannot be taken as prima facie evidence of discrimination without first considering alternative explanations. Only a few studies discuss the possibility that factors other than discrimination may contribute to the disparities. An obvious possibility is that if economically or culturally deprived students are more likely to have academic or behavioral difficulties, and if blacks are overrepresented in this deprived group, then they would be overrepresented on measures of remedial help and disciplinary action. The reliability of the data is also open to question: for example, disciplinary measures are sometimes unreported or labeled as something else. Many of the studies rely on data from the Office of Civil Rights, and there may be selective reporting to what is viewed as a policing agency (A. Taeuber, 1987). Additional research is needed to clarify these issues.

Blacks, Whites, and School Desegregation

Several analyses have found that desegregation leads to white flight from neighborhoods and schools affected by the desegregation. Such flight is especially likely to occur in school districts in the South, districts with a high degree of residential segregation, and those with a high percentage of black students (Armor, 1980; Coleman et al., 1975; Farley et al., 1980). However, one of the most sophisticated studies found that substantial white flight generally occurs only in the first year in which significant desegregation occurs and that the percentage of white students assigned to black-majority schools is the critical determinant of the degree of white flight (Rossell, 1978:193–194). White flight from a desegregated school is minimized when (1) black pupils are bused and white pupils are not; (2) the proportion of blacks in the school does not exceed one-third; (3) white's retain authority and control over decision making and operation of the school system; and

(4) government-mandated reductions in the number of predominantly black schools are not very large.

Perhaps because of these dynamics in the implementation of desegregation plans, black support for desegregation of schools declined from 78 percent in 1964 to 55 percent in 1978. Many blacks now complain that black children have had to bear the burden of being bused into hostile environments outside their own neighborhoods, where they may be subjected to discrimination at the hands of predominantly white faculty (Hochschild, 1985:11–12). Such eminent black educators as Benjamin Mays and Kenneth Clark have argued that blacks must focus on the quality of the education that black children receive rather than placing an overriding emphasis on desegregation (Bell, 1986a).

The last 40 years have seen a dramatic change in white attitudes toward school desegregation (see Chapter 3). Perhaps the most important recent findings are that majorities of white and black parents of children who are bused find busing partly or entirely satisfactory and that, in national polls of students, a majority see busing as improving race relations and black achievement (Hochschild, 1985:14; see Chapter 3). Thus, to the extent that schools have actually been desegregated, parents and students who have experienced the change give the process their approval.

PUBLIC ACCOMMODATIONS AND WORK ENVIRONMENTS

The 1964 Civil Rights Act prohibited discrimination in public accommodations related to federal government activities and interstate commerce. Covered were restaurants, cafeterias, lunchrooms, lunch counters, soda fountains, concert halls, theaters, gasoline stations, motion picture houses, sports arenas, stadiums, hotels, motels, and lodging houses (except for those with five or less occupants). Private clubs were specifically exempted.

By the mid-1970s, many Americans believed that through lawsuits, consent decrees, permanent injunctions, and voluntary compliance, the Civil Rights Act of 1964 had led to a broad-scale elimination of discrimination against blacks in public accommodations. However, systematic evidence, then as now, was scanty. The U.S. Commission on Civil Rights said in 1975 that the perception of success was due to "conventional wisdom" rather than a "careful survey of actual practices." As the Commission noted (1977:94):

> Much of the evidence in the field of public accommodations is to be found through such judicial review. These cases appear to point out a small and declining feature of public accommodations, and "it is known from observation" by many civil rights officials and black citizens generally that there is a high level of compliance with the law in the cities and urban areas of the South, especially among national business chains.
>
> Most complaints of discrimination in public accommodations now appear to originate in rural areas and smaller establishments, although exceptions persist. Documentation remains negligible, however, and many factors con-

tinue to influence the development of official complaints, the only adequate source of information. By all available accounts, then, the removal of legal support for segregation, and the enforcement of the law where needed, has accomplished the extensive desegregation of public accommodations throughout the Nation.

Workplaces

Black-white separation in places of employment was commonplace a few decades ago. It was achieved through the exclusion of blacks from employment within white firms. For example, NAACP Executive Secretary Walter White, writing in 1948, noted how difficult it was for a black person to obtain employment as a reporter, editor, or craftsman on a major newspaper or magazine (cited in Wolsely, 1971). This situation persisted throughout the next two decades (Stroman, 1986:23). The first black reporter on a major television network was Mal Goode, hired in 1962 by ABC. In 1965 the number of black people on the news staffs of the major networks was nine. There were no black officials, managers, or technicians employed by the networks at that time (Childs, 1987).

The 1968 Kerner Commission report criticized the mass media's failure to employ black reporters and editors and the exclusion of black professionals from the news gathering and editorial process (National Advisory Commission on Civil Disorders, 1968:Ch. 15:362–389). Edward Trayes's (1969) study of the previous two decades of black employment on white newspapers in the nation's 20 largest cities found that of 4,095 news executives, deskmen, reporters, and photographers, 108 (2.6 percent) were black. This percentage was itself an increase from zero in 1940, but it indicated the slowness of change.

In the 1970s, the extent of separation within workplaces was much less than in schools, colleges, or residential areas. Using a standardized measure of segregation (s), the indices were 19 for employment settings, 42 for 4-year colleges, 56 for elementary and secondary students, and 56 for residential parts within metropolitan areas (Becker, 1980:765, using national data reported by the Equal Employment Opportunity Commission).

Work separation varies greatly across major occupational categories, being least among professionals ($s=14$) and greatest among laborers ($s=40$) and service workers ($s=38$). Overall, because occupational segregation is relatively low and black workers are a small fraction of all workers, nearly all blacks work with some whites in the same occupational category. Thus, in a statistical sense, it is the white population that is isolated: that is, a smaller proportion of whites have any opportunity for interracial contact (Becker, 1980:767).

Labor Unions and Equal Employment

In a study conducted during World War II, Northrup (1944:2–5) found that 14 major national unions, including those as important as the machinists and railroad brotherhoods, explicitly prohibited black membership through their constitutions or rituals. Another eight unions, mostly in the building trades, usually refused admittance to blacks by "tacit consent," and nine others limited black participation to segregated "auxiliary" unions that were affiliated with all-white "parent" unions.

Black auxiliary unions generally did not control their own affairs or have influence on their parent unions, and their members did not have seniority rights equivalent to the rights of members in the affiliated "white" locals (Weaver, 1946:218). Black auxiliaries also did not usually receive a proportionate share of total employment (Northrup, 1944:6), and it was a common practice for the parent union to reserve the more desirable job categories in an industry for whites.

Major access to unions for blacks began with the organizing campaigns of the Congress of Industrial Organizations (CIO) in the 1930s. Unlike the craft unions of the American Federation of Labor (AFL), which obtained bargaining power through restricting access to jobs requiring a high skill level, the industrial unions could only succeed if they enlisted all of the workers in an industry (because employers could circumvent unionization by hiring the excluded workers). Thus, enrolling blacks and convincing them that they would be treated fairly was essential to organizing mass production industries such as automobiles and steel.

As the nation geared up for war in the 1940s, the need for manpower collided with the long-standing patterns of discrimination in the defense industries. There were numerous instances where white workers went on strike rather than accept desegregation of their work sites or upgrading of black employees. In just one 3-month period in 1943, the Bureau of Labor Statistics estimated that 101,955 person-days of war production were lost due to these so-called hate strikes (Foner, 1981:265). In some cases it was necessary for the Army to intervene to force strikers back to work. Despite some important victories, such as the desegregation of the Philadelphia transit workers, movement toward desegregation in many defense-related industries was grudging at best.

Intensive pressure from black community organizations, especially the threatened march on Washington in 1941, contributed to the issuance of *Executive Order 8802* by President Roosevelt. This order forbade discrimination in defense industries and created a Fair Employment Practices Commission (FEPC) to evaluate discrimination in industry. The development, limitations, and fate of the FEPC were indicative both of the influence that black organizations could bring to bear on the federal government and of the limitations of that influence. The FEPC lacked prosecutorial authority; it relied on moral persuasion and, as a last resort, presidential intervention to effect change. The FEPC asserted that even under these restrictions some progress was made. After hearings in 1941–1942 in which 31 firms were investigated, the percentage of minority workers rose from 1.5 to 5.1, or a total of 23,759 (Laney, 1986:13).

Gains that were viewed as modest by many black organizations were opposed by forces in the Congress. In 1942, authority for the FEPC was switched from the executive to the legislative branch of government. In 1943, a larger FEPC with greater enforcement powers was created. In 1945, the FEPC lost the power to issue directives or cease-and-desist orders to those firms and unions it found to be discriminating.

The FEPC became an important early model for governmental antidiscrimination practices and agencies (Laney, 1986). Analysis of data from 1940 to 1978 has shown in detail how numerous incremental changes in public policies eventually led Congress to the passage of Title VII of the Civil Rights Act of 1964. The beginnings of antidiscrimination policies are shown to date from the New Deal period. Although the civil rights movement and dramatic media coverage helped to produce congressional action, the 1964 act had been preceded by a long process of increasing support for public policies aimed at producing equal employment opportunity (Burstein, 1985). State legislation had provided precedents and models, and the principle of equal opportunity had gained substantial support in all regions of the nation before Congress finally enacted Title VII.

During the postwar years, the abolition of the FEPC and internal problems of the CIO impeded the unionization of black labor. During the early Cold War years, a concern with eliminating communist influence from the CIO diminished the influence of the left wing of the union movement, which had been most supportive of black interests in the industrial unions. The desire to unionize in the South also led the CIO to downplay its commitment to racial equality in order to avoid antagonizing white workers. Finally, the merger with the AFL (which was effected in 1955) implied some tacit acceptance of the more discriminatory practices long prevalent in the craft unions.

By the late 1960s, most of the cruder forms of segregation had disappeared from the labor movement. But black-white inequality still persisted in other guises. There were constant complaints that blacks were denied equal access to apprenticeship programs, the most important pathway to desirable jobs in the craft unions: a nationwide compliance survey of government contractors in 1964 found that only 1.3 percent of the apprentices were black (Marshall and Briggs, 1967:29).

Black participation in union governance was still minimal. As a consequence, standard arbitration procedures had little or no effect in ending discriminatory hiring and promotion, because "the union and the employer, who together select the arbitrator, are often precisely the parties who have participated in the discrimination" (Foner, 1981:397). The tradition of honoring seniority also made it difficult to improve black promotion opportunities, because it effectively froze into place the discrimination that had previously existed (Gould, 1977). In a number of industries, governing procedures, such as the practice of allowing pensioners to vote in union elections, enabled white leaders to remain in power even after blacks had become a substantial percentage of the union's working members. In response, blacks began to push for their advancement within unions by forming a number of black caucuses, such as the national ad hoc committee of black steelworkers in 1963 (Foner, 1981:Ch. 25).

In 1987, 22.6 percent of employed blacks were members of a union, compared with 16.3 percent of employed whites. Blacks were 14.4 percent of all employed union members, although they were 10.0 percent of all employed workers (Bureau of Labor Statistics, 1989:225). Some individual unions like the auto workers are one-fourth or more black. Blacks have now risen to positions of influence in a number of unions: Examples include William Lucy, international secretary-treasurer of the American Federation of State, County, and Municipal Employees, and Marc Stepp, vice president of the United Auto Workers. At the same time, blacks remain underrepresented in the unionized sector of the construction trades.

Ironically, black success in union management has occurred as the unionized sector of the labor market has been shrinking. In 1983, 27.2 and 19.3 percent of employed blacks and whites, respectively, were members of unions, 5 and 3 percentage points higher than in 1987. This shrinking membership has been occurring for many years. For example, in 1978, union workers were 23.6 percent of all nonagricultural employees; in 1968, they were 28.4 percent (Bureau of the Census, 1970, 1988).

RESIDENTIAL SEGREGATION

As blacks migrated to cities, they were excluded from white neighborhoods. Initial discrimination in the early twentieth century involved municipal ordinances that specified where blacks and whites could live, but these did not survive court tests as they were held to infringe on the rights of property owners (Bell, 1986a:64–65; Johnson, 1943:173). Later, restrictive covenants were written into the deeds of urban land parcels to keep Asian-Americans, Afro-Americans, and Jews out of the neighborhoods developed during the post–World War I building boom. These were originally approved by the Supreme Court but were ruled unenforceable in the 1940s (Bell, 1986a:64–65; Vose, 1959).

By 1940 cities in all regions had unwritten, but clearly understood, rules designating which neighborhoods were open or closed to blacks. Adherence to these understandings and rules produced a thorough segregation of public schools, parks, municipal facilities, churches, and shopping areas. The rules were enforced through both legal and extralegal practices, which included violence, real estate marketing that explicitly prohibited the sale of homes in white areas to blacks, federal housing policies that mandated segregation, municipal zoning ordinances, school board policies that designated separate attendance zones for white and black children, and the activities of thousands of neighborhood organizations that sought to keep certain minorities out of their areas (Conot, 1974:300–303; Helper, 1969; Hirsch, 1983; Kusmer, 1976:176; Shogan and Craig, 1964:20–21; Vose, 1959:50–55).

The migration of blacks during World War II led to a great increase in the demand for urban housing, but the established patterns of residential segregation were not removed. The post–World War II construction boom, which was encouraged by federal housing policies and governmental funds for expressways, produced millions of apartments and homes at the fringes of central cities or in their suburban rings. The outmigration of whites allowed blacks to occupy better quality housing in the cities, but it did not reduce racial segregation. By the late 1960s, the Kerner Commission on urban civil disorders described a city-suburban polarization that was rooted in racial and economic differences (National Advisory Commission on Civil Disorders, 1968:236–250). In the 1970s there was a rapid growth of the suburban black population as large numbers of blacks left central cities. However, much of the suburban black population was in areas adjacent to concentrations of urban blacks, creating many minighettos within these suburbs (Clay, 1979; Long and De Are, 1981).

METROPOLITAN AREAS

In 1980, 29 metropolitan areas had black populations of 150,000 or more. These ranged from New York, where 1.9 million blacks made up 21 percent of the population, to Milwaukee, where 151,000 blacks comprised 11 percent of the metropolitan population. Just over one-half of the total black population of the country lived within these 29 metropolitan areas. Table 2-5 (above) presents information about residential segregation and isolation in these metropolitan areas. Indices of black-white segregation are shown in the center of the table. These measures compare the distribution of blacks and whites across census tracts. They have a maximum value of 100 if every census tract is exclusively white or exclusively black; if blacks and whites were randomly distributed, the index would equal 0 (Taeuber and Taeuber, 1965; White, 1986; Zoloth, 1976).

Black-white residential segregation in U.S. metropolitan areas was very extensive at every time. In Chicago, for example, the index was 91 in both 1960 and 1970 and 88 in 1980; in Philadelphia, the index was 78 in both 1970 and 1980. In the Washington, D.C., metropolitan area, however, it fell from 81 in 1970 to 71 in 1980. In 1980, variation in black-white residential segregation across the country was small, although several southern locations—Norfolk, Richmond, Jacksonville, and Greensboro—were less segregated than places in the North. Among the 29 metropolitan areas, residential segregation did not decline in the 1960s, but it did decrease somewhat in the 1970s, by an average of four points per location. Decreases in the South exceeded those in the Midwest or Northeast. This change suggests that the suburbanization of blacks and open housing laws reduced segregation, but the change was modest.

The unique position of blacks can be clearly seen when black-white segregation is compared with that of other minority groups. The Asian-American and Hispanic populations have two characteristics that are relevant for this comparison: they have each grown more rapidly than the black population, and for the most part, they moved into metropolitan areas two to four decades after blacks. Because of their recent arrival, as well as their limited economic resources and their minority status, one would expect Asian-Americans and Hispanics (both black and white) to be segregated from (non-Hispanic) whites. Asian-Americans and Hispanics were indeed segregated, but much less than blacks. While the black-white residential segregation measure in 1980 averaged 77 in the 29 metropolitan areas with the largest black populations (see Table 2-5), the measure for Asian-Americans (compared with whites) and Hispanics (compared with non-Hispanic whites) averaged about 50 (Farley and Allen, 1987; Langberg and Farley, 1985). If black-white residential segregation continued to decline at the rate observed in the 1970s, it would take five or six decades for blacks to reach the levels of residential segregation now observed among Hispanics and Asian-Americans.

NEIGHBORHOODS

Using information about the racial composition of census tracts, one can measure racial isolation: the average percentage of blacks who live in a typically white census tract and the average percentage of whites who live in a typically black census tract. This measure of racial isolation is one of potential interracial contact; it does not assess the frequency with which blacks and whites actually meet (Lieberson, 1980:253–257). The data show that, regardless of the proportion of blacks in a metropolitan area, whites lived in neighborhoods that were almost exclusively white. For blacks, the data show greater variation from one metropolitan area to another in the racial composition of the census tract of the typical black. Measures of racial isolation for the largest U.S. metropolitan areas are shown in the right-hand columns of Table 2-5.

Whites typically live in census tracts that have few black residents. In 15 of the 29 metropolitan areas, whites were in neighborhoods that were 90 percent or more white. In the Chicago area in 1980, whites lived in census tracts that were 90 percent white and 4 percent black (the remaining 6 percent were Asian-Americans or Hispanics). Chicago blacks lived in neighborhoods that were 84 percent black and 15 percent white. The only places where blacks are 10 percent of the population of mainly white census tracts were several southern metropolitan areas. Blacks in Chicago, Detroit, and Cleveland lived in census tracts that were at least 80 percent black, but in the San Francisco area, on Long Island, and in Boston and Pittsburgh, blacks were about 50 percent of the population in their census tracts.

A study of changes for 1970–1980 in 60 metropolitan areas showed some decrease in black segregation in the South and West but little change in large urban areas in the Northeast and North-Central states. Segregation was much higher for blacks than for Hispanics and Asian-Americans (Massey and Denton, 1987). This racial isolation measure implies that when whites engage in neighborhood activities, they probably come into contact with very few blacks, since public schools, parks, municipal services, shops, and churches are designed to serve specific geographic areas. The residential isolation of whites ensures that they will seldom meet blacks as they go about their local activities, even if blacks make up one-fifth or one-quarter of the metropolitan population. In many neighborhoods, it must be quite unusual for a white to meet a black, except in the traditional occupational slots occupied by blacks.

In locations such as Detroit and Chicago where there are large black populations living in predominantly black areas, the geographic polarization of the races is almost complete. The parks, schools, city services, and churches for black neighborhoods attract few, if any, white patrons. The situation in San Francisco and on Long Island may be different, since blacks typically live in areas that have substantial white populations. These geographic differences affect the opportunity structure for blacks, meaning that solving the problems of poverty in Detroit or Chicago may not be the same as in Pittsburgh or Boston.

BLACK PARTICIPATION IN SOCIAL LIFE SINCE 1945

CHURCHES AND RELIGIOUS LIFE

Historically, predominantly white churches in the United States paid little attention to problems of discrimination or black-white relations in general. When they did, the interest was often in defense of slavery or, later, to assert the righteousness of segregation. Important exceptions to this have been the abolitionist movement of the mid-nineteenth century and the civil rights movement of the 1960s and early 1970s (Davis, 1975; Hammond, 1974:175; Simpson and Yinger, 1985:315–317).

Acquiescence to existing black-white relations reigned in most predominantly white American churches through the 1930s. At that time, the number of church-sponsored resolutions "decrying" racial injustice increased, but they tended to be quite general, with little attention to the effects of discrimination and segregation. In the post–World War II period, national denominational and interdenominational organizations began denouncing segregation more strongly; subsequently, there was "almost unanimous approval of the 1954 Supreme Court decision calling for the desegregation of schools" at top organizational levels (Yinger, 1986:33).

Many church organizations and individual church men and women became socially active. Some Protestant churches, many of which had left the inner city when white neighborhoods became black or Hispanic, set up new programs to aid community life and church activities in several cities. In addition, "thousands of Catholic, Jewish and Protestant ministers took part in the freedom rides, sit-ins, and protest marches of the civil rights movement in the 1960s" (Yinger, 1986:33–34).

In the late 1950s, Catholic and mainline Protestant churches increased their involvement in the civil rights movement. One announced goal was to increase the number of black ministers and other church officials in predominantly white churches. For example, in 1956, the United Presbyterian Church of North America voted for "complete integration of all churches, agencies, and institutions" (Mays, 1957:51–52). In 1962, the Episcopal House of Bishops issued a statement declaring "the church must affirm that any form of segregation or separation solely on the basis of race is contrary to the Divine will" (Sumner, 1983:34). The national governing bodies of many churches issued similar statements during this period (Yinger, 1986:24). To what extent has this stated resolve to include black Americans in the functioning of the nation's predominantly white religious institutions succeeded?

Predominantly black and predominantly white churches are still by far the norm in American society. Although segregation has been lessened considerably since 1940 and since the 1960s, it still persists within the religious world. In addition, while black-white coattendance at church and, to a lesser degree, coleadership have increased, separation of black and white worship continues for a number of reasons, many partly being the effects of past discrimination. It reflects differences in culture, in accustomed ways of worshipping, and denominational loyalty. Importantly, residential segregation as well as class and educational differences between blacks and whites strongly reinforce the continuance of church separation (Yinger, 1986:36–37). In the remainder of this section we elaborate on this conclusion.

The number of black ministers, priests, bishops, and other religious leaders in predominantly white denominations has increased in the post-1960s era, but the available data do not distinguish between blacks serving predominantly black churches within predominantly white denominations and those serving racially mixed congregations. The latter almost certainly constitute a minority within a small group. Yinger (1986:25–26) reports some illustrative figures: in the early 1980s, the Lutheran Church in America had 57 black ministers (of 6,748), of whom 3 served predominantly white congregations; the American Lutheran Church had 1 black bishop and 23 black ministers (of 7,550), and none served a white church. Of 3 million Episcopal Church members, 90,000 were black; in 1984 there were 10 black bishops in the United States, and black laymen served as delegates to the annual general convention. Increases in the number of black Catholics has outpaced increases in the number of black clergy: for example, while there is 1 priest for every 914 Catholics in the United States, there is 1 black priest for every 4,313 black Catholics. The small number of black Catholic bishops has been increasing during the past 10 years.

C. Eric Lincoln (1984:189) has compared the United Methodist Church, which has 7 black bishops, with other mainline Protestant and Catholic churches.

> . . . since 1964 has been routinely electing Blacks as bishops and assigning them with little regard to the racial composition of their jurisdictions. No

other denomination has gone so far in depth and determination as the Methodist, but a few others have taken steps which would be encouraging were it not for their obvious symbolic intent. . . . To endorse carefully selected Blacks for unusual appointments, or even to elect a few Blacks to high national office is one thing; it is quite another thing to bring about inclusiveness at the level of the local church.

What percentage of individuals attend church with members of the other race? Loescher (1948) reported in a study of 18,000 churches in six denominations that about 6 percent of black Protestants belonged to predominantly white denominations; and of these, not more than 8,000 attended mixed local congregations. This was less than one-tenth of 1 percent of black Protestants. In 1956, the Disciples of Christ reported that of 7,000 congregations, 464 (6.6 percent) were racially mixed to some degree (Lee, 1957, as cited in Yinger, 1986:21–22). La Farge (1956:22) reported that about one-third of black Roman Catholics attended mixed churches.

Most of these studies referred to "interracial" rather than to black-white mixing, so one cannot determine the degree of black participation in predominantly white churches precisely. Only one study of Congregational-Christian churches in standard metropolitan areas in the mid-1950s did designate separate racial groups (Long, 1958). The study found that almost 70 percent of the churches were all white, 12 percent were white mixed, but with no blacks ("Negroes"), 12 percent were white mixed with blacks, 3 percent were all black, and 2 percent were black mixed (with 1 percent "Oriental," "Spanish," or mixed).

The data from these studies suggest, although they do not conclusively document, that a slow increase in mixed black and white congregations began after World War II and that such congregations accounted for about 10 percent of all congregations by the mid-1950s. More recent data are available from only a few church research organizations. Of 36,430 Southern Baptist churches that furnished data to the national convention, 4,338 (11.9 percent) indicated that they had 1 or more black members. Of 5,784 congregations in the Lutheran Church in America, 1,529 (26 percent) had at least 1 black member. In the American Lutheran Church, 707 of the 4,548 predominantly white congregations (15.5 percent) had blacks who attended services.

The General Social Survey (GSS) included questions on black-white church attendance in 1978, 1980, 1983, and 1984. Excluding the "no church" respondents, Table 2-6 shows the results for the question about the church "you most often attend." Since nearly 4 of 10 whites report having attended church with blacks, blacks, who compose only one-ninth of the respondents (one-sixth of those in mixed congregations), could not be concentrated in a few mixed churches. These numbers should be interpreted carefully. Clearly, it is not credible that 40 percent of whites who attend church do so regularly with any significant numbers of blacks. Rather, we assume that the GSS data represent a measure of the percentages of white and black churchgoers who have at some time attended mixed services at their regular church.

TABLE 2-6 People Saying They Attend Church with People of the Other Race

Year	Whites		Blacks	
	Percent	Number	Percent	Number
1978	34.0	1,107	36.7	147
1980	41.0	1,103	50.0	128
1983	35.2	1,186	39.5	147
1984	42.9	1,053	57.3	157

Sources: Yinger (1986:16); see also Hadaway et al. (1984).

The extent of mixed congregations is greatly influenced by residential patterns. The GSS data show that among those surveyed who attend church, blacks and whites living in mixed neighborhoods are more likely to attend mixed church services than those who live in all-white or all-black areas. Among the same group, one-half of those who live in a mixed neighborhood have attended mixed churches; the number is slightly more than one-quarter for those who live in racially separate neighborhoods. Unfortunately, it is not possible to infer from the available data the proportions of blacks and whites attending individual churches or the precise relationship between residential desegregation and black-white coattendance in churches. Many of the important questions could only be answered with panel data and case studies. Furthermore, a substantial but undetermined number of the respondents who report coattendance are in congregations that are "turning over" from white to black (see Davis and White, 1980). For example, the Lutheran Church Missouri synod reported 163 chiefly black churches, 83 congregations with 20 percent or more blacks that were "changing to Black," and approximately 200 additional congregations with a few black members.

According to the GSS data, the proportion of Catholics who have attended mixed church services (whites, 50 percent; blacks, 92 percent) exceeds the proportion of Protestants who have done so (whites, 33 percent; blacks, 42 percent). Two reasons for this difference are that Catholic churches tend to be larger and to encompass larger areas, and Catholics are more likely to live in racially mixed neighborhoods. Also Catholics, like blacks, are more likely than white Protestants to live in central cities. Perhaps most importantly, independent black Protestant churches have played a more important role in black religious life than have independent black Catholic churches.

Blacks are approximately 14 percent of American Protestants and 3 percent of American Catholics. Blacks are overwhelmingly Protestant: according to various surveys, 82–86 percent are Protestant, 4–5 percent are Catholic, 7–8 percent are without religious preferences, and 1–2 percent belong to other religious groups (Yinger, 1986:4). How much cooperation and contact occurs between black and white churches and denominations?

Black-white interactions at the denominational level depend to a great extent on the national origins and history of Protestant churches. Southern

Baptists split from northern Baptists over the issue of slavery in 1845 (see Niebuhr, 1929), and that split is not completely repaired today. The predominantly white Methodist churches divided North and South in 1844 and did not rejoin to become the United Methodist Church until 1939. In 1952, that organization began the process of phasing out its segregated central jurisdiction for black churches, but official disbanding did not occur until 1972 (Richardson, 1976:492; Yinger, 1986:28). (Three major black Methodist denominations—The African Methodist Episcopal Church, the African Methodist Episcopal Zion Church, and the Christian Methodist Episcopal Church—belong to the separate Methodist Union.)

Opposition to the United Methodist national policy of desegregation continued for a number of years at the state and local levels. There was a reduction in the use of Methodist literature, less support for black-white relations work, and the formation of a Methodist Layman's Union to resist desegregation (see Kelley, 1972; Wood and Zald, 1966).

According to Yinger (1986:28), "The Southern Baptist Convention, the largest of the Baptist churches, and predominantly white, has long been regarded as among the least inclined toward an integrated denomination." Some of its leading ministers denounced desegregation sharply during the 1950s and 1960s. Three large black Baptist denominations (National Baptist Convention U.S.A., Inc., National Baptist Convention of America, and Progressive Baptist Convention, Inc.), with a total of 9 million members, are not members of a Baptist denominational union. Some predominantly white denominations are deeply split over the issue of having blacks as members of the Southern Baptist Convention. Recently, however, there has been some movement toward bringing black and white churches together; 941 black Baptist churches are dually aligned with the National Baptist Convention and the Southern Baptist Convention; and 12 percent of Southern Baptist churches report 1 or more black members.

Black church organizations are generally in favor of interracial cooperation. However, as Yinger (1986:29) notes, many blacks also emphasize the need for continuing differences in cultural and social approaches—emphasizing the need for "denominational pluralism" and black autonomy in determining styles of worship. These attitudes illustrate blacks' desire for both self-identity and interracial interaction (see also Chapter 4).

ORGANIZED SPORTS

Prior to 1945, organized sports in America were racially segregated by custom and in some places by law. The interwar period (1918–1940) was especially segregated. No blacks competed in major league baseball, basketball, and after 1933, in football. Blacks could not play in white-controlled tournaments in golf, tennis, or bowling. Many states and municipalities, primarily in the South, had laws prohibiting racially mixed athletic events, and high school and college teams in the North rarely included blacks. Prior to 1945, exclusion of blacks from sporting events with white participants generated parallel organizations such as black leagues, traveling exhibitions, and college teams (Eitzen, 1986:1).[1]

Since World War II, blacks have progressed significantly in participating in organized sports. The watershed years in professional sports—when the proportion of blacks in the sport approximated their proportion in the national population—coincided with the midpoint of the civil rights movement: for baseball, 1957; for basketball, 1958; and for football, 1960. The late 1950s and early 1960s were the years of many firsts in sports, but they continued through the 1980s. In 1985, 52 percent of the players in the National Football League were black, about 22 percent of major league baseball players were black, and approximately 80 percent of the players in the National Basketball Association were black. In collegiate basketball, 24 percent of female players and 49 percent of males were black (Eitzen, 1986: 6–8).

Despite the dramatic shift from no participation by blacks in major team sports prior to 1945 to the proportions listed above, blacks are underrepresented in positions of authority and control throughout organized sports. In collegiate ranks, the member institutions of the National Collegiate Athletic Association (NCAA) do not have black staff in numbers commensurate to blacks' participation rates as athletes. Among over 300 Division I schools, there are 2 black athletic directors, 3 head football coaches, and 29 head basketball coaches (Edwards, 1987:15). Sports officials and referees are also disproportionately white: in 1979, 5 of 27 (19 percent) NBA referees, 1 of 60 (1.67 percent) major league baseball umpires, and 8 of 100 (8 percent) NFL officials were black (Eitzen, 1986:37–38). In 1984, none of 24 major league baseball managers was black, and none of 28 NFL and 14 U.S. Football League (USFL) head coaches was black; 32 of 258 (12 percent) assistant coaches in the NFL and 11 percent in major league baseball were black. Representation of managers and coaches in basketball is somewhat greater, but still significantly below the proportion of black players. In 1986, the NBA had 3 black head coaches and 2 general managers; 15 percent of assistant coaches were black (Eitzen, 1986:38–39).

At the collegiate and high school levels, there were also few black coaches at predominantly white schools: as of 1986, there were no head football coaches in major colleges and just a small number of head basketball coaches. Division I college baseball had 1 black coach; furthermore, black assistant coaches are "basically seen as recruiters of black kids" (Edwards, 1987; Eitzen, 1986). The situation is similar for women: Alexander (1978), Coakley (1986:166), and Murphy (1980) reported that black women held fewer than 5 percent of college coaching positions for women's teams and less than

---

1. Black participation has varied throughout the history of professional sports. For example, blacks participated in professional baseball during the nineteenth century, but were driven out during the intense Jim Crow era of black-white relations of the late nineteenth and early twentieth centuries (see Ashe, 1988).

2 percent of college athletic directorships. The majority of the positions they held were in predominantly black schools.

Eitzen (1986:40–41) reports that few blacks are in executive positions in the organizations that govern sports.[2] There were no blacks with administrative authority in the NFL commissioner's office; among NFL teams, 5 blacks held executive positions (none was a general manager); on baseball teams, 32 of 913 (3.5 percent) front-office positions were held by blacks—26 of them were secretarial positions; and there was 1 black athletic director at a Division I NCAA school (Edwards, 1984b). Professional basketball is the leader in hiring blacks in authority positions: in the NBA in 1982, 3 of 124 (2.4 percent) of the persons listed as executives (presidents, vice presidents, board chairmen, and general managers) were black, and 12 of 399 (3 percent) lower level administrative and staff positions were held by blacks (Lapchick, 1984:240–241).

The differential positions of blacks in American sports is explained by a number of causes. For example, the dearth of black coaches and managers could be the result of two forms of discrimination. Overt discrimination occurs when owners ignore competent blacks because of their prejudices or because they fear the negative reaction of fans to blacks in leadership positions. The second form of discrimination is more subtle: blacks may not be considered for coaching positions because they did not, during their playing days, play at positions requiring leadership and decision making.

Scully (1974) has shown that in baseball, 68 percent of all the managers from 1871 to 1968 were former infielders. Because of the disproportionate numbers of blacks in the outfield, blacks often do not have the infield experience that traditionally has been a route to the position of manager. The situation is similar in football. Massengale and Farrington (1977) reported that 65 percent of head coaches at major universities played at the central positions of quarterback, offensive center, guard, or linebacker during their playing days. Blacks rarely play at these positions. The same pattern has been found for basketball, where two-thirds of professional and college head coaches played at guard. Once again, since black athletes in the past were underrepresented as guards, they are less likely than whites to be selected as coaches when vacancies occur (Chu and Segrave, 1980).

This pattern would suggest discrimination if blacks are "stacked" into nonleadership playing positions because of stereotypes about the comparative abilities of whites and blacks. Some studies indicate this pattern does exist. For example, Brower (1972) compared the requirements for the central and noncentral positions in football and found that the former require leadership, thinking ability, highly refined techniques, stability under pressure, and responsibility for the outcome of the game. Noncentral positions, on the other hand, require athletes with speed, aggressiveness, "good

---

2. Bill White, a former all-star first baseman, was named president of baseball's National League in February 1989. White thus became one of the highest ranking individuals in professional sports and the first black person to head a major sports league.

hands," and "instinct." These characteristics fit stereotypes of whites and blacks.

Differential rewards to black and white athletes in professional sports may also occur (as it does for retired military personnel) because of discriminatory reward structures in the larger society. Within the major sports, blacks appear to face no discrimination in pay. For example, the mean salaries of black outfielders, infielders, and pitchers exceed those of whites. Moreover, studies of salaries in professional baseball, basketball, and football report that once in the sport, blacks and whites are rewarded equally for athletic performance (Mogull, 1981). However, considering the total incomes of athletes (salary, endorsements, and off-season earnings), blacks do not have the same opportunities as whites when their playing careers are over. This outcome is reflected in radio and television sportscasting: in the early 1980s, of the 55 sportscasters for NBA teams only 5 (9 percent) were black (Lapchick, 1984:241).

There is indirect evidence of unequal opportunity for equal ability. On the basis of average performance, entrance requirements to the major leagues are more rigorous for blacks. Rosenblatt (1967) reported that during 1953–1957, the mean batting average for blacks in the major leagues was 20.6 points above the mean for whites; in the 1958–1961 period, the difference was 20.1 points; during 1962–1965, 21.2 points. He concluded (Rosenblatt, 1967:53):

> Discriminatory hiring practices are still in effect in the major leagues. The superior Negro is not subject to discrimination because he is more likely to help win games than fair to poor players. Discrimination is aimed, whether by design or not, against the substar Negro ball player. The findings clearly indicate that the undistinguished Negro player is less likely to play regularly in the major leagues than the equally undistinguished white players.

Rosenblatt's analysis was later extended to include the years 1966–1970 and 1971–1975. The discrepancy persisted: for those 5-year periods, blacks batted an average of 20.8 points and 21 points higher than whites, respectively (Eitzen and Yetman, 1977; Yetman and Eitzen, 1972; see also Pascal and Rapping, 1970, and Scully, 1974). The same pattern was found in professional football (Eitzen, 1986). Blacks outperformed whites in all positions in which they played. Lapchick (1984) confirmed this "unequal opportunity for equal ability" hypothesis for professional basketball.

At the college level, blacks who receive scholarships have higher athletic skills than most white recipients (Evans, 1979; Tolbert, 1975; Yetman and Eitzen, 1972). Blacks are also more likely to be recruited from junior colleges, which means that universities make a smaller investment in them and are relatively assured of getting athletes with proven athletic and academic abilities (Edwards, 1979; Tolbert, 1975). Compared with white players, blacks are also less likely to play in reserve roles (Eitzen, 1986:44).

ARTS AND ENTERTAINMENT

In the arts and entertainment, as in all other major areas of life, inclusion and recognition of blacks has been a continuing struggle. The large body of historical materials and contemporary evidence and analysis covering the place of blacks in these areas cannot be adequately reviewed in a necessarily brief account. However, some specific examples of change and continuity in several fields are discussed (see also Chapter 4). We have drawn three main conclusions from our study. First, to an extent not always fully appreciated by the general public, the black presence and active contributions have deeply influenced nearly all fields of art—music, dance, theater, painting, literature—and entertainment, whether on stage or in films, radio, or television. Second, black writers, artists, and performers have experienced a history of exclusion and discrimination. Historically, many artistic and cultural creations of blacks have been appropriated by white performers who benefited from the general public's unwillingness to accept black artists. Since the 1960s, acceptance and approbation have become increasingly widespread for black contributions to popular arts in the mass media. Third, exclusion and discrimination of black artists, although much less endemic than in the 1940s and 1950s, are still present and important.

From pre–Civil War times to the present, many white Americans have appreciated and enjoyed black cultural styles in arts and entertainment. The history of minstrel performances documents a recurring pattern in which blacks have originated cultural forms that were then taken over by whites. Beginning with the minstrel performances before the Civil War, white performers (in burnt-cork blackface) and white entrepreneurs produced stereotypes and burlesqued versions of black humor, dance, and music. Thus, "white blackface minstrels" were able to introduce to white Americans black artistic material "before blacks themselves could appear on Jim Crow stages" (Hughes, 1976:687; see also Ely, 1985). Later, genuine black minstrel troupes became famous in the American commercial theater. But for nearly all of that long history, blacks themselves had great difficulty in being accepted as artists and entertainers.

Exclusion of blacks from the "legitimate" dramatic stage in the nineteenth century produced the first of many famous black expatriates in the person of Ira Aldridge, acclaimed in Europe as one of the greatest Shakespearean actors of the time. Aldridge was never accepted as an actor in the United States, and he died in Poland in 1867. There is an Ira Aldridge chair at the Shakespeare Memorial Theatre at Stratford-on-Avon in England (Hughes, 1976:689). Another example is that of Bert Williams, who received top billing in the Ziegfield Follies in 1910 and who later performed before the king of England; but his only appearance (in a 1914 movie) without burnt-cork makeup, used to make him appear much darker than he really was, provoked a riot by whites (Bayles, 1985:25; Hughes, 1976:689).

Depictions of black culture by whites appeared early (in the 1920s and 1930s) in works such as Eugene O'Neill's *The Emperor Jones,* Paul Green's *In*

Abraham's Bosom, O'Neill's *All God's Chillun Got Wings,* and Marc Conelly's *The Green Pastures* (immensely popular on Broadway for years). Probably the most widely known depiction of Afro-American life on the stage during this era was George Gershwin's folk opera, *Porgy and Bess.* Such productions were frequently criticized by blacks as white caricatures of black culture.

The influence of Afro-American music has been pervasive and important, both nationally and internationally. From rural folk origins, spirituals, work songs, hymns, blues, and gospel music developed. Later came the distinctive contributions of ragtime and jazz, with their many and diverse variants and offshoots (see Whalum et al., 1976:791–826). Blues was a precursor of jazz, and its lyrics represent a major expression of folk poetry (Pinkney, 1969:143). Jazz has become a popular music form throughout much of the modern world.

Black musical performers have been prominent in both popular music and concert stage and opera. Roland Hayes, Paul Robeson, and Marian Anderson antedated the long roster of present-day operatic figures. When Marian Anderson, now recalled as one of the world's great contraltos, was denied the use of Constitution Hall in the nation's capital city in 1939, the impact of black exclusion and discrimination in the realm of art was internationally dramatized. (A group of citizens, including Eleanor Roosevelt, then arranged for her to sing at Lincoln Memorial; 75,000 persons attended.) When Anderson subsequently appeared in a small part at the Metropolitan Opera Association in 1955, the event was treated as sensational news (Franklin, 1976:85). In 1961 Leontyne Price sang the title role on opening night at the Met, and by the mid-1980s the contributions of such opera stars as Jessye Norman and Kathleen Battle were both acclaimed and taken for granted.

Since World War II, the list of prominent pianists includes George Walker, Eugene Haynes, Natalie Hinderas, Robert Pritchard, and Andre Watts. Other widely acclaimed performers of the concert stage have included Carol Brice, Mattiwilda Dobbs, Dorothy Maynor, William Warfield, Lawrence Withers, Dean Dixon, and Adele Addison.

Meanwhile, black musicians—in the traditions of blues, ragtime, jazz, and jazz derivations (from bebop to progressive jazz)—have become household names: King Oliver, Scott Joplin, Eubie Blake, Louis Armstrong, Jelly Roll Morton, Duke Ellington, Dizzy Gillespie, Charlie Parker, Count Basie, Miles Davis, John Coltrane, and many others. Worldwide audiences listen to music derived from black American sources.

Popular dances originating in the black community, beginning with the cakewalk, included the Charleston, the lindy hop, the jitterbug, and the twist, to name only the best-known early innovations. The close connection between black music and dance is suggested by the fact that Kerry Mills—originator of two-step ragtime (1893) and composer of *Meet Me in St. Louis, Louis* (1904)—is credited with popularizing the cakewalk.

Music of the concert stage and opera has drawn on themes of protest against discrimination to sound a message of resistance to oppression, as illustrated notably in Gunther Schuller's *The Visitation,* performed by the Hamburg State Opera in the 1967 Lincoln Center Festival. And themes from black music have been used by modern classical composers, including Igor Stravinsky and Anton Dvorak (George, 1966:747–749).

An unbroken line of black poets extends from Phyllis Wheatley in the mid-eighteenth century through Paul Lawrence Dunbar (died 1906), James Weldon Johnson, Claude McKay, Langston Hughes, Countee Cullen, Margaret Walker, Gwendolyne Brooks, Henry Hughes, Maya Angelou, and Imamu Baraka (earlier, LeRoi Jones) to the present. Audiences were quick to applaud popular versions of black life, but acceptance of serious drama by black authors came more slowly. Richard Wright's *Native Son* was produced on Broadway in 1947, and works by a few other black playwrights followed, including Langston Hughes's *Simply Heavenly,* Lorraine Hansberry's *A Raisin in the Sun,* and James Baldwin's *Blues for Mister Charlie.*

August Wilson's play *Fences* won the 1987 Pulitzer Prize, and in 1988 it was being performed on Broadway simultaneously with his *Joe Turner's Come and Gone.* Wilson's several plays illustrate the emergence in theater of serious drama about the inner experiences of black identity over the decades since the Civil War. His collaboration with Lloyd Richards, artistic director of the Yale Repertory Theater, has produced works that depict blacks' struggles to transcend experiences of uprootedness and oppression (Bernstein, 1988).

Although black prose writers produced notable works in earlier times, especially biographies and autobiographies, the first great efflorescence of creative writing appeared in the Harlem Renaissance of the 1920s (Bontemps, 1976:761–765; Huggins, 1971). Soon the black American as writer ceased to be a novelty, and by 1938 Richard Wright began his important works with *Uncle Tom's Children,* followed by *Native Son,* a Book-of-the-Month Club selection in 1940. The next black author to be hailed as a major novelist was Ralph Ellison, whose *Invisible Man* appeared in 1952. He was followed by a long roster of major novelists and essayists, including Ann Petry, Chester Himes, Roi Ottley, Lloyd Brown, Saunders Redding, and James Baldwin. By the 1960s there was a proliferation of works by proponents of social criticism and protest, including Malcolm X and Eldridge Cleaver; and black cultural nationalism once again found voice in the writings of authors such as Imamu Baraka, Henry Dumas, and Ishmael Reed (see Neal, 1976:772–784). In the 1970s and 1980s, a substantial body of novels and other creative writings by black women attained both popularity and favorable critical attention, including Alice Walker's *The Color Purple,* which was made into a controversial film, and Toni Morrison's award-winning novel *Beloved.*

Nine black American authors have been awarded the Pulitzer Prize in literature or a National or American Book Award, and in the last two decades black authors have appeared on best-seller lists in small but increasing numbers. Sales of the magnitude needed to make national best-seller lists indicate a wide appeal across the general public—a phenomenon that rarely existed in earlier decades for black authors writing primarily about black materials, characters, and culture. A few black authors, such as Frank Yerby and Willard Motley, attained success in the 1940s and 1950s with novels that were written about whites for a mainly white audience.

General popularity of black artists may best be exemplified in popular music. During the 1950s, many creative artists, such as Chuck Berry, Little Richard, and B. B. King, received rather limited commercial success relative to the influence of their music on other artists and popular culture in general. During the 1960s and 1970s, black performers increasingly gained popularity with white audiences as the "Motown sound" created by entrepreneur Berry Gordy produced widely popular performers such as the Supremes. The list of "crossover" or mass appeal artists has grown considerably since the 1950s and 1960s when performers such as Nat King Cole, Johnny Mathis, Ray Charles, Dionne Warwick, the Fifth Dimension, and Sam Cooke were reaching national top-ten charts. The largest selling album in history is Michael Jackson's *Thriller*, and two other black performers, Lionel Richie and Whitney Houston, have albums on the top-ten list for the 1980s. Perhaps exemplifying the emergence and increased acceptance of the black American performing artist in modern music was trumpeter Wynton Marsalis's winning of Grammy awards as both the top jazz soloist (1983–1985) and the best solo classical performance with an orchestra (1983–1984).

Popular music thus represents the field where the black presence has perhaps been most influential and is now most recognized and rewarded. Other areas—film, literature, and the visual arts—have a number of successful black artists, but barriers to black participation and recognition have not been removed to the same extent as in music (Powell, 1986; Stroman, 1986).

In film and television, for instance, the first appearances of blacks were as song-and-dance performers, musicians, and servants. Only in the late 1950s did major performers—Sidney Poitier, Sammy Davis, Jr., Harry Belafonte, Nat King Cole—begin to appear. Bill Cosby became the first black television performer in a costarring role in a regular television series, *I Spy* in the 1960s. In the 1970s, the black presence on television was widespread, although the relatively low rate of employment and limited types of roles in the industry evoked many protests and legal actions (Norford, 1976: 881–887).

Systematic reviews of research support several generalizations about blacks and television (Poindexter and Stroman, 1981). Blacks were initially greatly underrepresented in television portrayals, but the trend has been toward increased visibility. However, blacks are generally presented in minor roles and low status occupations; stereotyping and unfavorable characterizations continue to be presented. As consumers, blacks are more likely than whites to rely heavily on television for both information and entertainment, and blacks are more likely than whites, on average, to credit television portrayals with realism. Blacks have distinctive preferences for programs that feature black characters. Finally, there is an almost total lack of empirical study of the content and influence of television programs featuring black characters and themes.

CONCLUSION

There are great differences in patterns of historical change and current rates of black participation in American society. Despite these differences, two major conclusions emerge. First, whether one considers arts and entertainment, religious institutions, public schools, or a number of other major institutions, black participation has increased significantly, whether the baseline is pre–World War II or the mid-1960s. Second, with the exception of the Army, where there is considerable integration, increased rates of black participation have not resulted in the elimination of racial separation in American life.

Thus, while there has been increased access to housing for blacks in many areas of the nation, residential separation of whites and blacks in large metropolitan areas remains nearly as high in the 1980s as it was in the 1960s. This separation in housing underlies black-white patterns of separation in many other areas. For example, large-scale desegregation of public schools occurred in the South during the late 1960s and early 1970s and has been substantial in many small and medium-sized cities elsewhere; however, the pace of school desegregation has slowed, and black-white separation is still significant, especially outside the South. And because of the differential effects of educational tracking and differential social punishment rates, considerable separation of black and white students continues to exist even within desegregated schools.

Within desegregated settings throughout American society, blacks do not share equal authority and representation throughout an organization or institution. In major institutions with considerable numerical representation of blacks at some levels (e.g., sports and entertainment fields), blacks are conspicuously absent from decision-making positions. Gaining insight into why black participation varies so much across different spheres of social life requires analysis of the attitudes, values, and behavior of Americans that underlie the observed patterns. These dimensions of black-white relations are discussed in the next chapter.

REFERENCES

Alexander, A.
1978 Status of Minority Women in the Association of Intercollegiate Athletics for Women. Master's thesis, Temple University.
Allport, Gordon W.
1954 *The Nature of Prejudice*. Boston: Beacon Press, and Reading, Mass.: Addison-Wesley.
Armor, David J.
1980 White flight and the future of school desegregation. Pp. 187–226 in Walter G. Stephan and Joe R. Feagin, eds., *School Desegregation: Past, Present, and Future*. New York: Plenum.

Ashe, Arthur
  1988 *A Hard Road to Glory: The History of the African American Athlete.* Vol. I, *1619 Through 1918;* Vol. II, *1919 Through 1945;* Vol. III, *Since 1946.* New York: Warner Books.
Bayles, Martha
  1985 Television: the problem with post-racism. *The New Republic* (August 5):25–28.
Becker, Henry Jay
  1980 Racial segregation among places of employment. *Social Forces* 58(3)[March]:761–776.
Bell, Derrick
  1986a The Gyroscopic Effect in American Racial Reform: The Law and Race from 1940 to 1986. Paper prepared for the Committee on the Status of Black Americans, National Research Council, Washington, D.C.
  1986b Memorandum, an addendum to the paper prepared for the Committee on the Status of Black Americans, National Research Council, Washington, D.C.
Bernstein, Richard
  1988 August Wilson's voices from the past. *The New York Times,* March 22.
Bobo, Lawrence
  1987 Racial Attitudes and the Status of Black Americans: A Social Psychological View of Change Since the 1940s. Paper prepared for the Committee on the Status of Black Americans, National Research Council, Washington, D.C.
Bogart, Leo, ed.
  1969 *Social Research and the Desegregation of the U.S. Army.* Chicago: Markham Publishing Company.
Bontemps, Arna
  1976 The black contribution to American letters: part I. Pp. 741–766 in Mabel M. Smythe, ed., *The Black American Reference Book.* Englewood Cliffs, N.J.: Prentice-Hall.
Brisbane, Robert H.
  1976 Black protest in America. Pp. 537–579 in Mabel M. Smythe, ed., *The Black American Reference Book.* Englewood Cliffs, N.J.: Prentice-Hall.
Brower, Jonathan J.
  1972 The Racial Basis of the Division of Labor Among Football Players in the National Football League as a Function of Stereotypes. Paper presented at the Pacific Sociological Association, Portland, Oregon.
Bureau of the Census
  1970 *Statistical Abstract of the United States.* Washington, D.C.: U.S. Department of Commerce.
  1988 *Statistical Abstract of the United States.* Washington, D.C.: U.S. Department of Commerce.
Bureau of Labor Statistics
  1989 *Employment and Earnings* (Jan.). Washington, D.C.: U.S. Department of Labor.
Burstein, Paul
  1985 *Discrimination, Jobs, and Politics: The Struggle for Equal Opportunity in the United States Since the New Deal.* Chicago: University of Chicago Press.
Butler, John Sibley
  1980 Symposium: race in the United States military. *Armed Forces & Society* 6(4)[Summer]:594–600.
Childs, John Brown, ed.
  1987 Manuscript prepared for the Panel on Social and Cultural Change and Continuity, Committee on the Status of Black Americans, National Research Council, Washington, D.C.

Chu, Donald B., and Jeffrey O. Segrave
  1980 Leadership recruitment and ethnic stratification in basketball. *Journal of Sport and Social Issues* 5(Fall/Winter):13–22.
Clay, Phillip L.
  1979 The process of black suburbanization. *Urban Affairs Quarterly* 14(4)[June]:405–424.
Coakley, Jay J.
  1986 *Sport in Society: Issues and Controversies.* 3d ed. St. Louis: Mosby.
Cohen, E.
  1975 The effects of school desegregation on race relations. *Law and Contemporary Problems* 39:271–299.
Coleman, James S., Sara D. Kelly, and John A. Moore
  1975 *Trends in School Segregation 1968–1973.* Washington, D.C.: Urban Institute.
Conot, Robert
  1974 *American Odyssey.* New York: Bantam Books.
Cook, Stuart W.
  1979 Social science and school desegregation: did we mislead the Supreme Court? *Personality and Social Psychology Bulletin* 5(4)[October]:420–437.
Crain, Robert, Jennifer A. Hawes, Randi L. Miller, and Janet R. Peichert
  1986 Finding Niches: The Long-Term Effects of a Voluntary Interdistrict School Desegregation Plan. Department of Philosophy and Social Sciences, New York Teachers College.
Dalfiume, Richard M.
  1968 The forgotten years of the Negro revolution. *Journal of American History* 55(June):90–106.
Davis, David Brion
  1975 *The Problem of Slavery in the Age of Revolution.* Ithaca, N.Y.: Cornell University Press.
Davis, James H., and Woodwie W. White
  1980 *Racial Transition in the Church.* Nashville, Tenn.: Abingdon Press.
Davis, John P.
  1966 The Negro in the armed forces of America. Pp. 590–661 in John P. Davis, ed., *The American Negro Reference Book.* Englewood Cliffs, N.J.: Prentice-Hall.
Edwards, Harry
  1979 Sports within the veil: the triumph, tragedies and challenges of Afro-American involvement. *Annals* 445(September):116–127.
  1984 The black "dumb jock." *The College Board Review* 131(Spring):8–12.
  1987 Opportunity knocks. *Sports Illustrated* 67(November 16):15.
Eitzen, D. Stanley
  1986 Black Athletes in American Society Since 1940: Continuity and Change in Racial Barriers to Equal Participation. Paper prepared for the Committee on the Status of Black Americans, National Research Council, Washington, D.C.
Eitzen, D. Stanley, and Norman R. Yetman
  1977 Immune from racism. *Civil Rights Digest* 9(Winter):2–13.
Ely, Melvin Patrick
  1985 Amos 'n' Andy: Lineage, Life and Legacy. Ph.D dissertation, Princeton University. Ann Arbor: University Microfilms International.
Enloe, Cynthia
  1980 *Ethnic Soldiers: State Security Divided Societies.* Athens: University of Georgia Press.

Epstein, J.
1980 After the Bus Arrives: Resegregation in Desegregated Schools. Paper presented at the annual meeting of the American Educational Research Association, Boston, Massachusetts.

Evans, Arthur
1979 Differences in recruitment of black and white football players at a big-eight university. *Journal of Sport and Social Issues* 3(Fall/Winter):1–10.

Eyler, Janet, Valerie J. Cook, and Leslie W. Ward
1983 Resegregation within desegregated schools. Pp. 126–162 in Christine H. Rossell and Willis D. Hawley, eds., *The Consequences of School Desegregation*. Philadelphia: Temple University Press.

Farley, Reynolds
1987 Changes in the Status and Characteristics of Blacks: 1940 to Mid-1980s. Paper prepared for the Committee on the Status of Black Americans, National Research Council, Washington, D.C.

Farley, Reynolds, and Walter Allen
1987 *The Color Line and the Quality of American Life*. New York: Russell Sage Foundation.

Farley, Reynolds, Toni Richards, and Clarence Wurdock
1980 School desegregation and white flight: an investigation of competing models and their discrepant findings. *Sociology of Education* 53:123–139.

Fligstein, Neil D.
1980 Who served in the military, 1940–1973? *Armed Forces and Society* 6(2)[Winter]:297–312.

Foner, Philip Sheldon
1981 *Organized Labor and the Black Worker, 1916–1973*. New York: Praeger.

Franklin, John Hope
1966 A brief history of the Negro in the United States. Pp. 1–95 in John P. Davis, ed., *The American Negro Reference Book*. Englewood Cliffs, N.J.: Prentice-Hall.
1969 *From Slavery to Freedom: A History of Negro Americans*. 3d ed. New York: Vintage Books.
1976 A brief history. . . . In Mabel M. Smythe, ed., *The Black American Reference Book*. Englewood Cliffs, N.J.: Prentice-Hall.

George, Zelma
1966 Negro music in American life. Pp. 731–758 in John P. Davis, ed., *The American Negro Reference Book*. Englewood Cliffs, N.J.: Prentice-Hall.

Gerard, H., and N. Miller
1975 *School Desegregation*. New York: Plenum.

Gould, William B.
1977 *Black Workers in White Unions*. Ithaca, N.Y.: Cornell University Press.

Hadaway, C. Kirk, David G. Hackett, and James F. Miller
1984 The most segregated institution: correlates of interracial church participation. *Review of Religious Research* 25(March):204–219.

Hammond, John L.
1974 Revival religion and antislavery politics. *American Sociological Review* 39(April): 175–186.

Hawley, Willis D., ed.
1981 *Effective School Desegregation: Equality, Quality, and Feasibility*. Newbury Park, Calif.: Sage Publications.

Helper, Rose
1969 *Racial Policies and Practices of Real Estate Brokers*. Minneapolis: University of Minnesota Press.

Hirsch, Arnold R.
1983 *Making the Second Ghetto: Race and Housing in Chicago: 1940–1960.* New York: Cambridge University Press.
Hochschild, Jennifer
1985 *Thirty Years After Brown.* Washington, D.C.: Joint Center for Political Studies.
Horowitz, Eugene
1944 Racial attitudes. Pp. 141–147 in O. Klineberg, ed., *Characteristics of the American Negro.* New York: Harper & Row.
Houston, Charles Hamilton
1944 The Negro soldier. *The Nation* (October 21):496–497.
Huggins, Nathan Irwin
1971 *Harlem Renaissance.* New York: Oxford University Press.
Hughes, Langston
1976 Black influences in the American theatre: part I. Pp. 684–704 in Mabel M. Smythe, ed., *The Black American Reference Book.* Englewood Cliffs, N.J.: Prentice-Hall.
Johnson, Charles S.
1943 *Patterns of Negro Segregation.* New York: Harper & Row.
Kelley, Dean M.
1972 *Why Conservative Churches Are Growing.* New York: Harper & Row.
Kluger, Richard
1976 *Simple Justice: The History of Brown v. Board of Education and Black America's Struggle for Equality.* New York: Alfred A. Knopf.
Kusmer, Kenneth L.
1976 *A Ghetto Takes Shape: Black Cleveland, 1870–1930.* Urbana: University of Illinois Press.
La Farge, John
1956 *The Catholic Viewpoint on Race Relations.* New York: Harper & Row.
Laney, Garrine P.
1986 The Evolution of Equal Employment Programs, 1940–1985. Paper prepared for the Committee on the Status of Black Americans, National Research Council, Washington, D.C.
Langberg, Mark, and Reynolds Farley
1985 Residential segregation of Asian-Americans in 1980. *Sociology and Social Research* 70(1):71–75.
Lapchick, Richard
1984 *Broken Promises: Racism in American Sports.* New York: St. Martin's Press.
Letwin, Daniel
1986 Black Migration: 1940–1970. Paper prepared for the Committee on the Status of Black Americans, National Research Council, Washington, D.C.
Lieberson, Stanley L.
1980 *A Piece of the Pie: Black and White Immigrants Since 1980.* Berkeley: University of California Press.
Lincoln, C. Eric
1984 *Race, Religion, and the Continuing American Dilemma.* New York: Hill & Wang.
Loescher, F. S.
1948 *The Protestant Church and the Negro.* New York: Association Press.
Long, Herman H.
1958 *Fellowship for Whom? A Study of Racial Inclusiveness in Congregational Christian Churches.* New York: Department of Race Relations, Board of Home Missions.
Long, Larry, and Diane De Are
1981 Suburbanization of blacks. *American Demographics* 3(8)[September]:16–21;44.

Longshore, Douglas, and Jeffrey Prager
  1985 The impact of school desegregation: a situational analysis. Pp. 75–91 in Ralph H. Turner and James F. Short, Jr., eds., *Annual Review of Sociology,* Vol. 11.
MacGregor, Morris J., Jr.
  1981 *Integration of the Armed Forces, 1940–1965.* Washington, D.C.: Center of Military History, U.S. Army. U.S. Government Printing Office.
Marshall, Ray F., and Vernon Briggs
  1967 *The Negro and Apprenticeship.* Baltimore, Md.: Johns Hopkins University Press.
Massengale, John D., and Steven E. Farrington
  1977 The influence of playing position centrality on the careers of college football coaches. *Review of Sport and Leisure* 2(June).
Massey, Douglas S., and Nancy A. Denton
  1987 Trends in residential segregation of blacks, Hispanics and Asians: 1970–1980. *American Sociological Review* 52(6)[December]:802–825.
Mays, Benjamin E.
  1957 *Seeking to Be Christian in Race Relations.* New York: Friendship Press.
McAdam, Doug
  1982 *Political Process and the Development of Black Insurgency, 1930–1970.* Chicago: University of Chicago Press.
Meier, Kenneth J.
  1984 Teachers, students, and discrimination: the policy impact of black representation. *Journal of Politics* 46:252–263.
Meier, Kenneth J., and Robert E. England
  1984 Black representation and educational policy: are they related? *American Political Science Review* 78(June):392–402.
Mogull, Robert G.
  1981 Salary discrimination in professional sports. *Atlantic Economic Journal* 9(September):106–110.
Moskos, Charles C.
  1985 Blacks in the Army: an American success story. *Atlantic Monthly,* October.
Moskos, Charles C., and John S. Butler
  1987 Blacks in the Military Since World War II. Paper prepared for the Committee on the Status of Black Americans, National Research Council, Washington, D.C.
Murphy, M. D.
  1980 The Involvement of Blacks in Women's Athletics in Member Institutions of the AIAW. Ph.D. dissertation, Florida State University.
National Advisory Commission on Civil Disorders
  1968 *Report of the National Advisory Commission on Civil Disorders.* New York: Bantam Books.
Neal, Larry
  1976 The black contribution to American letters: part II, the writer as activist—1960 and after. Pp. 767–790 in Mabel M. Smythe, ed., *The Black American Reference Book.* Englewood Cliffs, N.J.: Prentice-Hall.
Niebuhr, Richard H.
  1929 *The Social Sources of Denominationalism.* New York: Holt, Rinehart & Winston.
Norford, George E.
  1976 The popular media: part II, the black role in radio and television. Pp. 875–888 in Mabel M. Smythe, ed., *The Black American Reference Book.* Englewood Cliffs, N.J.: Prentice-Hall.
Northrup, Herbert Roof
  1944 *Organized Labor and the Negro.* New York: Harper & Brothers.

Orfield, Gary
1983 *Public School Desegregation in the United States, 1968–1980*. Washington, D.C.: Joint Center for Political Studies.
Pascal, Anthony M., and Leonard A. Rapping
1970 *Racial Discrimination in Organized Baseball*. Santa Monica, Calif.: Rand Corporation.
Patchen, Martin
1982 *Black-White Contact in Schools: Its Social and Academic Effects*. West LaFayette, Ind.: Purdue University Press.
Pinkney, Alphonso
1969 *Black Americans*. Englewood Cliffs, N.J.: Prentice-Hall.
Poindexter, Paula M., and Carolyn A. Stroman
1981 Blacks and television: a review of the research literature. *Job* 25(2)[Spring]:103–122.
Powell, Richard J.
1986 The Visual Arts and Afro-America, 1940–1980. Paper prepared for the Committee on the Status of Black Americans, National Research Council, Washington, D.C.
Raper, Arthur
1933 *The Tragedy of Lynching*. Chapel Hill: University of North Carolina Press.
Richardson, Harry V.
1976 Afro-American religion: part I, the origin and development of the established churches. Pp. 492–506 in Mabel M. Smythe, ed., *The Black American Reference Book*. Englewood Cliffs, N.J.: Prentice-Hall.
Rist, Ray C.
1979 *Desegregated Schools: Appraisals of an American Experiment*. New York: Academic Press.
Rosenblatt, Aaron
1967 Negroes in baseball: the failure of success. *Trans-Action* 4(September):51–53.
Rossell, Christine
1978 School desegregation and community social change. *Law and Contemporary Problems* 42(3):133–183.
Sabrosky, Alan
1980 Symposium: race and the United States military. *Armed Forces & Society* 6(4)[Summer]:601–606.
Schexnider, Alvin J.
1980 Symposium: race and the United States military. *Armed Forces & Society* 6(4)[Summer]:606–613.
1983 Blacks in the military. Pp. 241–269 in *The State of Black America*. Washington, D.C.: National Urban League.
Schofield, Janet
1986 School Desegregation and Black Americans. Paper prepared for the Committee on the Status of Black Americans, National Research Council, Washington, D.C.
Scully, Gerald W.
1974 Discrimination: the cost of baseball. In Roger G. Noll, ed., *Government and the Sports Business*. Washington, D.C.: Brookings Institution.
Shogan, Robert, and Tom Craig
1964 *The Detroit Race Riot: A Study in Violence*. Philadelphia: Chilton Books.
Simpson, George E., and J. Milton Yinger
1985 *Racial and Cultural Minorities*. 5th ed. New York: Plenum.

Slavin, Robert E.
1978 *Effects of Student Teams and Peer Tutoring on Academic Achievement and Time-on-Task.* Report No. 253, Center for Social Organization of Schools. Baltimore, Md.: Johns Hopkins University.
1980 Cooperative learning in teams: state of the art. *Education Psychology* 15:93–111.
Stillman, Richard J., II
1976 Black participation in the armed forces. Pp. 889–926 in Mabel M. Smythe, ed., *The Black American Reference Book.* Englewood Cliffs, N.J.: Prentice-Hall.
Stouffer, Samuel A., Edward A. Suchman, Leland C. DeVinney, Shirley A. Star, and Robin M. Williams, Jr.
1949 *The American Soldier.* 2 vols. Princeton, N.J.: Princeton University Press.
Stroman, Carolyn A.
1986 The Mass Media and Black Americans. Paper prepared for the Committee on the Status of Black Americans, National Research Council, Washington, D.C.
Sumner, David E.
1983 The Episcopal Church's Involvement in Civil Rights, 1943–1973. Master's thesis, School of Theology, University of the South.
Taeuber, Alma F.
1987 Memorandum to the Committee on the Status of Black Americans, National Research Council, Washington, D.C.
Taeuber, Karl E., and Alma F. Taeuber
1965 *Negros in Cities.* Chicago: Aldine.
Tolbert, Charles M.
1975 The Black Athlete in the Southwest Conference: A Study of Institutional Racism. Ph.D. dissertation, Baylor University.
Trayes, E. J.
1969 The Negro in journalism: surveys show low ratio. *Journalism Quarterly* 46:5–8.
U.S. Commission on Civil Rights
1977 *Twenty Years After Brown.* Washington, D.C.: U.S. Government Printing Office.
Vose, Clement E.
1959 *Caucasians Only: The Supreme Court, the NAACP, and the Restrictive Covenant Case.* Berkeley: University of California Press.
Weaver, Robert
1946 *Negro Labor: A National Problem.* New York: Harcourt, Brace & World.
Whalum, Wendell, David Baker, and Richard A. Long
1976 Afro-American music. Pp. 791–826 in Mabel M. Smythe, ed., *The Black American Reference Book.* Englewood Cliffs, N.J.: Prentice-Hall.
White, Michael J.
1986 Segregation and diversity measures in population distribution. *Population Index* 52(2):198–221.
Williams, Robin M., Jr.
1947 *The Reduction of Intergroup Tensions.* Bulletin 57. New York: Social Science Research Council.
1977 *Mutual Accommodation: Ethnic Conflict and Cooperation.* Minneapolis: University of Minnesota Press.
Wolsely, Roland Edgar
1971 *The Black Press.* Ames: Iowa State University Press.
Wolters, Raymond
1984 *The Burden of Brown: Thirty Years of School Desegregation.* Knoxville: University of Tennessee Press.

Wood, James R., and Mayer N. Zald
   1966 Aspects of racial integration in the Methodist Church: sources of resistance to educational policy. *Social Forces* 45(December):255–265.
Yetman, Norman R., and D. Stanley Eitzen
   1972 Black Americans in sports: unequal opportunity for equal ability. *Civil Rights Digest* (August):20–34.
Yinger, J. Milton
   1986 Black Americans and Predominantly White Churches. Paper prepared for the Committee on the Status of Black Americans, National Research Council, Washington, D.C.
Zoloth, B.
   1976 Alternative measures of school segregation. *Land Economics* 52(August):278–398.

3

RACIAL ATTITUDES AND BEHAVIOR

Lev Mills
Le Roi? (1972)
Screenprint on paper
The Studio Museum in Harlem, New York City

F ar more research involving either systematic experimentation or large-scale sample surveys has been conducted on the attitudes of whites than on those of blacks. Some of the very earliest surveys on racial attitudes excluded blacks altogether. As one survey analyst wrote (Smith, 1987:441):

> The attitudes white Americans hold toward their black counterparts probably comprise the longest running topic in public opinion research. Yet, despite this prominence of race-relations topics in scientific sample surveys, until recently black Americans—long the minority group most identified with "racial matters" in the United States—were virtually invisible to serious students of American values.

In part this imbalance was due to small numbers of blacks in national survey samples. But in part it may also have reflected assumptions shared by many researchers, stated most clearly as Myrdal's "American dilemma": a contradiction between American democratic values and the actual discriminatory treatment of blacks. This view therefore posed American race relations as a problem fundamentally located in the minds of white Americans (Myrdal, 1944:lxxi), with black attitudes, perceptions, and beliefs as secondary reactions. This attention to white attitudes virtually ignored the important role of black self-determination, and it also drew attention away from the practical costs and advantages, to blacks and whites, of segregation and discrimination. But, the focus on attitudes of whites did have a substantive basis. In view of the economic and political power of the white majority, a change in some of their attitudes would be necessary if blacks were to succeed in their struggle for civil rights and equality.

In this chapter we present the data on white and black attitudes and then the explanations that have been offered for those attitudes. We trace change in the racial attitudes of white Americans, and we examine actual practices of discriminatory or equal treatment in black-white relations. The literature on the attitudes of whites is extensive, but is focused on a few particular types of issues: openness to integration, support for racially equalitarian treatment, and other matters involving evaluations of blacks, integration, or racial equality.

The focus on these issues in the survey data, at least implicitly, carries over much of the assumption that the American dilemma is a matter of whites' acceptance of blacks. We redress this emphasis wherever possible by comparing the attitudes of blacks to those of whites. Black attitudes often differ from those of whites. For example, blacks are far more likely than whites to believe that discrimination and prejudice are ongoing social problems that lie at the heart of black-white inequality and to place a stronger emphasis than do whites on equalitarian values. On many important issues, however, the attitudes of blacks and whites are very similar.

This chapter presents evidence supporting several important findings: growth in white acceptance of the goals of integration and equal treatment; white reluctance to accept the implementation of policies intended to change race relations; reluctance on the part of whites to enter social settings (e.g., schools) in which blacks are a majority; continuing discriminatory behavior by whites, especially in areas involving close personal contact; conflicting beliefs of whites with regard to the values of equality and individualism; and high levels of support among blacks for goals of integration and equal treatment.

In addressing both black and white perspectives, three points stand out: (1) blacks and whites share a substantial consensus, in the abstract, on the broad goal of achieving an integrated and equalitarian society; (2) their images of what constitute integrated, equalitarian, and racially harmonious conditions are often different or contradictory; and (3) black and white perceptions of the genesis and reproduction of group inequality are sharply divergent. The outcome of these patterns is a dynamic tension in which blacks are a self-aware and politically conscious group that resists a view of integration as complete assimilation, while many whites believe in and advocate equalitarian ideals but often express ambivalence and sometimes manifest open resistance and discriminatory behavior toward blacks.

THE EMPIRICAL RECORD: 1940–1986

CHANGE IN RACIAL ATTITUDES: AN OVERVIEW

Beginning in the late 1930s, the methodology and institutional base for conducting scientific sample surveys improved (see Rossi et al., 1983). This made it possible to develop an "attitudinal record" over time based on the recorded replies of sample survey respondents to questions concerning black-white relations (Schuman et al., 1985). In some cases, these questions have been asked in identical or near-identical form from the 1940s to the 1980s.

Several clear patterns emerge from these trend studies. Schuman and colleagues (1985) drew several conclusions regarding change in the attitudes of whites. We supplement their list with other conclusions regarding the attitudes of blacks.

- Black Americans have supported racially equalitarian principles as far back as there are data.
- There has been a steady increase in support among white Americans for principles of racial equality, but substantially less support for policies intended to implement principles of racial equality.
- Blacks also exhibit a gap between support for principles and support for policies intended to implement those principles, and blacks show recent decreases in support for policy implementation strategies.
- Whites are more accepting of equal treatment with regard to the public domains of life than private domains of life, and they are especially accepting of relations involving transitory forms of contact.
- Openness to equal treatment also varies by the number or proportion of blacks likely to be involved. Where blacks remain a clear minority, the data indicate growing white acceptance of racial equality. Where blacks approach a majority, change is less frequent and overall levels of pro equal-treatment response are low.
- Whites living in the North have been and remain more pro equal treatment than those living in the South. Patterns of change are usually the same in each region.
- Measures of black alienation from white society suggest an increase in black alienation from the late 1960s into the 1980s.
- The process of change during the 1960s and early 1970s appeared to involve both generational changes (cohort replacement effects) and individual change. For the late 1970s and into the 1980s, what change has occurred is almost entirely a product of cohort replacement.

What factors are responsible for changes in Americans' attitudes toward black-white relations? We identify three basic social forces: alterations in social context (historical change), individual modification of attitudes, and cohort replacement. Change over time in attitudes, whether positive or negative in direction, can be brought about through a process of demographic or cohort replacement, or it can be brought about by modifications in individual attitudes. In the former case, older generations who have one set of attitudes are replaced by younger people who hold a different set of attitudes. In the case of individual change, a person who expressed a particular attitude at one time changes to a different position at a later time.

For example, previous studies of white attitudes (Hyman and Sheatsley, 1964; Schuman et al., 1985; Taylor et al., 1978) found that change during the 1960s and early 1970s involved both cohort replacement and individual change. But Schuman and colleagues (1985) reported that positive change recorded in the late 1970s was mainly a product of cohort replacement. They also found that the difference between the very youngest cohorts and other recent cohorts had narrowed. Thus, recently, even cohort replacement was weakening as a mechanism for producing change in whites' attitudes toward blacks.

WHITE ATTITUDES

The Scientific American *Reports*

Until fairly recently the most widely known and best studies of change in racial attitudes were based almost exclusively on data collected in early surveys by the National Opinion Research Center (NORC) and reported in a series of articles published in *Scientific American*. The first of these articles (Hyman and Sheatsley, 1956) focused on issues of desegregation, reporting particularly on change between 1942 and 1956 in attitudes toward desegregation of schools, housing, and public transportation. On each of these issues there was evidence of increasing support for desegregation. Hyman and Sheatsley also reported that there were often large differences between North and South: there was majority sentiment for desegregation by northerners and for continued segregation by southerners. Also, younger people were more likely than older people to favor desegregation, and highly educated people were more open to desegregation than were people with low levels of education. The age differences and the apparent effects of education provided grounds for expecting that further change would occur as younger, better educated individuals "replaced" older, less educated individuals.

Hyman and Sheatsley suggested that attitudes were importantly linked to actual social conditions. Thus, where segregation existed without significant challenge, the attitudes reflected such conditions. They did not find that many Americans sensed a moral dilemma on race issues. They tried to examine Myrdal's (1944) concern with the contradiction between American values and the treatment of blacks by asking a question on whether or not blacks were being treated fairly. As they explained (Hyman and Sheatsley, 1956:39):

> Certainly a study of the comments people make in answering the questions reveals little soul-searching, hesitation or feeling of guilt. Many declare: "They're being treated too doggone good." Respondents remark: "Just look around you. They are being given every opportunity for progress that they never had before."

These results notwithstanding, there were two key reasons at that time to think that further change was probable. First, belief in the innate intellectual inferiority of blacks, a fundamental ideological factor in the case for segregation, had greatly declined between 1942 and 1956, falling from roughly 60 percent to just over 20 percent. Second, the survey findings suggested that positive change in attitudes followed the implementation of concrete social change.

The large sample sizes of the surveys allowed the analysts to divide southern communities into areas that had desegregated their schools, those that were moving in the direction of doing so, and those that were adamantly resisting change. They found the more change that had already taken place, the more positive were the attitudes toward school desegregation. Thus, 31 percent of respondents in areas with desegregated schools supported desegregation, compared with 17 percent in areas just beginning to take steps toward desegregation and only 4 percent in areas resisting desegregation. Some areas were probably more receptive to desegregation than others to begin with, but none even approached majority support. Hyman and Sheatsley did not argue that overwhelming opposition to change could be readily converted, but rather that where openness to racial change existed among at least a substantial minority of whites, it was likely that leaders could act to influence majority opinion.

The second article in the series (Hyman and Sheatsley, 1964) stressed many of the same points. In particular, it noted that the growing pace and intensity of the civil rights struggle had not slowed improvement in attitudes toward desegregating the schools, public transportation, and housing. The pace of change in attitudes from 1956 to 1963 was, in fact, faster than the pace of change had been between 1942 and 1956. For example, support among southern whites for school desegregation rose from 2 percent to 14 percent between 1942 and 1956, an increase of 12 points in 14 years; between 1956 and 1963, support for desegregation went from 14 percent to 30 percent, an increase of 16 points in just 7 years. Hyman and Sheatsley reported that change was not simply a function of younger, better educated people replacing older, poorly educated people: many people who had supported segregation at an earlier time had, at least in terms of their verbal replies to survey questions, changed to support for desegregation.

Hyman and Sheatsley again stressed that opinion bore an important connection to prevailing social conditions. Their 1963 data confirmed important differences among southern communities. Support for school desegregation ranged from a high of 54 percent in areas that had implemented desegregation, to 38 percent in areas that had made only token steps in that direction, to 28 percent in those areas where the schools remained segregated. In this case Hyman and Sheatsley were more certain than earlier that action by public officials had probably encouraged attitude change rather than the other way around.

In a subtle manner, the content and tenor of the *Scientific American* reports on racial attitudes changed as key social issues and events in the nation changed. While the first two articles stressed the strength of a positive trend in racial attitudes, the third article in the series (Greeley and Sheatsley, 1971) was also more directly and extensively concerned with the issue of "white backlash." Key questions used in the earlier analyses continued to show positive change, especially in the South. The overall level of support for desegregated public transportation was so high, 88 percent in 1970, that the question could not be used to elicit evidence of much further change. On the basis of these data, Greeley and Sheatsley saw little support for the idea that a white backlash against racial progress had arisen. Only among poorly educated "white ethnics" did they find any indication of a backlash, and even those effects were not large (Bobo, 1987a).

The fourth and most recent article in the series (Taylor et al., 1978) found little support for the white backlash hypothesis. Indeed, this article reported just the opposite, a remarkable "liberal leap" forward between 1970 and 1972 followed by steady positive change between 1972 and 1976. The sharp upturn in support for racial desegregation in the early 1970s was matched by similar upturns in positive attitudes on social and civil liberties. Thus, Taylor and colleagues argued that more favorable racial attitudes were part of a general and robust trend in public opinion. Although the replacement of older cohorts by younger cohorts and the increasing average level of education were important factors in the trend, much of the observed change involved individual changes in attitudes, not just cohort replacement.

In sum, from the early 1940s to the late 1970s there were important shifts in white attitudes, from widespread belief that blacks were born less intelligent than whites to the belief that the races were of equal intelligence and from majority support for segregation of public places, schools, and housing to majority support for equal treatment. Even assuming that social pressures for "correct" answers affected responses and that attitudes were only tenuously connected to behavior, the change had been impressive.

One analyst characterized this research as having shown such sweeping progress that questions on some issues, for example, desegregation of public transportation and of schools, had become obsolete; that the survey data provided no support for the white backlash hypothesis; that changes in racial attitudes were closely linked to the liberalization of public opinion on other issues; and that both cohort replacement and individual change in attitudes contributed to the trends documented in the *Scientific American* reports (Seeman, 1981:394).

However, the consistency, unambiguity, and comprehensiveness of the changes documented in these studies were not completely replicated by other studies. Condran's (1979) analysis of the NORC data for five questions asked in 1963, 1972, and 1977 suggested that change from 1972 to 1977 had not been as consistently positive as had the change from 1963 to 1972. He also found that on questions concerning residential integration and on those that asked if blacks should "push" themselves where they were not wanted, younger age cohorts were less positive than older cohorts. He concluded that much of the positive change in racial attitudes may have involved only verbal adherence to newly institutionalized racial norms and that certainly "the liberals of 1977 [had] less reason to be sanguine concerning white American racial attitudes than their counterparts of 1972" (Condran, 1979:475).

In addition, the widespread controversies over school busing, opposition to some affirmative action plans, and the continuing pervasiveness of residential segregation also raised questions about the meaning of the changes reported in the *Scientific American* reports. In an article published separately from the *Scientific American* reports, Greeley and Sheatsley (1974) directly addressed the extent and implications of whites' opposition to school busing. Fewer than one-fifth of whites in 1972 favored "the busing of black and white school children from one school district to another." Yet, Greeley and Sheatsley noted, blacks were far from uniform in their attitudes toward school busing, and whites' support for the principle of school desegregation continued to grow. They concluded that opposition to busing could not be reduced to simple racism. They did note that the crucial race issues had shifted from matters of broad principles to the far more problematic issues "of the practical policies which most effectively will achieve racial justice" (Greeley and Sheatsley, 1974:249).

Social Distance

Social distance preferences further complicate the picture of change. These questions pose hypothetical social settings that vary in racial composition. Respondents are asked to indicate whether they would take part in such settings, withdraw from such settings, or in other ways respond positively or negatively. Three of these questions pertain to willingness to allow one's children to attend schools with different numbers of black students, ranging from a few, to about half, to more than half. The National Opinion Research Center and Gallup have used nearly identical versions of these questions. The Gallup data provide the longer series, the questions having first been asked in a survey in 1958. At that point 75 percent of whites said they would not object to sending their children to a school in which a few of the students were black; 50 percent said they would have no objection to a school in which half of the students were black. Responses to all three questions show positive change over time. But, the increase in openness to desegregated schooling is much lower when the question specifies that most of the children in the school would be black. In addition, the educational and regional differentials are more pronounced for the "few" and "half black" questions than for the "most" question (see Table 3-1 and pages 125–127; see also Smith, 1981).

The patterns of results are largely similar when the questions pertain to residential areas and housing. Two questions address contact under circumstances in which blacks would be the clear minority ("next door" and "same block"); one implies a more substantial black presence in the neighborhood ("great numbers"). As is true for schools, the number of blacks mentioned in the question has an important effect on white openness to interracial contact.

Thus, when asked in 1958, "If black people came to live next door, would you move," 56 percent of whites said they would not move. But when

TABLE 3-1 Trends in Racial Attitudes

Whites

Type of Question	Question	First and Last Year Asked	Percent Change: Last Minus First Year	Percent Positive at Last Time Asked
Principle	Same schools	1942/1982	+58	90
	Equal jobs	1944/1972	+52	97
	Same transportation	1942/1970	+42	88
	Residential choice (NORC)[a]	1963/1982	+32	71
	Residential choice (ISR)	1964/1976	+23	88
	Same accommodations	1963/1970	+15	88
	Black candidate (Gallup)	1958/1983	+44	81
	Black candidate (NORC)	1972/1983	+12	85
	Against intermarriage laws	1963/1982	+28	66
	Intermarriage	1958/1983	+36	40
	General segregation[b]	1964/1978	+8	35
Implementation	Federal job intervention	1964/1974	−2	36
	Open housing	1973/1983	+12	46
	Federal school intervention	1964/1978	−17	25
	Busing (ISR)	1972/1980	0	9
	Busing (NORC)	1972/1983	+6	21
	Accommodations intervention	1964/1974	+22	66
	Spending on blacks	1973/1983	−1	26
	Aid to minorities	1970/1982	−4	18

Blacks

Type of Question	Question	First and Last Year Asked	Percent Change: Last Minus First Year	Percent Positive at Last Time Asked
Principle	Same schools	1972/1982	0	96
	Residential choice (ISR)	1964/1976	+1	99
	Black candidate (Gallup)	1958/1983	+4	96
	Black candidate (NORC)	1974/1982	0	97
	Intermarriage	1972/1983	+2	78
	General segregation[b]	1964/1978	+8	35
Implementation	Federal job intervention	1964/1974	−10	82
	Federal school intervention	1964/1978	−22	60
	Busing (ISR)	1972/1980	+3	49
	Busing (NORC)	1972/1983	0	56
	Accommodations intervention	1964/1974	+2	91
	Spending on blacks	1973/1983	−3	80
	Aid to minorities	1970/1982	−29	49

		Years	Change	%
Social distance	Few (Gallop)	1958/1980	+20	95
	Few (NORC)	1972/1983	+2	95
	Half (Gallup)	1958/1980	+26	76
	Half (NORC)	1972/1983	0	76
	Most (Gallup)	1958/1980	+9	42
	Most (NORC)	1972/1983	−6	37
	Next door	1958/1978	+30	86
	Great numbers	1958/1978	+26	46
	Same block	1942/1972	+49	85
	Black dinner guest	1963/1982	+26	78
Miscellaneous	Thermometer rating[c] of			
	blacks	1964/1982	+1	61
	Ku Klux Klan rating[d]	1965/1979	−13	71
	Intelligence	1942/1968	+30	77
	Civil rights push	1964/1980	+6	9
	Black push	1963/1982	+18	39
Miscellaneous	Thermometer rating[c] of			
	blacks	1964/1982	−13	76
	Ku Klux Klan[d]	1965/1979	−8	80
	Civil rights push	1964/1980	+18	45
	Civil rights progress	1964/1976	−28	32

Note: NORC, National Opinion Research Center; ISR, Institute for Social Research.

[a]This item uses a Likert scale response format. The percentages reported involve a combination of "disagree slightly" and "disagree strongly" responses.

[b]The trend for this item is probably affected by a contextual linkage to the federal school intervention implementation item.

[c]The feeling thermometer is a standard question used in the National Election Study. It calls for respondents to rank groups or individuals on a 100-point scale, where 0 indicates very cold feelings, 50 indicates neutral feelings, and 100 indicates very warm feelings.

[d]The rating scale runs from −5 to +5. The figures reported indicate the percentage of people giving "highly unfavorable" ratings of the Ku Klux Klan (scores of −4 or −5).

Sources: Data from Schuman et al. (1985) and Bobo (1987a).

123

asked about moving "if black people came to live in great numbers in your neighborhood," 20 percent said they would not move, 29 percent said they might move, and 51 percent said they definitely would move. This difference in levels of openness to interracial contact is present at the most recent time for these two questions (1978) and is slightly larger than it was in 1958. Although 86 percent in 1978 said they would not move if black people lived next door to them, only 46 percent said they would not move if large numbers of blacks were in the neighborhood.

All three of the social distance questions concerned with residential contact undergo positive change. This result is surprising for the "great numbers" question, which otherwise behaves very much like the question on majority black schools; both show low absolute levels of support and are not strongly related to level of education. For the two questions involving just a few blacks ("same block" and "next door"), people who have more education express greater openness to interracial contact than those with less education. In sum, the social distance questions that pertain to smaller numbers of blacks undergo change and relate to region and education in much the same way as do principle-type questions, such as "same schools." When larger numbers of blacks are mentioned—in particular, if blacks are stated to be a clear majority—the results more closely parallel those for the policy implementation-type questions, such as school busing (see below).

SOCIAL POLICY, SOCIAL CONTEXT, AND RACIAL ATTITUDES

Greeley and Sheatsley (1974) suggested that the shift in emphasis from matters of principle to matters of practical social policy was the decisive change in racial issues in the 1970s. The most recent of the *Scientific American* articles (Taylor et al., 1978) did not emphasize this important shift, however, presumably because the task was to trace change with items included in the early surveys. Thus, sustained attention to attitudes on policies on race issues was largely lacking until recently (Campbell [1971] is an exception). One trend study of black-white attitudes that did move beyond the types of questions relied on in the *Scientific American* reports to include questions on policy changes concluded that the basic patterns of change were indeed more complex.

This study (Schuman et al., 1985) differed from the *Scientific American* reports in three aspects. First, in addition to the NORC data, Schuman and colleagues also relied on data collected by the Institute for Social Research (ISR) at the University of Michigan and data collected by the Gallup organization. Thus, three major sources of trend data on racial attitudes were considered. Second, this more comprehensive coverage of data resources allowed consideration of two additional types of questions that played little or no part in the NORC surveys. Results for these additional questions differ from results obtained for the types of questions in the NORC surveys. Third, Schuman and colleagues also examined change in the racial attitudes of blacks and compared them with results for whites.

Schuman and colleagues examined trends for racial attitude questions that had been asked in national sample surveys in identical (or near identical) form at 2 or more times and spanned at least a 10-year period over the years from 1942 to 1983. These criteria resulted in a pool of 32 questions. The questions were placed into three groupings: those concerned with racial principles, those concerned with the implementation of principles, and those concerned with social distance preferences.

Racial principle questions addressed attitudes about the general goals of integration and equal treatment of the races; they did not cover what steps or policies should be undertaken to achieve these ends. Implementation questions addressed the steps that might be taken, usually by the federal government, to put the principles regarding black-white relations into concrete practice. The social distance questions—asked only of whites—concerned personal willingness to take part in social settings involving contact with varying numbers of blacks. The conceptual categories not only highlighted differences in the content of the questions, but also showed that different types of questions had different patterns of change over time. Table 3-1 shows the results for the main questions used by Schuman and colleagues for blacks and whites. Each question is given the same descriptive content label used by Schuman and colleagues.

The questions are organized into the three major conceptual categories and a residual miscellaneous category. Dates for the first and most recent times questions were asked are presented along with the percentage of respondents giving the more pro desegregation response at the most recent time questions were asked. Also shown is a difference score as a rough indicator of overall change. In some instances the most recent figures we report, and thus the difference scores, differ from those reported by Schuman and colleagues because more recent data are now available.

Focusing first on the results for whites, all of the racial principle questions show positive change. For example, the question labeled "same schools," which spans the period from 1942 to 1982, has moved 58 points in a pro desegregation direction. This change reflects substantial movement in a pro desegregation direction. This change occurred both in and outside the South. Furthermore, there is considerable narrowing of the gap between those with high and low levels of education.

This question can be treated as the prototypical racial principle item. The principle questions typically involved large positive change over time, regional convergence as the North reached a ceiling and the South continued to change, and a narrowing of educational differences over time. By the end of the series, most of these questions revealed very high absolute levels of support for the pro desegregation response.

The results do vary, however, by subject matter and by wording of the question. Support for school desegregation thus attains a much higher absolute level than does opposition to laws that forbid racial intermarriage. So it is clear that whites do not uniformly give the socially desirable response to racial principle questions. Still, the *Scientific American* reports are based almost exclusively on results for principle-type questions. An examination of trends in response to implementation questions qualifies the portrait of positive change.

Support for the implementation of principles of equalitarian black-white relations has been much less than support for the principles themselves. Moreover, support for implementation policies has seldom shown as much positive change as has support for the principles. Although the implementation questions usually do not span as many years as the principle items, there are several such questions that closely parallel several principle items in wording and that involve considerable overlap in the time points covered by the two types of questions.

The most striking case of divergence in trends between principle and implementation involves the questions of "federal school intervention" and "same schools": the former asks whether or not the federal government should become involved in efforts to desegregate the schools; the latter asks if black and white school children should attend the same schools. Although support for the principle of desegregated schools ("same schools") rose by 22 points from 1964 to 1977–1978 (the period of years for which there are data on both questions), support for federal efforts to implement this principle declined by 17 points. This decline occurred when the real-world context of the question was changing considerably. In 1964, desegregation of schools was primarily focused on the South and involved the dismantling of separate school systems that had been created and maintained under state laws. By the early 1970s, school desegregation was focused on the North, and federal involvement was symbolized by busing children to and from schools in segregated residential areas. These changes no doubt affected the 17-point decline. And, indeed, Schuman and colleagues reported that the decline was restricted almost entirely to the North, clearly involved change at the individual level, and occurred in the post-1972 period. The decline thus occurred after the introduction of mandatory desegregation and busing in the North. Further analysis showed that the decline in support for the implementation of school desegregation is not attributable to confusion between questions of the goal of school desegregation and of the use of federal authority; trust in the federal government, although it may contribute to the low absolute level of support for implementation, does not affect the trend (Bobo, 1987a).

A gap also exists between support for principles and support for implementation with regard to questions on job opportunities ("equal jobs" and "federal job intervention"), residential desegregation ("residential choice" and "open housing"), and access to public accommodations ("same accommodations" and "accommodations intervention"). None of these pairings show the sharp divergence in trends observed for the questions on schools. In particular, support for the implementation of rights for blacks to freely use hotels and restaurants and to live wherever they choose did increase over time. But the trends were not as strong as those for comparable principle items, and a substantial gap in support remained.

The importance of the distinction between principle and implementation is underscored by differences in the responses to these questions by educational level and region. Schuman and colleagues found that education usually had small or no effects on implementation questions (see also Jackman, 1978; Jackman and Muha, 1984). Two exceptions were the open housing question and the accommodations intervention question; as noted above, these were the two implementation questions that showed positive change. In addition, regional differences were usually smaller for questions of implementation than for questions of principle.

But as we observed earlier, attitudes may change if the social context changes. This holds for reactions to issues of policy implementation as well as to matters of principle. Recent reports have indicated that the degree of opposition to school busing among whites has declined (Harris, 1987; Schuman and Bobo, 1988). Our analysis confirms that resistance to school busing is less extreme than in the past. Table 3-2 shows the percentage of blacks and whites expressing opposition to school busing in General Social Surveys between 1972 and 1986. Blacks are always more likely to favor busing than whites, but both groups show a slight overall decline in opposition to school busing. This change occurs in the post-1978 period and to a larger degree among whites.

Table 3-3 shows the percentage of whites opposed to school busing by both region of the country and age. These data indicate that the change among whites occurred mainly in the post-1978 period, with the decline emerging most clearly in 1985 and 1986. The decline in opposition to school busing is somewhat larger among those in the 18- to 27-year-old age range. Among the youngest age group in both the North and South, more than one-third express support for school busing. The change is also larger in the South than in the North for three of the four age categories. A small tendency for greater opposition to school busing in the South has disappeared.

That these positive changes occur in response to a question that asks about "the busing of black and white school children from one district to another" should be underscored. This question poses one of the stronger versions of busing: it implies busing both blacks and whites and potentially crossing district boundaries. The positive trend may suggest considerable underlying attitude change. In general, it is a well-established finding that the exact wording of questions influences responses; that is, people do not respond to an abstract underlying issue or concept but to a question as posed (Schuman and Kalton, 1985; Turner and Martin, 1984). For example, Schuman and Bobo (1988) found in a 1985 national telephone survey that support for school busing among whites was higher than 40 percent when the question referred to busing blacks to predominantly white schools. That the observed change occurs disproportionately among younger and southern whites is consistent with the claim that actual experience with school desegregation and busing is weakening the previously solid wall of white opposition to this method of desegregating schools.

TABLE 3-2 Opposition to School Busing, by Race and Year (in percent)

Race	1972	1974	1975	1976	1977	1978	1982	1983	1985	1986	Change, 1986 – 1972
Black	45	37	53	48	52	48	44	44	43	38	–7
White	87	85	86	87	87	83	84	79	81	75	–12
Difference: black minus white	–42	–48	–33	–39	–35	–35	–40	–35	–38	–37	

Note: The question wording was as follows: "In general, do you favor or oppose the busing of (Negro/black) and white school children from one district to another?"

Sources: Davis and Smith (1987); data from 1972–1987 General Social Surveys.

TABLE 3-3 Opposition to School Busing Among Whites, by Region, Age, and Year (in percent)

Region and Age (years)	1972	1974	1975	1976	1977	1978	1982	1983	1985	1986	Change, 1986 – 1972
Non-South											
18–27	76	76	75	76	80	77	74	66	70	63	–13
28–39	85	88	86	89	83	81	85	77	78	71	–14
40–56	88	84	90	88	86	85	87	82	88	71	–17
57 and over	88	87	87	87	89	85	87	84	87	82	–6
South											
18–27	83	76	74	91	92	82	77	78	71	63	–20
28–39	95	90	85	89	96	87	85	84	74	72	–23
40–56	94	91	92	94	93	93	96	86	89	84	–10
57 and over	97	91	88	91	95	85	86	89	83	77	–20

Notes: The question wording was as follows: "In general, do you favor or oppose the busing of (Negro/black) and white school children from one district to another?" The following are classified as southern States: Alabama, Arkansas, Delaware, District of Columbia, Florida, Georgia, Kentucky, Louisiana, Maryland, Mississippi, North Carolina, Oklahoma, South Carolina, Tennessee, Texas, Virginia, West Virginia.

Sources: Davis and Smith (1987); data from 1972–1987 General Social Surveys.

BLACK ATTITUDES

Support for Principles and Implementation Policies

Data on the racial attitudes of blacks are sparser than those for whites in two respects. First, most national sample surveys contain only 150–250 black respondents, compared with 1,200 or more white respondents. As a result, data for blacks are not as statistically reliable as the data for whites, and it is usually impractical to examine differences by region and level of education. Second, many of the questions for which trend data are available were not asked of blacks until quite recently. However, the broad national trends themselves are important and reliable.

From the earliest point at which they were asked racial principle-type questions, nearly 100 percent of blacks have endorsed the principles of school integration, rights to free residential choice, and nondiscriminatory voting ("black candidate"). Only when questioned about their personal approval of interracial marriage did any appreciable number of blacks take the anti equal-treatment position, and even in this case, the overwhelming majority response was one of support for freedom of interracial marriage (Table 3-1).

In contrast, several of the implementation questions have undergone negative change from the early 1970s to the mid-1980s. Like whites, blacks show a decline in support for federal involvement in school desegregation efforts. But unlike whites (for whom no change took place), blacks show declines in support for federal efforts to prevent job discrimination ("federal job intervention")[1] (see Table 3-1). Schuman and colleagues (1985) also pooled the black data for several of the early surveys and compared them to pooled data for several of the later surveys. This procedure resulted in sufficiently large numbers of black respondents to allow breakdowns by region and education. The negative trends on implementation questions, by and large, occurred broadly rather than among any particular subgroup of blacks.

In addition to these declines in support for the implementation of racial policies concerning black-white relations, the principle-implementation gap in responses also holds for blacks. The clearest instance of this gap for blacks, outside the area of school desegregation (where other complexities arise), involves the "residential choice" principle question (asked in 1976) and the "open housing" implementation question (asked in 1983). When the free residential choice principle question was asked, virtually all blacks (99 percent) gave the positive response; in contrast, 75 percent of blacks expressed support for an open housing law. The gap of about 25 percentage points for

---

1. Two possible artifactual sources of these declines were ruled out through analysis: the composition of the black samples in terms of region of the country and rural versus urban areas of residence had not changed in ways that could have created the declines; race of the interviewer, which might well have varied systematically over time, did not affect responses to this type of question (Bobo, 1987a).

blacks compares with a gap of 42 points for whites. Among whites, 88 percent supported the principle question and 46 percent supported implementation through an open housing law.

It is premature, if not clearly mistaken, to conclude that blacks are repudiating government intervention in racial matters because they are basically satisfied with the civil rights accomplishments of the 1960s. For example, we suspect that declines in black support of implementation policies like school busing are related to white resistance and a feeling in the black community that costs of school desegregation are disproportionately borne by black pupils and their parents (see Chapter 2). Also, blacks increasingly express skepticism that progress in civil rights is being made. In survey questionnaires, fewer and fewer blacks perceive that "a lot" of progress has been made, although few blacks adopt the most pessimistic response that "no progress" has been made. This contrasts to the results for whites who have, since 1968, increasingly said that "a lot" of progress is being made (Bobo, 1987a).

Black Alienation from White Society

One of the clearest trends that emerges from studies of the attitudes of blacks is distrust and suspicion of white intentions and of predominantly white institutions. A litany of black grievances concerning the performance of various social and political institutions, as well as expectations of discriminatory or hostile treatment by whites, have been widely documented, especially since the urban riots of the mid-1960s. For example, Sears and McConahay (1973:68) concluded that their study of Los Angeles

> [residents] demonstrated the existence in the black community of serious grievances about police brutality, merchant exploitation, agency discrimination, poor service agency performance, local white political officials, and biases in white-managed communications media. These varied in intensity but in each case sizeable minorities expressed them. Each of the conventional mechanisms provided by our society to redress such grievances—individual striving, normal administrative procedures, conventional politics, and nonviolent protest—appeared blocked to almost half the community. Most important, those who felt most aggrieved were exactly those who felt the conventional channels of redress were denied to them.

Similarly, although with more attention to white intentions and interpersonal treatment, Campbell and Schuman (1968:26) commented on their results from a survey of blacks in 15 cities that had experienced rioting: "The majority of Negroes expect little from whites other than hostility, opposition, or at best indifference." Turner and Wilson (1976) analyzed data on 1,000 blacks surveyed in a large northern and a medium-sized southern city, and asked 50 attitude-perception questions. Their analysis found several distinct dimensions in these attitudes, the three strongest of which concerned "a general orientation expressing lack of trust and estrangement toward whites" (Turner and Wilson, 1976:145).

Many blacks express feelings of alienation from whites and predominantly white social institutions. Schuman and Hatchett (1974) created what they termed an "alienation from white society index," on the basis of data on the racial attitudes of Detroit-area blacks. The index is based on black responses to 11 questions dealing with whether individual whites and white institutions could be trusted, in particular, trusted to treat blacks fairly. Their analysis, based largely on 1968 and 1971 surveys conducted in Detroit and surrounding communities, indicated an increase in black alienation from 1968 to 1971. For example, the percentage of Detroit blacks thinking that most whites wanted to "keep blacks down" rose from 23 percent to 41 percent in those 3 years. Overall, they found fairly high levels of alienation, with the index scores for both years skewed toward high—though not extreme—black alienation.

In 1976, 5 of the original 11 questions were repeated in another Detroit-area survey (see Farley et al., 1979). Question wording and the percentage of blacks giving the most alienated response in each of three surveys are shown in Table 3-4. All five questions show increases in the more alienated response between 1968 and 1971, but only one shows a steady increase in the more alienated response through 1976 (i.e., the question labeled "progress").

Both the 1979–1980 National Survey of Black Americans (NSBA) and the 1982 General Social Survey (GSS) included questions similar to those used by Schuman and Hatchett (1974) and that, correspondingly, tap the extent to which blacks believe that white individuals and institutions can or cannot be relied on to treat them fairly. Responses to five questions from the 1979–1980 NSBA are shown in Table 3-5a, and responses to five questions from the 1982 GSS are shown in Table 3-5b. Nationwide, blacks were most optimistic about the trend in patterns of discrimination, with 65 percent believing there was less discrimination in the 1979–1982 period than 20 years earlier (NSBA "current discrimination"); 58 percent believing that there would be less discrimination 20 years later (NSBA "future discrimination"); 48 percent believing that opportunities for blacks had improved in the previous 5 years (GSS "current opportunities"); and 36 percent expecting opportunities to improve over the next 5 years (GSS "future opportunities").

These relatively positive assessments of trends in discrimination should not overshadow the fact of widespread belief by blacks that discrimination continues to be an important problem. One-third of blacks believed that blacks with qualifications comparable to those of whites could "almost never" expect to obtain as good a job as a white person, and another 54 percent thought that blacks could only "sometimes" obtain as good a job (GSS "job discrimination"). Similarly, 32 percent believed that blacks with the same qualifications as whites would "almost never" earn as much money as would whites, with another 55 percent responding that blacks would obtain comparable earnings only "sometimes" (GSS "earnings discrimination").

Several of the questions deal with more generalized orientations toward

TABLE 3-4 Black Alienation from White Society in the Detroit Area, 1968–1976

Question	Year of Survey			Change in Scores		
	1968	1971	1976	1971 – 1968	1976 – 1971	1976 – 1968
Keep Down						
On the whole do you think most white people in Detroit want to see (Negroes/blacks) get a better break, or do they want to keep (Negroes/blacks) down, or don't they care one way or the other?						
Percent responding "Keep down"	23	41	33	+18	−8	+10
Trust						
Do you personally feel that you can trust most white people, some white people, or none at all?						
Percent responding "None at all"	10	16	10	+6	−6	0
Progress						
Some people say that in the last 10 or 15 years, there has been a lot of progress in getting rid of racial discrimination. Others say there hasn't been much real change for most (Negroes/blacks) over that time. Which do you agree with most?						
Percent responding "Hasn't been much real change"	28	33	38	+5	+5	+10
Best Means						
As you see it, what's the best way for (Negroes/blacks) to try to gain their rights—use laws and persuasion, use nonviolent protest, or be ready to use violence?						
Percent responding "Ready to use violence"	6	11	4	+5	−7	−2
Neighborhood						
Would you personally prefer to live in a neighborhood with all (Negroes/blacks), mostly (Negroes/blacks), mostly whites, or a neighborhood mixed half and half?						
Percent responding "All" or "mostly black"	12	19	11	+7	−8	−1

Source: Data from Schuman and Hatchett (1974) and Farley et al. (1979).

TABLE 3-5a **Black Alienation from White Society**

Question	Response Categories	Percent
Current Discrimination		
Do you think there is more racial discrimination now (than 20 years ago just before the civil rights movement), less, or have things remained pretty much the same? (N = 2,007)	1. Less discrimination 2. Pretty much the same 3. More discrimination	65 24 11
Future Discrimination		
Twenty years from now, do you think there will be more racial discrimination than now, or will things probably remain the same? (N = 1,884)	1. Less discrimination 2. Remain the same 3. More discrimination	58 29 14
Keep Down		
On the whole, do you think most white people want to see blacks get a better break, or do they want to keep blacks down, or don't they care one way or the other? (N = 1,944)	1. Better break 2. Don't care 3. Keep blacks down	23 36 41
American or Black First		
Which would you say is more important to you—being black or being American, or are both equally important to you? (N = 2,010)	1. Being an American 2. Both equally important 3. Being black	9 71 20
Whites or Africans		
Who do you feel closer to—black people in Africa or white people in America? (N = 1,887)	1. Whites in America 2. Blacks in Africa 3. Volunteered answers: neither or both	24 56 20

Source: Data from 1979–1980 National Survey of Black Americans.

TABLE 3-5b Black Alienation from White Society

Question	Response Categories	Percent
Job Discrimination		
Do you feel that a black person who has the same education and qualifications can get as good a job as a white person? (N = 502)	1. Almost always 2. Sometimes 3. Almost never	13 54 33
Earnings Discrimination		
If a black person has the same qualifications as a white person, do you feel he or she can make as much money? (N = 503)	1. Almost always 2. Sometimes 3. Almost never	13 55 32
Current Opportunities		
Do you think the opportunities for blacks to get ahead have improved in the last 5 years, remained about the same, or gotten worse? (N = 502)	1. Improved 2. About the same 3. Gotten worse	48 32 20
Future Opportunities		
In the next 5 years, do you think that opportunities for blacks to get ahead will improve, remain about the same, or get worse? (N = 490)	1. Improve 2. About the same 3. Get worse	36 34 30
Trust Whites		
Do you feel you can trust most white people, some white people, or no white people? (N = 502)	1. Most white people 2. Some white people 3. No white people	7 82 11

Source: Data from 1982 General Social Survey.

135

whites. Responses to questions on feelings of trust and affinity with whites reveal many blacks expressing moderate to high levels of estrangement. Twenty percent of blacks put "being black" ahead of being an American, although the vast majority rank both memberships as important to them (NSBA "American or black first"); 56 percent said they felt "closer" to blacks in Africa than to whites in America (NSBA "whites or Africans"). Eleven percent of blacks said there were "no white people" who they felt they could trust, 82 percent trusted "some white people," and only 7 percent said that most white people could be trusted (GSS "trust whites"). And, on the one question that was also used by Schuman and Hatchett, 41 percent of blacks said that most white people want to "keep blacks down," 36 percent thought most whites "don't care" one way or the other, and 23 percent thought most whites wanted to see blacks get a "better break" (NSBA "keep down"). Although the NSBA and GSS sets of questions are heterogeneous, the responses have positive and small to moderate patterns of intercorrelation (Bobo, 1987b).

Substantively, an important change in the political context may have affected black attitudes by the time of the 1982 GSS survey. The Reagan administration was then perceived by many black leaders as the most aggressively anti civil rights administration since before the civil rights movement, and many polls at that time showed that blacks gave President Reagan extremely unfavorable ratings (Cavanagh, 1985). Thus, the greater coherence in black attitudes found in the 1982 data may be a result of a renewed sense of challenge or "threat" to black civil rights gains. This interpretation must remain speculative, however, because differences in question wordings and in question contexts might have contributed to the response patterns.

Alienation from contemporary white society is not concentrated within any particular segment of the black community. Alienation does not vary substantially between persons of low and high social status (as measured by education and family income), between younger and older people, northerners and southerners, or between men and women (Bobo, 1987b). However, black alienation from white society is related to several aspects of black cultural identity (see Chapter 4). Blacks who support affirming group bonds through various symbolic acts and those who support racially exclusive dating are more likely to feel alienated from white society. In addition, blacks who attribute more positive traits to blacks are also somewhat more likely to feel alienated from white society. In summary, black alienation from white society is a complex concept to measure. But available data do suggest some increase in black alienation from the late 1960s and into the early 1980s. Questions concerning white intentions or basic trust in whites elicit some of the most alienated responses.

BLACK AND WHITE PREFERENCES FOR BLACK-WHITE RELATIONS

Black and white preferences or attitudes toward black-white relations vary within each group and differ as the nature of the intergroup relation varies.

Whites' support for norms of equal treatment is highest when intergroup contact is random and impersonal, and it is lowest when such contact is persistent and intimate. For example, white respondents differentiate sharply among different areas of life, such as employment, schools, and intermarriage, depending on factors such as the proportions of whites and blacks involved. Thus, in one study of whites, 86 percent would "not mind at all" working with a black supervisor, while 49 percent gave this response toward a black family of equivalent income and education moving in next door (Seeman, 1981:383). This result represents an important continuity in preferences over time, and it is fundamental to understanding the structure of black-white relations in the United States.

In 1944, Myrdal hypothesized that for whites the importance attached to a type of social contact or black-white relation depended on its relevance to the "antiamalgamation" doctrine—the rule of no marriage or sexual intercourse between whites and blacks. Under this hypothesis, discrimination against and segregation of blacks were considered most important in areas of close personal contact. For blacks, the antiamalgamation doctrine played no special role in ranking areas of social contact or black-white relations. In fact, Myrdal's list had black and white rank orderings inversely parallel—those areas most important to blacks (jobs and civil rights) were least important to whites:

Whites' Rankings		Blacks' Rankings
1	Intermarriage and sexual intercourse involving white women	6
2	Personal relations: mixed neighborhoods, dancing, eating	5
3	Mixed schools, churches, public transportation	4
4	Political disfranchisement	3
5	Discrimination in the criminal justice system	2
6	Discrimination in employment	1

Something similar to a group rank ordering for whites is available from the attitudinal survey data. Table 3-6 lists various areas of possible social contact and relations. An area's ranking in these lists depends on the proportion of white respondents who desire inequality or differential treatment between the groups in that area. The higher the proportion espousing equal treatment, the lower is the area of contact on the rank ordering. Thus, types of group contact are ranked according to how large a proportion of whites desire unequal treatment.[2]

---

2. An alternative method, and the one Myrdal seemed to have in mind, would ask individuals to give their personal rank ordering and then attempt to construct a group ordering by aggregating over individuals. Even if data of this latter type were available, it is likely that no unambiguous group ordering could be constructed. Except under conditions of near unanimity, group orderings of preferences can seldom be unambiguously formed (Arrow, 1963; Sen, 1971).

TABLE 3-6 Whites' Opposition to Black-White Contact, by Rank Order

	Percentage of Respondents Opposed		
	1940s		
Type of Contact	North	South	1980s[a]
1. Intermarriage	96[b]	—	60
2. Residential	82	97	15
3. Schools	58	98	10
4. Jobs	30	75	3

[a] Data are for entire United States.
[b] The date for this percentage is 1958.

With respect to blacks, it is not possible to construct a meaningful ordering of this type with the available data. As mentioned above, blacks have overwhelmingly favored equal treatment as long as they have been asked these questions. This makes it very difficult to differentiate between types of contact, because so many are bunched within a small interval close to unanimity for equal treatment. (This situation is similar to that for white southerners in the 1940s on a range of contact areas, with differential treatment receiving near unanimity in most areas.)

These orderings are consistent with Myrdal's hypothesis for the 1940s. They also show that while the proportion of individuals desiring discriminatory behavior has declined over time, the rank orderings have been constant. According to these orderings, while few whites strictly desire unequal treatment in employment, school attendance, and residential living, a substantial majority would feel very uneasy or somewhat uneasy about intermarriage.

In light of the data reviewed, it is difficult not to conclude that at some fundamental level the attitudes of a majority of whites toward blacks are ambivalent. Whites express a desire for equal treatment, at least when small numbers of blacks are concerned, but when close intimate contact is involved, most whites do not yet accept blacks as social equals.

CONTEMPORARY BLACK-WHITE RELATIONS

As the attitudinal data just reviewed suggest, contemporary black-white relations fall somewhere between the overt racism of the past and an unambiguous commitment to full integration and equal opportunity. Anecdotal as well as systematic evidence of this state of race relations abounds. The "city of brotherly love" attracted national media attention when a black man, Wilson Goode, was elected mayor after a campaign that was largely free of racial overtones. Yet Philadelphia grabbed the national headlines again when a black family was driven from its new home in a traditionally white neighborhood. California, with a black voting-age population of only 7 percent, has twice almost elected a black Democratic nominee to the office of governor. Analysis of both voting and survey public opinion data suggest that negative racial attitudes were factors in George Dukemejian's victories over Tom Bradley in 1982 and 1986 (Pettigrew and Alston, 1988).

Such seemingly incongruent racial patterns are neither restricted to the realm of politics nor are they so rare and noteworthy that they always command media attention: they characterize mundane settings as well. Blacks in many social institutions, from sports and entertainment to business and government, have complained that the removal of absolute racial barriers has not eliminated all racial barriers and tensions. Some blacks working in corporate settings report that despite their demonstrated competence and commitment, the highest levels of management are rarely open to them (Jones, 1986).

Many companies in the private sector actively recruit blacks, and a large number have instituted programs and procedures to aid such recruitment efforts. Yet as the 1980s began, signs of resistance to black progress had intensified. For example, some corporations conducting equal employment training programs encountered greater resistance from management. Some white managers asked, "Why are we doing this when the outside environment has cooled to these equal opportunity programs? Why are we wasting our money?" A black manager at a major manufacturing company related that at a cocktail party during a regional sales meeting a ranking official in the company remarked in a group conversation that "most of my people would find it extremely difficult, almost counterproductive, to work for a minority individual" (*Wall Street Journal,* May 27, 1982, cited in Jones, 1988:19). The *Wall Street Journal* reported (cited in Jones, 1988:19) that there was "some evidence of a relaxation of efforts to recruit minority group members and women. We get the sense that companies aren't feeling the pressure anymore."

Many kinds of public and private interactions between blacks and whites that were once very infrequent and even illegal now occur frequently with little notice. Blacks and whites now enjoy meals together in public accommodations or their own homes in areas where this would have occasioned scandal and possibly violent reprisals just a few years ago. Their children attend school together, compete with and against one another in team sports, and they themselves associate freely and voluntarily in workplaces throughout the country. No amount of cynicism should be allowed to underestimate the significant gains in harmonious race relations made clear by these conditions.

Still, changes are sometimes more perceptual and psychological than tangible, and often a matter of subtle shifts in degree rather than a difference in kind. The forces behind these new and very complicated patterns of black-white relations are exceedingly difficult to separate.

PUBLIC ACCOMMODATIONS AND RETAIL ESTABLISHMENTS

Many blacks report hesitant and occasionally plainly differential treatment in searching for housing in predominantly white suburbs (Pearce, 1979) and when patronizing expensive stores, restaurants, or many other settings where blacks are infrequent participants (Schuman et al., 1983). We cite two examples of the latter type of behavior that are frequently reported by the news media throughout the country.

Local managers of a national hotel corporation settled out of court with U.S. Department of Justice officials to charges that their hotels, located in Alabama and Virginia, "tried to limit the number of black patrons in the hotels' lounges" (*Washington Post,* December 24, 1986:B6):

> According to the lawsuit, the techniques included imposing stringent dress codes on blacks and turning them away while admitting whites similarly dressed, requiring more identification for blacks than whites, and instructing employees to serve blacks only after all whites had been served.
>
> In the lawsuit the government also said the hotels instructed employees to be rude to blacks and served black customers drinks with less than the regular measure of alcohol. The lounges also discontinued special promotions, including free hors d'oeuvres, that attracted black business and played music meant to discourage black patronage, the government said.

In Greenbelt, Maryland, a 32-year-old male black social worker and his cousin, a 31-year-old male black attorney, were browsing in a dress shop looking for a birthday gift for the social worker's wife. Two white saleswomen became "nervous" and called the police to complain about two black men "loitering" in stores. While waiting in line to make a purchase at another store, the two men suffered the embarrassment of being confronted by two white police officers who "demanded that the men get out of the line, show identification and answer questions while background checks were run on them" (*Washington Post Magazine,* September 7, 1986:13).

In the 1980s most blacks in the great majority of places shop under conditions free of harassment. However, there are more than a few retail establishments and other places in which blacks are afforded access without overt harassment, but they must confront behavior—polite rudeness, overly aggressive attentiveness, or poor service—that lets them know they are not wanted. Many blacks avoid such establishments.

RACIAL ATTITUDES AND DISCRIMINATION IN HOUSING

A major factor in the differential treatment of blacks is white behavior that is motivated by attitudes and preferences against social settings in which a significant proportion of the people involved are black. One of the most important domains in which this behavior is prevalent is residential housing. The three strongest hypotheses put forward to explain the persistent residential separation of whites and blacks are discrimination, black and white preferences for ethnically homogeneous neighborhoods, and socioeconomic differences between the two groups. We discuss the first two interconnected hypotheses first.

The explanation most consistent with the data focuses on the attitudes of whites and the discriminatory real estate practices that such attitudes may foster. Near the turn of this century, DuBois (1899:389) wrote that most white people in Philadelphia preferred not to live near blacks, thus greatly curtailing blacks' housing choices. More contemporary studies show that almost all whites throughout the United States endorse the statement that minorities have the right to live in any residence they can afford. Such surveys show that white attitudes about racially mixed neighborhoods have changed considerably from attitudes of the 1940s (see Table 3-1 and Chapter 2). However, many whites also hold other beliefs that help to foster residential segregation.

For example, studies of residential segregation in the Detroit area (Farley et al., 1978, 1980) concluded that whites generally hold three beliefs about the effects of racial change on neighborhoods. First, stable interracial neighborhoods are believed to be rare; once a few blacks move in, whites believe more will follow and that the neighborhood is destined to become largely black (see Schelling, 1972). Second, many whites believe that residential property values are lowered by the presence of blacks; thus, they consider it risky to own housing in a racially changing neighborhood. Third, whites believe that crime rates are higher in black neighborhoods than in white neighborhoods. Whites also believe that if they were in an area with a black majority, they would be exposed to a high risk of victimization.

It can be inferred that at least partly as a consequence of these attitudes, whites did not want to purchase housing in neighborhoods where blacks were present or entering. In the Detroit metropolitan area, and presumably in others, residential areas were "color coded," and both buyers and sellers were aware of the neighborhoods that were open and closed to blacks (see also Molotch, 1972; Rieder, 1985:79–85; Taub et al., 1984).

One-quarter of the whites surveyed said they would be uncomfortable if blacks composed just 7 percent of the population in an area, and more than 25 percent said they would not consider purchasing a home in such a neighborhood. If blacks comprised 20 percent of the residents, over 40 percent of the whites surveyed said they would be uncomfortable and 24 percent would attempt to leave. Thus, the presence of even small numbers of black residents is very disturbing to a significant fraction of whites (Farley et al., 1978; see Figure 3-1 and Table 3-1).

The reluctance of whites to live in areas that blacks are entering or to remain in neighborhoods where blacks live offers real estate dealers financial incentives to steer blacks and whites to distinct areas. An extensive investigation into this problem in 1977 was done by the U.S. Department of Housing and Urban Development (HUD) (1979). In a sample of 40 large metropolitan areas, black and white customers, matched for their similarities in socioeconomic status, were often treated differently. Blacks who contacted four real estate agents faced a 72 percent chance of experiencing discrimina-

FIGURE 3-1 Attractiveness of neighborhoods with various racial compositions for (a) white and (b) black respondents.

(a) **White Respondents**

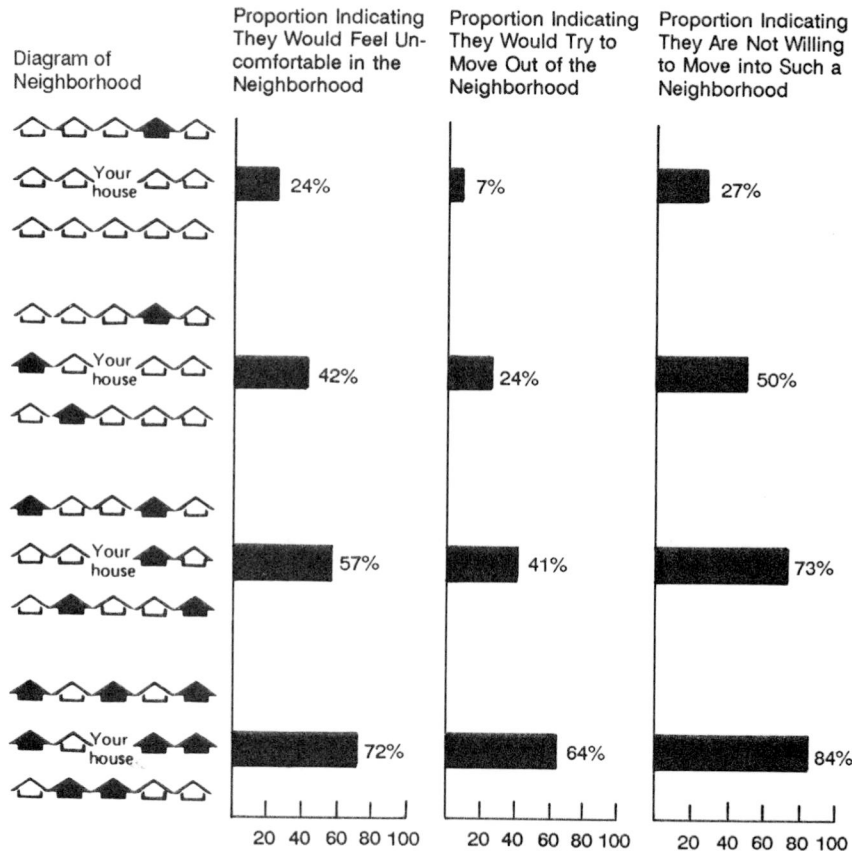

Diagram of Neighborhood	Proportion Indicating They Would Feel Uncomfortable in the Neighborhood	Proportion Indicating They Would Try to Move Out of the Neighborhood	Proportion Indicating They Are Not Willing to Move into Such a Neighborhood
	24%	7%	27%
	42%	24%	50%
	57%	41%	73%
	72%	64%	84%

Source: Reynolds Farley (1976) Detroit Area Study. Department of Sociology, University of Michigan.

tion in the rental market and a 48 percent chance in the sales market. The HUD report concluded that 70 percent of the whites and blacks who sought advertised rental housing in these metropolitan areas in the late 1970s were steered into separate neighborhoods. Among those who were buying, 90 percent were steered.

Earlier studies were consistent with HUD's housing market audit. In the late 1960s, HUD supported an investigation of the causes of residential segregation by race. This study was conducted by the National Research Council (Hawley and Rock, 1973). They reported that it was impossible to isolate one cause of the persistent isolation of blacks. Rather, there was a pervasive "web of discrimination" involving the actions and inactions of

FIGURE 3-1   (Continued)

(b)   **Black Respondents**

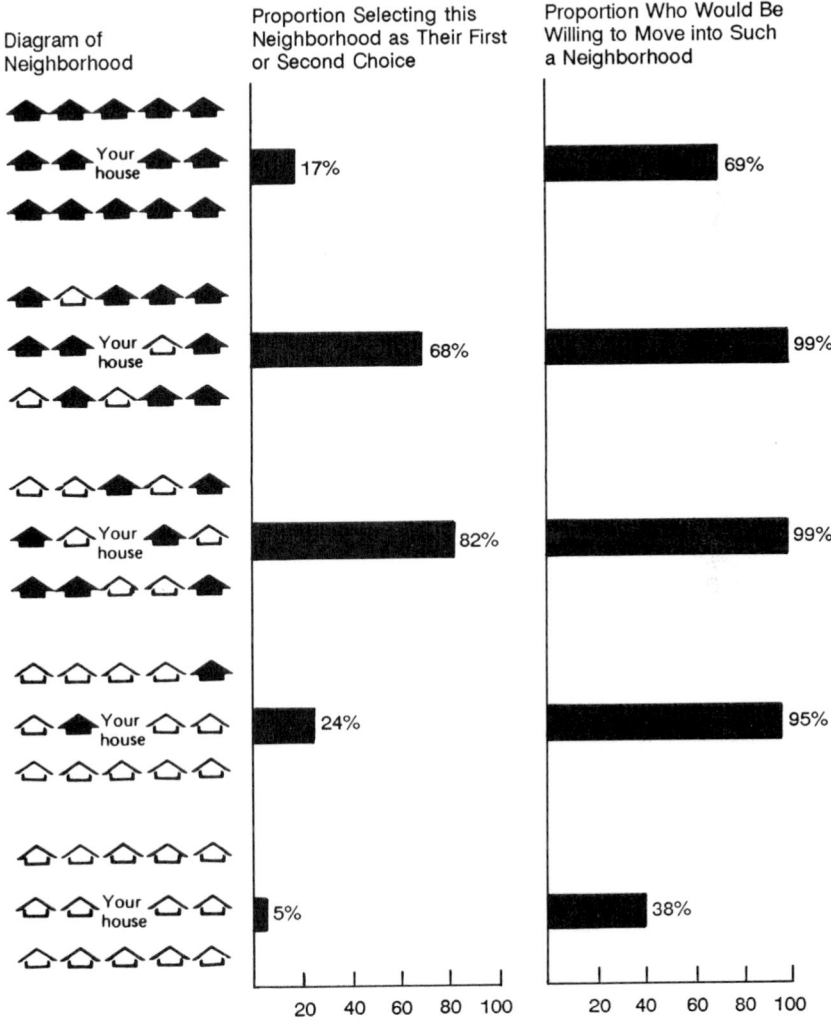

local government officials, federal agencies, financial institutions, and real estate marketing firms, which had the consequence of limiting housing opportunities for blacks and creating the segregated patterns of metropolitan America. These findings have been replicated in the 1980s (John Yinger, 1986).

Black attitudes are also important for assessing residential segregation. For close to 30 years, national samples of blacks have been surveyed about their preferences between racially mixed and black neighborhoods (Pettigrew, 1973). Two-thirds to three-quarters of black respondents have consistently chosen mixed neighborhoods. In the Detroit study (Farley et al., 1978), blacks' ideal choice was to live in an area that was about 55 percent white and 45 percent black. More generally, most blacks said they would be comfortable in any neighborhood except one in which they were the only black resident. Nearly all blacks were willing to be the third black to move into a predominantly white area, and many were willing to be second. However, blacks greatly resisted being the first black on a previously all-white block (see Figure 3-1). Their major reason was not due to a preference for racial homogeneity. Rather, some feared that crosses would be burned on their lawns or their homes would be stoned, and others believed that white neighbors would be unfriendly, make them feel unwelcome and out of place, and scrutinize their behavior (Farley et al., 1978:332). Thus, it is clear that the preferences and fears of whites as well as discrimination by the real estate industry—not black preferences—play a major role in the residential isolation of blacks.

HOUSING AND SOCIOECONOMIC STATUS

Residential segregation is often assumed to be mostly due to socioeconomic differences between blacks and whites. However, blacks of every economic level are highly segregated from whites of similar economic status.

For metropolitan areas with one-quarter million or more black residents in 1980, we computed measures of black-white residential segregation, controlling first for family income and then for the educational attainment of people age 25 and over. Average values for these segregation indexes for all 16 areas are shown in Table 3-7. As in Chapter 2, an index of 100 means total segregation, and an index of 0 implies a random distribution of blacks and whites in their residences. As an example, in the Washington, D.C., metropolitan area, the segregation index comparing black families with incomes of $10,000 to $14,999 in 1979 to similar white families was 70; for families with incomes of $35,000 to $49,999 in income, the segregation index was also 70. For all 16 metropolitan areas, the average segregation index for families with incomes of $10,000 to $14,999 was 75; for families with incomes of $35,000 to $49,999, it was 76. The segregation index for families with $50,000 and above equals that for families in poverty.

The lower part of Table 3-7 presents similar residential segregation indices using educational attainment as the measure of economic status or social class. Blacks and whites are greatly segregated irrespective of their income or education. Highly educated blacks also face barriers to locating housing in the same neighborhoods as well-educated whites. The segregation indices for black and white college graduates were 80 in Detroit, 76 in Chicago, and 72 in New York. The corresponding residential segregation indices for black and white high school dropouts were 77 in Detroit, 80 in Chicago, and 68 in New York.

An examination of Asian-white segregation shows the uniqueness of the

TABLE 3-7 Indices of Segregation by Income and Educational Level, 1980

Income or Educational Level	Black-White Segregation in 16 Areas[a]	Segregation in Three Metropolitan Areas[b]	
		Black-White	Asian-White
Family income in 1979			
Under $5,000	76	77	66
$5,000–$7,499	76	77	71
$7,500–$9,999	76	78	69
$10,000–$14,999	75	76	59
$15,000–$19,999	75	78	58
$20,000–$24,999	76	77	57
$25,000–$34,999	76	78	53
$35,000–$49,999	76	78	53
$50,000 or more	79	79	56
Educational attainment of persons aged 25 and over			
Less than 9 years	76	77	57
High school, 1–3 years	77	79	56
High school, 4 years	76	77	50
College, 1–3 years	74	74	48
College, 4 years or more	71	69	47

[a] These residential segregation scores are average values for 16 metropolitan areas (Atlanta, Baltimore, Chicago, Cleveland, Dallas, Detroit, Houston, Los Angeles, Miami, New Orleans, New York, Newark, Philadelphia, St. Louis, San Francisco, and Washington, D.C.) computed from census tract data. The index shown for an income of $20,000–$24,999, 76, compared the residential distribution of black families in this income category to that of white families in the identical category.

[b] These segregation scores are average values for those three metropolitan areas that contained at least one-quarter million blacks and one-quarter million Asians: Los Angeles, New York, and San Francisco–Oakland.

Source: Data from 1980 decennial census.

black situation. Three metropolitan areas—Los Angeles, New York, and San Francisco–Oakland—had at least one-quarter million black and one-quarter million Asian-American residents in 1980. For these locations, we can compare the segregation indices of both blacks from whites and Asian-Americans from whites. These segregation indices, computed after controlling for educational attainment, are shown in the two right columns of Table 3-7.

At every income and educational level, black-white residential segregation was substantially greater than Asian-white segregation. For example, in Los Angeles, for families with incomes of more than $50,000, the score comparing the distributions of Asian-Americans and whites was 58; for blacks and whites it was 83.

In contrast to the situation among blacks, residential segregation of Asian-Americans and whites declines as income and, especially, education increases. This implies that social and economic factors account for some of the residential segregation of Asian-Americans since segregation levels varied by status. It appears that Asian-Americans with high incomes or educations can move into high status white neighborhoods more easily than blacks can.

DISCRIMINATION IN THE WORKPLACE

The extent of discrimination against blacks in the workplace has apparently not been extensively investigated by direct tests similar in design to the audits of residential housing markets reported above. Consequently, the extent of employment discrimination must be inferred from less direct evidence. The two primary sources of evidence are estimates based on statistical models and on assessments of employment discrimination litigation and related activities of various government agencies, such as the Equal Employment Opportunity Commission (EEOC) and the U.S. Department of Justice.

From these sources, four major conclusions can be inferred: discrimination against blacks in the workplace continues; effects of discrimination on the earnings and occupations of employed blacks have declined; based on statistical estimates, there is no discrimination against black women in comparison with white women, but black (and white) women suffer considerable discrimination in comparison with men, and many individual cases of discrimination against black women continue to occur; current forms of discrimination in the workplace are less blatant than discrimination during past decades.

Methods of statistical estimation of discrimination vary somewhat but most are based on the same idea. Discrimination is defined as unequal treatment to individuals with equal productive characteristics. Statistical estimates of discrimination are computed from data on earnings or occupations and the presumed productive demographic characteristics of individuals. The statistical model estimates, separately for whites and blacks, the earnings or occupational status that would be obtained for a given set of demographic characteristics. Black earnings, occupations, and employment levels differ from those of whites partly because the demographic characteristics of the typical black worker (e.g., education, past work experience) differ from those of the typical white worker. Of course, a part of that difference is itself due to past and current discrimination against blacks. These estimates show different "payoffs" to blacks and whites. Part of the lower payoff to blacks is due to differences in the mean level of productive characteristics (e.g., lower education) and part is due to black-white differences in the market payoff to a given characteristic. Thus, the data can be used to estimate how much of the actual difference in payoffs to whites and blacks can be explained by differences in their productive characteristics. The proportion of the difference that cannot be explained by these characteristics is defined to be the measure of discrimination.[3]

---

3. An obvious pitfall in this procedure is that some productive characteristics may be incorrectly measured or some may not be included in the model. If so, the level of discrimination may be incorrectly estimated. In addition, there are other criticisms that argue that these methods underestimate the level of discrimination against blacks (see Featherman and Hauser, 1978).

Researchers who have used these techniques agree that discrimination against blacks has been reduced during the past 30 years (Farley, 1984; Featherman and Hauser, 1978; Haworth et al., 1975). For example, Farley (1984) found that from 19 percent to 35 percent of the difference between the earnings of black and white men in 1959 could not be explained by differences in productive characteristics. In 1979, the unexplained portion was 12–24 percent. The difference in the upper and lower estimates for both periods depended on whether one assumed that black mens' lower employment levels were due to discrimination or were mostly voluntary. Among women, the estimated effect of discrimination on earnings of blacks in 1959 was about 16 percent; in 1979, a black woman would have earned 8 percent more than a white woman with identical characteristics. In comparison with men, 47 percent of black womens' earnings deficit in 1959 could not be explained by productive characteristics; 36 percent was unexplained by the data in 1979.

Complementary evidence for the hypothesis that discrimination has declined is contained in a large literature showing the increase in rates of return to education for blacks. Prior to the mid-1960s, blacks received relatively much lower earnings or occupational status than whites for increased educational attainment. After the mid-1960s, returns to education rose faster for blacks than for whites (O'Neill, 1986; Smith and Welch, 1986; Weiss and Williamson, 1972). This evidence implies that discrimination has decreased, although it has not been eliminated.

This conclusion is consistent with the large number of discrimination cases alleged, won, and settled out of court in courts and in local, state, and federal government agencies responsible for adjudicating cases of employment bias. Since the mid-1970s, disparate treatment cases declined in significance as overt discrimination gave way to more subtle forms of discrimination (U.S. Equal Employment Opportunity Commission, 1984:215). Yet blatant cases of discrimination have apparently not been completely eradicated. An example is a case filed against a small bottling company in North Carolina by the EEOC in 1986. No blacks had been employed in any but the most menial positions in the company's 20-year history, a fact that the EEOC alleged was due to blatant discriminatory practices in job assignments and promotions for whites and blacks. Moreover, only one white had been employed in "black jobs" during this period. Overt segregation of plant facilities and disparate treatment of white and black employees in a number of other dimensions was also cited (Jacksonville *Daily News,* May 27, 1986; *Washington Post,* October 22, 1986).

Current discrimination is more likely to involve less overt forms of behavior that are far more difficult to detect. For example, Chapter 2 contained a discussion of employment exclusion in professional sports. A considerable literature reports that although black and white baseball players of given ability (as measured by performance) receive equal salaries, blacks apparently must have greater ability than whites to make the big leagues. Thus, occupational discrimination was found to exist for black baseball players of less than star talent. Employment discrimination of this type would be much more difficult to detect and prove in more typical occupations where clear-cut measures of productivity are not available (as they are in baseball); many allegations of discrimination are of a similar nature. On the basis of the statistical evidence and continued cases of private companies' regularly settling discrimination suits with large payments out of court to complainants, we infer that discrimination against blacks persists in the work force.

EXPLANATIONS OF BLACK AND WHITE ATTITUDES TOWARD RACE

In black-white relations, support among white people for general principles of equal treatment—norms or generalized statements of desirability—usually receives greater endorsement than specific proposals for implementing these principles. This gap between endorsement of principle and implementation of those principles occurs especially when the means of implementation involves governmental intervention. How is this finding to be interpreted? Schuman and colleagues (1985) have identified three broad types of interpretation of recent change in racial attitudes and behavior in the United States.

THREE INTERPRETATIONS

The "progressive trend" holds that the survey data indicating important and fundamental increases in white preferences for equality in black-white relations reflect real and consistent changes. A second line of interpretation, "underlying racism," maintains that many of the apparent changes indicated by these data are merely endorsements of general principles. Such endorsements represent an increasingly sophisticated rhetoric adopted by whites as a means of leaving intact their deeper commitment to group position and hardened resistance to realistic change while expressing symbolic concessions. The third approach, "meaningful patterns of progress and resistance," attempts to synthesize both the complex profile of change and resistance to change and the probable causes of that pattern.

The progressive trend accepts at face value the reported decreases in negative attitudes among whites. The underlying racism argument attempts to discount the apparent changes. Such discounting may refer to various lines of evidence: (1) lower proportions of whites approve the implementation than the principle items; (2) lower proportions of whites accept equal-treatment statements when large rather than small proportions of blacks are specified; (3) approval of equal treatment is less for close, personalized relations than for impersonal, public contexts; (4) whites are more likely to give pro equal-treatment responses to black than to white interviewers; and (5) responses vary greatly with changes in the specific wordings of the questions.

A prominent example used in making a case for the underlying racism explanation is provided by the public controversies concerning the use of busing as a means to bring about desegregation in the schools. Data on negative attitudes of white persons toward such busing have been interpreted as evidence of hidden or symbolic racism. And since many whites who oppose busing do not have children who are subject to busing, they are not acting out of pure self-interest.

Nevertheless, there is no plausible reason to doubt that whites' acceptance of blacks' rights to "equality of opportunity" have greatly increased during the past four decades. The great variations in apparent levels of acceptance do not belie the pervasive shifts in norms of legitimacy and appropriateness since the end of World War II. The changes are evident in overt behavior as well as in "testimony"—survey responses—and it is difficult to dismiss these forms of evidence as manifestations of hypocrisy, sophisticated tactics to maintain social peace, or as mere ritualistic lip service.

Furthermore, statistical analyses of survey data show that negative attitudes toward busing are positively correlated with overt expressions of racial prejudice (Sears et al., 1979). Hence, the inferred racism clearly is not merely symbolic, for many of those who oppose busing also voice expressions of overt racial prejudice and thus are not disguising their views. The real question concerns persons who endorse desegregation but reject measures intended to promote it.

COMPETING VALUES

Many Americans endorse a particular principle and then oppose a remedy designed to achieve that principle. This divergence has been notably true of attitudes toward civil liberties: support for abstract norms changes to expressions of intolerance of unpopular groups (McCloskey, 1964; Stouffer, 1955). Similarly, Americans who support black-white equality as an abstract goal often oppose particular civil rights measures.

In this context, the obvious observation is that generalized norms or values are, by definition, context-free, but the concrete implications of any implementation policy will be numerous and diverse. These implications may cause the principle to be constrained by competing values and situational realities, such as resource costs. The responses to direct questions as typically used in large-scale surveys rarely can be given a single clear-cut meaning. The meanings of terms are often numerous and ambiguous. Also, the taken-for-granted contexts within which respondents frame their replies are not always obvious or easily inferred. Hence, an important feature of measured attitudes is that analytic interpretation of their meaning depends heavily on knowledge of the context of assumptions, beliefs, and justifications that respondents have in mind. In ordinary social interaction when individuals express opinions, they often give reasons for those opinions. Analysis of such "reasons," in the form of accounts, explanations, justifications, elaborations, or qualifications, can aid interpretation of the meaning of responses, suggest new hypotheses, and help to specify the contexts and limits of particular attitudes. Accordingly, one line of interpretation is to examine how concrete policy implementation of general principles may entail contradictory or competing values.

Several of the important questions used in national surveys concerning implementation of principles of equality explicitly invoke action by the federal government. Hence, if respondents endorse the principle but reject the hypothetical governmental intervention, the responses might not indicate a "superficial" or merely symbolic orientation, but, rather, a principled objection to the use of federal power. More generally, it has been proposed that there is a genuine consensus among present-day American whites that racial discrimination should not be practiced or approved. For many Americans, however, this consensus does not extend to policies for implementation that involve compulsion. This situation is thought to express a contradiction between values of equality and values of individual freedom (Lipset and Schneider, 1978; Rokeach, 1983). This interpretation gains plausibility from the historical prominence of a clash between "equality" and "freedom" in American political attitudes and behavior.

Since at least the time of Alexis de Tocqueville (1835), commentaries on American life have stressed the prominence, and sometimes the complexity, of beliefs and values of individualism and concepts of liberty (Bellah et al., 1985; Williams, 1970:Ch. XI). The early traditions were those of religious and political individualism, with emphasis on individual moral value and responsibility, coupled with claims to freedom from imposed authority. These traditions were also subtly connected with a kind of utilitarianism that sometimes turned into a preoccupation with self-interest narrowly conceived (Davis, 1975:353–73). Hence, individualism can lead to easy justification of self-interest, to opposition to "welfare state" policies, and to rejection of affirmative action policies.

A plausible hypothesis is that American individualistic values favor universalistic competition—"May the best person win"—while regarding disadvantaged status as one's own fault. Attitudes of whites toward the condition of blacks and toward race-related public policies seem to be substantially related to how racial differences are explained. In general, Americans are sympathetic to inequality only to the extent that they perceive that inequality to be "undeserved." Whites tend to deny that race is currently a social problem and, therefore, believe that blacks themselves are responsible for the remaining socioeconomic differences between the races (Bobo, 1987a; Williams, 1988). Blacks, to a much greater extent, believe that race is still very much a social problem in America and therefore believe that systematic barriers limit their chances in life. These beliefs help explain why blacks and whites differ so sharply in levels of support for equal opportunity policies such as affirmative action and why, in particular, white opposition to such policies is so high.

In *The Anatomy of Racial Attitudes* Apostle and colleagues (1983) demonstrate that there is utility in grounding surveys of attitudes in a format that allows respondents to explain their reasons for holding given beliefs and attitudes. From a sample of 500 white persons in the San Francisco Bay area, their study elicited explanations of the racial attitudes expressed, which were then related to the respondents' beliefs and prescriptions. The hypothesis that competing values affect attitudes toward racial social policy was found to help explain a considerable amount of the difference between endorsement of principle and implementation of principle in such areas as employment and housing. In particular, those respondents who were classified as "individualists" by the researchers were the most likely to oppose institutional intervention against racial discrimination (Apostle et al., 1983:88–95, 110).

On the basis of surveys carried out in 1972, Sniderman and Hagen (1985) found that white Americans gave four main explanations for black-white inequality: individualistic (personal responsibility), fundamentalist (God's will), past discrimination (historical treatment), and deliberate economic exploitation (radical). The predominant view, held by about 60 percent of a nationwide sample, is individualistic. If asked spontaneously to explain the causes of social and economic inequality between blacks and whites, most whites emphasize a lack of effort by blacks (Kluegel and Smith, 1986; Schuman, 1971); if asked to choose the single most important reason among a set of possible causes, the individualistic factor is the one most likely to be chosen (Apostle et al., 1983; Sniderman and Hagen, 1985). These individualistic explanations of black-white inequality support the view that government has no role to play in improving the status of blacks. The individualistic emphasis also contributes to an underestimation of the extent of black-white inequality and to exaggeration of the effects of equal opportunity or affirmative action-type programs. For example, 53 percent of whites in a 1980 national survey perceived blacks to benefit from "some" or "a lot" of reverse discrimination (Kluegel and Smith, 1986).

The views of black Americans differ sharply. The 1980 national survey found that 53 percent of blacks but only 26 percent of whites believed that blacks face significant discrimination (Kluegel and Smith, 1986). A 1981 national survey found that 65 percent of blacks rejected the claim that a lack of motivation or effort was responsible for black-white inequality, compared with 40 percent of whites (Bobo, 1987a).

Blacks also appear to differ from whites in what they mean by discrimination. Even whites who think discrimination contributes to black-white inequality tend to view it as a problem created and maintained by prejudiced individuals. Blacks view discrimination as a result of both prejudiced individuals and broader social processes (Bobo, 1987a; Kluegel and Smith, 1986).

It is tempting to consider the competing values hypothesis as a resolution of the problem of the principle-implementation gap. However, it is not the entire story. First, and most important, it ignores the third basic finding from studies of white attitudes and beliefs concerning equal treatment in race relations: whites want considerable social distance from blacks. And, especially with regard to housing, the evidence shows that many whites will go to considerable efforts to maintain that distance. Thus, there is not only a gap between principle and implementation to be explained, but also a gap between support for principles and willingness to practice equalitarian principles on a personal level.

THE MEANING OF RACIAL EQUALITY

The explanation for the principle-implementation gap may depend on the question of what those who say they endorse the principles of racial equality and integration mean by those terms. One answer is that they have in mind some conception of American pluralism—the peaceful and equal participation of different groups in the democratic polity. But, as discussed above, pluralism in America carries with it claims for the primacy of liberty as well as equality. Some people surely would agree with the economist Milton Friedman that the principle of equal treatment should be endorsed and practiced but that individuals should have the personal right to practice differential treatment, because to compel them otherwise would be an infringement of their liberty (Friedman, 1962:111).

For example, two racial intermarriage questions asked of respondents in the 1982 and 1983 General Social Surveys illustrate this point, as well as the importance of specific question wording. Although 66 percent of whites (in 1982) said they opposed laws against intermarriage, only 40 percent (in 1983) said they personally "approved" of racial intermarriage. Analogously, about two-thirds of whites (in 1977) said that they would not favor laws against interracial marriage, but three-fourths of the respondents said they would be either "very uneasy" or "somewhat uneasy" if a close relative were planning to marry a "Negro" (J. Milton Yinger, 1986:12). The difference can be explained by noting that it is possible to personally object to a behavior or outcome without simultaneously feeling that others should be prevented from engaging in such behavior. Thus, it is possible that some whites may endorse the general principle that blacks have the right to live where they choose—and so reject the notion that groups of whites have the right to collectively prevent black desegregation of a neighborhood—and yet support each individual's right to live in a segregated neighborhood.

More concretely, objections to government coercion do influence people's reactions to the issue of open housing laws (Schuman and Bobo, 1988) and possibly school busing (Taylor, 1986). We might suppose, then, that there exists a three-directional ambivalence in the attitudes of many whites toward racial equality: support for it in principle, and support for it in practice, but only if certain preference boundaries are not overstepped—too many blacks or interracial contact is too close. The competing values hypothesis explains why whites can be in favor of equal treatment in principle but reject policies to implement it. But in using that hypothesis the issues have been too compartmentalized, for it ignores the expressed preferences of whites concerning black-white social distance.

"Implementation" has multiple, concrete implications. While a policy may introduce competing values and allow an objection on grounds of principle—"forced busing violates individual liberty"—the same policy may also create a solution that results in an overstepping of many whites' preference boundaries, such as too great a proportion of blacks in the schools. It is difficult with the data available to sort out the independent effects of each. Whites are likely to stress the clash of principles, but blacks will be inclined to agree with the Reverend Jesse Jackson that "it's not the bus, it's us."

GROUP STATUS

Changes in the status of one group often lead to intensified competition with another group (Brewer and Kramer, 1985:223–226). And some intergroup behavior in black-white contacts, especially public confrontations, is due to real or perceived advances in blacks' status and fears among whites of losing an established and superior group position.

The crucial role of defining and maintaining boundaries between groups has been documented in detail by experimental and observational studies (Brewer and Kramer, 1985; Stephan and Rosenfield, 1982). These social boundaries are accentuated by perceived oppositions, and by threats, including expressions of hostility or negative evaluations by members of outgroups. For instance, black activism to advance group position may have played an important role in raising group consciousness among many whites.

Jackman and Muha (1984) have focused the issue in terms of intergroup attitudes and ideologies as a mechanism of defending group status position. They hypothesize that claims based on group interests, as in preferential goals or quotas, are opposed by dominant groups (racial, gender, or class) on grounds of a principle of individual achievement. Jackman and Muha interpret the findings (from a national survey of 1,914 respondents) as revealing that well-educated whites show higher acceptance of racial integration and black rights as a sophisticated way of avoiding offense and confrontation by emphasizing individual rights, while evading commitment to group equality. "By upholding individualism as a guiding principle in the empirical and normative interpretation of social life, the rights of *groups* are thus rendered illegitimate and unreasonable" and the status quo can be protected (Jackman and Muha, 1984:760). This argument rests on a single (1975) survey in which there is little information on the contextual meaning of responses and no direct link between those responses and group-level or institutional factors. Still, the Jackman-Muha interpretation of the data cannot be summarily dismissed.

Some recent attempts to show a relationship between measures of individualistic values and measures of attitudes on issues such as affirmative action have produced unexpected results. Attitudes toward affirmative action policies tended to be more highly correlated with attitudes toward equalitarian values than with individualistic values (Bobo, 1989; Kinder and Sanders, 1987; Sears, 1988). This finding has been interpreted to mean that for many people low levels of support for affirmative action flow more from low levels of commitment to equality and a lack of awareness of social structural causes of inequality (coupled with prejudice) than from a high commitment to individualistic values. This research will doubtless be subjected to close review in the near future, and it will need replication in more studies before its full implications are understood.

Of relevance to these issues is a body of research in social psychology that provides explanations of how people explain a social phenomenon such as black-white inequality. Attribution theory (Fiske and Taylor, 1984; Heider, 1958) focuses primarily on how people develop explanatory accounts of interpersonal behavior. The two major types of causes are external, such as an environmental constraint or pressure to behave in a particular way, and internal, indicative of the underlying dispositions of the individual. Of course, many behaviors involve combinations of the two kinds of causes. The way in which a phenomenon is explained largely determines the meaning it has for a person. An outcome lacking a systematic, controllable cause differs from an outcome for which a clear social process or individual action can be pinpointed as the cause. Furthermore, outcomes rooted in a social force have different implications for ameliorative efforts than those rooted in a personal intention.

The views of both whites and blacks may reflect what has been termed the "fundamental attribution error" (Jones and Nisbett, 1972). Experimentally controlled studies of the attribution process routinely find that observers systematically overestimate the extent to which an actor's behavior is attributable to internal causes and systematically underestimate the importance of external causes. This tendency to overattribute to internal causes and to underestimate the importance of external environmental causes appears to be especially likely when judging a disliked out-group (Pettigrew, 1979).

This general psychological bias toward dispositional attributions when joined with possible self-interest motivations to protect a historically privileged group status may reflect a reasoned opposition of some whites to black advancement. In addition, the traditional American belief that the country is a land of abundant opportunity for those who want to work hard is another important contributor to low levels of support for equal opportunity policies (Kluegel and Smith, 1986). The fundamental attribution error may be more characteristic of societies with individualistic achievement orientations than those without such cultural beliefs. The crucial theoretical point is that long-standing and general beliefs about how society does and should allocate important social rewards affect both how racial inequality is perceived and how it is explained. As a result, attitudes toward policies to affect black inequality are also affected by these beliefs about why that inequality occurs. Beliefs that existing differences are based on individual merit may lead to opposition to policies such as affirmative action. Data do not allow us to determine whether the beliefs and perceptions of blacks or those of whites are more veridical. There is no doubt a measure of self-interest in the perceptions of both groups. The motivational factors behind the behaviors of whites and blacks are not a simple matter of values versus self-interest; both elements are at work.

CONCLUSIONS

These findings lead us to four general conclusions. The foremost conclusion is that race still matters greatly in the United States. Much of the evidence reviewed in this report indicates widespread attitudes of racism. This is not to gainsay convincing evidence of improving racial attitudes: a transformation of basic racial norms in the United States is the clearest finding from the survey trend data (Schuman et al., 1985; Smith and Sheatsley, 1984). The once widespread acceptance of segregation and discrimination as the guiding principles of black-white relations has given way to acceptance of the principles of desegregation and equal treatment. There are reasons to believe that this change extends beyond mere lip service or token and transitory forms of social contact. The second major conclusion regarding racial attitudes is thus a record of genuine progress.

Yet, a reluctance to live in racially mixed neighborhoods and interpersonal awkwardness and racially differential treatment across many situations all point to the persistence of race as an important factor in American society. Although each of the phenomena mentioned also has causes that are frequently unrelated to race, such as social status differences and political values, a direct concern with race is substantially implicated in each outcome. Our third major conclusion, then, is that in the midst of progress there remain significant forms of resistance to a variety of proposals for racial change.

It would be erroneous, however, to reduce the American racial pattern of progress and resistance to purely racial causes. A number of traditional values, which are not in and of themselves race related, play an important role. The values of liberty, equality, justice, and fairness are an inevitable component of any attempt to comprehend racial attitudes and relations in the United States. Values such as individualism affect not only how people perceive and explain black-white inequality, but also the likelihood of supporting policies aimed at affecting group statuses. Our fourth major conclusion is thus that a number of value-based concerns affect the observed patterns of racial progress and resistance.

The connections between attitudes and actual behavior are exceedingly complicated. White attitudes concerning black-white relations have moved appreciably toward endorsement of principles of equal treatment. Yet there remain important signs of continuing resistance to full equality of black Americans: principles of equality are endorsed less when social contact is close, of long duration, or frequent and when it involves significant numbers of blacks; whites are much less prone to endorse policies to implement equal participation of blacks in society.

These findings suggest that a considerable amount of remaining black-white inequality is due to continuing discriminatory treatment of blacks. However, direct evidence of systematic discriminatory behavior by whites is difficult to obtain. The best evidence is in the area of residential housing. Discrimination against blacks seeking housing has been conclusively demonstrated. How much the important example of the housing market indicates discrimination in other areas, such as the labor market, is tempered by the fact that residential segregation is very high on whites' "rank order of discrimination." Nonetheless, the overall preponderance of evidence indicates that the existence of significant discrimination against blacks is still a feature of American society.

REFERENCES

Apostle, Richard A., Charles Y. Glock, Thomas Piazza, and Marijean Suelzle
   1983   *The Anatomy of Racial Attitudes*. Berkeley: University of California Press.
Arrow, Kenneth J.
   1963   *Social Choice and Individual Values*. 2d ed. New York: John Wiley & Sons.
Bellah, Robert, Richard Madsen, William M. Sullivan, Anne Swidler, and Steven M. Tipton
   1985   *Habits of the Heart: Individualism and Commitment in American Life*. Berkeley: University of California Press.
Bobo, Lawrence
   1987a Racial Attitudes and the Status of Black Americans: A Social Psychological View of Change Since the 1940s. Paper prepared for the Committee on the Status of Black Americans, National Research Council, Washington, D.C.
   1987b Race in the Minds of Black and White Americans. Paper prepared for the Committee on the Status of Black Americans, National Research Council, Washington, D.C.
   1989   Memorandum to the Committee on the Status of Black Americans, National Research Council, Washington, D.C.
Brewer, M. B., and R. M. Kramer
   1985   The psychology of intergroup attitudes. *Annual Review of Psychology* 36:219–243.
Campbell, Angus
   1971   *White Attitudes Towards Black People*. Ann Arbor, Mich.: Institute for Social Research.
Campbell, Angus, and Howard Schuman
   1968   Racial attitudes in fifteen American cities. Pp. 1–67 in *Supplemental Studies for the National Advisory Committee on Civil Disorders*. Washington, D.C.: U.S. Government Printing Office.
Cavanagh, Thomas
   1985   *Inside Black America: The Message of the Black Vote in the 1984 Elections*. Washington, D.C.: Joint Center for Political Studies.
Condran, John G.
   1979   Changes in white attitudes towards blacks: 1963–1977. *Public Opinion Quarterly* 43(Winter):463–476.
Davis, David Brion
   1975   *The Problem of Slavery in the Age of Revolution*. Ithaca, N.Y.: Cornell University Press.
Davis, James A., and Tom W. Smith
   1987   General Social Surveys, 1972–1987. Machine readable data file. National Opinion Research Center, Chicago, Ill.
Denisoff, R. Serge, and Ralph Wahrman
   1979   *An Introduction to Sociology*. 2d ed. New York: Macmillan.

de Tocqueville, Alexis
  1835 *Democracy in America.* Reprinted 1966. New York: Harper & Row.
DuBois, William E. B.
  1899 *The Philadelphia Negro: A Social Study.* Reissued (1973), Millwood, N.Y.: Kraus-Thomson Organization Limited.
Farley, Reynolds
  1984 *Blacks and Whites.* Cambridge, Mass.: Harvard University Press.
Farley, Reynolds, Suzanne Bianchi, and Diane Colosanto
  1980 Barriers to the racial integration of neighborhoods, the Detroit case. *Annals of the American Academy of Political and Social Science* 444(January):97–113.
Farley, Reynolds, Shirley Hatchett, and Howard Schuman
  1979 A note on changes in black racial attitudes in Detriot: 1968–1976. *Social Indicators Research* 6:439–443.
Farley, Reynolds, Howard Schuman, Suzanne Bianchi, Diane Colosanto, and Shirley Hatchett
  1978 Chocolate city, vanilla suburbs: will the trend toward racially separate communities continue? *Social Science Research* 7(December):319–344.
Featherman, David L., and Robert M. Hauser
  1978 *Opportunity and Change,* New York: Academic Press.
Fiske, Susan T., and Shelley E. Taylor
  1984 *Social Cognition.* Reading, Mass.: Addison-Wesley.
Friedman, Milton
  1962 *Capitalism and Freedom.* Chicago: University of Chicago Press.
Greeley, Andrew M., and Paul B. Sheatsley
  1971 Attitudes towards racial integration. *Scientific American* 225:13–19.
  1974 Attitudes towards racial integration. In Lee Rainwater, ed., *Inequality and Justice.* Chicago: Aldine.
Harris, Louis
  1987 *The Harris Survey.* Orlando, Fla.: The Tribune Media Services, Inc.
Hawley, Amos Henry, and Vincent P. Rock
  1973 *Segregation in Racial Areas.* Division of Behavioral Sciences, National Research Council. Washington, D.C.: National Academy of Sciences.
Haworth, J. G., J. D. Gwartney, and C. Haworth
  1975 Earnings productivity and changes in employment discrimination during the 1960's. *American Economic Review* 65(2)[March]:158–168.
Heider, Fritz
  1958 *The Psychology of Interpersonal Relations.* New York: John Wiley & Sons.
Hyman, Herbert H., and Paul Sheatsley
  1956 Attitudes towards desegregation. *Scientific American* 195(December):35–39.
  1964 Attitudes towards desegregation. *Scientific American* 211(1)[July]:16–23.
Jackman, Mary R.
  1978 General and applied tolerance: does education increase commitment to racial integration? *American Journal of Political Science* 22:302–324.
Jackman, Mary R., and Michael J. Muha
  1984 Education and intergroup attitudes: moral enlightenment, superficial democratic commitment or ideological refinement? *American Sociological Review* 49:751–769.
Jones, Edward E., and Richard E. Nisbett
  1972 The actor and the observer: divergent perceptions of the causes of behavior. In Edward E. Jones, D. Kamouse, Harold H. Kelley, Richard E. Nisbett, S. Valins, and Bernard Weiner. *Attribution: Perceiving the Causes of Behavior,* Morristown, N.J.: General Learning Press.

Jones, Edward W., Jr.
  1986 Black managers: the dream deferred. *Harvard Business Review* (May/June):84–93.
  1988 Memorandum to the Committee on the Status of Black Americans, National Research Council, Washington, D.C.
Kinder, Donald R., and Lynn M. Sanders
  1987 Pluralistic Foundations of American Opinion on Race. Paper presented at the annual meeting of the American Political Science Association, Chicago.
Kluegel, J. R., and E. R. Smith
  1986 *Beliefs About Equality: American's Views of What Is and What Ought to Be.* Hawthorne, N.Y.: Aldine de Gruyter.
Lipset, Seymour Martin, and William Schneider
  1978 The Bakke case: how would it be decided at the bar of public opinion? *Public Opinion* 1(1)(March/April):38–44
McCloskey, Herbert
  1964 Consensus and ideology in American politics. *American Political Science Review* 58:361–382.
Molotch, Harvey Luskin
  1972 *Managed Integration.* Berkeley: University of California Press.
Myrdal, Gunnar
  1944 *An American Dilemma: The Negro Problem and Modern Democracy.* 2 vols. New York: Harper and Brothers.
O'Neill, June, James Cunningham, Andy Sparks, and Hal Sider
  1986 *The Economic Progress of Black Men in America.* Clearinghouse Publication 91. Washington, D.C.: U.S. Commission on Civil Rights.
Pearce, Diana
  1979 Gatekeepers and homeseekers: institutionalized patterns in racial steering. *Social Problems* 26:325–342.
Pettigrew, Thomas F.
  1973 Attitudes on race and housing: a social psychological view. In A. H. Hawley and V. P. Rock, eds. *Segregation in Residential Areas.* Washington, D.C.: National Academy of Sciences.
  1979 The ultimate attribution error: extending Allport's cognitive analysis of prejudice. *Personality and Social Psychology Bulletin* 5:461–476.
Pettigrew, Thomas F., and D. Alston
  1988 *Tom Bradley's Campaign for Governor: The Dilemma of Race and Political Strategies.* Washington, D.C.: Joint Center for Political Studies.
Rieder, Jonathan
  1985 *Canarsie: The Jews and Italians of Brooklyn Against Liberalism.* Cambridge, Mass.: Harvard University Press.
Rokeach, Milton
  1973 *The Nature of Human Values.* New York: Free Press.
Rossi, Peter H., James D. Wright, and Andy B. Anderson
  1983 *Handbook of Survey Research.* Orlando, Fla.: Academic Press.
Schelling, Thomas C.
  1972 A process of residential segregation: neighborhood tipping. Pg. 157–184 in Anthony H. Pascal, ed., *Racial Discrimination in Economic Life.* Lexington, Mass.: D. C. Heath and Co.
Schuman, Howard
  1971 Free will and determinism in beliefs about race. In Norman Yetman and C. Hoyt Steele, eds., *Majority and Minority: The Dynamics of Racial and Ethnic Relations.* Boston: Allyn & Bacon.

Schuman, Howard, and Lawrence Bobo
  1988 Survey-based experiments on white racial attitudes toward residential integration. *American Journal of Sociology* 94(2)[September]:273–299.
Schuman, Howard, and Shirley Hatchett
  1974 *Black Racial Attitudes: Trends and Complexities*. Ann Arbor, Mich.: Institute for Social Research.
Schuman, Howard, and Graham Kalton
  1985 Survey methods. In Gordon Lindzey and Elliot Aronson, eds., *Handbook of Social Psychology*. 3d ed. New York: Random House.
Schuman, Howard, Eleanor Singer, Rebecca Donovan, and Claire Selltiz
  1983 Discriminatory behavior in New York restaurants: 1950 and 1981. *Social Indicators Research* 13:69–83.
Schuman, Howard, Charlotte Steeh, and Lawrence Bobo
  1985 *Racial Attitudes in America: Trends and Interpretations*. Cambridge, Mass.: Harvard University Press.
Sears, David O.
  1988 Symbolic racism. Pp. 53–84 in P. A. Katz and D. A. Taylor, eds., *Eliminating Racism: Profiles in Controversy*. New York: Plenum.
Sears, David O., Carl P. Hensler, and Leslie K. Speer
  1979 Whites opposition to "busing": self-interest or symbolic politics! *American Political Science Review* 73:369–384.
Sears, David O., and John B. McConahay
  1973 *The Politics of Violence*. Boston: Houghton Mifflin.
Seeman, Melvin
  1981 Intergroup relations. Pp. 378–410 in Morris Rosenberg and Ralph H. Turner, eds., *Social Psychology: Sociological Perspectives*. New York: Basic Books.
Sen, Amartya
  1971 *Collective Choice and Social Welfare*. New York: Holden Day.
Smith, A. Wade
  1981 Racial tolerance as a function of group position. *American Sociological Review* 46:558–573.
  1987 Problems and progress in the measurement of black public opinion. *American Behavioral Scientist* 30:441–455.
Smith, James P., and Finis R. Welch
  1986 *Closing the Gap, Forty Years of Economic Progress for Blacks*, Santa Monica, Calif.: Rand Corporation.
Smith, Tom W., and Paul B. Sheatsley
  1984 American attitudes toward race relations. *Public Opinion* 6(October/November):14–15, 50–53.
Sniderman, Paul M., and Michael G. Hagen
  1985 *Race and Inequality: A Study in American Values*. Chatham, N.J.: Chatham House.
Stephan, Walter G., and David Rosenfield
  1982 Racial and ethnic stereotypes. Pp. 92–136 in Arthur G. Miller, ed., *The Eye of the Beholder: Contemporary Issues in Stereotyping*. New York: Praeger.
Stouffer, Samuel
  1955 *Communism, Conformity, and Civil Liberties*. New York: Doubleday.
Taub, Richard P., D. Garth Taylor, and Jan D. Dunham
  1984 *Paths of Neighborhood Change: Race and Crime in Urban America*. Chicago: University of Chicago Press.
Taylor, D. Garth
  1986 *Public Opinion and Collective Action*. Chicago: University of Chicago Press.

Taylor, D. Garth, Paul B. Sheatsley, and Andrew M. Greeley
  1978 Attitudes toward racial integration. *Scientific American* 238(6)[June]:42–50.
Turner, Charles F., and Elizabeth Martin, eds.
  1984 *Surveying Subjective Phenomena*. 2 vols. Panel on Survey Measurement of Subjective
       Phenomena, Committee on National Statistics, National Research Council. New
       York: Russell Sage Foundation.
Turner, Costellano B., and William Julius Wilson
  1976 Dimensions of racial ideology: a study of urban black attitudes. *Journal of Social
       Issues* (Spring):139–152.
U.S. Department of Housing and Urban Development
  1979 *Measuring Racial Discrimination*. Washington, D.C.: U.S. Government Printing
       Office.
U.S. Equal Employment Opportunity Commission
  1984 *A History of the Equal Employment Opportunity Commission, 1965–1984*, Washington,
       D.C.: U.S. Government Printing Office.
Weiss, Leonard, and Jeffrey G. Williamson
  1972 Black education, earnings, and interregional migration: some new evidence. *Amer-
       ican Economic Review* 62(3):372–383.
Williams, Robin M., Jr.
  1970 *American Society: A Sociological Interpretation*. 3d ed. New York: Alfred A. Knopf.
  1988 Racial attitudes and behavior. Pp. 331–352 in Hubert O'Gorman, ed., *Surveying
       Social Life: Papers in Honor of Herbert Hyman*. Middletown, Conn.: Wesleyan
       University Press.
Yinger, John
  1986 Measuring racial discrimination with fair housing audits. *American Economic Review*
       76(5):881–893.
Yinger, J. Milton
  1986 Black Americans and Predominantly White Churches. Paper prepared for the
       Committee on the Status of Black Americans, National Research Council, Wash-
       ington, D.C.

4

IDENTITY AND INSTITUTIONS

IN THE BLACK COMMUNITY

Jacob Lawrence
Rooftops (No. 1, This Is Harlem) (1943)
Gouache with pencil underdrawing on paper sheet
Hirshhorn Museum and Sculpture Garden, Smithsonian Institution,
Gift of Joseph H. Hirshhorn, 1966

The world of black Americans has always been a part of American society, but the black and white worlds have also always been mostly separate. The inevitable consequences have been distinctive features of black culture and social organization. In this chapter we sketch this society within a society, in which the social participation of most black Americans has been experienced. We focus on change over time in overall social structure, in black institutions, and in concepts of identity.

The communities and organizations created by blacks prior to the 1960s, as well as changing concepts of black identity during and afterward, were two crucial bases for the achievement of sweeping improvements in blacks' legal and political status during that decade. The activism facilitated by those black infrastructures led to improvements in the education, health, and economic position of many blacks and altered the social structure of black communities.

SOCIAL STRUCTURE

Major changes in black social structure have resulted from the rising incomes, better occupations, and increased educations of many blacks. But as higher status blacks have left inner-city areas, there has been increased racial stratification among blacks. The service needs of poorer blacks have placed strains on many black institutions, including schools, churches, and voluntary service organizations. These strains can be seen by the proliferation of activities devoted to the material needs of poor blacks by black organizations.

Further strains on black institutions and organizations resulted from the civil rights movement: improved access of higher status blacks to majority white institutions has led to alterations in black leadership structure, problems of recruitment and retention of black talent by black organizations, and reduced participation of higher status blacks in many spheres of black community life. In the process, the well-knit, if poor and underserviced, black communities of decades past have lost some of their cultural cohesion and distinct identity. Although there is some evidence that higher status blacks have somewhat less attachment to a need to preserve group identity, most blacks retain a high degree of racial pride and a conscious need to retain aspects of black culture as a significant component of their American identity. Because of these desires and needs, predominantly black institutions continue to play important roles in the lives of most blacks.

BEFORE THE CIVIL RIGHTS MOVEMENT

A Segregated Society

Five decades ago, black and white Americans inhabited parallel but connected societies. The common pattern was one of separate black and white communities that were socially and culturally distinctive. For example, partly because of ghettoization, social classes within black communities were frequently not spatially isolated from one another as was often the case in white communities (Drake and Cayton, 1945:659; Osofsky, 1971; Spear, 1967). This structure resulted partly from the residential restrictions imposed on blacks by segregation and discrimination and partly from the minute size of the black middle and upper classes.

Throughout the pre-1960 period, the black class structure was often described as being pyramid shaped, with a large lower class, a small middle class, and a tiny upper class. In contrast, the white class structure was described as being diamond shaped, with a small lower class, a huge middle class, and a small upper class—but the lower class being smaller than the black lower class and the other two classes being much larger (Drake, 1965:785; DuBois, 1903; Myrdal, 1944).

In 1940 the status of the vast majority of black Americans was well below middle class. More than 1 of every 2 black adults had no more than 8 years of education, and 62 percent of working black men and women were employed either in agriculture or in menial personal service jobs. In 1960, 31 percent of black workers were still employed in those industries. Throughout the 1950s, well over one-half of blacks lived in households with incomes below the poverty threshold (see Chapter 6). In 1953, for example, 1 of every 3 black families had incomes below $3,000 (in 1974 constant dollars), while just 1 of 50 had incomes above $15,000. Comparative figures for white families were slightly more than 1 of 8 and 1 of 10, respectively. As

FIGURE 4-1   Blacks in selected occupations, 1940–1980.

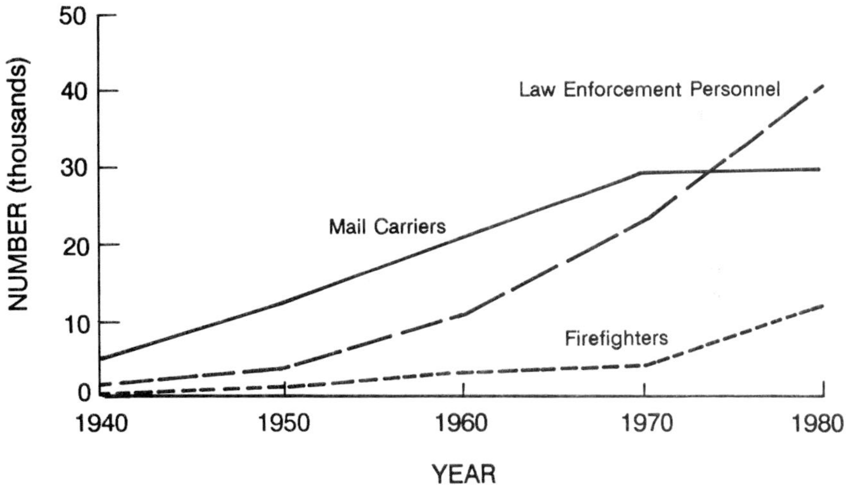

Source: Data from decennial censuses.

late as 1960, 13 percent of all black workers were in white-collar occupations, compared with 44 percent of whites.

The small black middle and upper classes prior to 1960 were primarily composed of small business owners and professionals, such as teachers, ministers, doctors, and lawyers. Between 1912 and 1938, 73 percent of all black college graduates became ministers or teachers (Halsey, 1938, cited in Bates, 1986:23). These professionals almost exclusively serviced the segregated black community. Most blacks were excluded from managerial, sales, and clerical positions in the wider society. Similar barriers to black employment as public servants led to small numbers of black police officers, firefighters, and postal workers (see Figure 4-1). Minimal employment in these occupations hindered the development of a potentially important non-college-educated black middle class.

Networks of churches and voluntary associations provided a major means of communication and support as well as lines of social division (Drake and Cayton, 1945:659; Frazier, 1963). Although voluntary associations and church memberships tended to be somewhat divided along class lines, there was also a general sense of community. The Chicago Commission on Race Relations's observation on community identity in 1922 held as true in the 1930s and through the 1950s as it had when published (Bracey et al., 1971:176):

> Living and associating for the most part together, meeting in the same centers for face-to-face relations, trusting to their own physicians, lawyers, and ministers, a compact community with its own fairly definite interests and sentiments has grown up.

Black parallel organizations were not imitations of white society as some have suggested (see Myrdal, 1944:43). While many black groups, such as the Prince Hall Masons and the National Medical Association, had organizational structures similar to those of white counterpart groups, they also imbued their activities with a distinctive world view. For example, the African Methodist Episcopal Church is a Methodist organization, but it also has its own mode of religious emphasis and a history of antislavery and civil rights activity that give it an identity of its own. Similarly, black newspapers provided, and still provide, a different perspective on the news: coverage by the black press of post–World War II Third World nations' struggles for independence, for example, frequently offered perspectives not generally available in the white American press.

Black parallel society was not autonomous: lack of black control over local governments and other important institutions made that impossible. The subordinate social status of the black community was apparent in the weak position of blacks in government and the small size of the black business community. For example, in 1941, there were 33 black elected officials in the entire United States. In 1965 the number was still less than 300 (see Chapter 5).

Black Cultural Life

From the 1940s through the 1960s, urban and rural black communities were in a constant state of flux, but they were connected by their racial identity and the continuing flow of rural to urban migrants. Such communities were transforming the cultural context of black and white America. Cultural expression in black communities was distinctive, imaginative, and often indicative of future trends in American popular culture. The arts as practiced by blacks were often linked with social activism and seen through the frame of reference with which blacks viewed American society. For example, key black visual artists—such as Richmond Barthe, Romare Bearden, Hale Woodruff, and Charles Johnson—frequently used realistic and naturalistic depictions of the world that gave their work social significance (Powell, 1986).

The quest for full participation and civil rights gave black writers an energy seldom rivaled in contemporary American literature. As in the other arts, the main emphasis in literature was on naturalism—"the literary depiction of environmental forces which shape and determine human behavior" (Gates, 1986:5). During the war years, black authors published works of fiction, drama, and poetry that spoke to social conditions of black Americans: William Attaway's *Blood on the Forge* (1941), Sterling Brown's *Negro Caravan* (1941), Saunders Redding's *No Day of Triumph* (1941), Margaret Walker's book of poetry *My People* (1942), Binga Desmond's *He Who Would Die* (1943), Frank Yerby's *Health Card* (1944), Melvin Tolson's book of poems *Rendezvous with America* (1944), and Gwendolyn Brooks's poetry *A Street in Brooklyn* (1945) were important examples.

Richard Wright's works of the 1940s and 1950s, including *Native Son* (1941), *Black Boy* (1945), and *The Outsider* (1953), were influential for other writers. Wright's emphasis had been the dulling impact of racism on blacks: "I sensed that Negro life was a sprawling land of unconscious suffering, and that there were but a few Negroes who knew the meaning of their lives, who could tell their [own] story" (cited in Gates, 1986:13).

In contrast, Ralph Ellison believed this approach gave an undue emphasis on the disintegrating effects of racism. Both Ellison and James Baldwin contested Wright's bleak view by concentrating on conscious and active black people, rather than blacks' actions as mere responses to racism. Blacks' experience of the rural to urban migration were depicted in Arna Wendell Bontemps and Jack Conroy's *They Seek a City* (1945) and James Baldwin's *Go Tell It on the Mountain* (1953). The complex connection of the black movement's relationship to white radicals and liberals was one theme depicted in Ralph Ellison's critically acclaimed *Invisible Man* (1952). Other works reflected on the racism that had permeated the military during the war, for example, Chester Hime's *If He Hollers Let Him Go* (1945). The dire realities of inner-city life for black youth were illustrated in Ann Petry's *The Street* (1946) and Claude Brown's *Manchild in the Promised Land* (1965).

A number of important works by black playwrights dramatizing black life, rebellion, and resilience under racial injustice appeared in the 1950s and 1960s. Few appeared on Broadway, and those that did seldom ran for very long. In general, the emphasis on social commitment and naturalistic depictions of reality "as it is" drama by black playwrights paralleled the works of many black novelists. Lorraine Hansberry, author of *A Raisin in the Sun* (1959), now a classic of the American stage, called for a politically relevant black art.

During the 1920s and 1930s, important musical developments had occurred in many cities, particularly Chicago, Kansas City, and New York. In the blues clubs of Chicago's Maxwell Street, musicians Muddy Waters, John Lee Williamson, Joe Williams, and Robert Nighthawk (among others) were developing a new urban blues; they also recorded in the white-owned studios of Victor Records and other companies. The World War II Chicago blues was a dynamic blend of country and developing city styles. By the end of World War II, this new urban music was becoming known as jump blues or rhythm and blues, R&B. It would soon have enormous impact on American popular music and then music worldwide. It was a musical manifesto of the urbanizing black population, most of whom, including the musicians, were from the South but who increasingly saw themselves as city people. As Robert Palmer (1981:146) notes:

> The new R&B or jump blues, appealed to black listeners who no longer wished to identify themselves with life down home, and the field offered attractive financial opportunity for skilled jazzmen willing to "play for the people." . . . By 1945 a number of Chicago clubs . . . were switching over to city R&B.

Meanwhile Duke Ellington, Coleman Hawkins, Count Basie, and Louis Armstrong had reached what Ralph Ellison calls "high artistic achievement" in the blues-jazz tradition (Ellison, 1964). In New York during the 1940s, the revolutionary music known as bop or bebop was being pioneered by Charlie Parker, John Birks Gillispie, Thelonious Monk, Bud Powell, Max Roach, and Kenny Clarke, among others. In the 1950s and 1960s, modern jazz became transformed into even more innovative forms under the tutelage of such musician-composers as Bud Powell, Miles Davis, and John Coltrane.

The development of bebop and rhythm and blues were testimonies to the ways in which urbanization was contributing to artistic expression. The city undoubtedly generated alienation and anomie, but black people transformed their urban experience in ways that drew from rural roots. And for many blacks, the revolution in music was just that, a revolution. As Marable (1984:52) wrote:

> [It was] on the "cultural front" what the Montgomery boycott, demonstrations and the new militant mood were in politics. It shattered established conventions; it mocked traditions; in form and grace, it transcended old boundaries to life and thought. It became the appropriate cultural background for their activities to destroy Jim Crow.

AFTER THE CIVIL RIGHTS MOVEMENT

The civil rights movement and the consequent changes in laws and social attitudes opened new opportunities for blacks. As many schools desegregated and as more resources were devoted to schools with black pupils, more young blacks completed high school and continued on to higher education. Many professions and businesses, anxious to overcome histories and reputations of white exclusiveness, recruited qualified black graduates. Racial discrimination, although far from being eradicated, became illegal and contrary to the nationally accepted ethos. Educated and economically successful black families could live in better neighborhoods of cities and in suburbs (although most were still segregated neighborhoods). As many did so, inner-city black neighborhoods lost many of their most affluent and skilled residents. Remaining are many blacks who have not "made it" and whose children will rarely do so either—hundreds of thousands of blacks in demoralized neighborhoods.

Thus, a monumental black poverty problem coexists with the growth of a substantial black middle class. Some of the more important consequences of the enlarged opportunities for black Americans and the increasing socioeconomic diversity within the black population have been a significant alteration in black leadership structure; problems in the recruitment and retention of talented blacks by black organizations and institutions; and the creation of new forms of black organizations.

The Black Middle Class

In terms of both occupations and incomes, the 1960s were a watershed decade for the growth of the black middle class. The proportion of black white-collar workers doubled from 13 to 26 percent, and unlike earlier decades, some of this growth occurred outside traditional black occupations, most notably in government employment. The proportion of black families with incomes above the white median family income also grew, from 13 to 21 percent.

Due to the structural barriers facing blacks in many occupations prior to World War II, the distribution of black white-collar workers was heavily skewed toward a handful of occupations. In 1940, teachers accounted for 36 percent of all blacks in white-collar occupations, self-employed business-men for 27 percent, and the clergy for 10 percent. By 1980, teachers accounted for 27 percent of blacks in white-collar occupations, while self-employed managers had declined to just over 1 percent and the clergy to 1 percent. Meanwhile, the share of salaried managers in the private sector increased from 6 to 18 percent, public sector managers from less than 1 to 12 percent, and social workers from slightly more than 1 to nearly 6 percent (see Table 4-1).

The prewar black middle class was drawn heavily from the salaried and managerial private sector; the post-1960s black middle class is much more rooted in the public sector. In 1940, 2 percent of black managers were employed by government; this percentage had risen to 27 percent by 1970 and to 37 percent by 1980. A majority of black professionals are government employees compared with less than 40 percent of white professionals. Overall, 27 percent of blacks were employed in government in 1980, compared with 17 percent of the total work force.

The growth of the new black middle class, contrary to some expectations, has created a black bourgeoisie that is more predisposed to align itself politically with the black lower class than was the case earlier. This pattern may be due to a "structural liberalism" stemming from a shared interest, reinforcing considerations of ideology or race solidarity, in seeing the public sector expand (Smith, 1982:36–38). It may be significant that a large proportion of lower status blacks receive public assistance and community services from programs that are disproportionately staffed by black professionals. Thus, the lack of a pronounced class differential in black attitudes toward the public sector can be partly attributed to the fact that the class structure and vested interest in the expansion of the public sector intersect in a very different way among blacks than among whites.

The Changing Black Elite

The trends of the black middle class in the occupational structure have had important implications for black leadership. For example, the occupa-

TABLE 4-1 Selected White-Collar Occupations Filled by Blacks, 1940–1980

Occupation	Number (Percent)									
	1940		1950		1960		1970		1980	
Managerial	62,220	(33.2)	112,020	(37.5)	121,762	(25.7)	170,035	(21.8)	487,432	(31.1)
Self-employed	49,760	(26.5)	73,560	(24.6)	63,357	(13.4)	34,893	(4.5)	21,781	(1.4)
Private salary	10,940	(5.8)	32,580	(10.9)	44,318	(9.3)	87,765	(11.2)	282,488	(18.1)
Government	1,240	(0.7)	5,250	(1.8)	12,282	(2.6)	46,388	(5.9)	181,847	(11.6)
Professional and technical^a	125,300	(66.8)	186,930	(62.5)	352,298	(74.3)	611,334	(78.2)	1,077,482	(68.9)
Clergy	17,920	(9.6)	19,110	(6.4)	14,530	(3.1)	12,850	(1.6)	16,195	(1.0)
Engineers	300	(0.2)	2,730	(0.9)	12,049	(2.5)	13,679	(1.8)	36,019	(2.3)
Lawyers and judges	1,000	(0.5)	1,530	(0.5)	2,970	(0.6)	3,728	(0.5)	15,277	(1.0)
Physicians	4,160	(2.2)	4,500	(1.5)	9,983	(2.1)	6,106	(0.8)	13,509	(0.9)
Social workers	2,720	(1.5)	6,750	(2.3)	15,345	(3.2)	40,791	(5.2)	88,512	(5.6)
Teachers	67,660	(36.0)	90,180	(30.2)	150,743	(31.8)	240,073	(30.7)	424,755	(27.1)
Total	187,520	(100.0)	298,950	(100.0)	474,060	(100.0)	781,369	(100.0)	1,564,914	(100.0)

^{a}Includes other professions not listed below.

Source: Data from decennial censuses.

tional distribution of the black elite, as measured by *Who's Who Among Black Americans* and its earlier equivalent, shows significant changes. Educators now constitute 32 percent of the black elite, up from 14 percent before World War II. The representation of medical doctors has dropped from 26 to 13 percent, and the clergy has dropped from 14 to 5 percent. The categories of government officials and business executives, apparently too scarce to merit tabulation before World War II, comprised 12 and 11 percent, respectively, of the black elite as of 1978 (Sites and Mullins, 1985:279).

Another way to analyze the composition of the black elite is to examine the institutional affiliations of the people represented on the list of the 100 most influential black persons compiled annually by *Ebony* magazine since 1963 (Smith, 1982:43–47). Black elected officials increased from 9 to 25 percent of *Ebony*'s black leaders between 1963 and 1980, while civil rights leaders dropped from 18 to 7 percent, and "glamour" personalities such as entertainers and athletes declined from 10 to 2 percent. Including black elected and appointed officials and black judges, the proportion of public officials among black leaders rose from 24 to 55 percent during this period.

As suggested by these changes in the composition of the black elite, new types of leaders in the black community are supplementing and to some extent supplanting the older leadership of the clergy, self-employed men and women in business, professionals, and people in the traditional black voluntary associations. The new leadership is composed of black elected officials, black managers of public and nonprofit institutions (such as foundations and colleges), black corporate executives and entrepreneurs, and black veterans of community organizing activities (see Broder, 1980:305–306, citing Vernon Jordan). The broader range of occupations and positions available to potential black leaders has had important ramifications for black organizations and for the ability of leaders to effect change.

INSTITUTIONS: INSTRUMENTS OF CHANGE

Important changes in both black institutions and organizations with black members have occurred since the 1960s. The two most important influences on black organizational life have been changes in blacks' socioeconomic status—education, incomes, occupations, and urban residence—and increases in black participation throughout American society. Some of the resulting alterations have been quite dramatic. Desegregation of baseball led to a complete disappearance of the professional black baseball leagues. Similarly, black theaters and cinemas such as the Apollo Theatre in Harlem and the Howard in Washington, D.C., which once drew top black performers to a segregated industry, have nearly vanished. The largest black newspapers, *The Chicago Defender*, *The Amsterdam News* (New York), *The National Afro-American* (Baltimore), and *The Pittsburgh Courier,* have experienced declines in circulation.

With the notable exception of the black baseball leagues, many such changes were partly due to general demographic change throughout the nation. For example, music halls and other places for live, large-scale entertainment declined everywhere during the age of television. Similarly, there has been a decline and disappearance of many large city newspapers, white and black. Meanwhile, largely due to rising living standards and literacy, the black newspaper tradition has continued in the increasing number of weekly newspapers, and the publication of periodicals and magazines aimed principally at black readers has grown (Childs, 1987).

Black voluntary and professional organizations such as the Elks, the Prince Hall Masons, the Knights of Peter Claver, the National Bar Association, the National Medical Association, and the National Dental Association continue to flourish. Similarly, the Greek letter fraternities and sororities, located mostly at black colleges, still hold national and regional conventions, and in many localities they contribute to black activity, both socially and in community building (Childs, 1987).

In this section we discuss some of the changes and adaptations made by black institutions and organizations during the past few decades. We also review briefly some important new developments in black organizational life. Throughout the discussion, the focus is on institutional structure and its relationship to changes in black status.

THE CIVIL RIGHTS MOVEMENT AND ITS LOCAL ROOTS

The civil rights movement emerged, to a large degree, from local communities and organizations that drew support from a wide range of people (Carson, 1986; Morris, 1984). National organizations such as the National Association for the Advancement of Colored People (NAACP) and the Congress of Racial Equality (CORE) played major roles; but, as Aldon Morris points out, for much of the organizing in the South, existing institutions, leaders, and organizations were critically involved in all phases of the movement, and they were especially important in the beginning stages, when the action was planned and resources mobilized. Even the new organizations that were formed (e.g., the Montgomery Improvement Association, the Southern Christian Leadership Conference [SCLC], the Albany Movement) grew out of a configuration of existing organizations (Morris, 1984:277–278). The problem was not the need to create organizations, but rather how to tie existing organizations into the civil rights movement. The existing structure of black organizations, much of it in the parallel society already described, was the base from which the civil rights movement grew to maturity.

Community efforts against discrimination involved a broad coalition of black organizations: churches, newspapers, the NAACP, the Urban League, and local black groups. They often worked in concert with the Congress of Industrial Organizations (CIO), the American Civil Liberties Union, the American Jewish Congress, and the National Lawyers Guild, among others. Such exclusively or predominantly white organizations provided money, people power, physical facilities, and their own organizing skills in efforts aimed at obtaining equal opportunity for blacks.

One example of the importance of the black social structure is found in the complementary activities of politically engaged churches and of students at the predominantly black colleges. In the late 1950s and early 1960s, the Nashville Christian Leadership Conference, a branch of the SCLC, was based both in the black churches and among students at Fisk University, Tennessee State College, American Baptist Theological Seminary, and Meharry Medical School. Black students, including many who were future civil rights leaders— including John Lewis, later chair of the Student Nonviolent Coordinating Committee (SNCC) and later a member of Congress from Georgia—were activists at these schools. The civil rights movement drew people and resources from black churches and black colleges throughout the South (Childs, 1987; Morris, 1984:183).

As a base for the civil rights movement, there was a long-established tradition of activism among people from many domains of community life. For example, when blacks arrived at the Highlander Center in Tennessee for training as civil rights organizers, there were beauticians in the groups. As Myles Horton, founder of the Highlander Folk School, recalled (quoted in Morris, 1984:145):

> A black beautician, unlike a white beautician, was at that time a person of status in the community. They were entrepreneurs, they were small businesswomen, you know, respected, they were usually better educated than other people, and most of all they were independent. They were independent of white control. . . . I noticed that some of the people that came to Highlander were beauticians, and I followed up that lead and used to run beauticians (community activism) workshops at Highlander, just for beauticians.

People learned community organizing skills in a movement dedicated to nonviolent struggle even in the face of violent white resistance. During the sit-ins, the freedom rides, and the marches and demonstrations, black students and church members mingled with people from indigenous community organizations. Those organizations were instrumental to the civil rights movement and improvements in blacks' status (see Chapter 5). And the movement and the changes it brought reverberated on the structure of those organizations.

RELIGIOUS INSTITUTIONS

Probably no other single institution has played such an important role in maintaining the cohesion of black society as the black church. As E. Franklin Frazier (1963:30) concluded: "An organized religious life became the chief means by which a structured or organized social life came into existence among the Negro masses." The church was an agency of moral guidance and social control. It was also an organizational network that laid the foun-

TABLE 4-2 Membership in Major Black Religious Denominations

Denomination (Year of Founding)	Membership	
	Early 1940s	Early 1980s
National Baptist Convention, U.S.A., Inc. (1895)	4,022,000	6,300,000
Church of God in Christ (1895)	300,000	3,710,000
National Baptist Convention of America (1917)	2,352,000	2,500,000
African Methodist Episcopal Church (1816)	869,000	2,210,000
African Methodist Episcopal Zion Church (1822)	489,000	1,202,000
Christian Methodist Episcopal Church (1870)	382,000	719,000
National Primitive Baptist Convention	44,000	250,000
Progressive National Baptist Convention (1961)	–	200,000

Sources: Data for early 1940s from Murray (1947:153–155); data for early 1980s from Jacquet (1987:Table 1-A) and Lincoln (1984:88).

dation for mutual aid societies, developed much of the black community's political leadership, and provided an impetus for educational advancement. The local church was often the center of black community life (Frazier, 1963:44; Lincoln, 1984:72).

The three largest black religious bodies are Methodist, Baptist, and Pentecostal. While independent black Baptist and Methodist churches can be traced back to eighteenth century South Carolina and Philadelphia (Lincoln, 1984), the first black American religious denominations, the African Methodist Episcopal (AME) Church and the African Methodist Episcopal Zion (AME Zion) Church, were founded in 1816 and 1822, respectively. The third major black Methodist denomination, the Colored Methodist Episcopal Church, was founded in 1870 and changed its name to the Christian Methodist Episcopal (CME) Church in 1954. These churches remain the three major black Methodist denominations to this day.

The three major Baptist denominations are of more recent vintage. The National Baptist Convention, U.S.A., Inc., known popularly as the "incorporated" convention, has probably been the largest single black denomination since its founding in 1895. The National Baptist Convention of America, the "unincorporated" convention, split from the first body in 1917. A second splinter church from the incorporated convention, the Progressive National Baptist Convention, Inc., was formed in 1961 (Childs, 1980; Simpson and Yinger, 1985:324).

The final major black denomination, the Church of God in Christ, is Pentecostal. Founded in 1895, it has shown the greatest growth of any black denomination since World War II, and it is now believed to be the second largest black church group in the United States. Self-reported estimates of the size of these churches are shown in Table 4-2.

With the beginning of the urbanization of the black population in the first decades of the twentieth century, many black churches began to deemphasize the "other-worldly outlook" characteristic of rural and lower status churches (Frazier, 1963:51). Urban black churches became primary links between thousands of black migrants from rural areas and their new and stressful urban environments. As black churches responded to urban problems with community aid and welfare work, many of them cooperated with organizations such as the NAACP and the National Urban League in the more secular affairs of the community.

The increasing secularism in the role of the church did involve some ambivalence and even resistance within individual church organizations. Especially in rural southern areas, where the emphasis of many black churches on the values of the afterlife pushed aside concerns with contemporary social affairs, the black church had gained a reputation as a conservative influence that helped to maintain black subordination in race relations (Johnson, 1941:135–136; see also Myrdal, 1944; Reed, 1986:Ch. 4). This resistance to involvement in civil affairs became increasingly unsuccessful as the 1950s progressed.

The split among black Baptists in 1961 illustrates the changing political role of the black church. The conservative leadership of the Reverend Joseph Jackson of the National Baptist Convention became increasingly controversial as activists sought to involve the church more directly in the civil rights movement. Jackson reflected an older tradition of leadership, that the major function of the black clergy is to minister to the religious needs of their flock, rather than to engage in political controversies (Nelson, 1987).

Since its founding in Atlanta in 1957, the SCLC has been the most important institutional framework for black church involvement in civil rights activity. The SCLC was established as a coalition of coalitions, that is, chapters consisting of church and other groups that were active at the local level in the South. Although it sometimes has been seen as little more than a paper organization dominated by the charisma of the Reverend Dr. Martin Luther King, Jr., it was in fact the most important institutional device for uniting the many diverse community-based civil rights organizations that emerged in the 1950s and early 1960s. Its leadership, both nationally and at the local level, was heavily dominated by the black clergy, but it also incorporated black lodges, labor unions, and women's groups as affiliates (Morris, 1984:Chs. 4–5).

The National Committee of Black Churchmen (NCBC), founded in 1967, has been described as the northern counterpart of SCLC, with one significant difference: most of its leadership was drawn from black clergy in the predominantly white denominations rather than those in the black denominations. It quickly established black caucuses in virtually all of the predominantly white denominations and emerged as a bridge between the religious establishment in the broader community and the black clergy (Lincoln, 1984:110–113).

Since its founding in 1978, the Congress of National Black Churches (CNBC) has played an increasingly important role in the direction of the affairs of the black church. The CNBC is a coalition of seven major black denominations: three major Baptist conventions (incorporated, unincorporated, and Progressive; see Table 4–2); the three major Methodist churches

(AME, AME Zion, and CME); and the Church of God in Christ. Under the leadership of its first chairman, Bishop John Hurst Adams of the AME Church, the CNBC established a Washington headquarters in 1982 and expanded its mission from an ecumenical focus to a pursuit of six broad priorities: theological education, employment, economic development, the media, evangelism, and human services (Lincoln, 1984:118–121).

The CNBC has been particularly active in the field of economic development. Black churchgoers contribute over $1 billion a year to their parishes, and the assets of black churches across the country are believed to exceed $10 billion. The CNBC has used some of these funds to benefit the black community through the establishment of credit unions, insurance programs, central purchasing plans, and the allocation of church funds to black-owned banks and small businesses. At the local level, black churches have been increasingly active in providing day care, health care, low-income housing, and other social services to their clientele (Lincoln, 1984:121–122; Nelson, 1987).

Despite the finding of a Gallup survey (1987) that 74 percent of the black population rated religion as "very important" in their lives compared with 55 percent of whites, formal black involvement in church affairs appears to be following a pattern similar to that of the rest of American society. Although religion is important to them, 40 percent of the surveyed blacks said they do not regularly attend a church or synagogue; among the whites surveyed, 44 percent gave this response.

American religious institutions, including black churches, are thus facing difficult times expanding the growth of their memberships. Increased social stratification within the black community, suburbanization of the middle class, and losses of worshippers as well as many talented ministers and other church officials to predominantly white organizations (see Chapter 2) make this trend especially difficult for black churches. Yet, for many blacks, particularly the poor, black religious organizations still supply a significant network of support services and spiritual sustenance.

COLLEGES AND UNIVERSITIES

History

The traditionally black colleges and universities have historically kept alive a tradition of scholarship about black concerns and also provided a means for improving the social and economic status of black Americans. The majority of black lawyers, dentists, and teachers in the United States today received their degrees from black institutions of higher learning (Hill, 1984:ix; Wilkinson, 1987:i).

The first three black institutions were founded in the North: Cheyney University (1837) and Lincoln University (1854), both in Pennsylvania, and Wilberforce University (1856) in Ohio. The majority of others, however, emerged in the South during and after Reconstruction. Given the refusal of local governments in many parts of the South to provide adequate public schooling for blacks, private charities, churches, and freedmen's societies performed much of this role. Many of today's black colleges began as private schools offering secondary-level instruction to blacks in the rural South and gradually added college-level courses to their curricula (Hill, 1984:1–3). By 1936, a total of 121 black institutions had an enrollment of 33,743 regular-term and 22,510 summer students at the college level. Most of these schools had by then phased out their secondary-level instruction, due in part to a rapid expansion of public schools in the South following World War I (Hill, 1984:Ch. 1).

The period between the two world wars witnessed the peak influence of black private colleges. Between 1936 and 1954, the number of private black institutions declined from 86 to 65, and they have continued to decline slowly, although their enrollments have grown gradually since 1954. The public black institutions have grown much more, doubling their enrollments since 1954. In the 1960s, "traditionally black institutions enrolled about one third of the approximately 434,000 black students in higher education" (Morris, 1981:8).

It was not until the 1970s that black students in large numbers began attending predominantly white public and private colleges and universities in the South. In the 19 states (and the District of Columbia) that have black institutions, the proportion of black students attending them declined from 62 percent in 1970 to 38 percent in 1980. Their total enrollment peaked at 222,220 in 1980 and has declined thereafter (Hill, 1984:xiv, xvi, 23, 45).

While the absolute number of degrees awarded by predominantly black educational institutions increased between the mid-1960s and mid-1970s, by the 1980s there was a decline in the proportion of blacks who graduated from the historically black institutions. Furthermore, in the 8-year period between 1976 and 1984, 5 of the 105 traditionally black colleges and universities closed. The political and demographic changes that have affected shifts in the student composition and educational missions of predominantly black colleges appear to have been inevitable (Blackwell, 1984:176–186; Egerton, 1971; U.S. Commission on Civil Rights, 1981:6–8). And recent decreases in financial aid and in enrollments of minority college students nationally have increased the difficulties of black institutions of higher education (Coleman, 1983; Cross and Astin, 1981; Newby, 1982; Tollet, 1981; Wilkinson, 1987).

The development of graduate programs at black educational institutions is a relatively recent phenomenon. In 1954, there were 16 institutions that conferred master's degrees in 10 disciplines. By 1982, master's degree programs had been established at 34 institutions in all 22 major disciplinary categories recognized by HEGIS (Higher Education General Information Survey). Howard University became the first historically black school to offer a doctoral degree in 1957, followed by Atlanta University in 1982. In addition, 3 other historically black universities granted a total of 12 doctoral degrees in 1982 (Hill, 1984:xv).

Current Patterns

As of 1984, there were exactly 100 predominantly black colleges and universities, including 11 2-year institutions. The 43 public black colleges supported by state governments accounted for more than two-thirds of the total enrollment. The other 57 black colleges are private institutions, 45 of which are affiliated with a religious denomination. The 100 colleges and universities, which are located in 19 states and the District of Columbia, still award more than one-half of all the bachelor's degrees earned by black students and employ two-thirds of the black college faculty. Although these institutions have been most important as teachers' schools, by 1981 business and management had replaced education as the most popular academic major among graduating seniors (Hill, 1984:ix–xiv).

Like most predominantly white universities, the traditionally black institutions continue to have primarily single-race enrollment as well as administration, staff, and faculty (Hill, 1984). In 1981, some 11 percent of the students at the black institutions were American whites, and 6 percent were nonresident aliens. There is a view that white student enrollments should not be increased in these institutions until enrollments of blacks increase at the predominantly white institutions, but some educators and public officials believe that this position contradicts the concept of integration in higher education as outlined in a 1981 report entitled *The Black/White Colleges* (U.S. Commission on Civil Rights, 1981).

However, that same document notes that the goal of enabling black youths to attain higher education might be diminished if white students enroll at black institutions without an increase in black enrollment at predominantly white schools. Thus, the U.S. Commission on Civil Rights (1981:34) has argued for a deferment of integration within predominantly black institutions until there is a substantial increase in black enrollment at traditionally white schools (see Wilkinson, 1987:2–3).

Four of the historically black colleges and universities now have majority white enrollments: Bluefield State in West Virginia, West Virginia State, Lincoln University in Pennsylvania, and Kentucky State (Wilkinson, 1987). Since the 1960s, the traditionally black institutions have been facing increased competition from predominantly white enrollment colleges and universities in trying to attract the most gifted black faculty and students, who in years past would have naturally gravitated to the black institutions, due to lack of opportunity elsewhere in the educational structure.

Enrollment declines and attrition have been recorded recently for blacks in predominantly white colleges and universities. Obstacles to successful completion of undergraduate training, however, are not merely characteristic of black students in predominantly white colleges and universities; those in the historically black institutions are affected as well (Wilkinson, 1987). Historically, black undergraduates in black institutions have had an attrition rate at least as high as that experienced by black undergraduates in predominantly white institutions between their second and fourth years of college. In addition, the attrition rate for black fourth-year students in black institutions has gone up considerably since 1976 (Office of Civil Rights, 1981). Concern over declining enrollment and rising attrition continued into the 1980s as the number of black students attending colleges and universities decreased (Wilkinson, 1987; see Chapter 7).

More recently, some public concern has been expressed about the academic missions, instructional functions, and research output of the nation's black colleges and universities. In Congress and in the media, considerable attention has been devoted to such issues as administrative leadership, salary structures, and program expenditure as they affect academic objectives (Jaschik, 1986:19–20), institutional productivity, and the nature of training of students (see Coleman, 1983; Frinberg, 1984, cited in Wilkinson, 1987; Hall, 1984; Muscatine, 1985). Furthermore, while black colleges are primarily teaching schools, many have either initiated or enhanced professional development and faculty research productivity (Billingsley, 1982), but administrative structures have remained virtually unchanged (see Blackwell, 1984:177; Griswold, 1983).

Financial problems have regularly plagued the traditionally black institutions. Many of them have only nominal endowments or none at all, making them dependent on students' ability to pay tuition and fees and on state appropriations, federal aid, and philanthropy. The low income levels prevailing among black students have exerted strong pressure to keep tuitions low, and the relatively low incomes of many graduates compared with those of their white peers has limited the institutions' fund-raising abilities, despite the activities of such groups as the United Negro College Fund. In recent years, the election of black state legislators in the South has generated some political influence to increase appropriations.

But the major outside assistance has come from the federal government. There are two sources of direct federal aid to these institutions. The Second Morrill Act in 1890 resulted in the establishment of 16 black land-grant colleges. Title III of the Higher Education Amendments of 1965 targeted federal funds to underfinanced colleges historically considered to be out of the mainstream of the higher education establishment (Hill, 1984:xviii; Wilkinson, 1987). In addition, the reliance of many black students on federal financial aid makes these programs vital to the financial stability of many black institutions (see Chapter 7).

BUSINESSES

From the Nineteenth Century to the Civil Rights Movement

Joseph Pierce (1944, cited in Bates, 1986) undertook the first large-scale quantitative study of the black business community. His survey of 3,866 black firms in 12 cities revealed an industry concentration reminiscent of black entrepreneurship in the antebellum South. Six lines of personal services and retailing dominated the sample of black firms: beauty parlors and barber shops, 26 percent; eating establishments, 19 percent; food stores, 8 percent; cleaning and pressing shops, 7 percent; shoeshine and repair shops, 5 percent; and funeral parlors, 3 percent. During the following 25 years, a number of less comprehensive studies reported similar findings: black businesses were primarily small-scale enterprises concentrated in a narrow range of low-revenue activities (Bates, 1986). These businesses were heavily, almost exclusively, dependent on the segregated black community for patronage. The poverty and small resources of that community necessarily meant that black firms were at a great commercial disadvantage. Black-operated firms had little growth potential and poor access to credit (Harris, 1936).

Despite these conditions, the segregated economy was able to support a small number of successful enterprises in industries in which white-owned firms had not been motivated to compete for black business. Among these were the banking and life insurance industries, hair-care products, and the mass media. A few black entrepreneurs were able to amass personal fortunes in these industries. A number of the most successful black businesses of the 1940–1985 period were started in these industries during the 1940s and 1950s: These examples are Johnson Publishing, founded by John Johnson in 1942; Johnson Products (hair care), founded by George E. Johnson in 1954; and Motown Industries, founded by Berry Gordy in 1958. Each of these companies continues to thrive today.

A number of black life insurance companies, many of which began as mutual aid burial societies in the late nineteenth and early twentieth centuries when many blacks found it difficult to obtain insurance from white companies, also continue actively today. Some of the oldest appear on *Black Enterprise* magazine's top 16 black-owned insurance firms, ranked by total assets in 1986 (*Black Enterprise*, June 1987:228–229): Southern Aid Life Insurance Company (ranked 16), founded in 1893 and located in Richmond, Virginia; North Carolina Mutual Life (ranked 1), founded in 1898 and located in Durham, North Carolina; Atlanta Life (ranked 2), founded in 1905 and located in Atlanta, Georgia; Mammoth Life and Accident (ranked 8), founded in 1915 and located in Louisville, Kentucky; and Chicago Metropolitan Mutual (ranked 5), founded in 1927.

Despite these exceptions, as late as 1969, 94 percent of black-owned firms were sole proprietorships; 84 percent had no paid employees; and average annual revenues per firm were a mere $27,000. At that time, one-half of black firms were located in the South (Bureau of the Census, 1979:Table 58). The total of 163,000 black-owned businesses in 1969 were 2.2 percent of all U.S. businesses. Most were concentrated in personal services and retail trade. Receipts from all black enterprises were $4.5 billion, less than 1 percent of all national business receipts.

Black-Owned Businesses Since 1970

In 1977 there were 231,203 black-owned firms, 70 percent of which were personal services and retail trade. The average receipts per black retail firm

FIGURE 4-2 Top 100 black-owned companies, by industry, 1987.

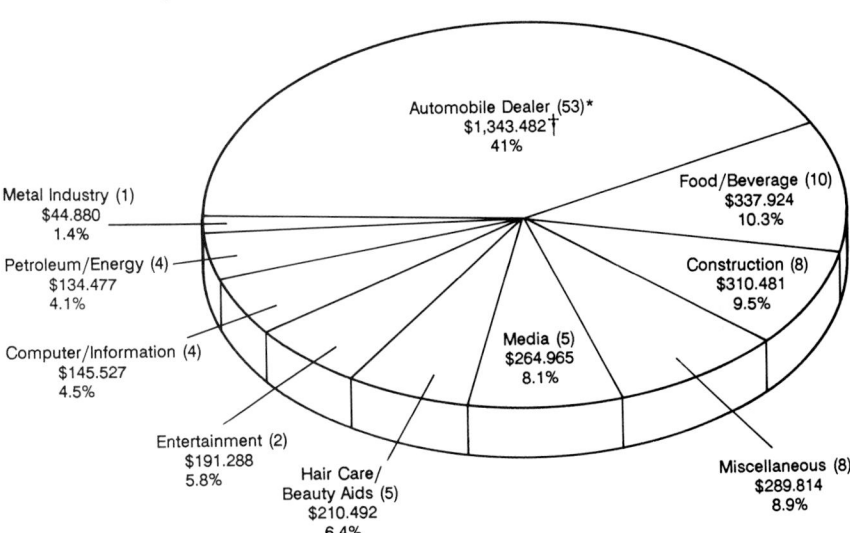

Notes: * = Number of companies. † = In millions of dollars, to nearest thousand.

Source: Reprinted with permission from *Black Enterprise* (1987:114).

were just 13.1 percent of average per-firm receipts of all U.S. retail firms, which was comparable for the service industries. In 1982, 339,239 black businesses in the nation had $12.4 billion in sales receipts, which represented about one-third of 1 percent of the total U.S. sales receipts of $4.12 trillion. Five years later, the share of black sales revenue was unchanged while the total was $18.1 billion. Thus, although blacks are 12 percent of the U.S. population, their businesses in the late 1980s still accounted for only one-third of 1 percent of the nation's total sales receipts.

In recent years, however, black businesses have grown faster than the nation's business sector as a whole—7 percent compared with 5 percent. They have also become less dependent on black consumers by expanding outside traditional black consumer markets. This modest diversification in the 1980s is illustrated by the changing industry distribution of *Black Enterprise* magazine's list of top 100 black firms, ranked by sales revenue.

Black Enterprise published the first 100 list for the year 1972. Total sales for the 100 firms were $473 million, and the list was dominated by manufacturers, auto dealerships, entertainment companies, and publishing and other consumer-service firms, each of which accounted for about 20 percent of all sales on the list. The 1987 list reflected the increased strength of black auto dealers: they accounted for 53 of the firms, a majority of the top 100 for the first time, and were responsible for 41 percent of sales. The distribution of sales revenues by industry for the *Black Enterprise* list of 100 is shown in Figure 4-2.

There has been an increasing number of financially skilled black entrepreneurs. Examples include C. Everett Wallace, who in 1985 acquired City & Suburban Distributors, Inc., a Chicago-based beer distributorship, with $41 million in sales; J. Bruce Llewellyn, who (with his partner former basketball star Julius Erving) owns the Philadelphia Coca-Cola Bottling Company (4 on the *Black Enterprise* list) with sales of $110 million; and Reginald F. Lewis, who in 1987 completed the largest financial transaction ever negotiated by a black American by the purchase of the International Foods Division of Beatrice, Inc., which has sales of $1.8 billion.

There are a number of reasons for the changes that are occurring among black-owned enterprises. Perhaps the most important are the general changes in black education and income (thus expanding black consumer markets), social attitudes toward race relations, and government policies aimed at aiding black business development. The civil rights movement created a new emphasis by the government and private sector to promote the advancement of black businesses. During the presidential primaries in 1968, Richard Nixon addressed the question of black participation in ownership of businesses. During the 1960s and 1970s, the Nixon administration created a number of subsidy and assistance programs, including those of the Office of Minority Business Enterprise, the Manpower Development and Training Program, and the Minority Enterprise Small Business Investment Company.

These programs, although beleaguered by charges of inefficiency and reverse discrimination, have enabled many successful black firms to get their start. However, they would probably have had little impact were it not for the increasing pool of black professional business men and women, many initially trained in major corporations, who have taken advantage of increased opportunities in American markets.

At the same time, mergers and acquisitions have also reduced the number of black-owned businesses. These firms often become part of a larger white firm, and this reduces the number of black firms. Smaller black firms are also being taken over by larger black firms: the insurance industry is an example of this kind of reduction. *Black Enterprise* (June 1987:223) reported that in the 1940s there were 69 black-owned insurance companies; that number was 42 in 1972 and 35 in 1987. Industry analysts project that if mergers continue at this rate, only a few large black insurers will be in operation in the next decade.

Many black businesses have engaged in joint ventures with larger white corporations by becoming franchises or subsidiaries of large firms: for example, the acquisition of a Michigan Pepsi-Cola bottling distribution center by Dr. William Harvey, the president of Hampton University, and the acquisition of a Coors beer distributorship by Willie Davis, a former Green Bay Packer. Another development in the 1980s is illustrated by the example of the Barfield Companies (43 on the *Black Enterprise* list), which became the second black-owned business to attract a major investment from a Fortune 500 company (Masco Industries, a metal-products company).

The lack of success of some black firms has been due to competition from larger, white enterprises. For example, over the years, black businesses have diversified into the communications industry. Notable acquisitions, such as the $65 million purchase of WKBW in Buffalo from Capital Cities Communications (CCC), have occurred. However, white-owned radio and television stations, noting the success of the urban-contemporary format of black radio stations, have begun to feature black artists who at one time could be heard only on black stations, enticing some listeners away from those stations. Another area that has been penetrated by white-owned companies, with big advertising budgets and the use of celebrity spokespersons, is the hair-care industry. Growth in sales of black hair-care products has prompted firms such as Revlon and Alberto Culver to introduce a number of products for black consumers. Black companies are attempting to compete by developing new products or opening up new markets.

The degree of penetration of black markets and businesses by white-owned firms can be seen in the fact that black firms' share of black consumer income has declined over the past 20 years. In 1969, the receipts of all black enterprises represented 11.7 percent of the $38.1 billion income of black consumers. The total fell to 10.8 percent in 1972; to 8.9 percent in 1977; and to 8.1 percent in 1986, when total black money income was $206 billion. It fell below 8.0 percent in 1987.

Increased competition from nonblack firms is a consequence of the same factors that are altering the composition of black firms, an expanding black consumer market and improved race relations. Overall, changes in the composition and viability of black-owned firms reflect the same basic social forces that have been transforming black institutions throughout the period since 1940: increased competition from white organizations for talented blacks and competition for black clients in the post–civil rights era.

THE NAACP AND THE NATIONAL URBAN LEAGUE

Since before World War II, virtually all observers have considered the two most prominent national black organizations to be the NAACP and the National Urban League (see, e.g., Myrdal, 1944:819; Smith, 1982:57; Wilson, 1973:171). The primacy of attaining basic civil rights as a black political objective was responsible for the long preeminence of the NAACP.

The NAACP, founded in 1909 as an interracial organization, grew out of the earlier Niagara movement (1905) of black intellectuals and social activists. As a mass membership organization concentrated in the larger urban centers, it was led for the most part by black professionals: W. E. B. DuBois and William Monroe Trotter in the early years, and Walter White and Roy Wilkins during the 1940s through the civil rights movement. The southern branches of the NAACP played a key role in organizing local voters leagues in the wake of the 1944 *Smith* v. *Allwright* decision (321 U.S. 649), which overturned white primary elections. But during the late 1950s, repression from local governments and the White Citizens' Councils depressed NAACP membership in the South and wreaked havoc with its organizational activi-

FIGURE 4-3 NAACP Legal Defense Fund litigation, 1940–1983.

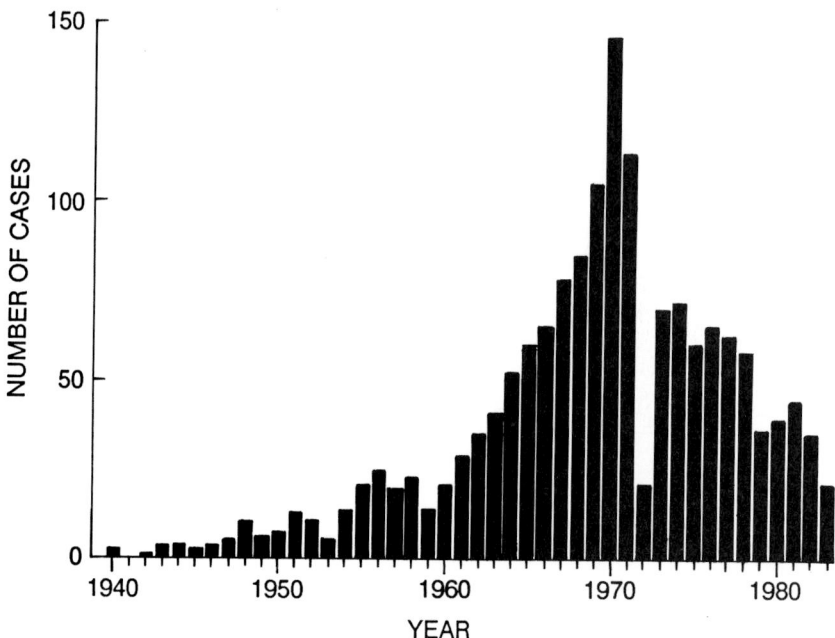

Source: Unpublished data from NAACP Legal Defense Fund.

ties. Much of the direct action associated with the civil rights movement in the South was channeled through new organizations (McAdam, 1982; Morris, 1984), leaving the NAACP southern chapters in older, more conservative hands. In the North, however, the NAACP faced less competition from the protest-oriented groups and came to be headed by insurgent leaders in many cities.

At the national level, the NAACP reached its peak influence during the years bracketed by the *Brown* school desegregation decision of 1954 and the passage of the Voting Rights Act in 1965. It had the reputation during that period of being the black organization with the greatest influence in Congress and in national politics generally. The NAACP still remains the premier black organization in terms of membership (450,000 in the late 1970s) and reputation, although there now exist a variety of specialized organizations devoted to social and economic development in the black community.

The NAACP Legal Defense Fund, Inc., known popularly as LDF, was organized as a separate entity in 1939 to handle litigation. It became fully independent of the parent organization in 1955 and had 25 full-time attorneys by the early 1960s. Although the LDF's activity has been reduced from the peak of 1970 (see Figure 4-3), it remains an important source of civil rights litigation in the American courts. The LDF's priorities can be seen

TABLE 4-3 Federal and State Litigation by NAACP Legal Defense Fund, by Category of Case, 1940–1983

Category of Case	Years			Total
	1940–1959	1960–1969	1970–1983	
All cases[a]	198	569	840	1,607
School desegregation	67	203	248	518
Employment discrimination	8	43	265	316
Prisons	3	12	72	87
Public accommodations	16	52	4	72
Housing and real estate	15	20	34	69
Demonstration rights	1	53	8	62
Voting rights	10	21	28	59
Habeas corpus	5	23	22	50
Jury procedures	7	21	16	44
Capital punishment	4	15	23	42
Social services	1	19	12	32
Police brutality	3	10	15	28

[a]Totals include cases not covered below.

Source: Unpublished data from the NAACP Legal Defense Fund.

from the cases it has filed during the past four decades: school desegregation and employment discrimination issues have dominated LDF litigation activities during the entire period, accounting for just over one-half of all litigation from 1940 to 1983 (see Table 4-3). Following schools (32 percent) and jobs (20 percent), cases dealing with criminal justice (16 percent), public accommodations (4 percent), and housing and real estate (4 percent) are distant third, fourth, and fifth place issues. This ranking is quite consonant with hypothesized rankings of major issues of importance to the black population in general (discussed in Chapter 3).

The National Urban League, founded in 1910, is the lineal descendant of a succession of social service agencies, dating back to 1906, that specialized in the problems of urban blacks. It has always been active in job training and placement activity, which has brought it into extensive contact with local businesses, social workers, and philanthropies. Thus, it has been regarded as the black organization with the closest ties to the white "power structure" in the private and nonprofit sectors (Parris and Brooks, 1971).

Unlike the NAACP, the Urban League has never been a mass membership organization, although it is organized into local affiliates (about 100 branches) that conduct the bulk of its programmatic activities. Having very nearly died of financial starvation in the 1950s, it achieved a renaissance under the leadership of executive directors Whitney Young, Jr., and Vernon Jordan from 1961 through 1980. Young's skill in pursuing a black agenda without alienating white support enabled the Urban League to raise greater resources than other black civil rights and social service groups amid the ferment of the 1960s. Due to its history of social work and cooperative ventures with business enterprise, the Urban League was well positioned to benefit from the funding made available at that time to deal with the problems of blacks in urban settings.

This combination of circumstances enabled the National Urban League to attain first rank among black organizations in terms of financial resources and program activities by 1970. The funds raised by the Urban League, which totaled only $265,000 in 1960, had increased almost 7 times in 1965 to $1,824,000, and another 8 times in 1970 to $14,542,000. During the same period, the comparable figures for the NAACP were $104,000 in 1960, $388,000 in 1965, and $2,665,000 in 1970 (Haines, 1984:Table 1). As of 1985, the National Urban League far surpassed all other black organizations in terms of donations and program expenditures; its outside revenues totaled $23,573,000, compared with $7,686,000 for the NAACP.[1]

POST-1960s ORGANIZATIONS

The very success of the NAACP in pursuit of ending de jure segregation stimulated new and more varied organizations in the black community, thereby lessening its once almost unique position as an exponent of the black condition in American life. With heightened interest in social and economic issues, many new organizations have arisen to play a major role in the organizational life of black Americans. Many of these organizations have a community-oriented agenda aimed at improving conditions at the local level. We identified more than 1,100 such organizations created since 1965 (Childs, 1987).

These new organizations reflect each of the post-1960s developments in black communities: the growth of the black professional class and changes in the black elite; increased black-white interaction; a growing concern with economic issues and the problems of the poor; and the proliferation of opportunities for educated blacks. In this section we do not attempt a thorough cataloging of these organizations, but only describe examples of a few kinds.

The Urban Coalition was the outgrowth of a 1967 meeting of large-city mayors trying to address the urban problems that were giving rise to ghetto riots. It attempts to enlist the public and private sectors in comprehensive communitywide efforts, with a special emphasis on the problem of minorities. Its major activities at present are in education, minority business development, and health care.

Although not defined as a black organization, the Children's Defense Fund (CDF) is prominent in black leadership circles (see *Ebony*, August 1988:128,130). Founded in 1968, it specializes in research and educational activity on the problems of children in poverty, a large proportion of whom are black. CDF stands at the center of a large cluster of loosely coordinated

---

1. The figures for the NAACP do not include the budget of the NAACP Legal Defense Fund.

groups that are active in domestic social policy that focuses on the problems of blacks and the poor.

Jesse Jackson has presided over a conglomerate of interlocking organizations. His first major program was the Chicago-based Operation Breadbasket, which originated as an SCLC enterprise and became independent after Martin Luther King's death. Operation Breadbasket concentrated on feeding the black poor and winning jobs through boycotts. It evolved into Operation PUSH (People United to Save Humanity), a nationwide organization with local chapters, devoted to black economic advancement. PUSH in turn gave rise to PUSH-Excel, a mass membership group that tries to motivate black parents, children, and school personnel to achieve excellence in education. In the wake of his 1984 presidential campaign, Jackson organized the Rainbow Coalition, Inc., a multiracial lobbying group, and the Citizenship Education Fund (CEF), a nonpartisan voter registration and candidate-training organization.

There are several summit coalitions of black leaders that play special roles in the black community. Among the most important are the National Black Leadership Roundtable, a coalition of about 125 national black organizations that convey local community sentiment from their chapters to the black congressional leadership and also assist in mobilizing the grass roots for lobbying campaigns on national issues; the National Black Leadership Forum, a coalition of the executives of 16 major black political, fraternal, and civic groups (Smith, 1982:64); and the "black leadership family," a more select and secretive group that played a key role in the strategy sessions over a black presidential candidacy in 1983 (Collins, 1986:94–98).

Another example of links among black organizations is TransAfrica, founded in 1977 as the result of discussions initiated at the 1976 black leadership conference of the Congressional Black Caucus. Its mission is to seek greater influence for black Americans in the foreign policy arena and to advocate greater attention to the views of African and Caribbean peoples in the conduct of American foreign policy. Today, it is most closely identified with the movement to protest apartheid by imposing sanctions on South Africa and reducing American investments in that country.

Multiracial coalition groups also have engaged in civil rights lobbying and litigation, and most of them predate the civil rights movement. A significant example is the Leadership Conference on Civil Rights, which is distinctive for the highly visible participation of representatives from many white and black religious denominations. The conference, founded in 1950, was active in the lobbying for various federal civil rights bills from 1957 to 1968. There are also local coalition groups in virtually every major city in the country. These local coalitions have frequently dominated the multiracial human relations committees (usually appointed by mayors) that have provided a forum for research, hearings, and public education on civil rights in many cities since the 1940s.

Three other multiracial groups have been particularly active in dealing with civil rights issues in the South. The Southern Regional Council helped to lay the groundwork for the Voting Rights Act through its long-continued investigations and statistical analyses of black registration patterns. The Lawyers' Committee for Civil Rights Under Law and the Southern Poverty Law Center have helped to make lawyers available at reasonable cost to blacks and their allies engaged in class-action suits and other forms of litigation or facing legal harassment from local authorities.

The Community Action Program (CAP) mandated by the "maximum feasible participation" clause of the 1964 Economic Opportunity Act has been an important source of black leadership. The CAP trained an entire generation of grass roots political activists in the black community (Peterson and Greenstone, 1977). Many of the black elected officials and community organizers of the 1980s gained their initial experience in this program in the 1960s.

Current areas of concern for local black activism include rent control, opposition to urban gentrification, bank services and loans, jobs in public works construction, and citizen action in crime prevention. Also, attorneys for the Legal Services Corporation (a federal agency started under the Economic Opportunity Act but now independent) have frequently participated in community activism, although they have been increasingly circumscribed by federal regulations restricting their involvement in class-action litigation. The bulk of their current activity is devoted to defending poor people who cannot afford an attorney on their own.

Caucus Organizations

Of the new organizations, caucus groups are prominent. By caucus group we mean an organization of black people within a predominantly white institution. A caucus seeks to protect and enhance black interests within an organization. Black caucus groups are found in nearly every organization with black and white members, including such diverse organizations as the Roman Catholic Church, the American Anthropological Association, the U.S. Department of State, the museum profession, and among advocacy groups concerned with the welfare of the aging.

Caucus organization indicates an important degree of black institutional participation. If there are enough blacks to form a caucus within an organization or a profession, then obviously more than token desegregation has occurred. Simultaneously, the self-identified need to establish such groups is indicative of a sense of black group identity within the larger group. A sense of racial identity is used by caucus groups as a base for transforming the wider institutional domain.

The Afro-American Museums Association (AAMA) is an independent body, but within the national museum profession, it is a good example of a black caucus. It seeks to increase professional black participation in museums, to serve the black community, and to make museums more responsive to the needs of that constituency.

Some museum professionals who belong to the AAMA also hold membership in the American Museum Association (AMA). The AAMA thus plays a dual role as both a parallel and a caucus organization. Many of the black museums and historical and cultural societies created since the 1960s have goals similar to those of the AAMA. The goals of such organizations usually include an emphasis on presenting a distinctive black American identity, showing its place in America, and educating the black population about its history while also emphasizing, to the wider public, black contributions in American history.

The Concerned Black Foreign Service Officers is a caucus group of black professionals within the U.S. Department of State. The objectives and mode of organization are typical of caucus formation. The group came to the attention of the media in January 1986 when it issued a report on racial discrimination in the Foreign Service. In December 1985, the group met to discuss the grade distribution, promotion, hiring, and attrition of black foreign service officers (FSOs). At this meeting the group discussed "statistical evidence of systematic discrimination against Black Foreign Service Officers" (private communication, January 3, 1986).

By organizing to address issues of apparent discrimination in the State Department, the black FSOs were acting as a caucus group. They soon decided to designate themselves as such. Their announced objectives were to fight for a completely open hiring and promotion system in the State Department and to protect the interests of black FSOs. Consequently, in October 1986, the organization filed a class-action suit in the U.S. District Court for the District of Columbia. The suit argued that the plaintiffs and members of the class of black FSOs "have been and continue to be discriminated against on the basis of race by means of an arbitrary and subjective performance evaluation and assignment system" (Complaint for Relief from Discrimination in Employment and Reprisal, Case No. 86–2850, October 17, 1986:2–3).

As with many other caucus groups the black FSOs did not proceed without difficulties. The issues of allegiance to the group, the wider community, and to the home institution, which are important in any caucus formation, are especially salient in government employment. From the point of view of the Foreign Service managers, caucus efforts could be construed as disloyal to the institution. From the perspective of black FSOs, their efforts were good for the service. The caucus argued that full integration of the black FSOs into the State Department would eliminate some ethnic and cultural biases in the foreign policy decision-making process and influence policy in ways that reflect broader Afro-American perspectives on world affairs.

The two caucus groups just noted are not unique; their basic features are characteristic of black caucuses. Organization-specific caucuses are subject to questions about their loyalty and allegiance: Is the caucus an instrument of the black community and thus suspect to the organization? Conversely, as a part of the organization, does the caucus really reflect black community concerns? Caucuses of black police, politicians, civil servants, and church officials face the same questions (Childs, 1987).

Organizations of Public Officials

One of the more significant black caucuses is that of black members of Congress, the Congressional Black Caucus (CBC), founded in 1971. The CBC receives information and opinion on policy issues from three major sources: committees of black academic experts that hold regional and national hearings to present their recommendations; the Congressional Black Caucus Foundation, which provides an in-house research capacity (although in its early years it suffered from financing problems and staff turnover); and an association with the National Black Leadership Roundtable (described above). The Roundtable's apparent capability to aggregate interests among its diverse membership is partly responsible for the wide acceptance the CBC has gained in speaking for black Americans (Smith, 1982:65). (This caucus group is discussed further in Chapter 5.)

The groups of black elected and appointed officials formed since 1970 are one of the most visible manifestations of black political participation. As the number of black officials increased during the late 1960s and early 1970s, they commonly found themselves shut out of existing networks of influence. Observers also saw an increasing need to assist newly elected black officials. Accordingly, the Ford Foundation helped to create the Joint Center for Political Studies in 1970. The Joint Center was established to determine where blacks were being elected to office, to help them organize into caucuses and more informal information-sharing networks, and to provide them with technical assistance and other forms of research support. By the early 1980s, the Joint Center had evolved into a major research organization specializing in issues concerning black Americans. While political research remains its major strength, it has recently expanded its coverage of economic and military policy.

The Joint Center has given birth to a cluster of related organizations, the most important of which is the National Coalition on Black Voter Participation (NCBVP), which was created in 1976. The NCBVP, more commonly known by the name of its ongoing voter registration and education project, Operation Big Vote (OBV), is a nonpartisan, nonprofit group. It operates by forming OBV units at the city and county level; these units are coalitions of NAACP and Urban League chapters, local black civic groups, churches, and fraternities and sororities that are devoted solely to spurring black voter participation.

For many years, the most important black voter registration group was the Voter Education Project (VEP), a spinoff from the Southern Regional Council. The VEP had emerged as the result of negotiations between the Kennedy administration and the Taconic Foundation in 1961, when federal officials were seeking to channel black activism away from sit-ins, boycotts, and other disruptive activities toward voting. Taconic took the lead in assembling a consortium of foundations to fund the project. VEP was extremely successful in its early years, accounting for the bulk of the massive increase in black registration in the South from 1962 to 1968. Thereafter, its funding became erratic, and it was forced to reorganize in 1985 because of financial difficulties and accusations of mismanagement (Hanks, 1986). The future of VEP remains tenuous in light of the expansion of OBV in the South since 1984.

BLACK IDENTITY

The black collective movements of protest and political action during the 1940–1970 period brought about important legal and political changes in America. For blacks, the social, cultural, and psychological processes that activated and maintained these movements reinforced collective and personal identities—"black" instead of "Negro" or "colored," black pride in addition to equality of rights or integration. Older techniques of avoidance, insulation, diversion, and individual adaptations were increasingly rejected in favor of direct social mobilization and political action (Simpson and Yinger, 1985:Ch. 7). To some extent the changes in social and institutional structure described in this chapter have altered individual concepts of identity and group cohesion.

As some blacks participated more fully in a desegregated society, what happened to their black identity? Black identity has never been a monolithic concept among the black population, but some systematic evidence suggests that variation in concepts of self-identity among blacks is related somewhat to socioeconomic status. These significant and widespread changes in social and institutional structure are described in this chapter as we discuss individual concepts of black identity and group cohesion.

DIVERGENT DEFINITIONS

Cultural Traditions

Tensions between desires to emphasize a unique self-identity and desires to participate fully in wider American society have always existed among black Americans (Huggins, 1971:Ch. 4). These tensions are clearly visible in the development of black cultural and artistic life during the period from 1940 to 1985. For example, the dramatic shifts of concern and emphasis within the Afro-American literary tradition since 1940 may be seen by comparing two diametrically opposed definitions of black American literature. The first, published in 1941 by Sterling A. Brown, Arthur P. Davis, and Ulysses Lee, is taken from the "Introduction" to their monumental anthology, *The Negro Caravan* (quoted in Gates, 1986:1):

> The editors . . . do not believe that the expression "Negro literature" is an accurate one, and in spite of its convenient brevity, they have avoided using it. "Negro literature" has no application if it means structural peculiarity, or a Negro school of writing. The Negro writes in the forms evolved in English and American literature. "A Negro novel," "a Negro play" are ambiguous terms. . . . [T]he editors consider Negro writers to be American writers, and literature by American Negroes to be a segment of American literature.

Three decades later, Larry Neal, a poet and literary critic and one of the cofounders, with Amiri Baraka, of the black arts movement, wrote (quoted in Gates, 1986:2):

> Black Art is the aesthetic and spiritual sister of the Black Power concept. As such, it envisions an art that speaks directly to the needs and aspirations of Black America. In order to perform this task, the Black Arts Movement proposes a radical reordering of the western cultural aesthetic. It proposes a separate symbolism, mythology, critique, and iconology.

Between 1940 and 1985, conceptions of what constitutes Afro-American literature have undergone major changes among black writers and critics. Today, the works of black authors are frequently viewed as part of a literary tradition with its own rules, history, themes, and structures. This transformation of definitions was a product of the black arts movement of the 1960s, whose agitation opened up traditional English departments to scholars of the black tradition (Gates, 1986:2).

Black writers were not alone in their efforts to exert an independent cultural voice in the nation. During the 1940s, there was an overall acceptance, within certain areas of the art world, of "Negro art." Two major schools of thought, one emphasizing the unique "Negroness" of the art and the other emphasizing its universality and race-blind nature, contended for primacy in cultural circles. As an example of the former, in 1941, the white art critic James Laue held that black artists used color with more resonance than did white artists. The black artist, he said, was apt to use wilder, more exotic colors that were also purer, deeper, and more unconventional. Similarly, the black philosopher Alain Locke (1925, 1969), one of the architects of the Harlem renaissance, agreed that there was a commonality in the works by black artists as a result of shared racial life (Childs, 1987).

In contrast, black artists such as Hale Woodruff, Richmond Barthe, Romare Bearden, and others emphasized universal aesthetic issues and dismissed racial ones. They argued that the works of black artists should be viewed as part of art in general and not racially distinct. In the immediate postwar years, a circle of black artists, including Woodruff, Barthe, Bearden, and James Herring, issued a manifesto enunciating the importance of viewing works by black artists through race-blind rather than race-conscious prisms. Yet, all the black proponents of this race-blind, universalistic approach emphasized black American themes in their work (Powell, 1986:14).

Self-Determination and the Nation of Islam

Even during the height of desegregation struggles, in many urban northern black communities the Nation of Islam presented an alternative to some of the underlying aims of the civil rights movement. Although the Nation's approach was not central in black American society, it became an important symbol of distinctively black cultural developments in the late 1960s.

The Nation of Islam had its origins among black Americans in Detroit during the 1930s. In 1945, Muslim mosques were established in Milwaukee and Washington, D.C. In 1946, Elijah Muhammed, the head of the Nation, organized a mosque in Chicago. From that time the Chicago Muslim community expanded. By 1959, the organization had grown to 50 temples in 22 states and the District of Columbia. All of the temples were in cities; only 7 were in the South.

The urban, and mostly nonsouthern, character of the Nation of Islam is important for understanding its social and cultural significance. Unlike the accelerating civil rights movement, the Nation was located in precisely the urban areas to which so many black people had moved during and after World War II. The Nation's message was best received by the urban poor of the black ghettoes, those who were most vulnerable to economic cycles and chronic unemployment and underemployment. The Nation appealed most to and drew from blacks who were cut off from, or dissatisfied with, existing black organizations, those who were alienated from any sense of participation in mainstream society—in short, those people who were least likely to benefit from an increase in black participation in the wider society.

It is within this context that the emphasis on black consciousness and the establishment of a separate autonomous black society was developed. The objectives of the Nation of Islam were quite different from those of the civil rights movement. Although the flag of the Nation proclaimed freedom, equality, and justice, these ideal goals were to be attained through establishment of an independent black nation within the United States. The Nation of Islam did not advocate increased black participation in the wider society, and it did not strive for a breaking down of barriers to that society. Its followers saw such efforts as diversions from the real necessity of community control, power, and autonomy. The United States would consist of many peoples, as it always had, but black people would control their own communities. Economic self-sufficiency and internal community power were viewed as necessary to racial advancement. From this perspective, the struggle to desegregate buses, other public accommodations, and white schools was unimportant.

Linked to the emphasis on autonomy was a focus on internal problems and solutions for black America. While the civil rights organizations addressed structural barriers of racism, the Nation of Islam emphasized the problems of ghetto life, crime, drugs, loss of family, and social alienation. To overcome these problems, the Nation offered strategies for the inner development of black communities under the umbrella of Islam. The Nation also demanded from its followers a rejection of what were seen as self-defeating behaviors. The Nation was very successful in reorienting many individuals with a history of involvement with drugs and other criminal activities, and in reaching those who were out of work and who were seeking a way to make life meaningful and rewarding (Childs, 1987).

AFRICAN-AMERICAN CULTURAL DUALITY

Social historian Clayborne Carson (1986:3) wrote: "Since the 1930s, an underlying assumption of scholarly studies of American race relations has been that black aspirations were mainly confined within the ideological boundaries of American progressivism and liberalism." Carson points out that this mainstream perspective does not attend to the full range of relevant aspirations and values held by blacks. For example, he argues (1986:3–4):

> Scholarly investigation of Afro-American political life was largely limited to those aspects of black politics that were concerned with participation in the white-dominated mainstream. To the extent that black institutions were studied at all, they were seen as declining in significance rather than as serving important political functions. The small number of social scientists of the period before 1966 who paid much attention to Afro-American traditions of racial separatism and nationalism generally saw them as apolitical or at least marginal to the dominant currents of black politics (see C. Eric Lincoln, 1961; John A. Morsell, 1961).
>
> Thus, it was hardly surprising that social scientists who observed the upsurge in black protest activity in the 1960s often interpreted it as an outgrowth of the process of assimilation rather than as a sign of increasing racial conciousness (see Ruth Searles and J. Allen Williams, 1962).

Carson's commentary represents an important criticism that many black Americans direct toward mainstream white American perspectives on black America.

In addition to the currents of emphasis on black cultural uniqueness and separateness, there is evidence that most blacks do not advocate separatism in their everyday lives. For example, black preferences, as reflected in surveys and other sources, clearly reveal a desire to live in neighborhoods with appreciable proportions of whites and to send their children to schools with white children, and a large majority of blacks respond that they have no objections to interracial marriage (see Chapter 3). These various observations exemplify the famous, and still relevant, characterization of the duality or "double-consciousness" contained in black American culture (W. E. B. DuBois, 1903:215):

> One ever feels his two-ness,—an American, a Negro; two souls, two thoughts, two unreconciled strivings; two warring ideals in one dark body, . . . The history of the American Negro is the history of this strife,—this longing to attain self-conscious manhood, to merge his double self into a better and truer self. . . . He would not Africanize America, for America

has too much to teach the world and Africa. He would not bleach his Negro soul in a flood of white Americanism, for he knows that Negro blood has a message for the world. He simply wishes to make it possible for a man to be both a Negro and an American, without being cursed and spit upon.

DuBois' conception of two-ness and of the conditions required for integrating blacks and whites in the United States represents an early and influential formulation of black pluralism. Recognition of Afro-American cultural duality is essential to the study of black Americans and black-white relations. Failure to use this concept has often created flaws in analyses of Afro-American culture and society (see, for example, Ellison's [1964] famous criticism of Myrdal's unguarded assimilationist approach in *An American Dilemma* [1944]).

As Carson points out, much research on black Americans has been concerned primarily with black-white relations and the mainstream half of Afro-American duality. It is also true that black nationalist thought has often been seen as an extremist and marginal element among black values, equating black nationalism with the extreme separatism and deprecation of whites found in some religious sects. But among blacks, varieties of "nationalism" hold many positions in the continuum of ideologies between extreme separatism and extreme cultural and biological assimilation (see, for example, Emerson and Kilson, 1965:1069; for textbook examples, see Simpson and Yinger, 1985:140–141, 319–325). The intensity of these convictions varies among individuals and for given individuals over time. Thus, cultural nationalism's popular strength depends on such factors as economic conditions and perceptions of changes in the degree of discrimination against blacks. Yet the preservation of black culture and group identity, and above all the realization of a society in which all groups interact in terms of social, political, and cultural equality, are important conditions that many blacks' definition of "integration" requires (see Farmer, 1966:126; Turner and Young, 1965:1156).

The importance of double consciousness and self-identity in the practical lives of black Americans may be illustrated by identity tensions created for many blacks who successfully seek the American dream. The pursuit of better housing and schools, higher incomes, and more prestigious occupations leads many blacks into unfamiliar environments and life-styles. In such situations social isolation at work, school, and home can lead to difficult adjustment problems (Jones, 1986, 1988; Schofield, 1986; see Chapter 7). The recollections of a 22-year-old black female college student highlights the social stress (Anderson, 1986):

> When I was 15, my dad was transferred from Baltimore to New Jersey. It was a big change for my family, including my mom, dad, and 8-year-old sister. We moved to this all-white suburban community. It was upper middle class Jewish and Italian, mainly. We were the only blacks around. A few people were friendly, but it wasn't Baltimore. One white woman, a

writer, was very friendly. At school, the students were very cold. It took a long time for me to make friends, but I managed it and graduated from the high school; it was a good school. My dad seemed not to mind so much being the only blacks there, but my mom really resented it. My parents didn't socialize or have a dinner party for two years. My mom began to meet black people on the commuter train, and so things got better. We used to get so excited when we saw another black person. It was lonely. My sister seemed to do all right. She had many white friends, and she goes to the bar mitzvahs and parties. Now my dad has been transferred back to Baltimore. My mom is happy. My sister misses her friends, and in Baltimore most of her friends are white.

Empirical validation of many of these points is somewhat problematical in view of a lack of direct data. However, it is possible to develop measures of black cultural pride and identity from survey data that are closely related to those topics. We must caution, however, that the survey data available do not fully reflect the depth and complexity of the views expressed in black literature, oratory, political commentary, or in ordinary discourse in the black community. In the next section we report the findings of a survey of recent analyses of black attitudes as they pertain to these issues (Bobo, 1987).

GROUP IDENTITY AND CONSCIOUSNESS

Black attitudes toward aspects of race relations other than issues of integration and equality fall into three interrelated groups: (1) black cultural and political consciousness, (2) black alienation from white society, and (3) attitudes related to black militancy. Studies of each group provide important and systematic data on the meanings blacks attach to race and race relations in the United States. In addition to drawing on this body of research, we have conducted secondary analyses of two national sample surveys of blacks. We use data from the 1979–1980 National Survey of Black Americans (NSBA), collected by researchers at the University of Michigan's Institute for Social Research (Jackson and Gurin, 1987), and from the 1982 General Social Survey.

How any group sees itself involves the use of labels and associated meanings (Hyman, 1968; Rosenberg, 1979, 1981). What do black people call themselves and what sorts of traits, qualities, and accomplishments do they believe to be attributes of group members? The labels used to designate black Americans have changed considerably over the past several decades, with popular usage of terms such as "colored" and "Negro" having all but vanished. Table 4-4 displays the responses of two national samples of blacks to questions on the group name they prefer. Depending on how the question is worded, these data show that between 52 and 72 percent of black Americans prefer the label "black." No other category, even one combining

TABLE 4-4 Blacks' Preferred Group Name

Surveys, Questions, and Responses	Percent
People use different words to refer to people of our race. What word do you use?	
Black (or black American)	72
Negro	9
Colored	12
Afro-American	1
Other positive	1
Other negative	3
None, don't know, don't care, doesn't matter	2
(Data from 1979–1980 National Survey of Black Americans: N = 2,069)	
Which would you most like to be called, "black," "Negro," "colored," or "Afro-American," or doesn't it make any difference?	
Black	52
Negro	6
Colored	5
Afro-American	6
Makes no difference	31
(Data from 1982 General Social Survey: N = 503)	

"Negro" and "colored," approaches "black" in level of preference.[2] The principal difference between the two questions involves a much higher use of the "makes no difference" response by those interviewed in the 1982 General Social Survey. The questions are sufficiently different that these results should not be treated as indicating change over time.

The labels themselves tell little about what people believe to be the traits and qualities that characterize group members. The 1979–1980 NSBA approached this issue in several ways. One was an open-ended question concerning "the things about black people that make you feel the most proud." A large and diverse set of responses were obtained; one coding of these responses is presented in Table 4-5. Very few black people responded by saying "nothing" or that there were no distinctive qualities about which blacks should be proud (3 percent). The bulk of responses fall into three categories: those concerned with the socioeconomic and scholastic achievements of group members (28 percent); those concerned with the degree of group pride and mutual support shown by blacks (24 percent); and comments concerning the general qualities of endurance, striving, and ultimate group progress (22 percent).

How do black parents socialize their children with regard to race? Sixty-three percent of blacks who have had children reported that they had spoken with their children about "what it is to be black." Table 4-6 displays responses to an open-ended question concerning the specific types of things

---

2. An interesting development in the late 1980s has been an announced preference for the label African-American by a number of prominent blacks. This illustrates the dynamic nature of black identity.

TABLE 4-5 Reasons for Feeling a Sense of Black Group Pride

Question and Responses	Percent
What are the things about black people that make you feel the most proud?	
Socioeconomic or scholastic achievements	28
Group pride, identity, togetherness, and mutual support	24
Endurance, striving, progress made	22
Impact on mass culture or athletics	5
Black cultural heritage	4
Morality and religiosity	4
Nothing or no difference	3
Miscellaneous	6
Not ascertained or inapplicable	3
(N = 2,107)	

Source: Data from the 1970–1980 National Survey of Black Americans.

TABLE 4-6 Black Parents' Attitudes Toward Socialization of Their Children

Question and Response	Percentage Saying "Yes"	As Percentage of Total Sample
In raising your children have you done or told them things to help them know what it is to be black? (If "Yes") What are the most important things you've done or told them?		
Necessity to excel and survive	23	12
Racial pride and heritage	26	12
Problem of racism and prejudice	9	4
Values of tolerance and equality	8	4
Social distance from whites	3	1
Religion and conventional values	9	4
Acceptance of self and blackness	13	6
Defer to or fear whites	1	—
Miscellaneous	3	1
Not ascertained or inapplicable	3	54
	(N = 1,003)	(N = 2,107)

Source: Data from the 1979–1980 National Survey of Black Americans.

TABLE 4-7 Black's Attitudes Toward Group Bonds and Dating Exclusivity (percent)

Question	Strongly Agree	Agree	Disagree	Strongly Disagree	Don't Care
Black parents should give their children African names.	3	17	56	10	14
Black children should study an African language.	14	42	29	6	9
Black people should shop in black-owned stores whenever possible.	16	47	30	4	3
Blacks should always vote for black candidates when they run.	13	26	51	7	3
Black women should not date white men.	13	26	51	7	3
Black men should not date white women.	13	18	48	8	13

Source: Data from the 1979–1980 National Survey of Black Americans; the number of respondents ranged from 2,058 to 2,073.

parents discussed with their children. Twenty-three percent of black parents indicated that they stressed the need to excel and work hard to survive, and another 26 percent indicated that they emphasized racial pride and black heritage to their children; only 9 percent emphasized the need to cope with racism and prejudice, although this issue may underlie many of the more frequently offered responses. Several analysts of riot-related attitudes in the 1960s were struck by evidences of positive group identity among blacks. This finding appeared to some analysts as an "unexpected" and important discovery because it contradicted theories of reactions to prejudice that predicted a low and deprecatory self-image for minority group members. This finding was important for at least two other reasons. First, it showed positive evidence that group identity coexisted with support for integration and intergroup harmony and with skepticism toward militant separatism. Second, this positive identity was an important factor in black support for political actions—including the ghetto uprisings of the 1960s—that had promise of drawing attention to black concerns and improving the status of blacks (Campbell and Schuman, 1968; Sears and McConahay, 1973:189).

In many ways, the 1979–1980 data tell a similar story about feelings of group bonds and separatism among blacks. Table 4-7 presents data on six questions, four of which concern symbolic and behavioral acts indicative of a sense of collective pride and identity and two of which speak to a desire for social distance from whites. Among the symbolic ways of expressing positive group bonds, 56 percent of blacks agreed with the statement that "black children should study an African language," and 20 percent agreed that "black parents should give their children African names." These responses probably index a general disposition to approve of emphasizing an African heritage rather than actual behavior patterns. The questions about behavior asked whether "blacks should always vote for black candidates when they run" (39 percent agreed) and whether "black people should shop at black-owned stores whenever possible" (63 percent agreed).

The two questions on separatism ask, first, whether "black women should not date white men" (39 percent agreed) and, second, whether "black men should not date white women" (31 percent agreed). Thus, between 3 and 4 of 10 blacks approved of group exclusivity in dating relationships. A small percentage of blacks strongly disagreed with either statement (7 percent for the question on black women and 8 percent for the question on black men). These results, when viewed in the light of stable and nearly unanimous black support for school integration and no race-based restrictions on housing choice as well as a majority preference for integrated neighborhoods (see Chapter 3), suggest that many blacks view integration in neighborhoods and public institutions as compatible with a continued sense of group affiliation and identity.

The two dating questions are highly intercorrelated (Bobo, 1987). An index composed of the dating questions and one composed of the remaining four symbolic and behavioral questions are modestly correlated, indicating that those blacks who oppose interracial dating are also more likely to favor other ways of affirming the group boundary. Still, the relatively low correlations of the indices indicate that many blacks who support various symbolic ways of expressing group ties do so while not endorsing racially exclusive dating.

Older blacks are more likely than younger blacks to oppose interracial dating and to support the several symbolic ways of affirming group boundaries. Better educated blacks and those with higher family incomes are less likely than other blacks to oppose interracial dating and the other group symbolic acts.

These data have implications for debates about the extent to which blacks have been effectively assimilated into an American cultural "melting pot" and about the effects of increasing class stratification within the black community. In particular, the age and education effects suggest some younger and better educated blacks do not feel as strong a sense of group boundaries as do older and less well educated blacks. Whether these differences reflect important cohort differences that might involve substantial change within the black population, or differences more properly attributed to aging per se, is not clear. Overall, these findings suggest two main implications. First, most black Americans experience and attach importance to a group cultural identity. Second, an interwoven set of qualities—such as group cohesion, striving, and endurance—and a perceived need to continue to instill such qualities in future generations appear to be key elements of this cultural identity. To the extent that these orientations treat race as an important social characteristic, involve a sense of obligation to blacks, and indicate a commitment to overcoming group disadvantages, these patterns of cultural identity indicate a high degree of race consciousness among black Americans.

REFERENCES

Anderson, Elijah
  1986 Of Old Heads and Young Boys: Notes on the Urban Black Experience. Paper prepared for the Committee on the Status of Black Americans, National Research Council, Washington, D.C.
Bates, Timothy
  1986 Paper prepared for the Committee on the Status of Black Americans, National Research Council, Washington, D.C.
Billingsley, Andrew
  1982 Building strong faculties in black colleges. *The Journal of Negro Education* 25:445–447.
Blackwell, James E.
  1984 *The Black Community: Diversity and Unity.* New York: Harper & Row.
Bobo, Lawrence
  1987 Race in the Minds of Black and White Americans. Paper prepared for the Committee on the Status of Black Americans, National Research Council, Washington, D.C.
Bracey, John H., August Maier, and Elliot M. Rudwick
  1971 *Black Workers and Organized Labor.* Belmont, Calif.: Wadsworth Publishing Co.
Broder, David S.
  1980 *Changing of the Guard: Power and Leadership in America.* New York: Simon & Schuster.
Bureau of the Census
  1979 *The Social and Economic Status of the Black Population in the United States, 1790–1978.* Current Population Reports: Special Studies: Series P-23; No. 80. Washington, D.C.: U.S. Department of Commerce.
Campbell, Angus, and Howard Schuman
  1968 Racial attitudes in fifteen American cities. Pp. 1–67 in *Supplemental Studies for the National Advisory Commission on Civil Disorders.* Washington, D.C.: U.S. Government Printing Office.
Carson, Clayborne
  1986 Paper prepared for the Committee on the Status of Black Americans, National Research Council, Washington, D.C.
Childs, John Brown
  1980 *The Political Black Minister: A Study in Afro-American Politics and Religion.* Boston: G. K. Hall.
Childs, John Brown, ed.
  1987 Manuscript prepared for the Panel on Social Change and Continuity, Committee on the Status of Black Americans, National Research Council, Washington, D.C.
Coleman, M.
  1983 Black colleges jeopardized by shrinking funds and enrollments. *The Washington Post,* June 20, A2.
Collins, Sheila D.
  1986 *The Rainbow Challenge: The Jackson Campaign and the Future of U.S. Politics.* New York: Monthly Review Press.
Cross, R. H., and H. S. Astin
  1981 Factors affecting black students persistence in college. In Gale Thomas, ed., *Black Students in Higher Education.* Westport, Conn.: Greenwood Press.
Drake, St. Clair
  1965 The social and economic status of the Negro in the United States. Pp. 3–46 in

Talcott Parsons and Kenneth B. Clark, eds., *The Negro American*. Boston: Beacon Press.

Drake, St. Clair, and Horace Cayton
1945 *Black Metropolis: A Study of Negro Life in a Northern City*. New York: Harcourt Brace.

DuBois, William E. B.
1903 *The Souls of Black Folk*. Reprinted (1965) in *Three Negro Classics*. New York: Avon Books.

Egerton, J.
1971 *The Public Black Colleges: Integration and Disintegration*. Nashville, Tenn.: Race Relations Information Center.

Ellison, Ralph
1964 *Shadow and Act*. New York: Random House.

Emerson, Ruppert, and Martin Kilson
1965 The American dilemma in a changing world: the rise of Africa and the Negro American. Pp. 626–658 in Talcott Parsons and Kenneth B. Clark, eds., *The Negro American*. Boston: Beacon Press.

Farmer, James
1966 *Freedom—When?* New York: Random House.

Frazier, E. Franklin
1963 *The Negro Church in America*. New York: Schocken Books.

Gates, Henry Louis, Jr.
1986 From Native Sons to Native Daughters: The Afro-American Literary Tradition, 1940–1985. Paper prepared for the Committee on the Status of Black Americans, National Research Council, Washington, D.C.

Griswold, C. L.
1983 Can Howard University take heat from within? *The Washington Post*, March 15, A19.

Haines, Herbert H.
1984 Black radicalization and the funding of civil rights: 1957–1970. *Social Problems* 32(October):31–43.

Hall, H. B.
1984 Executive salaries questioned. *The Hilltop* 67(April 6).

Hanks, Lawrence J.
1986 Black Voter Mobilization Since 1960. Paper prepared for the Committee on the Status of Black Americans, National Research Council, Washington, D.C.

Harris, Abram Lincoln
1936 The Negro as capitalist. Reprinted 1968. College Park, Md.: McGrath Publishing Co.

Hill, Susan T.
1984 *The Traditionally Black Institutions of Higher Education, 1960 to 1982*. Washington, D.C.: U.S. Department of Education.

Huggins, Nathan Irwin
1971 *Harlem Renaissance*. New York: Oxford University Press.

Hyman, Herbert H.
1968 Reference groups. Pp. 353–366 in David Sills, ed., *International Encyclopedia of the Social Sciences*. Vol. 13. New York: Macmillan.

Jackson, James S., and Gerald Gurin
1987 National Survey of Black Americans, 1979–1980. Inter-university Consortium for Political and Social Research, University of Michigan.

Jacquet, Constant H., ed.
1987 *Yearbook of American and Canadian Churches 1987*. Nashville, Tenn.: Abingdon Press.

Jaschik, S.
1986 Proposed college mergers, though not approved, are under fire in Texas. *The Chronicle of Higher Education* 33(November 19):19–20.
Johnson, Charles S.
1941 *Growing Up in the Black-Belt: Negro Youth in the Rural South.* Washington, D.C.: American Council on Education.
Jones, Edward W., Jr.
1986 Black managers: the dream deferred. *Harvard Business Review* (May/June):84–93.
1988 Memorandum to the Committee on the Status of Black Americans, National Research Council, Washington, D.C.
Lincoln, C. Eric
1961 *The Black Muslims in America.* Boston: Beacon Press.
1984 *Race, Religion, and the Continuing American Dilemma.* New York: Hill & Wang.
Locke, Alain
1925 *The New Negro: An Interpretation.* New York: Albert and Charles Boni.
1969 *The American Negro: His History and Literature.* New York: Arno Press.
Marable, Manning
1984 *Race, Reform and Rebellion: The Second Reconstruction in Black America: 1945–1982.* London: MacMillan Press.
McAdam, Doug
1982 *Political Process and the Development of Black Insurgency, 1930–1970.* Chicago: University of Chicago Press.
Morris, Aldon
1984 *The Origins of the Civil Rights Movement: Black Communities Organizing for Change.* New York: Free Press.
Morris, Lorenzo
1981 *Equal Educational Opportunity Scoreboard: The Status of Black Americans in Higher Education, 1970–1979.* Institute for the Study of Educational Policy. Washington, D.C.: Howard University. Washington, D.C.: Institute for the Study of Educational Policy.
Murray, Florence, ed.
1947 *Negro Handbook, 1946–1947.* New York: Current Books.
Muscatine, A.
1985 UDC wages an uphill struggle for respect. *The Washington Post,* May 11, A1, A8.
Myrdal, Gunnar
1944 *An American Dilemma: The Negro Problem and Modern Democracy.* 2 vols. New York: Harper and Brothers.
Nelson, William E., Jr.
1987 The Role of the Black Church in Politics. Paper prepared for the Committee on the Status of Black Americans, National Research Council, Washington, D.C.
Newby, J. E.
1982 Goals in teaching undergraduates in black colleges and universities: professional-centered or client-centered? *The American Sociologist* 17:113–118.
Office of Civil Rights
1981 An Analysis of Black Attrition in Traditionally-Black Institutions and in All Other Institutions. U.S. Department of Education, Washington, D.C.
Osofsky, Gilbert
1971 *Harlem: The Making of a Negro Ghetto, 1890–1930.* New York: Harper & Row.
Palmer, Robert
1981 *Deep Blues.* New York: Viking Press.
Parris, Guichard, and Lester Brooks
1971 *Blacks in the City: A History of the National Urban League.* Boston: Little, Brown.

Peterson, Paul E., and David J. Greenstone
  1977 Racial change and citizen participation: the mobilization of low-income communities through community action. Ch. 6 in Robert H. Haveman, ed., *A Decade of Federal Antipoverty Programs: Achievements, Failures, and Lessons*. New York: Academic Press.
Powell, Richard
  1986 The Visual Arts and Afro-America: 1940–1980. Paper prepared for the Committee on the Status of Black Americans, National Research Council, Washington, D.C.
Reed, Adolph L., Jr.
  1986 *The Jesse Jackson Phenomenon: The Crisis of Purpose in Afro-American Politics*. New Haven, Conn.: Yale University Press.
Rosenberg, Morris
  1979 *Conceiving the Self*. New York: Basic Books.
  1981 The self-concept: social product and social force. Pp. 593–624 in Morris Rosenberg and Ralph M. Turner, eds., *Social Psychology: Sociological Perspectives*. New York: Basic Books.
Schofield, Janet Ward
  1986 School Desegregation and Black Americans. Paper prepared for the Committee on the Status of Black Americans, National Research Council, Washington, D.C.
Sears, David O., and John B. McConahay
  1973 *The Politics of Violence: The New Urban Blacks and the Watts Riot*. Boston: Houghton Mifflin.
Simpson, George E., and J. Milton Yinger
  1985 *Racial and Cultural Minorities*. 5th ed. New York: Plenum.
Sites, Paul, and Elizabeth I. Mullins
  1985 The American black elite, 1930–1978. *Phylon* 46(September):269–280.
Smith, Robert C.
  1982 *Black Leadership: A Survey of Theory and Research*. Institute for Urban Affairs and Research. Washington, D.C.: Howard University.
Spear, Allan H.
  1967 *Black Chicago: The Making of a Negro Ghetto: 1890–1920*. Chicago: University of Chicago Press.
Tollet, Kenneth S.
  1981 *Black Institutions of Higher Learning: Inadvertent Victims or Necessary Sacrifices?* With 1981 prologue update. Institute for the Study of Educational Policy. Washington, D.C.: Howard University.
Turner, John B., and Whitney M. Young, Jr.
  1965 Who has the revolution or thoughts on the second reconstruction. In Talcott Parsons and Kenneth B. Clark, eds., *The Negro American*. Boston: Beacon Press.
U.S. Commission on Civil Rights
  1981 *The Black/White Colleges: Dismantling the Dual System of Higher Education*. Clearinghouse Publication 66(April). Washington, D.C.: U.S. Government Printing Office.
Wilkinson, Doris Y.
  1987 A Profile of the Nation's Resources: The Academic Missions and Cultures of Traditionally Black Colleges and Universities. Paper prepared for the Committee on the Status of Black Americans, National Research Council, Washington, D.C.
Wilson, James Q.
  1973 *Political Organizations*. New York: Basic Books.
Work, Monroe N.
  1937 *Negro Year Book: An Annual Encyclopedia of the Negro, 1937–1938*. Tuskegee, Ala.: Negro Year Book Publishing Company.

5

BLACK POLITICAL

PARTICIPATION

Jacob Lawrence
The 1920s . . . The Migrants Arrive and Cast Their Ballots (1974)
Serigraph
The Corcoran Gallery of Art, Gift of Lorillard Company

Until very recently, blacks have usually had to seek basic citizenship rights from outside the nation's electoral institutions. Thus, the frequent designation of political participation as voting, campaigning, and lobbying of elected and other public officials (see Verba and Nie, 1973:2–3) has not generally applied to black politics. For blacks, the struggle for basic citizenship rights—protection of person and property, equal treatment in the courts, the right to vote and hold public office, and equal treatment when seeking education and employment—has frequently involved litigation and protest.

Through litigation and protest, black political participation has been primarily a collective process throughout much of the period covered by this report. Therefore, we define political participation as activity directed toward the attainment, maintenance, or enhancement of collective aspirations regarding the rights of citizenship.

We analyze and discuss the political status of black Americans in three categories: civil, democratic, and allocational. Civil status refers to how well the government respects and enforces the liberty of the person; the freedoms of speech, assembly, religion, petition, and the press; the rights of property and contract; and the right of citizens to equitable justice by due process of law. Democratic status concerns the extent to which citizens participate in the governmental process through voting, selecting public officials, and holding public office. Allocational status denotes the degree to which citizens share in the provision of income, goods and services—including any public entitlements to an acceptable standard of social and economic security—and in educational and occupational opportunities.[1]

FROM RIGHTS TO RESOURCES

The transition from black Americans' concerns with civil and democratic status to their concerns with allocational status can be viewed as a move from the politics of rights to the politics of resources (Hamilton, 1986). For most of this century, black politics was a politics of rights. The objectives sought fell into two broad categories: the freedom to participate in the polity through the electoral process and the freedom to participate in the broader society through equal access to its institutions. In law, these objectives had been formally acknowledged by 1968: desegregation in public education was ordered by the Supreme Court in *Brown* v. *Board of Education* in 1954; equal access was extended to public accommodations by the Civil Rights Act of 1964 and to the housing market by the Fair Housing Act of 1968; and the Voting Rights Act of 1965 guaranteed the franchise to southern blacks for the first time in this century.

As a consequence, there was a broadening of black political objectives in the mid-1960s, a shift from the politics of rights to the politics of resources, a stronger emphasis on blacks' material status. The shift in emphasis did not mean that the civil and democratic status of black Americans had been fully resolved, as controversy continues over the nature and enforcement of those rights. Nor did it mean that blacks had previously been unconcerned about social and economic goals. Because of the poverty of the black community, the desire for an alternative distribution of resources has always figured prominently in black politics. What changed in the 1960s was the relative weighting of the two agendas (see Smith, 1982:39).

By the politics of resources, we refer to the pursuit of resources through political, and often, collective, means. As the politics of rights was concerned with securing improvements in civil and democratic status, the politics of resources is concerned with securing improvements in material well-being or allocational status. The politics of resources aims to increase government responsibility for the allocation of social and economic goods and services to benefit the disadvantaged. It is a strategy to direct political activity toward allocational decisions.

There are two distinct but interrelated controversies inherent in a politics of resources. One is ideological and the other operational. First, to what extent *should* the allocation of economic resources be a function of political decision making? Second, given the realities of private management in the American economy, to what extent *can* the allocation of resources be a function of political decision making? In this chapter we consider the empir-

---

1. Our use of these categories of political status is for organizational purposes only; for a conceptualization, see Marshall (1964:Ch. 4) or Parsons (1965).

ical aspects of the second question. How have blacks attempted to achieve more equal allocational status through a politics of resources? We consider several aspects of this question. We discuss how blacks mobilized to secure the civil and democratic status of citizenship, the prerequisite to participation in the competition for political voice ("The Struggle for Civil Rights").

We then examine voting and the election and appointment of black public officials ("Democratic Status"). The last major section discusses the organization and mobilization of the black community for collective action and the making of public policy ("Allocational Status"). But before we begin this examination of the politics of rights and the politics of resources, the next section ("Core Political Values") examines the ways in which the diverse sectors of the black community make sense of the political world and how those ideas are related to concrete programs for action.

CORE POLITICAL VALUES

Most Americans are not ideologues in the sense of possessing highly constrained belief systems that structure their political attitudes (Converse, 1972; Kinder, 1983). People do not make political evaluations on the basis of ideological reasoning, but on the basis of competing criteria, which include self-interest, group identification, and government performance. As people observe events, "policies and actions are simply judged right or wrong because of their implications for deeply held values" (Feldman, 1988). Thus, most people evaluate political issues and leaders while being "innocent of ideology" (Sears and Kinder, 1985).

In our usage, core political values are the basic criteria that underlie people's preferences for political action; they define what people expect from politics. They are "abstractions drawn from the flux of the individual's immediate experience," which are emotionally charged, and which "provide the criteria by which goals are chosen" (Williams, 1970:440).

Hanes Walton (1985:29) observed: "Many social scientists study black political ideologies to see why people adhere to them rather than to see how they affect and shape black political action." As Walton implies, the second question is at least as important as the first. In this section, we pursue that question, to explore why black Americans generate the specific political claims they do and how the beliefs of diverse groups within the black community are expressed in the forms of public opinion.

BLACK PRAGMATISM

The conventional framework for thinking about political values in American society does not adequately capture the spectrum of black political values. According to Gilliam (1986), the American left-right spectrum is articulated with reference to a constellation of issues concerning the role of the government in regulating the economy, the power of corporations and unions, the relations between federal and state governments, and the extent of civil rights and civil liberties. But in examining black core values, there are two different and distinct issues: the strategy, philosophy, and political meaning of the black experience, and the relationship of black priorities to the spectrum of political debate in the broader American polity.

Black Americans have never been united behind a single political philosophy (see Cruse, 1967). The labeling of blacks as "liberal" may help to illuminate the role of blacks in the coalition structure of American politics, but it is uninformative concerning the nature of political debate *within* the black community (Morris and Henry, 1978). Blacks have perennially debated the desirability of integration as opposed to black separatism and the strategic and tactical utility of accommodation and coalition as opposed to black self-determination (e.g., Carmichael and Hamilton, 1967; Holden, 1973; Walters, 1988). Another recurring debate concerns the relative importance of race and class as determinants of the black condition (e.g., Pinkney, 1984; Wilson, 1978). Which of these viewpoints to emphasize in a given strategic situation is critical to the articulation and pursuit of black political interests.

Blacks, like whites, evince a tendency to reject inflexible labels as irrelevant to the exigencies of politics. In a study of black elected officials in New Jersey, Cole (1976:93) observed:

> The difficulty of left-right labeling is compounded when it is applied to blacks. For blacks have been the have-nots of the system. Abstract ideologies for "all mankind" mean less to them than filling voids created by oppression.

Above all else, black political values concern the black community's perpetual struggle to succeed in a white-majority world. Thus, black core values are supple in their application: as the saying goes, blacks have no permanent friends and no permanent enemies, only permanent interests—a political tradition with regard to white allies that held sway as long ago as the Reconstruction era (see Jaynes, 1986:266). W. E. B. DuBois once framed this issue with the admonition, "We face a condition, not a theory." Or, as Vernon Jordan, former executive director of the National Urban League, greeted Ronald Reagan's victory in 1980:

> If the Reagan Administration protects black social and civil rights gains, and if it fulfills its promises to wipe out unemployment, it can add blacks to its emerging coalition. . . . Black people are not wed to any given political philosophy. Our needs are not bounded by liberal dogma. We are pragmatic. We want results, and if conservative means will move us closer to equality we will gladly use those conservative means.

As Hamilton (1981:250) notes, this language "is intended, one would assume, as a statement of how to function in the existing political environment—not a statement about what that environment ideally ought to be."

This political flexibility can be seen in other realms as well. For example,

TABLE 5-1 Attitudes Toward Capitalism, by Race (percent agreeing)

Statement	Blacks (N = 150)	Whites (N = 1,172)
The economy can run only if businessmen make good profits.	65	72
Generally speaking, business profits are distributed fairly in the United States.	29	36
In the United States, traditional divisions between owners and workers still remain. A person's social standing depends upon whether he/she belongs to the upper or lower class.	72	70

Source: Data from 1984 General Social Survey.

many blacks view the choice between "black power" and "integration" in instrumental or tactical, rather than philosophical, terms. For many black Americans, the desirability of a given mode of political activity (voting, lobbying, or protest) is often seen as being contingent on circumstance, rather than being considered intrinsically worthwhile. Or as Hamilton (1982:xix) noted: "People participate where, when, and how they think it matters."

In line with this preference for pragmatic goals and results rather than ideology, blacks use different criteria when evaluating political leaders. The authors of the most comprehensive survey of citizen evaluations of legislators report (Cain et al., 1987:420):

> Blacks ranked the roles of representatives very differently from the rest of the groups. They regarded policy as the least important activity and considered protecting the interests of the district and helping people as, respectively, second and third most important. As a group, blacks placed a higher priority on helping people than did any other group. To some extent this racial difference arises from educational and class differences, but even when such factors are taken into account, racial differences in representative priorities remain.

Similarly, when presented with a liberal-to-conservative scale and asked "Where would you place yourself on this scale, or haven't you thought much about this?," blacks are considerably more likely than whites to reject either ideological label, choosing instead to deny that they classify themselves in such terms. Controlling for education diminishes the gap a little, but a gap of over 10 percentage points remains.

However, blacks and whites hold similar views about basic tenets of our free enterprise system. As Table 5-1 shows, they substantially agree on the importance of profits as the motive force of capitalism. Just 7 percentage points separate blacks and whites on how fairly profits are allocated in the economy. And several questions about the rewards of "hard work" yield no racial differences (Kendrick, 1988:Tables 9–10).

Blacks are somewhat less willing to agree that "most people who don't get

TABLE 5-2 Attitudes Toward Equality, by Race and Income (percent agreeing)

Statement	Income Less Than $15,000		Income More Than $15,000	
	Blacks	Whites	Blacks	Whites
Our society should do whatever is necessary to make sure that everyone has an equal opportunity to succeed.	95	91	97	88
One of the big problems in this country is that we don't give everyone an equal chance.	83	57	81	45
If people were treated more equally in this country we would have many fewer problems.	87	66	87	53

Source: Data from 1986 National Election Study, reported in Kendrick (1988:Table 11).

ahead should not blame the system." The difference is markedly larger on other assessments of American society; see Table 5-2. Irrespective of income, more than 80 percent of blacks agree that all Americans do not have "an equal chance." This opinion is held by 57 percent of whites making under $15,000 a year and by 45 percent of more affluent whites; but higher income has no effect on blacks' skepticism about how well the country lives up to its ideals of equal opportunity. This pattern recurs in almost every comparison of black-white differences in political attitudes: if anything, middle-class blacks are more liberal and critical than less affluent blacks.

The distinctiveness of black political views is particularly notable on the question of government responsibility to aid the disadvantaged. Blacks are considerably more supportive than whites of the position that the government should guarantee a basic level of support to all citizens and protect people from the consequences of sickness, poverty, unemployment, and old age. As Table 5-3 shows, controlling for income actually enhances black-white differences on this subject (see also Gilliam, 1986; Gurin et al., 1988.) Blacks are also more willing to turn to the government for help with a pressing problem of any sort (Wolfinger, 1988:113).

More detailed and explicit responses on the role of government can be found in Table 5-4, which contrasts black and white views on spending for a variety of purposes. When asked about the adequacy of government spending on almost every specific category (e.g., health, environment, drug control, education, and crime control), majorities of both whites and blacks say that "too little" money is being spent. However, blacks invariably are more likely to favor increased spending on social services: the differences are 20 percentage points on "improving cities" and 41 percentage points on "welfare, but only 4 percentage points on crime control."

It appears that the political views of blacks also differ significantly from those of other racial minorities, although the data on this subject are fragmentary. A survey in California found that blacks were the most supportive

TABLE 5-3 Attitudes Toward Government Responsibility for Citizens' Welfare, by Race and Income (percent agreeing)

Statement	Income Less Than $15,000		Income More Than $15,000	
	Blacks	Whites	Blacks	Whites
The government must see to it that everyone has a job and that prices are stable, even if the rights of businessmen have to be restricted.	64	56	67	33
It is the responsibility of the government to meet everyone's needs, even in case of sickness, poverty, unemployment, and old age.	80	61	79	50
Personal income should not be determined solely by one's work. Rather, everybody should get what he/she needs to provide a decent life for his/her family.	64	45	30	22
The government in Washington ought to reduce the income differences between the rich and the poor, perhaps by raising taxes on wealthy families or by giving income assistance to the poor.[a]	69	54	62	39

[a] Responses to this item are pooled data from General Social Surveys in 1978, 1980, 1983, and 1984.

Source: Data from 1984 General Social Survey, reported in Kendrick (1988:Table 12).

TABLE 5-4 Attitudes Toward Government Spending, by Race (percent agreeing)

Item	Black (N = 510)	White (N = 1,323)	Difference: Black Minus White
Increase government spending on			
Education	78	55	23
Improving cities	67	47	20
Health	75	57	18
Environment	67	52	15
Crime control	79	75	4
Drug control	71	60	11
Welfare	58	17	41
Improving race relations	88	23	65
Decrease government spending on			
Defense	46	30	16
Space exploration	76	38	38

Source: Data from 1982 General Social Survey, reported in Seltzer and Smith (1985:Tables 1, 4).

of government social spending of all major racial and ethnic groups. Latinos ranked second, and Asian-Americans' views resembled those of whites (Cain and Kiewiet, 1986). Here we see the roots of the politics of resources. Many blacks are convinced that much of the progress in American society has come about, for them and others, because of the progressive role played by federal government policy. In tandem with black core values stressing fairness and equity in the allocation of society's goods and resources, this operational conclusion has given rise to the issues that now dominate the political agenda of blacks. It also explains the "liberalism" of black priorities when viewed through the prism of mainstream political categories (see, e.g., Nie et al., 1976:23–24, 253–255).

Black-white differences in values concerning redistribution are also reflected in the attitudinal differences between black and white elected officials. For example, 70 percent of black officials, compared with 26 percent of white officials, agreed with the statement: "True democracy is limited in the United States because of the special privileges enjoyed by business and industry." And 76 percent of black officials, compared with 30 percent of white officials, agreed: "It is the responsibility of the entire society, through its government, to guarantee everyone adequate housing, income, and leisure" (Conyers and Wallace, 1976:31).

A closely related attribute of black core political values is the emphasis on the polity as an arena for the pursuit of group equity, rather than a framework to assure the freedom of the individual. Blacks are well known for their use of collective actions such as boycotts, which are explicitly designed to advance collective goals for allocational status, and investing those claims with a moral significance. The black assertion of a moral claim to group entitlements is based on the view that discrimination and the economic structure produce an unfair and unequal distribution of resources. In contrast, the prevailing view of the white majority is that government is a means of nurturing the liberty needed for individual advancement, and whites see the prevailing economic distribution as the result of fair competition (Danzig, 1964; Huber and Form, 1973; Lane, 1986).

Blacks have often articulated a vision of maintaining a distinct black identity in the midst of American society (see Chapter 4). In Jesse Jackson's 1984 and 1988 presidential campaign speeches, the "rainbow" imagery was a rhetorical celebration of the group diversity in American society. In this respect, the "rainbow" is the very antithesis of the "melting pot" often seen as the American ideal. Blacks tend to be more responsive than whites or Asian-Americans to the distinctive cultural aspirations of Latinos on the issues of bilingual education and bilingual ballots (Cain and Kiewiet, 1986).

Well-educated blacks tend to be the most supportive of group solidarity in political action. Upper status blacks are also the most likely to possess the motivation and organizational ties to participate actively in electoral politics, as well as in other modes of political activity (Gurin et al., 1988). Thus, most members of the black middle class pursue group as well as individual goals when they attain positions of leadership. The sense of a "common

TABLE 5-5 Social Values, by Race (in percent)

Value	Black (N = 510)	White (N = 1,323)
Women's rights		
Approve women in politics	65	75
Approve married women working	70	76
Men better suited for politics	60	63
Approve abortion on demand	28	41
Approve Equal Rights Amendment	82	71
Vote for woman president	89	86
Morality and religion		
Approve sex education	87	85
Approve easier divorce law	47	20
Support Supreme Court on school prayer	21	41
Crime		
Courts too soft on crime	16	2
Oppose death penalty	53	18
Approve gun control	79	72

Source: Data from 1982 General Social Survey, reported in Seltzer and Smith (1985:Tables 2, 3, and 4).

fate," or identification with the shared experience of black Americans, is an important predictor of policy preferences. In addition to support for pro-black positions on race-related issues, such as affirmative action and South Africa, it is also associated with a desire for increased spending on education, jobs, and social welfare, and a desire to cut spending on defense. This support is consistent among all blacks, regardless of socioeconomic status or other demographic factors (Gurin et al., 1988).

Probably because of the rural southern heritage of so many blacks, a vein of social conservatism is manifested on certain kinds of issues among blacks. For example, blacks are less likely than whites to approve abortion on demand (by 28 to 41 percent). Blacks are also less likely than whites to approve of, married women working (by 70 to 76 percent), women in politics (by 65 to 75 percent)—although they are as willing to vote for a woman President (by 89 to 86 percent), or the Supreme Court's restrictions on school prayer (by 21 to 41 percent); see Table 5-5.[2]

A California study on racial minorities found blacks more favorable to school prayer and less favorable to banning handguns than whites, Asian-Americans, or Latinos; blacks were the least likely to favor the death penalty for murder (Cain and Kiewiet, 1986:31). However, views on such "social" issues do not appear to determine black political preferences; rather, views on spending for the disadvantaged appear to count more heavily in most blacks' voting decisions (Cavanagh, 1985).

---

2. These data are not broken down by education or income; we do not know if the black-white differences would remain if socioeconomic status differences were controlled.

BLACKS AND THE POLITICAL PARTIES

From Emancipation to the Great Depression, the black vote was heavily Republican. The GOP, the "party of Lincoln" that had freed the slaves, was seen as more receptive to black interests and black participation than the Democratic party with its segregationist southern wing. The New Deal policies of Franklin D. Roosevelt caused a large shift of blacks into the Democratic party in the 1930s. However, many blacks considered themselves "Roosevelt Republicans" during these years, and sizable pockets of black Republicanism persisted in many local areas (Weiss, 1983). A significant fraction of blacks continued to identify as Republicans, and Republican presidential candidates received from one-quarter to more than one-third of all black votes. (There were also substantial numbers of southern blacks who professed no interest in politics, doubtless a reaction to widespread denial of political freedom.) The shift from Republican loyalties was based on the Democrats' more generous and active social welfare policies; as late as 1960 the Democratic party's civil rights image was confused and ambiguous (Campbell, 1966; Hagen, 1989:Table 10). The landmark 1954 school desegregation decision, announced by a chief justice recently appointed by a Republican president, may have suggested that the Republican party still had much to offer blacks.

This transitional phase ended in 1964. Although that year's Civil Rights Act actually was supported in Congress by a higher proportion of Republicans than Democrats, the significant facts were its introduction by one Democratic president and its signing into law by another. Only six Republican senators voted against it, but one of them was Barry Goldwater, his party's presidential candidate. Goldwater's campaign ended Republican hopes of regaining a meaningful share of black support in national politics. Since then, blacks have been nearly unanimous in their Democratic affiliation, support for Democratic presidential and congressional candidates, and belief that the Republican party offers less to them. However, liberal or moderate Republicans opposing conservative Democrats in state and local elections have sometimes managed to attract significant black support.

A study on minorities in California offers comparative data on party identification among racial groups. The patterns roughly correspond to those with regard to political beliefs presented above. Blacks are by far the most Democratic in their allegiance (78 percent), followed by Latinos (54 percent). Among whites, Democrats have only a narrow margin of 37 to 35 percent over the Republicans, and Asian-Americans identify with Republicans over Democrats by 38 to 35 percent (Cain and Kiewiet, 1986).

Among whites, socioeconomic status is a strong predictor of party identification; lower status whites are much more likely to identify as Democrats and higher status whites as Republicans. Among blacks, this correlation has traditionally been much lower, and it was virtually absent in the mid-1980s. A Gallup survey commissioned for the Joint Center for Political Studies in 1984 found that "[lower and] upper status blacks are almost equally likely

TABLE 5-6 Black Delegates at National Political Conventions, 1912–1984

	Democratic Conventions			Republican Conventions		
	Black		Total	Black		Total
Year	Delegates	Percent	Delegates	Delegates	Percent	Delegates
1912	0	0.0	1,094	65	6.0	1,078
1916	0	0.0	1,092	35	3.5	985
1920	0	0.0	1,094	29	2.9	984
1924	1	0.1	1,098	39	3.5	1,109
1928	0	0.0	1,100	49	4.4	1,098
1932	0	0.0	1,154	26	2.2	1,154
1936	12	1.0	1,204	45	4.5	1,003
1940	7	0.6	1,094	32	3.2	1,000
1944	11	0.9	1,176	18	1.7	1,057
1948	17	1.3	1,234	41	3.7	1,094
1952	33	2.6	1,230	29	2.4	1,206
1956	24	1.7	1,372	36	2.7	1,323
1960	46	3.0	1,521	22	1.6	1,331
1964	65	2.8	2,316	14	1.0	1,308
1968	209	6.7	3,084	26	1.9	1,333
1972	452	14.6	3,103	56	4.2	1,348
1976	323	10.6	3,048	76	3.4	2,259
1980	481	14.4	3,331	55	2.7	1,993
1984	697	17.7	3,933	69	3.1	2,235

Sources: Data for Democratic conventions of 1912–1928 from Bain and Parris (1973) and Work (1937:102); for Democratic conventions of 1932–1984 from the Joint Center for Political Studies (1984a:Table 2); data for Republican conventions from the Joint Center for Political Studies (1984b:Table 1).

to identify with the Democratic party, whether the indicator of social status is education, income, or occupation" (Cavanagh, 1985:35). However, younger blacks were more likely to be Republicans than were older blacks. A follow-up study in 1987 found that 18 percent of blacks under the age of 30 identify as Republicans and 27 percent as "strong" Democrats. But among blacks over age 50, 6 percent are Republicans and 46 percent "strong" Democrats. Eddie N. Williams (1987) suggests that the Republicans may currently have an opportunity to target younger blacks to reduce the large Democratic majorities in the black community (but see Pinderhughes, 1986).

Civil rights issues have reinforced the economic interests underlying black partisanship. Lower status blacks, like lower status whites, support the Democrats for economic reasons. Upper status blacks often come from families with a history of poverty and view programs for the poor and for public sector employment as a basis of social mobility. They also support the Democrats' civil rights policies.

The only comprehensive time-series data on black participation in the national party organizations are statistics on black delegates to national party conventions (see Table 5-6). Black representation at Republican conventions was considerably higher in the early years of the century than it is today. It was also higher than the black proportion of Democratic delegates until 1952. The black share of Democratic delegates has increased from 0.6 percent in 1940 to 17.7 percent in 1984. The black share of Republican delegates declined from 3.2 percent in 1940 to 1.0 percent in the Goldwater convention of 1964 and rebounded to 3.1 percent in 1984.

The Democrats face a challenge in attempting to retain their black base. They must wrestle with the "special interest" perception in handling black priorities, but they must also accommodate the reality of the increased black presence in the party's shrunken coalition base and the demands for an increased leadership role that accompany that presence.[3] Despite the difficulties posed by most blacks' negative view of the Reagan legacy, the Republicans currently enjoy the best opportunity in a quarter of a century to compete for the black vote—particularly among younger blacks of the post-civil rights generation. This factor may encourage both parties to devise new strategies to compete for black votes.

BLACK NATIONALISM

Probably no other aspect of black political behavior is so thoroughly misunderstood by the broader society as black nationalism. Some commentators dismiss it as an aberrant form of racism. As Hanes Walton (1985:29) notes: "Most scholars have argued that black nationalism is *apolitical*," a romantic flight from the hard-nosed reality of American politics (see, e.g., Draper, 1970). Yet black nationalist movements have played leading roles in the election of such blacks as former mayor Kenneth Gibson of Newark, New Jersey, and former mayor Harold Washington of Chicago. Nationalist sentiments have also been instrumental in black protest and lobbying campaigns, conflicts over community control of schools and housing authorities, and most recently in the 1984 and 1988 presidential campaigns of Jesse Jackson.

Black nationalism is not a cohesive, unitary body of thought or action; it is probably more accurate to speak of black nationalisms (see Chapter 4). The major themes in black nationalist approaches to politics are racial pride and an emphasis on black control over the affairs of black communities. But there are major differences over such questions as the relevance of Christian religious traditions or leftist class analysis to an understanding of the black condition, as well as the conditions under which interaction and alliances with whites are acceptable (Smith, 1982). Moreover, there are regional variations in the black political experience; as Cole (1976:93) notes:

---

3. In late 1988 and early 1989, William Gray was elected chairman of the Democratic Caucus in the U.S. House of Representatives, and Ronald Brown was elected chair of the Democratic National Committee.

Neither black nationalism nor integration perch comfortably on a left-right spectrum. In much of the North black separatism is equated with radicalism, integration with conservatism; in the South, the reverse.

Systematic public opinion data on black nationalism are scarce. According to Smith (1982:69):

> At the peak of nationalist agitation in the late 1960s, support for the ultimate nationalist goal of a separate black state found support among only 7 percent of the national black population.

On the question of automatically voting for black candidates, blacks respond "no" by 81 percent. The contemporary level of support for a separate black political party has never exceeded the one-third of the black electorate recorded in 1972. The 1984 National Black Election Study found 24 percent in favor of a black party (Gurin et al., 1988). An earlier nationwide survey of black elected officials found that 9 percent considered "formation of an independent all-Black political party" to be "very important," and 15 percent considered it "fairly important" as a means of "achieving real progress for Blacks in America" (Conyers and Wallace, 1976:28).

Black separatism has historically been stronger among the black lower classes than among the middle class, which has tended to work more closely with mainstream, interracial political structures. Thus, Marcus Garvey was most popular with the urban black working class in the 1920s (Bracey, 1971), and the black independent parties of the 1960s and 1970s in Mississippi and Alabama were largely concentrated in impoverished, rural black communities (Frye, 1980; Walton, 1972).

Marx (1967:Ch. 5) found that black nationalists were disproportionately young, male, urban, and northern. Yet, like black conservatives, they were more likely to be lower than upper class, have low rates of social participation, lack knowledge about black leaders, and score high on a scale of authoritarian tendencies. Black attitude clusters about race relations during this period formed a monotonic scale. Black nationalists were the most pessimistic about the black condition and most likely to condone violence, conservatives voiced the opposite views, and militant integrationists were generally in the middle (Marx, 1967:114–115).

The 1984 National Black Election Study found that the least educated and least affluent blacks were most likely to support an all-black party and a vote-black strategy. Among higher status respondents, younger blacks tended to be much more nationalist than older blacks, but there was no significant age difference among lower status blacks. Partly because they lack economic and organizational resources, and partly because they are skeptical of the receptivity of the political system to black participation, supporters of black nationalists are much less likely to vote or engage in campaign activity than other blacks are (Gurin et al., 1988).

THE STRUGGLE FOR CIVIL RIGHTS:
PROTEST AND LITIGATION

Throughout the civil rights movement, two struggles were taking place simultaneously: a legal struggle and a protest struggle. The movement also had two goals: winning formal recognition of rights and ensuring that these rights would then be enforced. These goals were pursued through litigation and protest, and both were indispensable to the movement. Many rights successfully litigated in the courts, such as the right to equal treatment in interstate travel (*Morgan* v. *Virginia,* 1946), were not honored in practice until actual conditions of discrimination were shown to the nation and the world through mass media coverage of protest activity.

ANTECEDENTS TO THE CIVIL RIGHTS MOVEMENT

The use of protest as a political tactic has a long history among blacks. Developed as one of the few tactics available to them as slaves, organized protest was artfully used as a political and economic stratagem by the freed people during Reconstruction and afterward (Genovese, 1974; Jaynes, 1986:Ch. 7). During the first few decades of the twentieth century, black protest played a sporadic but important role. Between 1929 and 1941, northern blacks organized a series of "Don't Buy Where You Can't Work" campaigns in which white-owned ghetto businesses were boycotted unless they agreed to hire blacks. These "Jobs for Negroes" campaigns occurred in at least 35 cities, virtually all in the North (Brisbane, 1970:137–143; Meier and Rudwick, 1976:314–332).

Two other forms of economic grass roots protest were noteworthy in the 1930s. Blacks were active participants in the anti-eviction campaigns waged against landlords in large cities during the decade, and they also figured prominently in organized rent strikes later in the decade (Frank, 1982; Meier and Rudwick, 1976:336). A rural parallel to the urban anti-landlord activity was the attempt to unionize tenant farmers and sharecroppers during the 1930s in a number of cotton-growing areas of the South (Grubbs, 1971; Harris, 1982:102–103).

Schools were also an early arena for blacks' quest for equality, an arena in which complementary strategies of protest and litigation were highly effective. In the North during the 1920s and 1930s, the practice of keeping black students out of school to protest poor conditions in all-black schools "arose principally from the growing school segregation that accompanied the migration of Negroes to Northern cities" (Meier and Rudwick, 1976:312–313). Beginning with a movement in Springfield, Ohio, in the 1922–1923 school year, boycotts—sometimes accompanied by picketing—were seen in dozens of northern cities over the next three decades. This was one of the earliest examples of a recurring pattern of litigation and protest used as complementary modes of black political activity (Meier and Rudwick, 1976:313):

Legal action accompanied nearly all of these boycotts. The NAACP with its strategy of litigation was involved in the overwhelming majority of them; either parents received NAACP support after the boycott had started, or occasionally . . . NAACP leaders suggested the boycott in the first place. . . . [A]lthough most of these campaigns proved successful, victory came either through threatening court action or going to court, rather than through the boycott tactics.

In the South, one can observe the same pattern: school protests occurring alongside litigation to secure school desegregation (Kluger, 1976). This pattern would continue as the movement encompassed the desegregation of mass transit and public accommodations in the South.

THE CONTEXT OF THE POSTWAR YEARS

No single factor can be isolated as the overriding explanation of a civil rights movement that in many ways spanned the middle third of the twentieth century. Blacks have protested their status throughout American history. To understand why a successful, broadly based civil rights movement emerged when and where it did, one must look beyond the constant of racial inequality and focus on variables such as socioeconomic development, political opportunities, black organizational resources, and changing attitudes toward race relations in the population (see Chapters 2–4 above; McAdam, 1982; Morris, 1984).

Socioeconomic Changes

The opportunity for a comprehensive attempt to change black political status was facilitated by the rapidly changing socioeconomic structure of the postwar South. A very important factor was the restructuring of the cotton economy from labor-intensive agriculture to mechanized farming, which dramatically changed many social alignments among both black and white southerners. The migration of displaced black tenant farmers and sharecroppers into the manufacturing economy of the urban South and North improved wage levels for black adults, and black educational opportunities and attainment increased rapidly as well. As discussed throughout this report, these changes aided the growth and development of indigenous organizations in the black community. In addition, the long-standing unity of the southern business establishment in defense of segregation was fragmenting just as blacks were beginning to mobilize after World War II. Southern manufacturing and retail interests sought social modernization as a prerequisite to desperately needed economic growth. For some of the new white business leaders, the inadequacy of the black educational system and repression of black civil status represented an irrational underdevelopment of labor and consumer markets and a factor contributing to social disharmony (Bloom, 1987; Wright, 1986).

The restructuring of southern agriculture and the growth of other industries also had an impact on the white population. The urbanization of southern whites increased their incomes and educational opportunities and precipitated a slow restructuring of political preferences away from rural conservatism. Over time, the civil rights movement effected change with the aid of these social forces. Public opinion toward desegregation, even in the South, changed rapidly. As two students of public attitudes put it (Reed and Black, 1985:16–17):

> [S]upport for segregation in 1942 was virtually universal among white Southerners; no particular kind of white Southerner was less likely to support it than any other kind. By the 1950s, however, support for segregation had become less common among educated Southerners, less common among urban Southerners, less common outside the conventionally defined "Deep" South, less common among those who had lived outside the South or were often exposed to the mass media—less common, in short, among the kinds of Southerners being produced in ever larger numbers by urbanization and economic development.

As political opportunities arose, black organizations took advantage of them. Sit-ins and boycotts pressured the socioeconomic structure at its weakest link: its dependence on a black consumer market. Thus, at many critical junctures, typified by Birmingham in 1963, white retail merchants and manufacturers called for an accommodation with black community leaders that the local political establishment was reluctant to accept (Bloom, 1987; Morris, 1984; Juan Williams, 1987).

Political Effects

At the same time, black outmigration to northern cities expanded the size of the active black electorate, making it easier for blacks to get a hearing in national politics. The political thrust generated by the growing concentrations of black voters in northern industrial cities and states combined with black protest activity in the South to place black concerns on the national agenda. Ultimately, southern officials were forced to respond to decisions made in Washington by all three branches of the federal government, and this decisive federal intervention finally ended legal segregation in the South. Thus, socioeconomic change and the related shift in the structure of political opportunities determined the receptivity of the political process to the surge of black organizational activity.

This activity was initially generated by local leaders seeking to achieve local objectives. The bus boycotts in Baton Rouge, Montgomery, and Tallahassee in the 1950s originated among activists in those cities without much direction or encouragement from national civil rights leaders; the same was true of the student lunch counter sit-ins that began in the late 1950s (Carson, 1986; Morris, 1984). As these local activities became the focus of more and more national attention, the debate shifted to a broader plane. Black rights became an issue not just in Albany, Georgia, or Birmingham, Alabama; the demand grew to ensure such rights on a uniform, nationwide basis through the passage of federal legislation. Local protest activity created a climate in which such legislation could win a place on the national agenda, but its actual passage required extensive lobbying activity centered in Washington.

At the national level, black leaders hoped the media coverage of southern violence in the face of demonstrators would elicit sufficient outrage to overcome the long-standing federal reticence to interfere with the prerogatives of state and local governments. The Eisenhower and Kennedy administrations initially tried to limit federal involvement to the field of voting rights, which enjoyed more broadly based support than the emotional issue of desegregation. It was only after a racial crisis in Birmingham during 1963 that political pressure could entice Kennedy to propose a Civil Rights Act, which was passed early in the Johnson administration. The international uproar over brutal racial violence in Selma, Alabama, the following year was the spur to passage of the 1965 Voting Rights Act (Fleming, 1965; Garrow, 1978).

Public Opinion

By July 1963, a large majority of white Americans accepted the principles of equal voting rights and desegregation in employment and public accommodations (see Chapter 3). Support for congressional legislation mandating desegregated public accommodations grew rapidly from June 1963 to January 1964, a period encompassing the Birmingham crisis, the historic civil rights march on Washington, and nationally televised speeches in favor of such legislation by Presidents Kennedy and Johnson.

It was black claims on the public conscience made visible by disruptive public activism that forced national attention on civil rights. There is a striking correlation between the degree of movement activity and Gallup Poll figures on the proportion of the public identifying civil rights as the "most important problem facing the country." Both time series reach their peaks during the most intense period of movement activity from 1963 to 1965, which coincided with the adoption of the Civil Rights Act (1964) and the Voting Rights Act (1965) (see Figure 5-1).

But the pace of change was unsettling to many whites. Survey data show that most whites thought that the administration was "pushing too fast" for desegregation throughout this period. An even larger majority of whites thought that civil rights leaders were "pushing too fast." Blacks, however, increasingly thought that their leadership was "going too slowly" rather than "pushing too fast" (Burstein, 1985:59). Thus, the civil rights initiatives of the 1960s occurred in an atmosphere that might best be characterized as a mixture of empathy with the civil rights movement and growing acceptance of the notion that black Americans were entitled to the enjoyment of the most basic civil rights, counterbalanced by anxiety over the speed of change.

FIGURE 5-1 People's identification of civil rights as the most important problem confronting the country, 1962–1971.

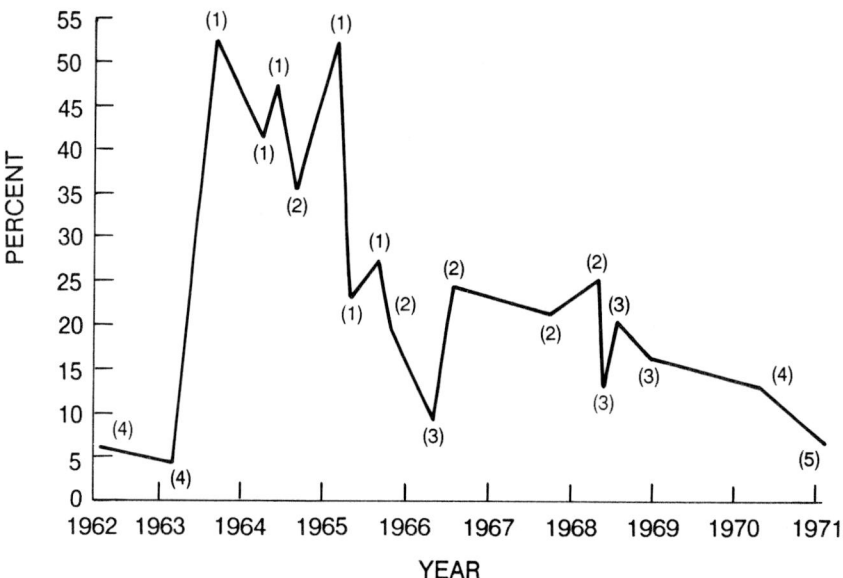

Note: The numbers in parentheses refer to people's rank of civil rights among the problems identified in that poll.

Source: McAdam (1982:198). Reprinted with permission.

ENFORCEMENT OF CIVIL RIGHTS

Following passage of the civil rights laws of the 1960s, emphasis in the field of civil rights shifted from the adoption of laws and policies to issues of enforcement. This section examines the evolution of civil rights enforcement in four areas: voting, education, employment, and public accommodations and housing.

In all four areas, the key issue in enforcement has been the conflict between the *intent* and *effect* standards of proof in discrimination cases (Bell, 1986a:37). Under an *effect* standard, discrimination is proven when the use of a procedural rule is shown to systematically reduce the representation of blacks that would otherwise be expected. This outcome can result even though the rule may appear racially neutral on its face. Under an *intent* standard, it is necessary to prove that any underrepresentation of blacks is a consequence of a deliberate action or desire for that outcome by a specific perpetrator.

The intent standard is more consistent with the common-law tradition of evidentiary proof than the effect standard, but it is very difficult to satisfy in discrimination cases (Freeman, 1978:1052–1055). An effect standard permits a clearer definition of guidelines for enforcement (Bell, 1986a). By the early 1970s, the enforcement practices in all four policy areas under examination had shifted from a reliance on intent to a reliance on effect; by the early 1980s, with the exception of voting rights, there had been a pronounced return to an intent standard in civil rights enforcement.

Voting

The voting rights that were to be protected by the voter registration provisions of the Civil Rights Acts of 1957 and 1960 could not be implemented in practice because of the necessity for case-by-case adjudication in the courts. This was remedied by the Voting Rights Act of 1965, which mandated the stationing of federal examiners in those individual southern counties with the worst history of abuse (see below). Counties with examiners showed the most dramatic black registration gains in the initial years of the act (U.S. Commission on Civil Rights, 1968:222–223). In addition, states with a long history of little black participation were required to submit all proposed changes in election procedures to the U.S. Department of Justice for "preclearance." Under this program, the proposed changes had to be approved by the department's Civil Rights Division before they were allowed to take effect. By 1970, blacks trying to register to vote infrequently encountered biased procedures or economic retaliation.

Education

Public school desegregation has also led to controversies about whether it is necessary to demonstrate intent in order to secure an encompassing court order that actually has an effect. The 1954 *Brown* decision declared segregated public schools unconstitutional, while the 1955 *Brown* ruling gave district federal courts the responsibility for implementing the decision if local officials did not do so. Most southern districts maintained their separate schools; in the North, school administrators often felt that the *Brown* decisions did not apply since school segregation resulted from the residential segregation of whites and blacks.

In the late 1950s and early 1960s, plaintiffs in the South demonstrated that school officials were maintaining separate schools. The early decisions relied on an intent standard: that is, if there was no demonstrable intent to segregate black and white students, the plans were acceptable. If southern school administrators could demonstrate that their procedures would, possibly, allow some black students to attend classes with whites, their plans were often accepted. Thus, there was the emergence of "freedom-of-choice plans," under which a few exceptionally motivated blacks attended formally white schools.

Then, in a series of unanimous and authoritative decisions between 1968 and 1972, the Supreme Court adopted an effects standard: that is, if the procedures adopted by school officials left most blacks and whites in racially homogeneous schools or classes, the plans were unacceptable. Federal courts were obligated to order strategies that actually desegregated the schools. In the precedent-making decision, involving schools in Charlotte, North Carolina, the Supreme Court approved the use of busing and racial ratios to achieve the desegregation required by the *Brown* decision (see pages 75–80).

In the early stages of post-*Brown* litigation outside the South, federal judges rejected plaintiffs' arguments and agreed with the contentions of school administrators that residential segregation caused school segregation. Later, plaintiffs demonstrated that city officials and school boards in the North and West took actions that exacerbated residential segregation and thereby caused school segregation. In *Keyes* v. *Denver School District No. 1* (1973), the Supreme Court ruled that there was no difference between the de jure school segregation of the South and the de facto segregation in the North. Because school board actions had played a role in residential segregation, the court approved an extensive busing program to desegregate Denver's schools. This decision served as precedent for decisions that affected many northern cities, including Detroit, Boston, Milwaukee, Buffalo, Columbus, and Dayton.

The city-suburban pattern of residential segregation that is found in many metropolitan areas guarantees that minority students in central-city public schools will attend classes with predominantly minority enrollments while white suburban students attend largely white schools. If the Supreme Court had used the effects standard, they might have approved the pooling of city and suburban students for purposes of desegregation. However, in 1974 decisions involving Detroit and Richmond, the court ruled that plaintiffs had not sufficiently demonstrated that the actions of city and state officials caused the residential segregation of blacks in the central cities and whites in the suburban rings. Because of the geographic separation of blacks and whites in separate city and suburban school districts, that decision appears to guarantee that public schools in many metropolitan areas will be as segregated as residential neighborhoods.

Many local elected officials and executive bodies have little power to merge black and white school districts. And the legislative and executive branches of the federal government have mostly left the issue of school desegregation to the courts. In general, legislators and executive officials have opposed busing, although it is frequently the only effective strategy for desegregation. Some officials, for example, have advocated a constitutional amendment to ban such busing. In the mid-1980s, the Civil Rights Division of the U.S. Department of Justice devoted much effort to end busing in some locations where it had been ordered by federal courts—Norfolk, Savannah, and Oklahoma City—or where it had been voluntarily adopted—Seattle. The Justice Department also argued, in the Bob Jones University case, that federal desegregation requirements should not apply to church-affiliated schools, a view that was rejected by both the courts and Congress.

In Atlanta, Detroit, Dallas, Portland (Oregon), and most recently in Norfolk, black community activists have recognized residential segregation patterns as deterrents to desegregated schools, and therefore they have moved toward a strategy of seeking to improve the quality of existing schools irrespective of the racial composition of their student bodies. The negotiation of agreements and programs along these lines has generally been opposed by the national civil rights organizations and their legal staffs, which remain committed to school desegregation as a primary objective for blacks (Bell, 1986a:17–18).

In higher education, efforts to recruit blacks have been widespread. The use of positive programs to open opportunities for blacks in educational admissions and in jobs has involved similar issues. Despite continuing controversy over quotas and goals, the Supreme Court has upheld the use of numerical remedies.

The law with regard to educational admissions appears to have stabilized around the standards proposed by Justice Powell in his pivotal opinion in the *Bakke* decision (438 U.S. 265 [1978]). Today, colleges and universities may use race as one of the factors considered in the admissions process, but it may not be the sole determining factor. Because racial "quotas" in education are tied to constitutional standards, they are invalid unless one of three conditions is met: they are based on a specific finding of past discrimination; the minorities receiving the actual benefit were themselves victimized by specific acts of discrimination; or the whites disadvantaged by the program either contributed to the discriminatory practices or directly benefited from them (Bell, 1986a:73).

Employment

Employment, as well as higher education, has been an important area of civil rights litigation during the past decade. To address job discrimination, the effect standard has taken the form of court decisions requiring numerical remedies to correct discriminatory patterns and agency-administered "affirmative action" mandating "goals and timetables" for the employment of blacks.

Employment quotas are not an altogether unprecedented phenomenon in federal employment policy. The Public Works Administration required contractors to meet black hiring quotas in public housing construction for some years beginning in 1936 (Weaver, 1942). In the 1940s, this policy was extended to Federal Works Agency projects (Kruman, 1975). For statutory standards now in effect, preferential hiring and promotion of blacks is legal and constitutional for manifestly segregated job categories so long as existing white employees are not fired or demoted, their rights are accommodated as part of the remedy, and the remedy is temporary.

The major enforcement arm of the federal government in employment discrimination is the Equal Employment Opportunity Commission (EEOC), created by Title VII of the 1964 Civil Rights Act. In its early years, the agency was relatively impotent. Its functions were limited to investigation, fact finding, and conciliation, and it had no powers of enforcement or prosecution. The EEOC could simply encourage the aggrieved party to initiate a civil suit in a U.S. district court against an employer or labor union. The U.S. Attorney General was also authorized to initiate actions when a "pattern or practice" of discrimination was found, although this authority was infrequently invoked.

After the enactment of Title VII, overt refusals to hire or promote for racial reasons became relatively rare, but employers made use of a wide range of seemingly neutral criteria in personnel decisions: education, training, experience, seniority, test scores, and arrest records. In response, the EEOC asserted as early as 1966 that Title VII prohibited the use of putatively racially neutral standards if they had an adverse impact on a disproportionate number of minorities and were not justified by business necessity. These principles were adopted by a unanimous Supreme Court in *Griggs* v. *Duke Power Co.* (401 U.S. 424 [1971]:429–431):

> [P]ractices, procedures, or tests neutral on their face, and even neutral in terms of intent, cannot be maintained if they operate to "freeze" the status quo of prior discriminatory employment practices. . . . Congress directed the thrust of the Act to the *consequences* [emphasis in the original] of employment practices, not simply the motivation.

In *Griggs,* the Court held that differential results were a violation of the 1964 act if they were produced by "employment procedures or testing mechanisms that operate as 'built-in headwinds' for minority groups and are unrelated to measuring job capability" (401 U.S. 424 [1971]:431).

Both the language of Title VII and the legislative history of the 1964 Civil Rights Act offered explicit assurances that employers would not be required to maintain quotas of employees. But the Court subsequently held that the antiquota language applied to proportional racial representation, not to the use of numerical remedies to correct past discrimination. During the debate over the 1972 amendments, the Senate defeated an amendment that would have prohibited federal agencies and officials from imposing numerical goals and timetables under Title VII or federal executive orders. This defeat provided a record of congressional intent for the Court (Days, 1984:317).

The EEOC's limited investigatory apparatus was swamped by a huge volume of complaints during its first years. When Congress amended the statute in 1972 to give EEOC authority to sue in court, the EEOC brought class-action suits to which the courts proved quite receptive (Laney, 1986; Rosenthal, 1973; U.S. Equal Employment Opportunity Commission, 1984:Ch. 3). In amending Title VII, Congress recognized that the initial congressional restrictions had had the unintended consequence of making the EEOC concentrate its resources on individually based actions rather than on class action suits that more efficiently deter discrimination.

The 1972 amendments also brought public employment under the coverage of Title VII and gave EEOC authority to sue employers in federal district courts. In 1976 Congress further amended the statute to protect pregnant women from discrimination, and in 1978 several new responsibilities were transferred to the EEOC, including implementation of the Equal Pay Act and the Age Discrimination Employment Act. An administrative reorganization in 1978 established a system for the rapid processing of complaints at the local level and eliminated the bulk of the backlog (Laney, 1986; U.S. Equal Employment Opportunity Commission, 1984:120).

While the enforcement machinery was improving, however, judicial interpretation was being restricted. A number of cases tightened the requirements for private parties bringing class actions. The Supreme Court held that Section 703(h) of Title VII exempting *"bona fide* seniority or merit system(s)" protects present job incumbents if granting preferences to blacks requires the denial of vested seniority rights. This ruling grants immunity from layoffs when seniority is involved, even when a policy of "last-hired, first-fired" incorporates past discrimination against newly hired black employees. In *Firefighters Local Union No. 1784* v. *Stotts* (104 S.Ct. 2576 [1984]), the Memphis firefighters case, the Supreme Court voided a lower court decree that would have protected from layoff those blacks hired specifically to remedy discriminatory hiring by the Memphis Fire Department.

Public Accommodations and Housing

Public accommodations and housing are the two polar ends of the compliance continuum in the civil rights field. Compliance with the public accommodations provisions of the 1964 Civil Rights Act has been relatively straightforward, although some legal ambiguities remain with regard to private clubs. In housing, however, continuing segregation and overt discrimination against blacks have been the norm, and there have been no effective legislative remedies. At the federal level, an ineffectual enforcement mechanism was created by design.

Virtually all observers concede that the Fair Housing Act of 1968 owes its existence to the assassination of Martin Luther King, Jr., and the subsequent riots. The act was actually an amendment to a highly popular bill to prosecute participants in riots and civil disorders, and the package was passed within a week of the national turmoil following King's assassination.

Enforcement is lodged with the secretary of the U.S. Department of Housing and Urban Development, who is empowered to hear and investigate complaints but cannot initiate them. The secretary may then refer the complaint to the requisite state agency, although the victim may also sue in federal court if no state court has jurisdiction. State governments have been reluctant to venture into this area since the repeal of several state fair housing laws in referenda during the 1960s. The "reliance on victims of discrimination to initiate compliance processes" has proved to be the "principal weakness" in fair housing enforcement (Bell, 1980:509–516; Newburger, 1988).

FIGURE 5-2 Reported voter participation in presidential elections, by race and region, 1952–1988.

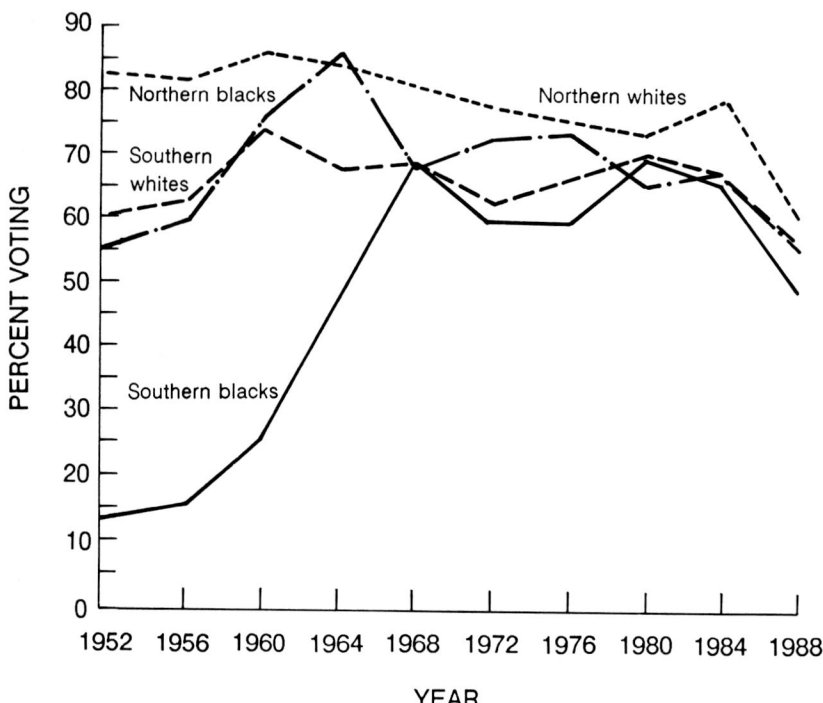

YEAR

Source: Data from Current Population Surveys.

DEMOCRATIC STATUS: VOTING AND HOLDING OFFICE

The Voting Rights Act of 1965 marked the beginning of a new era in contemporary American politics. Before 1964, black voter participation rates lagged behind white rates by a large margin; since then, they have approached the white rate (see Figure 5-2). After 1965, black concerns within electoral politics have primarily been over the consequences of electoral participation: political office, jobs, and public policy.

DETERMINANTS OF BLACK VOTER PARTICIPATION

The level of voter participation can be seen as the product of two sets of forces: the incentives to participate and the legal and political obstacles to fulfilling the desire (see Cavanagh, 1987; Wolfinger and Rosenstone, 1980; Walton, 1985:Ch.1). Higher status people are more likely to vote than lower status people because they are more likely to display political efficacy (the belief that one's participation can make a difference in the political process), citizen duty (the belief that voting is a civic obligation in a democracy), and a strong party allegiance (Campbell et al., 1960:Ch. 5).

Blacks are less likely than whites to have strong feelings of political efficacy or of trust in government. However, this relationship disappears or even reverses when socioeconomic status and feelings of personal trust and efficacy are held constant (Glaser, 1987). The apparent black alienation from politics has been due to two factors: socioeconomic disadvantage and a more broadly based distrust of other people's behavior. The latter factor is probably heavily conditioned by the generally subordinate position of blacks in American life. Yet lower status rural blacks are distinctive for a lack of political interest and a high degree of trust in political authorities—a combination of attitudes that tends to depress all forms of political participation (Gurin et al., 1988). With regard to legal requirements, the same socioeconomic factors that increase the incentive to vote also enable potential voters to overcome the hurdles of registration imposed by the political system (Wolfinger and Rosenstone, 1980). Changes in the legal and political environment have been an especially important determinant of black participation in the South.

The Fifteenth Amendment—adopted in 1870—said that voting rights could not be abridged on the basis of race or previous condition of servitude. For almost three decades, blacks participated in the political system of the South; many were elected to state legislatures and a few to Congress. However, many southern whites opposed black suffrage, and several strategies were used to get blacks off the voting rolls. In many areas of the South, the Ku Klux Klan and similar organizations used violence and economic sanctions to intimidate blacks who dared to go to the polls. But a series of Supreme Court rulings allowed southern states to disenfranchise blacks directly: the Court ruled that although the Fifteenth Amendment guaranteed blacks voting rights, individual states—not the federal government—determined who was eligible to vote.

In the last two decades of the nineteenth century, southern state legislatures created numerous obstacles (e.g., poll taxes and literacy tests) that discouraged blacks, and sometimes poor whites, from voting. Some states enacted "grandfather clauses"—that said that a person could vote if he were literate or if his grandfather had been eligible to vote. Such clauses disenfranchised blacks but not illiterate whites. Blacks in the South sued to overturn these laws, sometimes with the assistance of the Justice Department. In 1915 the Supreme Court ruled that grandfather clauses were unconstitutional.

Early in this century, southern states adopted a different technique to keep blacks from voting. In many states there was a one-party system, so winning the Democratic primary was tantamount to election. Southern legislatures declared that the Democratic party was a private organization with the ability to determine who could participate in its activities, including the primary election. The Supreme Court rendered a series of ambiguous decisions about the constitutionality of such an arrangement, but in 1944 held that whites-only primaries violated the Fifteenth Amendment. Following World War II, an increasing number of blacks in the urban South and in border states gained the franchise and began to influence politics at the local level.

President Eisenhower's U.S. Commission on Civil Rights (1961:23) found that "substantial discriminatory disfranchisement of Negroes" then existed in about 100 counties in eight southern states. That report played a crucial role in laying the groundwork for extensive federal intervention in the voter registration process. In reviewing the enforcement of the 1957 and 1960 Civil Rights Acts, the commission concluded that the tedious procedure of pursuing litigation on a county-by-county basis would not provide an adequate remedy (U.S. Commission on Civil Rights, 1961:100, 136).

The futility of this piecemeal litigation strategy was recognized in the 1965 Voting Rights Act, which authorized the appointment of federal officials to register voters in those counties that most egregiously denied blacks the right to vote. Moreover, literacy tests were forbidden in counties that apparently had applied them unfairly. Replacing biased local registrars with federal officials produced an almost immediate political revolution in the South. The most dramatic result was in Mississippi: in 1965, just 28,500 blacks, a mere 7 percent of the voting-age population, had been registered; 3 years later, 250,770 blacks were registered (Colby, 1984). In 11 southern states, black registration increased by 10 percentage points from 1964 to 1966, and by another 15 points in the next 4 years (Table 5-7).

Although southern blacks were able to register and vote, the meaning of that victory could be diminished by a variety of measures that local officials adopted to minimize black voting strength. Legislative malapportionment, one traditional method of giving more weight to some voters, had been prohibited by the Supreme Court's one-person, one-vote decisions in 1964. But a number of other methods were available to ingenious officials, including gerrymandering, use of at-large rather than district elections for local offices, adoption of runoff elections, annexation of neighboring communities to reduce the black proportion of city populations, and inconveniently located polling places.

These possibilities were anticipated in the Voting Rights Act. Title 5 of the law required that governmental units in "covered jurisdictions"—essentially, those jurisdictions to which federal registrars could be sent—had to get approval for any proposed changes in a "standard, practice, or procedure with respect to voting." This "preclearance" could be obtained either from the U.S. Department of Justice or the U.S. District Court in the District of Columbia. In contrast to Section 5, which applied to jurisdictions whose past history of abridging minority voting rights made their future conduct suspect, the new law's Section 2 applied to the entire country and was aimed at existing electoral procedures. It authorized litigation, either by public or private parties, to challenge any arrangements that might hinder a minority person's full use of the ballot.

These provisions were rooted in fears that some local officials would subvert black enfranchisement. But such an intent test proved difficult to apply in many cases. In *White* v. *Regester* (412 U.S. 755 [1973]), the Supreme

TABLE 5-7 Black Registration in Southern States, 1940–1984

Year	Blacks Registered	Black Voting-Age Population	Registration Rate (percent)
1940	151,000	4,843,000	3.1
1946	595,000	4,869,000	12.2
1952	1,006,000	5,019,000	20.0
1956	1,238,000	4,955,000	25.0
1958	1,304,000	4,994,000	26.1
1960	1,463,000	5,090,000	28.7
1962	1,481,000	5,148,000	28.8
1964	2,165,000	5,173,000	41.9
1966	2,689,000	5,208,000	51.6
1968	3,112,000	5,299,000	58.7
1970	3,506,000	5,243,000	66.9
1972	3,448,000	6,178,000	55.8
1974	3,842,000	6,562,000	58.6
1976	4,149,000	6,931,000	59.9
1978	—	7,305,000	—
1980	4,254,000	7,718,000	55.1
1982	4,302,000	8,077,000	53.3
1984	5,596,000	8,368,000	66.9
1986	5,796,000	8,957,000	64.7
1988	5,842,000	9,171,000	63.7

Sources: Data for number of blacks registered from Voter Education Project; black voting-age population estimated by the committee.

Court applied the far broader criterion of the likely effect of a particular provision. It called for an "intensely local appraisal" of the "totality of the circumstances" concerning whether minorities "had less opportunity than did other residents in the district to participate in the political process and to elect the legislators of their choice," thus violating the equal protection clause of the Constitution. Seven years later, the Court held that Congress had meant only to apply an intent test, rather than being concerned with the effects of any electoral arrangement (446 U.S. 55 [1980]). Two years later Congress in effect reinstated an effect test in the 1982 amendments to the Voting Rights Act.

By the 1980s the Voting Rights Act had become a major tool to advance the interests not just of blacks but of some other minorities as well: American Indians, Asian-Americans, and Hispanics. The key criterion is election of minority candidates (Thernstrom, 1987). When courts or the Justice Department have held that either proposed changes or existing arrangements might produce a lowered chance of victory for minority candidates, the remedy has been an alteration either of electoral arrangements or their application in particular cases. Thus, Los Angeles heeded a warning from the Justice Department and drew new boundaries for its city council districts to increase the election opportunities for Hispanics. In one of the most far-reaching decisions in March 1989, noting that a California city with at-large city council elections and a near majority of Hispanic residents had had only a single Hispanic council member in its history, the Supreme Court ordered that henceforth its council be elected from districts. This decision is likely to have major implications for the distribution of political power in hundreds of cities where at-large elections inhibit the full mobilization of black voting strength.

According to the University of Michigan's National Election Studies (NES), self-reported black general election turnout in the South has increased from 13 percent in 1952 to 65 percent in 1984. In the North, self-reported black turnout was 55 percent (27 percentage points below white turnout) in 1952, peaked in the 1964 Johnson-Goldwater contest at 85 percent, and has hovered between 65 and 73 percent since then. However, the NES regional data for blacks are subject to a relatively large sampling error (over 10 percentage points) due to small sample size. The most accurate estimates of black turnout are those of the Census Bureau's Current Population Survey (which are subject to a sampling error of only about 2 percentage points for both southern and nonsouthern blacks). This time series indicates a sharp drop in northern black turnout from 1964 to 1976, followed by a recovery in 1980 and 1984, with a less pronounced but similar pattern in the South; see Table 5-8.

Both the Census Bureau and NES estimates are subject to an additional source of error known as overreporting, the tendency of some survey respondents to report having registered and voted when they did not. Black nonvoters are consistently more likely to report voting than are white nonvoters. It is not yet clear whether this remains true after controlling for demographic characteristics, but the possibility should be kept in mind when considering the data reported.

The relationships linking race and other demographic variables to turnout have clearly changed over time, and these changes have had important consequences for the electoral inclusion of lower status black Americans. The demographic characteristics of the black voting-age population explained about one-third of the gap between black and white turnout prior to 1964. The remainder must be attributed to the systematic disenfranchisement of blacks in the South. Since that time, blacks have at times voted at a higher rate than whites of similar socioeconomic status: this occurred in the North in 1964 and in the South from 1968 to 1976; see Table 5-9 (see also Danigelis, 1978; Kleppner, 1982:117). It has become a nationwide phenomenon in the 1980s.

In order to examine these trends in more detail, we undertook an analysis of Current Population Survey samples from 1978 to 1984. Reported black turnout in 1984 was 5 percentage points *higher* than reported white turnout when demographic characteristics and state-level political and contextual variables were held constant (Hagen, 1988b:Table 21). This is a significant change from 1972, when black turnout was only marginally higher than white turnout after controlling for demographic factors (Wolfinger and Ro-

TABLE 5-8 Voter Participation (as a percentage of voting-age population), by Region and Race, 1964–1988

Region and Race	Presidential Election Years						
	1964	1968	1972	1976	1980	1984	1988
United States							
White	70.7	69.1	64.5	60.9	60.9	61.4	59.1
Black	58.5	57.6	52.1	48.7	50.5	55.8	51.5
Difference	12.2	11.5	12.4	12.2	10.4	5.6	7.6
North and West							
White	74.7	71.8	67.5	62.6	62.4	63.0	60.4
Black	72.0	64.8	56.7	52.2	52.8	58.9	55.6
Difference	2.7	7.0	10.8	10.4	9.6	4.1	4.8
South							
White	59.6	61.9	57.0	57.1	57.4	58.1	56.4
Black	44.0	51.6	47.8	45.7	48.2	53.2	48.0
Difference	15.6	10.3	9.2	11.4	9.2	4.9	8.4

	Mid-Term Election Years					
	1966	1970	1974	1978	1982	1986
United States						
White	57.0	56.0	46.3	47.3	49.9	47.0
Black	41.7	43.5	33.8	37.2	43.0	43.2
Difference	15.3	12.5	12.5	10.1	6.9	3.8
North and West						
White	61.7	59.8	50.0	50.0	53.1	48.7
Black	52.1	51.4	37.9	41.3	48.5	44.2
Difference	9.6	8.4	12.1	8.7	4.6	4.5
South						
White	45.1	46.4	37.4	41.1	42.9	43.5
Black	32.9	36.8	30.0	33.5	38.3	42.5
Difference	12.2	9.6	7.4	7.6	4.6	1.0

Source: Data from Bureau of the Census.

senstone, 1980:90–91). In addition, black women are now 4 percentage points more likely to vote than black men of comparable socioeconomic status. And black women who are heads of households are 11 percentage points more likely than similarly situated white men to vote (Hagen, 1988b:Table 10).

Since 1978 there has been a significant reduction in the impact of socioeconomic status as a determinant of black turnout (Kendrick, 1986). In 1984, blacks at the lowest levels of education and income outvoted similar whites by 9 to 12 percentage points; at the upper end of the status scale, black and white turnout was about equal. Blacks aged 35 or younger were 7 to 9 percentage points more likely to vote than whites of the same age (Hagen, 1988b:Tables 6–8).

Overall, the 1980s have seen a dramatic mobilization of lower status blacks with a previously marginal attachment to electoral politics. For example, first-time black registrants between 1982 and 1984 were disproportionately

TABLE 5-9 Differences Between Reported Black and White Voter Turnout, by Region, 1952–1980

Election and Year	Non-South		South	
	Unadjusted	Adjusted	Unadjusted	Adjusted
Presidential elections				
1952	−21.8	−14.6	−47.6	−35.9
1956	−25.7	−16.7	−41.1	−25.9
1960	−14.3	−10.8	−45.3	−28.7
1964	−3.1	+8.6	−22.4	−11.0
1968	−17.3	−10.8	+0.8	+14.9
1972	−2.5	+1.3	−7.1	+11.5
1976	−1.2	+3.5	−2.1	+12.4
1980	−11.4	−5.2	−6.1	−2.0
Congressional elections				
1958	−13.4	−4.0	−24.9	−16.7
1962	−20.7	−14.5	−14.2	−3.6
1966	−5.7	+5.0	−14.9	−0.9
1970	−17.3	−3.9	−9.0	−0.5
1974	−20.0	−15.8	−4.3	+3.8
1978	−12.0	−7.4	−9.7	−1.5

Notes: Values are differences (in percent), white minus black turnout. The adjusted difference was calculated by multiple classification analysis to remove the effects of age, education, income, and sex. Respondents below 21 years of age were excluded from the percentage base in all years.

Source: Data from Current Population Surveys, reported in Kleppner (1982:117).

composed of young people with high levels of racial consciousness (Cavanagh, 1985). The trend toward mobilization of lower status blacks is not mirrored in the white population: between 1978 and 1984, the determinants of white turnout remained fairly constant.

The role of race consciousness as a factor in political participation has received increased attention in some recent studies. Race consciousness among blacks involves (1) a feeling of closeness or identification with other group members; (2) dissatisfaction with group status, especially in the political arena; (3) an attribution of the unsatisfactory group status to illegitimate causes such as discrimination; and (4) a belief that group members must act collectively to improve the group's position. Studies using this set of attitudes have found that blacks are more likely than whites to express high levels of group consciousness on each dimension and that such patterns of belief are important correlates of political participation (Miller et al., 1981).

To explain why blacks had higher participation rates than whites of similar socioeconomic status, Verba and Nie (1973:158) concluded: "Consciousness of race as a problem or a basis of conflict appears to bring those blacks who are [racially] conscious up to a level of participation equivalent to that of whites." In a reanalysis of the Verba and Nie data, Shingles (1981:78–84) reported that a combination of feelings of political efficacy and mistrust seems to stimulate the desire to participate in policy-oriented activities among lower status blacks, while no comparable mechanism operates among lower status whites.

A comprehensive analysis of these issues was undertaken by the 1984 National Black Election Study (Gurin et al., 1988). In general, the study found that education is the most important positive correlate of feelings of racial solidarity. Although middle-class blacks exhibit the highest levels of group identity and political consciousness, racial solidarity is present throughout the black community to some degree. By motivating blacks to participate in community organizations, racial solidarity helps to mobilize lower status as well as upper status blacks for political activity (Gurin et al., 1988).

In contrast, other researchers believe that changes in the political environment is the major determinant of political participation. For example, Walton (1985:Ch. 5) argues that black participation rates have shown enormous variation over time despite the apparent existence of strong feelings of group consciousness among blacks throughout much of American history. Walton stresses such structural factors as the repression of black voting rights and the responsiveness of the major parties to black concerns as being more important determinants of black participation than other factors.

Registration practices make an important difference in voter participation. Compared to a system of election day registration, a closing date for registration 30 days prior to an election reduces black turnout by 10 percentage points and white turnout by 13 percentage points. For both whites and blacks, the availability of deputy registrars increases turnout by 2 to 3 percentage points, and the use of neighborhood registration locations (such as libraries, schools, and post offices) increases turnout by an additional 2 percentage points (Hagen, 1988b:Tables 14–15).

A number of factors in local political environments are also important determinants of black voter turnout. Many citizens only vote when they believe there is a worthy candidate. This factor is one explanation for the frequent finding that black voter turnout in municipal elections tends to be much more variable, and usually much lower, than white turnout. Black turnout tends to surge in the presence of a strong black candidate (see Hamilton, 1977; Nelson, 1982; Preston, 1984; for a review of case studies, see Cavanagh, 1987:Ch. 4). For example, the turnout of blacks in Chicago and Philadelphia in 1984 was about 11 percentage points higher than would have been predicted on the basis of the demographic characteristics of the population; whites in those cities were 10 percentage points more likely to vote than whites elsewhere. This turnout was probably a carryover from the intensity of the 1983 black mayoral campaigns in the two cities.

Turnout among both races was higher in states with the highest level of voter education activity in 1984. The difference in turnout in the states with the most and states with the least voter education money spent per capita was 7 percentage points for blacks and 6 percentage points for whites (Hagen, 1988b:35–39). Since nonprofit voter education activity was disproportionately directed toward blacks in 1984, it is possible that the effect was to spur

TABLE 5-10 Black Elected Officials, by Region, 1941–1985

Year	Northeast	North Central	South	West	Total
1941	10	20	2	1	33
1947	21	35	6	4	66
1951	29	31	16	6	82
1965	63	104	87	26	280
1970	238	396	703	132	1,469
1975	503	869	1,913	218	3,503
1980	570	1,041	2,981	298	4,890
1985	694	1,150	3,801	371	6,016

Note: Regions are those of the Bureau of the Census.

Sources: Data for 1941–1947 from Guzman (1947) and Murray (1947); for 1951 from Guzman (1952); for 1965 from *Ebony* (1965, 1966), U.S. Commission on Civil Rights (1968), and Weaver (1964); and for 1970–1985 from the Joint Center for Political Studies (1985).

a countermobilization of white voters in those states, as may have occurred in the South after passage of the Voting Rights Act (Hammond, 1977; Hanks, 1986; but see Stanley, 1987).

Two other contextual variables uniquely affect blacks. Black voter participation is 12 percentage points higher in states with a large black population (30 percent or more) than those with a negligible black population (1 percent or less); the black population percentage has no impact on white turnout, however. This finding probably reflects the importance of both plausible black candidate victories and black organizational activity at the local level in stimulating black turnout. Local economic conditions are also important factors. A 10-percentage-point increase in state unemployment boosts turnout in a state by 5 percentage points, regardless of race.

ELECTED OFFICIALS

The number of black elected officials increased from approximately 33 in 1941, almost all in northern cities, to about 280 in 1965. Thereafter it grew dramatically, especially in the South, where black candidates were generally not viable until the passage of the Voting Rights Act. Since 1965, black Americans have been elected to every major elective public office except those of chief executives: president, vice president, and governor. The national total of black elected officials was 6,829 in 1988.

From the perspective of the entire American political system, the number of black elected officials is still very small. As of 1985, 4.0 percent of all elected officials in the South were black, as were 0.7 percent of those outside the South, and 1.2 percent of those in the nation as a whole (Joint Center for Political Studies, 1985:Table 2); see Table 5-10. The annual rate of increase for black elected officials has dropped from a high of 26.6 percent in 1971 (the high point after the 1965 changes) to single-digit percentages in the 1980s.

The single most important determinant of black candidates' success is the racial composition of the electoral jurisdictions: the higher the black percentage of the voting-age population, the higher the probability of the election of a black to office (Conyers and Wallace, 1976:131–135; Engstrom and McDonald, 1981; Karnig and Welch, 1980:32). Thus, the largest increases have come at the lower levels of government. While the number of blacks in Congress increased from 10 to 22, between 1965 and 1985, the number of black state legislators increased from 102 to 392. And there were much larger increases among city council members (74 to 2,189), school board members (68 to 1,363), and mayors (3 to 286); see Table 5-11.

The relationship between racial composition of jurisdiction and black electability is mediated in important ways by intervening variables such as region, city size, districting procedures, and the use of partisan ballots in elections. Region and city size interact to produce what appears to be systematic black underrepresentation in small towns in the rural South. Among incorporated municipalities with a black population majority, 70 percent in the North had black mayors in 1985, compared with 31 percent in the South. Just over one-half of the municipalities outside the South with more than 2,500 people had black mayors if their population was 50 to 65 percent black. Southern municipalities were not likely to elect black mayors unless they were 80 percent or more black (Table 5-12). This pattern accounts for the low levels of black officials in southern county government as well. There are 82 black-majority counties in Alabama, Georgia, Louisiana, Mississippi, North Carolina, South Carolina, and Virginia: in 1985, the local governments were headed by whites in 61 of these counties; 23 of the 82 each had one black county commissioner; and in 15 others the county boards were completely white (Edds, 1987:11; see also M. Jones, 1976; Stekler, 1982).

The design of a local election system is an important determinant of the electability of black candidates. Election of blacks is more likely under a district election system than under an at-large election or a hybrid system combining aspects of the two (Engstrom and McDonald, 1981; Heilig and Mundt, 1983; Karnig and Welch, 1982; Latimer, 1979; Stekler, 1982:Ch. 3; Taebel, 1978). After controlling for other factors, election by districts yields a level of black representation on city councils that is roughly equal to the black share of the city population; an at-large system yields a black share of seats that is one-half the black population percentage; see Figure 5-3.

This factor accounts for a large part of the disparity between black population percentages and black representation in the South. At-large systems are much more common in the South. In examining 224 SMSA (standard metropolitan statistical area) central cities, Engstrom and McDonald (1981:1094) found 68 percent of southern cities had at-large elections, compared with 45 percent of nonsouthern cities (see also C. Jones, 1976; Karnig, 1976). Some investigators argue that the greater use of at-large elections in the South is partly due to an attempt to limit black representation (Davidson and Korbel, 1981).

Partisan municipal ballots have both positive and negative implications for

TABLE 5-11 Black Elected Officials, by Selected Office Categories, 1941–1985

Year	U.S. Offices		State Offices			City Offices			Total[a]
	Senate	Representative	Administrator	Senate	Representative	Mayor	Council	School Board	
1941	0	1	0	3	23	0	4	2	33
1947	0	2	0	5	33	0	18	8	66
1951	0	2	0	1	39	0	25	15	82
1965	0	4	1	18	84	3	74	68	280
1970	1	9	1	31	137	48	552	362	1,469
1975	1	17	5	53	223	135	1,237	894	3,503
1980	0	17	6	70	247	182	1,809	1,149	4,890
1985	0	20	4	90	302	286	2,189	1,363	6,016

[a] For 1965–1985 total includes all black elected officials, not just those in selected categories.

Sources: Data for 1941–1947 from Guzman (1947) and Murray (1947); data for 1951 from Guzman (1952); data for 1965, from Ebony (1965, 1966), U.S. Commission on Civil Rights (1968), and Weaver (1964); and data for 1970–1985 from Joint Center for Political Studies (1985).

TABLE 5-12 Incorporated Municipalities with Black Mayors, by Population, Racial Composition, and Region, 1985

Population of Municipality	Percent Black Population: South			Percent Black Population: Non-South		
	50–64%	65–79%	80–99%	50–64%	65–79%	80–99%
Less than 2,500	11	37	75	17	67	88
(N)	(176)	(78)	(84)	(6)	(6)	(16)
2,500 or more	12	45	100	58	75	78
(N)	(93)	(20)	(9)	(12)	(8)	(18)
Total	12	39	77	44	71	82
(N)	(269)	(98)	(93)	(18)	(14)	(34)

Source: Data from O'Hare (1986:7).

black candidates. On the positive side, black candidates often benefit from the endorsement and financial support a political party can provide its candidates. The party endorsement may also aid black candidates running on a party slate by drawing the votes of whites who might vote along racial lines in a nonpartisan ballot situation (Banfield and Wilson, 1963; Gordon, 1970; Karnig and Welch, 1980:26; Pettigrew, 1976; Pomper, 1966:79–97). A negative aspect is that incumbent party leaders frequently attempt to restrict access to party patronage and leadership positions, excluding blacks and other political newcomers. Blacks are more likely to run for mayor and city council in nonpartisan municipalities, presumably because under such a system there is no need to cultivate party ties. However, blacks are more likely to be elected mayor in partisan systems, leading the most thorough study of the subject to conclude that "once on the ballot, blacks benefit from the partisan system" (Karnig and Welch, 1980:146).

OTHER PUBLIC OFFICIALS AND EMPLOYEES

Many decision makers in the public sector are chosen by executive appointment, civil service procedures, or other means. For example, judges are often appointed to office. Prior to World War II, black judges were even more scarce than black elected officials. The first black federal judge was William H. Hastie, appointed by President Franklin D. Roosevelt in 1937 as judge of the District Court for the Virgin Islands. The number of black federal judges rose from 1 in 1941 to 98 in 1986, while the national total of black judges rose from 10 to 841 in the same time span; see Table 5-13. Thurgood Marshall became the first black justice of the Supreme Court in 1968.

The time series reveals the significance of the presidential appointment power with regard to black attainment of this particular public office. President Carter placed 37 blacks on the federal bench, more than all other presidents combined; President Reagan, as of early 1988, had appointed 6. As a consequence, the growth in the number of black federal judges has

FIGURE 5-3 Relationship between black percentage of city population and black percentage of city council, by election format.

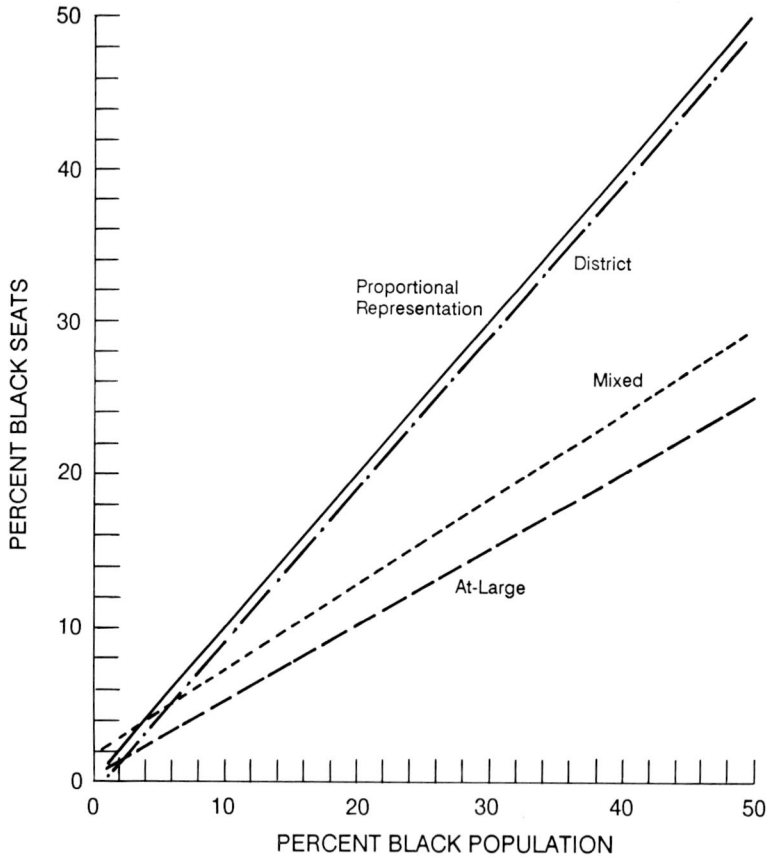

Note: The regression equations are: district = $-0.832 + 0.994$ BP% (S.E. 0.075); mixed = $1.748 + 0.556$ BP% (S.E. 0.061); at-large = $0.348 + 0.495$ BP% (S.E. 0.061).

Source: Engstrom and McDonald (1981:348). Reprinted with permission.

leveled off in the 1980s, rising from 94 to 98, while the number of black state and municipal judges continued to climb, from 505 to 743. The black share of federal judicial appointments dropped from 16.1 percent under Carter to 2.5 percent under Reagan.

The bulk of the recent growth has been in the South. The number of black state and municipal judges in the South rose from 38 in 1970 to 306 in 1986 (Table 5-14). Despite this growth, however, and the fact that the black population is disproportionately concentrated in the South, the black proportion of state judges remains lower in the South (3.4 percent) than in

TABLE 5-13 Black Judges in the United States, 1941–1986

Year	Federal	State and Municipal	Total
1941	1	9	10
1951	3	23	26
1961	4	54	58
1970	19	199	218
1980	94	505	599
1986	98	743	841

Sources: Data from Foster and Reid (1947:282), Guzman (1952:309–311), Toles (1970), Crockett et al. (1980), and the Joint Center for Political Studies (1986).

any other region. This may be due to the methods of judicial selection in the South. Black judges are least likely to be selected in a system of popular election; they are most likely to be selected where judges are appointed by the executive branch or selected through a merit system. The 11 states of the Old Confederacy use popular election to select judges (Henry et al., 1985:18–28).

There are few systematic trend data available on black appointed officials. The most detailed information is for the federal government, where the black share of total employment rose from 10 percent in 1938 to 17 percent in 1980 (Cavanagh, 1987:Table 19). For federal civil service executives, racial data have been collected since 1961: the black share of such positions (GS-12 and above) rose steadily from 0.7 percent in 1961 to 6.5 percent in 1984. The black share of the Senior Executive Service, the "supergrade" level of noncareer appointments, rose from 1.2 percent in 1969 to 5.0 percent in 1980 and dropped to 4.2 percent in 1984 (Cavanagh, 1987:Table 20). Systematic data on full-time presidential appointments are available only for the last two administrations: 12 percent of President Carter's appointees and 4 percent of President Reagan's were black.

TABLE 5-14 Black State and Municipal Judges, by Region, 1970 and 1986

Region	1970	1986
Northeast	66	157
North Central	72	169
South	38	306
West	23	106
Territories	0	5
Total	199	743

Note: Regions are those of the Bureau of the Census.

Sources: Data for 1970 from Toles (1970); data for 1986 from the Joint Center for Political Studies (1986).

The black share of federal managerial positions is highest in the agencies with sizable black constituencies, such as the Equal Employment Opportunity Commission, the U.S. Commission on Civil Rights, and agencies dealing with social services and personnel policy. Black managers are most rare in the "prestige" agencies dealing with economic policy, national security, and the sciences (Cavanagh, 1987:Table 22). In the foreign service, the black share of ambassadorships declined from 6.9 percent under Carter to 4.8 percent under Reagan. Blacks then held 1.8 percent of the 650 most senior policy-making positions in the State Department. The black percentage of entering junior officers in the foreign service declined from 18 percent in 1978 to 4 percent in 1985 (Jackson, 1987:47).

The black proportion of public administrators rose from 0.4 percent in 1940 to 7.8 percent in 1980. Since 1970, the overall black share of inspection and compliance officers has risen from 4.7 to 8.1 percent; many of these positions involve the administration of affirmative action programs for minorities and women. A curious anomaly is the position of postmaster; there were more black postmasters in 1950 than in 1980.

The black percentage of officials and administrators at the state and local levels rose from 5.3 percent in 1974 to 8.0 percent in 1984. The black proportion of new hires at the official and administrative levels was higher in both years (7.2 percent in 1974 and 9.9 percent in 1984), suggesting that the black share of such positions should continue to increase. However, the number of new hires at the state and local levels declined from 17,749 to 13,699 over the same time span (U.S. Equal Employment Opportunity Commission, 1986:Tables 5, 7). Thus, it seems probable that the rate of black increase will be lower in the immediate future than was the case in the last decade.

By government function, state and local governments have a concentration of black employees in social programs servicing a disproportionately black clientele. Thus, in 1984, the state and local agencies with the highest proportions of black employees were housing (38.4 percent), hospitals (24.6 percent), public welfare (23.4 percent), and health (20.7 percent), in addition to the agencies with a largely blue-collar work force, such as sanitation and sewage (32.7 percent), utilities and transportation (26.6 percent), and corrections (20.9 percent).

ALLOCATIONAL STATUS: INFLUENCING PUBLIC POLICY

POLITICAL LEADERSHIP AND PRIORITIES IN THE BLACK COMMUNITY

Prior to 1965, black electoral representation was largely restricted to a handful of black-majority districts in northern cities. As a consequence, black leadership generally "has not been an *elected* leadership, in the sense of a represented constituency choosing it at the polls" (Hamilton, 1981:240, emphasis in the original; see also Smith, 1982:27). In addition to the traditional lobbying organizations, many of the social institutions in the black community have also tended to take on more or less explicitly political roles, in the sense of aggregating and articulating black interests as well as providing a system of influence and control in directing the affairs of the black community (see Chapter 4; Carson, 1986:20; Holden, 1973:3–8). Thus, black fraternities, sororities, mutual-aid societies, and business and professional associations have played a central role in the recruitment of leadership and the mobilization of collective action in the black community. The black church provides the most familiar example of the political role often assumed by black social institutions. In recent times, however, the clergy's leadership role has diminished and many black ministers feel that their major duty to their congregations concerns religious rather than political needs (Nelson, 1987). Nonetheless, the church remains important in black politics as do the major civil rights organizations (see Chapter 4).

Since the early 1970s, the base of black leadership has been undergoing a major transformation. Structurally, this is due to the post-1960s growth in the black middle class, especially black professionals, which has provided an expanded base of black leadership outside the predominantly black institutions (see Chapter 4). In addition, and perhaps as a result of the structural change in leadership possibilities, the breakthroughs in the politics of rights inspired a major debate over the question of alternative strategies and alternative leadership frameworks for the pursuit of the politics of resources. In an influential article, Bayard Rustin (1965) argued that the era of protest was over and had to be succeeded by an era of black advancement through electoral politics. Similarly, Kilson (1987:17–18) argued that "the decline of civil rights groups is both inevitable and functional," and he agreed with Reed (1986) that black elected officials are destined to become the most important source of black political leadership.

In contrast, Carson (1986) and Nelson (1987) argued that the protest movement was part of a long historical process of institutional development in the black community and stress its continuity with the strategy and tactics of black politics throughout the century. According to their view, social movement activity will continue to retain an essential role in black politics in the years to come.

The existence of this controversy is itself a manifestation of black political progress. The emergence of a cadre of influential black elected officials obviously provides blacks with a broader base through which political objectives can be pursued. At the federal level, for example, members of the Congressional Black Caucus can provide political leadership not otherwise available to blacks. However, there are important limitations on the political change that can be effected by a relatively small number of elected officials. In particular, if the political goals sought by black Americans are substantially out of favor with key decision makers and their constituencies, then there will be obvious constraints on the ability of black officials to enact their black constituents' preferences into policy.

As we noted above (see Table 5-4), there is white support for an expanded federal role on many issues of interest to blacks, such as health, education, drug control, and the like. But whites may be less concerned about these issues. If blacks and whites have different priorities, blacks may have a difficult time placing their policy concerns on the federal government's priority list. The evidence is mixed on black-white differences on issue salience. A special study conducted by the Gallup Organization in 1984 for the Joint Center for Political Studies found different priorities. For blacks, the three most important issues in the presidential campaign were unemployment (65 percent), government programs to help the poor (45 percent), and civil rights (38 percent). Whites divided almost evenly among unemployment (42 percent), the federal deficit (42 percent), and inflation (40 percent). Only 6 percent of whites named civil rights as one of the three major issues (Cavanagh, 1985:4).

Of course, black priorities such as increased employment and aid to schools will not necessarily always remain low priorities to the general public. If so, black Americans and their political leaders will have a large stake and an important role to play in defining the policy agenda. No doubt black public officials, business elites, and other prominent professionals will have an instrumental position in the attempt to articulate issues of concern to blacks. However, this modern black leadership elite will also form partnerships with older black organizations (civil rights groups and churches), many of whom are in close touch with the political desires of the general black population.

In particular, the black church has often adapted more quickly to political events than other black institutions because its decentralized structure has made it flexible and responsive to demands for political activity. Black ministers frequently serve as "brokers," bringing together the diverse elements within a local black community to reach common ground for collective action (Nelson, 1987). The autonomy and reach of the black church made it the natural organizational framework for the civil rights movement in the South (see Chapter 4; Morris, 1984) and more recently enabled it to play a key role in Jesse Jackson's 1984 and 1988 presidential campaigns. The importance of the black church as an organizational base may be undergoing something of a renaissance at present, due to its participation in electoral politics, lobbying on South Africa, and local-level activity related to economic development in the black community.

The question of how to assert black interests through coalition activity, as opposed to more autonomous organization, is likely to spark intense political debate in coming years. At the federal level, coalition activity (within the black community and between it and the rest of society) appears both necessary and inevitable. It is aided by the political resources accumulated by black congressmen as they acquire seniority. And as blacks become more skilled and influential in presidential nomination politics, this arena may present an increasingly important outlet for black attempts to take a role in setting the national legislative agenda.

At the local level, however, blacks have shown signs of an increasing tendency to resort to protest politics. The fights over Howard Beach, the school chancellor position in New York, and the Chicago mayoral succession of 1987 suggest that church and community organization leaders may be trying to pursue a much more explicitly confrontational political strategy and thrust it on more mainstream black leaders. In recent years, these two forces have frequently coalesced in electoral campaigns (e.g., the Jackson presidential campaign of 1988, which drew much stronger support from black elected officials than did his 1984 campaign) and have helped to stimulate a dramatic increase in black voter participation. In Chicago in 1983, for example, social movement activity to protest cutbacks in welfare programs provided the nucleus of organizational support for Harold Washington's mayoral victory (Woods, 1987), and the same phenomenon of a social movement in electoral form could be discerned in Jesse Jackson's 1984 presidential campaign.

Protest has played a central role in black political activity precisely when aspirations crystallized at the grass roots level have not been given a favorable place on the agenda of the wider polity. As Lipsky (1968:1145) has said: "The 'problem of the powerless' in protest activity is to activate 'third parties' to enter the implicit or explicit bargaining arena in ways favorable to the protesters." Thus, black protest has often coincided with other, more conventional, forms of participation that serve to resolve conflicts that would not have been placed on an agenda without the protest activity.

The concept of confrontation to initiate negotiation was the strategic core of the civil rights movement. As the Reverend Dr. Martin Luther King, Jr., posed the question in his celebrated letter from the Birmingham jail (King, 1964:79):

> You are quite right in calling for negotiation. Indeed, this is the very purpose of direct action. Nonviolent direct action seeks to create such a crisis and foster such a tension that a community which has constantly refused to negotiate is forced to confront the issue. It seeks to dramatize the issue so it can no longer be ignored.

If disaffection with the slow pace of change accruing from electoral politics begins to set in at the grass roots level and if some leaders begin to cast increased doubt about the efficacy of mainstream participation as opposed to more confrontational strategies, the result could be a greater debate within the black community.

Black political interests are not exclusively concerned with gaining power in the public sector. Blacks have also shown disaffection with their pace of advancement in occupying positions of power in the corporate world, in influential law firms, and in other areas of the private sector. While data on this subject are difficult to obtain, we present some illustrative data on black participation in the private sector.

Law firms are an important link between the public and private sectors in America. The largest Washington, D.C., firms, in particular, specialize in a law practice that is virtually indistinguishable from lobbying (Green, 1975). The *Washington Post* surveyed the 14 Washington firms with more than 100 attorneys on staff and found that blacks were 18 of the 896 partners, or 2.0 percent, and 51 of the 1,367 associates, or 3.7 percent (Marcus, 1986). These percentages are similar to those for the United States as a whole. A survey of the nation's 250 largest law firms by the *National Law Journal* found that blacks accounted for 1,212 of the 16,530 partners, or 0.7 percent, and 499 of the 25,577 associates, or 2.0 percent.

Black law students are far less likely than white law students to enter private practice. A survey of 28,702 graduates from 160 accredited law schools in 1983 (Marcus, 1986) found the following:

Kind of Practice	All Graduates	Blacks
Private	58.9%	32.4%
Business	10.5	10.7
Government	11.4	23.3
Public interest	3.0	8.2

Corporate positions are not only important in directing economic affairs, but also as symbolic indicators of increasing black participation in the corporate sector. They represent points of access and influence on government and other private-sector activities. According to the annual survey of the nation's 1,000 largest business companies by Korn/Ferry International, a leading executive recruitment firm, the percentage of corporate boards with one or more minority members rose from 9.0 percent in 1973 to 29.5 percent in 1986. Minority members were most prevalent on the boards of retailers, 55 percent of which had minority representation, closely followed by banks and other financial institutions, 53 percent. Company size appears to improve minority representation: 51 percent of corporations with $5 billion or more in revenues, and 44 percent of those with $1 billion or more, had minority board members (Korn/Ferry International, 1987).

Brimmer (1985) estimated from the 1984 Korn/Ferry survey that about 19.7 percent of firms have at least one black director. There were approximately 125 black directors on the boards of the 633 firms responding. This was about 1.5 percent of the total number of directors. But the average black director holds 3.8 directorships. Thus, the entire universe of black corporate directors probably comprises no more than a few dozen individuals.

The EEOC estimated in 1982 that 4.3 percent of all corporate "officials and managers" were black. At the *Fortune* 1000 companies, however, black advancement into managerial ranks has been small. In 1979, only 3 of these companies' 1,708 senior executives were blacks; the number had risen to 4 of 1,362 in 1985 (Korn/Ferry International, 1987:Table 24). Black executives have been disproportionately laid off during corporate restructuring moves since 1984. One reason is that black executives often work in equal employment opportunity compliance and other minority-related areas; these jobs do not have much immediate impact on profits and are often the first to go during cutbacks.

LOCAL BLACK GOVERNANCE

For purposes of analysis, it is useful to distinguish the dynamics of black participation in the public policy process at the federal level from those prevailing at the local level. At the federal level, black interests are usually expressed in concert with white allies, making it difficult to assess the independent contribution of black political influence to the outcome. At the local level, blacks are increasingly situated in positions of authority that permit considerable discretion in policy decisions, although black mayors, like most mayors, often find significant limitations on their freedom to maneuver due to political and economic constraints.

A mayor may be a chief executive, but if patronage is controlled by a party chairman, or taxing authority is possessed by a board of estimate, then the mayor may be just one of many participants seeking a favorable outcome. The power of a mayor, whether black or white, is partially conditioned by the local governmental structure (e.g., a strong mayor or a council-manager form of government), but the unofficial channels of influence—such as campaign activists and contributors, downtown business interests, and the media—may be more important in affecting decisions. Thus, the mere existence of black elected officials cannot be equated with political power (Jones, 1978).

After an election, the forces responsible for mobilizing the black constituency in support of a black candidate often disband, leaving a black official with a fragile base to generate support for policy initiatives (Curvin, 1975; Nelson, 1978). At the same time, the fragmentation of authority within city governments and the leverage held by business interests and the media may be more powerful political forces with which a mayor must contend. Alienating these interests may lead to a mayor's appearing impotent and ineffective; catering to them leads to charges of "selling out" from black constituents. Either way, a policy-making base can be difficult to maintain over a sustained period of time even though an electoral base may appear to be secure.

Noting these considerations, most of the literature on black governance has stressed the limitations of black influence in the policy process (see, e.g., Nelson, 1978; Preston, 1976; Walton, 1972). These conditions are aggravated by the nature of the cities in which most blacks come to power. Although cities such as Washington and Newark have shown recent signs of some revival, most of the cities with black mayors have a declining employment and revenue base; inadequate educational systems, housing, and health care; and a large proportion of the population receiving public assistance.

Because local governments are in competition with one another to attract new businesses and residents while retaining existing ones, they are not inclined to increase taxes enough to pay for any significant degree of income redistribution (Peterson, 1981). The inadequacy of the revenue base constrains local officials from pursuing some policies—for example, tax increases—that might discourage businesses from locating in the jurisdiction;

indeed, attracting jobs to the local area is often considered the chief criterion of success for local officials. To the extent that black officials must heed such realities, black constituents may begin to fear cooption and reduced accountability on the part of black officials.

Black local officials must bargain not only with the private sector, they must also bargain with other public officials who often have access to a far superior revenue base. For example, state governments play a major role in welfare expenditures; the federal government is the primary source of funds for public housing; and most major redevelopment projects come about as a result of matching funds or tax subsidies from the federal government. Thus, the need to obtain resources constrains local black officials and requires accommodation with actors and interests independent of the black community. This complex of pressures gave rise to the seeming paradox by the early 1980s of increasingly conservative fiscal policies at the municipal level at a time when black electoral representation was surging in major cities across the country (Clark and Ferguson, 1983:144).

The clearest impact of black representation is on hiring and appointment policies in municipal governments. Having a black mayor increases both the black share of the municipal work force and the level of positions to which blacks are appointed (Eisinger, 1982; Moss, 1986). These changes are sometimes quite dramatic after the election of a black mayor. Between 1973 and 1980, for example, the black share of administrators rose from 13 to 35 percent in Atlanta and from 12 to 41 percent in Detroit (Eisinger, 1984:252).

It is almost universally believed that black representation improves the delivery of city services (such as police and fire protection, trash collection, schools, and road repair) in black neighborhoods, but most of the evidence is qualitative in nature (e.g., Keech, 1968; Lawson, 1976; Price, 1957; Wirt, 1970). Similarly, police harassment of blacks and the use of deadly force are believed to decline when black representation on the police force goes up. Several cities have seen large increases in the percentage of black police officers after a black mayor is elected (see Chapter 9).

In terms of municipal policy expenditures, black representation clearly results in increased spending on health care (Gruber, 1979; Peterson, 1981). Another study found that cities with black mayors and black city council representation spend more on health, housing, and education, although the findings were weak and somewhat inconsistent (Karnig and Welch, 1980:Ch. 6). A third study modeled the process underlying spending increases by city governments and found the critical link to be the presence of a strong mayor supportive of social programs. The presence of a sizable black electorate, and the level of black political activity, predicted the presence of such a mayor, but they were not independently associated with the spending outcomes (Clark and Ferguson, 1983:Ch. 5).

There is also considerable evidence from case studies that black mayors place a high priority on municipal contracting with minority firms (Kilson, 1987). The promotion of black-owned businesses was seen as "very important" by 86 percent of black elected officials, and 71 percent considered it "very important" to encourage the hiring of black corporate managers in white-owned businesses (Conyers and Wallace, 1976:28). This emphasis on black entrepreneurial opportunities is not without its detractors. Rich (1982:217) complained: "The new patronage system is a spoils system for the middle and upper classes. The benefits of the new system are not available to the working class." Noting this tension, Kilson (1987:111) predicted that the question of whether to emphasize opportunities for black professionals or more broadly based redistributive policies "will in time become a central focus of political contest in black politics." He also considered the development of a strong black economic base to be an essential ingredient for the growth of black political power (see also Hamilton, 1976).

Overall, fiscal and political constraints make large-scale spending programs unlikely at the local level. Black representation at the municipal level seems to have the greatest leverage over delivery of basic city services, which can improve the quality of life of black constituents in very straightforward (and relatively noncontroversial) ways. The major share of the benefits from black local governance may have helped produce the new black middle class through government employment opportunities and minority contracting. This is not a new pattern—it has been commonly observed among white ethnic groups as they made their first breakthroughs in local governance (Kilson, 1987; Wolfinger, 1973:Ch.3). To extend the benefits of the election of black officials more fully to black working-class people, Kilson (1987:131–132) saw a need for black political leaders to deal with three major problems: crime, public education, and housing.

Coalition activity has aided blacks and other minorities when congruent interests and preferences make it possible. A study of 10 cities in northern California found that black representation per se was not clearly related to policy outcomes; the critical factor was black participation in majority governing coalitions with white liberals and Hispanics on city councils. In cities with this feature of black and Hispanic "incorporation," there was serious consideration or adoption of policies favored by minorities with regard to police-civilian review boards, minority contracting, and minority hiring by city governments (Browning et al., 1984:Chs. 4–5).

The most fiscally healthy level of government—the states—is also the level at which blacks have tended to be least successful in exerting political influence. The southern states, where half of the black population resides, continue to spend the least on education and other basic social services. The election of black state legislators, and the expansion of statewide black lobbying efforts, is likely to be an increasingly important arena for black politics. Such a focus implies close attention to the redistricting and reapportionment to take place after the 1990 census.

THE FEDERAL POLICY PROCESS

It was not possible here to study comprehensively the entire range of federal policy. Rather, we have singled out four areas—foreign policy, antipoverty policy, minority business enterprises, and tax reform—for a brief examination in terms of recent black participation.

Foreign Policy

Concerns of the black population have traditionally been considered minimally important or excluded altogether from the realm of foreign and military affairs. Blacks were thought to exhibit little awareness of or desire to participate in foreign policy controversies (Hero, 1969; Morris, 1972). There has been a marked change in recent years. As Jackson (1987:2–3) noted:

> Blacks' growing interest and involvement in U.S. foreign policy—as political activists, diplomats, and especially as lobbyists—constitutes one of the genuinely new features of Afro-American development since 1940.

Blacks have sought to influence U.S. policy on Africa in much the same way that Jews have sought to influence policy toward Israel and Americans of Irish, Greek, and East European descent have tried to influence policy toward the areas of their interest. The three major objectives of black participation in foreign policy since 1940 have remained consistent: first, support for the national self-determination of African peoples; second, material assistance for the economic development of independent African nations; and third, a specific manifestation of the other two, elimination of the apartheid system in South Africa (Jackson, 1987:5–6).

One of the major policy breakthroughs for blacks during the 1980s has been the adoption of U.S. sanctions against South Africa. The success on this issue demonstrates the variety of avenues available for black political leverage in the face of a presidential administration that was strongly opposed to blacks' policy preferences. Success on this issue is all the more remarkable given the traditional latitude enjoyed by presidents in the conduct of foreign affairs. Blacks and their allies exerted pressure on four major fronts: during the 1984 presidential campaign, highlighting the significance of black participation in the Democratic coalition; in Congress, demonstrating the importance of senior black members; in city governments, which were responsive to the growing black electorate; and in grass roots activism.

The Reagan administration had pursued a policy of "constructive engagement" with the South African regime from 1981 to 1985. This policy became increasingly controversial as protests against apartheid escalated in South Africa and a state of martial law was declared. TransAfrica (see Chapter 4) had been laying the groundwork for congressional legislation with several years of lobbying after its success in persuading the Carter administration and Congress to support sanctions against Rhodesia (now Zimbabwe). The sanctions issue was given a major boost by Jesse Jackson's 1984 presidential campaign, which elevated support of sanctions to the status of mainstream Democratic party policy. The "Free South Africa" coalition, with its protests outside the South African embassy in Washington beginning in late

1984, also catalyzed grass roots activism at colleges and in cities throughout the country.

In recent years, there have been the congressional overrides of President Reagan's veto of sanctions and a rise of divestiture of South African-related holdings by government pension funds and university endowments. Several major corporations left South Africa in 1986 and 1987, partly because city governments have responded to lobbying by refusing to do business with firms that have a presence in South Africa. This exodus may accelerate as a result of the federal budget package passed in late 1987, which increased taxes on American corporate subsidiaries remaining in South Africa. The influence of black Congressman Charles Rangel of the Ways and Means Committee in the House-Senate budget conference was a crucial factor in securing the adoption of this measure. However, some observers believe that the antiapartheid campaign is beginning to suffer from the "lack of a popular post-sanctions agenda" (Jackson, 1987:32) and the dissipation of the movement's base of college students, clergy, and trade unions following the rapid initial victories on divestiture and imposition of sanctions.

Antipoverty Policy

Blacks have been stalwart members of a broad-based coalition to alleviate poverty through redistributive policies since the Great Depression. The federal government began to address the problems of poverty during the New Deal period and greatly expanded its activity in this sphere during the Great Society of the Kennedy-Johnson years (1961–1968). Today, there remains considerable controversy over the nature of this commitment as well as its scope.

Poverty is not merely an economic problem, but also a political problem related to the distribution of society's goods and resources by the public and private sectors. Given the widespread American belief in free enterprise, the private sector is expected to be the primary creator of jobs. Blacks advocated full employment as being preferable to relief during the New Deal, and recently that tradition was reflected in black support for the Humphrey-Hawkins bill mandating a federal full-employment policy (an ineffectual version of which became law in 1977; Hamilton and Hamilton [1986]).

In reviewing the public dialogue over antipoverty policy since the early 1960s, there is a striking continuity in the terms of the political debate. Three major problems have been continually addressed: structural unemployment (that is long-term job loss due to the disappearance of job categories, in contrast to the fluctuations of the business cycle); the inadequacy of public schooling; and the fear of creating poverty dependency or a permanent welfare class.

Four major kinds of social spending programs have been designed to alleviate poverty: social insurance, such as Social Security and Medicare; means-tested cash assistance, such as Aid to Families with Dependent Children (AFDC); means-tested in-kind benefits, such as food stamps; and human capital development programs, such as Head Start and the Job Corps. Social insurance payments have shown steady growth, with Medicare in particular showing dramatic increases since the mid-1970s. Means-tested cash assistance has declined in real terms since about 1970; for example, the inflation-adjusted level of AFDC benefits declined by 30 percent between 1972 and 1986 (see Chapter 6). However, this decline has been partly counteracted by an increase in the provision of in-kind benefits during the same time span. Because job training and other human capital benefits are not legally defined as entitlements, spending for them appears to be the most sensitive to the prevailing political climate. They were supported by most presidential administrations from 1961 until 1980 and then sharply reduced under President Reagan (Burtless, 1986; Ellwood and Summers, 1986).

There is a difficult trade-off between the political popularity of specific programs and their efficiency in alleviating poverty. Simply put, the most popular programs—the social insurance programs—are the most broadly based, the most expensive, and the least effectively targeted toward the poor. They are popular not merely because of their universal coverage, which diminishes the appearance of income redistribution, but also because they tap into a widely shared American core value: a sense of entitlement earned through personal contributions in the form of payroll taxes by employed workers.

The human capital programs—which take the form of education and job training—have enjoyed considerable support. The Head Start program is highly regarded by most policy experts as well as the public, and the Job Corps has also enjoyed some success. With these exceptions, the targeted education and training programs have been quite controversial, and at least one (the Comprehensive Employment and Training Act, CETA) became a favorite target of negative anecdotes about government scandal and inefficiency before it was terminated in 1981.

The most efficient programs for alleviating poverty, the means-tested transfer programs, are the least popular, probably because many people believe they violate core values about aiding the "undeserving poor." There is also the political problem posed by the programs' clientele: although most AFDC and food stamp recipients are white, a disproportionate percentage of blacks are recipients and have become a target of resentment for many taxpayers.

The antipoverty programs have relied on a politically fragile base of support. With the exception of the protest activity of the National Welfare Rights Organization in the early 1970s, and sporadic activities in various cities, there has been little organized grass roots demand for antipoverty programs from the recipients or potential recipients. This passivity is partly a function of the somewhat adversarial relationship between many clients and their local service bureaucracies; partly because the recipients have many socioeconomic characteristics that generally are associated with low levels of political participation and involvement; and partly due to the ambivalence many clients feel about welfare dependency, which makes many recipients less enthusiastic advocates for their programs than, say, Social Security beneficiaries.

As a consequence, the traditional "iron triangle" relationship of lobbyists, congressional committees, and federal bureaucracies has never flourished for antipoverty policy. A 1986 National Election Studies survey found 61 percent of whites and 49 percent of blacks agreeing that most recipients of public assistance could get along without it. Program advocacy has been dominated by organizations of social workers and networks of policy specialists in universities, think tanks, foundations, federal agencies, and the White House. Lacking a potent electoral base, the programs have attracted relatively little consistent congressional support (other than from the Congressional Black Caucus), leaving them highly vulnerable to reductions (Heclo, 1987; Levitan, 1969). The one major exception to this pattern is the Food Stamp program, which was enacted at the behest of farm-state senators George McGovern of South Dakota and Bob Dole of Kansas and has continued to enjoy strong support from a bipartisan bloc of big-city and rural members of Congress.

Minority Business Policy

Minority business enterprises have had more support within the political system than have the broad antipoverty programs. The early lodging of these activities in the Small Business Administration (SBA), a relatively popular agency, and the accession of a black chair of the House Small Business Committee (Parren Mitchell of Maryland) may have enhanced their ability to survive continuing controversy. While minority entrepreneurs are far less numerous and less affluent than their white competitors, they nonetheless contribute to the political support necessary to keep the program alive. To the extent that logrolling is involved in the passage of small business appropriations, minorities have enjoyed some bargaining leverage in the preservation of the targeted programs.

The impetus for the federal initiative in this area appears to have come from the National Urban League. Whitney Young, then the league's executive director, made black business opportunity a centerpiece of his "Marshall Plan for the cities" proposal in 1963. Shortly afterward, the federal government's small business activities were expanded to target minorities for the first time as part of the Johnson administration's "War on Poverty." As for other parts of the antipoverty effort, there appears to have been little congressional pressure or influence responsible for this innovation; White House staffers apparently devised the program on their own. The Economic Opportunity Loan Program was housed in the newly created Office of Economic Opportunity (OEO) in late 1964, and it targeted loans at businesses involved in hiring the socially disadvantaged, with particular emphasis on minority entrepreneurs. This program was transferred to the SBA in 1966, and the Minority Enterprise Small Business Investment Company (MESBIC) program was initiated the same year.

Expressing concern about the wave of civil disturbances in 1967, the Southern Leadership Conference proposed an increased federal role in stimulating the growth of black business. President Johnson responded with the test cities program, which directed the SBA to obtain contracts from federal agencies and subcontract them on a noncompetitive basis to firms that hired unemployed and underemployed workers. However, the contracts were not explicitly reserved for minority-owned firms.

To distinguish its program from what was termed the failure of the War on Poverty, the Nixon administration wished to devise an alternative to direct government hiring and training of minorities. Thus, federal policy became oriented toward fostering "black capitalism," and the early 1970s witnessed the most rapid expansion of the minority enterprise program (Bates, 1986). Through executive orders in 1969 and 1970, Nixon established the Office of Minority Business Enterprise (OMBE) and assigned it to the SBA. Unlike many of the antipoverty efforts that were abandoned when Nixon dismantled OEO, the minority enterprise program thereby became associated with an agency that enjoyed considerable support in Congress.

White owners of small businesses began to complain that the minority enterprise programs gave an unfair advantage to their minority competitors and lobbied to restrict the programs. Many minority enterprises, it was charged, were little more than white-owned and managed "front" firms with token black representation. Media exposés and congressional hearings brought to light accusations of fraud and mismanagement. Responding to these criticisms, the SBA suspended awards under the program in 1977 pending a comprehensive review.

At that time Congressman Parren Mitchell was emerging as a major force on the House Small Business Committee. Under his initiative, Congress passed a requirement in 1977 that 10 percent of federal contracts under that year's Local Public Works Act be set aside for minority business enterprises. The following year, a provision (Section 8[d]4) was added to the Small Business Act that requires all companies bidding on federal contracts of $1 million or more to submit a plan for subcontracting to small businesses owned by individuals from disadvantaged groups ("set-asides"); failure to submit such a plan automatically disqualifies the bid. This requirement vastly expanded the universe of federal contract work for which minority enterprises could successfully compete. In 1979, OMBE was replaced by the Minority Business Development Administration (MBDA), which provides management services and technical assistance to program participants.

A law passed in 1980 directed SBA to establish a system of "graduating" successful minority enterprises from the set-aside program after a certain period of participation. The program's advocates have generally opposed graduation provisions on the grounds that very few minority firms are economically viable without the set-asides. The Reagan administration attempted to emphasize the graduation process, but those attempts were opposed by Congress. Although the program remains controversial, its utility as a means of generating political support from black entrepreneurs is sufficiently plain to politicians of both parties that it is likely to survive for the foreseeable future.[4]

Tax Reform

The tax reform enacted by Congress in 1986 offers a different example of black policy activities. The basic fight was between the business lobbyists trying to retain specific tax "loopholes," and an improbable coalition of supply-side conservatives and liberal policy analysts who applauded the principles of lower marginal tax rates and the elimination of tax distortions in investment decisions (Birnbaum and Murray, 1987), but there were also important black interests at stake in the battle. Different black leaders reached opposing conclusions as to where those interests lay.

Two of the most influential black congressmen—Charles Rangel of Harlem and Parren Mitchell of Baltimore—played important roles on opposite sides of the debate. Rangel, one of the senior members of the House Ways and Means Committee, was one of the earliest and most vocal supporters of the concept of tax reform. Because many of his inner-city constituents depend on subsidized housing, he was instrumental in the inclusion of more advantageous depreciation rules for low-income housing in the House version of the bill (Rosenbaum, 1985), although this provision was deleted in the final legislation. But Rangel considered the main issue to be an opportunity to remove many lower income individuals from the federal tax rolls altogether through increasing the personal exemption and standard deduction. John E. Chapoton, then assistant secretary of the treasury, credited Rangel with persuading the Reagan administration that adjusting the earned income tax credit for inflation would make the bill more equitable and would improve its political prospects as well (Engelberg, 1985). The final version of the legislation incorporated these changes.

For Parren Mitchell, the benefit of reduced taxes was offset by the lower marginal rates on higher income taxpayers. The maximum effective rate in the final legislation was 33 percent, in contrast to the 50 percent rate prior to the 1986 reform. Mitchell reasoned that the difficulty in raising marginal rates in the future would make it impossible to fund major social spending programs, thus vitiating the ability of the public sector to meet the needs of the poor.

Each argument was credible among both black leaders and constituents. Black interest groups were generally not very active on either side of the issue, although some did testify in support of maintaining tax breaks for individual items deemed beneficial to blacks or those that would help governments serving black population centers (such as the deductibility of state and local taxes). In the final House vote on September 25, 1986, the

---

4. However, many observers believe that the Supreme Court's decision in *City of Richmond* v. *J. A. Croson Company* (Case 87-998, decided January 23, 1989) will place new limitations on the ability of local governments to operate minority business set-aside programs.

members of the Congressional Black Caucus voted in favor of the bill by a margin of 12 to 6.

SUMMARY

Black Americans did not seek their civil rights merely to enjoy equality on the basis of abstract principles of civic inclusion (see Barker, 1983). They sought those rights because they believed that direct access to political institutions and decision making through voting and increased elective representation would lead to greater equality between blacks and whites. In terms of civil status this belief has been generally realized.

There has been great improvement in blacks' civil status since 1940. Arbitrary harassment and intimidation of blacks by legal authorities, "hate" groups, and unorganized private citizens are much less prevalent than prior to World War II, and incidents today are usually publicized and investigated, rather than ignored. Equal access to public accommodations is generally accepted as a formal right throughout the country, in stark contrast to the legislated segregation that was nearly universal in the South until the 1960s. Enforcement of black contractual rights to rent and purchase housing remains ineffectual.

The democratic status of blacks has also seen dramatic change since 1940. Black voter participation in the South has risen from the negligible levels of the prewar period to a contemporary level that exceeds that of whites of similar socioeconomic status. As a result, the number of black elected officials in the United States rose from a few dozen in 1940 to more than 6,800 in 1988. The number of black public administrators and judges has shown comparable increases. Nevertheless, blacks comprise only 1.5 percent of America's elected officials.

Changes in black allocational status, although complex, have not led to equality with whites at levels commensurate to that achieved in civil status. Many of the changes stem from the evolution of the economy and the educational system (see Chapters 6 and 7), but political determinants have been important as well. The extensive development of equal opportunity law has improved the status of blacks (as well as that of women and other minorities) in education, employment, and business enterprises. Although blacks are disproportionately in the lower income brackets, they have also benefited from the extension of job training, health care, Social Security, and other cash and in-kind benefit programs provided by the public sector.

In Chapters 6–10 we discuss changes in blacks' allocational status in several specific areas. In each of those chapters it is clear that black political participation has been an important factor in the post-1940 determination of blacks' status. Equal access to schools, jobs, and medical facilities have frequently come to blacks only through political pressure on courts and legislatures. Yet it is also clear that increased civil and democratic status has not led to equal allocational status.

REFERENCES

Bain, Richard C., and Judith H. Parris
1973   *Convention Decisions and Voting Records.* 2d ed. Washington, D.C.: Brookings Institution.

Banfield, Edward C., and James Q. Wilson
1963   *City Politics.* New York: Vintage Books.

Barker, Lucius J.
1983   Black Americans and the politics of inclusion. *PS* 16(Summer):500–507.

Bates, Timothy
1986   Paper prepared for the Committee on the Status of Black Americans, National Research Council, Washington, D.C.

Bell, Derrick A., Jr.
1980   *Race, Racism, and American Law.* 2d ed. Boston: Little, Brown.
1986a   The Gyroscopic Effect in American Racial Reform: The Law and Race from 1940 to 1986. Paper prepared for the Committee on the Status of Black Americans, National Research Council, Washington, D.C.
1986b   Memorandum to the Committee on the Status of Black Americans, National Research Council, Washington, D.C.

Birnbaum, Jeffrey H., and Alan S. Murray
1987   *Showdown at Gucci Gulch: Lawmakers, Lobbyists, and the Unlikely Triumph of Tax Reform.* New York: Random House.

Bloom, Jack M.
1987   *Class, Race, and the Civil Rights Movement.* Bloomington: Indiana University Press.

Bracey, John H., Jr.
1971   Black nationalism since Garvey. Pp. 259–279 in Nathan I. Huggins, Martin Kilson, and Daniel M. Fox, eds., *Key Issues in the Afro-American Experience.* Vol. 2. New York: Harcourt Brace Jovanovich.

Brimmer, Andrew J.
1985   Black directors in the corporate boardroom. *Black Enterprise* (December):41.

Brisbane, Robert H.
1970   *The Black Vanguard: Origins of the Negro Social Revolution, 1900–1960.* Valley Forge, Pa.: Judson Press.

Browning, Rufus P., Dale Rogers Marshall, and David H. Tabb
1984   *Protest Is Not Enough: The Struggle of Blacks and Hispanics for Equality in Urban Politics.* Berkeley: University of California Press.

Burstein, Paul
1985   *Discrimination, Jobs, and Politics: The Struggle for Equal Employment Opportunity in the United States Since the New Deal.* Chicago: University of Chicago Press.

Burtless, Gary
1986   Public spending for the poor: trends, prospects, and economic limits. Ch. 2 in Sheldon H. Danziger and Daniel H. Weinberg, eds., *Fighting Poverty: What Works and What Doesn't.* Cambridge, Mass.: Harvard University Press.

Cain, Bruce E., John A. Ferejohn, and Morris P. Fiorina
1987   *The Personal Vote: Constituency Service and Electoral Independence.* Cambridge, Mass.: Harvard University Press.

Cain, Bruce E., and D. Roderick Kiewiet
  1986 *Minorities in California*. Pasadena: California Institute of Technology.
Campbell, Angus
  1966 The meaning of the election. In Milton C. Cummings, ed., *The National Elections of 1964*. Washington, D.C.: Brookings Institution.
Campbell, Angus, Philip E. Converse, Warren E. Miller, and Donald E. Stokes
  1960 *The American Voter*. New York: John Wiley & Sons.
Carmichael, Stokely, and Charles V. Hamilton
  1967 *Black Power: The Politics of Liberation in America*. New York: Vintage Books.
Carson, Clayborne
  1986 Paper prepared for the Committee on the Status of Black Americans, National Research Council, Washington, D.C.
Cavanagh, Thomas E.
  1984 *The Impact of the Black Electorate*. Washington, D.C.: Joint Center for Political Studies.
  1985 *Inside Black America: The Message of the Black Vote in the 1984 Elections*. Washington, D.C.: Joint Center for Political Studies.
Cavanagh, Thomas E., ed.
  1987 Manuscript prepared for the Panel on Political Participation, Committee on the Status of Black Americans, National Research Council, Washington, D.C.
Clark, Terry Nichols, and Lorna Crowley Ferguson
  1983 *City Money: Political Processes, Fiscal Strain, and Retrenchment*. New York: Columbia University Press.
Colby, David C.
  1982 A test of the relative efficacy of political tactics. *American Journal of Political Science* 26(4)[November]:741–753.
  1984 The Voting Rights Act and Black Registration in Mississippi. Paper delivered at the annual meeting of the Midwest Political Science Association, Chicago.
Cole, Leonard A.
  1976 *Blacks in Power: A Comparative Study of Black and White Elected Officials*. Princeton, N.J.: Princeton University Press.
Converse, Philip E.
  1972 Change in the American electorate. Ch. 8 in Angus Campbell and Philip E. Converse, eds., *The Human Meaning of Social Change*. New York: Russell Sage Foundation.
Conyers, James E., and Walter L. Wallace
  1976 *Black Elected Officials: A Study of Black Americans Holding Governmental Office*. New York: Russell Sage Foundation.
Crockett, George W., Jr., Russell R. DeBow, and Larry C. Berkson, eds.
  1980 *National Roster of Black Judicial Officers: 1980*. Chicago: American Judicature Society.
Cruse, Harold
  1967 *The Crisis of the Negro Intellectual*. New York: William Morrow.
Curvin, Robert
  1975 The Persistent Minority: The Black Political Experience in Newark. Ph.D. dissertation, Department of Political Science, Princeton University.
Danigelis, Nicholas L.
  1978 Black political participation in the United States: some recent evidence. *American Sociological Review* 43(October):756–771.
Danzig, David
  1964 The meaning of Negro strategy. *Commentary* 37(February):41–46.

Davidson, Chandler, and George Korbel
1981 At-large elections and minority-group representation: a re-examination of historical and contemporary evidence. *Journal of Politics* 43(November):982–1005.
Days, Drew S., III
1984 Turning back the clock: the Reagan administration and civil rights. *Harvard Civil
Rights-Civil Liberties Law Review* 19(Summer):309–347.
Draper, Theodore
1970 *The Rediscovery of Black Nationalism.* New York: Viking Press.
Ebony
1965 States boast record number of Negro lawmakers. 20(April):191–197.
1966 *The Negro Handbook.* Chicago: Johnson Publishing Company.
Edds, Margaret
1987 *Free at Last: What Really Happened When Civil Rights Came to Southern Politics.*
Bethesda, Md.: Adler & Adler.
Eisinger, Peter K.
1982 Black employment in municipal jobs: the impact of black political power. *Ameri-
can Political Science Review* 76(June):380–392.
1984 Black mayors and the politics of racial economic advancement. In Harlan Hahn
and Charles Levine, eds., *Readings in Urban Politics: Past, Present and Future.* New
York: Longmans.
Ellwood, David T., and Lawrence H. Summers
1986 Poverty in America: is welfare the answer or the problem? Ch. 4 in Sheldon H.
Danziger and Daniel H. Weinberg, eds., *Fighting Poverty: What Works and What
Doesn't.* Cambridge, Mass.: Harvard University Press.
Engelberg, Stephen
1985 Rangel and his relationships. *The New York Times,* June 30.
Engstrom, Richard L., and Michael D. McDonald
1981 The election of blacks to city councils: clarifying the impact of electoral arrange-
ments on the seats/population relationship. *American Political Science Review* 75
(June):344–354.
Feldman, Stanley
1988 Structure and consistency in public opinion: the role of core beliefs and values.
American Journal of Political Science 32:416–440.
Fleming, Harold C.
1965 The federal executive and civil rights: 1961–1965. *Daedalus* 94(Fall):921–948.
Foster, Vera Chandler, and Robert D. Reid
1947 The Negro in politics. Pp. 258–291 in Jessie Parkhurst Guzman, ed., *Negro
Yearbook: A Review of Events Affecting Negro Life, 1941–1946.* Tuskegee, Ala.:
Tuskegee Institute.
Frank, Dana
1982 No Work, No Rent: Eviction Protests in the 1930s. Unpublished paper, Yale
University.
Freeman, Alan
1978 Legitimizing racial discrimination through antidiscrimination law: a critical re-
view of Supreme Court doctrine. *Minnesota Law Review* 62(6):1049–1120.
Frye, Hardy T.
1980 *Black Parties and Political Power: A Case Study.* Boston: G. K. Hall.
Garrow, David J.
1978 *Protest at Selma: Martin Luther King, Jr. and the Voting Rights Act of 1965.* New
Haven, Conn.: Yale University Press.
Genovese, Eugene
1974 *Roll, Jordan, Roll: The World the Slaves Made.* New York: Pantheon Books.

Gilliam, Frank
  1986   Black America: divided by class? *Public Opinion* (February/March):53–57.
Gilliam, Reginald E., Jr.
  1975   *Black Political Development: An Advocacy Analysis.* Port Washington, N.Y.: Kennikat Press.
Glaser, James M.
  1987   The Paradox of Black Participation and Other Observations on Black Activism, 1952–1984. Paper prepared for the Committee on the Status of Black Americans, National Research Council, Washington, D.C.
Gordon, Daniel
  1970   Immigrants and municipal voting turnout: implications for the changing ethnic impact on urban politics. *American Sociological Review* 35(August):665–681.
Green, Mark J.
  1975   *The Other Government: The Unseen Power of Washington Lawyers.* New York: Grossman.
Grubbs, Donald H.
  1971   *Cry from the Cotton: The Southern Tenant Farmers' Union and the New Deal.* Chapel Hill: University of North Carolina Press.
Gruber, Judith
  1979   Political Strength and Policy Responsiveness: The Results of Electing Blacks to City Councils. Unpublished manuscript. Department of Political Science, University of California, Berkeley.
Gurin, Patricia, Shirley Hatchett, and James S. Jackson
  1988   *Hope and Independence: Blacks' Struggle in Two Party Politics.* New York: Russell Sage Foundation.
Guzman, Jessie Parkhurst
  1947   *Negro Yearbook.* Tuskegee, Ala.: Tuskegee Institute.
  1952   *Negro Yearbook.* New York: William H. Wise.
Hagen, Michael G.
  1988a Blacks and Liberalism. Paper prepared for the Committee on the Status of Black Americans, National Research Council, Washington, D.C.
  1988b Racial Differences in Voter Registration and Turnout. Paper prepared for the Committee on the Status of Black Americans, National Research Council, Washington, D.C.
  1989   The Salience of Racial and Social Welfare Issues. Unpublished paper, State Data Program, University of California at Berkeley.
Hamilton, Charles V.
  1976   Public policy and some political consequences. Ch. 8 in Marguerite Ross Barnett and James A. Hefner, eds., *Public Policy for the Black Community.* New York: Alfred Publishing.
  1977   Voter registration drives and turnout: a report on the Harlem electorate. *Political Science Quarterly* 92(Spring):43–46.
  1981   On black leadership. Pp. 239–265 in James D. Williams, eds., *The State of Black America, 1981.* Washington, D.C.: National Urban League.
  1982   Foreword. In Michael B. Preston, Lenneal J. Henderson, Jr., and Paul Puryear, eds., *The New Black Politics: The Search for Political Power.* New York: Longman.
  1986   Social policy and the welfare of black Americans: from rights to resources. *Political Science Quarterly* 101(2):239–255.
Hamilton, Charles V., and Dona C. Hamilton
  1986   Social policies, civil rights, and poverty. Ch. 12 in Sheldon H. Danziger and Daniel H. Weinberg, eds., *Fighting Poverty: What Works and What Doesn't.* Cambridge, Mass.: Harvard University Press.

Hammond, John L.
1977   Race and electoral mobilization: white southerners, 1952–1968. *Public Opinion Quarterly* 41(Spring):13–27.
Hanks, Lawrence J.
1986   Black Voter Mobilization Since 1960. Paper prepared for the Committee on the Status of Black Americans, National Research Council, Washington, D.C.
Harris, William
1982   *The Harder We Run*. New York: Oxford University Press.
Heclo, Hugh D.
1987   The political foundations of antipoverty policy. Ch. 13 in Sheldon H. Danziger and Daniel H. Weinberg, eds., *Fighting Poverty: What Works and What Doesn't*. Cambridge, Mass.: Harvard University Press.
Heilig, Peggy, and Robert J. Mundt
1983   Changes in representational equity: the effect of adopting districts. *Social Science Quarterly* 64(June):393–397.
Henry, M. L., Jr., et al.
1985   *The Success of Women and Minorities in Achieving Judicial Office: The Selection Process*. New York: Fund for Modern Cities.
Hero, Alfred O.
1969   American Negroes and United States foreign policy, 1937–1967. *Journal of Conflict Resolution* 13(June):220–251.
Holden, Matthew, Jr.
1973   *The Politics of the Black 'Nation.'* New York: Chandler.
Huber, Joan, and William H. Form
1973   *Income and Ideology*. New York: Free Press.
Jackson, Henry F.
1987   The Role of Black Americans in U.S. Foreign Policy: Search for New Power. Paper prepared for the Committee on the Status of Black Americans, National Research Council, Washington, D.C.
Jaynes, Gerald David
1986   *Branches Without Roots: Genesis of the Black Working Class in the American South, 1862–1882*. New York: Oxford University Press.
Joint Center for Political Studies
1984a   *Blacks and the 1984 Democratic National Convention: A Guide*. Washington, D.C.: Joint Center for Political Studies.
1984b   *Blacks and the 1984 Republican National Convention: A Guide*. Washington, D.C.: Joint Center for Political Studies.
1985   *Black Elected Officials: A National Roster*. Washington, D.C.: Joint Center for Political Studies.
1986   *Elected and Appointed Black Judges in the United States*. Washington, D.C.: Joint Center for Political Studies.
Jones, Clinton B.
1976   The impact of local election systems on black political representation. *Urban Affairs Quarterly* 11(March):345–356.
Jones, Mack H.
1976   Black officeholding and political development in the rural South. *Review of Black Political Economy* 6(Summer):375–407.
1978   Black political empowerment in Atlanta: myth and reality. *Annals* 439(September):90–117.
Karnig, Albert K.
1976   Black representation on city councils: the impact of district elections and socioeconomic factors. *Urban Affairs Quarterly* 12(December):223–242.

Karnig, Albert K., and Susan Welch
1980 *Black Representation and Urban Policy*. Chicago: University of Chicago Press.
1982 Electoral structure and black representation on city councils. *Social Science Quarterly* 63(March):99–114.

Keech, William R.
1968 *The Impact of Negro Voting: The Role of the Vote in the Quest for Equality*. Chicago: Rand McNally.

Kendrick, Ann
1986 The Dynamics of Black Electoral Participation. Paper prepared for the Committee on the Status of Black Americans, National Research Council, Washington, D.C.
1988 The Core Economic Beliefs of Blacks and Whites. Paper prepared for the Committee on the Status of Black Americans, National Research Council, Washington, D.C.

Key, V. O., Jr.
1949 *Southern Politics*. New York: Alfred A. Knopf.

Kilson, Martin
1987 Report on Black Politics in Comparative Perspective—A Study in the Politics of Inclusion. Paper prepared for the Committee on the Status of Black Americans, National Research Council, Washington, D.C.

Kinder, Donald R.
1983 Diversity and complexity in American public opinion. In Ada W. Finifter, ed., *Political Science: The State of the Discipline*. Washington, D.C.: American Political Science Association.

King, Martin Luther, Jr.
1964 *Why We Can't Wait*. New York: Mentor.

Kleppner, Paul
1982 *Who Voted? The Dynamics of Electoral Turnout, 1870–1980*. New York: Praeger.

Kluger, Richard
1976 *Simple Justice: The History of Brown v. Board of Education and Black America's Struggle for Equality*. New York: Alfred A. Knopf.

Korn/Ferry International
1987 *Korn/Ferry International's Executive Profile: A Survey of Corporate Leaders in the Eighties*. New York: Korn/Ferry International.

Kruman, Marc W.
1975 Quotas for blacks: the Public Works Administration and the black construction worker. *Labor History* 16(Winter):37–51.

Lane, Robert E.
1986 Market justice, political justice. *American Political Science Review* 80(June):383–402.

Laney, Garrine P.
1986 The Evolution of Equal Employment Opportunity Programs, 1940–1985. Paper prepared for the Committee on the Status of Black Americans, National Research Council, Washington, D.C.

Latimer, Margaret K.
1979 Black political representation in southern cities: election systems and other causal variables. *Urban Affairs Quarterly* 15(September):65–86.

Lawson, Steven F.
1976 *Black Ballots: Voting Rights in the South, 1944–1969*. New York: Columbia University Press.

Levitan, Sar A.
  1969 *The Great Society's Poor Law: A New Approach to Poverty.* Baltimore, Md.: Johns Hopkins University Press.
Lipsky, Michael
  1968 Protest as a political resource. *American Political Science Review* 62(December):1144–1158.
Marcus, Ruth
  1986 For black lawyers, path to top is slow. *Washington Post* November 16:A1, A12–A13.
Marshall, T. H.
  1964 *Class, Citizenship, and Social Development.* Garden City, N.Y.: Doubleday.
Marx, Gary T.
  1967 *Protest and Prejudice: A Study of Belief in the Black Community.* New York: Harper & Row.
Matthews, Donald R., and James W. Prothro
  1963 Political factors and Negro voter registration in the South. *American Political Science Review* 57(June):355–367.
McAdam, Doug
  1982 *Political Process and the Development of Black Insurgency, 1930–1970.* Chicago: University of Chicago Press.
Meier, August, and Elliott Rudwick
  1976 The origins of nonviolent direct action in Afro-American protest: a note on historical discontinuities. Ch. 14 in August Meier and Elliott Rudwick, eds., *Along the Color Line: Explorations in the Black Experience.* Urbana: University of Illinois Press.
Miller, Arthur, Patricia Gurin, Gerald Gurin, and Oksana Malanchuk
  1981 Group consciousness and political participation. *American Journal of Political Science* 25:494–511.
Morris, Aldon D.
  1984 *The Origins of the Civil Rights Movement: Black Communities Organizing for Change.* New York: Free Press.
Morris, Lorenzo, and Charles Henry
  1978 *The Chitlin' Controversy: Race and Public Policy in America.* Lanham, Md.: University Press of America.
Morris, Milton D.
  1972 Black Americans and the foreign policy process: the case of Africa. *Western Political Science Quarterly* 25(September):451–463.
Moss, Philip I.
  1986 Changing Public Sector Employment and the Occupational Advancement of Blacks, Women, and Hispanics. Paper prepared for the Committee on the Status of Black Americans, National Research Council, Washington, D.C.
Murray, Florence, ed.
  1947 *Negro Handbook, 1946–1947.* New York: Current Books.
Nelson, William E., Jr.
  1978 Black mayors as urban managers. *Annals* 439(September):53–67.
  1982 Cleveland: the rise and fall of the new black politics. Ch. 8 in Michael B. Preston, Lenneal J. Henderson, Jr., and Paul Puryear, eds., *The New Black Politics: The Search for Political Power.* New York: Longman.
  1987 The Role of the Black Church in Politics. Paper prepared for the Committee on the Status of Black Americans, National Research Council, Washington, D.C.

Newburger, Harriet B.
  1988 The Impact of Federal Housing Programs on Black Americans. Paper prepared for
       the Committee on the Status of Black Americans, National Research Council,
       Washington, D.C.
Nie, Norman H., Sidney Verba, and John R. Petrocik
  1976 *The Changing American Voter.* Cambridge, Mass.: Harvard University Press.
O'Hare, William
  1986 Racial composition of jurisdictions and the election of black candidates. *Population
       Today* 14(June):6–8.
Parsons, Talcott
  1965 Full citizenship for the Negro American? A sociological problem. *Daedalus*
       94(Fall):1009–1054.
Peterson, Paul E.
  1981 *City Limits.* Chicago: University of Chicago Press.
Pettigrew, Thomas F.
  1976 Black mayoral campaigns. Pp. 14–29 in Herrington J. Bryce, ed., *Urban Gover-
       nance and Minorities.* New York: Praeger.
Pinderhughes, Dianne M.
  1986 Political choices: a realignment in partisanship among black voters? Pp. 85–113 in
       The State of Black America, 1986. Washington, D.C.: National Urban League.
Pinkney, Alphonso
  1984 *The Myth of Black Progress.* Cambridge, England: Cambridge University Press.
Pomper, Gerald
  1966 Ethnic voting in nonpartisan municipal elections. *Public Opinion Quarterly*
       30(Spring):79–97.
Preston, Michael B.
  1976 Limitations of black urban power: the case of black mayors. Ch. 5 in Louis H.
       Masotti and Robert L. Lineberry, eds., *The New Urban Politics.* Cambridge, Mass.:
       Ballinger.
  1984 The resurgence of black voting in Chicago. Ch. 3 in Melvin G. Holli and Paul M.
       Green, eds., *The Making of the Mayor: Chicago, 1983.* Grand Rapids, Mich.:
       William B. Eerdmans.
Price, Hugh D.
  1957 *The Negro and Southern Politics.* New York: New York University Press.
Reed, Adolph L., Jr.
  1986 *The Jesse Jackson Phenomenon: The Crisis of Purpose in Afro-American Politics.* New
       Haven, Conn.: Yale University Press.
Reed, John Shelton, and Merle Black
  1985 How southerners gave up Jim Crow. *New Perspectives* 17(Fall):15–19.
Rich, Wilbur C.
  1982 The impact of public authorities on urban politics: challenges for black politicians
       and interest groups. Ch. 9 in Michael B. Preston, Lenneal J. Henderson, Jr., and
       Paul Puryear, eds., *The New Black Politics.* New York: Longman.
Rosenbaum, David E.
  1985 House panel votes to keep tax plan that aids housing. *The New York Times,*
       October 27.
Rustin, Bayard
  1965 From protest to politics: the future of the civil rights movement. *Commentary*
       39(February):25–31.
Sears, David O., and Donald R. Kinder
  1985 Whites' opposition to busing: on conceptualizing and operationalizing group
       conflict. *Journal of Personality and Social Psychology* 48(May):1141–1147.

Seltzer, Richard, and Robert C. Smith
1985 Race and ideology: a research note measuring liberalism and conservatism in black America. *Phylon* 46(June):98–105.

Shingles, Richard D.
1981 Black consciousness and political participation: the missing link. *American Political Science Review* 75(March):76–91.

Smith, Robert C.
1982 *Black Leadership: A Survey of Theory and Research*. Institute for Urban Affairs and Research. Washington, D.C.: Howard University.

Stanley, Harold M.
1987 *Voter Mobilization and the Politics of Race: The South and Universal Suffrage, 1952–1984*. New York: Praeger.

Stekler, Paul Jeffrey
1982 Black Politics in the New South: An Investigation of Change at Various Levels. Ph.D. dissertation, Department of Government, Harvard University.

Stille, Alexander
1985 Little room at the top for blacks, Hispanics. *National Law Journal* (Dec. 23).

Taebel, Delbert
1978 Minority representation on city councils: the impact of structure on blacks and Hispanics. *Social Science Quarterly* 59(June):142–152.

Thernstrom, Abigail M.
1987 *Whose Votes Count? Affirmative Action and Minority Voting Rights*. Cambridge, Mass.: Harvard University Press.

Toles, Edward B.
1970 Report of black lawyers and judges in the United States, 1960–1970. *Congressional Record* (Sept. 2):30786–30788.

U.S. Commission on Civil Rights
1961 *Voting*. Washington, D.C.: U.S. Government Printing Office.
1968 *Political Participation*. Washington, D.C.: U.S. Government Printing Office.

U.S. Equal Employment Opportunity Commission
1984 *A History of the Equal Employment Opportunity Commission, 1965–1984*. Washington, D.C.: U.S. Government Printing Office.
1986 *Minorities and Women in State and Local Government, 1974–1984*. Washington, D.C.: U.S. Government Printing Office.

Verba, Sidney, and Norman H. Nie
1973 *Participation in America: Political Democracy and Social Equality*. New York: Harper & Row.

Walters, Ronald W.
1988 *Black Presidential Politics in America: A Strategic Approach*. Albany, N.Y.: State University of New York Press.

Walton, Hanes, Jr.
1972 *Black Political Parties*. New York: Free Press.
1985 *Invisible Politics: Black Political Behavior*. Albany, N.Y.: State University of New York Press.

Weaver, Robert C.
1942 Federal aid, local control, and Negro participation. *Journal of Negro Education* 11(January):47–59.

Weaver, Warren, Jr.
1964 Democrats report record total of 280 Negroes in elective jobs. *New York Times*, December 23.

Weiss, Nancy J.
  1983 *Farewell to the Party of Lincoln: Black Politics in the Age of FDR.* Princeton, N.J.: Princeton University Press.
Williams, Eddie N.
  1987 The Republicans' image problem among blacks. *Focus* (November/December): 3–5.
Williams, Juan
  1987 *Eyes on the Prize.* New York: Viking.
Williams, Robin M., Jr.
  1970 *American Society.* 3d ed. New York: Alfred A. Knopf.
Wilson, James Q.
  1973 *Political Organizations.* New York: Basic Books.
Wilson, William Julius
  1978 *The Declining Significance of Race: Blacks and Changing American Institutions.* Chicago: University of Chicago Press.
Wirt, Frederick M.
  1970 *Politics of Southern Equality: Law and Social Change in a Mississippi County.* Chicago: Aldine.
Wolfinger, Raymond E.
  1973 *The Politics of Progress.* Englewood Cliffs, N.J.: Prentice-Hall.
  1988 Looking for Mr. Politicus. Pp. 109–122 in Ian Shapiro and Grant Reeher, eds., *Power, Inequality, and Democratic Politics.* Boulder, Colo., and London: Westview Press.
Wolfinger, Raymond E., and Steven J. Rosenstone
  1980 *Who Votes?* New Haven, Conn.: Yale University Press.
Woods, Daryl D.
  1987 The Chicago crusade. Ch. 2 in Thomas E. Cavanagh, ed., *Strategies for Mobilizing Black Voters.* Washington, D.C.: Joint Center for Political Studies.
Work, Monroe H.
  1937 *Negro Yearbook: An Annual Encyclopedia of the Negro, 1937–1938.* Tuskegee, Ala.: Negro Yearbook Publishing Co.
Wright, Gavin
  1986 *Old South, New South: Revolutions in the Southern Economy Since the Civil War.* New York: Basic Books.

6

BLACKS IN THE ECONOMY

Jacob Lawrence
Cabinet Makers (1946)
Gouache with pencil underdrawing on paper sheet
Hirshhorn Museum and Sculpture Garden, Smithsonian Institution,
Gift of Joseph H. Hirshhorn, 1966

F‌our decades ago Gunnar Myrdal sum-
marized the economic status of black Americans in dismal terms (1944:205):

> Except for a small minority enjoying upper or middle class status, the masses
> of American Negroes, in the rural South and in the segregated slum quarters
> in Southern and Northern cities, are destitute. They own little property:
> even their household goods are mostly inadequate and dilapidated. Their
> incomes are not only low but irregular. They thus live from day to day and
> have scant security for the future.

The 1940 census confirmed Myrdal's assessment. Crippled by the Great
Depression, America was poor, and blacks were very poor. The 1939 incomes of 48 percent of white families and 87 percent of black families are
estimated to have been below the federal poverty thresholds (Smith, 1988).[1]
And while a total of one-half of all white families were below the poverty
line, the per capita income of blacks was only 39 percent of white income
(Jaynes et al., 1986). In addition to cash income, much of the population—
including a slight majority of all blacks—lived on the land and depended on
home-grown food and fiber; one-third of southern blacks were sharecroppers
or tenant farmers, who scraped together a meager subsistence in primitive
conditions of work and life. Adding these "in-kind" products to cash in-

---

1. These calculations are based on the official 1964 poverty thresholds with all incomes
converted to 1984 dollars; see also note 2. As discussed below, the percentage of white and
black *individuals* who were poor was even higher.

come (if it were possible to estimate them) would not change the portrait of blacks' absolute and relative destitution.

A HALF CENTURY OF UNEVEN CHANGE

GAINS AND STAGNATION

World War II put America to work, and postwar prosperity and growth lifted living standards. Twenty years after Myrdal's study, 36 percent of black families and 9 percent of white families received incomes below poverty thresholds. Per capita black income was about 4 times higher than it had been in 1939, although it was still only one-half of white income.

By the 1960s, blacks were no longer concentrated in southern agriculture. Even as Myrdal was writing in the 1940s, they were migrating by the thousands to cities in the North and South, pulled by wartime industrial jobs and wages and pushed by the inexorable labor-saving mechanization of cotton plantations. The net emigration to the North eventually totaled 3.5 million blacks, more than one-quarter of the national 1940 black population of 13 million.

Myrdal viewed blacks' urbanization and industrialization with great optimism. He heralded it as the beginning of fundamental changes in American race relations after more than a half century of no fundamental change. Fundamental changes were indeed occurring in the 1960s, largely as a result of changing social conditions and blacks' own insistence on their civil and democratic rights.

During this period, black men moved from unemployment and farm labor to an array of blue-collar industrial jobs and a few white-collar positions. Comparing the employment situation of black men in 1973 with that of 1940 shows that the proportion of labor force participants who were unemployed, on public emergency jobs, or working on farms declined from 52 to 11 percent (Farley, 1987:42); those working as machine operators, factory laborers, or blue-collar craftsmen rose from 31 to 50 percent. During the same period, black women moved from domestic service and farm labor into factories, shops, offices, and some professional and managerial positions (see Table 6-1).

Moving from the rural or small-town South of 1940 to the nation's cities gradually brought to blacks the common comforts of American consumer technology—inside plumbing, electricity, refrigeration, telephones, automobiles, radio, and, eventually, television. They also gained much greater access to medical care, especially after President Johnson's Great Society inaugurated Medicare and Medicaid. Yet urban, industrial America, North or South, was not the promised land. In cities, unlike on farms, you cannot feed a family without cash income.

In the 1960s blacks deeply resented their continuing second-class status. Despite their gains since 1939, blacks in general did not share the affluent

TABLE 6-1 Occupation and Industry of Employment for Black Men and Women (in percent), 1939–1984

Sex and Occupation or Industry	1939	1949	1959	1969	1979	1984
Employed in major industry groupings						
Black men						
Agriculture, forestry, fisheries	42.5	24.9	12.7	5.3	2.8	3.4
Construction, manufacturing, mining	21.8	32.9	35.0	41.3	37.7	33.6
Transportation, communication, public utilities	6.5	9.0	8.2	9.9	12.6	12.6
Wholesale and retail trades	10.1	12.1	13.8	15.1	15.1	16.7
Service, including finance, insurance, real estate	15.8	15.6	17.4	21.1	24.7	27.5
Public administration	1.6	3.9	5.6	7.3	7.0	6.2
Black women						
Agriculture, forestry, fisheries	16.1	9.4	3.6	1.4	0.6	0.4
Construction, manufacturing, mining	3.7	9.4	9.3	16.1	18.1	16.5
Transportation, communication, public utilities	0.2	0.9	1.0	3.0	5.2	5.4
Wholesale and retail trades	4.2	10.3	10.1	12.2	12.6	14.3
Service, including finance, insurance, real estate	73.9	65.9	65.0	61.4	55.4	56.5
Public administration	0.6	2.2	3.8	5.9	8.0	6.9
Employed in major occupations						
Black men						
Professional	1.8	2.2	3.8	7.8	10.7	8.0
Proprietors, managers, officials	1.3	2.0	3.0	4.7	6.7	6.3
Clerical and sales	2.1	4.2	7.0	9.2	11.1	13.1
Craftsmen	4.4	7.8	9.5	13.8	17.1	15.8
Operatives	12.6	21.4	24.3	28.3	23.4	22.6
Domestic service	2.9	1.0	0.4	0.3	0.2	0.1
Other service	12.4	13.5	14.9	12.8	15.8	18.3
Farmers and farm workers	41.1	23.9	14.3	5.6	3.0	4.9
Nonfarm laborers	21.4	24.0	22.8	17.5	12.0	11.0
Black women						
Professional	4.3	5.7	6.0	10.8	14.8	13.9
Proprietors, managers, officials	0.7	1.4	1.8	1.9	3.7	5.2
Clerical and sales	1.4	5.4	10.8	23.4	32.4	33.1
Craftsmen	0.1	0.7	0.5	0.8	1.4	2.6
Operatives	6.2	14.9	14.1	17.6	14.9	12.0
Domestic service	60.0	42.0	35.2	17.5	6.5	5.9
Other service	10.5	19.1	21.4	25.7	24.3	24.8
Farmers and farm workers	16.0	9.3	9.6	1.6	0.6	0.5
Nonfarm laborers	0.8	1.5	0.6	0.7	1.4	1.8

Sources: Data from decennial censuses and the Bureau of Labor Statistics.

life-styles of the white majority. In one city after another, rising dissatisfaction and black consciousness erupted in violence and civil disorder. The blue-ribbon Kerner Commission, charged to help the nation understand the black rage, echoed *An American Dilemma* 25 years earlier (National Advisory Commission on Civil Disorders, 1968:253):

> Negro workers are concentrated in the lowest skilled and lowest-paying occupations. These jobs often involve substandard wages, great instability and uncertainty of tenure, extremely low status in the eyes of both employer and employee, little or no chance for meaningful advancement, and unpleasant or exhausting duties.

And now, two decades later, black-white differences are still large. These differences remain despite significant improvements since 1940 in the absolute and relative positions of blacks. But after initial decades of rising relative black economic status, black gains have stagnated on many measures of economic position since the early 1970s. Two important examples are poverty rates and per capita income. In 1985, 31 percent of black and 11 percent of white families lived below the federal poverty line; the 1974 poverty rates had been 29.3 percent of black families and 7.3 percent of white families. Black's real per capita income in 1984 was one-third higher than it had been in 1968 and about 6 times its 1939 level; but that income was only 57 percent of white income, the same relative position as in 1971.

The lack of progress in these important indicators of economic status during the past two decades is largely a consequence of two conflicting trends: rising average black wages relative to white wages but decreasing black employment relative to white employment. The rising weekly or hourly wages and occupational positions for employed blacks have been accompanied by falling and unstable employment patterns that have made employment increasingly unlikely for many blacks. The greatest share of this decreased employment has fallen on the least educated workers, who, faced with rising unemployment and stagnant or declining real wages, have often responded by dropping out of the labor force. The uneven distribution of employment and earnings losses has had consequences for the distribution of income among blacks.

BLACK INEQUALITY: THE POOR AND THE MIDDLE CLASS

Uneven change over time in the average economic position of blacks over the past half century has been accompanied, especially in the last quarter century, by accentuated differences in status among blacks. One of the most important developments since the 1960s has been that some segments of the black population gained dramatically relative to whites while others have been left far behind. During the 1960s, incomes were growing for most black (and white) families. Blacks in all income ranges gained relative to their counterparts in the white family income distribution. In fact, as the rate of poverty declined, the relative gains were greatest for black families with the lowest incomes (Jaynes et al., 1986). Then, during the 1970s, reductions in poverty rates slowed, leaving approximately one-third of black families with incomes below the poverty line throughout the decade and into the 1980s.

A major reason for the divergence in the economic status of black families is that the economy has been especially unstable with respect to the jobs and wages of black adult males. Their gains and setbacks, absolutely as well as relative to whites, are a major part of the economic experiences of blacks over the past 50 years. Conditions within the black community began to diverge sharply in the 1970s. This divergence can be seen very clearly in the experience of young men. By the early 1980s, black men aged 25–34 with at least some college earned 80–85 percent as much as their white counterparts. They also achieved some gains in private-sector white-collar positions. In terms of education, these black men represented the top one-third of their age group. At the other end of the group were the one-quarter of black men aged 25–34 who had not finished high school and who could not compete in the stagnant 1970s economy. An increasing number dropped out of the labor force altogether. These differing experiences lie behind the growing polarization that appears in economic statistics.

Earnings inequality has been increasing over the past 25 years for both white and black adult men, but especially among blacks (Jaynes et al., 1986). Since 1959, inequality among black men has been consistently greater than among white men. The lowest earning 40 percent of black men earned about 8 percent of the total earnings of black men in 1959, but 5 percent in 1984. The highest earning 20 percent of black men earned 50 percent of the total in 1959, but 60 percent in 1984. As noted above and discussed in detail below, a major source of the greater inequality is the increasing fraction of black men without any earnings. More generally, in 1984, about 40 percent of black men and 20 percent of white men (aged 25–55) earned less than $10,000. In 1969, approximately 10 and 25 percent of white and black men, respectively, had earnings below $10,000 (in 1984 constant dollars). This income was insufficient to maintain a family of four above the federal poverty threshold.

Polarization of the family income distribution has also taken place. In 1970, 15.7 percent of black families had incomes over $35,000; by 1986, this proportion had grown to 21.2 percent (in 1986 constant dollars). Similarly, the proportion of black families with incomes of more than $50,000 increased from 4.7 percent in 1970 to 8.8 percent in 1986 (22 percent of white families had incomes of more than $50,000 in 1986). During the same years, the proportion of black families with incomes of less than $10,000 also grew, from 26.8 to 30.2 percent.

An important aspect of this polarization in the incomes of black men and black families has been the growth, during the years since 1960, of female-headed black families. It is among such families that the incidence of poverty is highest. While some female-headed families are middle class just as some two-parent families are poor, it is not an exaggeration to say that the two most numerically important components of the black class structure have become a lower class dominated by female-headed families and a middle class largely composed of families headed by a husband and wife.

The divergent experiences of upwardly mobile blacks and those on the fringe or outside the economic mainstream are evident in statistics on education and earnings and on family composition and income:

• Among college graduates, the annual earnings of black males rose 6 percent relative to those of whites between 1969 and 1984; among persons with 1 to 3 years of post–high school education, the relative gain was 2 percent; but among high school graduates, blacks fell 5 percent further behind.

• Among two-parent households with children, black earnings rose 4 percent between 1973 and 1984, while white earnings fell 4 percent. Earnings of female-headed households fell for both blacks (9 percent) and whites (8 percent), but there are proportionately many more female-headed black households than white.

The divergent experiences of blacks are also evident in some comparisons of black and white economic statistics on wealth and poverty:

• The median wealth of black households is 9 percent of the white household median. However, among black and white households with incomes of less than $10,800 in 1984, the black median was 2 percent of the white. At all higher income levels, the relative median net worth of black households is more than 9 percent, but because the lowest income group contained a much larger fraction of black households (40 compared with 20 percent of white households), the median wealth of all white households was more than 11 times higher than the median of all black households.

• In 1969, 58 percent of all poor black children were in female-headed families (compared with 36 percent of white children); in 1984, 75 percent of poor black children were in female-headed families (compared with 42 percent of white children).

While much better off than blacks of lower status, middle and upper income blacks remain well behind comparable white households (see Landry, 1987). For example, although the absolute and relative gaps between average incomes of two-parent black and white families are not very large, black families need more members in the work force in order to approach the living standard of white families. Because the earnings gap between black and white women is smaller than the gap between men, black working wives contribute a greater share of total black income than do white working wives. In addition, black wives have a higher labor force participation rate than do white wives.

Even the most well-off black families in 1979 still had a difficult time meeting the standards set by the Bureau of Labor Statistics (BLS) as the income needed by an urban family of 4 to maintain middle-class living standards. The last year the data were published, the upper income standard was $34,317; intermediate, $20,517; and lower, $12,582. In 1979, approximately 24 percent of black families were in the middle-income range compared with 50 percent of white families. At the beginning of the 1970s, 23 percent of black and 47 percent of white families had been in the middle-income range (Hill, 1987:47). Thus, there was virtually no growth in the number of middle-income families during the 1970s by this measure. Although comparable data have not been published by BLS since 1979, all other economic statistics suggest that blacks are likely to have fallen further behind whites.

The rest of this chapter elaborates on these principal points concerning uneven changes in blacks' economic status over time, the divergence in wages and employment since the 1960s, and rising inequality. The next two sections discuss poverty and income and wealth: trends in poverty and the underlying social forces behind the trends, changes in the sources and sizes of the incomes received by whites and blacks, and the very large black-white differences in wealth and types of asset holdings. Blacks' labor market position is examined next through a description of their comparative earnings, employment, and occupational position. The last major section looks at equal employment laws and their enforcement, and then considers the special situation faced by black youth in the contemporary labor market.

POVERTY

TRENDS IN POVERTY SINCE 1939

In 1939, the poverty rates for black and white people were 93 and 65 percent, respectively (see Figure 6-1).[2] The odds that a black person would

---

2. In the late 1950s, the U.S. Department of Agriculture determined the minimum cost of a nutritionally adequate diet for families of various sizes. In the 1960s, officials at the Social Security Administration took these cost estimates and assumed that one-third of a household budget should be spent on food. This led to poverty "thresholds" or "lines" for households of different sizes, which are adjusted annually for inflation using the consumer price index. In 1986, the poverty threshold for an adult living alone was $5,701; for a family of two adults and two children, $11,203. If the pretax cash income of a person living alone or all members of a household falls below this poverty line, all members of that household are considered poor.

Some analysts argue that this procedure substantially overestimates poverty because of the access of farm and rural families to home-grown food and because of noncash federal transfer programs (such as food stamps) that have been available to the poor since the late 1960s.

Experimental work at the Bureau of the Census suggests that the widely cited poverty rates would be reduced by about 10 percent were households to receive credit for food stamps, school lunches, and subsidized housing. In 1985, for example, the poverty rate among blacks would have fallen from 31 to 28 percent; among whites, the change would have been from 11 to 10 percent.

However, other analysts argue that the official poverty rate is too low since it is challenging or impossible for a person to live on $5,700 or for a family of four to live on $11,000, especially in New York, Chicago, Detroit, and Los Angeles, where many of the minority poor reside. The Bureau of the Census has taken this into account by providing information about people in households whose incomes fall below 124 percent of the poverty line. If this definition is used, in 1986 the poverty rate for blacks would increase from 32 to 39 percent and from 11 to 15 percent for whites (see Levine and Ingram, 1988).

FIGURE 6-1 Poverty rates of blacks and whites and odds of being in poverty, estimated percentages, 1939–1985.

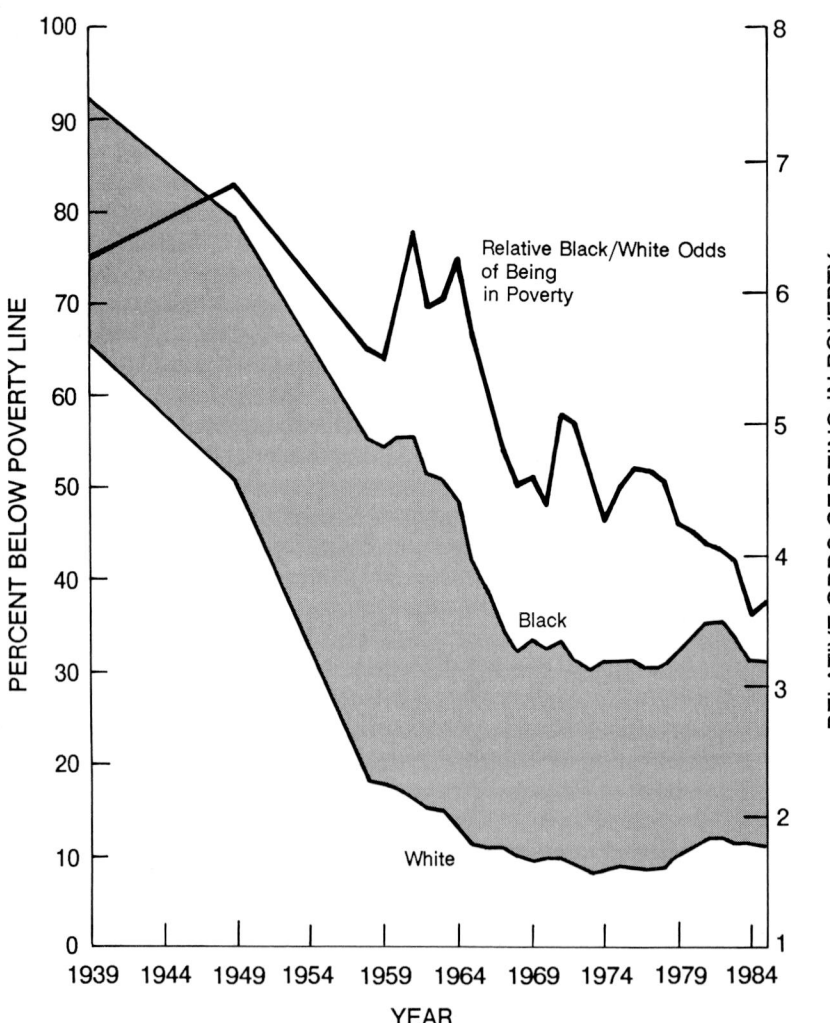

Source: Data from decennial censuses and Current Population Surveys.

be in poverty (the ratio of the poverty to the nonpoverty populations) were 7 times higher than those for a white. After that date, poverty rates fell rapidly for Americans. By 1974, poverty rates had declined significantly: 30 percent of blacks and 9 percent of whites lived in households whose incomes fell below the poverty line. The odds that a black would be poor (3 to 7) were more than 4 times those for a white (1 to 10). As for many economic measures, the early 1970s were a watershed, when progress, begun with recovery from the Great Depression, slowed or reversed. In 1986, both black and white poverty rates were higher, 31 and 11 percent, respectively, and the relative odds were similar to their levels in 1974.

The poverty of black children, in particular, is striking: 44 percent of black children lived in poor households in 1985. The comparable figure for white children was 16 percent. These figures were computed after family assistance benefits and other government transfers were added to household incomes (see note 2). Comparisons of pretransfer resources are even more distressing, especially for children in the decisive and vulnerable first 10 years of life. While a large majority of white children raised during the 1970s escaped poverty in their first 10 years, two-thirds of black children were not so fortunate. And 5 of 10 black children were poor for 4 of their first 10 years; only 1 of 12 white children knew that much poverty during the 1970s. One black child in 3, but only 1 white child in 33, was poor at least 7 of the 10 years (Ellwood, 1988).

Perhaps most important among the many contributing factors to the decline in poverty among blacks between 1939 and 1973 was the high rate of national economic growth sustained, with moderate cyclical interruptions, throughout the period. Per capita real gross national product (GNP, adjusted for price changes) grew at an average annual rate of 2.6 percent. During this period of sustained growth, blacks left the low-income rural South for cities and industries where wages were much higher. Between the census enumerations of 1940 and 1970, the percentage of blacks living in urban locations increased from 49 to 81 percent, and the percentage of blacks living in the South fell from 77 to 53 percent.

The adverse change in poverty trends after the early 1970s can be attributed to three major factors. First, again perhaps most important, has been the nation's economic growth. Between 1973 and 1986, per capita real GNP rose by only 1.5 percent per year. Second, while black men with jobs have continued to approach whites in the occupational ladder and in hourly wage rates, these gains have been offset by employment losses so great that relative per capita annual earnings of black men have stagnated. Third, changes in family structure have resulted in more black women and children in poverty. In 1985, 75 percent of the black children living in poverty were in female-headed households; 42 percent of poor white children were in such households.

The proportions of persons in poverty from 1959 to 1986, by family type (male or female headed) and race, are shown in Figure 6-2. Virtually all

FIGURE 6-2 Poverty rates of black and white families and odds of being in poverty, by household type, 1959–1986. (a) Family headed by a man.

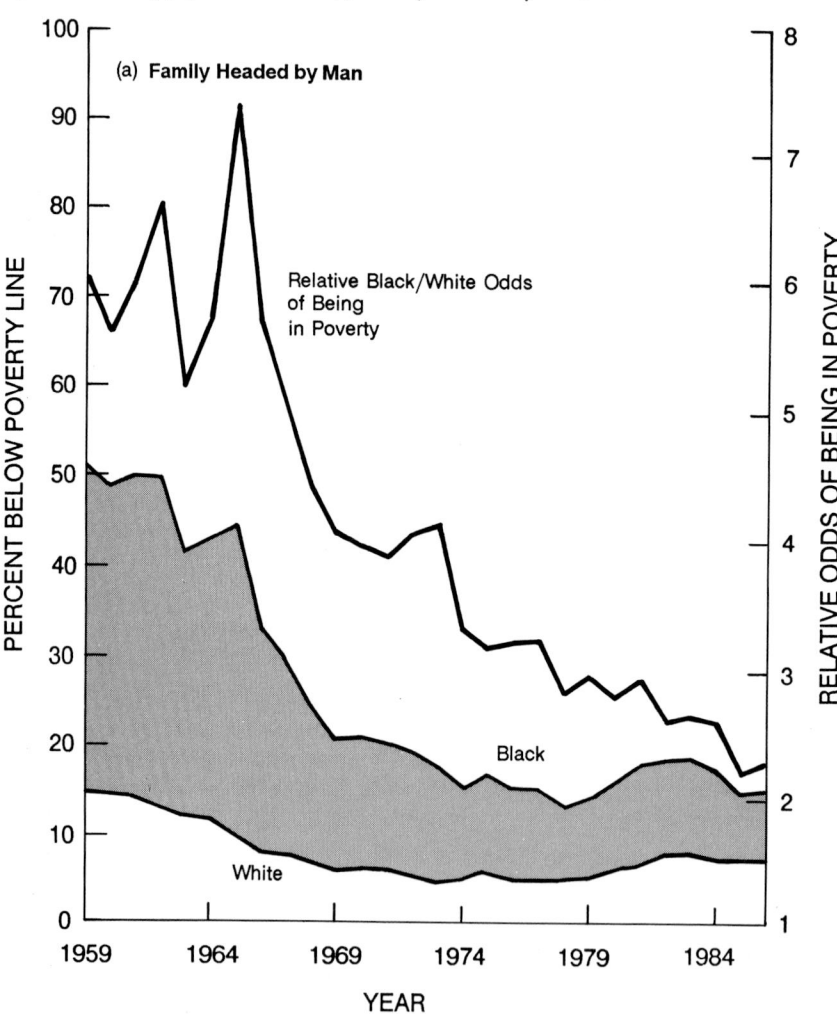

Source: Data from decennial censuses and Current Population Surveys.

families with an adult male include a second adult; very few female-headed families do. For both races and for both types of families, poverty rates declined between 1959 and 1973 and have fluctuated narrowly since then. For each family type, the odds of being impoverished have improved somewhat more for blacks than whites since the early 1970s. This good news was offset by bad news: the proportion of blacks in female-headed, single-parent families, always more prone to poverty than two-adult families, increased much more than among whites.

FIGURE 6-2 (b) Family headed by a woman.

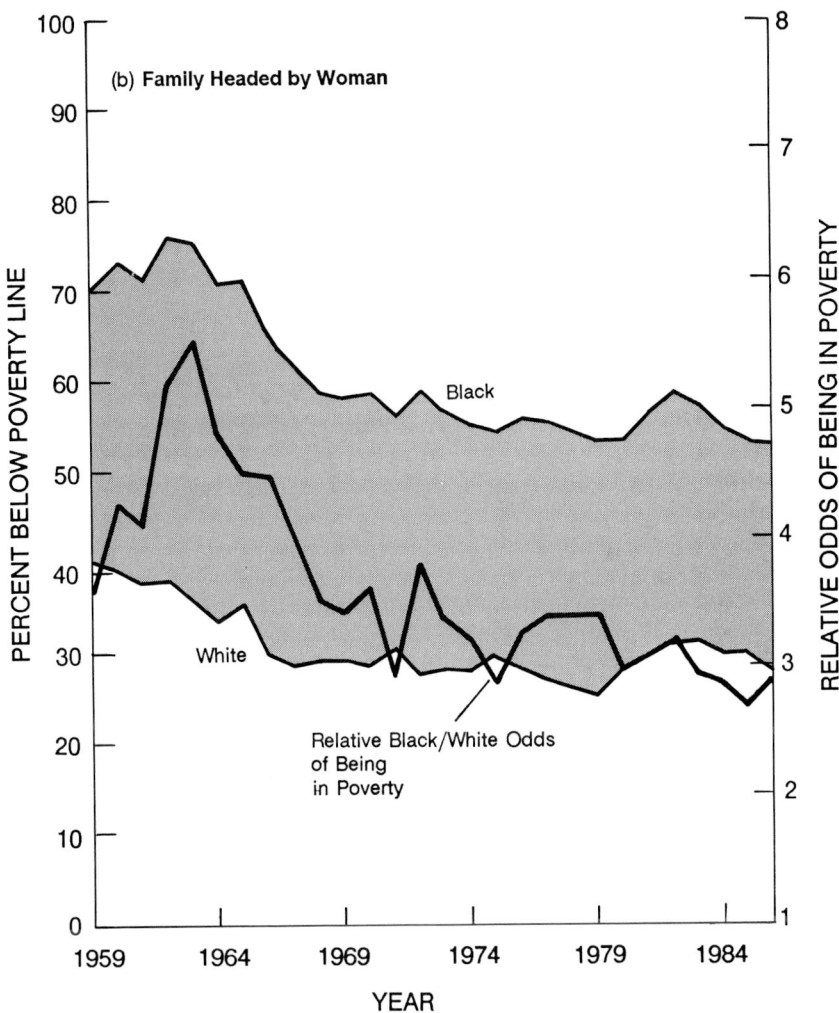

However, as serious as this trend is, it was not an arithmetically important factor in the overall increase in black poverty since the early 1970s. Had black family structure remained the same as in 1973, the percentage of poor black children would have fallen from 41 to 38 instead of rising to 43, and poverty among blacks aged 18–64 would have fallen from 24 to 23 percent instead of rising to 25 percent. Rather than family structure, it is low earnings that have led to increased poverty since the 1970s. Many intact black families are poor because the two adults heading them have very low earning capacities. Likewise, many single-parent families would remain poor if there were two adults present.

CURRENT CONDITIONS

Demographic Factors

Black-white differences and similarities in the demography and economics of poverty are noteworthy. In 1985, one-third of the black poor, compared with one-sixth of the white poor, were children in families headed by a woman. About 25 percent of the black poor, in contrast to less than 7 percent of the white, were adults—mostly women—in families headed by women. Compared with blacks, a high proportion of white poor live in husband-wife families or were persons aged 65 and over (Farley, 1987). Figure 6-3 shows the poor populations, black and white, by seven age-family characteristics.

Figure 6-3 also shows the distribution of the black and white poor populations in 1970. The changes illustrate the feminization of poverty and the shift to childhood poverty during the past 15 years. Children under age 18 made up less than 20 percent of the poor black population in 1970, but more than 45 percent in 1985. Among whites, the change was from about 10 percent to about 40 percent. These changes in the demographic structure of poverty were attributable to the sharp changes in family living arrangements, to modest declines in poverty among husband-wife families (see Figure 6-2), and to quite substantial declines in poverty among the elderly as Social Security benefits improved their living standards (see Danziger and Weinberg, 1986).

In 1986, median black family income was 57 percent of the white family median. However, as Table 6-2 indicates, the ratio varies considerably by type of family, with female-headed families behind two-parent families. Black married-couple families had nearly 3 times the income of black female-headed families, and white married-couple families had twice the income of white female-headed families. Among female-headed families, 52 percent of black and 27 percent of white were poor in 1984.

TABLE 6-2 Median Family Incomes, by Race and Family Type, 1986

Family Type	Black	White	Black/White Ratio
All families	$17,604	$30,809	0.57
Married couples	26,583	33,426	0.80
Wife in labor force	31,949	38,972	0.82
Wife not in labor force	16,766	26,421	0.63
Male head, no spouse present	18,731	26,247	0.71
Female head, no spouse present	9,300	15,716	0.59

Source: Data from Current Population Survey.

The Working Poor

Some forgotten victims of poverty are low-wage workers, who are also more vulnerable than other workers to periods of unemployment. Their numbers and their incomes are extremely sensitive to economic swings. Recent research suggests that a significant proportion of poor two-parent families have a full-time worker. No matter how poor they are, they do not qualify for much public aid. They may get food stamps, but the benefits are small (less than 60 cents per person per meal in 1986 for families with incomes one-half of the poverty line). Moreover, participation is low among eligible working poor families. These families seem to be helped by economic growth, but they have suffered disproportionately during the slow growth and severe recessions of the recent past (Danziger and Gottschalk, 1986a). Many have limited health protection, and most do not qualify for Medicaid. The United States is virtually alone among high-income countries in having no general provisions to protect the well-being and health of children.

Unemployment is becoming a more serious source of poverty and of medical indigency. A surprisingly large number of unemployed low-income workers get no unemployment insurance benefits. Danziger and Gottschalk (1986b) report that only 28 percent of unemployed household heads who had previously earned below $5.50 per hour received unemployment benefits in 1984, while 54 percent of those with higher wages received such benefits. The authors do not provide separate tabulations by race, but since blacks are disproportionately found in low-wage jobs, they are likely to be particularly affected. The unemployment insurance system seems to be providing less and less support over time: according to government figures, the fraction of unemployed workers who are covered has fallen from a high of 75 percent during the recession of 1975 to 34 percent in 1984. Danziger and Gottschalk conclude that low-wage workers have been hurt the worst. Two-parent families with an unemployed parent qualify for some welfare in half the states, but participation and benefits are low in most of those states.

Geographic Factors

The geographic distribution of black and white poor populations is not alike. Figure 6-4 presents information about the locations of the black and white poor in 1986. Compared with poor whites, poor blacks are more likely to live in central cities and in neighborhoods where a high proportion of residents are poor: approximately 57 percent of the black poor and 34 percent of the white poor resided in central cities. The majority of whites below the poverty line lived in suburban and nonmetropolitan areas. Figure 6-4 also shows that more than 2 of 5 of the black poor in 1986 were residents of census tracts in which one-fifth or more of the noninstitutional population lived in poverty. Fewer than 1 of 6 poor whites lived in census tracts with such high concentrations of poverty. As a consequence, poor blacks, to a much greater degree than poor whites, interact mainly with other

FIGURE 6-3 Poverty distribution, by race, age, and living arrangements, 1970 and 1985.

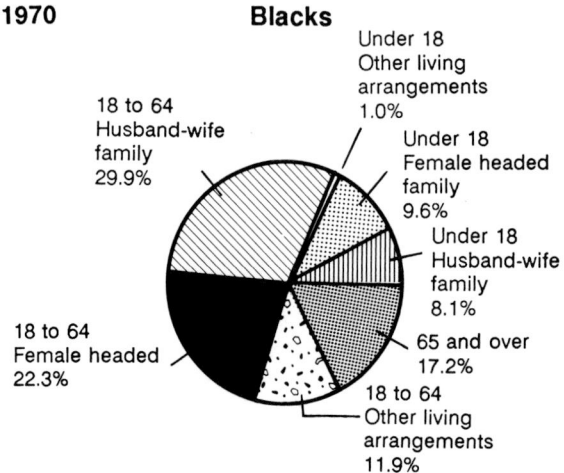

1970   **Blacks**

Under 18 Other living arrangements 1.0%

18 to 64 Husband-wife family 29.9%

Under 18 Female headed family 9.6%

Under 18 Husband-wife family 8.1%

18 to 64 Female headed 22.3%

65 and over 17.2%

18 to 64 Other living arrangements 11.9%

(Poverty Population, 7,680,000)

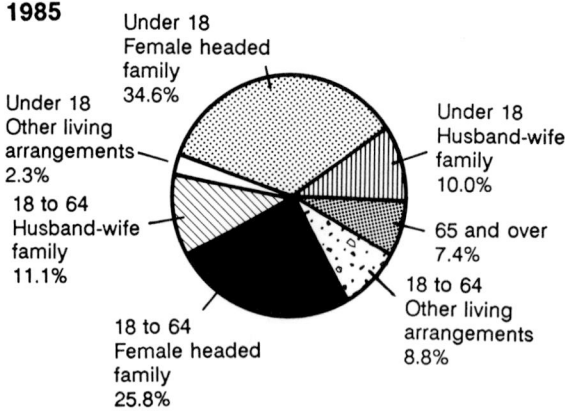

1985

Under 18 Female headed family 34.6%

Under 18 Other living arrangements 2.3%

Under 18 Husband-wife family 10.0%

18 to 64 Husband-wife family 11.1%

65 and over 7.4%

18 to 64 Other living arrangements 8.8%

18 to 64 Female headed family 25.8%

(Poverty Population, 8,926,000)

Source: Data from decennial census and 1985 Current Population Survey.

disadvantaged people. Black poor children attend schools with other poor children, go to churches with impoverished congregations, and deal with merchants geared to do business with a poor clientele. Racial segregation in residence reinforces the effects of economic separation.

Table 6-3 presents data for the 14 metropolitan areas with the largest black populations in 1980, a year in which the census reported that 30 percent of blacks and 9 percent of whites were below the poverty line. It shows the average proportion of the total population that is poor in the census tract of

FIGURE 6-3   *(Continued)*

1970   **Whites**

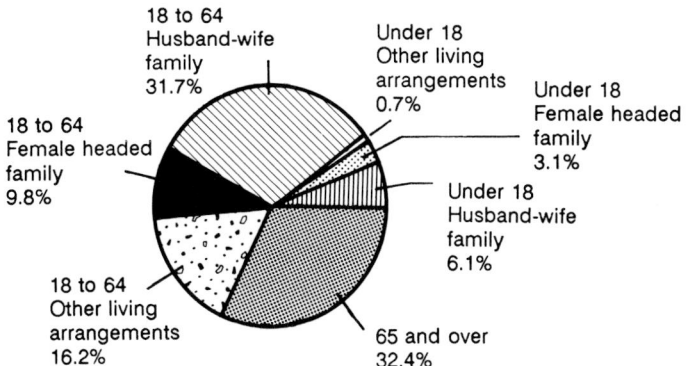

(Poverty Population, 18,935,000)

1985

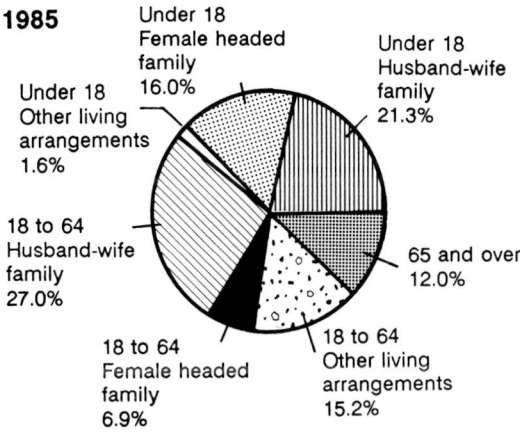

(Poverty Population, 22,860,000)

a typical poor black or white person. In Dallas, for example, poor blacks lived in areas where about one-third of the population was impoverished, poor whites in areas where about one-tenth was below the poverty line. Poor blacks face a density of poverty 3 to 4 times higher than that for poor whites. To the extent that escaping from poverty may be facilitated by living in more prosperous neighborhoods, poor whites have a great advantage over poor blacks.

Racial differences remain significant even for comparable family structures and residential locations. It could be that proportionately more blacks than whites are poor because relatively more blacks fall in demographic categories

FIGURE 6-4 Poverty distribution, by race and place of residence, 1986.

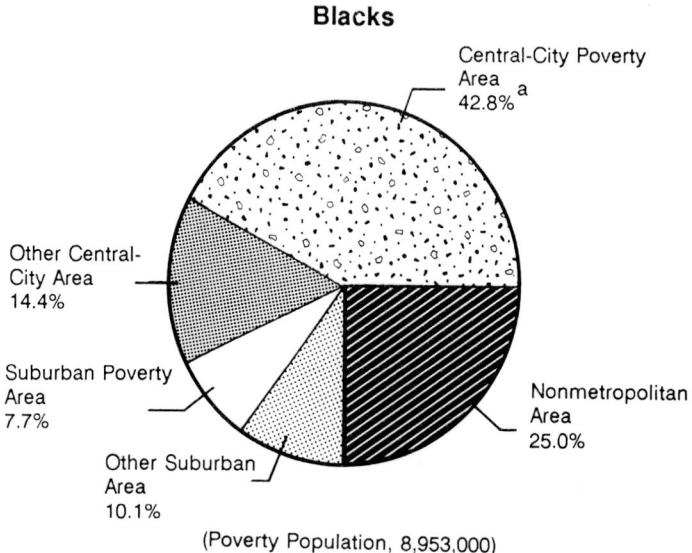

Blacks

Central-City Poverty Area [a]
42.8%

Other Central-City Area
14.4%

Suburban Poverty Area
7.7%

Other Suburban Area
10.1%

Nonmetropolitan Area
25.0%

(Poverty Population, 8,953,000)

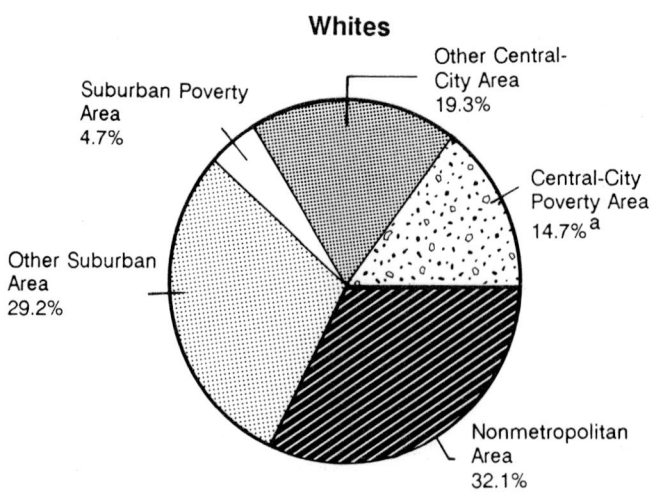

Whites

Suburban Poverty Area
4.7%

Other Central-City Area
19.3%

Other Suburban Area
29.2%

Central-City Poverty Area
14.7% [a]

Nonmetropolitan Area
32.1%

(Poverty Population, 22,183,000)

[a] Census tracts in which the poverty rate is 20 percent or higher.

Source: Data from Current Population Surveys.

TABLE 6-3 Concentration of Poverty in Major
Metropolitan Areas by Race, 1980

Metropolitan Area	Average Percentage of Population Poor in Census Tract of Typical Poor Person	
	Black	White
New York	36	20
Chicago	35	12
Los Angeles	29	16
Detroit	31	11
Philadelphia	37	12
Washington, D.C.	23	8
Baltimore	34	11
Houston	29	10
Atlanta	32	10
Dallas	33	11
Newark	35	13
San Francisco	29	12
St. Louis	32	10
New Orleans	38	11
Average	32	12

Source: Data from 1980 decennial census.

with high rates of economic deprivations—female-headed families, residents of central cities and poverty areas, and people with low educational attainment. Blacks do have these demographic characteristics more often than whites, but, in every category, the poverty rates for blacks are 2 to 3 times those of whites with similar characteristics (see Table 6-4).

The first two columns of Table 6-4 show that blacks, more often than whites, were young, lived in central cities, and were unemployed. These characteristics alone contribute to the poverty rate of blacks; however, the proportion below the poverty line in each category was much higher for blacks. Among those in central cities, 31 percent of blacks were poor, compared with 14 percent of whites. Of black households headed by an adult with only 1–3 years of high school education, 36 percent were poor, compared with 15 percent of similar white households. Of white households headed by a person who worked full time for 50 or more weeks in 1985, 3 percent were poor, compared with 7 percent of similar black households.

INCOME AND WEALTH

SOURCES OF INCOME

Total real income per person is the single most useful measure of the economic resources and the standard of living of a population. The 1984 per

TABLE 6-4 Poverty Rates and Distributions of Black and White Populations by Various Demographic Characteristics, 1985

Demographic Characteristic	Percent Distribution of Total Population		Percent Below Poverty Line, 1985	
	Black	White	Black	White
Age				
Under 6	11	9	46	18
6–15	18	13	43	16
16–21	11	9	35	13
22–44	37	37	23	9
45–54	8	10	20	7
55–64	7	10	25	8
65 and over	8	12	31	11
Region				
Northeast	17	21	24	9
Midwest	19	26	36	11
South	55	32	34	12
West	9	21	22	12
Place of residence				
Central cities	57	27	31	14
Suburban rings	25	50	22	7
Nonmetropolitan areas	18	23	42	15
Educational attainment of household heads (aged 25 and over)				
Less than 8 years	13	6	34	23
8 years	5	6	37	13
High school, 1–3 years	19	11	36	15
High school, 4 years	37	37	27	7
College, 1 or more years	26	40	11	3
Work experience of household head				
Worked 50 or more weeks				
Full-time	46	59	7	3
Part-time	4	3	31	12
Worked fewer than 50 weeks because of:				
Unemployment	10	8	38	20
Other reasons	10	8	36	14
Did not work in 1985	30	22	56	18

Source: Data from Current Population Surveys.

capita personal income (before taxes) of the black population was $6,277, which was 57 percent of the $10,939 per capita income of the white population. Although the black/white ratio was 18 percentage points higher than the 1939 figure of 39 percent, virtually all of this gain was achieved by the end of the 1960s. From 1969 to 1984, white income increased 22 percent, and black income increased 26 percent.

Total personal income includes wages and salaries, self-employment income, and "unearned" income. The last component is composed of income derived from property (interest, dividends, and rent) and transfer income (Social Security and other retirement benefits, family assistance benefits and supplemental security income, unfunded private pensions and annuities). Wage and salary income is the most important component of income for both blacks and whites, but the proportion of adults receiving this type of income has been increasing for whites and decreasing for blacks (Jaynes et al., 1986). The same is true of self-employment income. Those important sources of income are discussed below when we examine changes in blacks' earnings, employment, and occupations.

Unearned income has increased in importance for both whites and blacks. From 1967 to 1984, unearned income increased as a percentage of total income from 13 percent to 19 percent for blacks, and from 12 percent to 21 percent for whites. The proportion of blacks receiving property income has increased greatly over the past two decades, but black mean income from this source fell relative to whites by 6 percentage points from 1970 to 1984. In 1984, blacks, who are 11 percent of the population, received 2 percent of property income.

Blacks are relying increasingly on transfer payments, in particular on Social Security and other pensions. They are not increasingly dependent on family assistance benefits; such income has remained a fairly constant share of total black income, about 7.5 percent, since 1970. In 1984, 23 percent of black adults and 5 percent of white adults received some form of family assistance.

PUBLIC ASSISTANCE AND OTHER BENEFITS

Public assistance plays an important role in the support of some low-income families. Most of this support goes to single-parent families. For healthy nonelderly adults without children, there is little public assistance. Even poor two-parent families with children qualify for little help, mostly from food stamps and a few other federally sponsored programs. Family assistance benefits (chiefly Aid to Families with Dependent Children, AFDC) is virtually confined to single-parent families. This support expanded considerably in the late 1960s and early 1970s. But benefits are not indexed to inflation, and their real value has fallen by at least 30 percent since 1973. Benefits are below the poverty line in virtually every state, although there is considerable state-to-state variation. In 1986, for example, benefits for a family of 4 varied from a high of $698 per month in California to a low of $144 per month in Mississippi. In the median state, combined benefits averaged just over $500 per month for a family of 3 in 1986, less than 75 percent of the poverty line. In several southern states, benefits were roughly one-half the poverty level.

Recent research suggests that only a minority of those who ever use AFDC will do so for an extended period, but dependency appears to be quite long term among certain groups and has become a major public concern. Ellwood (1986a) reports that 20 percent of new white and 32 percent of new black recipients will receive AFDC for 10 years or more. This black-white difference is due to some extent to the higher proportions of black recipients in categories more likely to remain long-term beneficiaries. A never-married mother who enters the family assistance system when her child is very young seems particularly likely to receive benefits for a long time. Also, people with limited education or work experience tend to receive benefits longer than the average recipient. These two characteristics are obviously highly correlated.

A review of the large number of studies that have examined labor-supply effects of family assistance (Moffitt, 1985a, 1985b) suggests that those now on AFDC would increase their average hours of work from 9 hours per week to 14 hours if the program were abolished. Results of the negative income tax experiments (summarized in Burtless, 1987) show that a 10 percent increase in income leads to a 2 percent reduction in work by single parents. Unfortunately, there are no findings available from longitudinal studies that examined the impact of different programs on dependency and work behavior over the course of many years. Whether the reported effects are characterized as large or small obviously depends on one's point of view. A 5-hour-per week absolute change in labor supply may appear modest, but it does represent a 30 percent reduction in work. Still, the income for 14 hours of work per week, without family assistance, would leave a mother and her children very poor.

Single parents must both nurture their children and provide for them economically. While most married mothers now work, part-year or part-time jobs are the norm, with fewer than 30 percent of married mothers working full-time, all year.

For poor women, however, part-time work is not a feasible alternative to family assistance benefits, because it would raise net income very little, if at all. Even full-time work would leave a low-wage woman virtually no better off than receiving family assistance. Her benefits are on average 25 percent below the poverty line. If she works, she earns wages but faces benefit reductions and outlays for taxes, day care, transportation, and other work-related necessities. She is often no better off working unless she can earn $5, $6, or even $7 dollars per hour. A report from the U.S. House of Representatives (1987) Committee on Ways and Means shows that a woman working full time at a $5-per-hour job (and thus earning $10,000 in gross pay annually) will have only $1,500 more in disposable income than from family assistance benefits, and she will have lost her government medical protection (Medicaid). Women—or men—working at the minimum wage of $3.35 per hour have almost no additional disposable income.

It is not surprising, therefore, that earnings from work seldom provide an escape from family assistance programs. Only about one-fifth of the people who stop receiving AFDC do so because of increases in earnings. It is too hard for most single mothers both to earn an adequate living and to raise their children. As a consequence, marriage is the most common way in which women leave benefit programs. Some analyses suggest that the primary reason never-married mothers stay on AFDC longer than women who are divorced, separated, or widowed is that they are less likely to marry.

The results of recent experiments measuring the effects of work and training requirements on assistance programs have been generally favorable but quite modest. When the programs have been systematically evaluated, the benefits—including the increased earnings of recipients and the value of the work they perform in "workfare" plans—have exceeded the costs. In many experiments, the reductions in program expenditures and the taxes paid by those served were greater than the cost of serving program participants (see Gueron, 1986).

Unfortunately, the overall reductions in family assistance dependency and costs have been quite modest. For example, the job search and workfare programs instituted in San Diego County required family assistance recipients with no children under age 6 to participate in job search workshops designed to help them find work. Those participants who were unable to find private-sector employment were required to do public-sector work as a condition to receiving benefits for a period of 3 months. The benefits of this program exceeded the cost in a carefully controlled experiment, and the program has received national attention. Yet the total impact was quite modest when results for participants were compared with a randomly selected control group. The treatment group, those who participated in the program, earned $700 more per year; annual welfare savings were smaller, averaging $300. Experiments across the country have generated similar findings: annual earnings are raised $200 to $750; welfare savings are more modest. Moreover, since the programs typically serve only a small percentage of the people receiving benefits, the overall average reductions in benefit costs are even smaller (Gueron, 1986). Most workfare programs appear to be reasonable economic investments, but there are no carefully evaluated workfare programs that put more than a tiny dent in benefit caseloads.

One group that until recently was all but ignored in the family assistance debate is the absent fathers of the children in single-parent families. Almost two-thirds of all single mothers reported receiving no child support in 1985 from the fathers of their children, and only 11 percent of never-married mothers received such aid. The lack of child support payments essentially means that single mothers trying to be self-supporting must provide all the support for their family on their own. Lack of enforcement might also be seen as a signal that fathers, especially the unmarried fathers of children, bear little responsibility for their children. Many of these absent fathers no doubt have limited incomes themselves, but their problems and responsibilities have only recently become the focus of some discussion and research.

WEALTH

Comparisons of net worth or wealth—defined as total assets minus total debts—shows that black households compare less favorably to white households in terms of wealth than they do in terms of income. In 1984, per capita wealth for blacks was $6,837, compared with $32,667 for whites. Black householders had a median net worth of $3,397 and white householders $39,135, so for every $1 of wealth in the median white household, the median black household had $0.09.

Blacks, having lower incomes from which to save, can be expected to have accumulated less wealth. A less obvious finding is that, for comparable incomes, blacks have much less wealth than whites. In 1984, among households with a monthly income of less than $900, the ratio of black net worth to that of whites was 0.01; for those with monthly incomes between $900 and $2,000, the ratio was 0.14; for those with monthly incomes between $2,000 and $4,000, 0.32; and for $4,000 and over, 0.46. Because a much larger fraction of black households is in the lowest income group (40 percent compared with 20 percent of white households), the overall median wealth of white households is more than 11 times that of black households (Bradford, 1987:2).

Blacks with high educational attainment compare much more favorably to similar whites than do low-income blacks with modest educational attainments. In particular, among college-educated householders age 35 or less with incomes above $48,000 per year, the black/white ratio of median net worth is 0.93. Unfortunately, this group only composes about one-half of 1 percent of black households (Bradford, 1987:3). It cannot be determined to what extent this favorable comparison will be maintained as this age cohort becomes older. Estimates based on comparisons of older black and white householders with similar education and incomes suggest considerable deterioration over time, but such estimates probably underestimate black wealth accumulation possibilities for the younger cohorts.

Inequality of wealth among blacks and whites is greater than is inequality of income, and both income and wealth are more highly concentrated among black than white households. Most of the higher concentration of wealth among blacks is due to the greater fraction of black households with zero net worth: 13 percent compared with 2 percent for white households. Thus, measuring within groups inequality by the "Gini coefficient" (where $G = 1$ means complete inequality, all wealth owned by one household, and $G = 0$ means equality, all households have equal wealth) gives Gini's of 0.687 for black households and 0.616 for whites in 1984. Removing households with zero net worth reduces these measures to 0.629 for blacks and 0.608 for whites, showing that among households with positive net worth, wealth is distributed very similarly in the white and black populations (Bradford, 1987:8). Including households with negative net worth increases the inequality among blacks even more, in comparison with the inequality among whites, to 0.744 for blacks and 0.642 for whites.

Asset holdings among black and white households differ considerably (see Figure 6-5). The proportion of wealth held in interest-earning assets increases with income for both black and white households, but this proportion is higher among white households at all income levels (Bradford, 1987:10). Of

FIGURE 6-5 Wealth distribution, by race and asset type.

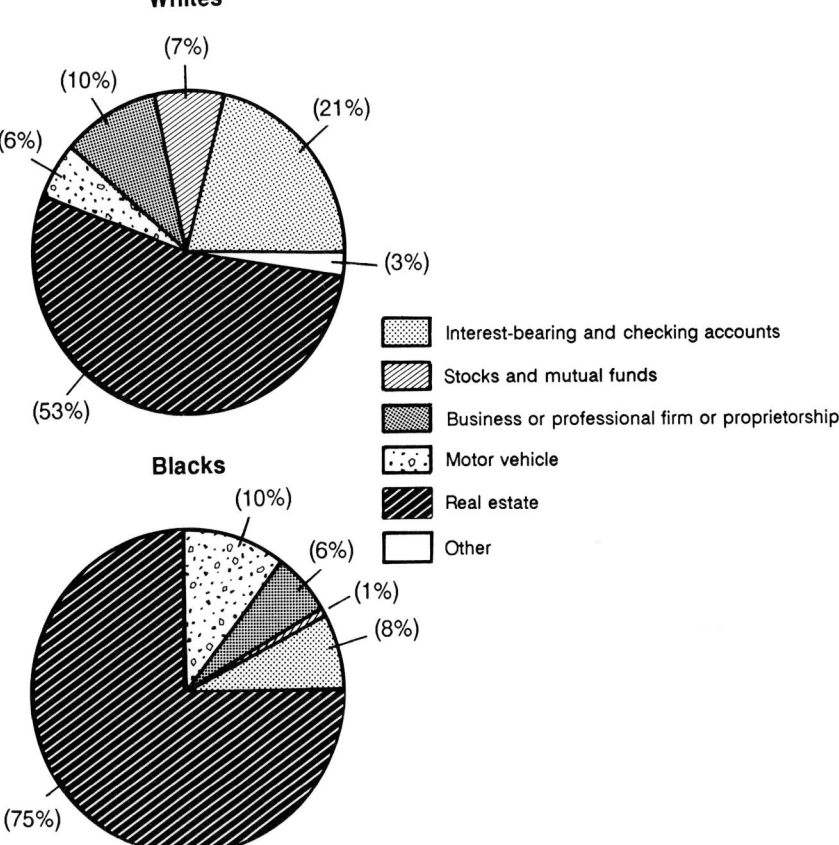

Whites

(7%)

(10%)

(6%)

(21%)

(3%)

(53%)

Blacks

(10%)

(6%)

(1%)

(8%)

(75%)

▢ Interest-bearing and checking accounts

▨ Stocks and mutual funds

▨ Business or professional firm or proprietorship

▢ Motor vehicle

▨ Real estate

▢ Other

Source: Data from 1984 Survey of Income and Program Participation.

black wealth, 75 percent was in real estate in 1984; 53 percent of white wealth was held in that asset. Less than 1 percent of black assets were in stocks and bonds. Although the comparative figures improve with household income, blacks still hold far less of their wealth in stocks or mutual funds and business equity.

Black households have a lower fraction of wealth in retirement assets, such as Individual Retirement Accounts (IRAs), at all income levels. And, interestingly, high-income blacks ($48,000 or more per year) hold the lowest fraction of wealth in such assets of all black households, nine-tenths of 1 percent (0.009). Among high-income white households, these retirement assets account for the highest fraction of wealth held (Bradford, 1987:11–

12). This difference may be due to the relative youth of higher income blacks, compared with both other blacks and higher income whites.

Overall, the net worth position of black households is very limited in comparsion with whites. One reason may be that more black families have been persistently, not just temporarily, poor, so that blacks have not benefited as much as whites from gifts and bequests given by parents and grandparents. Whatever the causes, the consequences are severe. Lacking assets and borrowing capacities, blacks are ill equipped to cope with economic adversities and to exploit economic opportunities.

BLACKS IN THE LABOR MARKET

NATIONAL ECONOMIC TRENDS

Blacks have a strong interest—stronger than the white majority—in national policies that hold unemployment low and keep the economy expanding vigorously. At the same time, their sensitivity to the nation's macroeconomic performance is a symptom of their continuing marginality and inferiority in economic status. The sustained rapid growth of the nation's economy during World War II and for a quarter century thereafter was extremely important to blacks' gains in economic status. This growth provided employment options for many blacks, upgraded their occupations, and facilitated their migration from rural poverty in the South. National and international economic trends since 1973 have been much less benign.

The principal data used to examine the labor market experiences of black men, women, and youth over the past 50 years are from the five decennial censuses (1940–1980) and, for 1985, the Current Population Survey. These data refer to individuals, not to families or households.

The U.S. economy grew rapidly and quite steadily in the first quarter century after World War II. It slowed down after 1973, battered by oil and energy crises, lagging productivity growth, stagflation, government-induced anti-inflationary recessions, high unemployment, high interest rates, financial disturbances, and international competition. Black economic gains were most substantial during the sustained booms of the 1940s and the 1960s. For example, black women's annual earnings, relative to white women's, gained 15 and 23 percentage points in those two decades, respectively, while black men gained 9 percentage points relative to white men during both decades; see Table 6-5. For both sexes, these two decades thus accounted for nearly all the relative gain of the 45 years. Since 1970, blacks' relative economic position improved only slowly, and since 1980 it has deteriorated.

Blacks are acutely sensitive to the expansions and recessions of business cycles. Blacks are disproportionately employed in low-wage jobs, unprotected by tenure and seniority, and in manufacturing and other goods-producing industries that are particularly sensitive to business cycles. The oldest plants in central cities are the most vulnerable. An economic down-

TABLE 6-5 Mean Earnings of Men and Women, by Race, 1939–1984

Sex and Type of Earnings	1939	1949	1959	1969	1979	1984
Men						
Hourly wage rate ($)						
Black	2.80	4.67	6.72	9.59	10.55	8.35
White	6.15	7.52	10.67	14.08	13.31	11.52
Ratio (percent)	45.5	62.1	63.0	68.1	79.3	72.5
Weekly earnings ($)						
Black	103	172	229	329	366	289
White	220	304	398	504	507	429
Ratio (percent)	46.8	56.6	57.5	65.3	72.2	67.4
Annual earnings ($)						
Black	3,833	6,655	9,540	14,177	15,160	13,218
White	8,745	12,596	18,079	22,860	23,032	20,457
Ratio (percent)	43.8	52.8	52.8	62.0	65.8	64.6
Ratio of per capita black/white earnings	42.4	45.3	49.6	56.7	57.3	56.1
Women						
Hourly wage rate ($)						
Black	1.81	3.65	5.14	7.68	8.78	7.10
White	4.19	5.33	7.32	9.43	8.37	7.75
Ratio (percent)	43.2	68.5	70.2	81.4	104.9	91.6
Weekly earnings ($)						
Black	59	115	139	232	271	227
White	143	187	217	271	256	233
Ratio (percent)	41.3	61.5	64.1	85.6	105.9	97.4
Annual earnings ($)						
Black	2,070	3,632	4,764	8,347	10,496	10,252
White	5,192	6,647	7,870	9,966	10,420	10,354
Ratio (percent)	39.9	54.6	60.5	83.8	100.7	99.0
Ratio of per capita black/white earnings	55.8	71.7	71.9	91.4	96.4	96.1

Notes: Data are for people 15 years old and over except for per capita earnings, which are for men and women aged 20–65. Amounts are in 1984 constant dollars.

Sources: Data from decennial censuses and 1985 Current Population Survey.

turn has an immediate impact on black blue-collar workers, especially the many blacks lacking skills, experience, and seniority.

Black unemployment rates are on average twice those of whites. Thus, for blacks the 1962–1969 expansion was very good and the recessions of 1970–1971, 1974–1975, 1979–1980, and 1980–1981 were very severe (see Danziger and Weinberg, 1986).

In an economy with high unemployment and stagnating or declining real wages, blacks have encountered greater difficulty escaping from poverty since 1973 than before. Recent structural changes in the U.S. economy have also worked against them. Foreign competition in "smokestack manufacturing" has destroyed jobs in the industries and regions where many blacks had found jobs at good wages from 1940 to 1970. The unions in these industries, notably automobiles and steel, had been particularly open to blacks. Since 1973, the pattern of employment in the U.S. economy has shifted to industries in which black penetration had been and remains lower, and to sectors and regions, especially the South and Southwest, where wages and fringe benefits are lower and unions are weak or absent. The movement of jobs, especially good jobs, from midwestern cities has stranded black residents in the very locations that once drew them, or their parents and grandparents, from the rural South.

The changing geographic location of jobs in the nation's metropolitan areas may also be hurting blacks. Nearly three-fifths (57 percent) of the nation's blacks live in inner cities. Many are poorly educated, and low-skill and blue-collar jobs have been leaving the inner cities for the suburbs. There remains considerable debate about the extent to which these geographic changes have had an impact on black employment (Ellwood, 1986b; Kain, 1968; Kasarda, 1985; Leonard, 1987).

The major sources of black gains in earnings and occupation status from 1939 to 1965 were South-to-North migration and concurrent movement from agricultural employment to nonagricultural industries. These shifts were facilitated by high rates of employment, job creation, and output growth (Gwartney, 1970:876; Smith and Welch, 1986). Wages in the South historically were much lower than in all other census regions for blacks and whites: this is still true for blacks, but not for whites. In addition, black/white relative wages have been lower in the South. Therefore, when a black migrated from South to North both the migrant's personal wage and blacks' average relative wage increased. Black gains in education also played a role during this period (O'Neill et al., 1986; Smith and Welch, 1986), but migration was much more important.

The special importance of migration can be seen in the earnings of males. Between 1939 and 1959, the black/white ratio of mean yearly male earnings rose 9 percentage points (44 to 53 percent) in the nation as a whole. However, in every Census Bureau region, relative black/white earnings rose less than 9 percent. Thus, if there had been no change in the regional distribution of blacks, black/white relative earnings could not have risen by 9 percent. The aggregate increase was due to the migration of blacks from low-wage to higher wage regions. Migration was not so singularly responsible for gains in black women's status. While the South-North wage differential was large for black women, they also made substantial relative occupational and earnings gains in every region from 1939 to 1965 (Jaynes et al., 1986).

Black economic gains from migration ended during the late 1960s. However, the decade of the 1960s was a period of great economic advancement for blacks. These gains were largely due to overall employment growth, increases in blacks' relative education, and reduction in racial discrimination (Haworth et al., 1975; Smith and Welch, 1986). For 1970–1980, black males lost relative ground in all regions except the South, where they continued to gain. Black women reached parity in annual earnings with white women by 1970 in all regions but the South (Farley, 1987).

EARNINGS

Black men and women have enjoyed substantial gains in relative earnings since 1939, by several measures (see Table 6-5). However, the magnitude of these gains and their persistence over time depend on the measure used. For example, two recent reports that focused on the hourly and weekly wages of employed men concluded that black workers made substantial progress in catching up with whites between 1939 and 1979 (O'Neill et al., 1986; Smith and Welch, 1986). By those measures, the ratio of black to white earnings has risen quite steadily. However, black/white earnings differences have changed less when measured on an annual basis: although the hourly wage rates of black men in 1984 were 72 percent of those of white men, black per capita annual earnings were 56 percent of white earnings. Black men's mean weekly earnings relative to whites' gained 20 percentage points during the 45 years, while their mean per capita earnings gained 14 points.

Each of these measures describes some important aspect of labor market status. In our view, however, the most meaningful indicators of general labor market status are annual per capita earnings or mean yearly earnings, because these statistics reflect employment status as well as wage rates. As noted above, blacks are often involuntarily stuck in part-time jobs and are more prone to unemployment than whites and therefore work fewer hours a week and fewer weeks per year. Most striking, the proportion of adult men with no work experience at all during a whole year is much greater for blacks than whites. Measures of earnings based on an entire year reflect these differences.

Black women began and ended the 45-year period with the lowest earnings of the four race-sex groups, but their relative position improved significantly. As can be seen from Table 6-5, the weekly wages and yearly earnings of black women grew faster than those of any other race-sex group. In 1939, the weekly wages of black women were 41 percent those of white women, 57 percent those of black men, and 27 percent those of white men; by 1984, the relative wages of black women were 97, 78, and 53 percent, respectively, of white women's, black men's, and white men's.

Relative wage gains occurred for black women at all levels of educational attainment, but they were largest at lower education levels, and college-educated women advanced the least. This pattern is the reverse of that for black men. By the 1970s, black women generally earned as much on an annual basis as white women of comparable education. However, as we have noted above, black women were more likely to work full-time, and they do not earn as much per week or per hour as comparable white women (Jaynes et al., 1986).

Black women's relative incomes have shown less improvement than their relative earnings. For example, in 1949, black women's mean yearly income of $2,189 was 72 percent of white women's mean of $3,031; 35 years later, black women's $8,622 mean yearly income was 89 percent of white women's $9,682 (Jaynes et al., 1986). One student of the subject summarizes the current situation as follows (Malveaux, 1986:19–20):

> Promising aspects of black women's economic status include improvements made since the 1960's, inroads into typically white male occupations, and increased business ownership. But there is a persistence of some patterns: of concentration in low-wage and part-time jobs, of spurts of progress followed by erosion (especially in educational arenas), and of persistent high unemployment.

Women's income and earnings in the South is a large part of the overall story, as it is for men (Jaynes et al., 1986). Gains have been large in the South, but black women's relative income is still below those in every other region. In 1949, the income of black women relative to white women was lowest in the South, 71 percent—compared with ratios of 88, 86, and 103 percent in other Census Bureau regions. By 1984, when white women in the South had reached virtual parity with white women elsewhere, southern black women's incomes were still considerably below the incomes of non-southern black and white women. The southern black/white ratio of 83 percent was still below every other region's 1950 ratio.

Lifetime Expected Earnings

Information on earnings over a period even longer than a year, indeed over a whole career, would also be valuable, but there are no individual wage and employment histories for cohorts who became adults in 1940 or 1950, and of course later cohorts are still of working age. However, from the data in each census (or survey) that relate annual earnings to age, as well as to race, sex, and other demographic variables in a given year, one can estimate how much a person would earn in a working lifetime if the person were to receive at each future age the average earnings reported in that year for that age. Summing average earnings for each age over the age groups 20 to 64 gives an estimate of "lifetime earnings." This number is best regarded as a useful summary statistic of earnings and labor market experience in the relevant year, enabling comparisons to be made between years and races. (All the earnings were converted into 1984 constant dollars.) The per capita averages automatically reflect differences in unemployment and labor force participation.

The estimates of lifetime earnings of men and women are shown in Figure 6-6. According to the census of 1940, a white man who survived from age 20 to 64 could expect to earn just over $300,000; a black man about $125,000. From 1939 to 1969, the earnings of men rose sharply. By 1969, the estimated lifetime earnings of white men reached about $1.1 million, an average of $24,000 for each year of the age span from 20 to 64; per capita earnings of black men increased even more rapidly, reaching about $600,000. The ratio of black/white expected lifetime earnings declined after the early 1970s, reflecting the higher rates of unemployment and slower growth of wage rates for blacks as the actual earnings of each declined.[3]

Women's lifetime estimated earnings should be interpreted with even more caution than those for men. Adult women are more likely than men to be voluntarily out of the labor force. Although this difference is diminishing, it still exists. Thus, comparisons of women's per capita earnings across ages, census years, and races will reflect different social changes in labor force participation as well as changes in job opportunities and wage rates.

Women earn much less than men, a difference accentuated by measuring lifetime earnings. After several decades of increases in the earnings of women, both white and black women in 1984 could expect to earn about 37 percent as much as white men and 64 percent as much as black men during work careers spanning the ages 20 to 64.

The black-white gap in per capita annual earnings has all but disappeared among women. In 1970, black women had estimated lifetime earnings that were 91 percent those of white women. The earnings of black women have continued to increase since then, and by 1984 the estimated lifetime earnings of black women were 96 percent those of white women. This near parity obscures some differences: white women are more likely to be out of the labor force, and black women more likely to be unemployed; black women work more hours per week, but about the same hours per year as white women.

Effects of Education

Black-white earnings differentials by educational attainment changed considerably in the 1969–1984 period, partly as a result of a dramatic downturn in pay rates. The mean weekly wages of black and white men and women have been lower in the 1980s than they were in 1970. Earnings losses have been greatest for those with the least education. For example, between 1969 and 1984, the real weekly earnings of black women with some

---

3. These numbers do not allow for probabilities of death. Since black men have always had, and still have, lower life expectancies than whites, if these were taken into account, blacks' expected lifetime earnings would be even lower relative to whites'. (For a different method of estimating lifetime earnings, see Note at the end of Chapter 1.)

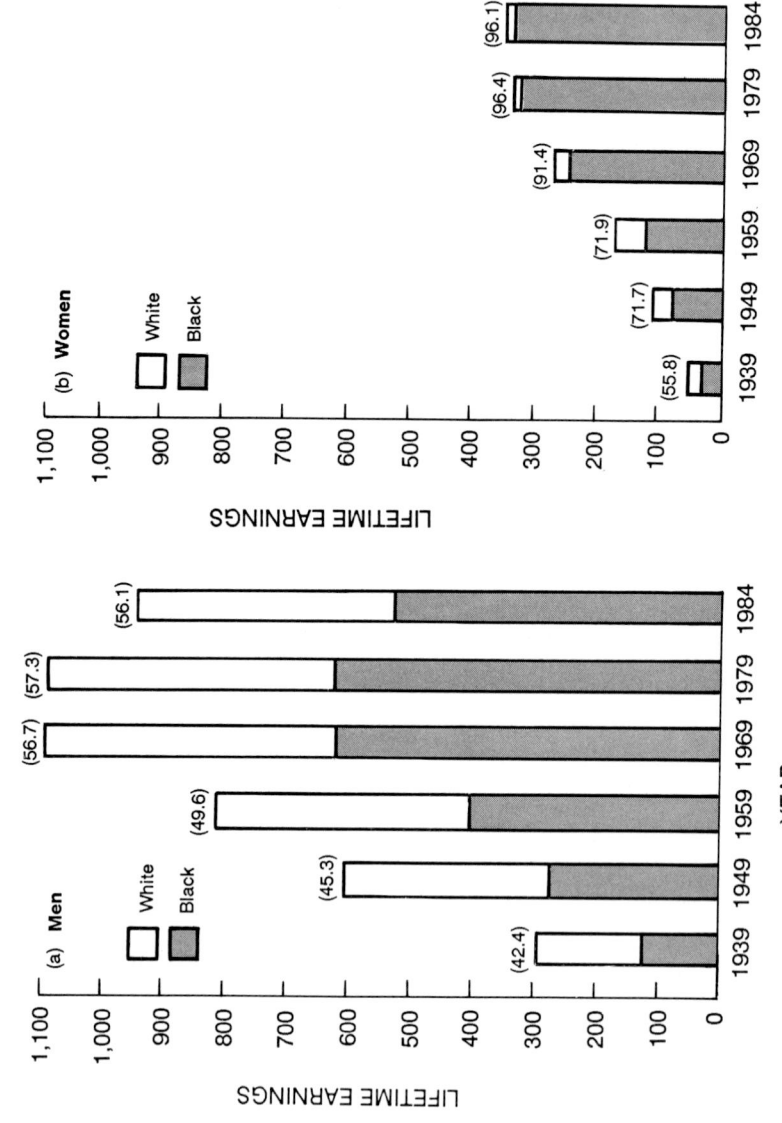

FIGURE 6-6 Expected lifetime earnings for black and white (a) men and (b) women.

Note: Lifetime earnings are given in thousands of 1984 dollars. Black earnings as a percentage of white earnings are in parentheses.

Source: Data from decennial censuses and Current Population Surveys.

high school education, but no diploma, fell 24 percent (from $201 to $152); the weekly earnings of black women with some college education, but no degree, fell 21 percent (from $308 to $242). Among black men with some high school education, but no diploma, weekly wages fell 32 percent (from $312 to $213); while among black men with college training, but no degree, weekly wages fell 20 percent (from $392 to $315) between 1969 and 1984. Decreases in the weekly wages of white men and women were also dramatic (see Table 6-5).

The earnings of well-educated black men rose relative to the earnings of comparatively educated white men during this period (see Smith and Welch, 1986). In the past, better educated black men earned more than other black men, but there was no evidence that they were closer to their white peers in earnings than those with fewer years of education. For example, in 1949, the average yearly earnings of black men with 8 years of education or less were 56 percent of those of similarly educated white men; the average yearly earnings of black male college graduates were 52 percent of those of white male college graduates. In 1984, in contrast, the average yearly earnings of black male college graduates was 74 percent of those of white male college graduates. Still, black men with college degrees have not attained earnings parity with white male college graduates. According to the 1985 census, the estimated average lifetime earnings of white male college graduates was $1.42 million, $450,000 more than those of black male college graduates.

EMPLOYMENT

Since 1940, decennial and monthly surveys conducted by the Bureau of the Census have classified adults by their work status. Individuals who held jobs in the survey week—even part-time positions or unpaid jobs in a family business or farm—are considered *employed*. Those who do not have a job but have made efforts to find work within the last month are considered *unemployed*. The labor force includes the employed and the unemployed. Those who neither had a job in the last week nor had looked for work in the last month are classified as *not in the labor force*. The latter is a heterogeneous group that includes full-time students, homemakers, and retirees; independently wealthy persons and others who simply choose not to work; and people who have become discouraged and have given up the search for work.

There are several measures of employment. The *employment rate* is the ratio of employed people to the total labor force. The *labor force participation rate* is the ratio of people in the labor force to the adult population. The *employment/population ratio* is the product of the employment rate and the labor force participation rate. Two groups with identical labor force participation rates would have different employment rates if their unemployment rates differed. For example, if the participation rate is 80 percent, the employment/population ratio will be 72 percent if the unemployment rate is 10 percent, but 76 percent if the unemployment rate is 5 percent.

Trends

During World War II and for a considerable time span thereafter, more than 9 of 10 black and white men aged 25–54 had jobs. Until about 1970, subsequent fluctuations in this proportion primarily reflected unemployment. Since the 1960s, however, there has been a substantial decline in employment among black men. By the early 1980s, the proportion of black men aged 25–54 who were employed had fallen to fewer than 8 in 10. Among women of that age, there has been a modest increase in the percent of blacks employed, but a much sharper increase among whites. At present, white women are more likely to be employed than black women, primarily because of higher unemployment among black women.

The employment/population ratio among all men has declined in recent decades, primarily because of increases in the proportion of men not in the labor force. However, while declining labor force participation is most responsible for the declining participation of both black and white men, the increased percentage of adult black men not working, relative to whites, since 1972 seems to be largely due to a general rise in unemployment. Unemployment has usually been about twice as severe for blacks as for whites. Black men's labor force participation rates were 3.5 points lower

FIGURE 6-7 Black and white men aged (a) 16–24, (b) 25–54, and (c) 55 and over who are employed, 1950–1986, and 3-year moving average of relative odds of employment, 1951–1985.

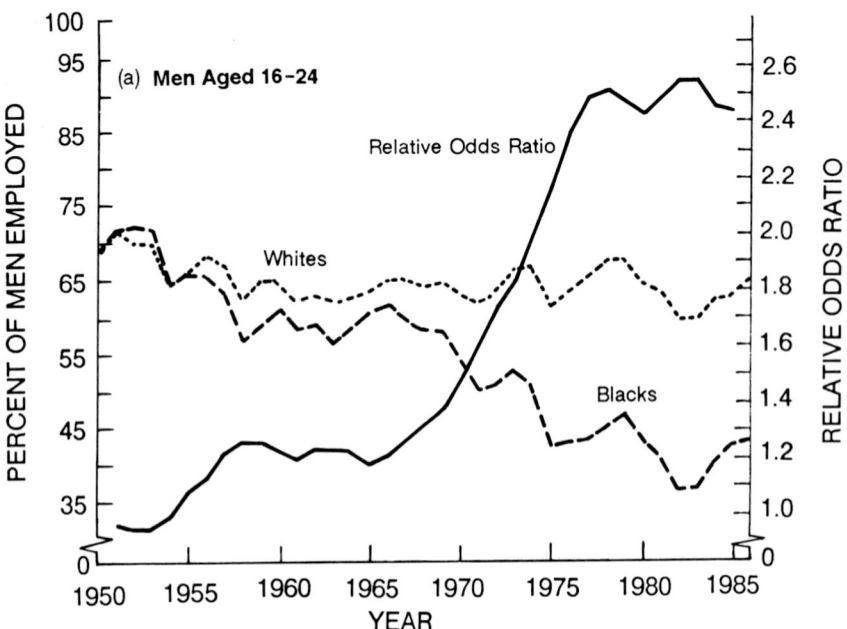

Source: Data from decennial censuses and Current Population Surveys.

FIGURE 6-7   *(Continued)*

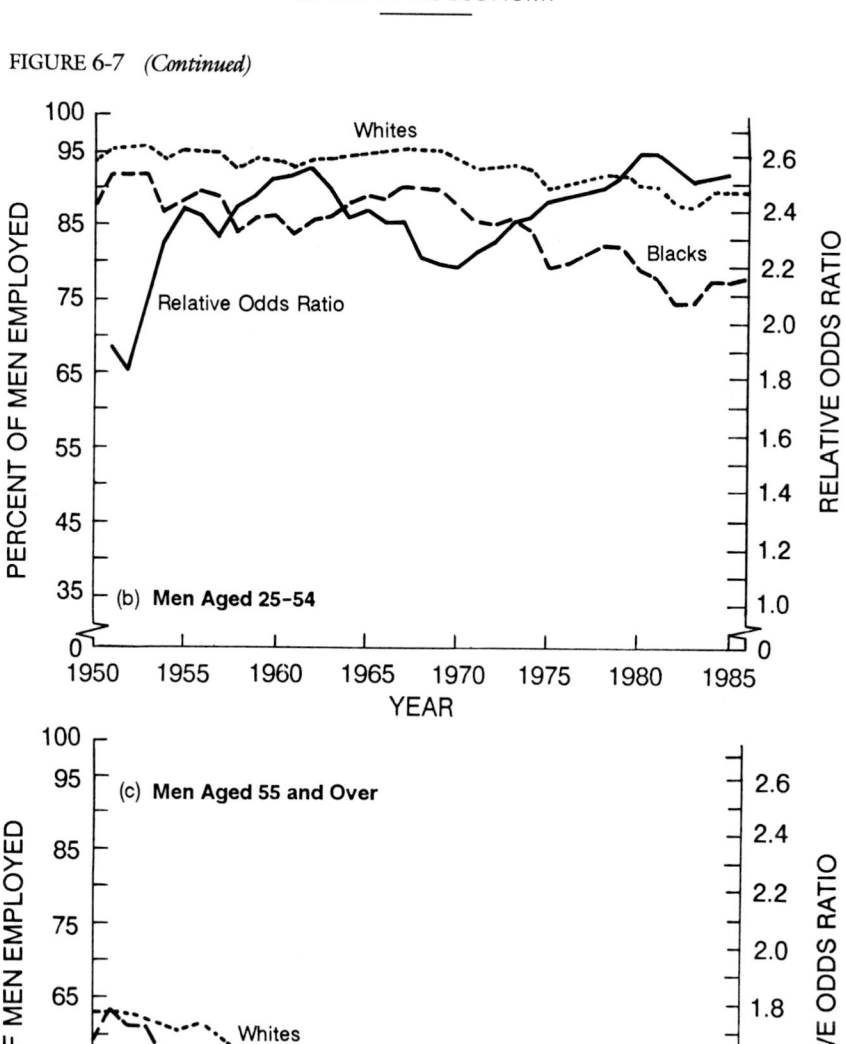

(b) **Men Aged 25-54**

(c) **Men Aged 55 and Over**

than white men's in both 1972 and 1986. However, over those years blacks' employment rates fell more than twice as much as whites'. Thus, the difference in unemployment rates is arithmetically why the black employment/population ratio fell 8 points while the white ratio fell 4.7 points.

Age-specific employment trends for black and white men and women from 1950 to 1985 are summarized in Figures 6-7 and 6-8. For each of three groups, those aged 16–24, 25–54, and 55 and over, the figures show the age-standardized employment/population ratio on the left scale. The same figures also present the relative black/white odds of employment, a 3-year moving average based on the percentage of white and black population at work. In 1950–1952, the relative odds of being employed to not being employed for men aged 16–24 was 1; that is, equal percentages of young white and black men were at work. In 1983–1985, the odds of having a job for young white men were about 2.5 times those for young black men. Among both young men and young women, the racial gap in employment has grown much larger. In particular, the relative odds of a young black person being employed deteriorated sharply from the mid-1960s to the early 1980s.

Figure 6-9 summarizes these dramatic changes in the work careers of men and women. It presents estimates of the lifetime labor force experiences of

FIGURE 6-8 Black and white women aged (a) 16–24, (b) 25–54, and (c) 55 and over who are employed, 1950–1986, and 3-year moving average of relative odds of employment, 1951–1985.

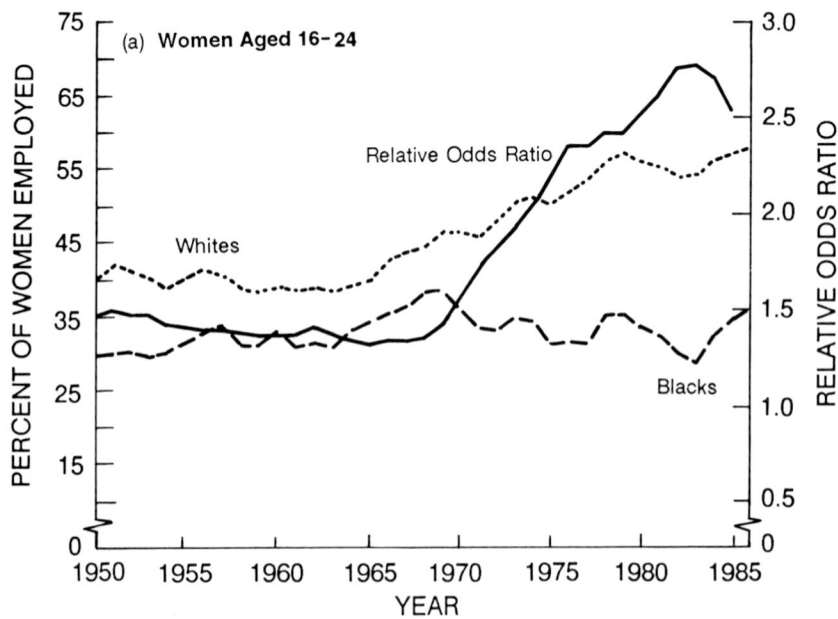

Source: Data from decennial censuses and Current Population Surveys.

FIGURE 6-8 *(Continued)*

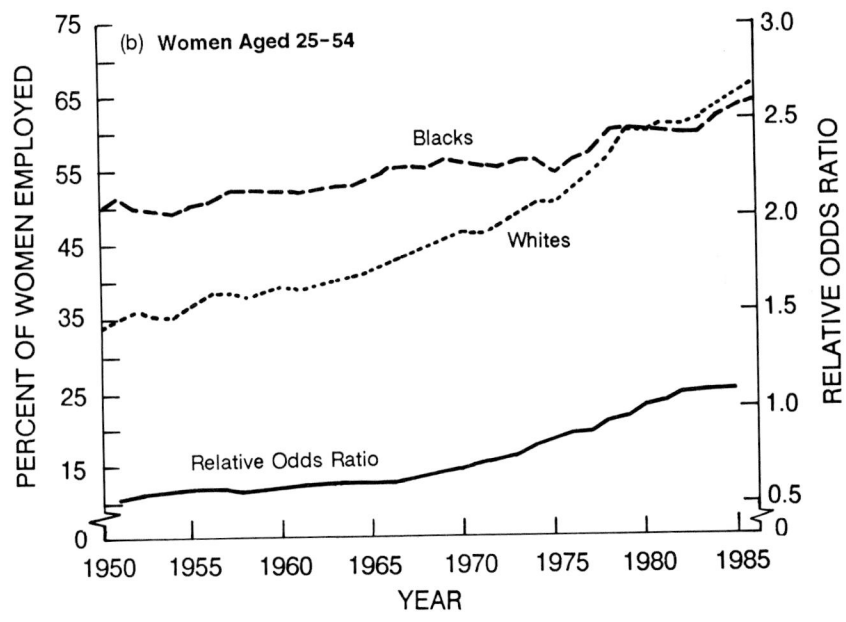

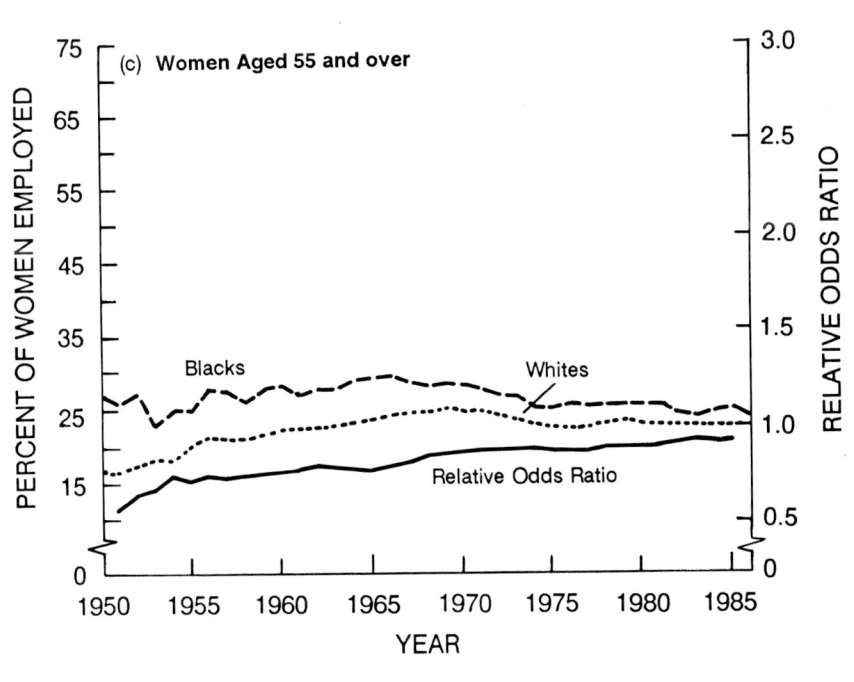

FIGURE 6-9 Estimated time spent employed and unemployed in a 45-year work career, by (a) men and (b) women, 1940–1985.

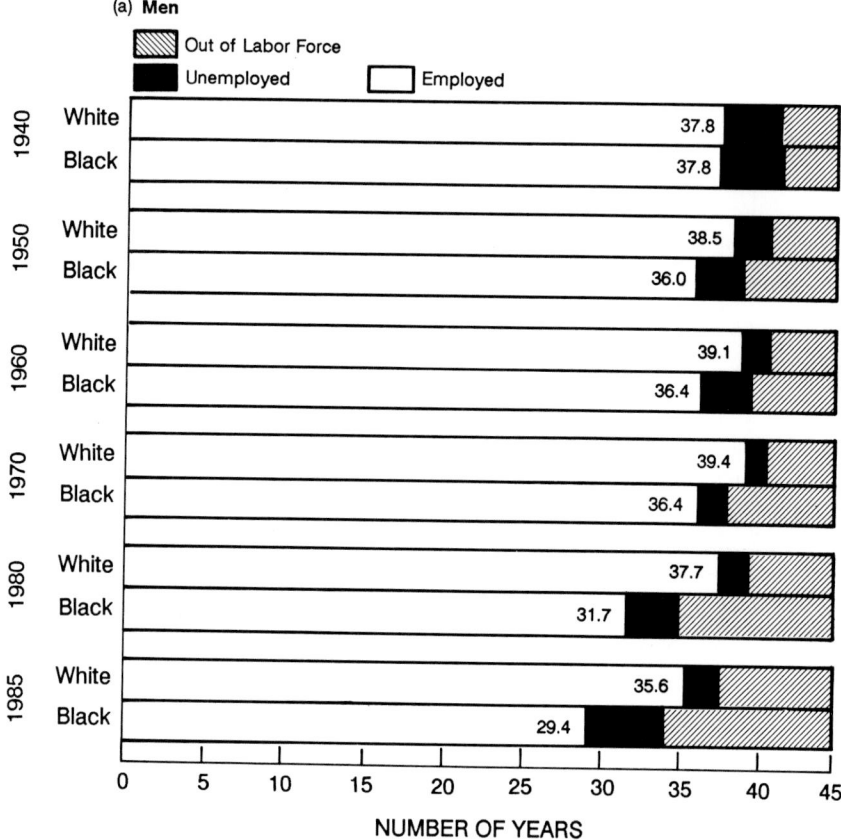

blacks and whites according to the rates of employment and unemployment observed from 1940 to 1985. These data show how many years a typical person could expect to be employed, unemployed, and out of the labor force from age 20 to age 65. (The estimates assume that a person lives for the entire 45-year span.) Again, these data are best viewed as summaries of the labor market conditions experienced by a group in a given year. They thus provide an excellent framework from which to compare such experiences in different years. In 1940, for example, a black man could expect to be employed for 37.8 years, unemployed for 4.0 years, and out of the labor force for 3.2 years.

Among men, the most substantial declines in years of employment have occurred since 1970, a change that is accounted for by higher rates of both unemployment and nonparticipation in the labor force. The decrease in employment has been greater among blacks. Between 1970 and 1985, the

FIGURE 6-9 *(Continued)*

(b) Women

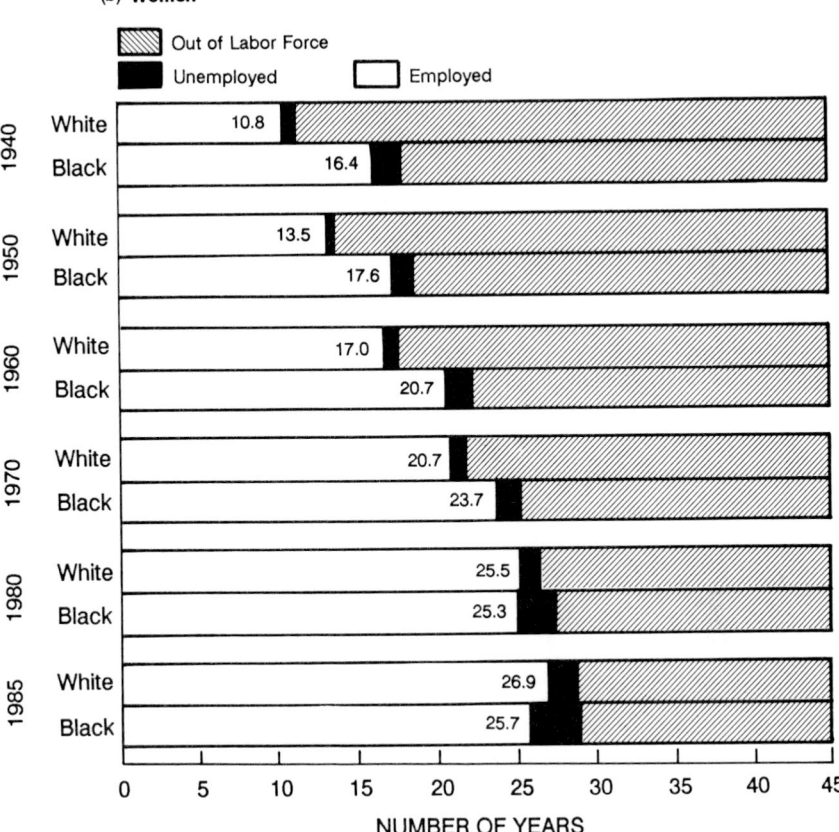

NUMBER OF YEARS

expected years of work for a white man fell from 39 to 36, but for a black man the change was from 36 to 29 years. According to the 1985 rates, black men will spend an average of 5 years unemployed and 11 years out of the labor force as they age from 20 to 65; white men will spend an average of 2 years unemployed and 7 years out of the labor force.

Women spent increasing time on the job and decreasing time out of the labor market for the 1940–1985 period. Historically, black women have had higher rates of employment than white women, but, as noted above, this changed by the early 1980s, and largely because of higher black unemployment, white women now spend more years at work.

College-educated blacks and whites differ substantially in years of employment, unemployment, and labor force participation, a difference that helps to account for the lower earnings of blacks. According to the rates of 1985, a black male college graduate would, if he survived to age 65, be employed for 36 years, a white for 40 years.

The employment of black women has increased dramatically over the 1939–1984 period. The percentage of black women with labor market earnings increased from 32 percent in 1939 to 56 percent in 1984. However, the employment gains were not evenly distributed among women of different educational attainment. The labor force participation rates of women of both races, and their increases, were greatest at the upper educational levels. Increases in participation have been smaller among black than white women, and black women's unemployment rates have risen in comparison with white women's. In all group comparisons except those for college-educated women, the black-white difference in unemployment rates was greater in 1985 than 45 years earlier. More black women are in the labor force, but their greater vulnerability to unemployment gives them a lower employment/population ratio than white women. On the basis of 1985 rates, black female college graduates surviving to age 65 could expect to work 36 years, white female college graduates 33 years.

Important differences in employment trends over time can be seen for specific age groups. For example, an increasing proportion of whites work while they are teenagers or in their early 20s, but among young blacks, the proportion with jobs has declined. Among adult men (aged 25–54) the decrease in employment has been greater for blacks than for whites, while among adult women the rise in employment has been greater for whites.

The Special Problems of Black Men

Men without employment or earnings have posed a serious obstacle to blacks' economic progress. Although the average weekly earnings of black men have risen much more than those of white men, black males work, on average, fewer weeks per year than whites, and this gap has been widening. Comparing 1979 with 1939, a gain from 47 to 72 percent in relative *weekly* earnings per worker effected a much smaller gain, from 42 percent to 57 percent in relative earnings per capita (Table 6-5, page 295).

In 1939, blacks' unemployment rates were generally 50 to 60 percent higher than those of whites, but since 1959 blacks' rates have been about double whites' rates. The percentage point differences in the unemployment rates of black and white adult males were at a minimum in the late 1960s. Many workers, black and white, are not in the labor force because they are discouraged by a scarcity of jobs. Quite likely, black participation in the labor force would be as high as white participation if their unemployment rates were comparable. As an illustration, the unemployment rate among black males in the state of Connecticut during 1984 was 7.6 percent, which was approximately the nationwide unemployment rate of white males in that year (7.4 percent). In Connecticut, the labor force participation rate of black males exceeded the national aggregate rate for white and black males. In general, labor force participation rates of black males are greatest in those states with the lowest black unemployment rates (see Table 6-6).

Unemployment and short-term work have affected disadvantaged blacks more than those able to gain from the opportunities opened by the civil rights revolution. The decrease in labor force participation and the increase in unemployment among men have been greatest among those with little education (Farley, 1987).

The plight of blacks in the bottom economic stratum, relative to whites and to more fortunate blacks, is dramatically shown in census figures on men reporting no annual earnings (Table 6-7). These are not teenagers or elderly men but men of prime working age. For both races, there was a large decline in the proportion of men reporting no earnings between 1939 and 1959.[4] Since 1959, the proportion of men reporting no earnings has risen, but the increase has been much steeper among blacks than whites. The increase in nonearners has been greatest among men with limited educations and among those approaching retirement.

Those men reporting no earnings[5] must be dependent on their relatives or on activities they do not report to census interviewers. Some may receive food stamps, unemployment compensation, locally provided benefits, or disability insurance. As suggested above, the reported lack of earned income of these men is likely to be a factor in the decline of stable marriages and two-parent households; men with no earnings are not good prospects as husbands and fathers.

Explanations for declining employment of black men confront an apparent anomaly. Improved wage and occupation opportunities for blacks would be expected, in theory, to increase their labor force activity; yet black labor force participation has declined, even for prime-age males (aged 25–54). An explanation that receives strong theoretical support but very weak empirical support is that the decline in black male employment is due to the growth in social transfer program benefits that made not working an attractive choice for low-wage workers.

---

4. Some of the early change occurred because of the inclusion in the 1950 census of a question about self-employment earnings, which was not asked in 1940. Macroeconomic changes and increasing employment opportunities also played an important role since the reported unemployment rate for adult black men declined from 14.7 percent in 1939 to 7.6 percent in 1949.

5. The existence of an extensive underground economy ranging from off-the-books cash deals and in-kind trading to more traditional criminal activity is well known, but there are no reliable data on the extent of this activity or the typical incomes involved. For black youths and young men (aged 16–24) the National Bureau of Economic Research (NBER) sample of more than 2,000 youths from the worst inner-city poverty tracks in Boston, Chicago, and Philadelphia indicate that criminal activities are an important alternative to legal employment for a minority of black youths in these very disadvantaged areas. While 58 percent of the survey group believed earnings opportunities were greater on a job, 10 percent believed opportunities for earnings from employment and "street" activities were equal and 32 percent perceived greater opportunities on the street. About one-fourth of the income reported by the sample of youths was from crime. However, most of the crimes were committed by a small minority of the sample. About 16 percent reported involvement in criminal activity (Freeman and Holzer, 1986:14; Viscusi, 1986:343). The most profitable of these criminal activities resulted in increased income of about $2,000 annually (Viscusi, 1986:333). We caution that this subsample was intentionally biased to survey the most disadvantaged black youths and, therefore, its findings cannot be extrapolated to the entire black population of males aged 16–24.

TABLE 6-6 Employment and Labor Force Participation Rate of Black Men in Selected States, 1984

| | Unemployed | | Labor Force Participation | | Difference: All Men Minus |
State	Black Men	All Men	Black Men	All Men	Black Men
Connecticut	7.6	4.2	78.0	78.8	0.8
South Carolina	9.8	5.5	68.6	74.7	6.1
Maryland	10.9	5.2	76.3	77.9	1.6
Virginia	11.0	4.5	76.0	80.5	4.5
Georgia	11.5	5.4	71.3	76.9	5.6
United States	16.4	7.4[a]	70.8	76.4	5.6

[a]The national unemployment rate for white males aged 25–54 was 5.2 percent.

Note: These five states have the lowest unemployment rates for black men, aged 16 and older, of those states that meet the Bureau of Labor Statistics' publication standards of reliability.

Source: Data from Bureau of Labor Statistics.

The Great Society of the 1960s stressed job training and employment policies, but it also increased social income transfers. The rate of growth of transfers in real per capita terms increased until the mid-1970s, and some of these programs are known to have affected labor force activity. For example, participation in disability payments programs—given to individuals who suffer from work-related disabilities—expanded greatly as benefit levels rose and eligibility standards were lowered. Barring cases of severe disability, those most likely to leave the work force are workers whose earnings are relatively low compared with benefit payments; thus, participation in these programs is proportionately higher for blacks than whites. However, the precise magnitude of disability transfers is not known and the evidence is not clear (Haveman and Wolfe, 1984; O'Neill et al., 1986:56–69; Parsons, 1980; Vroman, 1987). Furthermore, research by Brown (1984b) and Darity and Myers (1980) did not find that transfer programs caused blacks to leave the labor force at a greater rate than whites. Some scholars such as Becker (1981:Ch. 11) and Murray (1984) claim that government incentives have led to marital instability, more female family heads, and lower labor force attachment for males. (It is true that single men are less likely to work than married men.) However, the evidence supporting this position is also extremely weak (see Chapter 10).

In contrast to this proposed explanation of declining black employment is a more structural explanation. The shifting industrial base of the U.S. economy from blue-collar manufacturing to service industries, the slowdown in economic growth, and the consequent decline in real wages could be expected to produce a period of economic and social distress. For displaced and educationally or spatially misplaced workers, the rise in unemployment

TABLE 6-7 Men with No Earnings (in percent), by Age and Race, 1939–1984

Age	1939 Black	1939 White	1949 Black	1949 White	1959 Black	1959 White	1969 Black	1969 White	1979 Black	1979 White	1984 Black	1984 White
20–24	32	27	20	16	14	8	16	8	23	7	28	9
25–54	28	25	11	7	8	5	8	4	16	5	16	5
55–64	46	43	19	16	20	14	22	1	35	22	42	26
65+	72	74	55	9	63	61	68	65	78	71	81	78

Sources: Data from decennial censuses and Current Population Surveys.

and increased competition for moderate- to high-paying jobs might well lead to a rise in the number of discouraged workers. These men discontinue active job search for long periods of time. The rise in government transfer programs may have aided such decisions, but there are little theoretical or empirical grounds for believing that transfers were the major factor. The data clearly show that the adverse events had an earlier and more severe impact on the least educated workers and on blacks; thus, it is not surprising that black men with higher unemployment rates, more volatile occupations, lower wages, lower education, and disproportionate location in the urban areas of the most economically affected "snow belt" have lower labor force participation rates than white men.

OCCUPATIONS

Changes in Occupational Distribution

Concurrent with the distressing trends in black employment, the occupational distribution of employed blacks has dramatically improved since 1939. On the eve of World War II, blacks were concentrated in a very confined range of low-paying jobs: 75 percent of the employed black men in 1940 worked on farms as laborers or in factories as machine operators; 68 percent of black women were domestic servants or farm laborers. As blacks moved into cities they began to obtain better jobs (see Table 6-1, page 273); the proportion of employed workers who held professional or managerial jobs from 1950 to 1982 is shown in Figure 6-10. While the occupational distribution of whites improved as the economy shifted from blue-collar jobs to white-collar and service jobs, changes were somewhat greater among blacks as barriers to good jobs were lowered. For example, the percentage of employed white men with professional or managerial positions rose from 20 percent in 1950 to 32 percent in 1982; for nonwhite men, the increase was from 6 percent to 20 percent. Among women there is even clearer evidence of a narrowing gap in the occupational ranks: the percentage of employed white women holding these higher ranking jobs increased from 18 percent in 1950 to 26 percent in 1982; for nonwhite women, the percentage rose from 7 to 20 percent.

Numerous studies analyzing differences across the occupational distribution find that the proportion of employed workers in better jobs increased more rapidly for blacks than for whites and that this upgrading continued throughout the 1970s and 1980s (see e.g., Beller, 1984; Freeman, 1973). Studies of occupational mobility that take into account black-white differences in age, educational attainment, and place of residence also report a declining net effect of being black per se (Featherman and Hauser, 1976, 1978; Hout, 1984).

Nevertheless, large occupational differences remain and blacks are still greatly overrepresented in low-wage, low-skill jobs. In 1982, the percentage of black men employed as laborers or machine operators was greater than it

FIGURE 6-10 Professional and managerial workers, (a) men and (b) women, by race, 1950–1982.

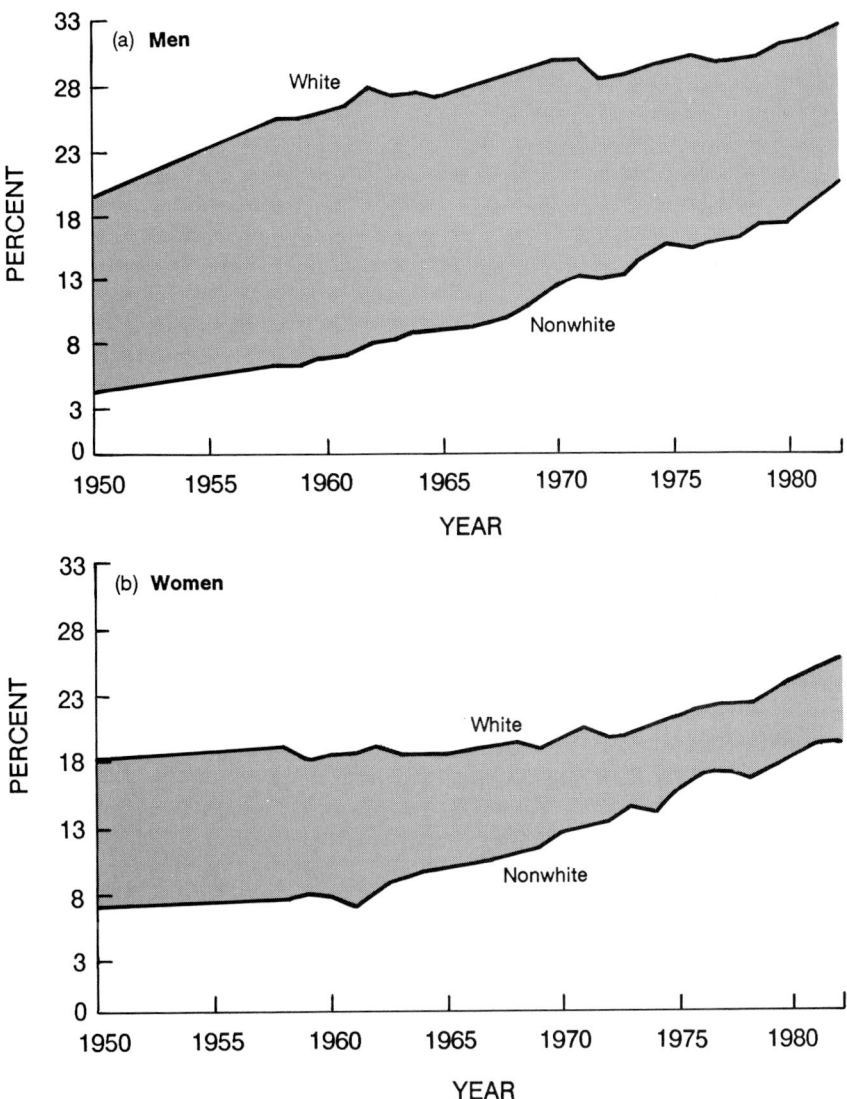

Source: Data from decennial censuses and Bureau of Labor Statistics.

was for white men in 1940. And the proportion of employed black men with professional or managerial jobs was barely equal to what it had been among white men three decades earlier. Among women, the corresponding lag in the proportion with professional or managerial jobs was about two decades. Several more decades of substantial change would have to occur before blacks and whites have similar occupational distributions.

As we noted above, occupational differences between black and white women have narrowed considerably since 1960, when 45 percent of working black women were in personal household service (see Table 6-1, page 273). In terms of broad occupational categories, blacks and whites are distributed similarly, although black women are twice as likely as white women to work in service occupations and more likely to work as laborers. White women are more likely to be professional or managerial workers and to work in sales. Moreover, 44 percent of black women are employed in lower paying, lower level, pink- and blue-collar occupations in manufacturing, service, and private households.

Malveaux (1986:11–13) points out that finer occupational breakdowns disclose that black women are occupationally separated into jobs that are not only "typically female" but also disproportionately black female. She defines "typically black female" occupations as those in which black women's representation is more than twice their representation in the labor force. In service jobs, for example, black women in 1981 were overrepresented by a factor of 3 or 4 as chambermaids, welfare service aides, cleaners, and nurse's aides: 41 percent of the black women who work in service occupations were employed in these four types of jobs. Nearly one-quarter of all black women were concentrated in just 6 of 48 clerical occupations. They are overrepresented by a factor of 4 as file clerks, typists, teacher's aids, keypunch operators, calculating machine operators, and social-welfare clerical assistants.

Self-Employment

Since the 1960s, market opportunities have induced blacks to create and expand businesses serving corporate and government clients. Government and private set-asides, preferential procurement policies, and other programs have often aided better educated and younger blacks to create and expand firms, particularly in finance, insurance, and real estate (see Chapter 4).

In 1959, self-employed blacks had, on average, less than 8 years of education, and their average earnings were lower than those of black employees. In contrast, by 1980, self-employed blacks under age 65 had more than 11 years of education, and their average earnings (from all sources) exceeded those of black employees. The average self-employment earnings of blacks also gained, relative to whites: in 1985, the self-employment earnings of black men relative to white men were roughly the same as relative wages and salaries, 64 and 66 percent, respectively; the same was true of women, 95 and 94 percent, respectively, but black women are self-employed at much lower rates than the other groups.

In 1960, two lines of business—personal services and retailing—accounted for more than one-half of all minority enterprises. The four most common fields were personal services, retail, construction, and other services. Between

1960 and 1980, however, all of the relative growth in minority enterprises occurred outside these four traditional lines of business, and especially in business services, finance, insurance and real estate, transportation and communication, and wholesaling (Bates, 1986:29–30). These are more skill-intensive lines of business, reflected in rising average years of education among self-employed blacks. Among all blacks self-employed in finance, insurance, and real estate in 1980, 66 percent had attended college (compared with 28 percent of all self-employed blacks) and most had degrees.

EMPLOYMENT AND EQUAL OPPORTUNITY

Although civil rights legislation, a general antidiscrimination ethos, affirmative action, and pressures from blacks and whites alike have greatly expanded opportunities for blacks, labor market discrimination has by no means completely disappeared. Rather, a very complicated picture has emerged. If a man or woman, regardless of race, manages to enter the labor market with a high-quality education or skill, he or she generally enjoys equal access to entry positions and to lower middle-status ranks. However, some evidence suggests that opportunities at the middle stage of a worker's career and at higher status positions are not equally available to blacks (see Chapter 3; Lazear, 1979); and, importantly, clearly race plays a decisive role in determining whether a man or woman will in fact reach the labor market with a quality education (see Chapter 7). This racial filter arises partly from black-white separation in residential, educational, and social networks and especially from the growing isolation of the black poor. Furthermore, these interactions between race and status result in employment network patterns that often vitiate the benefits of education for black male high school graduates.

EQUAL EMPLOYMENT OPPORTUNITY ENFORCEMENT

The idea of equal employment opportunity for black Americans gained highly visible support from the federal government for the first time during World War II. Policy in this area focused on the exclusion of blacks from good jobs in the expanding wartime industries and led to creation of the Fair Employment Practices Committee (see Chapter 2). Although Congress refused to extend enforcement of the principle of nondiscrimination in employment to the peacetime economy, blacks continued to pressure President Truman. In 1948, he followed the recommendations of his Committee on Civil Rights and proposed a federal policy of equal opportunities in employment. Thirteen years later, President Kennedy, whose election had resulted in part from black votes, issued *Executive Order 10925,* which banned racial discrimination by government contractors and established guidelines intended to promote the hiring of blacks.

The paramount achievement of the civil rights movement in this field was the Civil Rights Act of 1964, which outlawed discrimination in all aspects of employment. Title VII of the act created the Equal Employment Opportunity Commission (EEOC), a permanent, five-member bipartisan commission, to combat discriminatory employment practices in the private sector that are based on race, color, religion, sex, or national origin. Employers and labor unions with at least 100 employees or members and employment agencies were covered by the legislation. A 1972 amendment to the act extended the covered sector to organizations with more than 15 employees. The EEOC was empowered to investigate complaints, conciliate between employers and employees, and recommend to the U.S. Department of Justice that legal action be taken against violators of antidiscrimination laws. In the 1970s, the EEOC was given the power to sue alleged discriminators in court. The EEOC regularly collects compliance reports from the sector of the private economy covered by Title VII (see Chapter 5).

In 1965, *Executive Order 11246* established rules for nondiscrimination by federal contractors, first-tier subcontractors, and construction projects operating with federal assistance. Contractors with 50 or more employees and contracts of $50,000 or more are required to develop and submit affirmative action compliance programs with goals and timetables for the hiring and promotion of minorities. The executive order is administered by the Office of Contract Compliance Programs (OFCCP) within the U.S. Department of Labor.

Many people have attributed black economic gains in the 1960s and 1970s to these agencies' enforcement of antidiscrimination laws, and a number of studies have addressed this question. One body of research approaches the problem through statistical analysis of time-series data from a number of published sources. Another body of research attempts to measure the effect of federal employment discrimination programs through econometric analysis of cross-sectional data obtained from the EEOC and the OFCCP.

At the outset, we draw attention to an important distinction between these two categories of research. Time-series studies have been primarily concerned with the broad impact of equal employment opportunity (EEO) laws and their enforcement throughout the private and government sectors of the national labor market. Cross-sectional analyses focus specifically, and more narrowly, on the effects of federal government affirmative action requirements on private firms contracting with the government.

There is greater agreement among the findings from the latter research than among the research addressing the effects of general antidiscrimination laws. Nearly all of the cross-sectional research finds that blacks' employment share increased more in contractor firms subject to affirmative action requirements than in firms without federal contracts. In addition, some studies reported small or mixed results on occupational upgrading. Most of these studies analyzed data collected in the late 1960s and early 1970s. A more recent analysis by Leonard (1985) reported larger employment effects for the period 1974–1980. Leonard also reported that black males experienced occupational upgrading as a result of affirmative action compliance.

The first study on the race and sex composition of the work forces of government contractors and employers was that of Ashenfelter (1968). Subsequently, four studies covering the period 1966–1973 used EEO data to estimate the impact of OFCCP on the relative employment of blacks (Ashenfelter and Heckman, 1976; Burman, 1973; Goldstein and Smith, 1976; Heckman and Wolpin, 1976). All but Goldstein and Smith (1976) found positive effects on relative black male employment. There was only a small impact on relative occupational position in contractor establishments, although Burman (1973) found exceptions to that finding. These cross-sectional studies covered the late 1960s and early 1970s, before OFCCP had adequately specified how affirmative action was to be applied to contractor establishments (Wallace, 1984:11). Leonard (1985) used regression analysis to measure the effect of contractor and compliance review status on the change in the percentage employed according to demographic groups at 68,690 contractor establishments subject to affirmative action policies in the 1970s. He reported significantly larger black employment gains and net occupational upgrading than did studies of earlier periods.

There are two primary methodological difficulties in interpreting these studies (Heckman, 1987:14–15). First, estimates of black gains based on comparisons of employment or occupational status in firms with and without federal contracts at a point in time might be biased upward because firms hire in the same market. Thus, contractor firms bidding for black labor in order to meet federally mandated targets may simply hire blacks away from noncontractors. If contractor firms gain at the expense of noncontractor firms, comparisons of differences in employment status between the two types of firms will overstate actual gains in black employment status. Comparisons of contractor and noncontractor firms may overstate the effects of affirmative action when nothing has happened but a rearrangement of a given pool of labor.

Second, virtually all firms in given industries bid for government contracts. Winning a contract is partly chance, and firms may bid often. It is costly to hire and fire workers; thus, any noncontractor firm contemplating a bid may maintain a pool of black employees, and thus its work force may be similar to current contractor firms. In this event, although OFCCP could have had a large effect on government contractor industries, comparisons of contractor and noncontractor firms at a point in time would understate the effects of affirmative action.

Because of the importance of hiring and firing costs and of the robustness of the many studies finding positive effects, the second argument appears to be more plausible than the first. And thus, the findings of positive employment and occupation effects of the OFCCP activities are assessed to have been generally positive.

The time-series studies of EEOC in general have produced less agreement.

Freeman (1973) concluded that the improvements in the economic position of blacks during the late 1960s were largely consequences of government antidiscriminatory activity following the 1964 Civil Rights Act. Vroman (1975) reported similar findings, and Leonard (1985), using data on more than 1,700 class-action suits under Title VII, presented evidence that litigation under Title VII played an important and independent role in advancing the employment of blacks and had a relatively greater impact than affirmative action. But the research literature also contains studies that find very weak or nonexistent effects of government employment laws on black employment status; for a review, see Brown (1984a). Most notably, Smith and Welch (1977, 1986), the two strongest proponents of improvements in education as the major source of black economic gains, have reported either nonexistent effects or effects during the 1970s of short duration for equal employment policy.

Many of the latter studies suffer from a set of common problems. Given the ubiquity of the changes, studies that compare public-sector employers to private-sector employers have not been adequately specified to assess the impact of antidiscrimination activity or affirmative action that has been aimed at both sectors. In addition, if firms hire and fire within competitive labor markets, evidence of little difference in the relative wages between workers in contractor and noncontractor sectors is consistent with either strong or no effects of antidiscrimination programs: in a competitive market, the wages of identical labor would be equal in both sectors. Thus, the effects of equal employment opportunity programs cannot be measured by comparing wages across sectors as has been attempted in some studies (Smith and Welch, 1977).

A major problem is that it is difficult to measure the specific effects of general antidiscrimination laws. In addition, many programs, policies, and economic events occur contemporaneously. A recent study by Heckman and Payner (1989) overcomes many of these difficulties by using a variety of methods of empirical analysis on a single large and important industry, South Carolina textiles. Their analysis eliminates alternative hypotheses and strongly supports the conclusion that EEOC and OFCCP were major factors in the large increase in black employment during the 1960s in an industry that previously had barred almost all black workers. The Heckman and Payner study also illustrates, in a positive manner, how difficult it is to isolate the effects of a few programs or events when many of them are changing at the same time.

The changes in employment law occurred during a period when rapid changes in attitudes toward black-white relations were taking place across the entire nation (see Chapter 3). White Americans during the 1960s moved from significant verbal resistance of equal treatment of blacks in employment to overwhelming verbal acceptance. Many public and private institutions of higher and secondary education opened their doors to more than token numbers of blacks for the first time, and occupational and earnings upgrading escalated for many blacks. These signal events did not occur in a vacuum.

The civil rights movement had been waged long and hard to effect just such changes. It is beyond the scope of available data to determine unambiguously the precise numerical contribution of any one event, program, or executive order. Laws change and, if they are enforced, those laws change people's attitudes and behavior, as well as social institutions, or a social crisis emerges. Laws do not and cannot rely entirely on direct enforcement. If a society is to function, its justice system must depend to a large extent on voluntary compliance, although this must often be backed by governmental threat of sanctions.

Title VII has had a tremendous effect on behavior in the U.S. labor market. The EEOC and private individuals and organizations have taken hundreds of Title VII discrimination cases to the federal judicial courts. These cases have produced dozens of important judicial rulings that changed the behavior of employers and unions toward blacks and other discriminated groups (Jaynes et al., 1986). Many employers charged with discrimination modified their personnel procedures extensively even before the cases were decided. Other employers altered their procedures after observing companies in their industry being charged with violation of employment discrimination statutes. Major legal changes have occurred in seniority rules, hiring and promotion practices, and even in what constitutes labor market discrimination and have had wide-reaching effects on blacks' relative position in the labor market. These legal changes and their enforcement altered the social context of hiring, firing, and promoting. Firms in the private sector as well as local, state, and federal governments designed and instituted equal employment policies and affirmative action plans (Burstein, 1985; Marshall et al., 1978; Wallace, 1984:25).

Other important supporting evidence for the positive effects of EEOC laws and enforcement is contained in case studies of litigation involving unions and large employers. Cases producing consent decrees—such as a landmark agreement between AT&T, the EEOC, the U.S. Department of Justice, and the U.S. Department of Labor—provide specific examples of how equal opportunity employment has positively affected blacks' employment position (Wallace, 1985).

In summary, while we cannot determine with the available data the precise numerical effect of antidiscrimination programs, the evidence does show positive effects. General changes in race relations, educational improvement, the state of the economy, and government policies that facilitate these factors and provide incentives for the equal employment opportunity of minorities have each had an important role in determining blacks' labor market status.

SOCIAL NETWORKS AND JOB OPPORTUNITIES

Increases in the concentration of urban poverty among blacks (see above) has been especially damaging to the opportunities available for black youths. Highly concentrated poverty areas can be distinguished from other areas not merely by the race of the residents but, more importantly, by the kinds of access that the residents of these neighborhoods have to jobs and job networks, availability of marriageable partners, involvement in quality schools, and exposure to conventional role models (Anderson, 1986; Clark, 1965; Wilson, 1987). When urban analysts speak of the "ghetto underclass," they refer to these extreme areas of poverty. Very few whites, even poor whites, live in extreme poverty areas. The effects of adverse opportunities and perverse incentives on young black women and men can be seen in all of the data presented above.

The data analyzed from an early 1980s National Bureau of Economic Research (NBER) survey of young black men (aged 16–24; see note 5 above) identify many of the severe economic problems confronted by black youth in the most poverty-stricken areas of U.S. inner cities. As reported by Freeman and Holzer (1986:8), extensive analysis of these data found:

> [Black youths living in the poorest areas of inner cities were] much more likely to be unemployed and less likely to be employed than white youths or all black youths. They tend to have slightly lower wages than other youths and they work fewer weeks per year. In addition, those youths have far worse family backgrounds than others. One-third of them live in public housing; almost one-half of them have a family member on welfare. Only 28 percent of them have an adult man in their household.

Two particular effects stand out in relation to the employment of black youth. First, employment and labor force participation rates are especially low among inner-city black youths from households below the poverty income line (Freeman and Holzer, 1986). Second, young blacks with 12 or fewer years of education report earnings and occupations below those of equivalently educated whites. In contrast, the earnings and occupations of college-educated black youths are much more comparable to those of similarly educated young whites (Jaynes et al., 1986).

Investigators of the NBER data reported that much of the unemployment of the most disadvantaged black youths is due to two facts: they are frequently unemployed for long periods of time, and once out of work they have a very difficult time finding another job. Twenty percent of the young black men in the sample who were out of school experienced periods of joblessness that lasted longer than 1 year. And the durations of these periods of nonemployment do not appear to shorten with age (Freeman and Holzer, 1986:9; see also Clark and Summers, 1982). These employment problems are likely to continue as black youths age. Freeman and Holzer (1986:9) estimated that "if the rate of increase in employment with age remains at the level of the 1970s, the cohort of inner-city black youths 18 to 19 years old in 1979 will not achieve a rate of employment of 80 percent until they reach their mid-thirties."

Social networks and differential methods of job search are linked to the declining employment opportunities for poor black youths. Geographical dispersion of industry has probably contributed to an intensified competition for jobs at a time when the labor supply of women has increased and real wages have been generally falling (Borjas, 1986). As a result, the importance of social networks for gaining information about and access to jobs has probably been magnified. Many young blacks are outside the principal employment networks because of residential and educational segregation and resulting social separation.

A number of studies have found that young blacks and whites often use different techniques of job search. Blacks more often walk in and apply. Whites are more often referred by friends and relatives or public employment agencies. The search techniques of blacks are likely to lead to lower paying jobs. Higher paying positions for both high school graduates and college-educated youths are usually filled through informal social networks, to which blacks, especially those from poor inner-city neighborhoods, are not connected (Braddock and McPartland, 1987; Bradshaw, 1973; Culp and Dunson, 1986; Holzer, 1987). These different search techniques are related to the fact that blacks and whites have separate social ties and networks. Young blacks have ties to other blacks who, like themselves, have attended predominantly black schools and lived in black neighborhoods. Older black males— concentrated in blue-collar jobs in now-declining manufacturing industries— are of little help to young blacks seeking jobs in service industries today.

Braddock and McPartland (1987) report that the quality of employment blacks obtain is correlated with the racial composition of their social networks. Specifically, they found that blacks who attended racially mixed secondary schools are more likely to reside in racially mixed neighborhoods and work in racially mixed environments. They also earn more. If they go to college, they are more likely to attend racially mixed colleges. In short, they concluded that for blacks (Braddock and McPartland, 1987:11) "segregated networks lead to poor paying, more segregated jobs (it is better on the average to depend on some other job-search technique), and desegregated networks lead to better paying, less segregated work."

Interestingly, this association did not show up for black women. A possible explanation may be that black females gained access to expanding nonpersonal service employment and clerical opportunities during the 1950s and 1960s when fewer white females were in the labor force. The social employment networks of black females may therefore be more helpful to young black women attempting to gain access to clerical positions and other white- and pink-collar jobs.

Employers appear to devalue diplomas granted by predominantly black high schools. Employers may also associate young black males with "criminal behavior or aggression" (Braddock et al., 1986:21; see also Anderson, 1980, 1986). Such kinds of attribution may arise in social contexts in which a person has to decide on incomplete information whether to serve or hire or admit another. A job decision may go against a black youth, for example, simply because in the absence of specific evidence to the contrary, black youths are statistically more likely than whites or older adults to be poorly educated, inexperienced, unreliable, and even to have a criminal record. This sort of probabilistic prejudgment is unfair to an individual black to whom is incorrectly attributed the characteristics of others, and it can lead to self-perpetuating circles. The victims of such prejudgments in hiring lose the experience and the references that would make them employable. They may turn to activities and life-styles that justify the stereotype and raise the adverse odds that similar blacks encounter in the future (see Anderson, 1980, 1986; Freeman and Holzer, 1986:14).

Poor employment experiences of black youths are due to many factors: inadequate demand for black youths by employers offering "good" jobs; discrimination; increased competition from white women who entered the labor force in great numbers during the late 1970s; and the relatively poor educational preparation of many black youths. Many young blacks thus move in and out of low-paying jobs that offer little advancement potential. Black youth, like white youth, appear willing to accept these jobs only as a temporary relief. As Holzer (1986:65) noted, the potential of public- or private-sector programs that offer more low-paying, dead-end jobs cannot be effective as a means of improving the employment conditions among disadvantaged young blacks. Minimum-wage employment opportunities appear to be reasonably attainable. If the better employment opportunities to which many blacks aspire (see Chapter 10) are to be realized, there will need to be substantial improvements in the education and training opportunities available to black youth.

Several employment and training programs whose objectives are enhancing the long-term employment and earning opportunities available to disadvantaged people have been initiated by federal and local governments since the early 1960s. These programs have been very diverse in their approaches and in their targeted client groups. The same may be said for the research strategies used to evaluate such programs and their cost-effectiveness; for recent reviews of the large literature, see Bassi and Ashenfelter (1986), Betsy and colleagues (1985), Rees (1986), and Sawhill (1988).

Conclusions about the overall effectiveness of the large and diverse set of employment and training programs have been mixed. For example, Bassi and Ashenfelter (1986) concluded that, on the whole, the programs had been neither overwhelmingly successful nor a great failure. Two kinds of programs stand out as notably ineffective and notably effective. Short-term programs that emphasize work (on-the-job) experience alone appear to be among the least effective: clients' opportunities after such programs are virtually the same as they were before the program. Since low-skilled, disadvantaged workers are likely to be placed only in low-paying, non–career-oriented jobs, this finding seems unsurprising (Burtless, 1984; Sawhill, 1988).

In contrast, one kind of program that appears particularly effective has been those that provide very intensive remedial education and job training for youths, particularly the Job Corps. Although the Job Corps is quite expensive relative to short-term programs, it has frequently been found to have benefits significantly greater than its costs. The most positive effects have been on the employment and earnings of black participants. Positive effects are generally reported for black males and females, and especially young males, but not for whites (see Betsey et al., 1985; Burtless, 1984; Rees, 1986; Sawhill, 1988).

There are no satisfactory substitutes for a vigorous and expanding economy and an effective public school system to achieve an educated and employed work force. However, as complements to these important goals, intensive remedial education and job training programs are the most effective methods for ameliorating the very serious problems currently affecting the labor market condition of large numbers of poorly educated and disaffected black youths.

CONCLUSIONS

Changes in labor market conditions and social policies of governments have had great effects on the economic status of black Americans. Yet the current economic prospects are not good for many blacks. Adverse changes in labor market opportunities—falling real wages and employment, increases in one-parent families with one or no working adults—have made conditions especially difficult for those blacks from the most disadvantaged backgrounds. However, changes in family structure have not been a major cause of continuing high poverty rates since the early to mid-1970s; rather, lower real wages of men and women have increased the difficulty of rising from poverty through employment. This factor of lower real wages in recent years can be seen in the halt in reductions in poverty rates among all Americans.

Overall, from 1940 through roughly 1970, black Americans experienced sometimes erratic but generally significant improvements in their relative economic status: average earnings of men and women, per capita and family incomes, and measures of occupational status generally all rose relative to those of whites. While black women's earnings have reached near parity with those of white women, women's earnings lag behind men's. After the early 1970s, black gains in relative earnings and incomes slowed and then deteriorated for many indicators of average status (e.g., annual male earnings, per capita and family incomes). In particular, men's earnings and other aggregate measures of black income were, relative to white measures, lower in the mid-1980s than in 1970 and in many cases no greater than the levels reached in the 1960s.

An important explanation for these developments is that while the occupational positions and hourly wages received by employed blacks have continued to improve relative to whites, blacks' relative employment has fallen significantly. As a consequence, incomes and aggregate measures of earnings, being largely composed of the product of wages and employment, have not kept up with gains in wages. Reductions in relative levels of employment since 1970 for both black adult men and women have arithmetically been due primarily to higher unemployment rates. Although available data do not provide a definitive explanation for the particularly low employment rate of black men, the data do suggest that adverse changes in the demand for less educated workers had an especially important role in the employment status of black men.

One effect of the improvement in blacks' occupations and wages for those who are employed has been the development of an appreciable black middle class that exists in the presence of a large percentage of low-status blacks whose condition has persisted through periods of recession and prosperity. As this chapter shows, the economic fortunes of blacks are strongly tied (more so than those of whites) to a strong economy and vigorously enforced policies against discrimination. Without these conditions, the black middle class may persist, but it is doubtful it can grow or thrive. And the position of lower status blacks cannot be expected to improve.

Improvements in blacks' relative economic status have been primarily due to sustained economic growth and blacks' migration to higher wage sectors of the economy (1940–1973), rising levels of black education, vigorous enforcement of equal opportunity laws and employment programs that benefited blacks, and overall improvements in attitudes toward race relations in the economy. When these important factors have not been present, blacks have not generally made progress in their relative economic status.

REFERENCES

Anderson, Elijah
  1980 Some observations on black youth employment. Pp. 64–87 in Bernard Anderson and Isabel Sawhill, eds., *Youth Employment Issues and Policy*. Englewood Cliffs, N.J.: Prentice-Hall.
  1986 Of Old Heads and Young Boys: Notes on the Urban Black Experience. Paper prepared for the Committee on the Status of Black Americans, National Research Council, Washington, D.C.
Ashenfelter, Orley
  1968 *Minority Employment Patterns, 1966*. Princeton, N.J.: Industrial Relations Section, Department of Economics, Princeton University.
Ashenfelter, Orley, and James J. Heckman
  1976 Measuring the effect of an anti-discrimination program. Pp. 46–84 in Orley Ashenfelter and James Blum, eds., *Evaluating the Labor Market Effects of Social Programs*. Princeton, N.J.: Industrial Relations Section, Department of Economics, Princeton University.
Bassi, Laurie, and Orley Ashenfelter
  1986 The effect of direct job creation and training programs on low-skilled workers. Pp. 133–151 in Sheldon Danziger and Daniel Weinberg, eds., *Fighting Poverty: What Works and What Doesn't*. Cambridge, Mass.: Harvard University Press.
Bates, Timothy
  1986 Paper prepared for the Committee on the Status of Black Americans, National Research Council, Washington, D.C.
Becker, Gary
  1981 *A Treatise on the Family*. Cambridge, Mass.: Harvard University Press.
Beller, Andrea H.
  1984 Trends in occupational segregation by sex and race, 1960–1981. In Barbara F. Reskin, ed., *Sex Segregation in the Workplace*. Committee on Women's Employment and Related Social Issues. Washington, D.C.: National Academy Press.

Betsey, Charles L., Robinson G. Hollister, Jr., and Mary R. Papageorgiou
  1985 *Youth Employment and Training Programs: The YEDPA Years.* Committee on Youth
        Employment Programs. Washington, D.C.: National Academy Press.
Borjas, George J.
  1986 The demographic determinants of the demand for black labor. Pp. 191–232 in
        Richard B. Freeman and Harry J. Holzer, eds., *The Black Youth Employment Crisis.*
        Chicago and London: University of Chicago Press.
Braddock, JoMills Henry, II, Robert L. Crain, James M. McPartland, and Russell L.
Dawkins
  1986 Applicant race and job placement decisions: a national survey experiment. *Inter-*
        national Journal of Sociology and Social Policy 6(1):3–24.
Braddock, JoMills Henry, II, and James M. McPartland
  1987 How minorities continue to be excluded from equal employment opportunities:
        research on labor market and institutional barriers. *Journal of Social Issues*
        43(1)[Spring]:5–39.
Bradford, William D.
  1987 Wealth, Assets, and Income of Black Households. Paper prepared for the Commit-
        tee on the Status of Black Americans, National Research Council, Washington,
        D.C.
Bradshaw, Thomas
  1973 Jobseeking methods used by unemployed workers. *Monthly Labor Review*
        96(February):35–46.
Brown, Charles
  1984a The federal attack on labor market discrimination: the mouse that roared? In
        Ronald Ehrenburg, ed., *Research in Labor Economics.* New York: JAI Press.
  1984b Black/white earnings ratios since the Civil Rights Act of 1964: the importance of
        labor market dropouts. *Quarterly Journal of Economics* 99(February):31–44.
Burman, George
  1973 The Economics of Discrimination: The Impact of Public Policy. Ph.D. thesis,
        Graduate School of Business, University of Chicago.
Burstein, Paul
  1985 *Discrimination, Jobs, and Politics: The Struggle for Equal Employment Opportunity in*
        the United States Since the New Deal. Chicago: University of Chicago Press.
Burtless, Gary
  1984 Manpower policies for the disadvantaged: what works? *The Brookings Review*
        3(1)[Fall]:18–22.
  1987 The work response to a guaranteed income: a survey of experimental evidence.
        In Alicia H. Mannell, ed., *Lessons from the Income Maintenance Experiments.*
        Boston: Federal Reserve Bank of Boston.
Clark, Kenneth B.
  1965 *Dark Ghetto.* New York: Harper & Row.
Clark, Kim B., and Lawrence Summers
  1982 The dynamics of youth unemployment. In Richard B. Freeman and D. A. Wise,
        eds., *The Youth Labor Market Problem: Its Nature, Causes, and Consequences.* Chi-
        cago: University of Chicago Press.
Culp, Jerome, and Bruce H. Dunson
  1986 Brothers of a different color: a preliminary look at employer treatment of white and
        black youth. Pp. 233–260 in Richard B. Freeman and Harry J. Holzer, eds., *The*
        Black Youth Employment Crisis. Chicago and London: University of Chicago Press.
Danziger, Sheldon, and Peter Gottschalk
  1986a Do rising tides lift all boats? The impact of secular and cyclical changes in poverty.
        American Economic Review 76(2)[May]:405–410.
  1986b Unemployment Insurance and the Safety Net for the Unemployed. Discussion
        paper, Institute for Poverty, University of Wisconsin.

Danziger, Sheldon, and Daniel Weinberg, eds.
1986   *Fighting Poverty: What Works and What Doesn't.* Cambridge, Mass.: Harvard University Press.

Darity, William A., Jr., and Samuel L. Myers, Jr.
1980   Changes in black-white income inequality, 1968–1978: a decade of progress? *The Review of Black Political Economy* 10(4)[Summer]:354, 356–379.

Ellwood, David T.
1986a *Targeting the Would-Be Long Term Recipient of AFDC: Who Should Be Served?* Princeton, N.J.: Mathematica Policy Research.
1986b The spatial mismatch hypothesis: are there teenage jobs missing in the ghetto? Pp. 147–196 in Richard B. Freeman and Harry J. Holzer, eds., *The Black Youth Employment Crisis.* Chicago and London: University of Chicago Press.
1988   *Poor Support: Poverty in the American Family.* New York: Basic Books.

Farley, Reynolds
1987   Changes in the Status and Characteristics of Blacks: 1940 to Mid-1980s. Paper prepared for the Committee on the Status of Black Americans, National Research Council, Washington, D.C.

Featherman, David L., and Robert M. Hauser
1976   Prestige or socioeconomic scales in the study of occupational achievement. *Sociological Methods and Research* 4(4)[May]:403–422.
1978   *Opportunity and Change.* New York: Academic Press.

Freeman, Richard B.
1973   Changes in the labor market for black Americans, 1948–1972. *Brookings Papers on Economic Activity.* Vol. 1. Washington, D.C.: Brookings Institution.

Freeman, Richard B., and Harry J. Holzer, eds.
1986   *The Black Youth Employment Crisis.* Chicago and London: University of Chicago Press.

Goldstein, Morris, and Robert S. Smith
1976   The estimated impact of the antidiscrimination program aimed at federal contractors. *Industrial and Labor Relations Review* 29(4)[July]:523–543.

Gueron, Judith
1986   *Work Initiatives for Welfare Recipients: Lessons from a Multi-State Experiment.* New York: Manpower Demonstration Research Corporation.

Gwartney, James
1970   Changes in the nonwhite/white income ratio—1939–67. *American Economic Review* 60(5):872–883.

Haveman, Robert, and Barbara Wolfe
1984   The decline in male labor force participation comment. *Journal of Political Economy* 92(3)[October]:532–541.

Haworth, J. G., J. D. Gwartney, and C. Haworth
1975   Earnings productivity and changes in employment discrimination during the 1960's. *American Economic Review* 65(2)[March]:158–168.

Heckman, James J.
1987   The Impact of Government on the Economic Status of Black Americans. Unpublished paper, Department of Economics, University of Chicago.

Heckman, James J., and Brook S. Payner
1989   Determining the impact of federal antidiscrimination policy on the economic status of blacks: a study of South Carolina. *American Economic Review* 79(1)[March]:138–177.

Heckman, James J., and Kenneth I. Wolpin
1976   Does the Contract Compliance Program work? An analysis of Chicago data. *Industrial and Labor Relations Review* 29(July):544–564.

Hill, Robert B.
1987   The black middle class: past, present, and future. Pp. 43–64 in *The State of Black America 1986*. Washington, D.C.: National Urban League.
Holzer, Harry J.
1986   Black youth nonemployment: duration and job search. Pp. 23–65 in Richard B. Freeman and Harry J. Holzer, eds., *The Black Youth Employment Crisis*. Chicago: University of Chicago Press.
1987   Informal job search and black youth unemployment. *American Economic Review* 77(3)[June]:447–452.
Hout, Michael
1984   Occupational mobility of black men. *American Sociological Review* 49(3):308–322.
Jaynes, Gerald David, James Tobin, and Reynolds Farley, eds.
1986   Manuscript prepared for the Panel on Income, Employment, and Occupations, Committee on the Status of Black Americans, National Research Council, Washington, D.C.
Kain, John F.
1968   Housing segregation, Negro employment and metropolitan decentralization. *Quarterly Journal of Economics* 82(May):32–59.
Kasarda, John D.
1985   Urban change and minority opportunities. Pp. 33–67 in P. Peterson, ed., *The New Urban Reality*. Washington, D.C.: Brookings Institution.
Landry, Bart
1987   *The New Black Middle Class*. Berkeley: University of California Press.
Lazear, Edward
1979   The narrowing of black-white wage differentials is illusory. *American Economic Review* 69(4)[September]:553–564.
Leonard, Jonathan
1985   The Effectiveness of Equal Employment Law and Affirmative Action Regulation. Report to the Subcommittee on Employment Opportunities of the Education and Labor Committee and the Subcommittee on Civil and Constitutional Rights of the Judiciary Committee, U.S. Congress. School of Business Administration, University of California, Berkeley.
1987   The interaction of residential segregation and employment discrimination. *Journal of Urban Economics* 21:323–346.
Levin, Daniel B., and Linda Ingram, eds.
1988   *Income and Poverty Statistics: Problems of Concept and Measurement. Report of a Workshop*. Committee on National Statistics, Commission on Behavioral and Social Sciences and Education, National Research Council. Washington, D.C.: National Academy Press.
Malveaux, Julianne
1986   The Economic Status of Black Women: An Overview and Note on Interpretation. Paper prepared for the Committee on the Status of Black Americans, National Research Council, Washington, D.C.
Marshall, Ray, Charles B. Knapp, Malcolm H. Ligget, and Robert W. Glover
1978   *Employment Discrimination*. New York: Praeger.
Moffitt, Robert
1985a   Evaluating the effects of changes in AFDC: methodological issues and challenges. *Journal of Policy Analysis and Management* 4(Summer):537–553.
1985b   Work incentives in the AFDC system: an analysis of the 1981 reforms. *American Economic Review* 76(2)(May):219–223.
Murray, Charles
1984   *Losing Ground: American Social Policy, 1950–1980*. New York: Basic Books.

Myrdal, Gunnar
1944 *An American Dilemma: The Negro Problem and Modern Democracy*. New York: Harper & Row.
National Advisory Commission on Civil Disorders
1968 *Report of the National Advisory Commission on Civil Disorders*. New York: Bantam Books.
O'Neill, June, James Cunningham, Andy Sparks, and Hal Sider
1986 *The Economic Progress of Black Men in America*. Clearinghouse Publication 91. Washington, D.C.: U.S. Commission on Civil Rights.
Parsons, Donald O.
1980 Racial trends in male labor force participation. *American Economic Review* 70(December):911–920.
Rees, Albert
1986 An essay on youth joblessness. *Journal of Economic Literature* 24(June):613–628.
Ross, Christine, Sheldon Danziger, and Eugene Smolensky
1986 *The Level and Trend of Poverty in the United States, 1939–1979*. Madison, Wis.: Institute for Research on Poverty, University of Wisconsin.
Sawhill, Isabel V.
1988 Poverty in the U.S.: why is it so persistent? *Journal of Economic Literature* 26(3)[September]:1107–1119.
Smith, James P.
1988 Poverty and the family. In Gary D. Sandefur and Marta Tienda, eds., *Divided Opportunities: Minorities, Poverty, and Social Policy*. New York: Plenum.
Smith, James P., and Finis R. Welch
1977 Black-white male wage ratios: 1960–1970. *American Economic Review* 67(June):323–338.
1986 *Closing the Gap, Forty Years of Economic Progress for Blacks*. Santa Monica, Calif.: Rand Corporation.
U.S. House of Representatives, Committee on Ways and Means
1987 *Background Material on Programs Within the Jurisdiction of the Committee on Ways and Means*. Washington, D.C.: U.S. Government Printing Office.
Viscusi, W. Kip
1986 Market incentives for criminal behavior. Pp. 301–346 in Richard B. Freeman and Harry J. Holzer, eds., *The Black Youth Employment Crisis*. Chicago and London: University of Chicago Press.
Vroman, Wayne
1975 Changes in the labor market position of black men since 1964. Pp. 294–301 in James L. Stern and Barbara D. Dennis, eds., *Proceedings of the Twenty-Seventh Annual Winter Meeting*, Industrial Relations Research Association Series, December 28–29, 1974, San Francisco, California. Madison, Wis.: Industrial Relations Research Association.
1987 *Labor Supply and Black Men's Relative Earnings Since 1964*. Washington, D.C.: Urban Institute.
Wallace, Phyllis A.
1984 Title VII and the Economic Status of Blacks. Working paper of the Alfred P. Sloan School of Management, Massachusetts Institute of Technology, Cambridge, Mass.
1985 The Private Sector and Equal Employment Opportunity in the 1980s. Working paper of the Alfred P. Sloan School of Management, Massachusetts Institute of Technology, Cambridge, Mass.
Wilson, William Julius
1987 *The Truly Disadvantaged: The Inner City, the Underclass and Public Policy*. Chicago: University of Chicago Press.

7

THE SCHOOLING OF

BLACK AMERICANS

Jacob Lawrence
Graduation (1948)
Gouache on paper
The Evans-Tibbs Collection, Washington, D.C.

${B}$lack Americans have followed two major strategies to try to improve the educational opportunities made available to their children. At times, they have pursued high-quality schooling by insisting that segregated schools be provided equal educational resources. At other times, convinced that equal-quality education and segregated schools were incompatible, they have fought to integrate schools. At all times, blacks have sought educational excellence and equal educational opportunity. These goals are the principal concerns of this chapter. By educational excellence we mean high standards of academic performance for teachers and students (see Carnegie Forum, 1986; Holmes Group, 1986). By equal educational opportunity we mean that the support—both financial and in human resources—and the encouragement provided for education are equal for all students.

Equal educational opportunity is a complex concept. Prior to the mid-1960s, equality of educational opportunity was defined in terms of quantifiable resource inputs, such as physical facilities, teacher credentials, and racial mixture within the schools. But the Coleman-Campbell (1966) report *Equality of Educational Opportunity* shifted conceptions of equal educational opportunity to the achievement results produced by the schools. Equality came to be measured by school outputs, generally student scores on tests of achievement (see Coleman, 1968; Gordon, 1972; Mosteller and Moynihan, 1972). Implicit in this measure are the basic requirements for equal educational opportunity: equivalent resources for the education of all students, including equal curricular opportunities, teacher quality, and encouragement and expectation of learning. Missing from both measures are such factors as treatment within schools and the economic and social returns to schooling (see

Brookover and Lezotte, 1981; Ogbu, 1978). Because of the difficulty of finding direct measures for these factors, however, in this chapter we focus primarily on evidence about equal educational outcomes and changes over time in differences in these outcomes.

Many different indicators of educational status can be used. Examples include average years of school completed, average performance on achievement tests, representation in the population as a whole as compared to representation in institutions of higher learning, and group differences in attainment or achievement. We use a variety of such indicators to discuss how far the United States has moved from a society providing low-quality, unequal, and segregated schooling to blacks to a society providing excellent, equal, and integrated schooling. Our answer to this broad, evaluative question is based on an examination of four topics.

First, the chapter details changes in the basic outcomes of schooling such as levels of enrollment and attainment. Second, it describes changes in school performance, using achievement test scores and other indicators. Third, the chapter deals with factors internal to the schools that affect educational outcomes. It focuses on those aspects of the schooling process that are most important for achievement levels. Fourth, factors external to the schools that influence students' attainment and achievement are assessed: these include family, neighborhood, peer group influences, and the social and academic effects of desegregated schooling on blacks and whites.

ENROLLMENT AND ATTAINMENT

Trends in the enrollment and attainment status of blacks can be summarized by three important findings. First, there has been a substantial reduction in black-white inequality in the basic amount of schooling received. Second, noteworthy gaps between blacks and whites remain, especially in terms of high school completion and rates of college attendance. Third, there was a drop in college attendance by blacks from 1977 through 1982 and a divergence in the college enrollment chances of blacks and whites that has persisted through the mid-1980s.

EARLY CHILDHOOD EDUCATION

In the cohort of black males born in 1925, school enrollment rates exceeded 90 percent only when the cohort was between the ages of 10 and 12; but in the cohort born in 1965, the rates were greater than 90 percent from ages 7 to 14 and were greater than 95 percent from ages 9 to 12. Figure 7-1 shows the ratios of black/white school enrollment rates in the cohorts of black men who were 5 years old in 1930, in 1950, and in 1970. Black enrollment was less probable at every age than white enrollment in these

FIGURE 7-1 Black/white age-specific school enrollment rate ratios for boys aged 5 in 1930, 1950, and 1970.

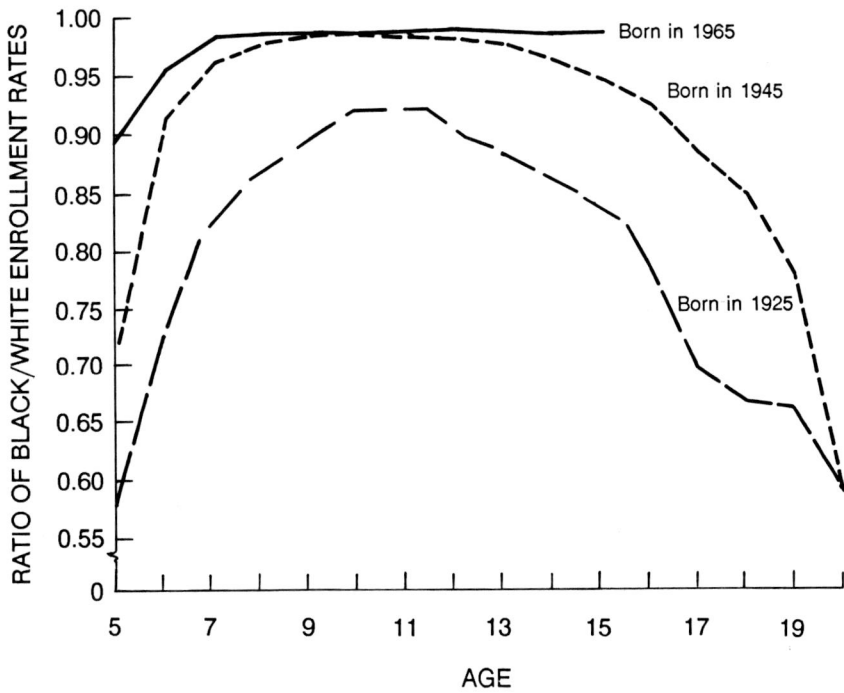

Sources: Data from decennial censuses and Current Population Surveys.

cohorts, but approached those of whites in a wider range of ages in each successive cohort.

The growth in formal schooling at younger ages continues as nursery school, Head Start, and kindergarten attendance has increased throughout the nation. Although the effects of participation in early schooling on academic achievement are mixed, the correlation of early school entry with later school leaving does point to continuing growth in educational attainment. Figure 7-2 shows age-specific school enrollment rates of cohorts of black and white children at ages 3, 4, and 5 from 1968 to 1985. During this period, for the first time, rates of participation in early schooling have not only grown dramatically among black and white children, but they have often been greater among blacks. The growth in schooling is most impressive at the youngest ages: among black children, participation between 1968 and 1985 grew from 69 percent to 93 percent at age 5, from 30 percent to 52 percent at age 4, and from 10 percent to 34 percent at age 3. The sensitivity of participation in early schooling to general social conditions and public policy is suggested both by the overall increase in participation since the late

FIGURE 7-2   School enrollment of black and white children aged 3–5, 1968–1985.

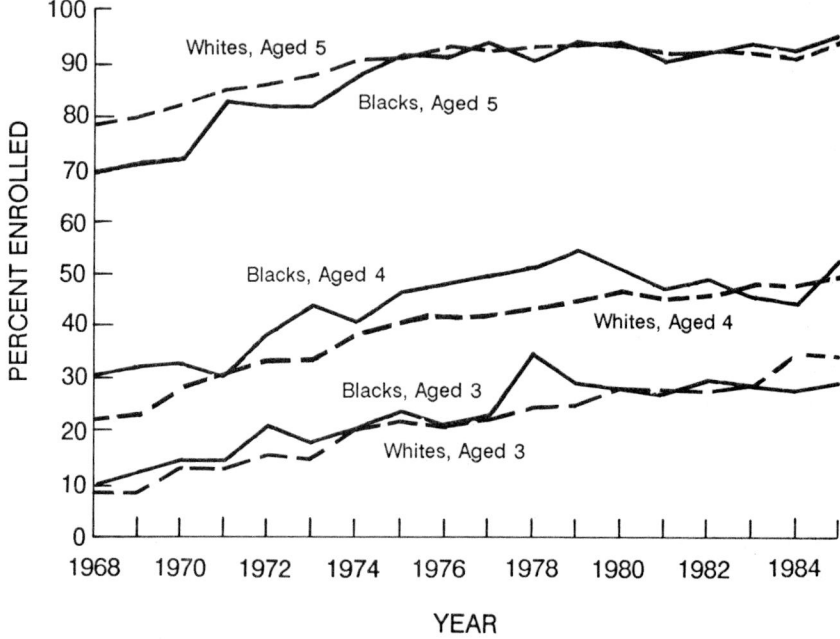

Sources: Data from decennial censuses and Current Population Surveys.

1960s and by the leveling off of growth in the late 1970s; there may even have been a decline in school participation of 3- and 4-year-olds after 1978.

HIGH SCHOOL ATTAINMENT AND DROPPING OUT

The median years of schooling for young blacks has risen sharply since before World War II, narrowing the gap between blacks and whites almost completely. In 1940, the median schooling for young black men was 6.5 years and for young white men it was 10.5 years, leaving a gap of 4 years; for black women it was 7.5 years and for white women it was 10.9 years, a gap of 3.4 years.[1] By 1980, the overall gap in median years of schooling had declined to less than one-half year: 12.6 years for blacks and 13.0 years for

---

1. It is more difficult to measure and interpret trends in schooling among people in their late teens and early 20s than among those at younger ages. The difficulty is partly because age and grade in school are not so tightly linked and partly because it is far more difficult to sample relevant populations by the later teen years (especially black males, who are missed by census enumerators at relatively high rates). Consequently, we rely on reports of schooling at ages 25–29 as our main source of information about high school completion. This age range is especially useful for comparisons of schooling because by age 25 most people have completed both secondary schooling and military service.

FIGURE 7-3 Schooling of adults aged 25–29, by race and sex (in median years), 1940–1980.

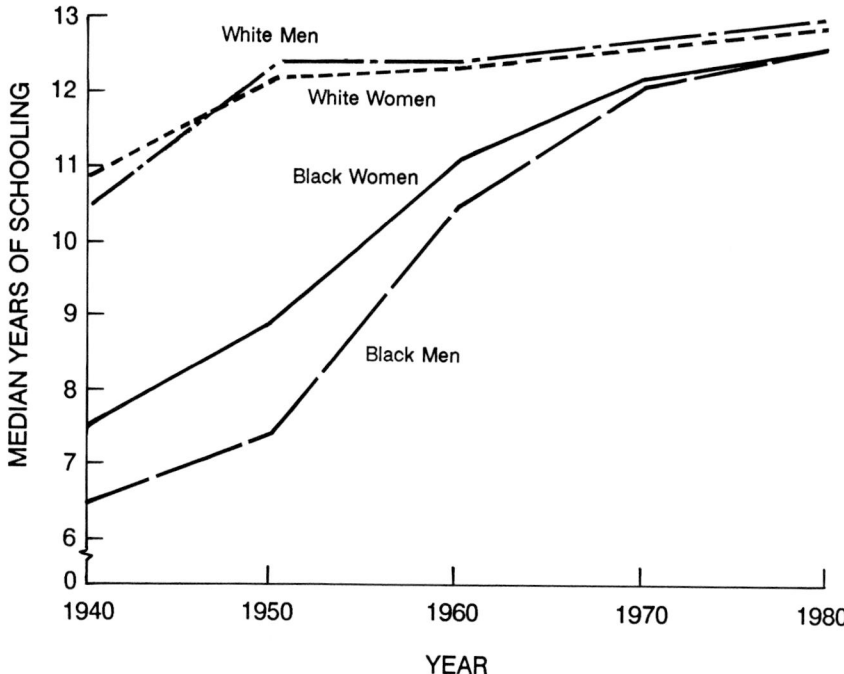

Sources: Data from decennial censuses and Current Population Surveys.

whites (see Figure 7-3). While useful, however, median years of education can be misleading as an indicator of group differences because educational attainments of blacks and whites have become so concentrated at several transition points in the schooling process, especially at high school graduation. Therefore, we also examined changes in the share of the population that has completed major schooling transitions.

In 1940, more than 70 percent of young black adults and fewer than 40 percent of whites had completed no more than 8 years of schooling. The percentage of adult Americans with this minimal level of schooling had declined markedly by 1980 (see Figure 7-4). Although there were still more blacks than whites with 8 or fewer years of schooling, fewer than 7 percent of blacks—or whites—were in this group. For the next transition, as recently as 1940, only 11 percent of black men and 14 percent of black women had completed high school, while white completion rates were at or near 40 percent. By 1980, high school completion had become almost universal among white men and women: more than 87 percent reported that they had completed high school (see Figure 7-4). Although there was very rapid growth in high school completion among blacks, by 1980, about one-

FIGURE 7-4 Adults aged 25–29 with (a) 8 or fewer, (b) 12 or more, or (c) 16 or more years of schooling, by race and sex, 1940–1980.

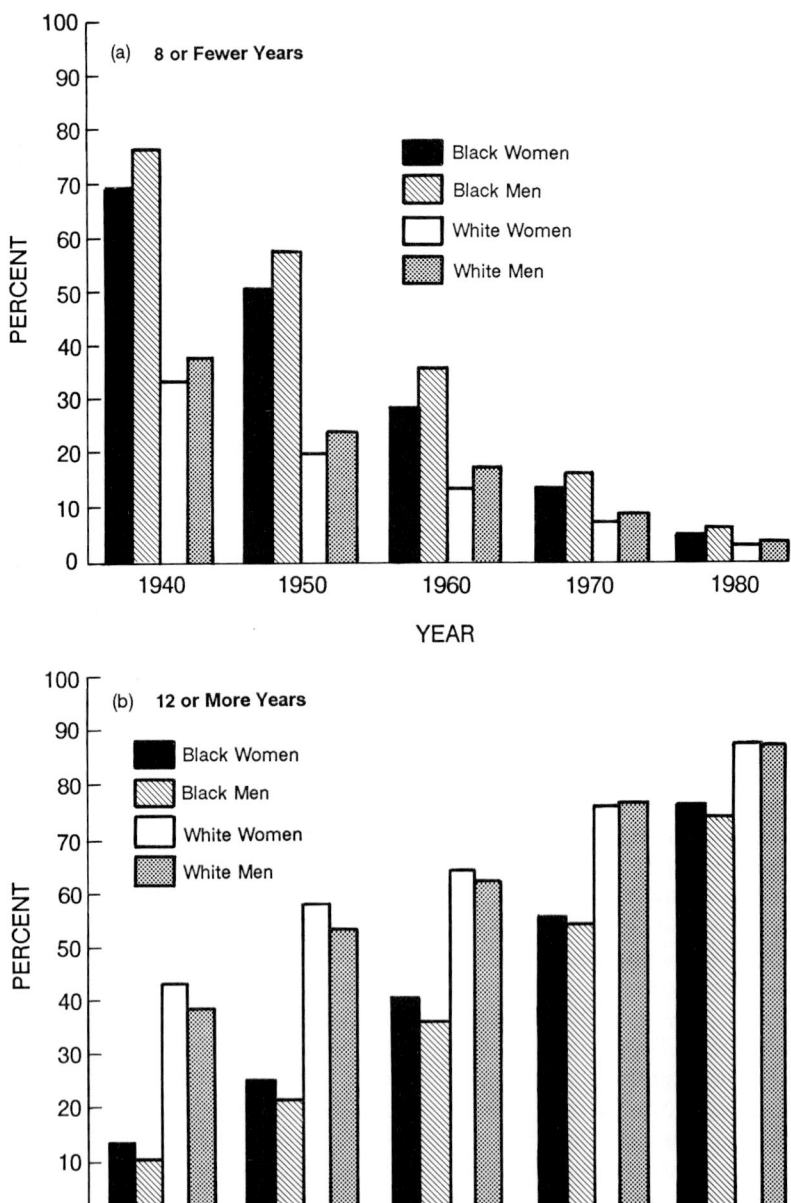

Sources: Data from decennial censuses and Current Population Surveys.

FIGURE 7-4 *(Continued)*

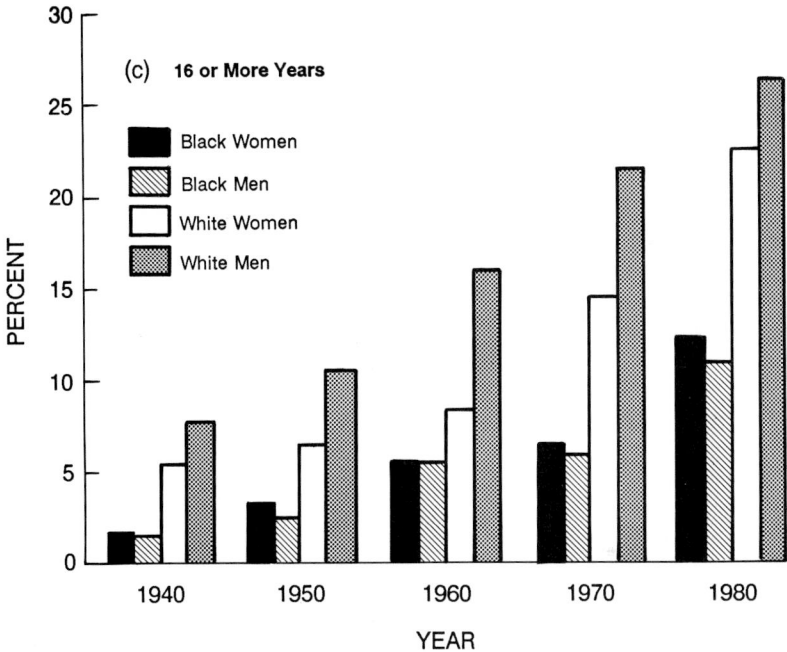

quarter of young black adults still did not complete high school: 76 percent of black women and 74 percent of black men reported high school completion.

It is difficult to reconcile estimates of 75 percent of blacks completing high school by ages 25 to 29 with common reports of black high school dropout rates approaching 50 percent. Such discrepancies may occur for many reasons. For example, there is significant variation in dropout rates from place to place. More important, there is little standardization of concepts or methods for the measurement of high school "dropout" or even of high school completion. For example, reports of high school completion by ages 25 to 29 may refer to certification by examination or the completion of other forms of high school equivalence. About 450,000 people each year achieve the equivalence of high school graduation by completing the GED (General Educational Development Test), and about 60 percent of these people are less than 24 years old. Blacks are overrepresented among those taking the GED; 18 percent of those taking the GED examination in a 1980 sample were black. If blacks are represented in this proportion among those taking and passing the GED at younger ages, then more than 40,000 young black adults could be completing high school in this way each year.

Finally, some members of relevant populations just do not appear in social surveys. By age 18, substantial numbers of youth with high school diplomas, as well as some without, have entered military service, and they are far less likely to be covered in the Census Bureau's Current Population Survey (CPS), which is the most standardized source of dropout measurements. Dropouts are defined as those who are not enrolled in high school or college and have not already completed grade 12. At the same time, after age 16, there are very serious, and perhaps growing, problems of surveying the black population, especially black men. The CPS data show the dropout rate as relatively low at age 16 among whites and blacks, with somewhat higher dropout rates among blacks (around 10 percent) than among whites (7–8 percent) in 1970–1971. They show a precipitous fall in the dropout rates among black men through 1978–1979 (with a very small rise subsequently) and among black women from 1974–1975 through 1982–1983. By the close of the period, the reported dropout rates of blacks of less than 6 percent are more than a percentage point below those of whites. It is fair to say that these reported trends are *not* credible, unless one is willing to disregard most common knowledge about high school completion. The rapid downward slide in reported dropout rates among blacks may reflect decreasing survey coverage of dropouts, rather than actual decreases in dropout rates. Dropout rates at age 18, which range from about 13 percent for white women to about 18 percent for black men, appear somewhat more credible, but they also show a sharp decline among blacks and substantial convergence with rates among whites.

For blacks and whites alike, there are essentially no sex differences in rates of high school completion. From the mid-1960s to the late 1970s, high school graduation grew from just over 70 percent to just under 90 percent among whites, and it has since leveled off. Among young black adults aged 25–29, high school graduation has grown dramatically and almost continuously, from about 50 percent in 1965 to nearly 80 percent in the early 1980s. Still, among young adults, high school graduation rates of whites exceed those of blacks by about 10 percent, so blacks are about twice as likely as whites not to graduate from high school.

COLLEGE ENTRY AND COMPLETION

Since 1977 there has been a marked decline in college entry among black high school graduates. No definitive explanations of this decline have been found. Little notice was taken of the decline until 7 years after it had begun; public interest increased in the wake of visible declines in black enrollment on the campuses of major universities and of occasional incidents of racial conflict. Black college entry declined during a period of unprecedented growth in the chances of white high school graduates to attend college (see Figure 7-5).

The rate of black high school graduates attending college rose from about 39 percent in 1973 to about 48 percent in 1977—when it was virtually equal

FIGURE 7-5 Odds of college entry among recent black and white high school graduates, 1969–1984.

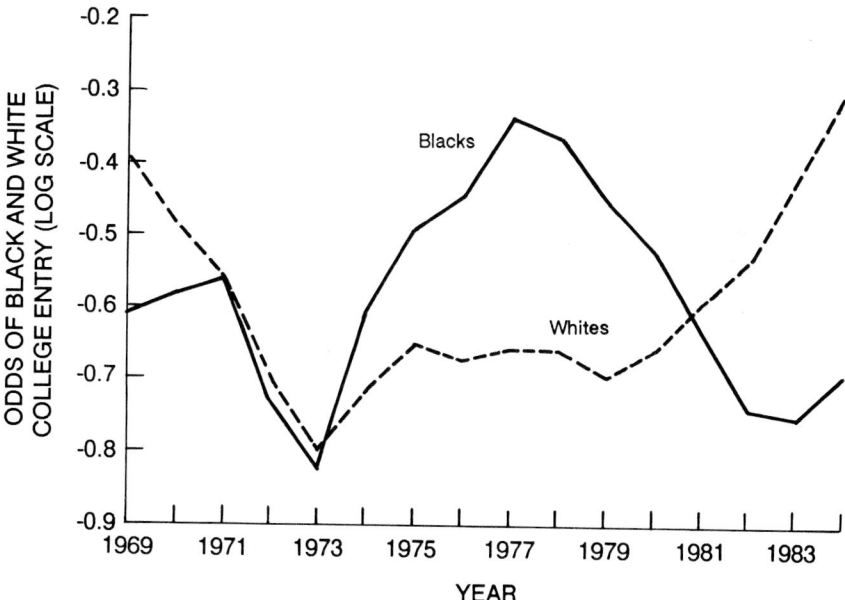

Note: Data are adjusted for family income, sex, region, and metropolitan location.

Sources: Data from decennial censuses and Current Population Surveys.

to those of whites—and then fell continuously to about 38 percent through 1983. In 1986, the latest year for which national data are available, 36.5 percent of black high school graduates entered college in the fall after high school graduation. In comparison, for 1973–1984, the college entry rate of whites rose almost continuously from about 48 percent to 57 percent. College entry rates rose most rapidly among whites after 1979, when blacks had experienced a sharp drop in their rate of college entrance.

Among blacks and whites, the odds of college entry declined from the late 1960s to the early 1970s. After 1973 college entry chances rose, especially among blacks, for whom they peaked in 1977. Among whites, college entry leveled off between 1975 and 1979, but it has risen continuously since then. Among blacks, a precipitous decline in college entry began in 1978. It appears to have leveled off after 1981, with black college entry chances lower than they were in the late 1960s.

In terms of college completion, blacks lagged far behind whites in 1940, and the gap has not been closed. In 1940, fewer than 2 percent of black women or men had completed college, compared with 5 percent and 7.5 percent of white women and men, respectively. By 1960, more than 5 percent of blacks had completed college; growth was slow between 1960 and

1970, and the most rapid period of growth in college completion among blacks was between 1970 and 1980: see Figure 7-4. In 1980, 12 percent of young black women and 11 percent of young black men had completed 4 years of college, compared with 22 percent of young white women and 25.5 percent of young white men. As recently as 1970, the share of college graduates among blacks was similar to that among whites in 1940. And today, the chances of a black youth completing college still lag about one-half behind those of a white youth.

EXPLAINING THE DECLINE IN BLACK COLLEGE ENTRY

One might think that the peak of college entry for blacks in the 1970s was abnormally high, given the other social and economic conditions of black Americans. At the same time, it is difficult to imagine that the "normal" level of continuation from high school to college among blacks in the 1980s should be lower than it was in the 1960s. Of course, the selectivity of high school graduation itself deserves to be considered as a possible source of decline in college entry. Rates of high school completion did increase among blacks during the 1970s and 1980s. As the selectivity of high school graduation declines (i.e., as increasing numbers of pupils from poor backgrounds graduate), one might expect continuation to college to decline. Yet, selectivity seems an unlikely source of declining college entry; there is no historic evidence for white cohorts that would suggest a negative correlation between rates of high school completion and rates of continuation to college. On the contrary, growth in college graduation among whites has been driven by a combination of increased rates of high school completion and stable or slightly increasing rates of continuation to college.

The causes of the decline in college enrollment among blacks are not easily pinpointed. Arbeiter (1986) considered four types of explanations: (1) short-comings of the available data; (2) shifts in the economic status of blacks relative to that of other groups; (3) the changing structure of financial aid; and (4) shifts in the outcomes of competition among schools, businesses, and the military for college-age black youth. A fifth possibility, advanced in two recent reports for the U.S. Department of Education (Chaikind, 1987; Myers, 1987), assert that differences in black-white college attendance rates result from differences in achievement.

Because the Census Bureau data used in most reports on black college attendance typically do not distinguish between part-time and full-time college attendance or between enrollment at 2- and 4-year institutions, it is possible that the observed decline could be attributable to decreases in numbers attending on a part-time basis or at 2-year institutions. If this were the case, then the overall trend would overstate the decline in black enrollment at 4-year institutions. But Arbeiter (1986:5), comparing data for 1980 and 1982, found that the largest decline in total black enrollment occurred at 4-year institutions, while there was an increase in black enrollment at 2-year institutions. For 1976 and 1982, there has been an absolute decline in full-time black enrollment at both 2- and 4-year institutions. And there has been a decline of 9.1 percent in the number of blacks taking the Scholastic Aptitude Test (SAT) from 1980 to 1985, suggesting a decline in the number of blacks planning to enroll in college, although there is no evidence of a decline in college aspirations among black high school seniors (see below).

Turning to economic status, the lower incomes of black families explain part of the black-white gap in college entry. But the college entry chances of blacks have fallen so far since 1980 that family income can no longer account for the black-white difference. The rise and decline of blacks' chances for college entry, absolutely and relative to those of whites, cannot be explained by changes in family income (or by changes in the college-going chances of men in comparison with women). Only the very highest income families in the black population experienced any improvement in college-going chances after 1980, and even this group lost ground relative to whites.

In Figure 7-6 the college-going chances of blacks and whites are compared. These changes are expressed as the odds of college entry among blacks, as given by the ratio of entrants to nonentrants, relative to the odds of college entry among whites.[2] The lower trend line shows a 2-year moving average of the natural log of the ratio of the odds of college entry among blacks to the odds of college entry among whites. Since the natural log of 1 is equal to 0, the zero point, shown near the top of the graph, is where the odds ratio for blacks and whites would be equal. There has been a long swing from the late 1960s to the middle 1980s, during which the college-going chances of black high school graduates first moved toward those of whites and then diverged, perhaps to a point more distant than in the late 1960s. In 1984, the odds that a black high school graduate would enter the first year of college within 1 year were less than one-half the corresponding odds for a white high school graduate. The upper trend line "adjusted" in Figure 7-6 is a comparable measure of the difference in the chances of college entry, but it is based on a statistical model in which the effects of sex, region, metropolitan location, and family income have been controlled.

Two features of the figure stand out. First, the two lines are virtually parallel throughout the period from 1969 to 1984. Thus, the observed trend in black-white differences in college entry is in no way a consequence of changes in sex composition, geographic location, or economic status. Specifically, changes in black family incomes do not explain the reversal in college chances. Second, the adjusted trend line always lies above the observed line. That is, once adjustments are made for the differing social composition of the black and white populations (on the variables included in the model), the differences in chances of college entry are more nearly centered around the zero point of equal chances. For example, during the 1970s, black high

---

2. The sample sizes for blacks are quite small, and the data have been smoothed in two ways. First, they were initially tabulated for pairs of years from 1968–1969 through 1984–1985. Second, the data shown are moving averages; thus, the data for 1970–1971 are actually an average for those 2 years, in which one-half weight is given to the adjacent years.

FIGURE 7-6 Relative odds of black and white college entry (log scale), 1969–1984.

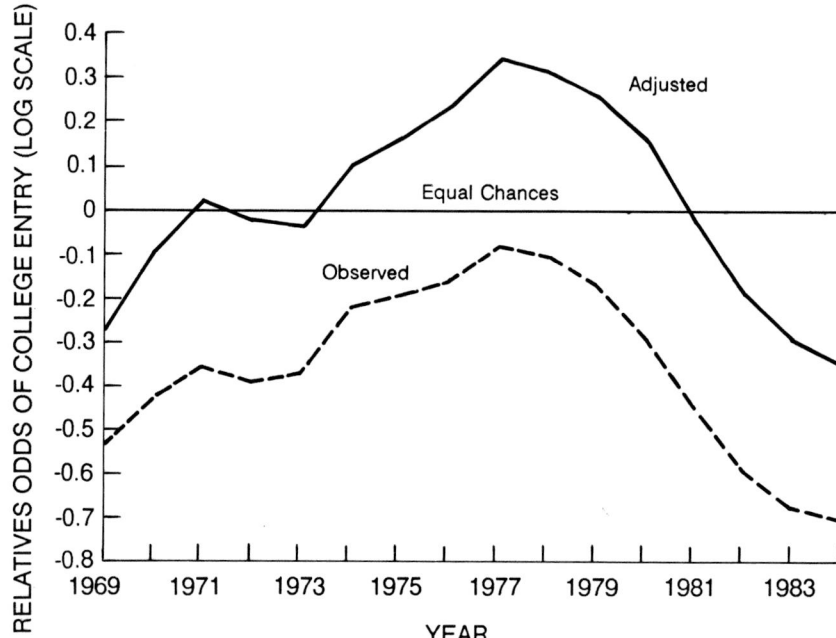

Note: Data are observed and adjusted for family income, sex, region, and metropolitan location.

Source: Data from decennial censuses and Current Population Surveys.

school graduates were more likely to enter college than whites with the same socioeconomic and geographic characteristics.

Two recent reports contend that a principal determinant of black college attendance is achievement test performance. The studies, conducted for the U.S. Department of Education, attempted to determine the impact of achievement levels and family income on black college attendance. Chaikind (1987) assessed change from 1970 to 1984 in black college enrollment rates; Myers (1987) focused on data from the High School and Beyond Survey (HSB) of 1982 seniors. Neither report directly relates actual changes in achievement or in family background to patterns of change in college attendance. Yet, by implication, these reports provide an account of change over time in black college attendance rates that emphasizes black-white differences in achievement (see, e.g., *Chronicle of Higher Education*, April 29, 1987).

The available evidence about *changes* in levels of academic achievement among black youth in the 1970s and 1980s suggests that their achievement levels are on the increase, absolutely and relative to those of whites. Thus, although black students continue to perform less well on tests than white students, it is unlikely that changes in academic achievement among blacks could explain either the trend in black college enrollment or the difference in trend between blacks and whites.

Another hypothesis that has been offered to account for the decline in black college entry is change in the educational goals of black youth. According to this hypothesis, black youth prefer attending vocational or technical schools, or 2-year colleges, to attending 4-year colleges or universities. This claim has no basis in fact. Annual surveys of the educational aspirations and plans of large national samples of black and white high school seniors by the Survey Research Center at the University of Michigan show that there has been little or no change in the plans or aspirations of high school seniors to attend technical or vocational schools or to complete a 2-year college program. Rather, the data show that the interest of black seniors in these two types of post–high school education has declined since 1982 (Bobo, 1987). At the same time, the aspiration to complete 4 years of college has grown almost as much among black as among white seniors, although after 1984 there may be a tendency for the collegiate aspirations of blacks to lag behind those of whites.

From 1980–1981 to 1985–1986, the total federal, state, and college "package" of financial aid declined 3 percent after controlling for changes in the consumer price index, but the real financial situation became worse than that because the costs of attending a state college or university rose faster than the general cost of living.

Over the 10-year period from 1975–1976 to 1985–1986, outright grants as a percentage of all financial aid declined from 80 percent to 46 percent, while loans increased from 17 percent to 50 percent as a percentage of financial aid. This change has probably reduced blacks' college-going chances more than those of whites. At equal levels of current family income, black youth are less economically secure than whites because black families are more vulnerable than white families to unemployment and are less wealthy than whites (see Chapter 6 and below). Consequently, as one recent report stated (Miller and Hexter, 1985:17): "Minority students are less likely to borrow than white students; fewer than one-third of low-income minority aid recipients secure a government secured loan, compared with more than two-fifths of low-income white aid recipients."

Why are black students less willing than white students to borrow funds to support their college attendance? In a purely economic analysis, a student's willingness to borrow will be affected by the economic return to his or her investment. Given the history of economic discrimination against blacks and the perception of fewer opportunities to enter good jobs, to be promoted, and to be retained in times of recession, a black student will not expect the same economic rewards with the same degree of certainty as a white student who makes the same investment of time and money in college education. If the expected rewards are less, then the amount of money that a student will borrow to invest are also likely to be less.

There is also a second, psychological factor affecting willingness to borrow. Black students are overwhelmingly from very low income families. During the period from 1968–1973 to 1980–1985, the percentage of recent black high school graduates with family incomes below $10,000 per year (in 1985

FIGURE 7-7 Plans of black and white male high school seniors to enter the armed services, 1976–1986.

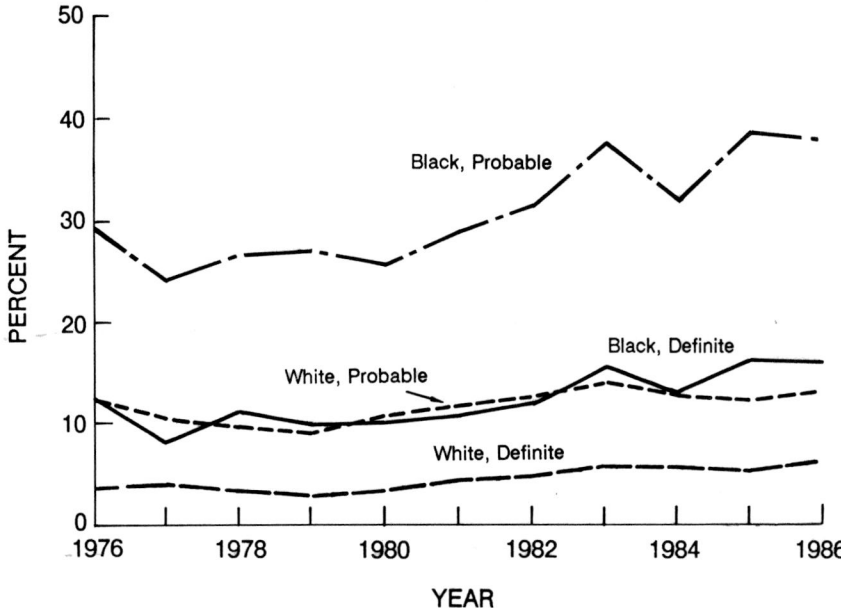

dollars) increased from 27 to 35 percent; the percentage of black graduates with family incomes higher than $40,000 per year increased from 6.1 percent to 8.5 percent. In contrast, among white graduates, the percentage of families with incomes below $10,000 grew from 9 to 10 percent, but the percentage of families with incomes over $40,000 grew from 25 percent to 35 percent. That is, the income distributions for families of black and white students are almost mirror images: 35 percent above $40,000 for whites and below $10,000 for blacks, 10 percent below $10,000 for whites and above $40,000 for blacks. A typical $10,000–12,000 college debt is much larger to a black student—relative to his or her family income—than to a white student (see Jaynes, 1986).

Changes in the attractiveness of military service is another proposed explanation of the decline in black college entry relative to that of whites. Plans and aspirations to enter military service after high school graduation have increased among black high school seniors of both sexes (see Figure 7-7). The percentage of black male seniors with definite or probable plans to enter the armed forces rose from 36.7 percent in 1977 to 50.0 percent in 1985; among black female seniors, the percentage with military plans rose from 15.9 percent to 29.0 percent during that period. Among white female seniors, intentions to enter the military are never larger than 5 percent and there has been no trend. Among white male seniors, plans to enter military service have grown from 16.6 percent in 1977 to 21.3 percent in 1985. Thus, the share of black female high school seniors who intend to enter the armed forces now exceeds that of white male high school seniors by a substantial margin.

These trends in plans to enter the military leave many questions unanswered. It is not clear to what degree military service competes for black seniors who would otherwise enter college, rather than choosing other forms of schooling or labor market entry after high school. It is also not clear whether black seniors choose military service because of the aggressive marketing of schooling entitlements that can be earned within the armed forces or for other reasons.

In conclusion, it appears that the decline in financial aid is the most important factor in the decline in black college enrollment. Increases in military enlistment may also be important. However, possible interactions between military enlistment and college enrollment decisions are not understood.

COLLEGE: DEGREE ATTAINMENT AND CHOICE OF MAJOR

Two recent assessments (Thomas, 1987; Trent, 1984) of black enrollment covering degree completion status, types of degree-granting institutions, and representation in the natural and technical sciences of undergraduate and graduate students found three major trends: (1) black students are no longer gaining ground in institutions of higher education and on some indicators they are losing ground; (2) on the key indicators of enrollment and degree completion, blacks remained underrepresented (especially in B.A. and advanced degrees in the natural and technical sciences); and (3) a small number of colleges, especially the nation's historically black institutions, made a disproportionate contribution to the pool of black degree recipients.

There has been a decline in black participation in graduate school. Thomas (1987:266) reported that between 1976 and 1982 "Black full-time enrollment in graduate schools declined by almost 20%, while white enrollment declined by about 8%." This decline did not reflect an increase in black college graduates seeking professional or technical degrees since the latter rates remained constant over the period. It also was not a result of a drop in the size of the pool of black B.A. recipients. In terms of degree completion, the percentage of M.A.'s awarded to blacks declined from 6.7 percent in 1976–1977 to 5.8 percent in 1980–1981. The figures for Ph.D. completion were stable, with blacks accounting for 3.8 percent in 1976–1977 and 3.9 percent in 1980–1981.

Black students (as with college students in general) appear to be majoring less in the areas of education and the social sciences and more in business (Trent, 1984), indicating a shift by black students away from programs leading to graduate school and toward fields that promise more direct entry to the labor market.

Despite the increasing enrollment of blacks in predominantly white colleges and universities, historically black institutions account for a disproportionate share of the black B.A. pool in the natural, biological, and technical sciences (Thomas, 1987; Trent, 1984). For example, although historically black colleges and universities accounted for 14 percent of the institutions granting B.A.'s in biology to blacks in 1980–1981, they accounted for 40 percent of the biology degrees awarded to blacks. These schools also graduate large percentages of blacks in engineering, mathematics, and the physical sciences.

ACHIEVEMENT

A preeminent concern in the area of race and education has been black-white differences in achievement test scores. Our examination of trends of school achievement of blacks—especially in terms of performance on standardized tests covering reading, math, and science—should be prefaced by several observations. First, achievement test performance is but one type of criterion of student success and school performance. Other outcomes of schooling are arguably as important as test achievement, such as the development of higher order reasoning ability, effective interpersonal and social skills, and the acquisition of basic cultural values and orientations. These other abilities are not readily measured, and thus, little systematic information is available on them. Second, achievement test performance is an imprecise indicator of ability to perform a wide range of nonschool work and social roles. Third, even carefully designed test instruments may include some degree of cultural bias that artificially lowers the tested performance of blacks relative to whites (see Taylor, 1980, and below). These limitations notwithstanding, achievement test performance remains an important measure of student ability and school performance. Such tests also play a part in determining access to higher education (Thomas, 1981).

EFFECTS OF PRESCHOOL AND COMPENSATORY PROGRAMS

During the 1960s, governments made a concerted effort to improve the educational achievement of children from poor households. The major programs for poor children, Head Start for preschool children and Chapter I funds (formerly, Title I funds) for remedial education, became popular quite early, despite reports that questioned their efficacy (see Skerry, 1983:18–39). There have since been more positive reports on their effects (see below), and these programs remain popular even in the cost-cutting climate of the 1980s (see *Education Week*, May 9, 1985:16–22; May 1, 1985:1, 12–13).

The research on these and other compensatory education programs suggests that some types of strategies, for example, early intervention efforts, produced more desired outcomes than others—"pull-out" or other special placement approaches. Early intervention efforts, which yield small long-term consequences for tested intelligence and achievement, do appear to have other noteworthy benefits. A set of longitudinal studies established in

1975, and known as the Consortium of Longitudinal Studies, reported on 14 studies of low-income families who participated in experimental and preschool programs prior to 1969. The more carefully designed of these studies found (1) students in preschool programs have significant gains in IQ followed by washout of the effect after termination of the program; (2) students in preschool programs are referred significantly less often to special education and are retained in grade less than those not in preschool programs; and (3) preschool participation had long-term benefits on math achievement (see Glazer, 1986; Karweit, 1986:41; Mullin and Summers, 1983). In particular, the two latter findings identify important outcomes of these programs.

Head Start centers tend to be small, serving an average of 56 students, and extremely flexible because there are no national standardized curriculum or performance standards. The centers are relatively efficient and inexpensive, thanks partly to reliance on donations and volunteer staff efforts. In addition, the lack of emphasis on credentials makes it possible to hire teachers and aides who do not have college degrees and so are paid much lower salaries than public school teachers. There is a strong emphasis on using parents at Head Start centers, as well as a more general ethic of neighborhood participation fostered by parental involvement in policy making. About one-half of Head Start students and personnel nationwide are black, but the proportion is much higher in many inner-city and rural areas, making the program an important institution of the black community (Skerry, 1983).

Although Head Start has been more publicized, the Chapter I (Title I) program is the most extensive federal effort in compensatory education, involving some 5 million children in 14,000 school districts. The Sustaining Effects Study of Compensatory and Elementary Education, mandated by Congress in 1975, remains the most comprehensive evaluation of Chapter I. This 3-year longitudinal study examined the achievement scores of 120,000 students in a representative sample of 300 schools and compared the scores of Chapter I recipients with those of a control group of "needy" students who were not included in Chapter I services. The findings were clearly positive (Carter, 1984:8):

> Statistical analysis showed significant gains for Title I [Chapter I] students, relative to needy students, for the Mathematics sections of the Comprehensive Tests of Basic Skills. This was true for grades 1 to 6. For the reading section . . . significant reading gains were found for grades 1 to 3, but not for grades 4, 5, and 6.

More striking was the finding that "in the beginning grades, school learning experiences are almost as effective as Initial Achievement and perhaps as important as Background." The impact of school learning experiences decreased, however, as grade level increased, until the effects were virtually nil by the sixth grade (Carter, 1984:11). The research on Head Start has also found that the benefits of the program, measured in terms of intelligence and achievement test scores, fade as the graduates advance through the primary grades (Skerry, 1983:21). Thus, while intervention at an early age can have a positive impact on achievement, it appears to lose much of its impact over time because of the increasing influence of other factors.

The annual budget for Head Start has risen to more than $1 billion, and the budget for Chapter I is approaching $4 billion. While millions of children are reached by these programs, considerably more are eligible and could be reached if additional funds were available. Federal spending on elementary and secondary education fell from $9.4 billion to $8.8 billion between 1980 and 1985, and the federal share of expenditures on elementary and secondary schools fell from 9.2 to 6.1 percent. During the same 5-year period, total state spending increased by approximately $20 billion, and total local spending increased by an additional $19 billion.

ELEMENTARY AND HIGH SCHOOL

Our analysis of data from the National Assessment of Educational Progress (NAEP) results in three key findings (also see Congressional Budget Office, 1986). First, school achievement scores of blacks have increased at a faster rate than those of whites. Second, despite gains by blacks, substantial gaps in school achievement remain. Third, among the youngest age group and birth cohort, there is evidence of a possible decline in black performance relative to that of whites; this trend, in particular, bears close scrutiny as more recent data become available.

Improvements in Black Achievement Scores

NAEP assessments of reading, math, and science performance have been conducted for 9-, 13-, and 17-year-olds since 1969–1970 and as recently as 1985–1986. Table 7-1 reports the percentage of correct answers for the reading assessment by race for the period 1969–1984. In each case, the improvement among blacks exceeded that among whites, resulting in a narrowing of the black-white gap at each age level. Similar patterns were obtained for the math assessments, and black gains relative to white gains on the science assessments occurred among 9-year-olds (4.7 percent) and 13-year-olds (2.1 percent). The science performance of 17-year-olds declined for both blacks and whites, falling from 47 percent correct to 41 percent correct for whites, and from 34.1 percent correct to 26.9 percent correct for blacks. These changes resulted in a slight increase in the black-white gap (0.09 percent) in science performance for 17-year-olds. However, the overall pattern is one of improvement among blacks and declines in the difference between blacks and whites.

The pattern of black improvement relative to whites can also be seen in the average black-white difference in percentage-correct reading scores by birth year. The difference remained in the range of 16–19 percent for cohorts

TABLE 7-1 Progress in Academic Achievement, by Race and Age, 1969–1984

Achievement Assessment	Correct Scores (percent)					
	9-Year-Olds		13-Year-Olds		17-Year-Olds	
	White	Black	White	Black	White	Black
Reading						
1969–1970	66.4	49.7	62.6	45.4	71.2	51.7
1974–1975	67.0	54.5	61.9	46.4	71.2	52.1
1979–1980	69.3	59.6	62.6	49.6	70.6	52.2
1983–1984	69.1	57.4	64.4	52.4	72.5	60.0
Change: 1969–1984	+2.7	+7.7	+1.8	+7.0	+1.3	+8.3
Most Recent White-Black Difference (1984)	+11.7		+12.0		+12.5	
Change in Difference (1969–1984)	−5.0		−5.2		−7.0	
Mathematics						
Most Recent White-Black Difference (1986)	+11.9		+10.1		+18.0	
Change in Difference (1973–1986)	−10.4		−11.8		−4.2	
Science						
Most Recent White-Black Difference (1982)	+14.5		+12.0		+16.4	
Change in Difference (1969–1982)	−4.7		−2.1		+0.4	

Sources: Data from Educational Testing Service (1985) and earlier National Assessment of Education Progress (NAEP) reports on reading; Albert E. Beaton, personal communication (1987), and earlier NAEP reports on mathematics; and Hueftle et al. (1983) and earlier NAEP reports on science.

born between 1954 and 1963, but declined to 10–13 percent for cohorts born between 1964 and 1974. These improvements in test performance occurred at all ability levels. NAEP has developed a classification of reading proficiency based on the complexity of the material used in the assessment, student familiarity with the material, and the types of questions asked. The broad pattern is one of improvement over time at each level of reading proficiency (those performing at the 95th, 75th, 50th, 25th, and 5th percentiles), with some age-group and time variation. For instance, 9-year-olds show improvements at each percentile level between 1971 and 1975, but level off or slightly decline thereafter. The results for 17-year-olds, however, are consistently upward (Bobo, 1987:Figures 8.23–8.25)

Improvements in test performance occur in all regions of the country. The NAEP data can be separated into four regions—Northeast, Southeast, Central, and Western. The broad pattern of improvement occurs in each of the four regions and at each age level. The one noteworthy deviation occurs among 9-year-olds in the Southeast, where the black-white difference increased between 1980 and 1984 (see below).

TABLE 7-2 High School Mathematics Enrollment Patterns, by Race, 1976

Number of Courses	Average Score	Black Students (percent)	White Students (percent)
0	47	29	18
1	59	37	24
2	70	21	26
3	82	13	32

Note: Average mathematics score (percent correct) for 17-year-olds by number of courses taken in algebra and geometry, 1976.

Source: Data from Jones et al. (1984).

The math and verbal SAT performance of blacks has also improved in absolute terms and relative to whites in the past several years. This indicator, however, is less useful: SAT takers are a self-selected group, and more low-performing blacks than whites take the SAT. Overall, the SAT results are consistent with other data. There is a fairly clear record of improving achievement test performance by blacks.

Accounting for change in achievement is difficult, but two contributing factors have been identified: patterns of course enrollment among blacks and whites, and policies aimed at improving the educational status of blacks, such as school desegregation and compensatory education efforts. The contributions of school desegregation and compensatory education programs are inferred on the basis of two observations. First, black students born in 1964 or later show the most striking improvements in achievement. These younger cohorts were more likely than earlier cohorts to have begun schooling in desegregated schools, and they are also more likely to have participated in the various preschool and compensatory education programs of the 1960s. Second, the largest gains in achievement occur in rural areas where school desegregation proceeded most effectively (Farley, 1984) and where funds for compensatory programs were often targeted. The one result that casts doubt on desegregation as a contributor to improving black performance is the uniformity of change across regions.

With regard to what has become known as the "differential course-taking" hypothesis, it seems clear that patterns of course enrollment are related to achievement test performance, especially in the area of mathematics (Davis, 1986; Johnson, 1984; Jones et al., 1984; Marrett, 1987; Matthews, 1984). For example, blacks are much less likely than whites to be enrolled in advanced mathematics courses. As the first two rows of Table 7-2 show, 66 percent of black 17-year-olds from the 1975–1976 NAEP data were enrolled in one or no algebra or geometry courses, in comparison with 42 percent of white students. The figures in the first two columns of the table show a strong positive relationship between the number of algebra and geometry courses taken and average mathematics score. Those with no algebra or geometry answered 47 percent of the mathematics assessment questions correctly; those who had taken three such courses answered 82 percent

TABLE 7-3 Advanced Mathematics Credits for High School Seniors, by Race and Sex (in percent), 1982

Number of Credits	Black		White	
	Male	Female	Male	Female
0	30.0	33.1	16.9	14.2
1	23.0	20.1	16.3	19.3
2	17.7	20.3	18.9	24.6
3	16.5	15.5	21.9	22.9
4	11.4	8.4	21.6	15.7
5	1.4	2.6	4.4	3.3
Sample size	538	616	3,030	3,277
Weighted N	85,530	118,733	764,754	879,600

Source: Data from Jones (1987).

correctly. In addition, there is a tendency for schools with larger proportions of black students to have a lower average number of these courses taken by students (Jones et al., 1984).

More recent data indicate both that blacks are less likely to be enrolled in advanced mathematics classes and that there is a strong relation between course taking and test performance. Information from the 1982 seniors in the HSB study on number of advanced mathematics credits is shown in Table 7-3. Black seniors were twice as likely as white seniors to have had no mathematics course at the level of algebra I or higher. The white seniors were approximately twice as likely as the black seniors to have taken four or more advanced mathematics courses. There is also a strong association between course taking and math test score performance for all four race-by-sex subgroups.

Several other factors known to contribute to mathematics achievement also differ between black and white students, including verbal skills, socioeconomic status, and mathematics achievement prior to high school. But even after accounting for the effects of these other variables, patterns of course enrollment still affect mathematics achievement. In particular, even after controlling for socioeconomic background, verbal ability, and prior mathematics achievement, having taken calculus improves scores—even among students with the same number of overall mathematics credits. Furthermore, average senior year mathematics achievement differences among the race-sex subgroups are accounted for by prior subgroup differences in socioeconomic status, verbal ability, and prior mathematics achievement, and differences in representation at the several levels of mathematics course taking (Jones, 1987).

In sum, over the relatively short period from 1970 to 1980, the gap between average academic performance of white and black school children narrowed appreciably. The effects are visible for all levels of ability and for all types of communities. The data suggest that the largest impact was in rural areas. It is not possible to conclude from the evidence that achievement gains of black students are due simply to school desegregation or to programs initiated in the 1960s that were designed to increase educational opportunities for minority students. However, the results do present a challenge to commentators who judge that these programs failed.

SIGNS OF SLIPPAGE AND REMAINING
BLACK-WHITE GAPS IN ACHIEVEMENT

There is some evidence of slippage among the younger age groups. When the NAEP achievement test data are divided into several types of communities, the likely extent and nature of this change can be seen. NAEP reports often display results by type of community, contrasting three categories in particular: extreme rural, disadvantaged urban, and advantaged urban. These categories are constructed so that they each contain about 10 percent of the nation's school children. The proportional representation differs for blacks, with 8 percent falling into the rural category, 30 percent in the disadvantaged urban category, and 5 percent in the advantaged urban category. Results examined by these categories both confirm the two overall patterns we stressed above, improvement among blacks and continuing black-white differences, as well as indicate possible deterioration among the youngest age group.

Black reading scores by birth cohort and type of community indicate a clear advantage in reading test score performance among the advantaged urban blacks over both their disadvantaged urban and their rural counterparts. In addition, at each age level and for each type of community shown—with one exception, rural blacks, aged 9—average reading scores among blacks have improved. The average black-white differences by birth cohort and type of community have consistently been larger in rural communities than in urban areas; the greatest decline in performance differences occurred in rural areas; however, there were increases in black-white differences in rural and urban disadvantaged areas between birth years 1970 and 1974.

A recent study of literacy in the United States conducted by NAEP (Kirsch and Jungeblut, 1986) concludes that there are large black-white gaps in performance on average, especially at medium and higher levels of proficiency. Perhaps most telling, as the report emphasizes (Kirsch and Jungeblut, 1986:5): "These differences appear at each level of education reported." The differences are thus not entirely the result of lower educational attainment among blacks, although disparities in family socioeconomic background and level of attainment are a component of these differences.

The NAEP literacy study involved a large, nationally representative sample of young adults, aged 21–25; developed innovative measures of literacy; and focused on levels of proficiency rather than on arbitrary points that distinguish the "literate" from the "illiterate." This is an important point inasmuch as definitions of literacy have changed considerably over time. The nineteenth century standard was the ability to write one's name. The early twentieth century standard was a fourth-grade level of reading ability, and more recent conceptions have suggested an eighth-grade level of reading

TABLE 7-4 Results of Three Literacy Tasks by Adults Aged 21–25, by Race, 1985

| | Percent Performing at or Above Indicated Score | | | | | |
| | Prose | | Documents | | Quantitative | |
Scores	White	Black	White	Black	White	Black
150	100.0	97.7	99.9	98.6	99.8	98.3
200	98.0	86.2	97.9	82.3	98.0	87.4
250	88.0	57.5	89.9	55.5	89.4	60.4
300	63.2	23.7	65.4	19.8	63.3	22.0
350	24.9	3.1	24.3	2.5	27.2	2.4
375	10.8	0.7	10.5	0.9	11.5	0.8

Note: Each scale ranges from a minimum of 0 to a maximum of 500, with a standard deviation of approximately 50.

Source: Data from Kirsch and Jungeblut (1986).

ability. In lieu of specifying some arbitrary standard, the NAEP approach defined literacy as "using printed and written information to function in society, to achieve one's goals, and to develop one's knowledge and potential" (Kirsch and Jungeblut, 1986:3).

In addition, the NAEP study devised tasks that simulated real-world behaviors and activities—for example, reading newspaper articles, writing a letter, completing applications, interpreting pay stubs, balancing a checkbook, using bus schedules, and reading maps. The tasks focused on proficiency with prose, with documents—using information contained in forms, tables, and charts—and with quantitative tasks. The tasks varied in difficulty in terms of the amount of information required, the abstractness and complexity of the interpretations needed to obtain the correct answer (from entering one's name in a blank space to summarizing the theme of a poem), and the amount of extraneous information that had to be filtered out.

The levels of proficiency exhibited by blacks and whites on the prose, documents, and quantitative tasks are shown in Table 7-4 for selected levels of performance. Each scale ranges from 0 to 500 and has a mean of approximately 305 and a standard deviation of 50. Black-white differences are small at the low end, but begin to emerge at the 200-score level. A prose score of 200 is roughly equivalent to being able to identify a single piece of information from a moderate-length sports article; a similar documents score is roughly an ability to select and match store coupons on the documents scale; and for the quantitative scale the score is roughly equivalent to being able to add simple checkbook entries. At this level, there is about a 12 percent difference between blacks and whites.

This difference widens to about 30 percent on average at the 250-score proficiency level and to an average of 40 percent at the 300-score level. A prose score of 250 is roughly equivalent to an ability to match two discrete pieces of information from a sports article, and a documents score of 250 is roughly equivalent to an ability to locate an intersection on a road map. A score of 300 on the quantification tasks is equivalent to entering and calculating more complex checkbook account entries. For prose, a score of 300 is equivalent to locating more complex information from a news article. For documents, a score of 300 is equivalent to an ability to use a map and follow directions to a particular location.

After introducing controls for family background (such as parents' education and occupation), high school curriculum, and educational attainment, the average difference between blacks and whites declined substantially for all three literacy scales. Prior to these controls, average black-white differences ranged from 51 to 60 scale points. The difference declined to between 41 and 45 points after these controls were taken into account.

There is reason to believe that the differences are smaller than in the past. A recent Census Bureau study of literacy, which involved a sample of all adults rather than just young adults, found smaller differences in performance among younger blacks and whites than among older blacks and whites.

Among the possible causes of these patterns and group differences are family background, differences in ability, test bias, differences in motivation, and differences in the educational resources and climates of schools and communities. In the next section, we focus on those institutional practices and policies and individual behaviors that can be manipulated through social policy. Specifically, the next section addresses the part that the schools themselves play in keeping blacks in the educational pipeline and encouraging high achievement. Following consideration of "intraschool" factors in achievement and attainment, we explore in greater depth the literature on nonschool or "extraschool" factors.

SCHOOL FACTORS IN ATTAINMENT AND ACHIEVEMENT

THE EFFECTS OF SCHOOLS AND BETWEEN-SCHOOL DIFFERENCES

What the schools can do to affect student achievement outcomes has been a source of controversy since the Coleman-Campbell report (1966). That study reported two major unexpected findings: despite extensive segregation, inequality in the measured resources and facilities available to students of different races within regions was small; and aggregate school resources had trivial effects on achievement scores after students' family backgrounds and schools' student body compositions were taken into account.

The latter result, in particular, has been interpreted to imply that there is little the schools can do to reduce black-white differences in performance, and that school quality—conventionally understood to mean such resources as modern facilities and highly trained teachers—has little to do with how much students learn. The report also found large black-white differences in achievement test performance at the time of school entry, and these differences were substantially maintained throughout the years of schooling. Some interpreters read the report to suggest that achievement differences between blacks and whites were not produced by the schools and probably could not be reduced by the schools (see Mosteller and Moynihan, 1972). These conclusions, the subject of intense controversy and scrutiny, continue to influence the questions addressed by educational researchers.

The efficacy of attempts to change the schools in ways that would aid blacks—for example, through compensatory education programs—has also been the subject of controversy. Early evaluation efforts concluded that at best small gains were made. More recent assessments of program effectiveness, although more encouraging (Glazer, 1986), apply less demanding criteria for success than original expectations for these programs would have envisioned (Jencks, 1986). Thus, initial appraisals of attempts to intervene directly to improve the educational status of blacks seemed also to indicate limited results.

On the basis of all the information now available, we find that the negative interpretations of the Coleman and Campbell study have been overstated (see Hanushek, 1986). The finding of only small, between-school difference effects on pupil's achievement levels was often the major item of contention. Criticisms have been made of (1) biases in the sample used in the study, (2) shortcomings of the measures used, (3) the criteria for designating significant effects, (4) the conceptual assumptions about the ordering of variables (Should the variance shared by family background and school variables be attributed to one or the other?), and (5) what, if any, legitimate policy implications might be derived from the study. But after substantial reanalyses (see Mosteller and Moynihan, 1972) of the data, and extensive work on different data sets by others (Hauser et al., 1976), the basic finding of small, between-school differences remains intact (Mullin and Summers, 1983; Spady, 1973).

There are three principal findings concerning school factors. First, there do not appear to be substantial differences in achievement that are traceable to between-school differences in such factors as facilities, teacher qualifications, and class size. However, there do appear to be considerable differences in the socioeconomic status, background, and school performance of black and white teachers (see below). Importantly, one aspect of this observation is that as a result of an intractable data problem—selectivity on an independent variable—there is no credible evidence that private schools are better institutions than public schools.

Second, contrary to much prior literature, we find grounds to infer that what the schools do substantially affects the amount of learning that takes place. Differences in the schooling process as experienced by black and white students contribute to black-white achievement differences. Much research on between-institution differences has focused on a limited number of the most tangible inputs to the schooling process—such as expenditures per pupil and teacher test scores. Other between-school differences that are related to within-school practices do matter. These differences are closely tied to teacher behavior, school climate, and the content and organization of instruction.

Third, early intervention compensatory education programs, such as Head Start, have had salutary effects on the educational performance of blacks. However, other compensatory education strategies, such as remedial instruction classes and other "pull-out" type programs, may do as much to reinforce and even widen performance gaps as they do to reduce them (Karweit, 1986).

The studies that have produced these findings share an emphasis on the need for effective teaching. Karweit (1986:13) notes:

> Achievement of black children will probably be best enhanced through the same avenues that achievement for all children will be enhanced—by good instruction emphasizing active involvement, by good school management which enables good instruction and by increased parent involvement in the day-to-day instructional activities of their children.

Yet, it is important to stress at the outset that, because of a lack of theoretical development in these areas and certain methodological limitations (such as small effects, cross-sectional as opposed to longitudinal data, and small samples), some of our findings concerning schooling effects and school climate are advanced more tentatively than findings presented in the previous sections.

THE SCHOOLING PROCESS

There is an important distinction between schools as organizations and the schooling process (Barr and Dreeben, 1983; Bidwell and Kasarda, 1980). Readily measured institutional attributes such as average classroom size and number of library books do not index the extent and quality of student utilization of these school resources. In particular, several within-school factors warrant close consideration: ability grouping and tracking and other aspects of school and classroom organization and the actual material used and covered in instructional settings.

Teacher Expectations, Characteristics, and Behavior

Tracking and teacher expectations are two of the main concerns of educators who argue that schools can impede minority achievement. Low teacher expectations in combination with practices, such as ability grouping and tracking, frequently sort black students into a "hidden curriculum" (Clark, 1963; Leacock, 1970; Rist, 1970). This hidden curriculum is usually less demanding and is believed to allocate and socialize blacks toward lower levels of attainment and achievement. Research on ability grouping does show that blacks are disproportionately located in low-ability groups and non-college preparatory tracks (Oakes, 1982, 1983), where the pacing and dynamics of low-ability groups and classrooms are substantially different from those of high-ability groups and classrooms.

Teacher characteristics and behavior, as well as differences in classroom dynamics, have been the focus of a large number of small-scale studies. While none of these studies yields definitive conclusions, their cumulative findings suggest that teachers and their classroom behaviors do make a difference.

Qualitative studies by Rist (1970) and others showed how teachers in kindergarten and the early elementary levels tend to stereotype and sort young children according to their demeanor, dress, and other class-related characteristics. One result was that the groupings into which pupils were placed tended to perpetuate and reinforce any performance differences that were initially present. In another study, Pederson and colleagues (1978) found vastly superior later test scores and occupational achievement levels among students who were exposed, in first grade, to teacher A, compared with those who had teachers B and C. Since the students had been randomly assigned to teachers and a large number of different age cohorts were involved, the outcome could not be due to "chance" factors. Interviews with teacher A's students revealed a picture of a dedicated teacher, with uniformly high expectations, and one with the ability to motivate students to persist in their efforts. This kind of teacher is also described anecdotally in other case study accounts (e.g., Sowell, 1972) and in the "effective schools" literature. Unfortunately, however, the research provides few clear guides for identifying such teachers.

Available quantitative studies show varying but generally weak relationships between teachers' academic background characteristics and students' performances (Bowles and Levin, 1968; Coleman and Campbell, 1966; Murnane, 1975; Summers and Wolfe, 1977). But an often neglected factor may prove important: the teacher's socioeconomic status background (Alexander et al., 1987).

Given the evidence to this point, perhaps it is wise to conclude, with Hanushek (1972), that it is much easier to recognize effective teachers than it is to predict their behaviors on the basis of objective indicators. Even so, however, it may be possible to assign such teachers to early grade levels and to classrooms that have large proportions of students with low socioeconomic status so that their positive influences on students at this critical stage may have a cumulative effect on their subsequent performance.

Classrooms

Classroom organization and student-student interactions have also been identified as critical conditions for learning. Some researchers (Aronson, 1978; Sharan and Sharan, 1976; Slavin, 1978, 1980) have instituted and evaluated a series of cooperative learning experiments as an alternative or supplement to standard competitive classroom procedures. These cooperative learning experiments have involved small teams of four to six students selected to maximize internal heterogeneity with respect to gender, race, and ability levels. The intent was to encourage faster students to help slower ones and then to reward the teams in such a way that slower students could contribute equally to the team score. Such techniques have produced uniformly favorable results with respect to friendships and interracial interaction patterns, while they may have somewhat improved the relative performance of the slower learners. There have now been a sufficient number of successful replications of these small-scale cooperative experiments to justify their application on a wider scale and a more sustained basis (see Bossert, 1979). A different line of work by Epstein (1980) suggests that classroom devices that encouraged increased decision-making responsibilities, as students mature, positively affect students' coping skills and performance.

Finally, several studies, summarized and evaluated by Karweit (1983, 1986), have dealt with the use of classroom time and how it affects performance. There are substantial differences in the ways in which individual teachers use their classroom time, and common sense would suggest that an efficient use of time would have a major impact on how much students learn. Thus far, however, the relationships between time use in the classroom and student performance levels have turned out to be weaker than anticipated, but encouraging enough to warrant further examination of these relatively easily manipulated variables. As Karweit notes, however, we know too little about the "receiving" side of the equation, namely what factors affect the attention and motivational levels of students, although some clues do exist. For example, a study in Chicago's first-grade classrooms shows that differences in vocabulary acquisition can be traced to the amount of classroom time used in actual daily reading and to differences in the readers used (Dreeben and Gamoran, 1986; see Hayes, 1988:584).

SCHOOL CLIMATE AND "EFFECTIVE SCHOOLS"

Educators associated with the "effective schools" movement (Brookover et al., 1979; Edmonds, 1979, 1986; Lezotte and Bancroft, 1985) are sharply critical of the view that variations in school quality do not affect the educational performance of black or other disadvantaged students. The effective schools research emphasizes aspects of the school culture or climate that can either enhance or undermine the goal of high achievement and proper social development.

Effective schools research started explicitly (Klitgaard and Hall, 1974; Weber, 1971) as a critique of the assertion that family factors were more important than school factors for the achievement of minority and low-income children. Edmonds (1986:94–95) summarized this line of research as establishing that "variability in the distribution of achievement among school-age children in the United States derives from variability in the nature of the schools to which they go." Although this research has weaknesses and sometimes overstates the case for school effects, it has begun to identify processes that contribute to high achievement among students attending low-income and black schools and to suggest ways of translating research results into specific intervention strategies (Purkey and Smith, 1985). Work on effective schools began as a search for "outliers" or schools whose objective characteristics—serving low-income, urban, minority populations—would suggest low levels of performance, but where many students exhibited exemplary performance. These schools were contrasted, at least implicitly (e.g., Weber, 1971) with schools exhibiting poor performance. The factors apparently differentiating the two types were then designated as traits of effective and ineffective schools.

Weber (1971) identified four very successful schools (reading test performance above the national norm) serving low-income populations. He attributed the apparently effective schooling to a set of eight characteristics. Most important were the leadership of a strong principal, high expectations for student performance, a "good school climate," and regular monitoring of student progress. In short, the character, culture, or climate established in some schools promoted high achievement. Klitgaard and Hall's (1974) analysis of four large data sets from the Michigan State schools and New York City school system identified a handful of schools that regularly produced high achievement, net of socioeconomic status of the school population. Success in those schools was attributed to factors similar to those identified by Weber (1971).

Notions such as school culture or climate are difficult to define and measure. Anderson's (1982) review identified four broad dimensions of school culture and climate: (1) the norms, beliefs, values, and cognitive structures that characterize a school; (2) the organizational structure or social system, which includes the formal and informal rules of organized activity; (3) the school ecology or the physical and material attributes of the school facility; and (4) the social context in which the school is located, including the social class, race, and other background characteristics of the population. It is the first two of these that have been stressed in the effective schools literature.

Among the most important attributes of the culture of effective schools are a belief among school administrators and teachers that all students, regardless of race or social class background, can achieve to some high minimum level of competence and a strong school leader, usually a principal, who continually reinforces the idea that the schools' highest priority is academic achievement.

Purkey and Smith's (1983) review distilled a set of nine school characteristics and four subsequent school dynamics that make up an effective school culture:

1. school site management at the building level, so that a principal and group of teachers have latitude to respond to their particular needs;
2. instructional leadership on the part of a principal or group of teachers that initiates and sustains a commitment to high achievement;
3. stability in staffing in order to provide school continuity;
4. instructional planning involving the careful development of curriculum and teaching plans to make the most effective use of classroom time;

5. continuous staff development to ensure adaptation to new needs;

6. parental involvement and support to tighten the home-school link in a way that reinforces high achievement goals;

7. schoolwide recognition of success that reinforces the central place of academic achievement in the schools' mission;

8. maximized learning time so that disruptive behavior and nonteaching bureaucratic activities intrude as little as possible on classroom time; and

9. district support in maintaining staff stability and initiatives.

These characteristics set in motion four dynamic aspects of school culture: (1) a greater emphasis on collaborative planning among administrators and teachers, (2) a stronger sense of community, (3) well-articulated and shared goals for the school, and (4) improvements in school discipline and order.

Lightfoot's (1983) ethnographic study of six exemplary high schools concluded that a key accomplishment of these schools was to be "good enough." The schools did not conform to a highly routinized and idealized image of the "excellent" school. Instead, these schools were effective at changing, adapting, and institutionalizing a capacity to respond to the inevitable problems and imperfections of the schooling process. A basic mission of such good schools and the first step toward establishing an effective school culture was the development of a safe, orderly, and disciplined atmosphere in the school. This requires that teachers and administrators demand of students that they become self-regulating, disciplined, and industrious. If students are not responsive to the authority of teachers and school administrators, if misbehavior, vandalism, violence, absenteeism are rife, progress toward the achievement of even basic competencies will be difficult.

At the center of efforts to develop an effective school culture, Lightfoot concluded, are the school principal and the ideology or vision for the school that the principal attempts to put in place. Effective leadership by a principal requires a mixture of the instrumental qualities of the stereotypical principal and a more expressive, symbiotic, nurturant partnership with the teachers and students at the school.

The research base that has led to the identification of the characteristics of effective schools has some weaknesses (Brophy and Good, 1986; Purkey and Smith, 1983): use of small samples; ignoring of important confounding factors in identifying outlier schools; reliance on schoolwide averages that may mask poor performance among particular groups of students; and a frequent use of subjective criteria in designating "effective schools." The students in schools designated as effective in some studies still are not performing as well as students in middle-class suburban schools.

Ethnographic and longitudinal studies also suggest that there are important differences between low-income effective schools and effective schools serving middle-class students. Lightfoot (1983) found that the effective school serving a low-income black population stressed the maintenance of order, disciplined student behavior, and the learning of basic skills and competencies. Hallinger and Murphy (1986) similarly found that the effective schools serving low-income minority groups emphasized the acquisition of basic skills. Both studies indicated, however, that effective schools for higher income groups stressed "open" instruction formats and development of higher order reasoning abilities. Purkey and Smith (1983) are especially critical of the view that the effective schools literature provides a simple formula for school improvement. In particular, many schools, especially those serving predominantly low-income or black students, may be lacking in most or all of the nine characteristics of an "effective school" (Karweit, 1986).

The effective schools research is important, however, because of the diversity of researchers and methods that have produced similar conclusions and because of the common-sense power of its principal claims. Intervention strategies that attempt to accomplish many of the recommendations of the effective schools approach have been tried. The Baldwin-King schools project in New Haven, Connecticut, is an exemplar of a promising strategy that has produced sustained improvement in the achievement and interpersonal social skills of black students (Comer, 1980, 1984). This project, which began in 1968 in two New Haven elementary schools serving a largely low-income black population (Baldwin and King), was designed as a collaborative effort of university researchers, school administrators and teachers, and parents of children attending the schools. The intervention was premised on the idea that schools work best when there is a clear and effective authority structure. But this authority structure has to establish and reinforce positive ties between the school environment and the families and communities of the children they serve. And beyond creating an orderly environment and encouraging parental involvement, the school must also respond to the social, emotional, and developmental needs of children.

Comer's (1980, 1984) research indicated that the implementation of this model of school activity was difficult and uneven, but ultimately successful. The strategy builds stronger and more trusting ties between parents and schools; this is an important accomplishment since there is often a component of mutual distrust, suspicion, and conflict between black parents and the schools as institutions (Lightfoot, 1983; Ogbu, 1974; Sieber, 1982).

Lightfoot (1983:349) identified an institutionalized capacity to assist students experiencing behavioral problems as one of the key features of a "good" school. Similarly, the Baldwin-King project stressed using knowledge derived from research on child development and mental functioning in responding to students. These efforts were so effective at integrating previously disruptive students that some of the services were discontinued.

This type of program and the curriculum changes that developed from it led to improved "school attendance, academic achievement, and improved social behavior and school climate" (Comer, 1980:203). Indeed, scores on tests of math and reading ability showed that students at the King School performed better than students attending other schools with low-income minority student bodies in New Haven; students who had been at the King school under the intervention program for the most sustained length of time

(2 to 5 years) did better than students who had been at King for less than 2 years.

MINIMUM COMPETENCY TESTING AND TEACHER TESTING

In 1986, about 40 states had some test of basic skills acquisition—generally known as minimum competency tests. Karweit (1986) and Serow (1984) reported that movements were under way in 23 states to require a minimum level of proficiency for high school graduation. Advocates view the tests as making schools accountable for demonstrating that students meet some basic standards. The diploma sanction is justified on the grounds that it reinforces the importance of the test, encourages students to take it seriously, and helps to identify students in need of remedial assistance.

Critics of minimum competency testing charge that such tests, especially when passing is made a condition for receiving a diploma, will negatively and disproportionately affect black students, and evidence supporting this claim is accumulating. Linn and colleagues (1982) reported on a 1977 reading communications test in Florida: 3 percent of white students but 24 percent of black students failed. The failure rates were higher for both races on a mathematics test, but the black-white gap was even larger: approximately 20 percent for whites and approximately 75 percent for blacks. Data assembled by Serow (1984) showed the patterns of disproportionate black failure rates in California, Florida, North Carolina, and Virginia.

These differences in passing rates translate into differences in rates of diploma denial by race. Serow (1984:72) examined data from North Carolina and found that 0.5 percent of whites were denied a diploma because of failing a minimum competency test, and 4.4 percent of blacks were denied a diploma on these grounds. Such results may encourage earlier dropout, increase the likelihood that black students will be retained in grade (Karweit, 1986), and increase the overall dropout rate for blacks.

Doubts have also been raised about the usefulness of minimum competency tests as a diagnostic tool for identifying students needing remediation (Linn et al., 1982; Karweit, 1986; Serow, 1984). Karweit (1986) noted that the use of the examinations has emphasized selection for grade promotion or graduation rather than diagnosis of learning difficulties, and that in many ways the basic content of the test lends itself to mechanical learning of discrete bits of information. Thus, even if students are assigned to a remedial program, the work is likely to emphasize passing a particular examination (Karweit, 1986:30; Madaus and Greaney, 1985:288).

Many of the problems with minimum competency testing may be more matters of implementation than fundamental flaws in the desire to increase performance and accountability. In particular, immediate problems and disadvantages introduced by the tests may ultimately be outweighed by clearer standards of performance for students and teachers. One method of dealing with the immediate problem of black failure rates on such examinations is to adopt educational programs aimed at closing performance gaps rather than at remediation. Levin (1986) and others have proposed "accelerated" curriculums for minority students. The program draws on promising teaching and classroom organization strategies (e.g., cooperative learning arrangements and peer tutoring), timetables and deadlines for bringing students up to appropriate grade-level performance, and other innovative steps such as parental involvement and pupil engagement. Research on the success of such programs is still at an early stage. However, if testing and minimum performance standards policies continue, then steps toward accelerated programs of this kind seem necessary if the pattern of lower black performance is to be improved.

Teacher testing is also on the rise. As many as 39 states now have some form of teacher testing. The examinations also frequently have proficiency criteria and sanctions for failure attached to them. According to Gifford (1986:251):

> In most cases, as a result of their own initiative or the insistence of governors and legislatures, state departments of education have instituted a standardized examination, established a cutoff score, and prohibited teacher candidates from employment as teachers until they have passed the test. In a few instances (Arkansas, Texas, and Georgia), state education departments have mandated that licensed, working teachers pass an examination to retain their certification; and at least one state educational agency (Florida) has linked merit pay increases to teacher testing.

Black teachers have experienced a disproportionate failure rate on these examinations (see Table 7-5). For example, on the California Basic Educational Skills Test (CBEST) in 1983, 26 percent of blacks and 76 percent of whites passed. Similarly, 35 percent of black but 90 percent of white test takers passed the Florida teacher competency examination in 1983 (Gifford, 1986:255).

Such results appear to have had a discouraging effect on the number of blacks aspiring to become teachers (Baratz, 1986). For example, in 1978, the first year of Louisiana's program, 31 percent of the teacher examination takers were black; that percentage had declined to 13 percent by 1982. The overall passing rate for blacks during the time period was 15 percent.

Universities that train large numbers of black teachers and other professional associations have responded to this problem by modifying their training and preparation programs. These changes sometimes produce dramatic increases in how their graduates perform on teacher competency examinations (Baratz, 1986). The results substantially improved pass rates for black teachers attempting these tests. For example, Gifford (1986) reported improved black performance on the CBEST between 1983 and 1985.

TABLE 7-5 Pass Rates on Teacher Competency Tests in 10 States, 1982–1983

State	All	Whites	Asians	Blacks	Hispanics	Native Americans
Alabama	81	86		43		
Arizona						
January 6, 1983	66	73	50	24	42	22
July 9, 1983	59	70	25	41	36	19
California	68	76	50	26	38	67
Florida						
June 1982	85	92	67	37	57	90
February 1983	84	90	63	35	51	100
Georgia	78	87		34		
Louisiana	77	78		15		
Mississippi		97[a]		54[a]		
		100[b]		70[b]		
Oklahoma	78	79	82	45	71	70
Texas	54	62	47	10	19	47
Virginia (trial testing)						
Communication skills		97		56		
General knowledge		99		69		
Professional knowledge		99		83		

[a]Pass rates at predominantly white public institutions.
[b]Pass rates at predominantly black public institutions.

Source: Data from American Association of Colleges of Teacher Education.

HIGHER EDUCATION: INSTITUTIONAL CLIMATE, SOCIAL ADJUSTMENT, AND ACADEMIC SUCCESS

Black students on white campuses frequently express feelings of alienation and social isolation (Allen et al., 1984; Fleming, 1984; Gibbs, 1973; Smith, 1981; Willie and Cunnigen, 1981). In a survey of entering black undergraduate and graduate students at eight predominantly white state universities located throughout the nation, Allen and colleagues (1984) found black students to be ambivalent about their status. The students tended to report lukewarm relationships with white students, faculty, and staff, and they did not feel strongly engaged with campus activities. Many turned to black organizations and activities and reported very positive interactions with other black students and black faculty. Indeed, one of the most consistent recommendations for change made by the students surveyed was that the number of black faculty and students be increased.

In the surveys by Allen and colleagues (1984), 65 percent of the black undergraduates and 73 percent of the black graduate students reported having encountered discrimination. The discrimination sometimes took the form of treatment by university staff or employees that implied the black students did not belong on campus at all (e.g., excessive requests for proof of identification at campus events) or that the black students had gained access to the university through illegitimate means (such as special admission programs). Some of the students who said they faced discrimination reported patronizing or explicitly derogatory remarks by faculty members. The most frequently reported form of discrimination involved the use of racist epithets, symbols, or mimicry by white students (see also Willie and Cunnigen, 1981:194).

Events since the late 1970s suggest that discrimination and tensions on college campuses are persistent and possibly increasing problems. Direct acts of aggression and violence have occurred at many college campuses (Smith, 1981:30; *The Chronicle of Higher Education,* January 1, 1988). The National Institute Against Prejudice and Violence estimated that 70 of the nation's college campuses experienced significant racial or ethnic violence in 1987.

A recent study based on a large sample of black and white students from 30 southern and eastern colleges confirmed the importance of social adjustment factors to black success in college (Nettles et al., 1986). Several of the social adjustment factors had statistically significant interactions with race, usually having larger effects on black academic performance than on white performance. Results of this research are noteworthy because of the large sample size, use of reasonably reliable measures, and formal tests for interactions between the relevant social psychological factors and race of the student (see also Fox, 1986; Getzlaf et al., 1984). Future research in this area needs to more systematically address how the black student experience differs from that of whites, to develop longitudinal designs, and to consider a wider and more complex array of student outcomes.

EXTRASCHOOL FACTORS IN ATTAINMENT AND ACHIEVEMENT

THE SOCIAL CONTEXT OF THE SCHOOLS

Schools do not exist in a vacuum. What happens in them is affected by what children bring to and receive from the schools. It is well known that children from higher socioeconomic status backgrounds are more likely than those from low socioeconomic status backgrounds to score high on achievement tests, to receive persistent encouragement from adults, and to form high educational aspirations. They are also more likely to complete college and pursue advanced or professional degrees. These outcomes, in turn, have powerful effects on occupational positions and, thereby, on earnings.

These differences in educational attainments are to a substantial degree not due to differences in measured ability. As Sewell and Hauser (1980:69) summarized in their studies of Wisconsin high school students:

> Among students in the top quarter in ability, a student from the lowest quarter in socioeconomic status is approximately half as likely to attend college or to graduate from college as a student from the highest quarter in socioeconomic status. The chances of a high ability student obtaining graduate or professional education, where one would presume ability would be determinant, are approximately 3.5 times greater if he comes from a family with high socioeconomic status than from a low socioeconomic status family.

Although these Wisconsin data pertain mainly to white students, recent analyses suggest that the same processes are at work among blacks (see below).

To a substantial degree, black-white differences in educational status can be traced to average social class differences between the two groups. For example, we report below that differences in socioeconomic status explain the entire black-white difference in dropout rates and account for at least 20 percent of the difference in achievement test performance. The more significant point, however, is that black-white differences in school performance are likely to persist so long as differences in the socioeconomic status of the two groups remain.

Socioeconomic status alone, however, does not explain all black-white educational differences. Direct racial discrimination in the provision of education has a long history in the United States. A degree of national consensus on the idea that schooling for blacks should be of high quality and be provided on an equal and integrated basis is a recent phenomenon. Historically, discrimination in education has included exclusion from the schools, shorter school days and shorter school years for blacks, lower qualifications and poorer pay for black teachers, and plainly inferior facilities and materials (Bond, 1934; Bullock, 1967).

The broader experiences of labor market discrimination, of residential segregation, and of antiblack attitudes and beliefs are also relevant to black-white differences in schooling. All of these are likely to affect the in-school behavior of both whites and blacks as students and as teachers. Racial discrimination and separation are thus of fundamental importance for understanding the educational status of blacks. The one event that has had overarching significance for the schooling of black Americans was neither a pedagogical innovation nor a shift in population characteristics. Rather, it was legal and political: the 1954 Supreme Court ruling in *Brown* v. *Board of Education*.

BLACK-WHITE SIMILARITIES AND DIFFERENCES

Families, neighborhoods and communities, and peer groups affect student performance by influencing patterns of school-related behavior and underlying orientations toward education. We report two main research findings. First, contrary to the conclusions of a large literature, the same factors that affect schooling outcomes for whites also affect blacks. Consequently, important differences between blacks and whites on factors such as socioeconomic background, early levels of achievement, beliefs about discrimination, and time spent on homework compared with time spent watching television have important roles in generating educational outcome differences between the two groups.

A second and related conclusion is that blacks' particular minority group status affects their experiences within, and adaptations to, the schools. Black children frequently live in social environments that make them less likely to perceive high educational achievement as an unambiguously desirable goal. High achievement may also not be regarded as leading to important rewards or as essential to the adult social roles they perceive as open to them (Ogbu, 1978, 1986). Consequently, black youth may view themselves as having limited opportunities, and they may feel ambivalence about the probable returns to educational success. Such expectations may explain why black children expend less effort in academic activities than do white children.

The Educational Attainment Process

A large number of studies have concluded that the process of educational attainment differs for blacks and whites.[3] Variables used to explain educational outcomes were routinely found to be less powerful in accounting for the educational attainment of blacks than that for whites. Moreover, socioeconomic status exerted less powerful effects at each stage of the attainment process for blacks. In addition, social psychological factors were found to play a larger role in the attainment process among blacks, especially educational aspirations (Portes and Wilson, 1976), beliefs regarding the need for conformity to conventional norms (Porter, 1974), and fatalism regarding the likelihood of receiving economic rewards for education (Kerckhoff and Campbell, 1977b). The general explanation for these differences stresses black-white differences in access to educational goals, rewards, and preparatory experiences—as well as differential treatment and evaluation within educational institutions.

Recent research using more sophisticated and powerful statistical techniques questions the conclusions of much of this body of work. On the basis of analyses of nationally representative samples with large numbers of black high school students, both Gottfredson (1981) and Wolfle (1985) have rejected the claim that the educational attainment process works differently for blacks and whites. There are two bases for their refutations. First, the previous literature used inappropriate tests for black-white differences in attainment "process" effects, either not correcting for sample design com-

---

3. These studies have used nationally representative data (Allen, 1980; Epps and Jackson, 1985; Porter, 1974; Portes and Wilson, 1976); city, state, or school district samples (DeBord et al., 1977; Hout and Morgan, 1975; Kerckhoff and Campbell, 1977a,b); and samples of students in integrated and segregated schools (Falk, 1978; Howell and Frese, 1979; Wilson, 1979).

plexities, failing to perform formal tests of any kind, or relying on data with such small numbers of black students that reliable inference was impossible. Second, the measurement characteristics of key factors in the statistical models used differ by race, thus creating the appearance of black-white differences when corrections for differential reliability are not made. Using statistical techniques that allowed formal tests for black-white differences and adjustment for differential reliability of measurement, neither Gottfredson nor Wolfle found any important differences in the educational attainment process by race. Gottfredson analyzed the data used in several of the earlier studies, but omitted variables such as self-esteem, conformity orientations, and fatalism. Wolfle tested a model (see Heyns, 1974; Thomas et al., 1979) that omitted the social psychological factors altogether, but included school factors such as curriculum placement. Wolfle (1985:516) succinctly summarized both sets of results when he concluded: "The process of educational attainment is not different for blacks and whites."

Analyses of the High School and Beyond survey data for 1980 sophomores carried out expressly for this report (Pallas, 1986, 1987) extended these results in two ways: by focusing on the scholastic outcomes of schooling—achievement test performance and grades—in the students' senior year (1982) rather than ultimate educational attainments, and by examining the impact of school input and social background differences on the causes of differences in achievement between blacks and whites. Even if the same variables predict achievement performances for blacks and whites, different mean levels of the predictors (e.g., family income) may account for much of the observed group differences in achievement.

One major result of these analyses was that there were minor, but statistically discernible, group differences in the impact of socioeconomic status on high school dropout rates, on senior-year academic achievement, and on senior-year levels of aspirations. Although higher socioeconomic status reduced dropping out among blacks and whites and increased aspirations, achievement, and grades, these effects were somewhat stronger among whites. Also, sophomore-year aspirations exerted a weaker influence on senior-year outcomes among whites than among blacks. On the whole, the results indicate greater similarities than differences between blacks and whites in the achievement process.

Another major result was that differences in social background, sophomore-year levels of achievement, curriculum placement, and a set of behavioral and social-psychological indicators measured in the sophomore year account for significant portions of the black-white difference in senior-year scholastic outcomes. In particular, differences in socioeconomic status entirely explain blacks' higher dropout rate. In addition, most of the difference in senior-year achievement levels reflected prior differences in achievement.

Families, Socialization, and School Performance

An enormous body of research has addressed the link between experiences within families, a child's cognitive development, and school success. Much of this research attempts to identify social class and black-white differences in child-rearing behaviors that may cause achievement differences. Two observations are frequently made: there is substantial variation by social class and race in child-rearing practices, principally in language usage, parental teaching strategies, and other forms of cognitive stimulation; and these differences, which operate in favor of those with high social status, affect cognitive development and school performance.

Several possible effects of family structure on cognitive development have been identified: family size, family composition (one or two parents), and birth order. For example, family size is held to be inversely related to cognitive development, especially for later siblings, because there is less time for parental supervision and instruction as the available time is necessarily spread among more children. Family composition is important because burdens that might be shared by two adults fall on the shoulders of one in a single-parent household.

Both family size and composition do affect cognitive development and educational outcomes. However, net of family size effects, birth order and spacing do not have important consequences for schooling outcomes (Hauser and Sewell, 1985; Olneck and Bills, 1979). The evidence on family composition is less decisive than that concerning family size: several recent reports emphasize that effects of one-parent or two-parent status on achievement are small and traceable to associated differences in socioeconomic status (Johnson, 1987; Scott-Jones, 1987a; Svanum et al., 1982). In addition, some research suggests that the negative effects of one-parent households on educational outcomes among blacks are mitigated by support from extended family members (Brackbill and Nicholls, 1982).

Studies of family interaction typically assume that within families a climate is produced that crucially affects cognitive abilities and academic development (Johnson, 1987:10). A number of studies have focused on how low-income black families encourage or discourage school achievement (Clark, 1983; Norman-Jackson, 1982; Scheinfeld, 1983; Scott-Jones, 1987b; Shade, 1978; Slaughter, 1969). Clark's (1983) ethnographic study of 10 black low-income families reported that families of high-achieving children tended to be warm and nurturing, set clear academic and behavioral standards, and monitored their children's actions and schoolwork. Families with a low-achieving child were characterized by feelings of depression, lack of personal control, and low emotional spirit. This climate had adverse consequences for parental guidance and monitoring of children and for a child's performance in school. Thus, socioeconomic status does affect child-rearing behaviors that, in turn, have consequences for cognitive development and school performance. To the extent that blacks on average are of lower socioeconomic status than whites, their schooling performance is thus likely to be lower.

But there are some black-white performance differences even after controlling for socioeconomic status. In part, this occurs because most efforts to control for socioeconomic status are based on cross-sectional information about family income, occupation, and the like. To the extent that black families experience more and longer periods of extreme poverty or unemployment, such data provide at best a lower limit estimate of the effect of socioeconomic conditions on differences in black-white achievement.

Another possible reason for black-white achievement differences net of socioeconomic status is a black-white cultural difference in socialization. Studies of transracially adopted children provide empirical support for this hypothesis. Scarr and Weinberg (1978) and Moore (1982, 1986, 1987) studied transracially adopted black children and found that these black children perform about as well as white children on intelligence tests.

Moore's research examined a group of 46 black children, 23 of whom were given traditional placements with another black family and 23 of whom were placed with a white family. All 46 adopting families were of high socioeconomic status, although the white adoptive families were slightly higher. The results showed that transracially adopted black children performed better on the WISC-IQ test than black children adopted by black families. Measured differences in performance were related to differences in behavioral style in the test situation, in mothers' teaching strategies, and in the racial mix of friends and of the community of residence. Moore's research and that of Scarr and Weinberg found that scores in measured intelligence were directly related to greater proximity to a white middle-class cultural standard. Moore (1982:142) concluded that variation in the tested intelligence of black children on the basis of rearing in a black middle-class or white middle-class environment is difficult to explain on any basis other than black-white cultural differences.

This cultural difference research has been careful in design and persuasive in findings. The research should be replicated and extended to explain the social origins of black-white cultural differences in child-rearing and cognitive development.

Some serious efforts to account for the social origins of black-white achievement differences emphasize a distinctive black American cultural and cognitive style. A number of scholars contend that there are unique elements in black learning styles and cognitive processes (Baratz and Baratz, 1970; Blau, 1981; Boykin, 1986; Cole and Bruner, 1971; Gay and Abrahams, 1973; Hale-Benson, 1982; Massey et al., 1982; McDermott, 1974; Mercer, 1974; Shade, 1978, 1982; Shade and Edwards, 1987; Valentine, 1971). The data are often drawn from small and unrepresentative samples, and the research has not as yet explained why other minority groups, such as Asian-Americans, with their own cultural distinctiveness, attain high academic achievements. Several lists of specific types of black-white differences now exist, particularly those offered by Shade (1978) and Boykin (1986). More work needs to be done on this important issue.

Social Status and Ambivalence About Education

Another explanation of the causes of black-white achievement differences emphasize the importance of racial stratification on black orientations toward performance in school. As formulated by Ogbu (1978), this perspective contends that as a result of racial stratification there is often sharp discontinuity between the home and community experiences of black students and the middle-class values, standards, and expectations of the schools.

Ogbu's cross-cultural research proposes that any minority group, even if of the same "race" as the dominant social group, will exhibit lower school achievement and measured intelligence when compared to the dominant group if the minority group occupies a "caste-like" social status. Caste-like minority group status is defined by involuntary incorporation into the dominant society and by extreme discrimination during an extended period of relegation to society's least valued occupational roles. The black American experience fits this definition.

Ogbu (1986) identified several groups outside the United States that occupied a caste-like status: West Indians in Great Britain, Maoris in New Zealand, Buraku outcasts in Japan, Harijans in India, and Oriental Jews in Israel. In each case, when compared with more privileged groups, those groups with caste-like status were 1–2 years behind in reading, disproportionately concentrated in remedial reading programs, and underrepresented in higher education. Minority group caste-like status, rather than race, was the important factor since the minority group did less well than the dominant group even when they were of the same race (as in India, Israel, and Japan).

To the extent that adults in U.S. communities do not hold social and occupational positions that expose them to various middle-class skills, orientations, and behaviors, they are less able to pass onto their children the skills, competencies, and orientations necessary to attain high levels of achievement. As a result of location in different social structural positions and environments, therefore, blacks and whites develop different orientations to schooling and bring different orientations to that institution.

Ogbu's (1974) ethnographic research in Stockton, California, found that black parents were emphatic in saying that they valued schooling and wanted their children to do well and get a good education. They even held public demonstrations to demand more and better education for their children. But at the same time the parents' own lives helped to create ambivalent attitudes toward schooling in their children. Parents told their children to get a good education and encouraged them verbally to do well in school, and those who could helped with homework; meanwhile, the actual texture of their own lives in terms of menial jobs, underemployment, and unemployment conveyed a second kind of message powerful enough to undo their exhortations.

Among black students themselves, the negative messages conveyed by the textures of their parents' lives and community responses were reinforced by their own observations of the employment and unemployment status of older people around them. These other sources of information included older siblings, relatives, and other adults who had finished or left school, their own inability to get part-time and summer jobs, observations of and even participation in public demonstrations for more jobs, and reports in the mass media about the employment difficulties of blacks. Under these circumstances, black students did not try to maximize their school performance; they said they did not persevere in their schoolwork because they did not think that they would have equal opportunity to get good jobs when they finished school.

Among the principal consequences of caste-like minority status is the adoption of a perspective that attributes the groups' low status to unfair discrimination and prejudice. In the United States, this perspective becomes a component of how blacks evaluate encounters with schools. Blacks often have feelings of suspicion, distrust, conflict, and resistance to full assimilation (McDermott, 1974). Boykin (1986) suggested that black students confront a triple quandary that involves the need to simultaneously master mainstream American culture, black American culture, and the critical perspective of a low-status minority. When the mainstream culture in the schools is experienced as alien and hostile, many black children attempt to assert the value and integrity of the experiences of their homes and communities by rejecting the standards of the schools.

Recent ethnographic work by Fordham and Ogbu (1986) suggests that black student peer culture undermines the goal of striving for academic success. Among eleventh graders at a predominantly black high school in Washington, D.C., many behaviors associated with high achievement—speaking standard English, studying long hours, striving to get good grades—were regarded as "acting white." Students known to engage in such behaviors were labeled "brainiacs," ridiculed, and ostracized as people who had abandoned the group. Interviews with a number of the high-achieving students—who showed a conscious awareness of the choices they were making—indicated that some had chosen to put "brakes" on their academic effort in order to avoid being labeled and harassed. The students premised these choices on what they saw as their own limited economic chances in life. The burden of peer disapproval was often not perceived as worth the likely limited benefits perceived to accrue to academic success (see also Petroni, 1970; Petroni and Hirsch, 1970). This pattern is also documented by some experimental and survey-based research. Banks and colleagues (1977) compared the responses of black and white children concerning, first, the sorts of tasks they found enjoyable or likeable and those they disliked and, second, whether they would be willing to expend considerable effort at these tasks.

The white students rated as likeable more of the tasks likely to be rewarded in school (e.g., doing well enough in school to make the honor roll) than did blacks. But the black and white students did not differ in the amount of energy they intended to expend toward those tasks they valued.

Hare and Castenell (1986) concluded that black students, in particular black males, form stronger attachments to the peer group. Their data on 500 Champaign, Illinois, fifth graders showed black males to have lower achievement orientations and sense of internal control than white males, but to have higher ratings on measures of perceived social abilities and peer group attachment. Using the same data, but this time focusing on gender differences, Hare (1985) found that black males expressed a greater attachment to peer group culture than black females.

Broader social experience with racial stratification influences teachers and school administrators as well. Ogbu (1974) reported that the teachers and school administrators he observed did not reward (and thereby discouraged) children's classroom performance, resisted parents' efforts to help their children, and did not provide information that would help black youngsters plan their future.

More systematic exploration of these ideas about how family and community processes affect schooling as experienced by black students needs to be undertaken. Research based on assessments of statistical models leads to the conclusion of substantial similarity in the process of educational achievement and attainment for blacks and whites, while a growing body of ethnographic observations of behavior and interaction within the schools suggests that some special factors may be operating for blacks. These additional factors need further empirical testing. Future research would do well to focus on whether and to what extent the educational aspirations and plans of black students are developed and expressed with greater ambivalence or uncertainty compared with those of whites.

SCHOOL DESEGREGATION AND ACADEMIC ACHIEVEMENT

We reported above that school desegregation modestly improves the academic performance of black pupils and has no substantial effect on white pupils' academic achievement. We now elaborate on this conclusion. We also report mixed findings pertaining to the effects of school desegregation on students' self-esteem and educational aspirations.

Studies of the relationship between educational and occupational aspirations of blacks and whites in segregated schools have been reviewed by a number of researchers, all of whom concluded that the level of aspiration of segregated blacks is as high or higher than that of segregated whites (Cook, 1979:424; Epps, 1975; Weinberg, 1977). Reported findings on the self-esteem and educational aspirations of black children in desegregated schools are so diverse that overall generalizations are not warranted. Effects evidently depend on variables not adequately accounted for in the available research (Longshore and Prager, 1985:85).

Reviewing 25 studies of racially mixed schools encompassing natural and planned desegregation, St. John (1975) reported that blacks' occupational and educational aspirations either remained equal to those of whites or became lower after desegregation. Some studies find a trend for minority aspirations to decrease as the percentage of white students in the school increases (Cook, 1979:426). St. John (1975) and Stephan (1978) concluded that blacks in desegregated schools have lower self-esteem than blacks in segregated schools. Epps (1978) and Zirkel (1971) found the existing studies too inconsistent to reveal a trend. Weinberg (1977), after examining 60 studies, concluded that in 29 of the 60, desegregated blacks have the higher self-esteem (Cook, 1979:426-427).

Research on the effects of desegregation on the achievement of white students has consistently concluded that their achievement has been unaffected (Cook, 1979:429; St. John, 1975). A number of major reviews of the desegregation achievement literature agree that small gains in black achievement from attendance for 1-2 years in mixed-race schools do occur (Crain and Mahard, 1978; St. John, 1975; Stephan, 1978; Weinberg, 1977). However, they differed in their estimates of the frequency of such gains. St. John (1975) summarized 64 studies with the conclusion that they provide no assurance of achievement gains. Bradley and Bradley (1977) reached the same conclusion. Stephan (1978) stated that of the 34 studies he examined, two-thirds showed no positive effect. Weinberg (1977), concentrating on 49 studies of planned desegregation (omitting studies of other mixed-race schools), judged that 60 percent of them showed achievement gains for blacks. Assessing 73 studies of this type, Crain and Mahard (1978) found positive effects in from one-half to two-thirds of the cases. Cook (1979:428) concluded that positive gains were more frequent than negative ones, and achievement gains were most consistent "(1) when desegregation is required by official policy; (2) when students begin their education in desegregated schools; (3) when cumulative rather than short-term gains are emphasized" (see also Crain and Mahard, 1978; Weinberg, 1977).

An analysis by Crain and Mahard (1983) of the relationship between desegregation and achievement test scores dealt with 323 samples from 93 studies in 67 cities. Gains for black students on standardized achievement test scores (or grade equivalents) outnumbered losses, 173 to 98. Both the percentage of samples showing positive changes in academic achievement and the size of the effects were larger in the studies that had the more rigorous research designs (e.g., random assignment, longitudinal data). The findings imply that many studies have underestimated the positive effects because of methodological defects in sampling, design, or techniques of analysis. Such problems may well account for the large variation in findings. Further support for positive effects comes from what to date is probably the most thorough analysis of the available research literature (see Wachter, 1988).

BLACK FACULTY IN HIGHER EDUCATION

Underrepresentation of black faculty at predominantly white colleges and universities continues to be significant. A recent report noted that in 1960, blacks comprised 3 percent of all college and university faculty and were heavily concentrated in the historically black institutions; in 1968–1969, the percentage had fallen to 2.2 percent of all college and university faculty. In the early 1980s, blacks were less than 5 percent of the full-time faculty at predominantly white universities (Exum, 1983:385). Figures for 1977–1983 show a drop of 6.2 percent in the number of full-time black faculty at public 4-year institutions and of 11.3 percent at private institutions. Black underrepresentation is greatest at elite universities and at 2-year colleges. There is little prospect for growth in black representation in light of the declines in both the percentage of blacks going on to college and the percentage pursuing graduate and professional degrees.

Black faculty are concentrated in certain fields. Despite a shift toward majors in business and other fields, black faculty remain concentrated in education and the social sciences. Yet, even in these areas of greatest concentration, blacks remain underrepresented.

Career development, evaluation, and promotion of black faculty have faltered since the early 1970s. In the 1980s, the percentage of blacks holding doctorates who have pursued academic careers is on the decline, and black promotion rates among those pursuing academic careers are lower than those for whites or other minority groups. Recruitment efforts falter for many reasons. Menges and Exum (1983) noted that efforts to recruit faculty from groups traditionally underrepresented in academia tend to focus on setting goals and making an initial appointment. Yet both the setting and meeting of such goals are problematic: the information needed to estimate the size of the pool of possible candidates is often lacking, and there may be great variability in whether any goal set is viewed as a minimum or a maximum target, whether goals are to be applied university-wide or on a department-by-department basis, and whether goals are accompanied by effective advertising and recruiting techniques.

Once blacks are added to the ranks of tenure-track faculty, problems of career development, evaluation, and promotion arise. Menges and Exum (1983) reported that black faculty are likely to encounter six types of problems that put them at a special disadvantage: lack of seniority, greater non-teaching responsibilities than whites, dual appointments, different research interests, lack of social networks, and conflict over affirmative action.

First, as a result of lack of seniority, black faculty are in vulnerable positions if faculty reductions take place. Second, black faculty members often face greater service demands than whites, for counseling black students, working on professional groups and activities, and serving on various departmental and university committees. Such demands on the time of black faculty can reduce the time available for work on research and teaching. Because many of their duties are similar, black and white faculty shared several career-related sources of stress, such as high personal expectations for research productivity. But black faculty reported a larger number of sources of stress, and the largest black-white differences concerned administrative duties and the lack of institutional rewards for administrative and service work. Thus, black faculty were more likely than whites in the matched sample to report that administrative and student counseling work reduced their time for research and teaching, and that the institution did not provide enough formal rewards for the service activities they were performing. This poses a dilemma for many black faculty because they were often recruited with the idea that they would perform a larger service role, or were expected to do so, yet ultimately few rewards accrued to such activities. Third, blacks in addition often must divide their energies between a major disciplinary appointment and an appointment in a black or Afro-American studies program or department.

Fourth, among the most consistent observations made about black graduate students and faculty, at least in the social sciences and humanities, are a distinctive set of research interests and a degree of dissatisfaction with prevailing research paradigms. For example, Prestage (1979:768) noted that black political scientists are likely to bring an "out-group" perspective to their research; Mommsen (1974:109–111) noted that black sociologists tended to concentrate on social problems and race relations issues; and two large edited volumes have attempted to systematize the work and perspectives of black psychologists (Boykin et al., 1979). These differences in perspectives are accentuated by the recency of a significant black presence in academia, which is related to a fifth problem: blacks tend to lack the support networks crucial to career development and promotion (Menges and Exum, 1983).

Sixth, there is often a value clash over affirmative action (Dingerson et al., 1985; Elmore and Blackburn, 1983; Exum, 1983; Menges and Exum, 1983; Steele and Green, 1976). Affirmative action pressures have sometimes been interpreted as a challenge to university and departmental autonomy and as a threat to merit standards of evaluation. But the often heated debates over affirmative action have been overdrawn according to some observers: Exum (1983) concluded that most monitoring and compliance evaluation efforts focused on issues of access (e.g., applicant searches and recruitment), but did not extend to departmental procedures for evaluation and promotion (Berry, 1983; Prestage, 1979).

Research indicates no recent change in the rate of faculty and staff hiring of minorities. Dingerson and colleagues (1985) found no evidence of increased hiring of blacks for academic administrative positions. In a study of listed positions, their data indicated that blacks and women of either race were hired when additional resources were committed to recruitment and search efforts. The average cost of the hiring process when the position was filled by a nonwhite male exceeded the cost of a traditional hire by about $2,000.

Affirmative action goals are sometimes treated as maximum quotas rather than minimum targets. A case study by Steele and Green (1976) of a major research university found that the estimated size of the pool of potential minority applicants was related to the number of offers eventually made to minority candidates only among departments that already "had a good track record," and that in many departments minority hiring ceased after reaching the goal level. As Steele and Green explained, "In the case of minorities, the effect of the policy was limited to quota maintenance" (1976:431–432).

POLICY CONTEXT AND CONCLUSIONS

Education in the United States has historically been a state and local obligation. With the exception of its important role in the funding of land-grant colleges and black colleges, the federal role in education, until the mid-1950s, was generally miniscule. Three developments increased the federal role in the field of education. First were civil rights obligations as required by the Supreme Court in the *Brown* decision of 1954. This was supplemented by many lower federal court rulings requiring desegregation and by the Civil Rights Act of 1964. Second was concern for the quality of American education, accelerated by the Soviet success in orbiting the satellite *Sputnik* in 1957. This concern led to the National Defense Education Act and to several types of federal assistance encouraging higher quality in American education, particularly in science and mathematics. Third was the concern for poverty that led to the Economic Opportunity Act of 1964, which launched a number of programs that attempted to improve the educational performance of the poor.

The first and third of these factors bear directly on the education of black children. Desegregation was an attempt to fulfill constitutional requirements and to improve the educational environment for black children. Because of the economic differences between blacks and whites, programs designed for poor children were in some part programs for black children. However, federal intervention in state and local school systems never was great enough to alter decisively the administration of those systems. In this context, actions at all three levels of government have affected and will continue to affect the schooling of black Americans.

Are black Americans receiving an excellent and equal education? We have six major conclusions that pertain to these questions. First, substantial progress has been made toward the provision of high-quality, equal, and integrated education. Whether the baseline period is the 1940s, the 1950s, or even as recently as the mid-1960s, the amount, achievement outcomes, and intergroup context (integrated versus segregated) of black schooling have greatly improved. Second, compensatory education programs—Head Start and Chapter I—have overall positive (although sometimes short-term) effects on the academic achievement of disadvantaged students. Programs for pre-school children have a number of positive and long-term effects on subsequent educational enrollment, achievement, and attainment.

Third, however, there remain persistent and large gaps in the schooling quality and achievement outcomes of education for blacks and whites. Black high school dropout rates remain higher than those for whites, black performance on tests of achievement lags behind that of whites, and blacks remain less likely to attend college and to complete a college degree. After the mid-1970s, the college-going chances of black high school graduates have declined, and the proportion of advanced degrees awarded to blacks has decreased.

Fourth, what the schools do substantially affects the amount of learning that takes place. Differences in the schooling process as experienced by black and white students contribute to black-white achievement differences. These differences are closely tied to teacher behavior, school climate and peer group influences, and the content and organization of instruction.

Fifth, blacks' status in higher education, as undergraduates, graduates, and faculty, has worsened or stalled since the mid-1970s. Several indicators, in particular college attendance rates, show signs of slippage, with blacks' status deteriorating relative to that of whites and of other minorities.

Finally, separation and differential treatment of blacks continue to be widespread in the elementary and secondary schools and, in different forms, in institutions of higher learning.

These conclusions are based on many kinds of findings. Foremost among these is the fact that measures of educational outcomes (attainment and achievement) of students and teachers reveal substantial gaps between blacks and whites. Blacks on average enter the schools with substantial disadvantages in socioeconomic backgrounds and tested achievement levels. The schools do not compensate for these disadvantages. On average, American students leave the schools with black-white achievement gaps not having been appreciably diminished. At the pinnacle of the educational process, blacks' lower life opportunities are manifest in the fact that the odds that a black high school graduate will enter college within a year of graduation are less than one-half the odds of those for a white high school graduate.

The large differences in socioeconomic background between blacks and whites are perhaps the most significant factors in accounting for these black-white disparities in educational status. When background differences are combined with such factors as residential separation of blacks and whites, the cumulative impact is very great. Socioeconomic background differences account for significant percentages of the educational achievement and attainment differences between blacks and whites—and virtually all of the difference in high school dropout rates. Furthermore, many of the differences in learning among schools has been attributed to differences in the social background of student populations. Blacks' much lower mean social status levels combined with high levels of school segregation (especially among lower status urban blacks) compounds the negative effects of low socioeconomic status on black attainment and achievement levels.

Thus, although substantial progress has been made toward the provision of educational resources to blacks, there remain persistent and large gaps in the schooling quality and achievement outcomes of education for blacks and whites. Black high school dropout rates remain higher than those for whites, black performance on tests of achievement shows relative gains but lags behind that of whites, and blacks remain less likely to attend college and to complete a college degree.

Since the late 1970s, the college-going chances of black high school graduates have declined, and the proportion of advanced degrees awarded to blacks has decreased. While we cannot conclude with certainty that the cause has been the significant decline in (real) financial aid grants to students, other reasonable hypotheses can explain only a negligible component of this change.

Segregation and differential treatment of blacks continue to be widespread in schools. This segregation has several consequences for students: although school desegregation does not substantially affect the academic performance of white students, it modestly improves black performance (particularly reading); when several key conditions are met, intergroup attitudes and relations improve after schools are desegregated; and desegregation is most likely to reduce racial isolation as well as to improve academic and social outcomes for blacks when it is part of a comprehensive and rapid program of change.

REFERENCES

Alexander, Karl L., Doris Entwisle, and Maxine S. Thompson
  1987 School performance, status relations, and the structure of sentiment: bringing the teacher back in. *American Sociological Review* 52:665–682.
Allen, Walter R.
  1980 Preludes to attainment: race, sex, and student achievement orientation. *Sociological Quarterly* 21(Winter):65–79.
Allen, Walter R., Lawrence Bobo, and Paul Fleuranges
  1984 Preliminary Report: 1982 Undergraduate Survey of Black Undergraduate Students Attending Predominantly White, State Supported Universities. Center for Afro-American and African Studies, Ann Arbor, Mich.
Anderson, Carolyn S.
  1982 The search for school climate: a review of the research. *Review of Educational Research* 52(3):368–420.
Arbeiter, Solomon
  1986 Minority enrollment in higher education institutions: a chronological view. *Research and Development Update*. New York: College Board.
Aronson, Elliot
  1978 *The Jigsaw Classroom.* Beverly Hills, Calif.: Sage Publications Inc.
Banks, W. Curtis, Gregory McQuarter, and Janet L. Hubbard
  1977 Task-liking and intrinsic-extrinsic achievement orientations in black adolescents. *Journal of Black Psychology* 3:61–71.
  1979 Toward a reconceptualization of the social-cognitive bases of achievement orientations in blacks. Pp. 294–311 in A. Wade Boykin, Anderson J. Franklin, and J. Frank Yates, eds., *Research Directions of Black Psychologists*. New York: Russell Sage Foundation.

Baratz, Joan C.
1986 Black Participation in the Teacher Pool. Paper prepared for the Task Force on Teaching as a Profession, Carnegie Forum on Education and the Economy, New York.

Baratz, Stephen S., and Joan C. Baratz
1970 Early childhood interventions: the social science base of institutional racism. *Harvard Educational Review* 40:29–50.

Barr, Rebecca, and Robert Dreeben
1983 *How Schools Work*. Chicago: University of Chicago Press.

Berry, Mary Frances
1983 Blacks in predominantly white institutions of higher learning. Pp. 295–318 in James D. Williams, ed., *The State of Black America 1983*. New York: National Urban League.

Bidwell, Charles E., and John D. Kasarda
1980 Conceptualizing and measuring the effects of school and schooling. *American Journal of Education* 88(4):401–430.

Blau, Zena S.
1981 *Black Children-White Children: Social Competence, Socialization and Social Structure*. New York: Free Press.

Bobo, Lawrence, ed.
1987 Manuscript prepared for the Committee on the Status of Black Americans, National Research Council, Washington, D.C.

Bond, Horace Mann
1934 *Education of the Negro in the American Social Order*. New York: Prentice-Hall.

Bossert, Steven T.
1979 *Tasks and Social Relationships in Classrooms*. New York: Cambridge University Press.

Bowles, Samuel, and Henry H. Levin
1968 The determinants of scholastic achievement—an appraisal of some recent evidence. *Journal of Human Resources* 3(1):3–24.

Boykin, A. Wade
1986 The triple quandary and the schooling of Afro-American children. Pp. 57–92 in Ulric Neisser, ed., *The School Achievement of Minority Children: New Perspectives*. Hillsdale, N.J.: Erlbaum.

Boykin, A. Wade, Anderson J. Franklin, and J. Frank Yates, eds.
1979 *Research Directions of Black Psychologists*. New York: Russell Sage Foundation.

Brackbill, Y., and P. L. Nicholls
1982 A test of the confluence model of development. *Developmental Psychology* 18:192–198.

Bradley, L., and G. Bradley
1977 The academic achievement of blacks in desegregated schools. *Review of Educational Research* 47:399–499.

Brookover, W. B., and Lawrence Lezotte
1981 Educational equality: a democratic principle at a crossroads. *Urban Review* 13(2):65–71.

Brookover, Wilbur, Charles Beady, Patricia Flood, John Schweitzer, and Jose Wisenbaker
1979 *School Social Systems and Student Achievement: Schools Can Make a Difference*. New York: Praeger.

Brophy, Jere, and Thomas L. Good
1986 Teachers behavior and student achievement. Pp. 238–375 in Merlin C. Wittrock, ed., *Handbook of Research on Teaching*. New York: Macmillan.

Brown, Shirley Vining
1987 *Minorities in the Graduate Education Pipeline*. Princeton, N.J.: Educational Testing Service.
1988 *Increasing Minority Faculty: An Elusive Goal*. Princeton, N.J.: Educational Testing Service.
Bullock, Henry A.
1967 *A History of Negro Education in the South from 1619 to the Present*. New York: Praeger.
Carnegie Forum
1986 *A Nation Prepared: Teachers for the Twenty-First Century*. New York: Carnegie Forum on Education and the Economy.
Carter, Launor F.
1984 The sustaining effects study of compensatory and elementary education. *Educational Researcher* 13(7):4–13.
Chaikind, Stephen
1987 College Enrollment Patterns of Black and White Students. Washington, D.C.: Decision Resources Corporation.
Clark, Kenneth B.
1963 Educational stimulation of racially disadvantaged children. Pp. 142–162 in Harry Passow, ed., *Education in Depressed Areas*. New York: Teachers College Press, University of Columbia.
Clark, Reginald M.
1983 *Family and School Achievement: Why Poor Black Children Succeed or Fail*. Chicago: University of Chicago Press.
Cole, Michael, and Jerome S. Bruner
1971 Cultural differences and inferences about psychological processes. *American Psychologist* 26:867–876.
Coleman, James
1968 The concept of equality of educational opportunity. *Harvard Educational Review* 38(1):7–22.
Coleman, James S., Ernest Q. Campbell, and others
1966 *Equality of Educational Opportunity*. Washington, D.C.: U.S. Government Printing Office.
Comer, James P.
1980 *School Power*. New York: Free Press.
1984 Home-school relationships as they affect the academic success of children. *Education and Urban Society* 16:323–337.
Congressional Budget Office
1986 *Trends in Educational Achievement*. Washington, D.C.: U.S. Congressional Printing Office.
Cook, Stuart W.
1979 Social science and school desegregation: did we mislead the Supreme Court? *Personality and Social Psychology Bulletin* 5(4):420–437.
Crain, Robert L., and Rita E. Mahard
1978 Desegregation and black achievement: a review of the research. *Law and Contemporary Problems* 42(Summer):17–56.
1983 The effect of research methodology on desegregation-achievement studies: a meta-analysis. *American Journal of Sociology* 88(5):839–854.
Davis, Josephine D.
1986 The Effect of Mathematics Course Enrollment on Racial/Ethnic Differences in Secondary School Mathematics Achievement. Draft report. Princeton, N.J.: Educational Testing Service.

DeBord, Larry W., Larry J. Griffin, and Melissa Clark
  1977 Race and sex influences in the schooling processes of rural and small town youth. *Sociology of Education* 50C(April):85–102.
Dingerson, Michael R., John A. Podman, and Debra Burns
  1985 The hiring of underrepresented individuals in academic administrative positions: 1972–1979. *Research in Higher Education* 23(2):115–134.
Dreeben, Robert, and Adam Gamoran
  1986 Race, instruction, and learning. *American Sociological Review* 51(October):660–669.
Edmonds, Ronald
  1979 Effective schools for the urban poor. *Educational Leadership* 37(October):15–24.
  1986 Characteristics of effective schools. Pp. 93–104 in Ulric Neisser, ed., *The School Achievement of Minority Children: New Perspectives*. Hillsdale, N.J.: Erlbaum.
Educational Testing Service
  1985 *The Reading Report Card*. Princeton, N.J.: Educational Testing Service.
Elmore, Charles J., and Robert T. Blackburn
  1983 Black and white faculty in white research universities. *Journal of Higher Education* 54(1):1–15.
Epps, Edgar G.
  1975 Impact of school desegregation on aspirations, self-concept, and other aspects of personality. *Law and Contemporary Problems* 39:300–313.
  1978 The impact of school desegregation on the self-evaluation and achievement orientation of minority children. *Law and Contemporary Problems* 42:57–76.
Epps, Edgar G., and Kenneth W. Jackson
  1985 *Educational and Occupational Aspirations and Early Attainment of Black Males and Females*. Atlanta, Ga.: Southern Education Foundation.
Epstein, Joyce L.
  1980 A Longitudinal Study of School and Family Effects on Student Development. Report No. 301. Center for Social Organization of Schools, Johns Hopkins University, Baltimore, Md.
Exum, William H.
  1983 Climbing the crystal stair: values, affirmative action, and minority faculty. *Social Problems* 30(4):383–399.
Falk, William W.
  1978 School desegregation and the educational attainment process: some results from rural Texas schools. *Sociology of Education* 51(October):282–288.
Farley, Reynolds
  1984 *Blacks and Whites: Narrowing the Gap?* Cambridge, Mass.: Harvard University Press.
Fleming, Jacqueline
  1984 *Blacks in College: A Comparative Study of Students' Success in Black and in White Institutions*. San Francisco: Jossey-Bass Publishers.
Fordham, Signithia, and John U. Ogbu
  1986 Black students' school success: coping with the burden of 'acting white.' *Urban Review* 18(3):176–206.
Fox, Richard N.
  1986 Application of a conceptual model of college withdrawal to disadvantaged students. *American Educational Research Journal* 23(3):415–424.
Gay, Geneva, and Roger D. Abrahams
  1973 Does the pot melt, boil, or brew? Black children and white assessment procedures. *Journal of School Psychology* 11(4):330–340.

Getzlaf, Shelly B., Gordon M. Sedlacek, Kathleen A. Kearney, and Jane M. Blackwell
1984 Two types of voluntary undergraduate attrition: application of Tinto's model. *Research in Higher Education* 20(3):257–268.

Gibbs, Jewell Taylor
1973 Black students/white university: different expectations. *Personnel Guidance Journal* 51(7):463–469.

Gifford, Bernard R.
1986 Excellence and equity in teacher competency testing: a policy perspective. *Journal of Negro Education* 55(3):251–271.

Glazer, Nathan
1986 Education and training programs and poverty. Pp. 152–173 in Sheldon H. Danziger and Daniel H. Weinberg, eds., *Fighting Poverty*. Cambridge, Mass.: Harvard University Press.

Gordon, Edmund W.
1972 Toward defining equality of educational opportunity. Pp. 423–434 in Frederick Mosteller and Daniel P. Moynihan, eds., *On Equality of Educational Opportunity*. New York: Random House.

Gosma, Erica J., Betty A. Dandridge, Michael T. Nettles, and A. Robert Thoeny
1983 Predicting student progression: the influence of race and other student and institutional characteristics on college student performance. *Research in Higher Education* 18(2):209–236.

Gottfredson, Denise C.
1981 Black-white differences in the educational process: what have we learned? *American Sociological Review* 46(October):542–557.

Hale-Benson, Janice E.
1982 *Black Children: Their Roots, Culture, and Learning Styles*. Baltimore, Md.: Johns Hopkins University Press.

Haller, Emil J., and Sharon A. Davis
1981 Teacher perceptions, parental social status and grouping for reading. *Sociology of Education* 54:162–174.

Hallinan, Maureen
1984 Summary and implications. Pp. 229–240 in Penelope L. Peterson, Louise Cherry Wilkinson, and Maureen Hallinan, eds., *The Social Context of Instruction*. New York: Academic Press.

Hallinger, Philip, and Joseph F. Murphy
1986 The social context of effective schools. *American Journal of Education* 94(3):328–355.

Hanushek, Eric
1972 *Education and Race: An Analysis of the Educational Production Process*. Cambridge, Mass.: Heath-Lexington.
1986 The economics of schooling: production and efficiency in the public schools. *Journal of Economic Literature* 24(September):1141–1177.

Hare, Bruce H.
1985 Reexamining the central tendency: sex differences within race and race difference within sex. Pp. 139–155 in Harriette Pipes McAdoo and John Lewis McAdoo, eds., *Black Children: Social, Educational, and Parental Environments*. Beverly Hills, Calif.: Sage Publications Inc.

Hare, Bruce R., and Louis A. Castenell
1986 No place to run, no place to hide: comparative status and future prospects of black boys. Pp. 201–214 in Margaret B. Spencer, Geraldine K. Brookins, and Walter R. Allen, eds., *Beginnings: The Social and Affective Development of Black Children*. Hillsdale, N.J.: Erlbaum.

Hauser, Robert M., and William H. Sewell
  1985 Birth order and educational attainment in full sibships. *American Educational Research Journal* 22(1):1–23.
Hauser, Robert M., William H. Sewell, and Duane F. Alwin
  1976 High school effects on achievement. Pp. 309–341 in William H. Sewell, Robert M. Hauser, and David L. Featherman, eds., *Schooling and Achievement in American Society*. New York: Academic Press.
Hayes, Donald P.
  1988 Speaking and writing: distinct patterns of word choice. *Journal of Memory and Language* 27:572–585.
Heyns, Barbara
  1974 Pupil selection and stratification within schools. *American Journal of Sociology* 79(6):1434–1451.
Holmes Group
  1986 *Tomorrow's Teachers: A Report of the Holmes Group*. East Lansing, Mich.: Holmes Group, Inc.
Hout, Michael, and William R. Morgan
  1975 Race and sex variations in the causes of the expected attainments of high school seniors. *American Journal of Sociology* 81(2):364–394.
Howell, Frank M., and Wolfgang Frese
  1979 Race, sex, and aspirations: evidence for the 'race convergence' hypothesis. *Sociology of Education* 52(January):34–46.
Hueftle, S. J., S. J. Rakow, and W. W. Welch
  1983 *Images of Science: A Summary of Results from the 1981–82 National Assessment in Science*. Minneapolis: Minnesota Research and Evaluation Center.
Jaynes, Gerald D.
  1986 Gramm-Rudman and black education. *Black Enterprise* (May):39.
Jencks, Christopher
  1986 Comment. Pp. 173–179 in Sheldon H. Danziger and Daniel H. Weinberg, eds., *Fighting Poverty*. Cambridge, Mass.: Harvard University Press.
Johnson, Martin L.
  1984 Blacks in mathematics: a status report. *Journal for Research in Mathematics Education* 15(2):145–153.
Johnson, Sylvia T.
  1987 Extra-School Factors in Achievement, Attainment, and Aspirations Among Junior and Senior High School-Aged Black Youth. Paper prepared for the Committee on the Status of Black Americans, National Research Council, Washington, D.C.
Jones, Lyle V.
  1987 The influence on mathematics test scores, by ethnicity and sex, of prior achievement and high school mathematics courses. *Journal for Research in Mathematics Education* 18:180–186.
Jones, Lyle V., Nancy Burton, and Ernest C. Davenport
  1984 Monitoring the mathematics achievement of black students. *Journal for Research in Mathematics Education* 15(2):154–164.
Karweit, Nancy
  1983 Time-on-Task: A Research Review. Report No. 332. Center for Social Organization of Schools, Johns Hopkins University, Baltimore, Md.
  1986 Elementary Education and Black Americans: Raising the Odds. Paper prepared for the Committee on the Status of Black Americans, National Research Council, Washington, D.C.

Kerckhoff, Alan C., and Richard T. Campbell
  1977a Black-white differences in the educational attainment process. *Sociology of Education* 50(January):15–27.
  1977b Race and social status differences in the explanation of educational ambition. *Social Forces* 55(3):701–714.
Kirsch, Irwin S., and Ann Jungeblut
  1986 *Literacy: Profiles of American's Young Adults.* Princeton, N.J.: Educational Testing Service.
Klitgaard, Robert E., and George R. Hall
  1974 Are there unusually effective schools? *Journal of Human Resources* 10(1):90–106.
Leacock, Eleanor
  1970 Education, socialization, and the 'culture of poverty.' In Annette T. Rubinstein, ed., *Schools Against Children: The Case for Community Control.* New York: Monthly Review Press.
Levin, Henry M.
  1986 The educationally disadvantaged are still among us. *Educational Leadership* 44(6):19–21.
Lezotte, Lawrence, and Beverly A. Bancroft
  1985 Growing use of the effective schools model of school improvement. *Educational Leadership* (May):23–27.
Lightfoot, Sara Lawrence
  1983 *The Good High School: Portraits of Character and Culture.* New York: Basic Books.
Linn, Robert L., George F. Madaus, and Joseph J. Pedulla
  1982 Minimum competency testing: cautions on the state of the art. *American Journal of Education* 91:1–35.
Longshore, Douglas, and Jeffrey Prager
  1985 The impact of school desegregation: a situational analysis. *Annual Review of Sociology* 11:75–91.
Madaus, George F., and Vincent Greaney
  1985 The Irish experience in competency testing: implications for American education. *American Journal of Education* 93:268–294.
Marrett, Cora Bagley
  1987 Black and Native American students in precollege mathematics and science. Pp. 7–32 in Linda S. Dix, ed., *Minorities: Their Underrepresentation and Career Differentials in Science and Engineering, Proceedings of a Workshop.* Office of Scientific and Engineering Personnel. Washington, D.C.: National Academy Press.
Massey, Grace C., Asa G. Hilliard, and Jean Carew
  1982 Test-taking behaviors of black toddlers: an interactive analysis. Pp. 163–179 in L. Feagans and D. C. Farran, eds., *The Language of Children Reared in Poverty.* New York: Academic Press.
Matthews, Westina
  1984 Influences on the learning and participation of minorities in mathematics. *Journal for Research in Mathematics Education* 15(2):84–95.
McDermott, R. P.
  1974 Achieving school failure: an anthropological approach to illiteracy and social stratification. Pp. 82–118 in George O. Spindler, ed., *Education and Cultural Process.* New York: Holt, Rinehart & Winston.
Menges, Robert J., and William H. Exum
  1983 Barriers to the progress of women and minority faculty. *Journal of Higher Education* 54(2):123–144.

Mercer, Jane R.
1974 Latent functions of intelligence testing in the public schools. Pp. 77–94 in L. Miller, ed., *The Testing of Black Students*. Englewood Cliffs, N.J.: Prentice-Hall.

Miller, Scott E., and Holly Hexter
1985 *How Low Income Families Pay for College*. Washington, D.C.: American Council on Education.

Mommsen, Kent G.
1973 On recruiting black sociologists. *American Sociologist* 8(August):107–116.
1974 Black Ph.Ds in the academic marketplace: supply, demand, and price. *Journal of Higher Education* 45(4):253–267.

Moore, Elsie G. J.
1982 Language behavior in the test situation and the intelligence test achievement of transracially and traditionally adopted black children. Pp. 141–162 in L. Feagans and D. C. Farran, eds., *The Language of Children Reared in Poverty*. New York: Academic Press.
1986 Family socialization and IQ test performance of traditionally and transracially adopted black children. *Developmental Psychology* 22:317–326.
1987 Ethnic social milieu and black children's intelligence test achievement. *Journal of Negro Education* 56(1):44–52.

Mosteller, Frederick, and Daniel P. Moynihan
1972 A pathbreaking report. Pp. 3–66 in Frederick Mosteller and Daniel P. Moynihan, eds., *On Equality of Educational Opportunity*. New York: Random House.

Mullin, S. P., and Anita Summers
1983 Is more better? The effectiveness of spending on compensatory education. *Phi Delta Kappa* 64:339–347.

Murnane, Richard. J.
1975 *The Impact of School Resources on the Learning of Inner City Children*. Cambridge, Mass.: Ballinger.

Myers, David E.
1987 Changes in Achievement Levels and Attendance in Postsecondary Schools: A Technical Note. Washington, D.C.: Decison Resources Corporation.

Nettles, Michael T., A. Robert Thoeny, and Erica J. Gosman
1986 Comparative and predictive anaylses of black and white students' college achievement and experiences. *Journal of Higher Education* 57(3):289–318.

Norman-Jackson, Jacquelyn
1982 Family interactions, language development, and primary reading achievement of black children in families of low income. *Child Development* 53:349–358.

Oakes, Jeannie
1982 Classroom social relationships: exploring the Bowles Gintis hypothesis. *Sociology of Education* 55(4):197–212.
1983 Limiting opportunity: student race and curricular differences in secondary vocational education. *American Journal of Education* 91(3):328–355.

Ogbu, John U.
1974 *The Next Generation: An Ethnography of Education in an Urban Neighborhood*. New York: Academic Press.
1978 *Minority Education and Caste: The American System in Cross-Cultural Perspective*. New York: Academic Press.
1986 The consequences of the American caste system. Pp. 19–56 in Ulric Neisser, ed., *The School Achievement of Minority Children: New Perspectives*. Hillsdale, N.J.: Erlbaum.

Olneck, Michael R., and David B. Bills
  1979   Family configuration and achievement: effects of birth order and family size in a
         sample of brothers. *Social Psychology Quarterly* 42(2):135–147.
Pallas, Aaron M.
  1986   Extra-School Factors in the Achievement of Black Adolescents. Paper prepared
         for the Committee on the Status of Black Americans, National Research Council,
         Washington, D.C.
  1987   Black-White Differences in Adolescent Educational Outcomes. Paper prepared
         for the Committee on the Status of Black Americans, National Research Council,
         Washington, D.C.
Pederson, Eigil, Therese Annette Faucher, and William W. Eaton
  1978   A new perspective on the effects of first-grade teachers on children's subsequent
         adult status. *Harvard Educational Review* 48:1–31.
Petroni, F. A.
  1970   Uncle Toms: white stereotypes in the black movement. *Human Organization*
         29(4):260–266.
Petroni, F. A., and E. A. Hirsch
  1970   *Two, Four, Six, Eight, When You Gonna Integrate?* New York: Behavioral
         Publications.
Porter, James N.
  1974   Race, socialization and mobility in educational and early occupational attain-
         ment. *American Sociological Review* 39(June):303–316.
Portes, Alexandro, and Kenneth L. Wilson
  1976   Black-white differences in educational attainment. *American Sociological Review*
         41(June):414–431.
Prestage, Jewel L.
  1979   Quelling the mythical revolution in higher education: retreat from the affirmative
         action concept. *Journal of Politics* 1:763–783.
Purkey, Stewart C., and Marshall S. Smith
  1983   Effective schools: a review. *Elementary School Journal* 83(4):427–452.
  1985   School reform: the district policy implications of the effective schools literature.
         Elementary School Journal 85(3):353–389.
Rist, Ray C.
  1970   Student social class and teacher expectations: the self-fulfilling prophecy in ghetto
         schools. *Harvard Educational Review* 40(3):411–451.
Scarr, Sandra, and Richard A. Weinberg
  1978   The influence of 'family background' on intellectual attainment. *American Socio-
         logical Review* 43(October):674–692.
Scheinfeld, Daniel R.
  1983   Family relationships and school achievement among boys of lower-income urban
         black families. *American Journal of Orthopsychiatry* 53(1):127–143.
Scott-Jones, Diane
  1987a Black Families and the Education of Black Children: Current Issues. Paper pre-
         pared for the Committee on the Status of Black Americans, National Research
         Council, Washington, D.C.
  1987b Mother-as-teacher in the families of high- and low-achieving low-income first
         graders. *Journal of Negro Education* 56(1):21–34.
Serow, Robert C.
  1984   Effects of minimum competency testing for minority students: a review of expec-
         tations and outcomes. *Urban Review* 16(2):67–75.

Sewell, William H., and Robert M. Hauser
1980 The Wisconsin longitudinal study of social and psychological factors in aspirations and achievements. Pp. 59–99 in Alan C. Kerckhoff, ed., *Research in Sociology of Education and Socialization*. Vol. I. Greenwood, Conn.: JAI Press.

Shade, Barbara J.
1978 Social-psychological characteristics of achieving black children. *Negro Educational Review* 29(2):80–86.
1982 Afro-American cognitive style: a variable in school success? *Review of Educational Research* 52(2):219–244.

Shade, Barbara J., and Patricia A. Edwards
1987 Ecological correlates of the educative style of Afro-American children. *Journal of Negro Education* 56(1):88–99.

Sharan, S., and Y. Sharan
1976 *Small Group Teaching*. Englewood Cliffs, N.J.: Educational Technology Publications.

Sieber, R. Timothy
1982 The politics of middle-class success in an inner-city public school. *Journal of Education* 164(1):30–47.

Skerry, Peter
1983 The charmed life of Head Start. *The Public Interest* 73(Fall):18–39.

Slaughter, Diane
1969 Maternal antecedents of the academic achievement behaviors of Afro-American Head Start children. *Educational Horizons* (Fall):24–28.

Slavin, Robert E.
1978 Effects of Student Teams and Peer Tutoring on Academic Achievement and Time-on-Task. Report No. 253. Center for Social Organization of Schools, Johns Hopkins University, Baltimore, Md.
1980 Cooperative learning in teams: state of the art. *Education Psychology* 15:93–111.

Smith, Donald H.
1981 Social and academic environments of black students on white campuses. *Journal of Negro Education* 50(3):299–306.

Sowell, Thomas
1972 *Black Education: Myths and Tragedies*. New York: McKay.

Spady, William G.
1973 The impact of school resources on students. Pp. 135–177 in Fred N. Kerlinger, ed., *Review of Research in Education*. Vol. I. Itasca, Ill.: F. E. Peacock.

Steele, Claude M., and Stephen G. Green
1976 Affirmative action and academic hiring: a case of a value conflict. *Journal of Higher Education* 47(4):413–435.

Stephan, Walter G.
1978 School desegregation: an evaluation of predictions made in Brown vs. Board of Education. *Psychological Bulletin* 85:217–238.

St. John, N. H.
1975 *School Desegregation: Outcomes for Children*. New York: John Wiley & Sons.

Summers, Anita A., and Barbara J. Wolfe
1977 Do schools make a difference? *American Economic Review* 67(September):639–652.

Svanum, Soren, Robert G. Bringle, and Joan E. McLaughlin
1982 Father absence and cognitive performance in a large sample of six- to eleven-year-old children. *Child Development* 53:136–143.

Taylor, Howard F.
1980 *The I.Q. Game: A Methodological Inquiry into the Heredity-Environment Controversy*. New Brunswick, N.J.: Rutgers University Press.

Thomas, Gail E.
   1987 Black students in U.S. graduate and professional schools in the 1980s: a national and institutional assessment. *Harvard Educational Review* 57(3):261–282.
Thomas, Gail E., Karl L. Alexander, and Bruce K. Eckland
   1979 Access to higher education: the importance of race, sex, social class and academic credentials. *School Review* 87:133–156.
Trent, William T.
   1984 Equity considerations in higher education: race and sex differences in degree attainment and major field from 1976 through 1981. *American Journal of Education* 41(May):280–305.
Valentine, Charles A.
   1971 Deficit, difference, and bicultural models of Afro-American behavior. *Harvard Educational Review* 41(2):137–157.
Wachter, Kenneth W.
   1988 Disturbed by meta-analysis. *Science* 241(Sept. 16):1407–1408.
Weber, G.
   1971 *Inner-City Children Can Be Taught to Read: Four Successful Schools.* Washington, D.C.: Council for Basic Education.
Weinberg, M.
   1977 *Minority Students: A Research Appraisal.* Washington, D.C.: National Institute of Education.
Willie, Charles V., and Donald Cunnigen
   1981 Black students in higher education: a review of studies, 1965–1980. *Annual Review of Sociology* 7:177–198.
Wilson, Kenneth L.
   1979 The effects of integration and class on black educational attainment. *Sociology of Education* 52(April):84–98.
Wolfle, Lee M.
   1985 Postsecondary educational attainment among whites and blacks. *American Educational Research Journal* 22(4):501–525.
Zirkel, Perry A.
   1971 Self-concept and the disadvantage of ethnic group membership and mixture. *Review of Educational Research* 41:211–225.

8

BLACK AMERICANS' HEALTH

William H. Johnson
Convalescents from Somewhere (1941–1942)
Gouache, pen and ink
National Museum of American Art, Smithsonian Institution,
Gift of the Harmon Foundation

W̲ho will live and who will die and how much handicap and disability will burden their lives depend in large part on conditions of education, environment, and employment as well as on access to adequate medical services. Health is not only an important "good" in itself, it is also a determinant of life options during the entire life span. For example, lack of prenatal care leads to greater likelihood of infant death, neurological damage, or developmental impairment; childhood illnesses and unhealthy conditions can reduce learning potential; adolescent childbearing, substance abuse, and injuries cause enormous personal, social, and health effects; impaired health or chronic disability in adults contributes to low earning capacity and unemployment; and chronic poor health among older adults can lead to premature retirement and loss of ability for self-care and independent living. Health status is therefore an important indicator of a group's social position as well as of its present and future well-being.

OVERVIEW

This chapter provides data describing trends in black health status and the differential rates of illness, disability, and death that persist between black and white Americans. The discussion focuses on conditions that sustain the continuing health differentials between blacks and whites. We consider biomedical, environmental, and social factors that contribute to the health outcomes for blacks within defined periods of the life span, giving particular attention to poverty and those sociocultural factors that influence access to health services.

Although multiple factors contribute to the persistent health disadvantages of blacks, poverty may be the most profound and pervasive determinant. There has been a consistent finding across communities and nations that persons of the lowest socioeconomic status have higher death rates. In a classic study, Kitagawa and Hauser (1973) found that there was a gradient of mortality rates with steady increases from the highest to the lowest social classes. Mortality rates were higher as socioeconomic status declined for both whites and blacks, whether that status was measured by family income, educational level, or occupation. For people of the lowest status, overall mortality was 80 percent greater than for those at the highest socioeconomic level. In addition to increased mortality, almost every form of disease and disability is more prevalent among the poor.

Because of the relationship between poverty and health, and because poverty has been a persistent problem for blacks in the United States, it is to be expected that blacks' greater poverty is responsible for much of the black-white health disparity. Poverty rates among children cause special concern for their future health status. Poverty in childhood often means lack of proper nutrition, unsafe housing, and poor access to health care or other resources needed for healthy growth and development.

During much of the period covered in this study, there was open segregation of medical facilities in the United States. In the 25-year period before 1965, persistent barriers to access to preventive, primary, and hospital care influenced the quality of life and the patterns of illness observed among blacks.

Organizations such as the Medical Committee on Human Rights, the National Medical Association, and the Student National Medical Association played important roles in efforts to end discrimination in health care facilities and in health professional schools. Following the 1954 *Brown* Supreme Court decision, which declared segregation in public schools unconstitutional, efforts to desegregate health care facilities intensified.

Important events that led to more equal access to medical care for blacks were the Civil Rights Act in 1964 and the Medicaid and Medicare legislation in 1965. Title VI of the Civil Rights Act prohibited racial discrimination in any institution receiving federal funds, thus giving hospitals a powerful incentive to alter their practices. Hospitals receiving federal funds were forbidden to deny admission to patients, to subject patients to separate treatments, or to deny admitting privileges to medical personnel solely on the basis of race. Access to health care was further increased when litigation in the 1960s explicitly defined the obligation of hospitals using federally provided construction funds to meet their "free care" requirements and to serve those unable to pay.

A second method of addressing blacks' unequal access to health care concerned their underrepresentation in the medical care professions. During the 1960s and 1970s many efforts were mounted to enlarge the representation

FIGURE 8-1 Life expectancy at birth, by race and sex, 1950–1985.

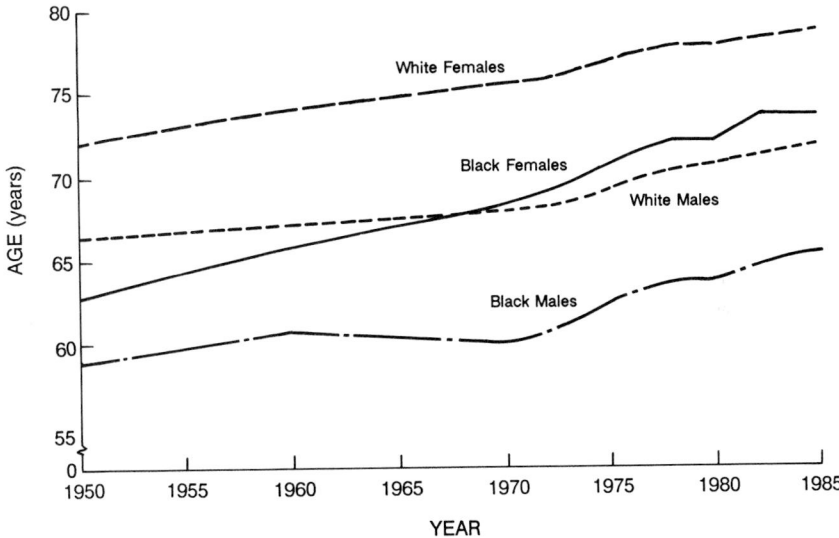

Source: Data from the National Center for Health Statistics.

of blacks and other minorities in the health professions. It was believed that access to health care for poor blacks would improve if there were more black physicians. This belief prompted some medical schools to recruit more black and other minority students and to channel them into primary care specialties.

While the chapter presents facts about past and current health disadvantages of blacks compared with whites, the focus on problem areas should not leave the impression that most black Americans are unhealthy. Over the past 50 years, blacks' health status and life expectancies have improved a great deal. A general overview of this point can be made by considering trends in mortality and life expectancy.

A useful summary index of the effects of differing mortality rates is the average (mean) life expectancy at birth. It is calculated on the basis of age-specific death rates as of a given date, and it estimates the number of years that will be lived on the average by individuals born in a particular year, assuming a constancy of then-current age-specific mortality rates.[1] Figure 8-1 summarizes trends in black-white differences in life expectancy at birth. In the 1950–1985 time span, death rates fell for both races, particularly for black females, but whites continued to enjoy an advantage over blacks. The difference in life expectancy of black and white men decreased from a gap of about 11 years in 1940 to a 6-year difference in 1960 and has shown little

---

1. Mean life expectancy at birth is calculated by methods analogous to the calculation of mean lifetime earnings and employment used in Chapter 6.

improvement since then. Among women, there has been a consistent pattern of relative improvement for blacks, and the racial gap in the mid-1980s was less than one-half its size in 1940. As a result, the advantage in life expectancy black women enjoy over black men increased during this period. The life expectancy of a black male in 1985 (65.3 years) is lower than that already achieved by white males in 1950, 66.5 years (National Center for Health Statistics, 1988:80–81).

Projections of mortality rates into the future are necessarily uncertain, particularly given the current epidemic of acquired immune deficiency syndrome (AIDS). Nonetheless, we estimate that if the 1950–1985 trends continue, life expectancies for black and white women will converge in the first half of the twenty-first century, but no convergence to white rates can be foreseen for black men (R. Farley, 1985).

These summary statements conceal a complex pattern of age-specific and cause-specific changes (Farley and Allen, 1987; U.S. Department of Health and Human Services, 1985e). Among children under age 15, there have been consistent and large decreases in the risk of death, but the death rates for black children are 30 percent to 50 percent higher than those for white children. Between 1950 and the late 1960s, mortality rates actually rose among adult men, especially black men, and fell at a very slow rate among adult women of both races. The last two decades have been characterized by rapid declines in mortality rates, declines that were not foreseen by health experts. Rates have fallen for almost all race-sex groups, but the decline at the older ages, 60 and above, has been unusually sharp, reflecting, perhaps, improvements in the income level of the elderly and the government's assumption of many health care costs with Medicare (Crimmins, 1981). Contagious and infectious diseases were more common causes of death among blacks than among whites in 1940, but that specific cause of disparity has been reduced.

Mortality from heart disease declined slowly between 1940 and the mid-1960s and more rapidly afterward. The pace of change was more rapid for women than men among both races. Improved detection and treatment of hypertension, and changes in smoking, diet, and exercise were factors influencing the reductions. There is still a large disparity and excess of black deaths from heart diseases. Mortality from suicide remains much higher for whites than blacks, while cirrhosis and diabetes death rates, although declining rapidly since the late 1960s, remain higher for blacks (R. Farley, 1985).

Two causes of death merit special attention, cancer and homicide. If data from the 1930s and early 1940s are accurate, then blacks formerly had considerably lower cancer mortality rates than whites (Lilienfeld et al., 1972). This has changed in a dramatic manner. Since the 1940s, there have been particularly sharp increases in death rates from lung cancer for both races, but the rise has been greater among blacks, especially black men. Mortality from other types of cancer has held steady or declined among whites in the last two decades but has increased among blacks. Thus, there is now a substantial excess in cancer mortality among blacks. Homicide has a particularly large impact on average life expectancy since its usual victims are young adults. Although recent trends show lower homicide rates among blacks, it remains a leading cause of death for black men.

The U.S. Department of Health and Human Services (HHS) *Report of the Secretary's Task Force on Black and Minority Health (1986b)* identified six medical conditions for which the gaps in mortality between whites and blacks are the greatest. The six causes of death, taken together, account for about 86 percent of the excess black mortality in relation to the white population: accidents and homicides (35.1 percent), infant mortality (26.9 percent), heart disease and stroke (14.4 percent), cirrhosis (4.9 percent), cancer (3.8 percent), and diabetes (1.0 percent).[2] The report did not attempt to encompass the full dimensions of disparities in health status; while the mortality data for these six conditions are important, they do not capture the full personal and societal costs of deaths from other causes and of chronic or acute illness. In particular, this methodology has omitted important health problems of black children.

In the rest of this chapter we analyze the health status of black Americans across the life span, using the following divisions: pregnancy and infancy; childhood (ages 1–14); adolescents and young adults (ages 15–24); adulthood (ages 25–65); and older adults (over age 65). For each period of life, a few conditions of highest concern have been selected for analysis. In making these choices consideration has been given to magnitude, severity, distribution, and knowledge of contributory factors. We also emphasize the potential for prevention.

The black population has benefited from advances in medicine, but not equally with whites. From birth to advanced old age, blacks at each stage of the life cycle still die at higher rates (except for adult black women since 1970) and suffer disproportionately from a wide range of adverse health conditions. When national health objectives for 1990 were established by the Public Health Service (U.S. Department of Health and Human Services, 1980), the black-white disparity in the late 1970s was so great that it did not appear possible to overcome it in the short term. In the areas of infant mortality and deaths by injury, separate and unequal goals for blacks and whites were set. For many of the objectives set by the Public Health Service, the national targets were achieved before 1990 for whites but not for blacks (U.S. Department of Health and Human Services, 1986d). Based on recent trends, blacks are not projected to achieve equality in health by 1990 or in the near future.

PREGNANCY AND INFANCY

Infant mortality, the rate at which children die before their first birthday, serves both nationally and internationally as an indicator of the overall status

---

2. *Excess death* expresses the difference between the number of deaths actually observed in a minority group and the number of deaths that would have occurred if that group had experienced the same death rates for each age and sex as in the white population.

TABLE 8-1 Infant Mortality Rates in Various Countries, 1984

Country	Infant Mortality Rate
Japan	6
Sweden	6.4
Finland	6.5
Switzerland	7.5
Denmark	7.7
France	8.2
The Netherlands	8.3
Norway	8.3
Canada	8.5
Singapore	8.8
Australia	9.2
United States, white	9.4
Federal Republic of Germany	9.6
Great Britain	9.6
Spain	9.7
German Democratic Republic	10.0
Belgium	10.7
Austria	11.4
Italy	11.6
New Zealand	11.6
Israel	12.8
Greece	14.1
Cuba	15.0
Czechoslovakia	15.3
Bulgaria	16.1
United States, black	18.4

Notes: The infant mortality rate is deaths per 1,000. Rankings are from lowest to highest infant mortality rates based on the latest data available for countries with at least 1 million population and with complete counts of live births and infant deaths, as indicated by the United Nations (1985).

of the health of a community or a nation. Infant mortality in the United States, 10.6 deaths per 1,000 live births in 1985, remains persistently higher than the rate in many other developed nations; Finland, Japan, and Sweden enjoy the world's lowest rates, less than 7 deaths per 1,000 live births (National Center for Health Statistics, 1987c:94); see Table 8-1.

Black rates of infant mortality have remained at approximately twice the rate for whites over the course of this century despite impressive improvements for all groups in reduced infant mortality. In 1985, the infant mortality rate for whites was 9.3, for blacks 18.2. After relative stagnation in the 1960s, the infant mortality rate began a rapid decline (see Figure 8-2). The accumulating evidence (McCormick, 1985) indicates that a major factor in

FIGURE 8-2 Infant mortality rates, by race, 1940–1985.

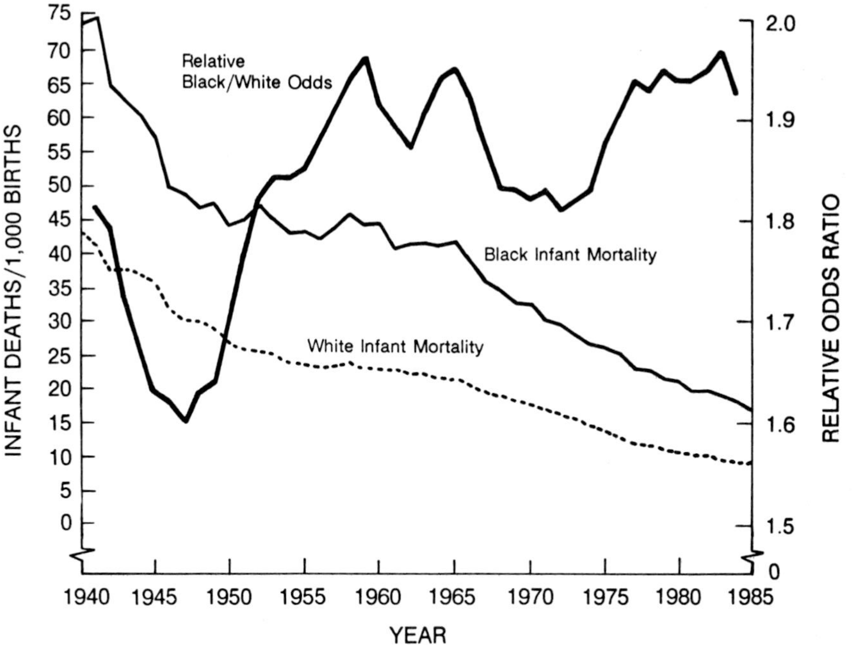

Source: Data from the National Center for Health Statistics.

the rapid decline after the 1960s has been the increased survival of low-birthweight infants, largely attributed to high-technology, hospital-based management and regional neonatal intensive care units.

The national average figures for infant mortality do not show all the disparities between blacks and whites in infant mortality rates across the United States. Black infant mortality rates show considerable variations by region. During 1982–1984, the black infant mortality rate was lowest in the Mountain and Pacific states (15.4 and 16.2 deaths per 1,000 live births, respectively), and highest in the East North Central states (21.7), particularly in Illinois (23.3) and Michigan (23.7) (National Center for Health Statistics, 1987c:Table 14). Across states, the lowest state mortality rate for black infants (12.5) was higher than the highest state mortality rate (10.1) for white infants.

NEONATAL AND POSTNEONATAL MORTALITY

During the first half of this century most of the infant mortality was postneonatal (deaths between 28 days and 1 year) and was caused by low living standards and infectious disease. After 1960, with improved living standards and major advances in control of infection, neonatal mortality (death prior to 28 days) became the major component of infant mortality. Low birthweight, 2,500 grams (5.5 pounds) or less, is the major predictor of neonatal mortality and accounts for 60 percent of all infant deaths. Currently, 20 percent of postneonatal deaths are attributed to low birthweight (Institute of Medicine, 1985:29).

The relationship between birthweight and infant mortality has been repeatedly documented. For infants born weighing less than 2,500 grams, the mortality rate rapidly increases with decreasing birthweight until infants weighing less than 1,000 grams (1.5 pounds) have only a 20 percent chance of survival under optimal care. Compared with normal birthweight infants, low-birthweight infants are almost 40 times more likely to die in the neonatal period; for very low birthweight (1,500 grams or less) infants, the relative risk of neonatal death is much greater.

The marked gap in the infant mortality rate between whites and blacks mirrors the more than twofold difference in the rates of low birthweight and very low birthweight between the two groups. Blacks are twice as likely as whites to have low-birthweight infants: black rates are 12.4 per 1,000 live births, and white rates are 5.6 (National Center for Health Statistics, 1987c:27). This increased risk for blacks also occurs for very low birthweight babies: 2.56 percent for blacks and 0.92 percent for whites (National Center for Health Statistics, 1987c:77). Blacks account for 16.2 percent of all live births but 30 percent of all low-birthweight newborns and 34 percent of very low birthweight newborns. In the neonatal period there is a survival advantage of black infants in the low-birthweight range, but it is overwhelmingly offset by the high percentage of low-birthweight black infants.

Some low-birthweight babies are very small but born at full term. However, most low-birthweight infants are born prematurely (preterm). An analytic review of the trends, causes, and preventive approaches to low birthweight (Institute of Medicine, 1985) identified a high-risk profile that included such demographic factors as poverty, low educational level, unmarried status, and black race; medical factors such as poor obstetrical history, very young or very old age of childbearing, and urogenital infections; and behavioral factors such as use of tobacco, alcohol, or illegal drugs, exposure to toxic substances, and absent or inadequate prenatal care. The report highlighted the importance of black race as a high-risk factor and emphasized the urgent need for research to investigate causes of racial differences in birthweight.

The Institute of Medicine (IOM) study showed that babies born in the United States have the best chance, worldwide, for survival at low birthweights, a condition attributed to the excellence of sophisticated perinatal medical services. However, these medical triumphs are offset by the fact that the United States has continued to have a far higher percentage of low-birthweight babies over the past 25 years than other comparable industrialized nations.

A national study of low-birthweight births to 2 million white women and 418,000 black women for 1973–1983 showed that the racial disparity in birthweights is increasing (Kleinman and Kessel, 1987). Births of infants with moderately low birthweights (between 3.3 and 5.5 pounds) decreased much more among whites (16 percent) than among blacks (6 percent). Rates of very low birthweights (less than 3.3 pounds) decreased 3 percent among whites but increased 13 percent among blacks. The study emphasized that preterm birth, not low birthweight per se, is the primary cause of perinatal mortality. Over the decade studied, preterm low birthweight has remained constant and low birthweight at term declined.

During the decade of study, blacks were found to be more highly concentrated than whites in high-risk socioeconomic groups. Furthermore, even blacks who were at low risk in terms of age, marital status, and education had a somewhat higher incidence of preterm delivery than whites who were at high risk in terms of the same factors (17.2 for blacks and 15.1 for whites per 1,000 live births). Causes of this persistence of black-white differences in birthweight even among black mothers at lower risk were not completely explained. This study also found that the overall contribution of teenage births to low birthweight has been overemphasized: if all teenage births had been prevented in 1983, the low-birthweight rates would have decreased by only 8 percent for whites and 3 percent for blacks.

Lieberman and colleagues (1987) concluded that race is not an independent risk factor and that the black-white differences in prematurity rates are attributable to specific medical and socioeconomic characteristics. This study of a hospital-based cohort of 8,903 black and white women found the rate of prematurity to be a function of the number of risk factors present regardless of which particular risk was present. When single marital status, age under 20 years, on welfare, high school not completed, and maternal anemia were included as factors, essentially all the racial variation in prematurity was explained. A prospective study of a cohort of 29,415 Asian, black, and white pregnant women in a Kaiser-Permanente health maintenance organization considered patterns of mean birthweight and low birthweight; after examination of 22 variables, it was concluded that ethnicity is not an independent risk factor (Shiono et al., 1986).

It is likely that intergenerational effects of socioeconomic conditions on the growth and development of a mother from prebirth to childhood may influence the intrauterine growth of her child. Since many middle-class blacks are the first generation in their family to achieve that status, the designation by current income may mask the effects of maternal childhood poverty. A research project is planned to track the birth histories of a cohort of blacks who have an intergenerational history of sustained economic advantage. This group will be drawn from descendants of black physicians who were graduates of Meharry Medical College early in the century (Samuel Kessel, personal communication, 1988). Since the highest infant death rates are associated with preterm birth, research is increasingly being directed to this problem. However, on the basis of existing knowledge, a great many medical conditions that predispose to prematurity could be prevented by appropriate prenatal care.

PRENATAL CARE

Prenatal care is clearly related to positive pregnancy outcome. Many of the risks associated with low birthweight can be identified in a first prenatal visit, and steps can be taken to prevent or correct them. Conversely, late care or no care is associated with low birthweight, increased prematurity rates, increased stillbirths, and increased newborn mortality. A pregnant woman who receives no prenatal care is 3 times as likely as others to have a low-birthweight baby. Neonatal, postneonatal, and infant death rates are 4 times higher for babies born to women who received no prenatal care than for those receiving at least some care (Centers for Disease Control, 1986a:272; Institute of Medicine, 1985; Office of Technology Assessment, 1988).

Despite shortcomings in many evaluations of prenatal care, the evidence of more than 55 studies confirms the medical effectiveness and cost benefits of timely prenatal care. Yet, one-quarter of all pregnant women still receive none or only belated prenatal care. These percentages are significantly higher among poor, black, adolescent, and unmarried women, those in rural areas, and those over 40—the groups most likely to be at high risk from other causes. In 1984, 20 percent of white women and 38 percent of black women received no prenatal care in the first trimester of pregnancy (National Center for Health Statistics, 1987c:77).

The provision of prenatal care can have a demonstrable effect on pregnancy outcomes among high-risk populations. In New York City, for example, publicly supported Maternity and Infant Care (MIC) projects have provided prenatal care for eligible poor residents for 15 years, and perinatal mortality rates have been consistently lower for MIC patients than for otherwise comparable patients living in the same districts, and they have also been lower than average rates for New York City as a whole (Kessner et al., 1973).

Diet and nutrition of mothers during pregnancy affect the birthweight, growth, and development of their infants. Despite awareness of the risks of poor nutrition and a public policy for food supplementation for poor mothers, a sizable percentage of pregnant black women exhibit nutritional deficiencies of protein, calories, and especially iron (Lieberman et al., 1987). Nutritional problems are especially serious for the youngest teenage mothers, who must nourish their own rapid development as well as that of the fetus.

Preventive care programs have shown positive results in assuring adequate nutrition. For a targeted population of poverty mothers, the U.S. Department of Agriculture's (USDA) Supplemental Food Program for Women, Infants, and Children (WIC) provides food supplements for pregnant and lactating women and infants and children up to 5 years of age. A positive impact on weight gain during pregnancy, on increased birthweight, and on infant survival has been found in studies of its effects. In addition to the direct benefits of more and better nutrition, WIC eligibility requires medical prescription and thus itself provides entry into the health care system as an additional benefit and contributor to the positive outcomes of the WIC program (Kennedy et al., 1982; Kotelchuck et al., 1984).

Substance abuse by mothers is another important factor in the health of infants. Low birthweight is associated with maternal cigarette smoking, which may be a significant factor in 20 to 40 percent of low-birthweight infants born in the United States (Institute of Medicine, 1985:68). Low-income and less educated women have the highest rates of smoking, thus adding to their total risk. Studies also indicate that mothers who consume substantial amounts of alcohol are at risk for low-birthweight babies and fetal alcohol syndrome that can include birth defects or mental retardation (Institute of Medicine, 1985:69).

AIDS is becoming an increasing problem in the area of black infant mortality and morbidity. Recent assessments of the pattern and spread of the AIDS outbreak confirm the heavy and increasing prevalence of AIDS and human immunodeficiency virus (HIV) infection among blacks (and Hispanics) (Centers for Disease Control, 1986b). The impact on infants is due to maternal intravenous drug use and heterosexual transmission and the resulting prenatal or perinatal infection of babies. It is estimated that 30 to 50 percent of HIV-infected mothers will give birth to an infected infant. Among AIDS cases in children where race is known, between June 1981 and July 1988, approximately 55 percent have occurred in blacks (and 14 percent in Hispanics) (Centers for Disease Control, 1988a).

MATERNAL MORTALITY

Maternal mortality is defined as the number of deaths to women per 100,000 live births from complications of pregnancy or childbirth or within 90 days postpartum. The disparities between black and white maternal mortality rates are greater than the infant mortality differences, and although rates have fallen significantly for both groups, the disparities have barely changed in more than 30 years. In 1950, the rate of maternal mortality for whites was 60, and the rates for nonwhites, 200 (R. Farley, 1985:7); in 1984, the maternal mortality rate for whites was 5.4 and that for blacks was 19.7 (National Center for Health Statistics, 1987c:111); thus, the black rate remains more than 3 times the white rate. National figures may understate maternal deaths because in many states the information on the death certificate does not indicate whether the woman was pregnant or had recently been pregnant. Some recent evidence suggests that the recent steep decline in maternal mortality related to infection is largely due to the reduction in septic abortion and reflects legalization of abortion in 1973, combined with improved obstetrical care.

Many of the same factors that influence infant mortality also influence maternal mortality. One-third to one-half of the maternal deaths studied in Massachusetts between 1954 and 1985 were judged to have been preventable, the deaths having resulted from the high rate of teenage pregnancy, late or no prenatal care, "inadequate" prenatal care (judged to be a factor in 50 percent of the nonwhite maternal deaths), and a high rate of unintended births. It seems clear that black-white disparity in maternal mortality could be sharply reduced by efforts to ensure early and adequate prenatal care.

While all of the determinants of infant and maternal mortality and morbidity between blacks and whites described here are not understood by medical science, many specific programs and practices are known to be beneficial in reducing the risk of infant and maternal mortality, especially the preeminent role of low birthweight in determining infant mortality. There is consensus in the medical field about the importance of the following (see Institute of Medicine, 1985):

• Pregnancy risk identification, counseling, and risk reduction; health education related to pregnancy outcome generally and to low birthweight in particular; and full availability of family planning services, especially for low-income women and adolescents.

• Ensuring that all pregnant women in the United States, especially those at medical or socioeconomic risk, are given access to and receive high-quality prenatal care.

• A public information program to call the problem of low birthweight to the public's attention and to reinforce its importance with the nation's leaders and to help reduce low birthweight by conveying a set of ideas to the public about avoidance of important risk factors.

CHILDHOOD

DEMOGRAPHY AND HEALTH STATUS

In 1987, there were 5.3 million black American children aged 5–14; they represented 16 percent of the nation's children in this age group. Although there is a declining proportion of children in the total population, because of differential birthrates the percentage of black children will represent an increasing percentage of the nation's future population of children. Black children are much more likely to live in a single-parent household, often with an adolescent mother, and they are somewhat more likely to have parents who have not completed high school. Nationwide, black children are overrepresented among the poor, and the youngest black children are the most likely to live below the poverty level (see Chapters 6 and 10).

The links between poverty and poor health in childhood have been well established. For example, research done in Boston, where there is wide access to hospital care, found substantial socioeconomic and racial disparity in mortality rates. The socioeconomic effects varied across different ages and causes of death but were prominent throughout childhood (Wise et al., 1985). Other studies have confirmed that poor children are more frequently ill, more seriously ill, and are more likely to have severe health consequences (Dutton, 1981; Egbuonu and Starfield, 1982). Although poor education is often associated with poverty, it does exert an independent effect on health

TABLE 8-2 Mortality Rates for Children Aged 1–14, by Race, 1985

Children	1–4	5–14
Male		
White	52.4	29.9
Black	89.0	41.3
Female		
White	39.7	19.4
Black	70.3	28.1

Note: Mortality rate is deaths per 100,000 children aged 1–14.

Source: Data from National Center for Health Statistics.

status. Children born to parents who are poorly educated also suffer health disadvantages. Using indirect estimation procedures for 1975 data, Mare (1982) found that childhood mortality is highly associated with family income and educational attainment of parents as independent effects. Survival rates of children whose mothers had less than a high school education were as much as one-third lower than those whose mothers were high school graduates.

Black children have benefited from the impressive health gains for all American children since 1950. The rate of death from all causes for children aged 1–4 was 139.4 in 1950 and 51.4 by 1985. For children aged 5–14, the comparable rates were 60.1 in 1950 and 26.3 in 1985 (National Center for Health Statistics, 1988:80). However, black children have not shared equally in the overall health gains, and their death rates are much higher than those for white children.

Despite dramatic overall mortality gains, death rates for black children are from 30 percent to 50 percent higher than for whites, and the rate of decline in black children's mortality has slowed in recent years. The mortality disparities are strikingly high for black male children, approximately 50 percent higher than for white males and 100 percent higher than for white females of comparable ages (see Table 8-2). Injury is the leading cause of death in childhood. Accidents cause 3 times more deaths than either of the next two leading causes of childhood death (cancer and congenital anomalies). Nearly all of the dramatic decline in childhood mortality since 1950 was due to reduction in infections and other deaths from natural causes. In contrast, deaths from injuries are rising.

Automobile passenger injuries have taken their greatest toll among white children. For black children, the highest rates of injuries occur in or near the home. Injuries are related to socioeconomic status: poor children are very likely to live in areas in which heavy traffic patterns lead to pedestrian injury, streets need repair, there are dilapidated or abandoned structures, and there is dangerous uncollected trash or litter. Within the house, unrepaired stairwells and inadequate or absent screens or window guards expose children to the risk of falls. Missing smoke detectors along with defective heaters and other household appliances pose fire hazards. Poor homes are also more likely to contain toxic substances such as chemicals for pest control or peeling lead paint.

RISKS TO HEALTHY GROWTH, DEVELOPMENT, AND LEARNING

During childhood there is an important interaction between physical status and healthy development. This section briefly discusses the factors—apart from acute or chronic illness per se—that have a significant impact on healthy growth development and learning. These factors include malnutrition, anemia, lead poisoning, lack of immunization, lack of dental care, and child neglect and abuse. All of these factors affect poor, black children disproportionately. Each of them exerts an independent influence, but unfortunately, they tend to occur together and thus to multiply the adverse effects.

Malnutrition

Good nutrition is an exceedingly important aspect of brain growth and learning. The most rapid brain growth occurs in the unborn fetus and during early infancy. Head circumference at birth and in early life is an important proxy measure for brain growth and development in early infancy. This early brain growth and development is heavily dependent on nutrition (Engle et al., 1979; Winick, 1970).

Literal starvation, the extreme of malnutrition, is not common in the United States. However, there is hunger and malnutrition among poor children. Current studies emphasize the interaction between malnutrition and environmental influences, particularly the amount and type of early stimulation. Cravioto and Delacardie (1978) pointed out that apart from direct effects on brain growth and development, chronic marginal malnutrition influences mental functioning in three other ways: the chronically malnourished child loses learning time because of chronic or repeated illnesses; there is apathy and inattentiveness that relate to lack of energy (calories); and the malnourished child tends to develop a pattern of lack of engagement with persons and objects in the environment, with a resulting lack of needed attention or stimulation.

Height in less than the 10th percentile is defined as linear growth retardation and is used as a measure of marginal nutrition for children. The Centers for Disease Control (CDC) (1983) reported that from 10.9 to 23.6 percent of low-income black and other minority children showed linear growth retardation. (The population surveyed was children who were eligible for WIC and EPSDT [Early Periodic Screening, Diagnosis, and Treatment] programs, which are designed to overcome child malnutrition.) There is a "national health objective" (U.S. Department of Health and Human Services, 1980) that growth retardation of infants and children caused by inadequate diets should be eliminated by 1990, but many eligible children are not served by current programs (see below). Under current programmatic efforts, the 1990 goal will not be met.

Anemia

Iron-deficiency anemia is a specific indicator of nutritional deficiency in infants and young children. Iron-deficiency anemia affects many organ systems (Lanzkowsky, 1978; Smith and Rios, 1974). Fatigue, weakness, anorexia, pica (eating nonfoods such as dirt), and acute gastrointestinal blood loss are not uncommon in anemic children. Severe anemia may result in intestinal inflammation, malabsorption, and cardiovascular pathology. Recently, iron deficiency even in the absence of overt anemia has been implicated in effects on the brain that cause irritability, attention deficits, and distractibility (Leibel, 1977; Oski and Stockman, 1980); these conditions obviously may affect learning. Studies show that these symptoms can be reversed by giving diets rich in iron and that the brain symptoms disappear earlier than measurable changes in blood iron.

Infants are particularly prone to anemia because their rapid growth and development deplete body iron stores at a time when a largely milk diet contains insufficient iron for growth requirements. Current studies show that among poor black children, the young children are most at risk. According to the Nutrition Surveillance Annual Summary for 1983–1985 (Centers for Disease Control, 1985), 8.2 percent of black children fell below the 5th percentile for hematocrit measure (packed red cell volume) of anemia. According to the report of the Joint Nutrition Monitoring Committee (U.S. Department of Health and Human Services, 1986e:9), the highest prevalence of iron deficiency (20.6 percent) was observed among poor children aged 1–2 years; the diets for 96 percent of this group were reported to be inadequate in iron.

Diagnosis of anemia is accurate and inexpensive; it only requires a finger prick. Anemia can be prevented by starting an iron-fortified diet in infancy. The efficacy of iron therapy is well documented (Starfield, 1977). The newly discovered relationship of iron deficiency to enhanced lead absorption and higher body lead levels makes this health problem even worse. Although WIC programs have reached 2.8 million children and nursing mothers since it was established in 1970 and has reduced anemia for those whom it served, only 25 to 30 percent of eligible infants and mothers are reached by the program.

Lead Poisoning

Lead poisoning is one of the most prevalent health problems among children in the United States. It is increasingly clear that children are highly susceptible to the toxic effects of lead, even at the very lowest levels. With

TABLE 8-3 Immunization of Children Aged 1–4, by Race, 1976 and 1985 (in percent)

Children	Measles		Rubella		DPT[a]		Mumps		Polio	
	1976	1985	1976	1985	1976	1985	1976	1985	1976	1985
White	68.3	63.6	63.8	66.3	75.3	70.0	50.3	61.8	66.2	58.9
Nonwhites	54.8	48.8	61.6	47.4	68.7	48.7	61.8	47.0	39.9	40.1

[a]Diphtheria, pertussis, tetanus.

Source: Data from National Center for Health Statistics.

repeated exposure, lead accumulates in the body. Until about 1970 a level of 60 micrograms of lead per deciliter or lower was considered nontoxic. Beyond that cutoff level, lead encephalopathy occurs and causes vomiting, convulsions, delirium, coma, and even death. However, recent research has shown that levels as low as 25 to 30 micrograms per deciliter are toxic to the nervous system, and they are being adopted as the new cutoff standard for treatment. The most recent data suggest that even lower levels are damaging.

Lead toxicity symptoms include irritability, slowed nerve conduction rates, attention deficits, fatigue, loss of appetite, weakness, sleep disturbance, and sudden appearance of atypical behavior. Needleman and colleagues (1979) report deficits in classroom performance associated with elevated levels of lead in children. The child's nutritional status is significant in determining risk. Deficiencies in iron, calcium, and phosphorus enhance absorption and retention of lead. Therefore, children in poverty are likely to have nutritional deficiencies that render them more vulnerable to even low-level lead exposure, and they also tend to live under conditions that can give rise to heavy exposures to lead. A national survey (Mahaffey et al., 1982) reported that an estimated 675,000 children 6 months to 5 years of age had lead levels of 30 micrograms or higher. They found that 2 percent of white children had elevated blood levels, compared with 12.2 percent of black children. Among black children living in inner-city areas and in families at or below the poverty level, 18.6 percent had lead levels above the toxic level. This is 9 times the rate in white children.

There is a screening test (free erythrocyte porphyrin [FEP]) for lead levels that is accurate and inexpensive (Centers for Disease Control, 1985:10; Piomelli, 1973). This test has the added advantage of screening for iron deficiency along with lead levels.

Lack of Immunization

Immunization rates for many of the preventable serious infectious diseases of childhood have grown only slowly or have fallen since 1976 (see Table 8-3). Measles is considered the most threatening of the preventable childhood contagious diseases. Its frequent complications include pneumonia, ear infections, and deafness. Brain inflammation (encephalitis) occurs in about 1 of every 1,000 cases, often producing permanent brain damage and mental

TABLE 8-4 Decayed, Filled, and Missing Teeth, Children Aged 5–17, by Race, 1979–1980

Children	Mean No. of Decayed, Filled, or Missing Teeth	Percent Distribution of			
		Decayed Teeth	Filled Teeth	Missing Teeth	Total
White					
Male	4.57	14.9	79.8	5.3	100.0
Female	5.24	13.1	80.8	6.1	100.0
Nonwhites					
Male	3.79	37.1	46.8	16.1	100.0
Female	4.50	31.5	53.3	15.2	100.0

Source: Data from National Center for Health Statistics (1982b).

retardation. About 1 of every 10,000 children afflicted with measles dies as a result of complications. There has been a recent rise in measles, from 1,497 reported cases in 1983 to 2,704 reported cases in 1985. A national health goal is to reduce reported cases below 500 by 1990 (National Center for Health Statistics, 1987b:30). Rubella (German measles) remains an important problem, with 20,000 reported cases in 1977, and actual cases are estimated to be as much as 20 times the reported number. There is a national health goal for a reported rubella incidence of less than 1,000 cases by 1990 (National Center for Health Statistics, 1987b:30).

The striking benefits that intensive systematic immunization can achieve are perhaps most dramatically demonstrated by the worldwide elimination of smallpox. The postvaccination decline in paralytic polio in the United States from 20,000 cases a year to 5 cases in 1985 is another example (National Center for Health Statistics, 1987b:31). The current decline in immunization rates and rising black-white disparities argue for national and local campaigns on a sustained basis to increase both access to immunization and parental awareness of the importance of immunization.

Lack of Dental Care

Dental care is an often ignored but important area of health. Dental decay (caries) and periodontal disease start in childhood and cause progressive destruction leading to extensive tooth loss in adult life. Repeated national surveys and a detailed collaborative study (Robert Wood Johnson Foundation, 1983) have shown that black children have much higher rates of untreated dental disease than whites. Table 8-4 shows the results of the 1979–1980 National Dental Caries Prevalence Survey: it can be inferred that once a tooth begins to decay, black children have a lower likelihood that it will be filled and a higher likelihood that it will become a missing tooth.

Reductions in dental caries are accomplished by use of fluorides in drinking water, dental sealants, and toothpastes; education of children in oral hygiene and noncariogenic dietary practices; and regular visits to the dentist for prevention and remedial care. Dental care is typically not covered by private or public health insurance, public dental insurance for the poor is limited, and poor children have very low rates of dental visits. The EPSDT program for Medicaid children has increased its early dental care for poor children very slowly. In the early 1980s, only 20 percent of the target population had been screened, and of those screened only 25 percent were referred for treatment.

Child Neglect and Abuse

Child neglect and abuse appear to have increased significantly in the past few decades. A review of the 50 states and the District of Columbia found that abuse reports and numbers of deaths attributed to abuse increased by 180 percent (to 1.9 million cases) in the period from 1976 to 1985 (U.S. Congress, 1987). This reported increase is partly related to the establishment of a universal absolute legal mandate for the reporting of suspected child abuse in the United States during that period. Local laws are typically vague and open to broad interpretation. For many reasons, abuse is more likely to be reported among poor and minority families than among the affluent ones. Reports show that 85 percent of the perpetrators of abuse and neglect are the child's biological or stepparents. Types of abuse are categorized as physical abuse, physical neglect, psychological abuse, psychological neglect, and sexual abuse. The available data indicate that child neglect is twice as prevalent as child abuse.

High-risk families range from those who are obviously deeply troubled and chronically disorganized, often already known to the social agencies, police, or other community resources, to otherwise stable families temporarily under stress. Some child abuse is related to drug-abusing parents, and alcohol is implicated in many cases. Abuse and neglect have been found to rise with chronic unemployment. Physically or mentally handicapped children can be targets of abuse by parents frustrated by the difficulties in coping with the handicaps. Teenage parenthood or parental ignorance and immaturity can be critical factors in child neglect and abuse.

When parents are immature, dependent, or unable to handle responsibility, their feelings of stress may cause them to direct their anger and frustration at a child. They often have strong beliefs about the value of physical punishment and often expect children to perform according to unrealistic wishes. Abusing parents often are isolated socially and have difficulty seeking help even when they are troubled about their parenting behaviors.

Efforts to reduce child abuse will have to be multifaceted. Some promising approaches involve preventive parent education and skills training; enhancement of community and social support systems, including home visits to high-risk mothers; and assistance to abusing parents through collaborative efforts of the public and private sectors. Projects designed to create an integrated health and social service delivery system for multiproblem families offer promise. Such programs help ensure that families at risk or involved in neglect or child abuse have continuing contact and follow-up care from a health or social services agency from the prenatal through the school years. The use of home visitors has had more rigorous evaluation than any other preventive approach, and four of five programs that were evaluated were found to be effective in reducing rates of maltreatment (Armstrong, 1981; Gray et al., 1979; Lutzker and Rice, 1984; Olds et al., 1986).

ADOLESCENTS AND YOUNG ADULTS

The youth population of the United States peaked in 1980 as a result of the post–World War II baby boom and is now declining. Because of the slower rate of decline among blacks, the proportion of youths who are black will rise from 13.7 percent in 1980 to 15.2 percent in 1996. At current fertility rates, and with a smaller childbearing cohort, the total population aged 15–24 is expected to show only moderate growth after 1996. Relative to whites, blacks and other minorities will be a significantly larger proportion of American youth in the coming cohorts.

Mortality rates for youths aged 15–24 are among the lowest for any period of life, and their health is considerably better than it was for people of that age 40 years ago. In recent years, however, male adolescents and young adults have not shown the sustained health gains seen in other segments of the population. Among male youth in the 1970s and 1980s, death rates due to accidents, homicide, and suicide were higher than they were in 1950. The HHS special report on minority health (U.S. Department of Health and Human Services, 1985e) identified injuries as one of the six causes of excess deaths among blacks. This increased risk occurs over the entire age range, but it is most prominent in the late adolescent and young adult groups. Deaths from auto accidents, suicide, homicide, and other injuries now account for more than three-quarters of all mortality among people aged 15–24.

Since 1950 there has been a shift in the burden of adolescent illness away from the traditional medical etiologies of disease toward newly defined health problems that arise from environmental factors and health-related personal behaviors. For black youth, several conditions are of major concern: teenage pregnancy and reproductive health; substance abuse (tobacco, alcohol, illegal drugs); injuries (accidental and nonaccidental); and glaucoma.

Adolescents are the most medically underserved sector of the population. The 1986 National Access Survey found that black youth is heavily represented in the profile of persons experiencing cutbacks in the availability of health care. Preventive health care is especially important to adolescents, and these services are least likely to be covered by insurance of any kind. The national health objectives were stated by the surgeon general to reduce deaths for youth 15–24 years of age to fewer than 93 per 100,000 by 1990. In 1985 the death rates were 136.3 for white males, 174.1 for black males,

48.4 for white females, and 59.5 for black females. Clearly, the stated objectives will not be met for white or black males.

TEENAGE CHILDBEARING AND REPRODUCTIVE HEALTH

For adolescent and young adult women, pregnancy and reproductive health-related conditions are the leading causes of hospital admission and sick days. Teenage childbearing is one of the major issues confronting black youth. It has profound, immediate, and long-term health implications for the young mother and her children, and also represents a challenge to black family structure and functioning.

Birthrates among teenage black women have been dropping since the 1960s (see Chapter 10). However, because the total number of black adolescent women increased by 20 percent, there were substantial increases in the total births to black teenagers, despite the declining birthrates. In addition, because birthrates to black teenagers remain 2 to 3 times higher than those for whites, a higher proportion of all black births occur among teenage mothers: in 1984, 20 percent of all black births were to teenagers, compared with 11.1 percent among whites (Hofferth and Hayes, 1987). Because black teenage women represent only 14 percent of the U.S. adolescent female population, the overwhelming majority of all teenage births nationally are to white adolescent girls. Nonetheless, special attention to teenage childbearing among blacks is needed because of the adverse medical, personal, and social consequences of those teenage births.

The higher birthrate for black teenagers can be accounted for by earlier initiation of sexual intercourse (on average 2 years earlier than whites); less use of contraception; less likelihood of abortion; and almost universal decision to keep and rear children who are born, rather than offering them for adoption (Newcomer et al., 1983; Smith and Udry, 1985; Zelnick et al., 1981). Black teenagers are slightly less likely than whites to terminate an unintended pregnancy by abortion. However, because of their higher rate of pregnancy, black abortion rates per 1,000 women are double those for whites. In 1981, abortion rates for girls 15–19 were 69 per 1,000 for blacks and 39 per 1,000 for whites (Hayes, 1987).

As discussed above, black teenage mothers are at risk for bearing low-birthweight infants for whom neonatal mortality and postneonatal mortality and morbidity rates are very high. Among the babies who are low-birthweight survivors, there is greater likelihood of experiencing long-term neurological, developmental, or learning problems. The youngest mothers are also at increased risk for obstetrical complications or death in comparison with older mothers. Late or inadequate prenatal care, poor nutrition, and poor self-care are factors in low birthweight and infant mortality as well as in maternal death. In 1984, 46 percent of teenage mothers had not received early prenatal care.

Adolescent motherhood, regardless of race, predicts lower educational and occupational attainment, lower wages, and increased risk of living in chronic poverty compared with peers who postpone parenthood. The children of teenage mothers face higher health risks as well as greater risks of lower intellectual and academic achievement and of social behavior problems. They may also be more likely to become adolescent parents themselves than are the children of adult mothers (Hofferth and Hayes, 1987).

Social status, family structure, and neighborhood were studied by Hogan and Kitagawa (1985) as factors influencing age of initiation of intercourse and likelihood of pregnancy among urban disadvantaged blacks. They found that young age of initial intercourse is the best predictor of teenage pregnancy. Early sex initiation and pregnancy were found to be linked to several family factors: having a single parent, five or more siblings, a sibling who is an adolescent parent, and lax parental control of dating. Additional risk factors were living in a ghetto neighborhood and low educational aspirations or achievement.

In addition to risking pregnancy, the early onset of unprotected intercourse among blacks places them at high risk of contracting sexually transmitted diseases. These diseases increasingly threaten the health and well-being of millions of adolescents and young adults. Although there has been some recent decline in the incidence of gonorrhea and syphilis in the population as a whole, both diseases continue to increase among adolescents: the 15–24 age group represents about 75 percent of all reported cases. Moreover, newer sexually transmitted diseases such as genital herpes, chlamydia, papilloma virus, and venereal warts have risen sharply in the general population. Chlamydia, most common in the 15–24 age group, is now the most prevalent venereal disease. These infections may be without apparent symptoms, and many young people can suffer serious permanent complications from unrecognized and untreated disease. Even when aware of symptoms, adolescents are reluctant to seek care (O'Reilly and Aral, 1988). AIDS, through heterosexual transmission, poses a special threat to minority youth.

SPECIAL HEALTH RISKS

Drugs, Tobacco, and Alcohol Use

Substance abuse, particularly alcohol and stimulant drugs, increases risk of accidents, suicides, and homicides; family disruption; and poor school and job performance and may lead to acute and chronic medical conditions. Drug abuse among adolescents is highly correlated with adolescent pregnancy, poor grades, dropping out of school, and delinquency (Jessor and Jessor, 1982). Prior to the early 1960s, experience with illicit drugs was probably limited to less than 2 percent of the general population. However, even at that time, rates of use were high in some black urban ghettos: in St. Louis, half of black, urban-born 30-year-olds surveyed in 1962 had tried marijuana (Robins and Murphy, 1967).

At present, black adolescents have a lower reported use of illicit drugs and alcohol than whites. For example, a 1985 household survey reports that for illicit drugs, any use in the past year among those aged 12–17 was 25 percent for whites and 19 percent for blacks, and among those aged 18–25 it was 44 percent for whites and 39 percent for blacks. For cocaine the figures for those aged 12–17 were 4.4 percent among whites and 2.5 percent among blacks. For those aged 18–25, cocaine use was reported as 18 percent among whites and at 11 percent among blacks (National Institute on Drug Abuse, 1987). However, these data may suffer from unrepresentative sampling. Surveys are usually based on high school student samples or household surveys, thus excluding school dropouts and institutionalized and street youths, and underrepresenting students with high absentee rates.

The true dimensions of drug use for blacks may be underreported. This hypothesis is supported by a 1979 survey that found mortality from drug-related deaths increased steeply in nine major metropolitan areas, and about one-third of those fatalities occurred among black youth in the 15–24 age group (National Institute on Drug Abuse, 1980). Currently, cocaine, and its potent derivative "crack," show increased use among all youth. In 1986, the first national data report of high school seniors found that 4.1 percent had used crack in the past year and 17 percent had tried cocaine (Johnston et al., 1987). By any measure, drug problems have greatly increased over the past 40 years, and although that increase may now have slowed, a majority of adolescent blacks and whites have experimented with illicit drugs. The drug problem is potentially far more serious now because of the AIDS risk associated with the sharing of needles or "drug works." Although heroin use is minimal among adolescents, there is an increasing trend toward intra-venous injection of cocaine. Cocaine injection poses a higher risk of HIV infection because cocaine's effects are of short duration, and so users inject far more frequently than do heroin users.

Tobacco smoking patterns for both whites and blacks occur at a median age of 17 years for males and about 18.5 years for females. A 1985 household survey reported that cigarette use in the past month for those aged 12–17 was 18 percent for whites and 9 percent for blacks; for those aged 18–25, cigarette use was reported by 39 percent of whites and 35 percent of blacks (National Institute on Drug Abuse, 1987). These survey data may suffer from unrepresentative sampling problems similar to those of survey data on drug use. Cigarette advertising has been found to be targeted to women and youthful black populations (Davis, 1987). These campaigns often include free distribution of sample cigarettes. Health education programs can include awareness of these commercial pressures and teach techniques of consumer resistance. There are current models of school-based, peer-mediated inter-vention programs that are effective in reducing rates of initiation of smoking (Botvin et al., 1980; McAllister et al., 1979).

Alcoholism and alcohol-related mortality and morbidity are leading con-tributors to the total burden of illness. It is estimated that alcohol is impli-cated in about one-half of all homicides and in a substantial percentage of adolescent and adult unintentional injuries (e.g., burns, falls, drownings, auto accidents). Cirrhosis of the liver and cancers of the esophagus are direct consequences. Among young blacks and whites, alcohol is frequently associated with abuse of other drugs and magnifies their adverse consequences (U.S. Department of Health and Human Services, 1985a,c,d). The 1985 household survey reported that among persons aged 18–25, use of alcohol in the past month was reported for 76 percent of whites and 58 percent of blacks (National Institute on Drug Abuse, 1987).

The dangers associated with alcohol use are not well understood by adolescents. In 1986, only 25 percent of high school seniors perceived any risk of harm from one or two drinks daily, and only 39 percent perceived "great risk" of harm from regular drinking of 5 or more drinks once or twice each weekend. While 67 percent perceived great risk in consuming 4 or 5 drinks nearly every day, this means that 33 percent did not view this as harmful (Johnston et al., 1987). Evidently, there is a place for programs that educate adolescents about the dangers of alcohol use and that teach skills for responsible use and resisting pressures to drink.

Injuries

As noted above, injuries are the leading cause of death for adolescents, and there are very large disparities in death rates for blacks and whites (see Figure 8-3). Among both blacks and whites, the total rates are 3 to 4 times higher for males than for females. In 1984, the rates for major causes of deaths per 100,000 for males aged 15–24 were homicide: blacks, 62 and whites, 11; motor vehicle accidents: blacks, 32 and whites, 59; and suicide: blacks, 11 and whites, 22.

Drownings, falls, and burns are important causes of death by unintentional injury in this age group. Injuries also figure prominently as a source of morbidity, with those in the 15–19 age group accounting for as many as 44 percent of hospitalizations and 48 percent of emergency room visits for injuries. For every death, there are many other adolescents who are impaired or disabled by nonfatal injuries.

Homicide (intentional injury) is the major cause of death and disability among black male adolescents (see Figure 8-4). The black homicide rate decreased by 22 percent between 1970 and 1985, from its peak of 102.5 to 66.1; white homicide rates increased by 30 percent, from 7.9 to 11.2, in the same time period (Centers for Disease Control, 1986a). Although the disparity has narrowed, black homicide rates in 1985 for those aged 15–24 were still 6 times greater than white rates (National Center for Health Statistics, 1988). The CDC analysis was unable to ascertain the contribution of socioeconomic status to the risk of homicide. The study did find that the highest risk of homicide is faced by young males, who are killed by friends or acquaintances using firearms (usually handguns) in the course of an argument.

Accident (nonintentional injury) data are derived from death certificates, hospital discharge abstracts, emergency room reports, National Health Interview Survey reports, and traffic accident data. There is no national reporting

FIGURE 8-3 Death rates from (a) homicide, (b) residential fires, (c) drowning, and (d) pedestrian accidents, by race and age group.

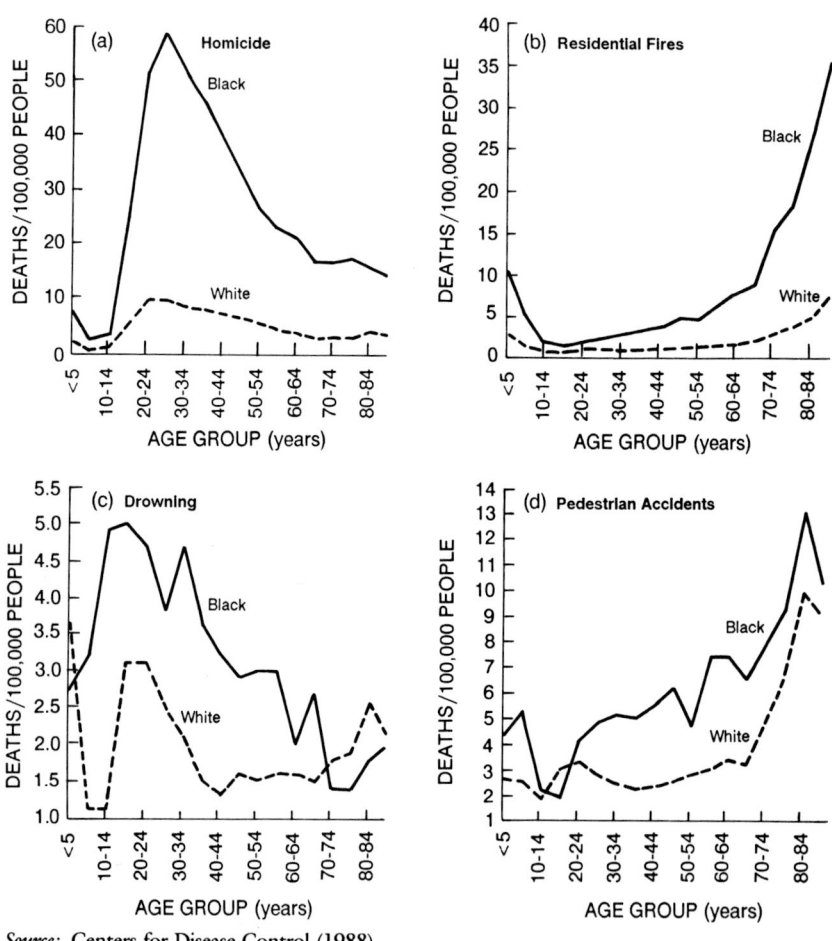

Source: Centers for Disease Control (1988).

system for the accidents that do not result in death. Some studies have found that deaths due to fires are strongly income-related for urban children. Investigations into the clusters of human and environmental factors that account for specific injuries to specific cohorts of persons are an emerging research area for clarifying the epidemiology of the black-white disparities in mortality and morbidity due to injuries.

Glaucoma

Glaucoma is a disorder of increased fluid pressure within the eye that causes damage to the retina and the optic nerve. It is the leading cause of blindness

FIGURE 8-4 Homicide rates for people aged 15–24, by race and sex, 1950–1985.

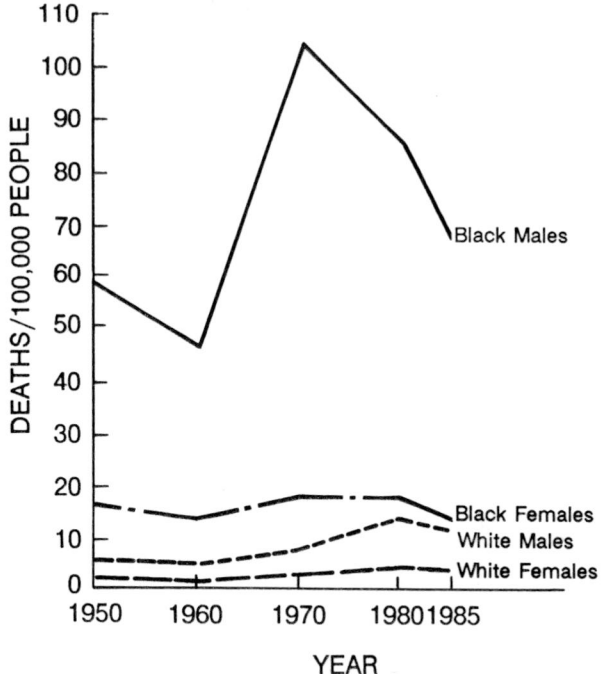

Source: Data from Centers for Disease Control.

among blacks in the United States. Recent clinical evidence has called attention to the fact that the prevalence of blindness from glaucoma in black children and young adults is much higher than it is for whites. For adults aged 45–64 years, excess rates of blindness due to glaucoma are even higher for blacks. In 1984, the American Academy of Ophthalmology issued a special announcement alerting clinicians to glaucoma as a major health problem for blacks. Irreversible vision loss is often extensive by the time the patient seeks health services. Early detection is possible through a simple intraocular pressure measurement test (tonometry). Black children who are near sighted (myopic) are at particularly high risk. Currently, little is known of the determinants of this disorder or reasons for high risk for blacks. There are no data regarding diet, stress, health habits, toxic exposures, or other factors that could act singly or in combination to cause the heightened glaucoma and blindness experienced by blacks.

ADULTHOOD

Younger people are expected to be healthier than the elderly, and the differential is usually explained as a result of the aging process. There are

FIGURE 8-5 Leading causes of death, by race and age group, 1984.

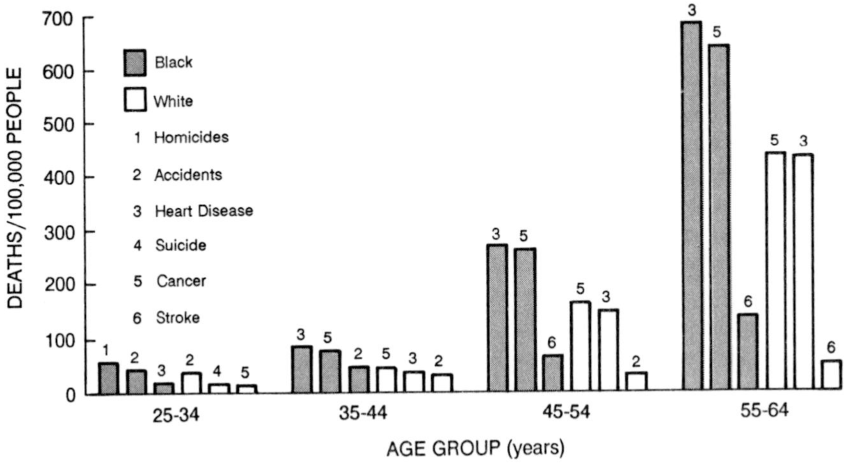

Source: Data from U.S. Department of Health and Human Services.

some sex differences in mortality. The greater longevity of women has been partly explained by a lesser exposure to environmental hazards and less participation in hazardous life-styles, including use of firearms, speeding, heavy substance abuse, and promiscuity. To the extent that these differences are reduced, there is the prospect that men will approach more closely the life expectancy of women.

Biological differences appear to explain very little of the difference in health status between blacks and whites. There were 58,942 excess deaths for blacks in 1980. Only 379 of these deaths, less than 1 percent, were attributable to hereditary conditions such as sickle cell anemia, for which genetic patterns among blacks have been established (U.S. Department of Health and Human Services, 1985e). Instead, the major factors appear to be socioeconomic and physical environments, personal health habits, and life-styles (see Figure 8-5). In this section we focus on five of the problems that contribute to health disparities between white and black adults—homicide, AIDS, substance abuse, hypertension, and cancer. This list is very different from what it would have been in 1940; tuberculosis and many other infectious diseases are no longer high on the list. But the current problems pose as many challenges today as did infectious diseases in 1940.

MAJOR HEALTH RISKS

Homicide

Intentional injury has only recently been recognized as a public health problem. Intentional injury includes a wide spectrum of assaultive behaviors:

child abuse, spouse abuse, rape, suicide, and homicide. Our discussion is focused primarily on homicide because it contributes so heavily to the differential in mortality between blacks and whites during the middle years of life.

Homicide is the leading cause of death for black males aged 15–34. There are 8,000 black victims of homicide a year. Although blacks were 11.5 percent of the population in 1983, they were 43 percent of the homicide victims. The black-white differentials for homicide are higher than for any other leading cause of death. And because the typical homicide victim is young, every homicide accounts for an average 30.6 years of potential life lost prior to age 65; in comparison, the potential average time of life lost is only 2.1 years for death due to heart disease (Centers for Disease Control, 1986a). Although homicide risk is greatest among males in the 25–34 age group, the gap between black and white risks is evident for both sexes in all age groups (see Figure 8-3). In both blacks and whites, most homicides are intraracial and inflicted by young male acquaintances and relatives as a result of a quarrel, not as part of another crime (Jason et al., 1983).

Homicide rates fluctuate a great deal over time, suggesting that societal factors play a significant role. Brenner (1983) reported an association between the homicide rate and unemployment. In recent years, there has been a significant decline in the black homicide rate, and of the five race-specific health objectives stated for 1990, this is the only one which seems likely to be met (U.S. Department of Health and Human Services, 1986d). The decline cannot be explained as due to any specific intervention.

The causes of homicide are complex. They are associated with three separate sets of risk factors: biological, psychological, and sociological. Biological risk factors for involvement in homicide as a victim or perpetrator relate to being male and being young. Psychological factors relate to violence that is learned from role models or is the result of disturbed developmental patterns and the failure to develop adequate inhibitions against inappropriate and excessive expression of anger and frustrations. Sociological risk factors relate to American culture and the structure of American society (National Commission on the Causes and Prevention of Violence, 1969). For example, it is estimated that about one-half of all homicides in the United States are related to the use of alcohol. Between 10 and 20 percent of homicides nationwide are associated with the use of illegal drugs (U.S. Department of Health and Human Services, 1986a:163).

For attempted homicides, the outcome is influenced by the lethality of the instruments to which the individuals may have access. Access to handguns, used most frequently by people aged 25–34, has been considered to be a major cause of homicide. The evidence for this is not conclusive and indeed is difficult to establish (Wright et al., 1983). Further studies of fatal and nonfatal outcomes may increase understanding of the problem (see Chapter 9).

At present there are no scientifically proven efficacious interventions that would lead to the reduction of homicide. Under the circumstances, limiting

TABLE 8-5 Cumulative Incidence of AIDS and Relative Risk, by Race and Ethnic Groups, Age, and Transmission Category, 1981–1987

Category	White	Black	Hispanic	Other
Adults, total[b]	380.8 (1.0)	1,068.1 (2.8)[a]	1,036.3 (2.7)[a]	141.0 (0.4)[a]
Adult men	188.9 (1.0)	578.2 (3.1)[a]	564.4 (3.0)[a]	74.4 (0.4)[a]
Adult women	12.2 (1.0)	161.1 (13.2)[a]	104.6 (8.6)[a]	11.1 (0.9)
Homosexual men	298.6 (1.0)	413.8 (1.4)[a]	513.9 (1.7)[a]	94.7 (0.3)[a]
Bisexual men	46.8 (1.0)	177.7 (3.8)[a]	126.3 (2.7)[a]	24.9 (0.5)[a]
Heterosexual IV drug users	10.1 (1.0)	201.2 (19.9)[a]	195.1 (19.3)[a]	4.2 (0.3)[a]
Hemophiliacs	2.6 (1.0)	1.4 (0.6)[a]	2.7 (1.0)	1.7 (0.7)
Transfusion recipients	5.1 (1.0)	7.5 (1.5)	6.5 (1.3)	5.0 (1.0)
Pediatric, total[c]	3.8 (1.0)	46.3 (12.1)[a]	26.1 (6.8)[a]	3.2 (0.8)
Mother, IV drug user	0.8 (1.0)	21.8 (26.4)[a]	13.9 (16.9)[a]	1.3 (1.6)
Mother's partner, IV drug user	0.2 (1.0)	5.5 (25.8)[a]	6.2 (29.2)[a]	0.0 (0.0)
Transfusion-associated	1.1 (1.0)	2.7 (2.3)[a]	2.1 (1.9)	0.0 (0.0)
Hemophiliacs	0.6 (1.0)	0.7 (1.0)	1.3 (2.0)	0.6 (1.0)

[a] Relative risk significantly different from 1.0 ($P < 0.05$).

[b] For all men, homosexual men, and bisexual men, the denominator consisted of all men ≥15 years; for all women, the denominator was all women ≥15 years; for other adult categories, the denominators included all men and women ≥15 years.

[c] For pediatric categories, the denominators consisted of all children <15 years.

Notes: Cumulative incidence is given per 1 million population. Relative risk is given in parentheses. Relative risk is the ratio of the cumulative incidence in each race or ethnic group to the incidence in whites.

Source: Data from Curran et al. (1988). Reprinted with permission.

access to handguns and training in conflict resolution have been recommended. But perhaps the most important aspect of the situation is that the subject of violence is now accepted as a legitimate public health concern.

AIDS

AIDS has created an international challenge of enormous proportions for the society in general and the medical profession in particular. Persons at greatest risk are homosexual males, intravenous drug users, recipients of blood transfusions, those who have had heterosexual contact with infected individuals, and children born to women who are infected. Women who are infected with the virus can transmit it during pregnancy to their prospective children. AIDS is a special problem for blacks: 25 percent of all reported cases and more than 50 percent of the children under the age of 15 who have AIDS are black (Centers for Disease Control, 1986b); see Table 8-5. Blacks with AIDS are more likely to be IV drug users, most of whom identify themselves as heterosexuals. The epidemiologic patterns of viral transmission in blacks suggest greater incursion into the heterosexual population. The greatest source of new infections is infected persons who presently show no symptoms and do not know they are infected.

The AIDS epidemic can be devastating to people who face large medical bills without adequate insurance (see section on Provision of Health Care). The financial costs for the care of persons with AIDS are enormous, ranging from $23,000 to $168,000 per patient over a lifetime (Bloom and Carliner, 1988). The cost of treatment with azedothymine (AZT), an antiviral agent, can range from $10,000 to $20,000 a year per patient.

Although there is as yet no vaccine and no effective cure, enough is known about methods of transmission of the virus (HIV) that causes AIDS so that almost all future infections with the AIDS virus could theoretically be prevented (Francis and Chin, 1987). The use of condoms inhibits the sexual transmission of the virus (Conant et al., 1986), and in the case of intravenous drug users, the use of sterile needles can prevent transmission. The overwhelming need is for public education to change behaviors with respect to safer sex and drug-use practices. A recent report (Turner et al., 1989) detailed how education must be culturally sensitive to blacks and other minorities and initiate comprehensive interventions at various levels of personal and community involvement.

Substance Abuse

Substance abuse includes the excessive use of tobacco, alcohol, or illicit drugs. The abuse of these substances is conceptually linked by the addiction, the compulsion, loss of control, and continued use despite adverse consequences. In general, the use of cigarettes, alcohol, and drugs is learned at an early age (during high school and college) and continued during the adult years, when most of the effects on health and mortality begin to be seen. The National Health Survey (National Center for Health Statistics, 1987c) indicates that in 1985, among the age group 20 and over, 41 percent of blacks and 32 percent of whites smoked tobacco.

The magnitude of this problem in blacks can be judged by deaths related to substance abuse. The mortality rate per 100,000 people for lung cancer is 95 for black males and 70 for white males. These deaths are largely due to smoking. It is also estimated that cigarette smoking is responsible for 30 percent of cancer deaths and that smoking-related deaths are particularly high among blacks. The mortality from cirrhosis of the liver—which is closely related to alcohol consumption—is 29 for blacks and 15 for whites. Alcohol and drugs are also important factors in many cases of intentional and unintentional injury. It is this combination of circumstances that gives substance abuse its high priority among problems for black adults.

It appears that genetic and social factors play an important role in the case of alcoholism. For example, it has been shown that adopted children with an alcoholic biological parent are at 4 times higher risk of alcoholism than control subjects (Bohman et al., 1981; Goodwin et al., 1974). Schuckit

(1985) has concluded that genetic influences are important in alcoholism and reflect multiple genes interacting with environmental factors.

Apart from genetic influences, children living in a home in which parents use alcohol as a means of coping with problems may learn that model. Ease of access to the various substances also constitutes a considerable risk. Research is needed to clarify the contributions of heredity and environment to all addictive processes and to provide a sound scientific basis for the development of preventive strategies.

Hypertension

It has been recognized for a long time that blacks experience higher rates of hypertension than whites. It has been estimated that hypertensive disease is responsible for more than 5,000 excess deaths a year in the black population (National Center for Health Statistics, 1987c). Hypertension is an important risk factor for stroke, especially stroke due to cerebral hemorrhage. The age-adjusted death rate for stroke among blacks is almost twice that for whites (National Center for Health Statistics, 1984). End-stage renal disease is another consequence of hypertension, and it has been estimated that its incidence is 3 to 4 times higher among blacks than among whites (Easterling, 1977).[3]

Although the cause of hypertension and the racial differences in its incidence are not known, increased awareness of the disease and early diagnosis and treatment have been shown to be effective in reducing hypertension among blacks. Indeed, hypertension control among blacks is one of the success stories of modern public health (see Table 8-6).

In the period from 1960 to 1980, the proportion of people with hypertension found in epidemiologic surveys who had had no medical contact for their disease has declined significantly, and the decline among blacks was much greater than the decline among whites. Greater awareness has increased the chances of early diagnosis and prompt treatment (National Center for Health Statistics, 1982a). Limited use of salt, an adequate supply of foods containing potassium, abstinence from smoking, and weight control are usually recommended as first steps, with medication recommended if these steps are insufficient.

The success of the hypertension program can be attributed not only to individual action but also to a comprehensive national strategy of research and education. There has been the coordinated effort of the National Heart, Lung, and Blood Institute, the American Heart Association, the American

---

3. The cause of hypertension is not known, nor is there a satisfactory explanation for the much higher rates for blacks (Gillum, 1979). The epidemiological evidence does not seem to support a genetic basis (Tyroler and James, 1978). Other theories, still unsupported, include racial differences in sodium and potassium metabolism (Luft et al., 1977; Page, 1976) and effects of weight gain. Socioeconomic status and stress have also been considered as possible causal factors.

TABLE 8-6 Prevalence Rates of Hypertension for Persons Aged 25–74 (in percent) by Treatment History, Race, and Sex, 1960–1980

Hypertension Prevalence	All People[a]	White Men	White Women	Black Men	Black Women
In the population					
1960–1962	20.3	16.3	20.4	31.8	39.8
1974–1976	22.1	21.4	19.6	37.1	35.5
1976–1980	22.0	21.2	20.0	28.3	39.8
Hypertension never diagnosed[b]					
1960–1962	51.1	57.6	43.9	70.5	35.1
1974–1976	36.4	42.3	29.7	41.0	28.9
1976–1980	26.6	40.6	25.2	35.7	14.5
On medication					
1960–1962	31.3	22.4	38.2	18.5	48.1
1974–1976	34.2	25.9	48.5	24.0	36.4
1976–1980	56.2	38.3	58.6	40.9	60.6
On medication and controlled[c]					
1960–1962	16.0	11.8	21.9	5.0	20.2
1974–1976	19.6	15.1	28.1	12.7	22.3
1976–1980	36.1	20.9	40.3	16.1	30.9

[a]Includes all other races not shown separately.

[b]Reported that was never told by physician that he or she had high blood pressure or hypertension.

[c]Subset of "on medication" group; those taking antihypertensive medication whose blood pressure was not elevated at the time of the examination.

Notes: Hypertension is defined as elevated blood pressure, that is, a systolic measurement of at least 160 mm Hg or a diastolic measurement of at least 95 mm Hg, or as taking antihypertensive medication. Populations are age adjusted by the direct method to the population at the midpoint of the 1976–1980 National Health and Nutrition Examination Survey.

Source: Data from U.S. Department of Health and Human Services.

Red Cross, the National Black Health Providers' Task Force on Blood Pressure Education and Control, and other organizations. It is an example of how community action combined with individual responsibility can improve individual and public health.

Cancer

Most blacks have learned that hypertension is a problem, but most blacks are believed to be unaware of the magnitude of the problem of cancer in the black population. From 1978 to 1981, the average annual age-adjusted cancer mortality rate per 100,000 population for all sites of cancer was 163.6 for whites and 208.5 for blacks. In 1930, white females had the highest and nonwhite males the lowest cancer mortality in the United States; by 1970–1975 their relative positions were reversed (Greenberg, 1983). There are several possible statistical explanations for the reversal, such as increased completeness of diagnosis among blacks and underestimates of the rate among black males because of greater underenumeration of black males in earlier censuses. But even making allowances for these possible errors, the evidence for an increase in the cancer rate for blacks seems indisputable.

Blacks experience higher incidence, higher mortality, and poorer survival from cancer than whites. The overall rate of incidence exceeds that of whites by 10 percent. Much of the difference can be attributed to black males, whose rate of incidence is 25 percent higher than that of white males. Cancers of the lung and prostate account for many of the cancers in males and are largely responsible for the higher rates for blacks. The esophagus is another site at which the black excess is relatively great.

It has been known for a long time that lung cancer is associated with cigarette smoking (U.S. Department of Health, Education, and Welfare, 1979). The risk of cancer is related to the duration of tobacco use, the amount of daily smoking, the tar and nicotine content of the tobacco, and the depth of inhalation. Even passive smoking has been shown to be harmful to one's health (Sandler et al., 1985). It has been estimated that 90 percent of the risk of bronchogenic carcinoma can be attributed to smoking. Both tobacco and alcohol are known to contribute to cancer of the esophagus.

Cancer of the cervix is more common in black than in white women. Where diagnosed early, this is a highly treatable form of cancer. The continuing deaths for black women from cervical cancer is a marker of the inadequate prevention and treatment they receive. A number of risk factors have been associated with cervical cancer, but there is still a great deal to be learned about its causes (Hulka, 1982; Kessler and Adams, 1976). The predominant view is that it is related to sexual behavior and probably precipitated by genital infection with the papilloma virus and herpes virus. Evidence concerning possible causes of prostate cancer other than age is still scanty. Dietary and hormonal factors are thought to be possible contributors.

Socioeconomic factors have been shown to be strongly related to the incidence, survival, and mortality from cancer (Nomura et al., 1981; Page and Kuntz, 1980). It is suspected that a significant portion of the higher rates in blacks is due to the higher proportion of persons in the lower socioeconomic positions who are less likely to receive such preventive services such as Pap smears and breast examinations, but a great deal of research is still needed.

Prevention strategies include cessation of smoking, reduction of alcohol use, and periodic Pap smears for early detection of cervical cancer. At the present time, the most important strategy for reducing prostate cancer is to work toward a better understanding of the causes and toward more effective means of early detection. Progress in the reduction of cancer will require more emphasis on prevention research and on education of the black community with respect to the early signs and to the necessary changes in health behavior.

OLDER ADULTS

DEMOGRAPHIC CHARACTERISTICS AND HEALTH

Black adults reach age 65 with life histories of disproportionate prevalence of acute and chronic disease, illness, and disability. They have had poorer quality of health care from conception and birth, continuing exposure to greater and more severe environmental risk factors, and the stress of prejudice and discrimination (Cooper et al., 1981). Cohort data for cause-specific mortality and morbidity over the past four decades suggest the presence of accumulated deficits across the early years of the life course. These deficits place black older people at greater risk for morbidity and mortality than whites of comparable ages.

Older age among blacks, as in the general population, is not a time of inevitable decline (Katzman, 1985; Rowe, 1985). Changes in life-styles, reductions in environmental risks, and medical interventions can positively affect the quality of late life of older black adults. Survey data (Gibson and Jackson, 1987) reveal that many of the black oldest old (80 years and older) are free from functional disability and limitations of activity due to chronic illness and disease. Health care improved tremendously with the passage and implementation of Medicare and Medicaid in 1965, and consecutive cohorts of older blacks are better educated and thus more likely to take advantage of available health resources.

The changing age structure of this society will have important effects on the health of older blacks. Over the past 40 years, the percentage of the population in the 65 and older age group has grown, and this increase will continue over the next several decades (see Table 8-7). It is projected that by the year 2020, blacks and whites over age 65 will constitute approximately 12 and 19 percent of the total black and white populations, respectively. The greatest proportionate growth for both blacks and whites will be in the oldest old-age categories.

Disproportionate growth of the older segment of the population, particularly among the very old, will create severe cost and support burdens to care for frail individuals (Davis, 1986; Siegel and Taeuber, 1986; Soldo, 1980). An increasingly elderly society is already placing strains on public sources of health care financing (Davis, 1986; Davis et al., 1987). Black older adults are more dependent than whites on public health care resources because their past lower earnings and greater job instability have made many ineligible for private pension plans, decreased their ability to accumulate personal savings, and restricted their Social Security accumulations. New limitations on public programs and the increased privatization of health care delivery systems will make it relatively more difficult for older blacks to meet rising health care costs.

TABLE 8-7 Elderly Population by Race (percentage of total population), 1950–2020

Race and Age	1950	1960	1970	1980	1990	2000	2010	2020
White								
65+	8.4	9.6	10.2	11.9	13.6	14.0	14.9	18.6
70+	5.0	6.0	6.7	7.9	9.3	10.4	10.5	12.7
75+	2.7	3.3	3.9	4.7	5.9	7.0	7.3	7.9
80+	1.2	1.5	1.9	2.5	3.2	4.1	4.7	4.7
85+	0.4	0.5	0.7	1.1	1.5	2.7	3.4	3.5
Black								
65+	5.7	6.3	6.8	7.8	8.2	8.4	8.9	11.6
70+	3.0	3.7	4.1	4.9	5.6	6.0	6.1	7.4
75+	1.6	1.9	2.2	2.8	3.5	3.9	4.1	4.5
80+	0.8	0.9	1.1	1.4	1.8	2.3	2.6	2.7
85+	0.3	0.4	0.5	0.6	0.9	1.2	1.4	1.5

Sources: Data from decennial censuses and Census Bureau projections.

Significant improvement in the social and economic status of older blacks has occurred over the past four decades (Jackson, 1981). Since 1950, individuals over the age of 65 have enjoyed an increase in unadjusted median income. Older black adults in comparison to whites, however, continue to experience relative disadvantages (Jackson, 1981). Family income for people aged 65 years and older does not vary much by type of household. As in the general black population, female-headed households are relatively disadvantaged. Although 39 percent of blacks over 65 lived in poverty in 1981, it represented a large decrease from 1959, when 63 percent of black older adults had incomes below the poverty line. If slightly more generous criteria for poverty are used—designating poor persons as those whose incomes are less than 125 percent of the poverty level—then in 1980 approximately 52 percent of blacks over the age of 65 were poor (Chen, 1985). Among female-headed households, some 69 percent of blacks over the age of 65 were below 125 percent of the poverty level.

An examination of sources of income clearly indicates why elderly blacks are in poverty: 22 percent of the black population over age 65 receive support from Supplemental Security Income, reflecting their prior poor earning status. Only 5 percent receive any income from savings; in contrast, 36 percent of the white older adult population has income from savings. The largest sources of income for blacks, in and out of poverty, is from government programs such as Social Security and Supplemental Security Income. Of special note is the fact that for every family type and living arrangement, black older adults receive approximately $2,000 less Social Security income than comparable whites (Jackson, 1985). Jackson and Gibson (1985) found in 1980 that the black elderly were more likely to be working and to be dependent on single sources of funds, largely public, for their support. Few reported receiving any financial support from relatives or friends. Given the general poverty rates and financial status across the adult life spans of blacks, family and friends have few resources to share with older black adults.

The longer survival of females than males means that there are few males relative to females for middle-aged and older adults. In 1985, for example, in the total population aged 65 and older there were 67 males for every 100 females. For the ages over 75, there were 54 males for every 100 females. The sex ratios for blacks were not significantly different: 64 males for every 100 females aged 65 to 74 and 56 males for every 100 females among those 75 years of age or older. The projections to the year 2020 suggest a decrease in the black sex ratio, while the white sex ratio is projected as remaining constant and even showing a slight increase.

MORTALITY AND MORBIDITY

Although there is disagreement regarding the extent of the change, most observers find that the health status of older blacks has improved considerably over the past few decades, particularly with the advent of Medicaid and Medicare in the mid-1960s. Among indicators of this improvement are an increase in private physician care and a slight increase in nursing home placements for older black adults. The latter improvement is particularly relevant given the increasing numbers of oldest old blacks, the largest prospective users of nursing home care.

Although both blacks and whites have made gains in life expectancy, there has been a persisting lag in gains for blacks. Between 1900 and 1984, the expected remaining years of life at age 65 increased from 11.5 to 14.8 for white men; from 10.4 to 13.4 for black men; from 12.2 to 18.8 for white women; and from 11.4 to 17.5 for black women.

A crossover in expected remaining years of life between blacks and whites occurs in the oldest ages (Manton et al., 1979). At about age 80, black men and women can expect to outlive their white counterparts. It has been suggested, but not established, that this crossover in expected years of life is due to the weeding out of all but the hardiest blacks by very old age as a result of their earlier greater susceptibility to illness and violent death (Siegel and Davidson, 1984).

Omran (1977) reported that the largest increment in life expectancy extension occurred with the eradication of infectious diseases. The current major killers in middle and older ages for both black and white men in 1980 were heart disease (including arteriosclerosis), cancer, accidents, cerebrovascular disease, and homicide. For black and white women, the rank ordering of the leading causes of death is similar to that of males, the only difference being that cerebrovascular disease ranks third rather than fourth. For black women, pneumonia is no longer among the four leading causes of death, while accidents now play a larger role than in earlier periods. For black men, there has been an increase in cancers and a reduction of cerebrovascular disease as causes of death.

Only a few categories of causes account for the majority of the individual deaths in the total population over 65 years of age (Brody and Brock, 1985; Jackson, 1981; Siegel, 1980; Siegel and Davidson, 1984). Diseases of the heart accounted for 44 percent of all deaths in 1980, and the combination of diseases of the heart, malignant neoplasms, and cerebrovascular diseases accounted for 75 percent of all deaths. While there has been a decrease in heart disease for both black men and women since 1950, this decrease has not been as steep as the decrease for white males. Jackson (1981) notes that the general decline in death rates from heart disease is undoubtedly due to better medical care and greater efficiency in diagnosing and managing hypertension. There have also been reductions in cerebrovascular disease as a cause of death in all race and sex groupings at each decade over the 30-year period. The rates for white men and women are higher than the rates for blacks over this period only in the over age 85 groups (Kuller, 1985).

The importance of cardiovascular disease (diseases of the heart, cerebrovascular diseases, and arteriosclerosis) as a cause of death for older blacks can be estimated by calculating what the remaining years of life would be if a particular cause of death was totally eliminated (Siegel, 1980; Siegel and Davidson, 1984; Siegel and Taeuber, 1986). For the total population over the age of 65 in 1978, an average of 14.3 years would have been added to the existing life expectancy if these diseases were totally eliminated. White and black men would have gained the fewest years (10.1 and 11.2, respectively), white women would have gained 17.4 years, and black women would have gained an additional 22.1 years of life. The relative importance of cardiovascular disease for black females is emphasized by noting that the elimination of malignant neoplasms in 1978, in contrast, would have added only 2 years to their life expectancy.

Measures of morbidity (including health self-assessments, reports on restrictions in minor and major activities, and work days lost) have consistently shown that the black elderly have greater morbidity than older whites (Gibson, 1986; Shanas, 1980; Siegel and Davidson, 1984). While good trend data comparing blacks and whites are not available prior to 1965, the findings since then reveal diminishing but continued race differences in the major morbidity indicators (Shanas, 1980). Table 8-8 shows the race by sex differentials for 1978–1980. These differences are representative of the trends over the past two decades.

BARRIERS TO HEALTH UTILIZATION AND HEALTH CARE

It has often been claimed that older blacks suffer perceived and actual psychological, social, and structural barriers to health care (Haywood, 1984; Jackson, 1981; James et al., 1984; Kasl, 1984; Myers, 1984; Woodlander et al., 1985). The usual explanation offered is that low social status is a major impediment to good health care. Recent writings on this topic, however, suggest that other factors may be involved (Davis and Lillie-Blanton, 1987; Davis and Rowland, 1983; Neighbors and Jackson, 1986, 1987). James and colleagues (1984) found that blacks with hypertension of all social classes

TABLE 8-8 Selected Morbidity Indicators for Elderly People, by Race, 1978–1980

Selected Morbidity Indicator	White				Black			
	All Ages		65 and Over		All Ages		65 and Over	
	Male	Female	Male	Female	Male	Female	Male	Female
Limitation in major activity due to chronic condition (percent)	11.2	10.5	42.5	34.2	12.7	12.2	56.5	46.5
Restricted activity (days per year)	16.6	20.6	34.1	41.4	19.0	20.5	54.3	58.7
Bed disability (days per year)	5.5	7.6	11.4	13.9	8.0	10.7	24.8	21.5
Time (days) lost from work	4.6	5.1	3.5	4.9	7.1	8.3	3.5	6.5

Source: Data from National Center for Health Statistics (1984).

report less frequent use of medical care, more difficulties in getting into the health care system, and greater dissatisfaction with medical care services than do similarly afflicted whites. Woodlander and colleagues (1985) estimated that one-third of the excess of black over white deaths in Alameda County, California, in 1978 were preventable, and they proposed that inequalities in health services reinforce broader social inequalities and are in part responsible for disparities in mortality. Cooper and colleagues (1981) reached a similar conclusion.

Lack of financial resources is clearly implicated as a major barrier to good medical care (Davis and Rowland, 1983; Jackson, 1981, 1985). In analyses of 1980 national survey data, Neighbors and Jackson (1986, 1987) found that both lack of insurance coverage and perceived barriers to health care contributed to blacks' perceptions of a lack of quality care available to them. Other factors, however, including racial discrimination in treatment, lack of knowledge of racial and ethnic group life-styles, and cultural factors, also seem to act as barriers to effective treatment (Cooper et al., 1981; Haywood, 1984; James et al., 1984; Kasl, 1984).

Following the introduction of Medicare and Medicaid, many people have argued that financial resources are no longer a serious barrier to care (Siegel and Davidson, 1984). However, recent analyses (Davis, 1986; Palmer and Gould, 1986) suggest that extensive copayment requirements and facets of needed health care that are not covered by government programs necessitate the contribution of significant personal financial resources in order to obtain quality care at older ages (Berk and Wilensky, 1985).

PROVISION OF HEALTH CARE

As already noted, access to health care has improved considerably for black Americans since the early 1960s. However, on several indicators of access, black-white differentials have remained constant, and those gains that have been made have not been shared evenly among blacks. Data on health insurance coverage, sources of care, use of health services, and quality of care provide evidence of access to and entry into the health care system. In this section we review each of these areas as well as data concerning minority professionals and current trends in the minority work force.

INSURANCE COVERAGE

Funding sources for health care services in the United States have changed enormously in the past four decades. The proportion of the population with health insurance for hospital care increased from 57 percent in 1953 to 68 percent in 1963 (U.S. Department of Health, Education, and Welfare, 1979). Since then health coverage has been broadened to cover outpatient services, and with the enactment of Medicaid (for the poor) and Medicare (for the elderly) in 1965, the number of poor and elderly black and white Americans with health coverage under public programs increased greatly. Since 1970, Medicaid has provided health coverage for about one of every five blacks under age 65. Approximately one-third of all Medicaid beneficiaries are black, and Medicare's coverage of the elderly has assured minimum benefits for blacks aged 65 or older. The gap between the number of blacks and whites with no health coverage has declined, although the trend since 1978 has been toward an increase in the percentage of both black and white Americans with no health coverage. Black Americans are still much less likely to have health coverage than whites.

In 1984, an estimated 22 percent of blacks and 14 percent of whites under age 65 were not covered by either public or private health insurance (National Center for Health Statistics, 1987c), and those figures have been rising since then. Children's risk of being uninsured is slightly higher, 25 percent of black and 17 percent of white children in 1984 (Sulvetta and Swartz, 1986); those figures have also been rising. Current Population Survey data show that in 1986, 61 percent of all children who were uninsured came from poor and near-poor families. The Office of Technology Assessment estimates that 19 percent of children under age 13 were uninsured in 1986. This is an increase from the 17 percent who were uninsured in 1980 (Swartz, 1986).

Between 1978 and 1986 federal appropriations for maternal and child health services declined (in 1978 dollars) by 43 percent, for Community Health Centers by 11 percent, and for migrant health centers by 33 percent (Office of Technology Assessment, 1988). Medicaid eligibility has been restricted and payments to physicians have been reduced along with other reforms of Medicaid designed to reduce expenditures. As a result of these changes, more than one-third of physicians in obstetrics, pediatrics, and other specialties refuse to participate. Low fees are the chief reason for nonparticipation, but payment delays and paperwork are also cited.

Uninsured blacks and whites continue to face serious problems in obtaining ambulatory care comparable to that obtained by those with health coverage. Data from metropolitan areas (averaged for 1978–1980) show that about one-third of uninsured blacks and whites under age 65 had not seen a physician in the past year, compared with about one-fourth of blacks and whites with private coverage and one-sixth of blacks and whites covered by Medicaid (Trevino and Moss, 1983).

Previous research generally has characterized black older adults as having greater morbidity and, thus, greater need for health care than white older adults (Kovar, 1980). Yet, they have typically received less health care than whites. Davis (1986) reported racial disparities in service utilization under Medicare during the initial years of the program. An examination of the program in more recent years found that although differences had narrowed, blacks were still receiving less care than whites (Ruther and Dobson, 1981). A 1980 survey (Robert Wood Johnson Foundation, 1983) found that approximately 12 percent of the total population reported problems in getting access to health care—and the problems were greater among poor blacks and other racial minorities. Other work has shown less health insurance coverage among blacks, less continuity of insurance coverage, and more dissatisfaction with health care (Neighbors and Jackson, 1986).

Barriers to access to care are also experienced by a substantial number of blacks who are underinsured, a number estimated to be between 1 million and 2 million in 1984 (P. Farley, 1985). Counting these and the more than 6.4 million blacks who are uninsured, at least one in four black Americans faces a potential barrier in access to ambulatory and hospital care (Davis and Lillie-Blanton, 1987).

SOURCES OF CARE

Blacks are twice as likely as whites to be without a regular source of medical care or to have no regular source other than a hospital outpatient department or emergency room. Some reversals in these patterns have been achieved in the past 20 years, but in 1983, 27 percent of blacks, compared with 13 percent of whites, reported a hospital outpatient department or emergency room as their usual source of care (National Center for Health Statistics, 1986). In 1985 blacks used emergency services at about twice the rate that whites did (Table 8-9).

The use of hospital outpatient departments and emergency rooms has implications for both quality and continuity of care. Diagnosis and treatment are enhanced by a provider's knowledge of a patient's history, by patient follow-up, and by a good provider-patient relationship. The potential for each of these is greatly reduced in hospital outpatient departments and emergency rooms. The consequences of not having a health care provider who serves as an entry point into the health care system or who monitors the care received can be serious. The U.S. health care system is highly decentralized and complex, with many specialties and subspecialties. For this large and often impersonal system, a primary provider who can facilitate the

TABLE 8-9 Physician Visits per Capita, by Race and Source of Care (in percent), 1964–1985

Year and Place of Visit	Visits per Capita		Black/White Ratio
	Whites	Blacks	
Year			
1964	4.7	3.6	0.77
1980	4.8	4.6	0.96
1983	5.1	4.8	0.94
1985	5.3	4.9	0.92
Source of care			
Doctor's office, clinic, or group practice			
1964	71.0%	56.2%	0.79
1985	58.4%	47.6%	0.82
Hospital outpatient department or emergency room			
1964	10.2%	32.7%	3.21
1985	13.1%	24.8%	1.89

Note: Values for source of care do not add to 100 percent because they do not include all sources or places of care (e.g., house calls and telephone visits).

Source: Data derived from National Health Interview Surveys.

linkage with the most appropriate form of care can make a difference in access to and receipt of health services.

One indicator of access to health care can be found in the number of physician visits per year. In the early 1960s, blacks were more likely than whites to report their health as poor or fair and to suffer from chronic conditions, but they saw physicians less frequently than whites did. In 1964, blacks (and other minorities) saw physicians an average of 3.6 times per year, compared with an average of 4.7 times per year for whites (see Table 8-9). By 1985, the gap between whites and blacks had narrowed, with blacks averaging 4.9 visits per year and whites 5.3 visits per year (National Center for Health Statistics, 1987c). However, there are subgroups of the black population that appear to face continued barriers in access to health care. For example, striking racial differences in the use of physician services are evident in data for blacks and whites who are uninsured, under age 17, living in the South, living in rural parts of the country, or seeking care for specific medical conditions (Davis and Rowland, 1983; Trevino and Moss, 1984; U.S. Department of Health and Human Services, 1985b).

In 1980 older blacks and whites differed little in their number of physician contacts. In fact, older black men and women reported slightly more contacts on average (Davis and Rowland, 1983). Overall, the difference between blacks and whites in the use of various physician specialties has narrowed over the past 10 years. Some data also suggest a decrease in racial differences in the "quality" of physician visits for the same time period. In 1981, there was a decrease in racial differences in reported first visits, the length of visits, and the average number of rescheduled visits. In all categories of quality of care, blacks show improvement between 1964 and 1983. Nearly three-quarters

TABLE 8-10 Elderly Residents of Nursing Homes and Personal Care Homes (number per 1,000 population), by Race and Age, 1963–1977

Race and Age[a]	1963	1969	1973–1974[b]	1977[c]
White				
65 and over	26.6	38.8	47.3	49.7
65–74	8.1	11.7	12.5	14.2
75–84	41.7	54.1	61.9	70.6
85 and over	157.7	221.9	269.0	229.0
Black				
65 and over	10.3	17.6	21.9	30.4
65–74	5.9	9.6	10.6	16.8
75–84	13.8	22.9	30.1	38.6
85 and over	41.8	52.4	91.4	102.0

[a]For data for the years 1963–1969, Hispanic origin was not designated; therefore, Hispanics may be included in either the white or all other category. For data for the years 1973–1974 and 1977, Hispanics were included in the white category.

[b]Excludes residents in personal care or domiciliary care homes.

[c]Includes residents in domiciliary care homes.

Source: Data from National Center for Health Statistics (1987c).

now report having seen a physician within the past year, and the percentages reporting no visits over 2 years have decreased appreciably, from 21.8 percent in 1964 to 12.6 percent in 1983. For the period 1978–1980, black and white older adults do not differ in the intervals since last physician visits.

In 1980, 5 percent of the total population over 65 was in nursing homes (Kovar, 1980). Rates of nursing home use, however, differ greatly by age and sex. Rates are 11 times higher for men over 85 than for men aged 65–69 and 16 times higher for men over 85 than for women aged 65–69 (Rice and Feldman, 1983). The use of nursing homes by both males and females has increased progressively since 1963 (see Table 8-10). Although there has been less use of nursing homes by blacks than other racial groups, blacks have experienced a similar increase over time.

It is estimated that by the year 2040, persons in the over-85-year group will constitute over 50 percent of the demand for nursing home beds or other long-term services (Soldo and Manton, 1985). By the year 2040 there will be 13.3 million Americans over the age of 85, 4 million of whom will require some type of personal assistance in daily living. These numbers could translate into a total need for 2.7 million nursing home beds.

Preventive Care

Preventive care and access to it are critical components of long-range efforts to reduce illness or disability within a population. In the recent past, blacks had far fewer general physical examinations than did whites. Since 1970, this situation has considerably improved (U.S. Department of Health and Human Services, 1985e, 1986a). By 1984, 62 percent of black women, com-

TABLE 8-11 Hospital Discharges per 100 Persons, by Race and Poverty Status, 1964–1979

	Poor				Nonpoor			
Race	1964	1973	1976	1979	1964	1973	1976	1979
White	15	20	19	21	13	13	13	13
Black (and others)	10	15	17	17	10	12	12	12
White/black ratio	1.50	1.33	1.12	1.24	1.30	1.08	1.08	1.08

Source: Data from President's Commission for the Study of Ethical Problems in Medicine and Biomedical and Behavioral Research (1983).

pared with 80 percent of white women, began prenatal care in the first trimester of pregnancy (Anderson et al., 1987). Immunizations for preventable diseases show a similar pattern.

Difficulties of access and issues of confidentiality, consent, and ability to pay pose barriers that make adolescents reluctant to seek care. Black youth like black children and adults chiefly receive care in emergency rooms, public clinics, and hospitals rather than in office-based facilities. In 1986, the Robert Wood Johnson Foundation found that 20 percent of blacks and 16 percent of whites reported no regular source of care. In addition to the conditions discussed in this chapter, mental health problems and chronic and handicapping conditions also represent significant unmet needs.

Adolescents tend to seek care only when they are acutely ill, injured, or pregnant. However, preventive health care and health promotion are especially important for them. This is the age group when many adult patterns of health behavior will be established. The reluctance of adolescents to seek health care makes outreach an important component of health care delivery. Adolescent health problems are often multiple and intercorrelated. Most health settings are not prepared at a single site to offer services for drug or alcohol abuse, sexually transmitted diseases, prenatal care, assessment of learning disorders, and so on. Community-based comprehensive adolescent health services, including school-related clinics, seem to offer promise for meeting the special needs of adolescents.

Hospital Care

Hospital care or at least access to it can be indicated by hospital discharge rates. From 1964 to 1979, hospital discharge rates (hospital discharges per 100 persons) of blacks and other minorities increased, reducing the black-white gap almost entirely among the nonpoor (President's Commission for the Study of Ethical Problems in Medicine and Biomedical and Behavioral Research, 1983); see Table 8-11. More recent data, unadjusted for income or health status, indicate that the progress achieved by blacks has been maintained. Excluding deliveries, hospital discharge rates in 1985 were 10.7 for blacks and 11.1 for whites (U.S. Department of Health and Human Services, 1986a).

Several studies, however, report black-white differences in the use of hospital services by Medicaid beneficiaries. One study found hospital discharge rates for black Medicaid beneficiaries of 224 per 1,000 compared with 400 per 1,000 for white beneficiaries even after adjusting for socioeconomic characteristics and health conditions (O'Brien et al., 1985). Studies of blacks in the general population provide contradictory evidence. The studies differ methodologically in so many ways that the varied findings could well be a result of differences in the study designs. Further research will be required to evaluate gains in access to hospital care.

Among people aged 65 and older, black-white differences in the use of hospital inpatient services declined substantially between 1965 and 1982. Rates for blacks and other minorities, unadjusted for health status, were fairly similar to those of whites (Ruther and Dobson, 1981). Evidence regarding access to long term care facilities is less reassuring. In 1977, elderly blacks were about half as likely as whites to receive care in nursing homes. As noted above, however, this finding reflects a considerable narrowing of the gap observed in 1963. The factors that account for differential use of nursing home services are unclear, but continuing racial and economic barriers have been identified and are under investigation (Lief, 1985; National Senior Citizens Law Center, 1980).

QUALITY OF CARE

Little research has been conducted on quality of care by race (or any other demographic characteristic). It cannot be assumed that the greater equity in the quantity of care obtained is matched by an increasing equity in quality of care. Varying population needs, ill-defined standards, and unsystematic evaluation have made the assessment of differences in quality difficult.

While the evidence is by no means definitive, there are ample data to suggest that some black-white differences in quality exist. For example, Mitchell and Cromwell (1980) found that physicians with large Medicaid practices were less qualified (as measured by board certification, age, and hospital-admitting privileges) than physicians with a small percentage of Medicaid patients. Janzen (1973) reported that the quality of care (as measured by interpersonal aspects of care received by patients in 19 Michigan hospitals) was lower for blacks than for whites, even though there were few differences in the technical aspects of care. Similar findings were reported by Gottesman and Bourestom (1974) on the basis of a survey of nursing home residents.

Differences in source of care are one indicator of likely differences in quality of care. Egbert and Rothman (1977) found that between 1952 and 1972, black patients and Medicaid patients in a Maryland hospital were significantly more likely to be operated on by a surgical resident than by a staff surgeon. And, as noted above, current survey data also show that blacks are more likely than whites to obtain care from emergency rooms and hospital outpatient departments. While the technical care rendered in these situations cannot be assumed to be of lower quality, the interpersonal aspects of care are in question.

But other studies report no inequities in quality of health care by race. Furthermore, most of the studies on quality are from a single locality or health care setting, and their findings cannot necessarily be generalized. After a critical assessment of the available literature, Wyszewianski and Donabedian (1981) concluded that there are few studies that have shown that any one population group disproportionately receives poor quality care.

The lack of research and data that can be used to answer questions about the appropriateness or adequacy of care has seriously hindered the assessment of differences in the quality of care received. Although empirical evidence of inequities in quality is minimal, it is unlikely that the economic and racial stratifications that historically existed in this country have been fully reversed in 20 years. Some of the Medicaid systems of payment or financial incentive (e.g., reimbursement at prevailing rates in an area) probably help to maintain some of the differences in care provided in higher income and white neighborhoods in contrast to lower income and black neighborhoods. Whether the differences result in lower quality care still needs to be examined in well-designed research.

HEALTH PROFESSIONALS AND WORK FORCE

There are relatively few black health professionals. In 1950, 2.1 percent of all the physicians in the United States were black, and in 1983, the number had barely increased, to 2.7 percent. In 1981, less than 2 percent of the faculties of U.S. medical schools were black (Sullivan, 1983:807). Black women in medicine were more underrepresented than black men or white women in the profession: in 1980, 11.6 percent of all physicians were women, a mere 0.8 percent of all physicians were black women. Aggregate national data on dentists, registered nurses, optometrists, and pharmacists also show ratios of the number of black professionals in these areas to black population to be well below similar ratios for the nonminority population (U.S. Department of Health and Human Services, 1985b). Table 8-12 shows the percentages of blacks in selected health occupations.

During the 1960s and 1970s efforts were made to increase the representation of blacks and other minorities in the health professions. These efforts were motivated by a desire to improve access to health care on the assumption that minority health personnel would be more likely to serve minority patients and the poor. Although more than 80 percent of black patients report having a white physician as their primary provider, the assumption is supported by the fact that more than 80 percent of the clients of black physicians are black (McKinney, 1986:214; see also Keith et al., 1985; U.S. Department of Health and Human Services, 1985b:383). The location and practice patterns of minority health professionals are significantly different from those of majority health professionals (Hanft et al., 1985:8; Keith et al., 1985). Black practitioners are more likely than whites to locate in areas

TABLE 8-12 Black Employment (as percentage of total employment) in Selected Health Occupations, 1983

Occupation	Black Percentage of Total
Physicians	2.7
Dentists	3.2
Registered nurses	6.7
Physician's assistants	7.7
Licensed practical nurses	17.7
Health technologists and technicians	12.7
Nursing aides, orderlies, and attendants	27.3
Therapists	7.6

Source: McKinney (1986:204).

with high percentages of poverty and in urban areas with significant black populations (Hanft et al., 1985:8–9).

The proportion of black health professionals serving black populations is not likely to change appreciably in the near future. In virtually none of the states considered in a relatively recent study does the percentage of black graduates of medical, dental, and pharmacy schools (the three disciplines examined) approach the percentage of blacks in the population. Thus, even if the numbers of black graduates continue to rise, it is not likely that they will significantly alter black professional-to-population ratios in the near future (U.S. Department of Health and Human Services, 1985b:384).

Black students in medical schools increased most in the late 1960s and early 1970s: the percentage of black first-year students rose from 2.7 percent to 7.5 percent. But the percentage then fell to under 7 percent and remained at that level throughout the rest of the 1970s and into the 1980s (see Figure 8-6). The percentages of minorities enrolling in and graduating from medical school have changed little since the mid-1970s, even though the percentage of minority applicants to medical schools increased 12 percent between 1974–1975 and 1981–1982 (U.S. Department of Health and Human Services, 1984:21, 36). Because of decreased funds for student financial aid (Sandson, 1983) and because most black medical students come from families with annual incomes below $20,000 (Hanft et al., 1983), there is a very real possibility that the number of blacks enrolling in medical schools in the future will drop precipitously (see Association of American Medical Colleges, 1983).

Comparisons of first-year enrollment for minority women in schools of medicine since 1971 show that minority women have increased their representation in medical schools at a faster rate than all women or minority males. Black women were 20.4 percent of black medical students in 1971–1972, 38.2 percent in 1977–1978, and 44.9 percent in 1983–1984 (U.S. Department of Health and Human Services, 1984:35, 39).

The contribution of the predominantly black medical schools to the education of black physicians is significant. Despite considerable expansion in medical education in the United States during the past 25 years, in 1981–

FIGURE 8-6 Blacks as a percentage of the U.S. population, of undergraduate students, and of first-year enrollees in schools of medicine, 1970-1971 to 1983–1984.

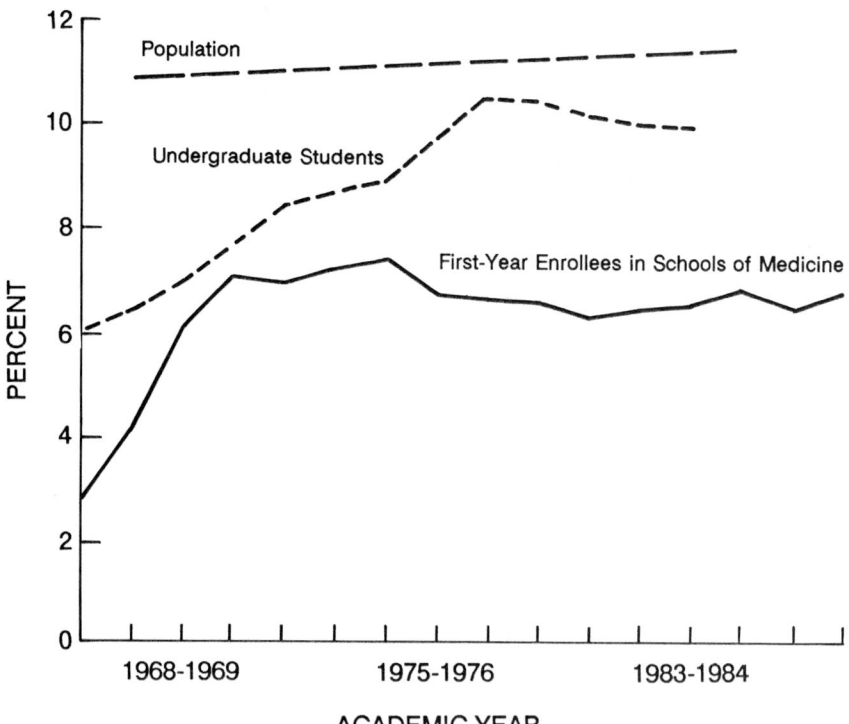

Source: Data from U.S. Department of Health and Human Services.

1982 the four predominantly black medical schools (Morehouse, Meharry, Drew, and Howard) had almost 25 percent of the black students in the nation's 127 medical schools. Six of the nation's medical schools had no black students, and 75 (61 percent) had a black student enrollment of less than 5 percent. Other studies have shown that more than 60 percent of the graduates of Meharry and Howard medical schools practice in inner cities and rural areas (Lloyd et al., 1978; Sullivan, 1983).

Black nonphysician health employees are concentrated in the lower wage health occupations of aides, practical nurses, and technicians. Blacks hold 24 percent of health service jobs. These same occupations are also female dominated. Given changes taking place in the industry, earnings are not likely to grow as rapidly as they did in the 1970s. In fact, licensed practical nurses, nursing aides, custodial workers, dieticians, and kitchen workers, as well as other support workers, are expected to experience significant reductions in demand for their services by the nation's hospitals (McKinney, 1986:202–206, 212).

CONCLUSIONS

Over the past 50 years there has been enormous progress in the health statuses of both blacks and whites. This progress has been most striking for females. However, a considerable relative disadvantage for blacks remains. A common hypothesis is that the difference is mainly due to the higher proportion of blacks in the lower income groups. This is a plausible argument based on the well-known association between income and health. Poverty limits access to medical care. Medicare and Medicaid have been identified as factors that have contributed to improved health statuses for both blacks and whites.

While available data do not provide conclusive evidence, it does appear that access to care by minorities and the poor increases with the availability of minority providers. The recent trends of stabilization or decline in numbers of black health professional students, particularly in medicine, thus signal continuation in the future of access problems, especially in poor rural areas.

With many public hospitals in financial crisis, private hospitals experiencing higher uncompensated care debts, and an increase in for-profit health care providers, the uninsured and underinsured are likely to encounter greater rather than fewer barriers in access to care. The data suggest that black Americans are at a relative disadvantage in obtaining quality health care, because they are more likely than whites to be uninsured and to rely on hospital-based providers for their primary care.

Over the past two decades, there had been significant progress in reducing the prior inequities and assuring that poor and minority children had adequate access to health care. This was accomplished through a number of policy actions that included the targeting and expansion of maternal and child health services under Title V of the Social Security Act, the development of Head Start, the formation of community health centers, and the establishment of Medicaid as health insurance for the nation's poor. By the mid-1970s, based on medical visits per year, indicators showed major gains in access for the poor. However, the pattern of care has differed. Poor and minority children obtain care in hospital emergency rooms and hospital clinics rather than from a private physician. This care results in little continuity for poor black children and imposes hardships in terms of the conditions of obtaining care. In general, these visits represent serious medical conditions; parents do not tend to bring children for routine or preventive care.

The use of medical care by children has been found to be highly sensitive to the cost of obtaining care. The Medicaid program offers care for many of the very poorest children but typically in settings that make access more burdensome for Medicaid children and serve to reduce access. When parents cut back on health visits, they have not discriminated well between visits that are highly effective and those that are not (Leibowitz et al., 1985). Poor children and minority children are disproportionately affected by these erosions of access to care. Some of the sensitive indicators such as low birthweight in neonates, as discussed, have already shown slowed decline or reversals. There are concerns that the adverse effects are pervasive across the life course.

Many of the problems responsible for the current gap in health conditions between blacks and whites are problems for which medical knowledge is deficient, for example, knowledge of the causes of hypertension, low birthweight, or cancer of the prostate. But progress in health status does not always depend on full knowledge of causation. There has been significant recent progress in reducing rates of hypertension among blacks, without further knowledge of its primary causes.

Preventive health services and systematic programs of outreach have demonstrated their effectiveness in prenatal and infant care. The same concepts apply to other periods of the life span and to such problems as teenage pregnancy, hypertension, AIDS, and to the long-term care that is likely to be a major health problem of the black elderly in the near future.

There is also growing awareness of the importance of interventions that provide early treatment or prevent health-damaging personal behaviors relating to sexually transmitted diseases, smoking, drugs, and alcohol. In the specific *Objectives for the Nation* (U.S. Department of Health and Human Services, 1980), the overall goal set by the surgeon general was to improve the health habits of youth and by 1990 to reduce deaths among people aged 15–24 by at least 20 percent, from a 1977 baseline of 115 to fewer than 93 per 100,000. Progress has been made but the goals have not yet been met. A midcourse review by HHS of the status of these objectives in 1986 showed that none of them were met for black youth regarding sexually transmitted diseases, smoking, drugs, or alcohol (U.S. Department of Health and Human Services, 1986b).

Many of the problems that contribute to the differentials in health status are not subject to a simple medical solution, but require an understanding of social and individual behavior and an appreciation for comprehensive interdisciplinary approaches. The disparities in black and white rates of homicide, teenage pregnancy, or AIDS are not likely to be eliminated purely by medical science even with the best public health expertise available.

Due to progress in the prevention and cure of most infectious diseases, chronic diseases are now a significant source of illness in the United States and other developed countries. For both blacks and whites, behavioral factors are crucial in the development and management of these chronic diseases. The combination of these behavioral factors with fewer resources to meet daily needs, less opportunity to obtain these resources, and less power to overcome disadvantaged circumstances largely accounts for blacks' poorer health status.

REFERENCES

Andersen, R., M. Chen, L. Aday, and L. Cornelius
1987 Health status and medical care utilization. *Health Affairs* 6(Spring)(1):136–156.
Armstrong, K. A.
1981 A treatment and education program for parents and children who are at risk of abuse and neglect. *Child Abuse and Neglect* 5:167–175.
Association of American Medical Colleges
1983 *Minority Students in Medical Education: Facts and Figures.* Washington, D.C.: Office of Minority Affairs.
Berk, M. L., and G. R. Wilensky
1985 Health care of the poor elderly: supplementing Medicare. *Gerontologist* 25:311–314.
Bloom, D. E., and G. Carliner
1988 The economic impact of AIDS in the United States. *Science* 239:604–609.
Bohman, M., S. Siquaardsson, and R. Cloninger
1981 Material inheritance of alcohol abuse. *Archives of General Psychiatry* 38:965–969.
Botvin, G. J., A. Eng, and C. L. Williams
1980 Preventing the onset of cigarette smoking through life skills training. *Journal of Preventive Medicine* 9:135–143.
Brenner, M. H.
1983 Mortality and economic stability: detailed analysis for Britain and comparative analysis for selected industrialized countries. *International Journal of Health Services* 13(4):563.
Brody, J. A., and D. B. Brock
1985 Epidemiologic and statistical characteristics of the United States elderly population. In C. E. Finch and E. L. Schneider, eds., *Handbook of the Biology of Aging.* New York: Van Nostrand Reinhold.
Centers for Disease Control
1983 *Nutrition Surveillance.* DHHS Pub. No. 8. Washington, D.C.: U.S. Department of Health and Human Services.
1985 *Preventing Lead Poisoning in Young Children.* DHHS Pub. No. 99-2230. Washington, D.C.: U.S. Department of Health and Human Services.
1986a *Morbidity and Mortality Weekly Report* 35:272.
1986b Acquired immunodeficiency syndrome (AIDS) among blacks and Hispanics—United States. *Morbidity and Mortality Weekly Report* 35(42):655–666.
1987 Human immunodeficiency virus infection in the United States. *Morbidity and Mortality Weekly Report* 36:1–20.
1988a Distribution of AIDS cases by racial/ethnic group and exposure category: United States, June 1, 1981–July 4, 1988. *Morbidity and Mortality Weekly Report* 55(3):1–10.
1988b Differences in death rates due to injury among blacks and whites. *Morbidity and Mortality Weekly Report* 55(3):25–32.
Chen, Y.
1985 Economic status of aging. Pp. 641–665 in R. B. Binstock and E. Shanas, eds., *Handbook of Aging and the Social Sciences.* New York: Van Nostrand Reinhold.
Conant, M., D. Hardy, J. Sernatinger, D. Spicer, and J. A. Levy
1986 Condoms prevent transmission of AIDS-associated retrovirus. *Journal of the American Medical Association* 255:1706.
Cooper, R.. M. Steinhauer, A. Schatzkin, and W. Miller
1981 Improved mortality among U.S. blacks, 1968–1978: the role of antiracist struggle. *International Journal of Health Services* 11:511–522.

Cravioto, J., and E. R. Delacardie
   1978 Nutrition, mental development and learning. In F. Faulkner and J. M. Tanner, eds., *Human Growth*. New York: Plenum Press.
Crimmins, Eileen M.
   1981 The changing pattern of American mortality decline, 1940–77, and its implications for the future. *American Journal of Sociology* 844(6):839–854.
Curran, J. W., H. W. Jaffe, A. M. Hardy, W. M. Morgan, R. M. Selik, and T. J. Dondero
   1988 Epidemiology of HIV infection and AIDS in the United States. *Science* 239(4840):610–616.
Davis, K.
   1986 Aging and the health-care system: economic and structural issues. *Daedalus* 115:227–246.
Davis, Karen, and Marsha Lillie-Blanton
   1987 Health Care for Black Americans: Trends in Financing and Delivery. Paper prepared for the Committee on the Status of Black Americans, National Research Council, Washington, D.C.
Davis, K., M. Lillie-Blanton, B. Lyons, F. Mullan, N. Powe, and D. Rowland
   1987 Health care for black Americans: the public sector role. Pp. 213–247 in David P. Willis, ed., *Currents of Health Policy: Impacts on Black Americans, Part 1. Milbank Quarterly* (Suppl.)65.
Davis, K., and D. Rowland
   1983 Uninsured and underserved: inequities in health care in the United States. *Milbank Quarterly* 61:149–176.
Davis, R. M.
   1987 Current trends in cigarette advertising and marketing. *New England Journal of Medicine* 316:725–732.
Dischinger, P. C., A. Y. Apostolides, G. Entwisle, and J. R. Hebel
   1981 Hypertension incidence in an inner city black population. *Journal of Chronic Diseases* 34:405–413.
Dutton, D. B.
   1981 Children's health care: the myth of equal access. Pp. 357–440 in *Better Health for Our Children: A National Strategy. Vol. IV, Background Papers*. DHHS Pub. No. 79-55071. Washington, D.C.: U.S. Department of Health and Human Services.
Easterling, R. E.
   1977 Racial factors in the incidence and causation of end-stage renal disease. *Transactions of the American Society for Artificial Internal Organs* 23:28–33.
Egbert, L. D., and I. L. Rothman
   1977 Relations between the race and economic status of patients and who performs their surgery. *New England Journal of Medicine* 297:90.
Egbuonu, L., and B. Starfield
   1982 Child health and social status. *Pediatrics* 69(S):550–557.
Engle, P. L., M. Irwin, R. E. Klein, C. Yarbrough, and J. W. Townsend
   1979 Nutrition and mental development in children. Pp. 291–306 in M. Winick, ed., *Human Nutrition: A Comprehensive Treatise*. Vol. 1. New York: Plenum Press.
Farley, Pamela
   1985 Who are the underinsured? *Milbank Memorial Fund Quarterly/Health and Society* 63(3):476–503.

Farley, Reynolds
1985 An Analysis of Mortality, 1940 to the Present. Paper prepared for the Committee on the Status of Black Americans, National Research Council, Washington, D.C.
1986 Racial Trends and Differentials in Mortality: 1940 to 1984. Revision of 1985 paper prepared for the Committee on the Status of Black Americans, National Research Council, Washington, D.C.

Farley, Reynolds, and Walter Allen
1987 *The Color Line and the Quality of American Life.* New York: Russell Sage Foundation.

Francis, D. P., and J. Chin
1987 The prevention of acquired immunodeficiency syndrome in the United States: an objective strategy for medicine, public health, business and the community. *Journal of the American Medical Association* 257:1357–1366.

Gibson, R.
1986 Blacks in an aging society. *Daedalus* 115:349–372.

Gibson, R. C., and J. S. Jackson
1987 The black aged. In Davis P. Willis, ed., *Currents of Health Policy: Impacts on Black Americans,* Part 2. *Milbank Quarterly* (Suppl.) 65.

Gillum, R.
1979 Pathophysiology of hypertension in blacks and whites: a review of the basis of racial blood pressure differences. *Hypertension* 1:468–475.

Goodwin, D. W., F. Schulsinger, and N. Moller
1974 Drinking problems in adopted and non-adopted sons of alcoholics. *Archives of General Psychology* 31:164–169.

Gottesman, L. E., and N. C. Bourestom
1974 Why nursing homes do what they do. *Gerontologist* 14:501.

Gray, J. D., C. A. Sutler, and J. G. Dean
1979 Prediction and prevention of child abuse and neglect. *Journal of Social Issues* 35(2):127–139.

Greenberg, M. R.
1983 *Urbanization and Cancer Mortality: The United States Experience 1950–1975.* New York: Oxford University Press.

Hanft, R. S., L. E. Fishman, and W. J. Evans
1983 *Blacks and the Health Professions in the 80's: A National Crisis and a Time for Action.* Washington, D.C.: Association of Minority Health Professions Schools.

Hanft, R. S., L. E. Fishman, and C. C. White
1985 Minorities and the Health Professions: An Update. Draft of August 1985, Association of Minority Health Professions Schools, Washington, D.C.

Hayes, Cheryl D., ed.
1987 *Risking the Future: Adolescent Sexuality, Pregnancy, and Childbearing.* Vol. I. Panel on Adolescent Pregnancy and Childbearing, Committee on Child Development Research and Public Policy, National Research Council. Washington, D.C.: National Academy Press.

Haywood, J. L.
1984 Coronary heart disease mortality/morbidity and risk in blacks. II. Access to medical care. *American Heart Journal* 3:794–796.

Hofferth, Sandra L., and Cheryl D. Hayes, eds.
1987 *Risking the Future: Adolescent Sexuality, Pregnancy, and Childbearing.* Vol. II. Working Papers and Statistical Appendixes. Panel on Adolescent Pregnancy and Childbearing, Committee on Child Development Research and Public Policy, National Research Council. Washington, D.C.: National Academy Press.

Hogan, D. P., and E. M. Kitagawa
  1985 The impact of social status, family structure and neighborhood on the fertility of black adolescents. *American Journal of Sociology* 90:825–855.
Hulka, B.
  1982 Risk factors for cervical cancer. *Journal of Chronic Disease* 35(1):3–11.
Institute of Medicine
  1985 *Preventing Low Birthweight*. Committee to Study the Prevention of Low Birthweight, Division of Health Promotion and Disease Prevention. Washington, D.C.: National Academy Press.
Jackson, J. S.
  1981 Urban black Americans. Pp. 37–129 in A. Harwood, ed., *Ethnicity and Medical Care*. Cambridge, Mass.: Harvard University Press.
  1985 Race, national origin, ethnicity, and aging. Pp. 264–303 in R. B. Binstock and E. Shanas, eds., *Handbook of Aging and the Social Sciences*. New York: Van Nostrand Reinhold.
Jackson, J. S., and R. C. Gibson
  1985 Work and retirement among the black elderly. Pp. 193–222 in Z. S. Blau, ed., *Current Perspectives on Aging and the Life Cycle*. Vol. I. Greenwich, Conn.: JAI Press, Inc.
James, S. A., E. H. Wagner, D. S. Strogatz, S. A. Beresford, D. G. Kleinbaum, C. A. Williams, L. M. Cutchin, and M. A. Ibrahim
  1984 The Edgecombe County (NC) high blood pressure control program. II. Barriers to the use of care among hypertensives. *American Journal of Public Health* 74:468–472.
Janzen, E.
  1973 Paper prepared for an institute on quality assurance for nursing care. American Nurses' Association and the American Hospital Association, Kansas City, Missouri.
Jason, J., M. Flock, and C. W. Tyler, Jr.
  1983 Epidemiologic characteristics of primary homicides in the United States. *American Journal of Epidemiology* 117(4):419–428.
Jessor, R., and S. Jessor
  1982 Adolescence to young adulthood: a twelve year prospective study of problem behavior and psychosocial development. In S. A. Mednick and M. Harway, eds., *Longitudinal Research in the United States*. Boston: Martinus Nijhoff.
Johnston, L., P. O'Malley, and J. G. Bachman
  1987 1986 Senior High School Survey. University of Michigan Institute of Social Research. Ann Arbor, Mich.
Kasl, S. V.
  1984 Social and psychologic factors in the etiology of coronary heart disease in black populations: an exploration of research needs. *American Heart Journal* 108:660–668.
Katzman, R.
  1985 Aging and age-dependent disease: cognition and dementia. In *America's Aging: Health in an Older Society*. Committee on an Aging Society, Institute of Medicine and National Research Council. Washington, D.C.: National Academy Press.
Keith, Stephen N., Robert M. Bell, August G. Swanson, and Albert P. Williams
  1985 Effects of affirmative action in medical schools: a study of the class of 1975. *New England Journal of Medicine* 313(24):1519–1525.

Kennedy, E. T., S. Gershoff, R. Reed, and J. E. Austin
1982 Evaluation of the effect of WIC supplemental feeding on birthweight. *Journal of the American Dietetic Association* 80:220–227.

Kessler, J. L., and E. Adams
1976 Human cervical cancer as a venereal disease. *Cancer Research* 36:783.

Kessner, D., J. Singer, C. Kalk, and E. Schlesinger
1973 *Contrasts in Health Status. Vol. 1: Infant Death: An Analysis by Maternal Risk and Health Care.* Institute of Medicine. Washington, D.C.: National Academy of Sciences.

Kitagawa, Evelyn M., and Philip M. Hauser
1973 *Differential Mortality in the United States.* Cambridge, Mass.: Harvard University Press.

Kleinman, J. C., and S. S. Kessel
1987 Racial differences in low birth weight. *New England Journal of Medicine* 317:749–753.

Kotelchuck, M., J. Schwartz, M. Anderka, and K. Finison
1984 WIC participation and pregnancy outcomes: Massachusetts statewide evaluation project. *American Journal of Public Health* 74(October):1086–1092.

Kovar, M. G.
1980 Morbidity and health care utilization. In S. Haynes and M. Feinleib, eds., *Epidemiology of Aging.* NIH Pub. No. 80-969. Washington, D.C.: U.S. Government Printing Office.

Kuller, L. H.
1985 Stroke report. Pp. 477–584 in *Report of the Secretary's Task Force on Black and Minority Health. Vol. IV: Cardiovascular and Cerebrovascular Disease.* Washington, D.C.: U.S. Department of Health and Human Services.

Lanzkowsky, P.
1978 Iron metabolism and iron deficiency anemia. Pp. 173–211 in D. R. Miller, H. A. Pearson, and C. H. Smith, eds., *Smith's Blood Diseases in Infancy and Childhood.* 4th ed. St. Louis: Mosby.

Leibel, R. L.
1977 Behavioral and biochemical correlates of iron deficiency. *Journal of the American Dietetic Association* 71:398–404.

Leibowitz, A., W. G. Manning, and E. B. Keeler
1985 Effect of cost-sharing on the use of medical services by children: interview results from a randomized controlled trial. *Pediatrics* 75(5):942–951.

Lieberman, E., K. J. Ryan, R. R. Monson, and S. C. Schoenbaum
1987 Risk factors accounting for racial differences in the rate of premature birth. *New England Journal of Medicine* 317:743–748.

Lief, Beth
1985 Legal and administrative barriers to health care. *New York State Journal of Medicine* 85(4):126–127.

Lilienfeld, Abraham M., Morton L. Levin, and Irving Kessler
1972 *Cancer in the United States.* Cambridge, Mass.: Harvard University Press.

Lloyd, S. M., Jr., D. G. Johnson, and M. Mann
1978 Survey of graduates of a traditionally black college of medicine. *Journal of Medical Education* 53:640–650.

Luft, F. C., C. E. Grim, J. T. Higgins, Jr., and M. H. Weinberger
1977 Differences in response to sodium administration in normotensive white and black subjects. *Journal of Laboratory and Clinical Medicine* 90:555–562.

Lutzker, J. R., and J. M. Rice
   1984   Project 12-ways: measuring outcome of a large in-home service for treatment and prevention of child abuse and neglect. *Child Abuse and Neglect* 8:519–524.
Mahaffey, K. R., J. Annest, J. Roberts, and R. Murphy
   1982   National estimates of blood lead levels: United States 1976–1980: association with selected demographic and socioeconomic factors. *New England Journal of Medicine* 307:573–579.
Manton, K., S. S. Poss, and S. Wing
   1979   The black/white mortality crossover: investigation from the perspective of the components of aging. *Gerontologist* 19:291–300.
Mare, R. D.
   1982   Socioeconomic effects on child mortality in the United States. *American Journal of Public Health* 72:539–547.
McAllister, A., C. Perry, and N. Maccoby
   1979   Adolescent smoking: onset and prevention. *Pediatrics* 63:650–658.
McCormick, Marie C.
   1985   The contribution of low birth weight to infant mortality and childhood morbidity. *New England Journal of Medicine* 312(2):82–90.
McKinney, Fred
   1986   Employment implications of a changing health-care system. Pp. 199–215 in Margaret C. Simms and Julianne M. Malveaux, eds., *Slipping Through the Cracks: The Status of Black Women*. New Brunswick, N.J.: Transaction Books.
Mitchell, J. B., and J. Cromwell
   1980   Medicaid mills: fact or fiction. *Health Care Financing Review* 2:37.
Myers, H. F.
   1984   Summary of workshop III: working group on socioeconomic and sociocultural influences. *American Heart Journal* 108:706–710.
National Center for Health Statistics
   1982a *Blood Pressure Levels and Hypertension in Persons Aged 6–74. United States 1976–80.* DHHS Pub. No. (PHS) 82-1250. Washington, D.C.: U.S. Department of Health and Human Services.
   1982b *The Prevalence of Dental Caries: The National Dental Caries Prevalence Survey*. NIH Pub. No. 82-2245. Washington, D.C.: U.S. Department of Health and Human Services.
   1984   *Monthly Vital Statistics Report*. 33(3) Supplement. U.S Department of Health and Human Services.
   1986   *Health United States: 1985*. DHHS Pub. No. (PHS) 86-1232. Washington, D.C.: U.S. Department of Health and Human Services.
   1987a Advance Report of Final Mortality Statistics, 1985. *Monthly Vital Statistics Report* 36(5). Washington, D.C.: U.S. Department of Health and Human Services.
   1987b Annual Summary of Births, Marriages, Divorces, and Deaths: United States, 1986. *Monthly Vital Statistics Report* 35(13). Washington, D.C.: U.S. Department of Health and Human Services.
   1987c *Health United States: 1986*. DHHS Pub. No. (PHS) 87-1232. Washington, D.C.: U.S. Department of Health and Human Services.
   1988   *Health United States: 1987*. DHHS Pub. No. 88-1232. Washington, D.C.: U.S. Government Printing Office.
National Commission on the Causes and Prevention of Violence
   1969   *To Establish Justice, to Insure Domestic Tranquility, Final Report*. 13 vols. Washington, D.C.: U.S. Government Printing Office.
National Institute on Drug Abuse
   1980   *Drug Abuse Deaths in Nine Cities: A Survey Report*. Research Monograph 29. Washington, D.C.: U.S. Department of Health and Human Services.

1987 *Population Estimates: National Survey on Drug Abuse.* DHHS Pub. No. (ADM) 87-1539. Washington, D.C.: U.S. Department of Health and Human Services.

National Senior Citizens Law Center
1980 Race discrimination in nursing homes. *Nursing Home Law Letter* No. 39 and 40.

Needleman, H., C. Gunnoe, A. Leviton, R. Reed, H. Peresie, C. Marker, and P. Barrett
1979 Deficits in psychological and classroom performance in children with elevated dentine lead levels. *New England Journal of Medicine* 300:689–693.

Neighbors, H. W., and J. S. Jackson
1986 Uninsured risk groups in a national survey of black Americans. *Journal of the National Medical Association* 78:275–282.
1987 Barriers to medical care among adult blacks: what happens to the uninsured? *Journal of the National Medical Association* 79(5):489–493.

Nomura, A., L. Kolonel, W. Rellahan, J. Lee, and E. Wegner
1981 Racial survival patterns for lung cancer in Hawaii. *Cancer* 48:1265–1271.

O'Brien, M. D., J. Rodgers, and D. Baugh
1985 *Ethnic and Racial Patterns in Enrollment, Health Status, and Health Services Utilization in the Medicaid Population.* Washington, D.C., Health Care Financing Administration.

Office of Technology Assessment
1988 Children's access to health care. Pp. 52–70 in *Healthy Children: Investing in the Future.* U.S. Congress. Washington, D.C.: U.S. Government Printing Office.

Olds, D. L., C. R. Henderson, and R. Chamberlin
1986 Preventing child abuse and neglect: a randomized trial of nurse visitations. *Pediatrics* 78(1):65–78.

Omran, A. R.
1977 Epidemiologic transition in the U.S. *Population Bulletin* 32:3–42.

O'Reilly, K. R., and S. Aral
1988 Adolescence and sexual behavior: trends and implications for STD. *Journal of Adolescent Health Care* 2:43–51.

Oski, F., and J. Stockman
1980 Anemia due to inadequate iron sources or poor iron utilization. *Pediatric Clinics of North America* 27:237–252.

Page, L. B.
1976 Epidemiologic evidence on the etiology of human hypertension and its possible prevention. *American Heart Journal* 91:527–534.

Page, W. F., and A. J. Kuntz
1980 Racial and socioeconomic factors in cancer survival: a comparison of Veterans Administration results with selected studies. *Cancer* 45:1029–1040.

Palmer, J. L., and S. G. Gould
1986 The economic consequences of an aging society. *Daedalus* 115:295–324.

Piomelli, S.
1973 A micromethod for free erythrocyte porphyrins: the FEP test. *Journal of Laboratory and Clinical Medicine* 81:932–936.

President's Commission for the Study of Ethical Problems in Medicine and Biomedical and Behavioral Research
1983 *Securing Access to Care.* Vol. 1. Washington, D.C.: U.S. Government Printing Office.

Rice, D. P., and J. J. Feldman
1983 Living longer in the United States: demographic changes and health needs of the elderly. *Milbank Memorial Fund Quarterly/Health and Society* 61:362–396.

Robert Wood Johnson Foundation
  1983 *Updated Report on Access to Health Care for the American People*. Princeton, N.J.: Robert Wood Johnson Foundation.
Robins, Lee Nelkens, and G. E. Murphy
  1967 Drug use in a normal population of young Negro men. *American Journal of Public Health* 57:1580–1596.
Rowe, J. W.
  1985 Health care of the elderly. *New England Journal of Medicine* 312:827–835.
Ruther, M., and A. Dobson
  1981 Unequal treatment and unequal benefits: a reexamination of the use of Medicare services by race, 1967–1976. *Health Care Financing Review*. HCFA Pub. No. 03090. Washington, D.C.: U.S. Department of Health and Human Services.
Sandler, D. P., A. J. Wilcox, and R. B. Everson
  1985 Cumulative effects of lifetime passive smoking on cancer risks. *Lancet* 1:312.
Sandson, J. I.
  1983 A crisis in medical education: the high cost of student financial assistance. *New England Journal of Medicine* 308(21):1286–1289.
Schuckit, M. A.
  1985 Genetics and the risk of alcoholism. *Journal of the American Medical Association* 254:2614–2617.
Shanas, E.
  1980 Self-assessment of physical function: white and black elderly of the United States. In S. Haynes and M. Feinleib, eds., *Epidemiology of Aging*. NIH Pub. No. 80-969. Washington, D.C.: U.S. Government Printing Office.
Shiono, P. H., M. A. Klebanoff, B. I. Granbard, H. W. Berendes, and G. G. Rhoads
  1986 Birth weight among women of different ethnic groups. *Journal of the American Medical Association* 255:48–52.
Siegel, J., and Davidson, M.
  1984 *Demographic and Socioeconomic Aspects of Aging in the United States*. U.S. Bureau of the Census, Current Population Reports, Series P-23, No. 138. Washington, D.C.: U.S. Government Printing Office.
Siegel, J. S.
  1980 Recent and prospective demographic trends for the elderly population and some implications for health care. In S. Haynes and M. Feinleib, eds., *Epidemiology of Aging*. NIH Pub. No. 80-969. Washington, D.C.: U.S. Government Printing Office.
Siegel, J. S., and C. M. Taeuber
  1986 Demographic perspectives on the long-lived society. *Daedalus* 115:77–118.
Smith, E. A., and J. R. Udry
  1985 Coital and non-coital sexual behaviors of white and black adolescents. *American Journal of Public Health* 75:1200–1203.
Smith, N., and E. Rios
  1974 Iron metabolism and iron deficiency in infancy and childhood. *Advances in Pediatrics* 21:239–280.
Soldo, B.
  1980 America's elderly in the 1980's. *Population Bulletin* 35:3–47.
Soldo, B., and K. G. Manton
  1985 Changes in the health status and service needs of the oldest old: current patterns and future trends. Pp. 286–323 in R. Sugman and M. W. Riley, eds., *Milbank Memorial Fund Quarterly/The Oldest Old* 63.

Starfield, B.
1977   Iron-deficiency anemia. Pp. 77–120 in *Children's Medical Care Needs and Treatments*. Cambridge, Mass.: Ballinger.

Sullivan, Louis W.
1983   Special report: the status of blacks in medicine: philosophical and ethical dilemmas for the 1980s. *New England Journal of Medicine* 309(13):807–808.

Sulvetta, M., and K. Swartz
1986   *The Uninsured and Uncompensated Care, a Chartbook*. Washington, D.C.: Urban Institute.

Swartz, K.
1986   *Statistical Analysis of the Bureau of the Census' Current Population Survey 1980, 1984, 1986*. Prepared for the Office of Technology Assessment, U.S. Congress. Washington, D.C.: Urban Institute.

Trevino, F. M., and A. J. Moss
1983   Health insurance coverage and physician visits among Hispanic and non-Hispanic people. In *Health United States: 1983*. DHHS Pub. No. (PHS) 84-1232. Washington, D.C.: U.S. Department of Health and Human Services.

Turner, Charles F., Heather G. Miller, and Lincoln E. Moses, eds.
1989   *AIDS: Sexual Behavior and Intravenous Drug Use*. Committee on AIDS Research and the Behavioral, Social, and Statistical Sciences, Commission on Behavioral and Social Sciences and Education, National Research Council. Washington, D.C.: National Academy Press.

Tyroler, H. A., and S. A. James
1978   Blood pressure and skin color. *American Journal of Public Health* 68:1170–1172.

United Nations
1985   *Demographic Yearbook: 1985*. Table 20. New York: United Nations.

U.S. Congress, House of Representatives
1987   *Abused Children in America: Victims of Official Neglect*. HR 100-260. Select Committee on Children, Youth, and Families. Washington, D.C.: U.S. Government Printing Office.

U.S. Department of Health, Education, and Welfare
1979   *Smoking and Health: A Report of the Surgeon General*. DHEW Pub. No. (PHS) 79-50066. Washington, D.C.: U.S. Department of Health, Education, and Welfare.

U.S. Department of Health and Human Services
1980   *Promoting Health/Preventing Disease, Objectives for the Nation*. Public Health Service, Office of the Assistant Secretary for Health. Washington, D.C.: U.S. Department of Health and Human Services.

1984   *Minorities and Women in the Health Fields*. DHHS Pub. No. (HRSA) HRS-DV 84-5. Washington, D.C.: U.S. Department of Health and Human Services.

1985a   *Health Status of Minorities and Low Income Groups*. DHHS Pub. No. (HRSA) HRSA-P-DV 85-1. Washington, D.C.: U.S. Department of Health and Human Services.

1985b   Minority and other health professionals serving minority communities: report of the working group on health professionals. Pp. 375–549 in *Report of the Task Force on Black and Minority Health. Vol. II: Crosscutting Issues*. Washington, D.C.: U.S. Department of Health and Human Services.

1985c   *Secretary's Task Force on Black and Minority Health*. Office of the Secretary of Health. Washington, D.C.: U.S. Department of Health and Human Services.

1985d   *Report of the Secretary's Task Force on Black and Minority Health. Vol. I: Summary*. Washington, D.C.: U.S. Department of Health and Human Services.

1986a   *Current Estimates, 1985*. DHHS Pub. (PHS). Washington, D.C.: U.S. Department of Health and Human Services.

1986b *Report of the Secretary's Task Force on Black and Minority Health. Vol. IV: Cardiovascular and Cerebrovascular Disease. Part 1.* Washington, D.C.: U.S. Department of Health and Human Services.

1986c *The 1990 Health Objectives for the Nation: A Midcourse Review.* Office of Disease Prevention and Health Promotion, Public Health Service. Washington, D.C.: U.S. Department of Health and Human Services.

1986d *Prevention of Disease, Disability and Death in Blacks and Other Minorities.* Annual Program Review, 1986. Centers for Disease Control, Public Health Service. Washington, D.C.: U.S. Department of Health and Human Services.

1986e *Nutrition Monitoring in the United States: Progress Report.* DHHS Pub. No. (PHS) 86-1255. Washington, D.C.: U.S. Department of Health and Human Services.

Winick, M.
1970 Nutrition and mental development. *Medical Clinics of North America* 54(6):1413–1429.

Wise, P. H., M. Kotelchuck, and M. L. Wilson
1985 Racial and socioeconomic disparities in childhood mortality in Boston. *New England Journal of Medicine* 313:360–366.

Woodlander, S., D. U. Himmelstein, R. Silber, M. Bader, T. Harnly, and A. A. Jones
1985 Medical care and mortality: racial differences in preventable deaths. *International Journal of Health Services* 15:1–22.

Wright, James D., Peter H. Rossi, and Kathleen Daly
1983 *Under the Gun: Weapons, Crime, and Violence in America.* New York: Aldine Publishing Company.

Wyszewianski, L., and A. Donabedian
1981 Equity in the distribution of quality of care. *Medica*

Zelnik, M., J. Kanter, and K. Ford
1981 *Sex and Pregnancy in Adolescence.* Beverly Hills, Calif.: Sage Publications Inc.

9

CRIME AND THE

ADMINISTRATION OF CRIMINAL JUSTICE

James Lesesne Wells
Ethiopia at the Bar of Justice (1928)
Linoleum cut
Collection of the artist

Crime and punishment cannot be properly analyzed apart from the larger social, political, and economic contexts from which they emerge. Black crime and the position of blacks within the nation's system of criminal justice administration are related to past and present social opportunities and disadvantages and can be best understood through consideration of blacks' overall social status. Thus, although this chapter focuses on post-1940 developments, the review considers a broader historical record.

The chapter assesses crime and the criminal justice system in terms of three major topics: blacks as defendants and offenders, blacks as victims, and blacks as criminal justice personnel. The investigation begins with a historical sketch of the status of blacks within the criminal justice system. Next, we describe trends in black and white arrest and imprisonment rates over the past few decades and the status of black and white victims of crime. The treatment of blacks arrested and processed through the criminal justice system is then compared with the treatment accorded to whites. Finally, we consider the presence and impact of blacks as personnel in the agencies and institutions of the criminal justice system.

CRIME AND PUNISHMENT

Much of the discussion examines the treatment of blacks arrested and processed for violations of the law. Great inequalities in the treatment of blacks and whites in the legal system have been present throughout most of the nation's history (Bell, 1980; Higginbotham, 1978; Mangum, 1940). Our discussion of such inequalities focuses primarily on the past four decades. Changes during this period indicate that previous levels of differential treatment are no longer prevalent. The post-1965 "due process and equal rights revolution" within the criminal justice system and related civil rights reforms have led to substantial scrutiny of alleged racial inequalities in the administration of justice.

During the past 25 years there has been an increase in the presence of blacks as criminal justice personnel. This increased presence has a number of important ramifications. The simplest is its indication of the extent to which previous practices that excluded blacks have been altered. Since this change has implications beyond equal employment opportunity, we report on the relation between the increased presence of black personnel and the treatment of blacks as victims, suspects, and defendants.

SCOPE AND LIMITATIONS OF THE REVIEW

It is important to note what is left out of this review. Nothing is said here concerning civil actions in the legal system. In most instances, the racial and social class inequalities found in the administration of criminal justice have also been evident in "the civil side of the court" (Carlin, 1966). Like crime, many of the behaviors regulated by such civil proceedings pose significant threats to individual lives and security as well as to the public welfare.

Our analysis depends on the availability of reliable data sources, and we focus on a rather limited range of criminal law violations. Much of the statistical analysis uses the crime index of the Federal Bureau of Investigation (FBI), which includes homicide, rape, assault, robbery, larceny, burglary, and automobile theft. The persons who are arrested for these crimes come disproportionately from lower socioeconomic backgrounds. An exclusive focus on these so-called "street crimes" may divert attention from the large volume of crimes that is disproportionately committed by whites and members of the middle and upper classes, for example, corporate crime, tax evasion, fraudulent financial dealings, and similar offenses (see J. Farley, 1988:271–273).

Because index crimes are salient objects of popular fears and are relatively easy to detect, they attract much public attention—a situation that historically has encouraged attributions of criminality to ethnic and racial minorities. Such observations are not meant to underemphasize the racial disproportions in arrests of persons for index offenses. Rather, we note that equal attention to white-collar crimes and corporate crime might produce a considerably different image of the "typical" criminal offender.

Our analysis is further affected by the nature of the available empirical investigations. Very few studies of either crime or the administration of justice are longitudinal. In some studies, there are methodological flaws, many of which are noted in our assessment. In addition, few studies consider more than one or two of the decision points of the criminal justice system.

For example, analysts who study arrest decisions often do not examine the behavior of judges and juries. These limitations also emphasize the need for caution in assuming causal links between race and criminal behavior (see Pope, 1979; Wolfgang and Cohen, 1970). They also make it difficult to provide definitive answers to the question of the extent of racial bias in the administration of justice.

This chapter also does not consider or review certain theoretical issues such as the literature on the correlates and presumed "causes" of criminal behavior (except for a brief discussion of the role of alcohol, drugs, and guns in criminal acts). Nevertheless, we emphasize that a majority of the empirical investigations on which we rely acknowledge a linkage between the etiology of crime among blacks, their treatment in the criminal justice system, and their low socioeconomic status.

A HISTORICAL PERSPECTIVE

During all periods for which systematic data are available, blacks have been overrepresented both as victims and offenders. Before 1940, there is substantial evidence that blacks were disproportionately singled out for arrest and punishment. Although such practices have abated over time, the effects of past disproportions extend into the present, influencing both the etiology of crime and negative reactions among blacks toward the criminal justice system. There are also instances of racial bias in the administration of criminal justice even today.

Relatively little is known about black or white crime rates or the comparative treatment of black and white offenders prior to the Civil War (Franklin, 1980:138). Although similarities between slavery and modern criminal justice practices have been noted (Blassingame, 1977; Sellin, 1976), the relative statuses of blacks and whites within the nation's criminal justice system are generally products of the late nineteenth and early twentieth centuries. The modern criminal justice system, especially the elaborate penal system, did not begin to develop in the United States until the early decades of the nineteenth century.

During the decades between the end of Reconstruction and 1940, scholarly discourse centered on three observations: (1) the disproportionate representation of blacks within the nation's prisons and jails, especially in the South; (2) the frequent lynching of blacks by white mobs; and (3) the brutal treatment of black prisoners, most often within the chain-gang system. Although arrest statistics are not readily available for this period, imprisonment data show that in most southern states blacks comprised from 70 to 95 percent of the imprisoned populations (Adamson, 1983:561,565). For example, in Georgia in 1878, 1,122 of the 1,239 convicts (90.6 percent) were black (Adamson, 1983:565; Green, 1969:282). Similar ratios were found in South Carolina (Zimmerman, 1947:62) and in North Carolina (Hawkins, 1985:191).

Not only were high rates of imprisonment the rule, but methods of punishment within the penal system also varied by race. In the South, chain-gang labor was used primarily as a punishment for black convicts (Hawkins, 1985; Wharton, 1965:235,240). It was also a source of cheap black labor for private employers (Daniel, 1972; Jaynes, 1986:270–271, 306–307). The mortality rate for all prisoners was high during this period, but it was exceptionally high for black inmates, who were more likely than whites to be exposed to adverse weather conditions and to be beaten and abused by guards (Zimmerman, 1947). High rates of imprisonment of blacks relative to whites were not confined to the South; they were found in all other major regions and have continued to the present (Christianson, 1981, 1982; Dunbaugh, 1979; Hawkins, 1985).

These and similar data have evoked a persistent question: How much of the gap between black and white rates of reported crime and levels of punishment for crime has been the result of white racial discrimination? Against the background of a long history of lynchings and many publicized instances of miscarriages of justice, many scholars came to question the accuracy of reported levels of black crime. The presence of overt bias in arrests, trials, and sentencing was acknowledged by leading criminologists (e.g., Sellin, 1935). Nevertheless, by the time of the Myrdal study (1944), a scholarly consensus held that allowing for the effects of discrimination, the rate of criminal activity among blacks was considerably higher than that found among whites. This view was shared by both black and white analysts (see DuBois, 1904; Johnson, 1941; Sellin, 1928).

CRIMINAL OFFENDERS AND VICTIMS

TRENDS IN SERIOUS CRIMES AND IMPRISONMENT

Much crime goes unreported by victims and is otherwise undetected. Furthermore, even when crime is detected and brought to the attention of the police a large number of cases are never "cleared" (solved). The clearance rate for some offenses (e.g., burglary, minor assaults, and auto theft) is frequently 30 percent or less (Reid, 1979:63)—which means 70 percent or more of known offenses are never cleared by an arrest. Obviously, for unreported crimes and for the vast majority of known offenses that are not cleared, there is no arrest and thus little is known about the social character-istics of the offender. Consequently, to the extent that race or racial bias may be factors in the detection or clearance of crime, official arrest statistics may distort the level of race differences in actual criminal activity.

The use of surveys of crime victims is one method that helps to overcome some of the limitations of official arrest statistics. Comparisons of official black-white arrest rates for specific crimes with victims' reports of the race of their assailants do indicate that discrepancies exist. For example, in 1986, 47 percent of rape arrestees were black, but only 35 percent of surveyed victims said their attackers were black. However, blacks accounted for 62 percent of robbery arrests, and 63 percent of surveyed robbery victims identified their assailants as black. It is not known whether the discrepancies that exist are due to biases in survey samples or in arrest statistics, to differential reports of crime to police, or to biases that make blacks more prone to arrest than whites.

Beginning in 1930, the federal government began to publish the *Uniform Crime Reports* (*UCR*), the first annual, nationwide compilation of arrest data. These annual reports have become the cornerstone of research on crime and criminal justice.[1] The *UCR* has provided data on the race of arrestees since 1933. Between 1933 and 1940, data from the *UCR* were used to appraise many widely held presumptions about race, ethnicity, and criminal behavior. In the North, the rate of crime among recent white immigrants was thought to be and sometimes was reported (for local areas) to be substantially higher than that of native whites (see Ferdinand, 1967; Powell, 1966; Warner, 1934; Willbach, 1938, 1940–1941). Thus, it is not surprising that the initial editions of the *UCR* contained comparisons among foreign-born whites, blacks, and native-born whites. The data show a steady increase in the rate of crime for all three groups during this period (Myers and Sabol, 1987). A part of the increase (and of fluctuations) is attributable to changes in the FBI's data-gathering techniques. But the Great Depression era was characterized by both an actual increase in reported crime and the use of more extensive social control measures. And the relative synchronization in the rates of arrests for blacks and whites suggests that the causal forces that underlie the statistics are very similar for both groups.

For this period, the data fail to support the commonly held belief that foreign-born whites were much more likely than native whites to be charged with criminal conduct. Although there were some individual offenses for which foreign-born whites had higher rates at the beginning of the period (homicide, assault, stolen property, weapons possession, and gambling), by 1940, the arrest rates for these offenses for native whites were higher than those of foreign-born whites. However, the data do show higher rates of arrests among blacks than among whites. By 1940, the total rate of arrests for blacks was more than 10 per 1,000 higher than the rate for whites (17 and 6 per 1,000, respectively). Figure 9-1 shows the trends for total arrest rates to 1985 for blacks and whites. Because of changes in recordkeeping practices during the period, caution should be exercised in comparing pre-1952 and post-1952 rates.

The contrast between black and white arrest rates in these data is striking. There is a strong positive upward movement in both the black and white trends, but whether one looks at the pre- or post-1952 trends, the results are similar: black arrest rates are higher than white rates, and the gap between the two has been widening. In 1978, the arrest rate per 1,000 whites was

---

1. Recent surveys of criminal victimization indicate that the *UCR* underestimates the amount of criminal activity in the United States. Although such criticism continues, the *UCR* remains the most important *official* source of data on criminal activity in the United States.

FIGURE 9-1   Total arrest rates, by race, 1933–1985.

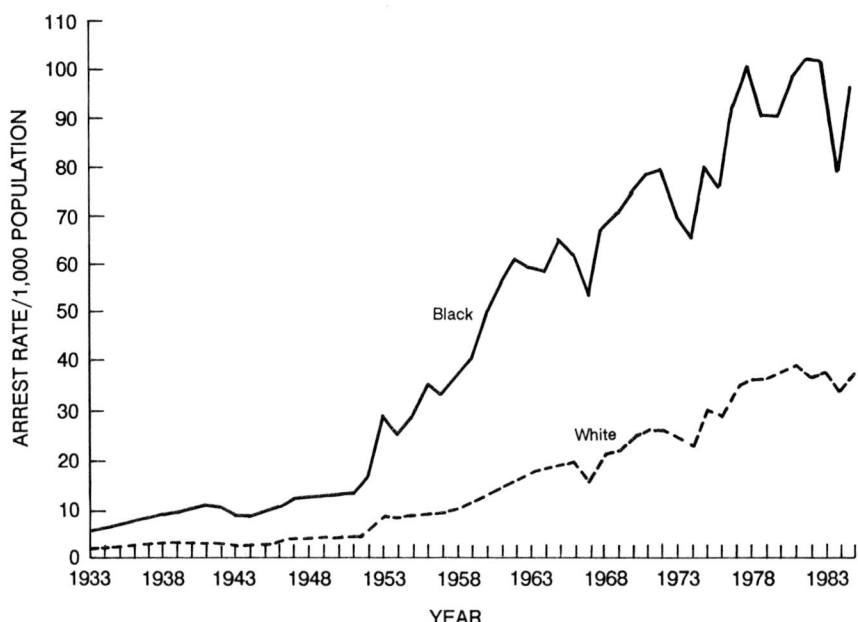

Source: Myers and Sabol (1987).

around 35 while the black rate was almost 100; thus, the white rate in 1978 was comparable to that for blacks during the late 1950s and early 1960s.

Trends in arrests for the major index crimes of homicide, rape, robbery, assault, burglary, larceny, and auto theft do not give a comprehensive picture of all black and white crime, but they reveal much about the changing levels of racial differences. As an example, consider the patterns for homicide shown in Figure 9-2.

Homicide arrest rates for whites have been relatively stable for much of the entire 1933–1985 period. Black homicide rates, while significantly higher than those for whites, have fluctuated widely from year to year, particularly in recent years (see Brearley, 1932; Farley, 1980; O'Carroll and Mercy, 1986; Shin et al., 1977). Moreover, black arrests for murder (and nonnegligent manslaughter) have oscillated around two plateaus. One plateau spanned the period from 1933 to 1952 and the second is seen in the 1970s and 1980s. Rape, robbery, and assault arrest rates also rose sharply for blacks after 1952 (Myers and Sabol, 1987). Moreover, for most of the period from 1953 until around 1978, the racial gap in arrest rates for these offenses grew. There was also a widening of the racial gap in arrests for burglary, larceny, and auto theft. These economic crimes showed substantial increases for both blacks and whites.

During the last decade of this 50-year period, there is evidence that for

FIGURE 9-2 Homicide arrest rates, by race, 1933–1985.

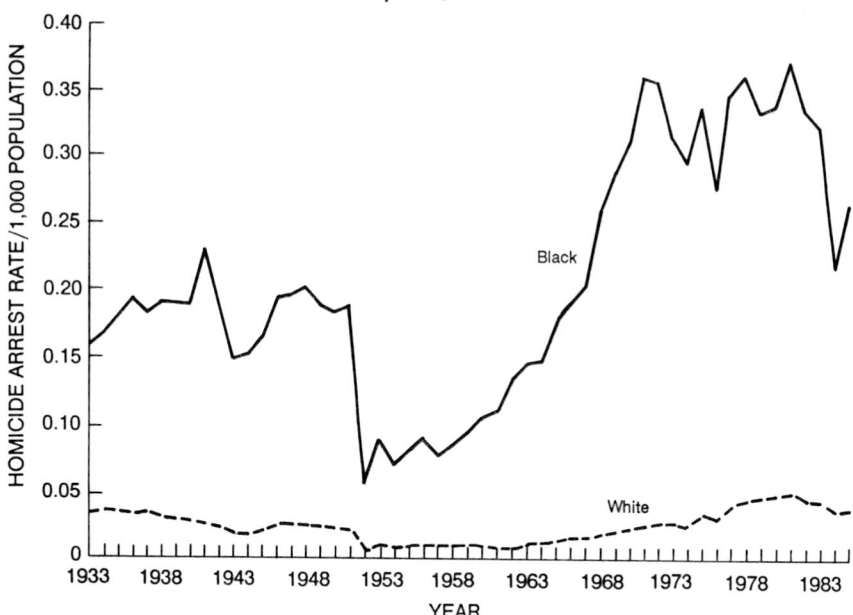

Source: Myers and Sabol (1987).

some offenses the black-white gap may have peaked and is now constant or narrowing somewhat. This observation applies to homicide, forcible rape, larceny, and robbery. Also, the motor vehicle arrest rate differential has narrowed continuously since the 1970s, and the black-white difference for burglary arrests has decreased since 1975. These changes suggest the possibility that the long-term trend of a widening gap between arrests of blacks and whites for serious (index) offenses may be ending (Hawkins, 1987; Myers and Sabol, 1987).

These data suggest several major periods of nonlinear change in the rate of arrests for serious crime among blacks. One period was 1933–1951, which coincided with great upheavals in American social and economic conditions: high unemployment in the Great Depression, unprecedented mobilization of the nation in World War II, and then postwar instability as the economy shifted from military production to the manufacture of consumer goods. There was also a continuation of the migration of blacks to urban centers outside of the South.

The second major change occurred during the 1950s. This was a period of rapid black urbanization. Changes in crime data for this period, however, are suspect because of changes in the method of recording arrests. It is difficult to determine whether the downward trend in arrests for both blacks and whites observed during the years immediately after 1951 represents a change in actual criminal behavior or is an artifact of recordkeeping. From about 1968 through the late 1970s, there was increased professionalization of police forces and greater expenditures for law enforcement, largely as a result of federal support of such efforts through the Law Enforcement Assistance Administration (LEAA). One result was a dramatic increase in the rates of incarceration for all races, particularly after 1970.

There were notable changes in the distribution of black arrests during the five decades between 1933 and 1985. For 1933–1951 and 1968–1985, index crimes accounted for a significant fraction (about one-third) of all black arrests; during the 1950s and early 1960s those crimes accounted for only about 15 percent of total criminal activity. There appears to be a recent shift from the violent crimes of murder, rape, and assault toward economic crimes of robbery, burglary, larceny, and auto theft, also placing the most recent period in line with the earliest one. Between 1933 and 1951, arrests for those economic crimes accounted for 25 percent of total black arrests, and from 1968 until 1985, they accounted for 23 percent of all black arrests; for 1952–1967, they accounted for less than 12 percent of all black arrests. For whites, the index crimes accounted for 28 percent of all arrests for 1933–1951, for 11 percent for 1952–1967, and for 19 percent for 1968–1985 (Myers and Sabol, 1987). The distribution of arrests among blacks in the post-1968 period is almost exactly the same as the pre-1950s arrest distribution among whites, with more than 70 percent of arrests for nonindex crimes. Nonindex crimes continue to represent a far greater proportion of white arrests than of black arrests.

Arrest rates among males of specific ages show some important aspects of the arrest data. For many of the criminal activities discussed (e.g., robbery, burglary, aggravated assault), the average period of individual participation in criminal activity begins during adolescence and lasts only 5–10 years. Indeed, for robbery and burglary, arrest rates peak at about age 17 and then decrease rapidly, falling to one-half the peak rate for people in their mid-20s and to one-quarter for people in their late 30s (Blumstein et al., 1986). These data imply that overall trends in arrest rates for index crimes are importantly influenced by birth rates and the black-white differences in arrest rates are affected by black-white differences in the age distribution of the respective populations. Thus, the upward trend in arrest rates during the 1960s and 1970s is explained in part by the fact that the baby boom cohorts born in the late 1940s through the 1950s were reaching adolescence during those decades. The decline in fertility rates after 1960 is consistent also with the fall in arrest rates during the early 1980s. In addition, since the black population is younger than the white population, part of the higher arrest rate among males is due to the fact that there is a higher proportion of males aged 15–25 in the black population than there is in the white population.

National data reporting incarceration rates in prisons and jails and disaggregated by race were not systematically collected for much of the period covered by our study. Available sources also differ in how the data are presented: only prisoners sentenced for felonies are counted during certain

TABLE 9-1 Prison Population, by Race, 1939–1985

Year	White	Black	Percent Black
1939	47,971	17,324	26
1949	38,155	15,640	29
1960	108,920	67,781	38
1974	97,700	89,700	48
1979	161,642	145,383	47
1985	260,847	227,137	46

Notes: Data for 1939 are for all court-received prisoners or flows during each year. Data for 1949 are for male felony prisoners received from courts during each year, including federal and state courts but excluding data for Georgia, Michigan, and Mississippi. Data for 1960 include all nonwhites and are the year-end felony population. Data for 1974–1985 are for the year-end stock population.

Source: Hawkins (1987).

years; some statistics represent a count of admissions during a given year; other data are a count of populations—all prisoners confined at the end of a given year. The latter figure is larger, of course, because it represents the cumulative effects of many years of admissions. Each set of data can be used for documenting the status of blacks in comparison to whites.

Table 9-1 shows various indices of the racial composition of the nation's prison population for selected years between 1939 and 1985. The data reveal an increase in the percentage of blacks among the nation's prison population since 1960. Between 1933 and 1939, blacks accounted for 24–26 percent of all prisoners received from the courts. For 1943–1950, the percentage of black felony admissions ranged from 27 to 31 percent. By 1960, blacks were 39 percent of the stock felony population, and from 1974 to 1985, blacks accounted for about 47 percent of all persons confined at the end of the year.

ALCOHOL, DRUGS, HANDGUNS, AND CRIME

Because of the connections among drugs, guns, and criminal behavior, differential drug use and gun (especially handgun) availability have been frequently discussed as reasons for the black-white gap in crime rates. Recently, drug use and trafficking in the black community have received considerable media attention. Researchers are divided, however, as to the role played by alcohol and drug use in the etiology of criminal behavior (see Collins, 1981; Goode, 1984; Inciardi, 1986). And although the United States has a rate of gun ownership higher than those of most other industrialized nations (Wright et al., 1983), criminologists remain skeptical about how this condition affects the nation's high level of criminal violence. In this section we assess some possible impacts of alcohol, drugs, and handguns on black-white crime differences.

Drugs and Alcohol

Drug and alcohol use may relate to criminal behavior in several ways. First, people may be more likely to engage in criminal behavior when they are under the influence of drugs or alcohol than when they are not. Such behavior is often attributed to a loss of self-control that results from drug intoxication. Alcohol and some illegal drugs, such as marijuana, hallucinogens, and "angel dust" (PCP), have been related to violent behavior, including sexual aggression (see Goode, 1984:67,124).

Second, people who engage in repeated drug use are believed to be more likely than nonusers or casual users to be involved in criminal activity (Collins, 1981:154–206; Wish and Johnson, 1986). The view that drug use promotes criminal careers is based in part on the belief that heavy drug users are likely to be found in deviant subcultures that promote criminal activity. It is also based on the idea that drug users have to resort to crime to pay for their habits, a pattern shown to exist for many heroin addicts (Goode, 1984:222–223; Inciardi, 1986:115–132). This perspective provides much of the current impetus for the mandatory testing for drugs of persons arrested for crime. Such testing has shown that arrestees are disproportionately involved in drug use: for example, more than one-half of the people arrested for serious crimes in Washington, D.C., and New York City during 1985 and 1986 tested positive for drugs (Wish, 1987, 1988). Wish reported that many active offenders use drugs and that high rates of drug use are associated with high rates of criminal activity.

In an examination of studies that have explored the linkage between alcohol use and criminal behavior among blacks, Roizen (1981:207) reported that estimates of the proportion of offenders drinking immediately before or at the time of the crime vary from one-third to two-thirds of black offenders. Yet after a careful review of such findings, mainly from survey research, she concluded (Roizen, 1981:252):

> Drinking, even heavy and problem drinking, is relatively common. Crime is not. Men and women committing serious crimes are a relatively small, statistically and socially deviant population. They are also among those people most likely to elude the survey net. There is little in this research that directly links drinking behavior to criminal behavior . . . criminal offenders drink more and have more drinking problems than those of relatively comparable status in the general population. There is little support, however, . . . for the proposition that a disproportionate amount of Black crime is a consequence of drinking.

Violent behavior associated with the trafficking of drugs is now receiving considerable media coverage, but it has not been the subject of substantial research. Most analyses of trafficking have looked at international implications or the involvement of organized crime (e.g., Inciardi, 1986:175–198; Moore, 1988). None has thoroughly examined drug trafficking within the black community of the sort that appears to be associated with high rates of homicide among black teenagers and young adults.

Recent increases in gang-related violence can be linked to drug trafficking and other crime in black and Hispanic communities. For example, it was reported that 17 percent of the District of Columbia's 148 homicides in 1985 were connected to dealing in narcotics. By 1986, that figure had climbed to 33 percent of 197 homicides; and by 1987, it was 57 percent of 228 homicides. Police estimated that in the first 2 months of 1988, 67 percent of the city's 34 homicides were due to local drug wars (*Time*, March 14, 1988:22). Control of the market for "crack," a form of cocaine, is reportedly the reason for escalated drug wars. Most of the violence and much of the actual trafficking in crack is concentrated in black neighborhoods.

One response to trafficking in crack and other drugs within black communities has been an increase in self-help activities directed at drug dealers and purchasers. During January and February of 1988, the *New York Times* reported that black Muslims had begun a 24-hour patrol of the Bedford Stuyvesant section of Brooklyn in an effort to rid the community of drugs, particularly crack (*New York Times*, January 23, 1988:29,31; February 25, 1988:A1,B4). Similar Muslim patrol efforts were later begun in Washington, D.C. In both cities, these groups have received significant community support and the tacit approval of the police. In some instances they have joined patrolling policemen in areas of high-volume drug sales.

Fruitful investigations might study specific connections between drug trafficking and drug use and black crime. In black communities, trafficking in drugs is a source of tremendous rivalry and conflict between competing sellers. The sale of drugs has become an available source of income for unemployed black youth and adults who sell drugs to residents of lower class communities and also to middle-class and affluent blacks and whites (see Chapter 6).

Handguns

Handguns are the weapon of choice and convenience for a variety of criminal offenses, notably robberies, major assaults, and homicide. Rose and Deskins (1986:85) estimated that guns are used in 43 percent of all robberies. Of special interest here is the extent to which ownership of handguns and other types of guns may or may not contribute to the black-white difference in crime rates. Surveys and other evidence of gun ownership show no sharp or consistent differences in weapons ownership across racial groups (Wright et al., 1983:108). A 1973 National Opinion Research Center (NORC) survey analyzed by Wright and Marston (1975) showed that whites were slightly, but not substantially, more likely than nonwhites to own a weapon. But the data revealed no difference in rates of handgun ownership. On the basis of these and other findings, Wright and colleagues (1983:108–109) concluded:

> Because some studies report ownership being higher among whites (by small margins), others report ownership higher among blacks (by small

margins), and still others report no significant difference, the most prudent conclusion is very probably that weapons ownership is not linked in any important way to race.

Of course, such conclusions do not disprove a linkage among gun use, race, and crime. It is still possible that blacks who commit crimes are more likely than whites to have access to or to use guns. Rose and Deskins (1986) document the extensive use of guns of all types among black homicide offenders in major urban areas, and they also report a growing reliance on the use of handguns. In each of six cities investigated, guns (of all types) represented the most frequently used homicide weapon for black offenders, ranging from a high of 88 percent of all cases in Atlanta to 76 percent in Detroit and Pittsburgh.

Alcohol, drugs, and guns are significant correlates of criminal behavior among Americans. But their wide distribution among the entire American population raises questions about how much they contribute to overall crime rate differences across socioeconomic and racial groupings. For example, Wright and colleagues (1983:107) reported the highest rate of private gun ownership among affluent and middle-class people. Nonetheless, drug trafficking, drug abuse, and violent behavior are having an especially damaging impact on black communities.

THE COSTS OF CRIME: BLACKS AND BLACK COMMUNITIES AS VICTIMS

Despite much attention to crime and justice in race relations, few studies have examined the impact of crime and punishment on black communities themselves. Modern-day victims of crime received little attention, whether white or black until very recently. This lack of attention may be the result of the way that cases are processed in the criminal justice system; it may also stem from the fact that the victims of common law crimes have been concentrated among people of lower socioeconomic status. The effects of crime on black victims and black communities have aroused comparatively little public concern.

Given the high rates of black criminal offending, patterns of residential segregation, and the intraracial character of most crime, blacks are about twice as likely as whites to be victims of robbery, vehicle theft, and aggravated assault (McGarrell and Flanagan, 1985:294–312). They are also disproportionately victims of homicide: deaths due to homicide among blacks have ranged between 6 and 7 times those for whites during the past 50 years (Brearley, 1932; O'Carroll and Mercy, 1986; Shin et al., 1977). In short, blacks are subject more frequently than whites to violent death, injuries, and property losses by criminal actions. Victimization surveys also show that blacks suffer greater injuries and also lose a greater proportion of their personal wealth to crime than do whites and Hispanics; see Table 9-2.

Most black criminal offenders victimize other blacks. This pattern is true

TABLE 9-2 Victimization Rates per 1,000 Persons, by Race or Ethnic Group, 1981

Race or Ethnic Group	Robbery	Assault	Burglary	Household Larceny	Total
White	6	26	83	119	234
Black	17	31	134	142	324
Other	10	27	68	118	223
Hispanic	12	25	104	148	289

Source: Data from U.S. Department of Justice (1983:20).

for most crimes of violence (O'Brien, 1987) and for many property offenses. The greater level of economic resources that is found within white communities has led to a portion of property offenses by blacks that is directed at whites. Such interracial criminal activity appears to be limited partly by black-white residential separation. Recent evidence suggests that most offenders tend to commit crimes in areas near to where they live; hence, a pattern of intraracial victimization is evident for all racial-ethnic groups (see Illinois Criminal Justice Information Authority, 1987).

The high volume of criminal activity in black communities has meant that their victimization rates exceed those found in other communities. Furthermore, since the incidence of victimization is highest for persons who have incomes of less than $10,000 a year, the blacks in the lower socioeconomic classes suffer especially.

But the economic impact of crime on the black community goes far beyond its effects on individual victims. For example, as Andrew Brimmer (1975) has argued, crime losses experienced by minority firms represent a significant drain on these firms' net earnings. Their economic viability is lessened by the continued threat and reality of robbery and burglary. Urban economists also argue that such threats and reality deter many businesses from locating in ghetto areas. It is plausibly argued that the threat of crime increases the cost of doing business even if the firm experiences no criminal victimization (Fusfield and Bates, 1984:166–169): insurance rates are higher in ghetto areas; commercial lenders may restrict credit or charge higher interest rates; and delivery patterns of cautious distributors may be more uncertain and erratic. To the extent that these patterns prevail, the results are a loss of jobs for black residents, more expensive goods and services, decreased livability of neighborhoods, and the loss of other benefits of locally operated businesses (Caplovitz, 1968). At the same time, much of the income from illegal activities does not stay in the ghetto (Fusfield and Bates, 1984:167).

Given that high rates of crime reduce the likelihood of profitable businesses in the black community, one must ask why and how some firms have survived and prospered. Some of the variation may be due to the type of business, the hours of operation, the level of consumer interaction, and the method of transactions used. Many businesses survive by adopting protective measures that add to the "armed camp" mentality that often pervades inner-city black communities. These measures, though needed to ensure the survival of businesses, convey strong messages about the quality of life in such environments.

There are few studies of the costs and benefits of crime for any group. Yet some aspects of these largely unexplored questions can be researched with data from the national annual survey of the victims of crime, the National Crime Survey (NCS). This source provides information on the race, family structures, income, and the employment characteristics of households in sampled neighborhoods. It also gives detailed information about the characteristics of heads of households and individuals in the sample and contains data on the incidence of commercial or business victimization.

Begun in 1974, these annual surveys of personal and household victimizations are conducted for a nationally representative sample of more than 10,000 individuals from 59,000 housing units and other living quarters in 6-month rotation groups. Although a variety of criminal acts are included among the count of victimizations—assault, burglary, larceny, motor vehicle theft, rape, and robbery—three important classes of crimes are generally excluded. First, drug transactions, prostitution, and related crimes are excluded because these are classified as "victimless" crimes. Second, "series victimizations," or the occurrence of three or more essentially identical criminal events among which the police cannot distinguish, are excluded. And finally, crimes against most businesses are excluded, except for households in which a commercial enterprise is conducted or when a victimization occurs in a commercial enterprise. As a result of these survey problems, the NCS can give only a truncated picture of victimizations in the black and white communities.

To understand the impact of criminal activity on communities, it is useful to focus on the costs incurred by victims. These costs include dollar losses from property crimes, expenses related to injuries sustained in violent attacks, and time lost from work in the aftermath of crime. Looking at the broad patterns of these costs for 1974–1985, the costs of crime are consistently greater for blacks than they are for whites. When the data are examined in greater detail, race differences remain, although some of these differences may be the result of the greater incidence of poverty among blacks.

The National Crime Survey includes questions to victims about the dollar losses (theft and damages) associated with criminal incidents. The U.S. Department of Justice calls these monetary costs "economic losses." In 1985, the majority of the more than 14 million personal victimizations in the United States resulted in losses of less than $50. The estimate is derived by including the loss categories of "no monetary value" (1 percent), "not known and not available" (8 percent), and "less than $50" (45 percent). Whites were slightly more likely than blacks to have small losses from personal victimizations, which include robberies and assaults. For example, for victims reporting some economic loss in 1985, 46 percent of whites and 40 percent of blacks claimed amounts of less than $50 (Myers and Sabol, 1987).

A black-white gap is apparent for household victimizations, which include burglaries, larcenies, and motor vehicle thefts. While the economic losses for blacks and whites in amounts over $250 have been rising (partly due to price inflation), there is a nearly constant excess of the black loss over the white loss; see Figure 9-3a. For personal victimizations, however, the excess of black losses is not observed for every year, although both these measures of victimization were rising; see Figure 9-3b. Throughout the mid- to late 1970s, blacks were more likely than whites to have economic losses over $250. The reverse was true for 1979–1980 and for 1983–1985. Since blacks report far more household than personal crimes, relative to whites, the pattern of comparatively greater losses experienced by blacks seems persistent.

Blacks also experience greater medical costs (Figure 9-4) and more time lost from work (Figure 9-5) due to personal victimizations (e.g., rapes, robberies, and assaults) than do whites. First, as Figure 9-4 depicts, greater proportions of blacks than whites had medical expenses in excess of $250 as a result of injuries sustained in violent attacks. And as detailed in Table 9-3, blacks lose more time from work as a result of crime. Blacks who required inpatient medical care as a result of their injuries spent more days in the hospital than hospitalized whites.

The distribution of criminal incidents by the race of the victim and characteristics of the neighborhood in which the victim's household is located and the dollar losses from robbery and theft are given in Tables 9-4 and 9-5. For the selected years 1973, 1977, and 1981, the majority of black victims of criminal incidents lived in mixed neighborhoods with less than 45 percent black populations in 1977 and 1981, while the majority of white victims lived in essentially all-white neighborhoods. Only about one-fifth of criminal incidents with black victims involved persons who lived in households in all-black neighborhoods in 1973, and that proportion dropped to 16–17 percent in later years.

As expected, given the differing rates of poverty among blacks and whites, the poverty status of neighborhoods also differed between black and white victims. About 70 percent of white victims lived in neighborhoods with poverty rates of less than 10 percent. Black victims, in contrast, were disproportionately found in near-poverty and high-poverty areas, mostly in the former: about 40 percent were in near-poverty neighborhoods (poverty rates from 11 to 25 percent), much more than in high-poverty neighborhoods (rates above 25 percent).

A relatively small proportion of criminal incidents occurred in commercial buildings. The highest rates of commercial victimizations occur in all-white neighborhoods—where most of the commercial establishments exist. Poor black neighborhoods, where the majority of the residents are black and the poverty rate exceeds 25 percent, experience business victimizations at about the same rate as poor white neighborhoods (Myers and Sabol, 1987:113).

For household losses due to thefts, blacks who live in nonpoor neighborhoods report significantly higher total monetary losses than blacks in poor

FIGURE 9-3 Economic losses from (a) household and (b) personal crimes, by race of victim, 1974–1985.

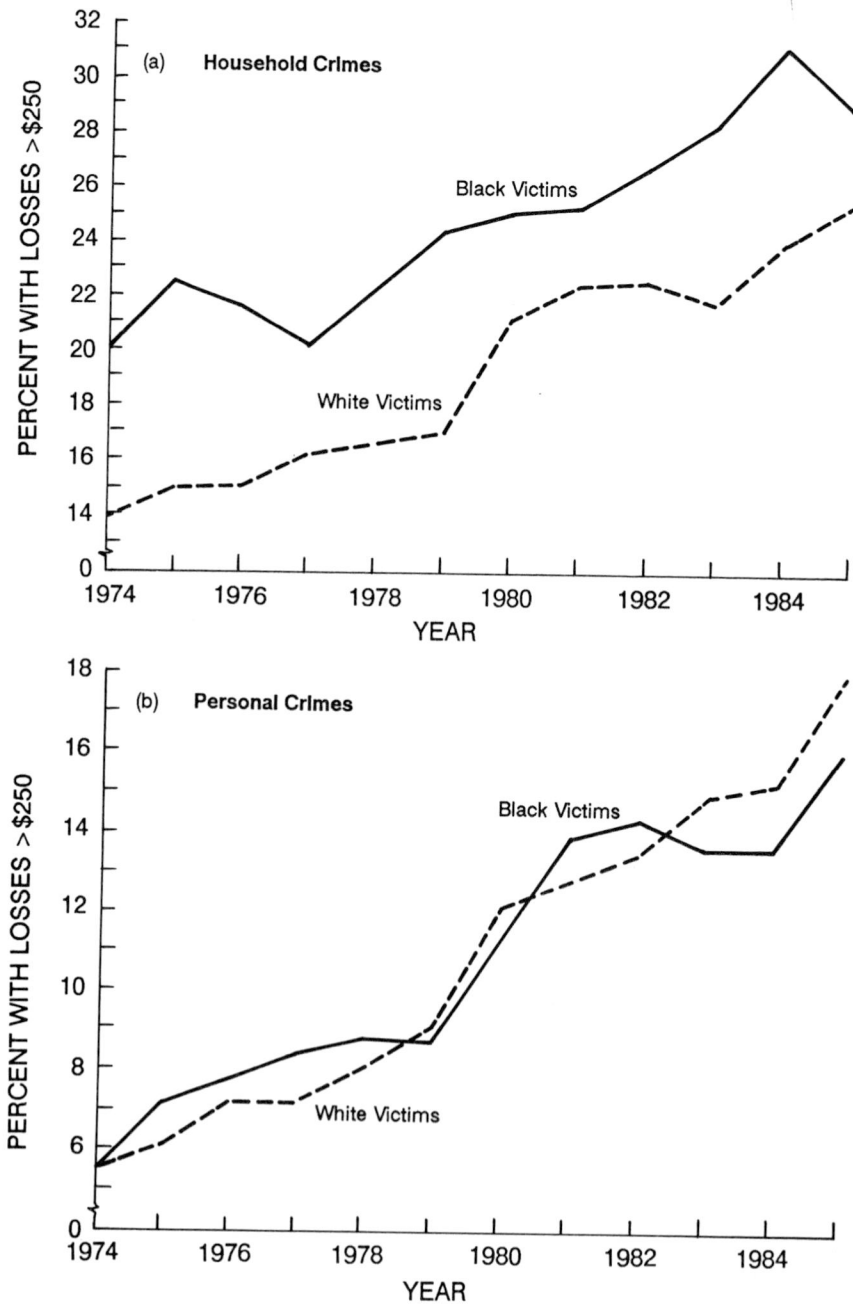

Source: Myers and Sabol (1987).

FIGURE 9-4 Medical expenses of violent crime victims, by race of victim, 1974–1985.

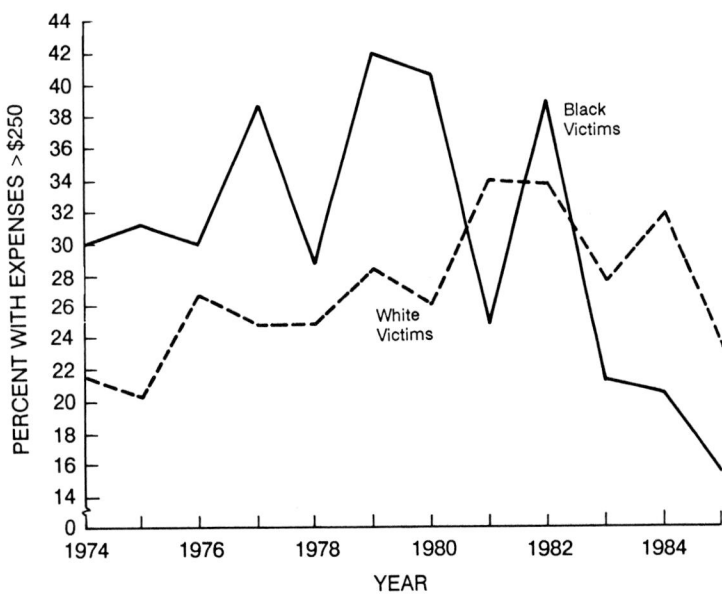

Source: Myers and Sabol (1987).

FIGURE 9-5 Time lost from work because of personal victimization, by race, 1974–1985.

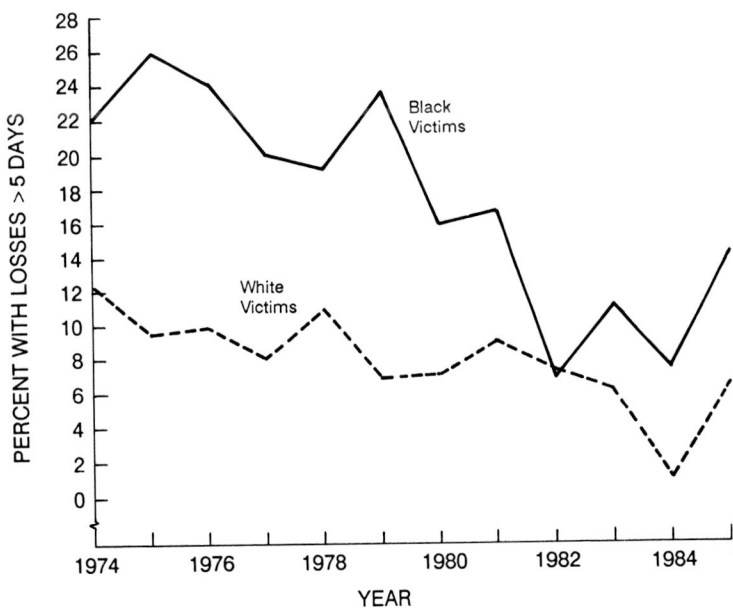

Source: Myers and Sabol (1987).

TABLE 9-3 Days Lost from Work, by Race of Victim and Type of Victimization, 1974–1985

Year	Days	White Victim		Black Victim		All Households & Persons	
		Household	Personal	Household	Personal	Household	Personal
1974	0–5	94.00%	84.30%	92.00%	74.00%	92.00%	82.80%
	≥6	4.20	14.30	8.10	24.10	8.10	15.40
	N.K.	1.80	1.50		1.90		1.80
1975	0–5	92.40	87.20	93.70	69.20	92.80	84.00
	≥6	6.60	11.40	4.70	27.90	6.10	14.40
	N.K.	1.00	1.30	1.60	3.00	1.10	1.60
1976	0–5	93.30	86.20	92.90	72.80	93.30	84.30
	≥6	4.70	11.90	3.90	26.10	4.50	13.80
	N.K.	2.00	1.90	3.20	1.00	2.20	1.90
1977	0–5	91.70	87.70	95.80	75.70	92.20	85.70
	≥6	6.80	10.10	4.10	22.00	6.50	12.10
	N.K.	1.50	2.10	0.00	2.30	1.20	2.10
1978	0–5	93.00	86.00	91.80	77.60	92.90	84.90
	≥6	4.50	12.90	8.20	21.20	5.30	13.80
	N.K.	2.40	1.10	0.00	1.10	1.90	1.30
1979	0–5	95.10	88.90	98.70	72.40	95.50	86.30
	≥6	3.70	8.90	0.00	25.60	3.40	11.30
	N.K.	1.10	2.20	1.30	2.00	1.20	2.20
1980	0–5	94.20	90.00	88.90	76.50	93.60	88.10
	≥6	4.40	9.10	7.50	17.90	4.70	10.50
	N.K.	1.40	0.90	3.60	5.60	1.70	1.40
1981	0–5	96.60	87.90	93.40	77.40	96.00	86.60
	≥6	1.70	11.00	4.50	18.70	2.30	11.70
	N.K.	1.70	1.10	2.10	3.90	1.70	1.60
1982	0–5	94.90	89.60	95.80	89.10	95.10	89.70
	≥6	4.10	9.30	2.50	8.80	3.80	9.20
	N.K.	1.00	1.10	1.70	2.10	1.10	1.20
1983	0–5	93.10	86.40	93.00	79.50	89.30	89.30
	≥6	1.00	8.10	2.90	13.10	0.90	4.70
	N.K.	5.10	5.50	4.10	7.40	9.70	6.30
1984	0–5	81.30	87.00	87.10	81.30	86.40	81.50
	≥6	9.60	3.10	3.10	9.60	3.50	10.50
	N.K.	9.10	9.90	9.90	9.10	10.10	8.00
1985	0–5	85.20	84.50	90.80	72.80	87.80	85.60
	≥6	4.30	8.50	1.00	16.30	2.20	6.80
	N.K.	10.50	7.40	8.30	10.80	10.10	7.70

Notes: N.K.: not known. Total percent for each year does not always equal 100 because of rounding.

Source: Myers and Sabol (1987).

TABLE 9-4 Criminal Incidents by Racial Makeup of Neighborhood and Race of Victim, 1973–1981

Racial Makeup of Neighborhood (percent black)	1973 Victim		1977 Victim		1981 Victim	
	Black	White	Black	White	Black	White
0	4.8	49.8	6.1	50.5	10	50.3
1–10	11.8	36.5	15.3	36.4	15.5	36.9
11+	83.4	13.7	78.3	13.1	74.5	12.8
Total	100%	100%	100%	100%	100%	100%
≤45	44.8		51.8		54.5	
≥46–89≤	34.3		32.5		28.6	
≥90	20.9		15.7		16.9	
Total	100%		100%		100%	

Note: Total percent does not always equal 100 because of rounding.

Source: Myers and Sabol (1987).

neighborhoods. Such a finding is not consistently evident among whites during the years between 1973 and 1981. Blacks in nonpoor and near-poor neighborhoods report losses that are twice as high as those reported by whites in nonpoor and near-poor neighborhoods. While the losses of blacks and whites in poor neighborhoods are comparable, the losses of blacks in neighborhoods with poverty rates of less than 10 percent are among the very highest rates reported of any group. Looking at family income, this finding is strengthened considerably. The major monetary losses from personal and household victimizations in recent years were borne by the black middle class and near poor.

While many larcenies and assaults are black male-on-male offenses and violent attacks are increasingly becoming the source of significant mortality among young inner-city black males, measures of monetary losses from thefts, burglaries, and other household crimes suggest that economic crimes are occurring across class lines and are not simply an instance of poor blacks stealing from other poor blacks. However, the losses due to crime among the black poor should not be underemphasized since these victims have fewer resources and methods of compensating for those losses.

Our broad conclusion is that blacks bear a disproportionate share of the costs of criminal victimizations, but that they do not share these costs equally. Middle-class and near-poor blacks seem to suffer significantly greater losses than poor blacks or than whites of any income level. Thus, blacks living in near-poverty or nonpoverty areas lose more on average from thefts, robberies, and burglaries than blacks or whites living in high-poverty areas.

These findings run counter to two popular misconceptions: that the white community suffers disproportionately from black crime and that poor blacks suffer disproportionately from all types of black crime. The repeated appeals for law and order frequently found in black middle-class newspapers and popular magazines provide further indication of the actual pattern of crime against blacks.

TABLE 9-5 Financial Losses (in dollars) Because of Robbery and Theft, by Race of Victims, 1974–1985

Year	Value	White		Black		All Races	
		Robbery	Theft	Robbery	Theft	Robbery	Theft
1974	0–$249	77.80%	91.80%	81.40%	90.60%	77.40%	91.70%
	≥ $250	15.80	5.10	11.70	5.10	14.70	5.00
	N.K.	6.40	3.10	7.90	4.30	7.90	3.30
1975	0–$249	78.30	91.30	79.60	89.00	78.70	90.90
	≥ $250	13.70	5.60	15.10	6.50	13.90	5.70
	N.K.	6.90	2.50	5.30	4.70	6.70	2.70
1976	0–$249	76.00	89.60	79.10	85.20	79.70	89.30
	≥ $250	11.00	6.70	10.70	7.50	13.00	6.70
	N.K.	14.00	3.00	7.20	5.30	7.20	3.20
1977	0–$249	77.70	89.00	74.80	85.10	75.90	89.10
	≥ $250	14.40	6.70	16.40	8.10	15.20	6.90
	N.K.	7.10	3.10	8.90	5.90	7.60	3.40
1978	0–$249	68.00	90.90	84.80	86.50	71.60	88.00
	≥ $250	22.80	3.40	11.70	8.20	19.80	7.80
	N.K.	7.90	7.90	3.80	4.40	6.80	3.50
1979	0–$249	75.60	85.70	66.10	84.10	72.90	85.40
	≥ $250	16.30	9.00	18.20	7.00	16.50	8.90
	N.K.	8.60	4.90	15.70	8.20	10.30	5.30
1980	0–$249	67.00	84.00	68.50	82.40	67.60	84.90
	≥ $250	22.00	11.80	19.70	10.50	21.30	22.00
	N.K.	9.80	4.40	11.80	7.00	10.30	9.80
1981	0–$249	67.30	83.30	67.50	82.60	67.50	83.20
	≥ $250	21.70	12.70	25.40	12.60	22.60	12.60
	N.K.	11.10	3.80	7.10	4.20	9.90	3.90
1982	0–$249	70.30	82.50	64.00	82.00	68.40	82.20
	≥ $250	20.00	13.30	28.40	12.30	22.50	13.20
	N.K.	8.90	4.00	7.00	5.60	8.40	4.30
1983	0–$249	63.50	82.00	68.20	81.00	80.50	93.10
	≥ $250	26.00	14.10	24.40	13.60	8.60	2.70
	N.K.	11.50	3.90	7.50	5.40	10.60	4.10
1984	0–$249	61.10	80.50	69.50	77.60	62.90	80.50
	≥ $250	26.20	14.60	17.60	13.50	25.10	14.60
	N.K.	11.80	4.10	11.80	8.60	11.60	4.60
1985	0–$249	67.30	79.20	61.20	78.00	65.50	79.00
	≥ $250	24.20	15.70	27.10	14.40	24.70	15.60
	N.K.	9.80	4.70	11.80	7.30	9.90	5.10

Note: N.K.: not known.

Source: Myers and Sabol (1987).

THE CRIMINAL JUSTICE PROCESS

The findings presented to this point have documented the magnitude of arrests and of victimization among blacks, and the persisting gaps between blacks and whites. We now discuss the treatment accorded to blacks and whites at various stages of the criminal justice process.

POLICE BEHAVIOR AND THE DECISION TO ARREST

Extensive investigations of racial bias in the decision to arrest have not been conducted. Most police behavior, unlike that of judicial personnel, is not easily visible to would-be researchers, and the sheer volume of police activity makes it difficult to assess. It is not surprising, therefore, that much of the direct evidence supporting allegations of bias in arrest decisions has been anecdotal. Also, the higher rates of black arrests across many types of offenses sometimes have been interpreted as indirect evidence of bias.

The enforcement of most criminal laws allows substantial discretion by the police—discretion that could lead to rates of arrest that do not reflect "actual" criminal behavior. However, the role of the police in initiating the arrest of persons is more limited than sometimes thought. The vast majority of cases that enter the criminal justice system do so as a result of the efforts of victims or other complainants rather than through the initiative of the police (Reiss and Bordua, 1967:29–32).

Most investigations of crime by police are reactive rather than proactive (Black, 1973), but sometimes the police are the complainants: for example, police surveillance may result in observation of criminal activity. Thus, one possible source of bias could be differential police surveillance of persons by race. This could be a result of the attitudes of individual policemen, or of policy, if police departments differentially patrol neighborhoods based on the race of their residents.

Empirical investigations during the 1950s and 1960s often concluded that white police officers frequently held opinions that were prejudiced toward blacks. In a study of police behavior in a California city, Skolnick (1966:80–90) reported that "a negative attitude toward Negroes was a norm among the police studied." Similarly, in a study of police behavior in Boston, Chicago, and Washington, D.C., Black and Reiss (1967:132–139) found that 72 percent of the white officers displayed attitudes toward blacks that were classified as either "prejudiced" or "extremely prejudiced." Quinney (1970:130, citing Kephart, 1957:88–93) reported that 75 percent of police officers studied in Philadelphia during the 1950s overestimated the percentage of arrests involving blacks made in the districts to which they were assigned (see Banton, 1964).

Some writers have argued that these attitudes were translated into discriminatory behavior (e.g., Mendelsohn, 1971:167). Others took a more cautious view. Skolnick (1966:84), Black and Reiss (1967), *Yale Law Journal* editors (1967:1645,n.9), and Bayley and Mendelsohn (1969) all argued that prejudice did not necessarily lead to discriminatory behavior on the part of police officers (Cooney, 1987:5–6).

Several more recent studies show some differences in the behavior of the police toward white and black citizens who make complaints. Friedrich (1977:302–303) found a differential: 61 percent of white complaints and 52 percent of black complaints were written up as crimes. Pursuing the matter further, Friedrich (1977:310–313) discovered that although black and white officers were equally likely to record incidents as crimes, both were more likely to record incidents against members of their own race as crimes. The differential was greater for white officers than for black officers: white officers officially recorded 26 percent more of the white complaints than of the black complaints, and black officers wrote up 7 percent more of the black complaints than of the white complaints. One difference in crime reports across the races can thus be traced to a greater tendency of white policemen to treat the complaints of people of their own race as more legally serious than those of people of the other race (Cooney, 1987).

Such studies as those reported above have been rare. We do not know for certain how generalizable the results are across the more than 40-year period covered by this review, or to different settings (e.g., South and non-South, small towns and large cities).

RACE PREJUDICE AND VICTIM RACIAL CHARACTERISTICS

The focus of the empirical literature on race prejudice in the administration of justice has primarily been on the race of the offender. A now sizable literature reports that prejudice may serve to either overpenalize or underpenalize black offenders in comparison to their white counterparts. The choice of alternatives is believed to depend on the race of the victim.

Prejudice toward blacks may result in black offenders who victimize other blacks being treated more leniently than black or white offenders who victimize whites (Baldus et al., 1983; Garfinkel, 1949; Gross and Mauro, 1984; Johnson, 1941; LaFree, 1980; Paternoster, 1983, 1984; Radelet, 1981; Thomson and Zingraff, 1981). Most of these observations have involved the behavior of non–law enforcement personnel (e.g., judges and juries). The logic underlying their arguments has recently resulted in a review by the U.S. Supreme Court of the differential allocation of the death penalty on the basis of the race of the victim (*McClesky* v. *Kemp*, 107 S.Ct. 1756 [1987]). The studies of Quinney (1970), Friedrich (1977), and Hawkins (1983, 1986) suggested that the police may also respond differentially to incidents involving black and white offenders and victims. The race of both the victim and offender have not been controlled in most studies of police behavior. But when the race of both parties to an alleged crime is included in the analysis, there does appear to be a difference in the police response to intraracial and interracial incidents.

Intraracial arrest rates do not vary much in locations outside of the South. A three-city (Boston, Chicago, and Washington, D.C.) observation study of police behavior during 1966 (Black, 1971) found that blacks were arrested more frequently than whites for intraracial crimes. Black proposed that this difference was not the result of race prejudice on the part of the police officer and was not primarily a race-of-victim effect. Rather, he concluded that the difference in arrest rates disappears once the "degree of respect" shown the police officer by the suspect is included in the analysis. Black suspects were found to display greater antagonism toward the police than white suspects, and this fact, rather than race per se, was said to account for their higher arrest rate. One of the major criticisms of Black's conclusion is the lack of explanation as to why black suspects were "more disrespectful" toward the police than their white counterparts. The disrespect of black suspects toward the police may be a product of the volatility of police-civilian encounters in black communities and the documented prejudice of policemen. There appears to be a cycle of disrespect generated by the interactions between black communities and the police toward each other. And of course, racial tensions characterized the entire country when this research was conducted in 1966 (Hawkins, 1987).

More recently, in a study of arrests in Rochester, New York; St. Louis, Missouri; and Tampa–St. Petersburg, Florida, Smith and colleagues (1984) reported little difference in the way police handled intraracial crimes in black and white communities. Similar conclusions were reached in a study of interpersonal disputes by Smith and Klein (1984) and of family violence by Berk and Loseke (1980–1981:333). But another study of interpersonal violence (Smith, 1987) found that cases of violence between whites are significantly more likely to end in arrest than similar cases between blacks.

Interracial arrest rates produce somewhat different patterns. A study of all sexual assault cases handled by the police in a large midwestern city during 1970, 1973, and 1975 (LaFree, 1980) reported three major findings. First, the race of the suspect and victim did not significantly predict arrest before 1973, when sexual assault cases were dealt with by the homicide and robbery unit of the police department. Second, after the formation in 1973 of a special police unit to deal with sex offenses, cases between blacks became less likely to result in arrest than those between whites or those between a black suspect and a white victim. (There were too few cases of white offenders and black victims to be meaningfully included.) Third, throughout the period of the study, cases of black suspects alleged to have offended against white victims attracted legally more serious charges than cases involving any of the other offender-victim combinations of race.

Smith and colleagues (1984) found that for cases of black suspects and white victims the probability of arrest was .336; for cases of black suspects and black victims it was .218; for cases of white suspects and white victims it was .189; and for cases of white suspects and black victims the probability was .107. However, after controlling for a number of other variables (e.g., the suspect's "level of respect toward the police"), the differences between these probabilities diminished to statistically nonsignificant levels. Nevertheless, the authors found that arrests were more likely for property crimes against whites than against blacks, and that the requests of white complainants for arrests were complied with more frequently than those of black complainants (Cooney, 1987:9).

Victimless offenses do not present clear evidence of black-white disparities. A study of 195 cases of public drunkenness (the largest single category of arrestees during the past several decades) revealed no significant difference in the arrest rates of black and white offenders (Lundman, 1974). A larger study of the same offense in another city arrived at the same conclusion (Pastor, 1978). Similarly, Friedrich's (1977:301–302) analysis of 319 traffic cases failed to uncover any systematic difference in the treatment of black and white drivers. On the other hand, Lundman's (1979) study of 293 moving traffic violations reports that black drivers were somewhat more likely than white drivers—55 percent to 47 percent—to receive a citation from the police.

Juvenile arrest patterns lead to more definite conclusions with respect to black-white arrest rate differences. The first observational study of this issue suggested that black juveniles were more vulnerable to arrest than white juveniles (Pilavin and Briar, 1964). This result was confirmed and elaborated in a three-city study by Black and Reiss (1970), who presented a set of related findings: (1) Only 15 percent of all police-juvenile encounters ended in arrest. (2) Black juveniles were more likely to be arrested than white juveniles for the same conduct. (3) When only a suspect was present, the difference in arrest rates for black and white juveniles was negligible (14 percent for blacks and 10 percent for whites). (4) When complainants and suspects were present, black juveniles were arrested 2.5 times more frequently than white juveniles (21 percent for blacks and 8 percent for whites). (5) When complainants were present, the police comply with their expressed preferences to a significant degree. In the sample of cases analyzed, a request for leniency never resulted in arrest; requests for arrest were granted in a majority of cases. (6) There were differences in the preferences expressed by black and white complainants: black complainants sought arrest slightly more frequently than white complainants (21 percent for blacks and 15 percent for whites), but white complainants expressed a preference for the informal disposition of cases considerably more frequently than black complainants (58 percent for whites and 31 percent for blacks). (7) The great majority of suspects and complainants were of the same race. (8) The higher arrest rate of black juveniles was therefore largely a function of police officers complying with requests from white complainants for lenient dispositions for white juveniles (Cooney, 1987).

Black and Reiss's findings were subsequently replicated by Lundman and colleagues (1978), cited in Cooney (1987). These authors also concluded that differences in the preferences of black and white complainants explain cross-racial variation in juvenile arrest rates. Neither of these studies could explain the racial difference in complainants' preferences. Cooney (1987) suggests that a plausible hypothesis is that the difference in complainants' preferences are related to the greater prevalence of female-headed families in the black population. Two-parent families are likely to be able to exert a more secure system of authority over children and protect them from external influences (see Matsueda and Heimer, 1987). It is known that recourse to legal solutions is least likely when nonlegal authority is strong (Black, 1976:107–111); it is quite possible that more effective controls generated by two-parent families leads to a relatively lower demand for formal legal action against juvenile offenders in the white community (Cooney, 1987).

POLICE ORGANIZATION

Modern police departments are complex organizations. Arrest rates are an organizational outcome as well as a reflection of criminal activity. Such factors as the availability and allocation of financial resources, the extent and nature of resource allocation, and various political exigencies affect police arrest rates. In this section we report findings on police organization in relation to racial differentials in police-citizen encounters.

Jacobs (1979) reported that metropolitan areas with larger numbers of blacks had stronger law enforcement agencies than areas with fewer blacks in 1970, but not in 1960 (with "strength" estimated by indices such as expenditures for personnel and number of personnel). Other studies have explored whether this relationship is a result of higher crime rates among blacks or of other factors. Jackson and Carroll (1981) used the racial composition of the city, the level of black mobilization activity, and the frequency of riots in the 1960s as predictors of police strength in a sampling of 90 nonsouthern cities during 1971. They concluded that police expenditures were mobilized or expanded when blacks appeared threatening to the dominant group. Liska and colleagues (1981) looked at police department strength in 109 U.S. municipal areas between 1950 and 1972. They reported that the apparent effect of racial composition depends on geographical region and year (before or after the civil disorders of the 1960s). The greatest increases in police strength were noted first for the South and then in all regions after the 1960s. The large increases in police forces during the late 1960s and early 1970s could not be accounted for by a rise in reported crimes alone.

Liska and colleagues (1985) looked at data on arrests for 77 U.S. cities with populations of 100,000 or more. They found that the percentage nonwhite and a measure of segregation were significantly correlated with the number of arrests per 100,000 known crimes. However, they did not find that the certainty of arrests was greater for blacks than for whites. Rather, they suggest that a high percentage of nonwhites and a low level of segregation increase the perceived threat of crime. These perceptions then increase pressure on the police to control crime, which in turn increases the certainty of arrests for both whites and nonwhites.

Police organization and policy have important effects on the number of shootings of civilians by police officers. Police use of deadly force results in a sizable number of citizens being killed every year. Since there is some underreporting, precise figures are not available. Nevertheless, it has been estimated that police killings represent about 1.5–4 percent of all homicides each year (Sherman and Langworthy, 1979:559).

Of those killed by the police, disproportionate numbers are black (Sherman, 1980:95):

> According to official statistics, blacks constituted forty-six percent of people killed by official police action in 1975, while they constituted only 11.5 percent of the population.

Takagi (1979, cited in Hawkins, 1987) calculated that in the years from 1950 to 1968 blacks were killed by police at least 9 times as frequently as whites. The overrepresentation of blacks among victims of police killings could be due to either or both of two causes (Goldkamp, 1976). The first is that blacks expose themselves to being killed by the police by engaging more frequently than whites in dangerous criminal activity. The second possibility is simply that there is a greater willingness of the police to shoot blacks.

Examining data on police homicide from the 50 states for the period of 1961–1970, Kania and Mackey (1977) found that the best predictors of killings by police were the police exposure to violent crime and the overall rate of homicide. However, the authors did not analyze the data by race. Of more direct relevance is the study by Milton and colleagues (1977:11) of police shootings in seven cities. They concluded:

> The number of blacks and other minorities shot by police is substantially greater than their number in the general population, but is not inconsistent with the number of blacks arrested for serious criminal offenses (index crimes).

It is not clear, however, how well this measure of police-citizen contact (arrests for serious crime) can serve as a predictor of another form of contact (killings).

Methodological problems also reduce the plausibility of a number of studies that have concluded that police racial bias does exist. For example, Harding and Fahey (1973) concluded that a credible alternative to the official police version of the killing existed in 11 of the 79 cases from Chicago that they analyzed. The authors found also that the percentage of blacks killed per 10,000 arrests was higher than the percentage of whites so killed. But neither of these findings can be taken as direct evidence of racial discrimination. As noted above, comparing death and arrest rates proves little because arrest rates do not directly measure differences in the kind of conduct (by the citizen or officer) that plausibly will lead to the use of deadly force (see, e.g., Knoohuizen et al., 1972).

Several studies have sought to control more adequately for the conduct of the people killed by the police. Meyer's (1980) analysis of shootings by Los Angeles police from 1974 to 1979 found that a greater percentage of blacks than whites who were shot at by the police were subsequently found to have been unarmed. However, Meyer also reported that more of the shootings that involved blacks were preceded by suspects' disobeying police orders to halt or by suspects' appearing to reach for weapons. Given these ambiguous results, it is not surprising that one of the main points made by Meyer's paper is the need for more research.

Sherman (1980) reached different conclusions: he stated that changes in police policy toward gun use by officers reduces the number of blacks killed by police. Fyfe (1981, 1982) reached similar conclusions concerning police shootings in Memphis and New York City. Police records of all shootings by officers in New York City from 1971 to 1975 showed that blacks were overrepresented among those shot at by the police, but that they also made up a greater percentage of shooting opponents armed with guns and a greater percentage of those involved in robberies at the time of the shooting. Furthermore, more whites (16 percent) than blacks (8 percent) had no gun when shot at by the police. Fyfe (1981) therefore concluded that the racial disparity in shootings was a function of the greater involvement of blacks in crimes that precipitated police-citizen violence. But Fyfe (1982) arrived at a different conclusion when he conducted similar research in Memphis. There he found that the disproportionate shooting of blacks could not be explained by their greater criminal activity. He attributed the difference between the findings in New York and Memphis to the difference in stringency of the policy on use of firearms in the two departments. The police shootings in New York, but not those in Memphis, were subject to strict review procedures. Thus, the deterrent against unlawful or improper shooting presumably was greater in New York than in Memphis.

In sum, blacks far more often than whites are killed by police, and some part of the differential may arise from the more frequent involvement of blacks in violent crimes. But the most concern among blacks has been over the disproportionate number of unjustified killings of blacks. In this regard, the relatively large number of police killings of all citizens, especially during the past, is partly a consequence of permissive gun-use policy in many police units. Greater variation in local police procedures leave open the possibility of racial discrimination by individual police officers in some cities.

Police-citizen review boards have been a response to the problems created by racial tensions over police shootings of blacks and other minorities. The use of force by the police against blacks was identified to be one of the factors precipitating many of the civil disturbances of the 1960s (see, e.g., the National Advisory Commission on Civil Disorders, 1968). (More recent disturbances in Miami [in 1980] have also involved allegations of police misconduct vis-à-vis blacks.) A major observation of the commission report was the lack of adequate mechanisms for black communities to redress grievances against the police. The commission's recommendation led to the establishment of police-civilian review boards in many cities.

During the past two decades, many such boards have ceased to exist. This trend may be due to greater acceptance of the idea that the most effective way to control police misconduct is through internal administrative procedures. As Skolnick (1968) noted, this belief was widely adhered to even when external review boards were first established. Alternatively, the trend could represent an effort to avoid police accountability. Little research has been conducted on the relative merits of alternative methods of controlling police use of deadly force. Much of the impetus for reform of police behavior appears to have shifted to the hiring and promotion of black police officers.

PRETRIAL BARGAINING AND PROSECUTION

Prosecutors may be the most important decision makers in the criminal justice process because prosecutors determine whether to press criminal charges against defendants or to dismiss a case. If a decision is made to go forward with a case, a prosecutor must determine the appropriate charge and decide whether or not to negotiate a plea with the defendant. If a decision to plea bargain is made, the terms of the bargain must be specified, and the prosecutor can change the charge, drop one or more counts, or recommend a mitigated sentence to the judge. If a prosecutor chooses not to bargain, then the case must be prepared for trial and argued in court (Alschuler, 1968, 1979).

Yet the role of prosecutors is perhaps the least known of all official roles in the administration of justice, and analyses focusing on racial disparities in prosecutorial decision making are especially scarce. Despite the popular image of the jury trial as the method of fact determination and sentencing for criminal law cases, most criminal cases are plea bargained. Guilty pleas obtained through bargaining account for approximately 95 percent of the convictions in U.S. courts (Zatz and Cameron, 1987:5). Thus, along with the decision to arrest, prosecutorial decisions are a major factor in the treatment accorded criminal suspects.

The decision to prosecute necessarily involves a large amount of discretion, but there are some limits. The decisions that are made must maintain harmonious relations with judges and defense attorneys (Church, 1976, 1978; Eisenstein and Jacob, 1977; Maynard, 1984; Nardulli, 1978). Prosecutors must also balance courts' need for efficiency, their own desire for high conviction rates, and the dispensing of "justice." Despite these real limits, prosecutors' discretionary power has been described as "unchecked," "subject to abuse," and "unconstitutional" (e.g., Blumberg, 1967; Davis, 1971; 1976; Michalowski, 1985). Yet plea bargaining is likely to remain an indispensable means of helping to clear crowded court calendars, especially in urban areas.

In addition, the recent national trend toward determinate sentencing has enhanced the role of prosecutors. Determinate-sentencing statutes seek to reduce the discretion of judges and parole boards. Discretion then reverts to the prosecutor (McCoy, 1984; Miethe, 1987). Once a legislature has set the presumptive sentence for each offense, including specified increases or decreases in sentence severity for aggravating and mitigating circumstances, the judge has considerably less room within which to act. Prosecutors, through changes in charges, and in some cases in the number of counts, may then determine the sentence. In most instances, such changes result from plea bargaining.

From defendants' perspective, possible avoidance of jail or prison time is the primary consideration in deciding whether to plead guilty and, if so, to what charge (Church, 1976; Neubauer, 1974). Almost invariably, plea bargaining results in a lighter sentence than would result from conviction by a jury. This apparent leniency for plea bargaining may be a reward for saving the court time and money and showing evidence of contrition. Alternatively, it may simply be a built-in response to a policy of initial overcharging in expectation of a plea bargain. Prosecutorial discretion may not be equally advantageous to all defendants. In particular, it may operate in ways that are detrimental to poor and minority defendants (Uhlman, 1979:14).

Generally, prosecutorial discretion may be said to be potentially biased if any of the following three conditions are met (Zatz and Cameron, 1987:8): dismissals by the prosecutor are more likely for one racial or ethnic group than another; rates of plea bargaining differ for members of different racial or ethnic groups; or members of one group receive consistently better deals than members of another group. Racial disparities in prosecutorial decisions may be due to a number of factors, including: (1) reluctance to proceed with the case if police disproportionately arrest minorities without sufficient evidence for conviction; (2) reluctance of prosecutors to bargain with minority defendants; (3) perception by prosecutors that minorities would not have the financial resources necessary to delay case processing to the point at which a trial would be unduly costly to the state; (4) differences in the perceived credibility of minority and white witnesses, including victims; (5) perception by prosecutors that a given offense and defendant fit or do not fit certain stereotypical images, particularly concerning dangerousness; (6) racial differences in patterns of overcharging by prosecutors in anticipation of plea bargaining; (7) the racial or ethnic composition of the courtroom actors; and (8) the racial or ethnic composition of the jurisdiction.

The decision to charge or dismiss is pivotal, and the severity of the initial charge is also very important. If prosecutorial decisions are biased against black defendants, one hypothesis would be that cases involving black suspects would have lower rates of dismissals and more severe initial charges. Different studies support or question this hypothesis. For example, in a study of racial disparities in California, Michigan, and Texas, Petersilia (1983:vii) found that blacks in California were more likely than whites to be released without charges. This finding may reflect a response by prosecutors to disparities in arrest practices by police. The supposition that police are more likely to arrest minorities without sufficient evidence or probable cause is supported by the fact that police were more likely to use warrants, which require more stringent evidentiary criteria, when arresting whites than blacks (Petersilia, 1983:26,92–93). As a consequence, prosecutors were more likely to release minorities without filing criminal charges, because the evidence would not support pursuing the case. Another possible reason for the higher dismissal rates for minorities is that prosecutors anticipated difficulties in obtaining convictions at trial if they believe minority victims and witnesses may refuse to cooperate or if they suspect that white victims would have trouble identifying minority suspects (Petersilia, 1983:92–93).

White suspects were more likely than blacks or Hispanics to have felony charges filed against them by police upon arrest, but a greater percentage of whites were subsequently charged with misdemeanors. Blacks were least likely to have the seriousness of their case reduced (reduction rates for Hispanics were between those for whites and blacks). Once charged, offenders of all races had about the same chance of being convicted of a felony, but white defendants were more likely than minorities to be convicted by plea bargain. In contrast, minority defendants were more likely than whites to have their felony cases tried by jury (Petersilia, 1983:xv–xvi; see below).

Other researchers have analyzed precourt and court processing decisions. Hepburn (1978) found that blacks were more likely than whites to be arrested on insufficient evidentiary grounds, but if a warrant was issued, minorities were more likely than whites to be held for prosecution. Similarly, Uhlman (1979) noted that blacks were subjected to more scrutiny by police, which contributed in turn to higher arrest rates for blacks. These higher arrest rates were compounded by an increased likelihood of prosecution rather than dismissal and by more limited opportunities to post bail and plea bargain (Uhlman, 1979:13).

Bernstein and colleagues (1977), Welch and colleagues (1984), and Albonetti (1986) also explored the possibilities of racial bias in prosecutors' decisions to charge or dismiss defendants. They found some results that are consistent with Petersilia's study and others that differ. The racial differences were quite small and in most cases did not attain statistical significance. Welch and colleagues (1984) concluded that the major contribution of their study was to test, and generally to reject, previous hypotheses that discrimination is greater in the less visible prosecutorial decisions in comparison with more visible court proceedings. Similarly, Albonetti (1986) found higher, but not statistically significant, prosecutorial dismissal rates for minorities than for whites.

Plea bargaining may be the method of disposing of a case once the decision to charge has been made. As noted above, Petersilia reported higher rates of plea bargaining for whites than for blacks or Hispanics. In interpreting this finding, Petersilia (1983:101) wrote:

> Racial differences in plea bargaining and jury trials might help explain why minorities receive harsher sentences. This study did not control for plea bargaining in analyzing racial differences in sentence severity. If future research establishes that plea bargaining does contribute to these differences, the next important research task would be to discover why minority defendants are less likely than whites to plea bargain and more likely to have jury trials. Do prosecutors consistently offer less attractive plea bargains to minority defendants, or do minority defendants simply insist more on jury trials?

Whatever the reasons, a large number of investigators have reported that minorities consistently plea bargain less than do whites (LaFree, 1980;

Mather, 1979; Uhlman, 1979; Welch et al., 1985; Zatz and Lizotte, 1985). Most attempted explanations for this phenomenon have emphasized the alienation and suspicion that lower class minorities feel in judicial systems operated by middle-class officials who are usually white. While relatively little research has been conducted that focuses on whether white and minority defendants receive the same quality of bargains, preliminary evidence suggests that whites receive systematically better deals than do blacks and other minorities (Welch et al., 1985; Zatz, 1985).

SENTENCING

Given the widespread public perception of sentencing as punishment for crime, the sentencing decision is "the symbolic keystone of the criminal justice system" (Blumstein et al., 1983:1). In this section we consider several reviews of sentencing studies (Blumstein et al., 1983; Hagan, 1974; Hagan and Bumiller, 1983) and other sources to assess the treatment of blacks during the past four decades.

Sentencing Outcomes and Imprisonment Rates

In reviewing sentencing studies over the past several decades, Hagan and Bumiller (1983:1) noted that such research has become increasingly sophisticated in its use of multivariate statistical techniques. This increased level of sophistication has occurred concurrently with a growing diversification of both research methods and conclusions about the existence of discrimination in sentencing. Many studies report findings of racial bias while others do not.

Controversy in this area of research was less apparent several decades ago. Investigations conducted during the 1940s and 1950s (Johnson, 1941; Johnson, 1957; Lemert and Roseberg, 1948) generally reported findings of racial bias. However, Hagan (1974) noted that these studies and numerous others conducted during the 1960s often did not include tests of statistical significance or summary measures of association. In addition, the study designs often failed to control for legal variables that are known to affect sentence severity (e.g., prior record, offense type, number of charges, characteristics of the offense, and other aggravating or mitigating factors). Those studies were also vulnerable to problems associated with sample selection bias (Hagan and Bumiller, 1983; Klepper et al., 1983).

Hagan and Bumiller (1983) reviewed 51 studies of race and sentencing. In order to assess the possible impact of the civil rights movement on racial differentials, the studies were divided into two groups, pre- and post-1968. Among the pre-1968 studies that controlled for type of offense and prior record, 3 of 11 reported discrimination in sentencing. Of those studies that did not control for these factors, 11 of 14 reported discrimination. This analysis suggested that controlling for these legal variables greatly reduced the likelihood of a finding of racial bias.

Hagan and Bumiller also reported that one-half (10 of 20) of the post-1968 studies reported discrimination. During this period, four of the six studies that did not control for the legal variables reported a finding of discrimination. Hagan and Bumiller (1983:20) conclude:

> While in both time periods studies with these controls have fewer findings of discrimination than studies without such controls, this does not lead in the second time period to any marked decline in the tendency to conclude that discrimination has occurred.

Other reviews of the literature on race and sentencing have produced similar mixed findings (Hardy, 1983; Kleck, 1981; Spohn et al., 1981–1982).

Evidence of both bias and nonbias are also reported in a longitudinal study of the treatment of black and white offenders at several decision-making points in the criminal justice systems of California, Michigan, and Texas (Petersilia, 1983). After controlling for other major factors that might influence sentencing and time served, Petersilia found that blacks and Hispanics received harsher sentences and served longer times in prison than whites. However, she suggested that racial differences in plea bargaining and jury trials (rather than in the sentencing process itself) may have explained some of the differences in length and type of sentence. Plea bargaining resolved a higher percentage of felony cases involving white defendants; jury trials resolved a higher percentage of cases involving minorities. As noted above, conviction by jury results in more severe sentencing.

Petersilia (1983:94) notes, however, that even if these differences accounted for some of the racial differences in sentencing, explanations must still be provided for the decisions that result in black defendants getting jury trials at rates higher than those found among white defendants. In response to this question Petersilia (1983:95) suggests:

> Other studies have shown that blacks are less able than whites to make bail and are more likely to have court appointed lawyers. Research has shown that under those circumstances defendants are more likely to be convicted and to get harsher sentences. Apparently, both circumstances result in weaker cases for the defendant.

These findings and conclusions are similar to those found in several other recent studies, which generally conclude that racial differences in sentencing are less attributable to overt racial bias than to socioeconomic status differences between blacks and whites. Socioeconomic status differences may affect access to competent counsel, the posting of bail, or knowledge of the system and how to make it work to one's benefit. By definition, low socioeconomic status is associated with high rates of unemployment, sporadic work histories, unstable family units, and other forms of perceived risk of continued engagement in criminal activity. Such characteristics are frequently barred from formal use as a part of presentencing reports, but they are used to estimate a convicted person's potential for rehabilitation or recidivism; hence, they may affect decisions concerning probation and parole. They may also be used informally during sentencing despite restrictions on their use. It is frequently argued that these legally relevant, though race-related, factors, rather than race discrimination per se, help to explain black-white sentencing differentials in the post–civil rights movement era.

Determinate sentencing laws may also have an impact on racial inequality in the criminal justice system because of blacks' lower socioeconomic status. A common belief among both scholars and policy makers has been that the flexible sentencing guidelines of the past fostered racial discrimination by permitting judges so inclined to make decisions based on their individual biases toward various racial groups. For example, DuBois (1904) long ago argued that such discretion and the fact that judges were often influenced by public opinion contributed to racial disparities in the administration of justice.

Blumstein and colleagues (1983:1–12) noted that the decade of the 1970s was characterized by a variety of efforts at sentencing reform. These included efforts to modify existing sentencing practices, to establish more detailed criteria for sentencing, and to establish new sentencing institutions and procedures. In various states these reforms took the form of rules and guidelines for plea bargaining, mandatory minimum sentences, statutory determinate sentencing, presumptive or prescriptive sentencing guidelines (requiring judges to provide reasons for sentences), and the establishment of sentencing councils. This movement toward so-called "fixed" sentencing largely reflected an effort to curb somewhat the wide discretion given judges (U.S. Department of Justice, 1978).

Petersilia and Turner (1985) report that the use of the new sentencing guidelines appeared to widen racial disparities in sentencing, supervision, and parole decisions. They report that recent sentencing, probation supervision, and parole release guidelines inevitably reflect such concerns as "just deserts," incapacitation of offenders who pose the most serious threat to public safety, and the most effective use of prison space. Thus, guidelines must be developed to include factors that indicate characteristics of the criminal offender that might correlate with recidivism. Racial inequalities then result because many of those factors are socioeconomic factors that are highly correlated with race. For example, two frequently used predictors of recidivism in California are "having served time in a juvenile institution" and "having a conviction before age 16." In addition, various "status" factors, while not formally used during sentencing, affect probation and parole decisions; such factors include noncriminal characteristics of the offender (e.g., employment history, education, living arrangements, and alcohol or drug abuse). In California, employment history in particular was found to work to the disadvantage of blacks (Petersilia and Turner, 1985:viii).

Noting the strong opposition by civil libertarians to the use of various noncriminal status factors in sentencing, Petersilia and Turner (1985:ix) succinctly explained the complexity of the problem of reducing racial disparities in sentencing:

Our findings suggest that a basic truth must be acknowledged if sentencing reform is to go forward. Guidelines are intended to overcome racial *discrimination*—and they probably do. However, they cannot be expected to overcome racial *disparities* in sentencing *where serious criminality is disproportionately high in the black population* [italics in original]. Non-criminal status factors related to race can be eliminated, and the guidelines will still identify high-risk criminals about as well as they now do. But it is not possible to omit racially correlated factors that reflect criminal seriousness unless society is willing to have all serious offenders treated less severely because many of them are black.

Racial imprisonment differentials showing that blacks are incarcerated in numbers disproportionate to their representation in the general population are often cited as evidence that there is racial discrimination in sentencing. With regard to such statistics, Blumstein and colleagues (1983:13) wrote:

> The overrepresentation of blacks in prison is evidence that some interaction of individual behavior patterns and societal response leads to the imposition of severe punishments on one group of people at rates that are disproportionate to their numbers in the population; however, it is *not* [italics in original] by itself evidence of racial discrimination at the sentencing stage in criminal courts.

This conclusion concerning sentencing is consistent with an earlier investigation by Blumstein (1982) that used a statistical model to estimate the extent to which black overrepresentation in prison populations could be explained by factors other than race discrimination. Similar methods were used by Langan (1985). Both investigators concluded that the disproportionate representation of blacks in prisons is primarily attributable to the overrepresentation of blacks among arrestees and, more specifically, among those arrested for the types of crimes having a higher certainty and greater severity of punishment: 80 percent of the black-white imprisonment differential was statistically explained by such "nondiscriminatory" variables in the Blumstein study.

In discussing the unexplained 20 percent, the study acknowledged the possibility of discrimination. But the report emphasized that there may be "nondiscriminatory" race-related variation in criminal activity that was not adequately reflected in the data. For example, within given categories of criminal offenses (e.g., robbery or homicide), blacks may be more likely than whites to have committed crimes with less mitigating characteristics; blacks may have longer criminal records than whites; and low levels of education and occupational status may affect perceptions (by the courts) of the ability of offenders to function within the legitimate economy.

On the basis of examinations of black-white imprisonment differentials and an extensive review of sentencing practices in the United States, Blumstein and colleagues (1983:13) concluded:

> The available research suggests that factors other than racial discrimination in sentencing account for most of the disproportionate representation of

blacks in U.S. prisons, although racial discrimination in sentencing may play a more important role in some regions or jurisdictions, for some crime types, or in the decisions of individual participants.

Although methodological flaws have been evident in most sentencing studies, Austin (1984) argued that there is a tendency among current researchers to more fully examine studies that find racial bias than those studies that report no bias. Hagan and Bumiller (1983) acknowledged that the focus of their own critical analysis was on the studies that reported a finding of discrimination. Austin has also observed that studies finding no bias also have methodological flaws and problems of interpretation that call their conclusions into question.

Beyond these considerations is the question of whether the measures of racial bias used in many studies of sentencing are adequate. For example, racial bias in the post–civil rights era is substantially less overt than during earlier years. Such obvious changes have led Wilbanks (1987) to conclude that today it is largely a myth that there is "racism" in the administration of justice. On the basis of a review of past sentencing research, Zatz (1987) challenges such an assertion.

Zatz analyzed findings from research on sentencing disparities for four time periods. Particular attention was given to changes in research methodologies and data sources, the social contexts within which the research was conducted, and the various forms in which bias can appear. Zatz reached several general conclusions on the basis of that review. First, research designs may inadvertently fail to detect discrimination by concentrating on overt bias and generally ignoring or labeling as "nondiscriminatory" more subtle manifestations of bias. Second, since overt racial bias, in addition to being illegal, casts doubt on the legitimacy and rationality of the criminal justice system, it is not likely to be evident in today's criminal justice procedures. Third, subtle biases are no less systematic than overt biases. These subtle forms may be described as those that exist when membership in a particular group influences decision making indirectly or in interaction with other factors. Thus, as noted above, some aspects of determinate sentencing can represent institutionalization of criteria (e.g., prior record) that reflect past discrimination. The logical problem is that if one "controls" for all conceivable background factors associated with criminal behavior other than racial category, the residual variance associated with race is bound to be small. But if many of the more important background predictors are themselves products of past racial status, it is unwarranted to conclude that all discrimination is absent.

A conclusion that discrimination against blacks in the criminal justice system is absent is not justified on the basis of the current data. Yet, few criminologists would argue that the current gap between black and white levels of imprisonment is mainly due to discrimination in sentencing or in any of the other decision-making processes within the criminal justice system. The higher rate of crime among blacks explains much of the differential.

The Death Penalty

It is widely agreed that use of the death penalty in the South has been affected by racial prejudice. Some prima facie indication of bias is seen in the extremely disproportionate rates of execution of blacks. Between 1930 and 1962, 54 percent of all prisoners executed under civil authority in the United States were black (2,049 of 3,812). Blacks were 49 percent of all persons executed for murder (1,619 of 3,298) and 46 percent of those executed for all other crimes (31 of 68), excluding rape; 19 of those 31 black offenders were executed for armed robbery. The greatest disproportion was observed for those executed for rape. Blacks comprised 89.5 percent of all persons executed for rape (399 of 446): 392 of those 399 executions occurred in the South; the other 7 occurred in the North Central states (U.S. Department of Justice, 1963, as cited in Bedau, 1964:103–120). Brown (1988:98) reports that as of March 1, 1987, 42 percent (777 of 1,974) of prisoners under sentence of death were black.

Statistics of this sort have shaped public and scholarly discourse on the subject of the death penalty for more than half a century. Two important early studies of discrimination in the imposition of the death penalty were conducted by Johnson (1941) and Garfinkel (1949). They raised issues that have been explored by subsequent investigators and formed the basis for a recent unsuccessful challenge to the constitutionality of the death penalty (*McCleskey* v *Kemp*, 107 S.Ct. 1756 [1987]). The issue in that case was the differential treatment of offenders charged with killing whites in comparison with those charged with killing blacks.

Both Johnson (1941) and Garfinkel (1949) reported that punishment varied on the basis of both victim and offender characteristics. From the most to least serious in terms of predicted punishment, Johnson (1941:98) listed the following homicide pairs: (1) blacks killing whites, (2) whites killing whites, (3) blacks killing blacks, and (4) whites killing blacks. Johnson examined murder indictments issued between 1930 and 1940 in North Carolina, Georgia, and Virginia and reported that the order of severity of punishment matched the predicted order listed above. These findings have resulted in a vast body of literature that has documented differential levels of punishment for offenders based on the race of the victim.

In Florida in 1977, 94 percent of the 114 men on death row had killed white victims while 4 percent had killed blacks (2 percent had killed both blacks and whites). Thus, race of victim appeared to affect the odds of a murderer's receiving the death penalty (Zeisel, 1981:460–61). This finding was clarified by the analysis of Radelet (1981:918), again with Florida data, that found that those accused of killing whites were more likely than those accused of killing blacks to be indicted for first-degree murder. Once the race of the victim was controlled, the race of the defendant did not strongly affect the probability of a death sentence.

The possible effects of race need to be separately assessed at the point of indictment, sentencing, and subsequent action. In the study by Radelet

(1981), it was the indictment decisions by prosecutors and grand juries that resulted in disproportionate severity of sentencing for those who killed white victims (see also, Baldus et al., 1983; Bowers and Pierce, 1980; Green, 1964; Gross and Mauro, 1984; Hawkins, 1983; Myers, 1979; Myrdal, 1944; Paternoster, 1983, 1984; Radelet, 1981; Radelet and Pierce, 1985; Wolfgang and Riedel, 1973; and Zimring et al., 1976).

BLACK CRIMINAL JUSTICE PERSONNEL

It has been proposed that the real and presumed differential treatment of blacks in the criminal justice system might be lessened if there were more black policemen, prosecutors, judges, jurors, and other decision makers within the system (see Owens, 1987:45). The position of blacks as personnel of the criminal justice system also represents another dimension of the overall status of blacks. Accordingly, we now review changes in the status of black criminal justice officials and assess their impact on the status of blacks throughout the system.

POLICE OFFICERS, PROSECUTORS, AND JUDGES

Black police officers were very scarce prior to the early 1970s. In 1940, blacks were about 1 percent of such personnel in the United States. The proportion grew steadily but slowly to 8 percent in 1984. As a matter of custom and administrative policy, the token black police officers hired in many cities of the South prior to the 1970s were not permitted to detain or arrest white citizens. This practice appears to have been the case in many northern cities as well. Among the few blacks hired as officers, even fewer were ever promoted to higher ranks of authority.

Much of the impetus for an increase in the number of black law enforcement officials came in response to the civil disorders of the 1960s. A major concern was the prevention of future disorders. For example, in discussing the need for more black police officers in urban areas, the report of the National Advisory Commission on Civil Disorders (1968:315) said:

> The Crime Commission Police Task Force found that for police in the Negro community to be predominantly white can serve as a dangerous irritant; a feeling may develop that the community is not being policed to maintain civil peace but to maintain the status quo. It further found that contact with Negro officers can help avoid the stereotypes and prejudices in the minds of white officers. Negro officers also can increase departmental insight into ghetto problems and provide information necessary for early anticipation of the tensions and grievances that can lead to disorders. . . . There is evidence that Negro officers also can be particularly effective in controlling any disorders that do break out. In studying the relative performance of Army and National Guard forces in the Detroit disorder, we concluded that the higher percentage of Negroes in the Army forces con-

tributed substantially to their better performance. As a result, last August, we recommended an increase in the percentage of Negroes in the National Guard. The need for increased Negro participation in police departments is equally acute.

Detailed information regarding the racial composition of police departments during the period between 1965 and 1968 is found in the report. Of the 28 departments that responded to a commission survey, the percentage of blacks during these years ranged from less than 1 percent to 21 percent. The median figure for all cities was 6 percent. In no case was the proportion of blacks in the police department equal to the proportion in the population. It is reasonable to assume that the 28 departments responding to the survey had better black representation than the national average.

Among the 7,046 black officers employed in the 28 departments, 30 held the rank of captain or above; blacks held 2 percent of those positions overall and had attained these higher ranks in 12 of the 28 departments reporting (see Table 9-6). The absence of black supervisory officers was evident even in many nonsouthern cities that had reputations for good race relations. For example, San Francisco with a 14 percent black population and a police force of 1,754 officers, named its first black sergeant in April 1968 (Knowles and Prewitt, 1972:15).

Concerns for the prevention of civil disorders and for equal employment opportunity after 1970 led to a marked increase in the number of blacks in sworn ranks in some departments, but other departments showed little change. Lewis (1987) assessed the level of black representation in police departments across the United States. He studied 46 cities in 1975 and 72 cities in 1985, comparing the percentage black within each department to the equal employment opportunity (EEO) compliance index, a measure derived from a comparison of police employment and general labor force availability for blacks. For purposes of interpretation, the EEO compliance index can be divided into four levels: an index of .75 or higher is considered "high compliance"; an index of between .50 and .75 is considered "moderate compliance"; an index of between .25 and .50 is considered "low compliance"; and an index of .25 or below is considered "noncompliance." Racial parity on the EEO index is 1.00.

Among the 46 cities surveyed in 1975, the percentage of blacks in sworn police ranks ranged from 1.3 in Lubbock, Texas, to 29.9 in Atlanta (see Table 9-7). The mean index was .57, slightly more than one-half of racial parity, and barely in the moderate compliance category. Five cities had a level of high compliance (.75 or higher). In 1985, the mean EEO index for the same 46 cities had risen to .75, indicating high compliance. There were 17 cities with a rate above .75, 10 of which were above 1.00, racial parity. Among the larger sample of 72 cities, the mean EEO index in 1985 was .70; 26 cities achieved high compliance, with 11 exceeding racial parity. However, only one city in the South—Lexington-Fayette, Kentucky—had achieved racial parity in 1985.

The most striking finding was the large increase in the percentage of black police officers in those cities that were headed by black mayors, had black police chiefs, or whose hiring practices were subject to affirmative action consent decrees. During the entire period between 1970 and 1985, 17 cities had been led by black mayors, 16 had black police chiefs, and 28 had been under consent decrees. Through the use of regression analysis, Lewis found that the proportion of blacks in the city's labor force and the presence of black mayors were the most significant variables positively associated with black representation in combined sworn and police patrol ranks in 1975. However, in 1985, in addition to these variables, the presence of black police chiefs and the presence of affirmative action consent decrees emerged as significant variables (Lewis, 1987:5).

Black prosecutors and judicial personnel are not represented in the criminal justice system in proportions similar to those of blacks in police departments. However, the presence of blacks is considerably greater than it was two or three decades ago. For example, Knowles and Prewitt (1972:16,24) report that in the early 1960s black representation within most courthouses in the United States was primarily in janitorial service. In North Carolina, for instance, no blacks were employed in the judicial system, and 31 of 2,000 employees in the state prison department were black. Such patterns were typical of states both in and outside the South during this period.

THE IMPACT OF BLACK PERSONNEL

The influence of black criminal justice professionals on the operation of the system and the quality of treatment afforded blacks and whites is a complex issue, and limited research has been conducted on it. Because of the belief that an increase in the proportion of blacks as personnel in the criminal justice system would have "positive" effects, there have been expectations from the black and white communities that black personnel would be more sensitive and responsive to black needs. Simultaneously, the major expectation from the criminal justice system itself has been that black personnel would perform their jobs effectively.

Black policemen have traditionally been assigned to high-crime areas where residents are dissatisfied with the police protection, and it is unlikely that such conditions could be remedied by a mere increase in the proportion of black police officers (Owens, 1987). Similarly, black correctional officers have been placed in institutions in which blacks comprise a sizable percentage of the prison population; they enter an environment where inmate and guard codes and cultures are well entrenched and clearly delineated. Yet black criminal justice personnel are expected to bring a special sensitivity to the job, especially with regard to matters involving fellow blacks. In the few existing studies, researchers have attempted to assess this presumed sensitivity by comparing the actions of black and white personnel.

Black policemen have been studied more than other justice personnel in the system. Smith and Klein (1983) observed more than 5,000 contacts

TABLE 9-6 Black Police Representation
(a) In Selected City and State Police Departments

City or State	Percent Nonwhite		Ratio of Sergeants to Officers		Ratio of Lieutenants to Officers		Ratio of Captains to Officers		Ratio of Captains and Above to Officers	
	Population	Police Officers	NW	W	NW	W	NW	W	NW	W
Atlanta	38	10	1:49	1:73	1:33	1:16	0:98	1:58	0:98	1:145
Baltimore	41	7	1:30	1:7	1:69	1:27	1:208	1:167	1:208	1:135
Boston	11	2	1:49	1:11	0:49	1:31	0:49	1:123	0:49	1:205
Buffalo	18	3	1:37	1:22	1:37	1:14	0:37	1:56	0:37	1:42
Chicago	27	17	1:21	1:9	1:921	1:35	1:1,842	1:127	1:307	1:140
Cincinnati	28	6	1:27	1:12	1:27	1:25	0:54	1:64	0:54	1:120
Cleveland	34	7	1:28	1:13	1:165	1:26	0:165	1:79	0:165	1:121
Dayton	26	4	1:16	1:7	0:16	1:30	0:16	1:67	0:16	1:100
Detroit	39	5	1:25	1:12	1:114	1:26	No such rank		1:227	1:66
Hartford	20	11	0:38	1:10	1:38	1:20	0:38	1:34	0:38	1:152
Kansas City	20	6	1:7	1:6	0:51	1:24	0:51	1:80	1:51	1:63
Louisville	21	6	1:35	1:13	1:35	1:18	0:35	1:53	1:35	1:75
Memphis	38	5	No such rank		1:12	1:4	0:46	1:18	0:46	1:19
Michigan State Police	9	—	0:1	1:11	0:1	1:63	0:1	1:79	0:1	1:500
New Haven	19	7	0:31	1:21	0:31	1:26	0:31	1:35	0:31	1:69
New Orleans	41	4	1:8	1:12	1:54	1:25	0:54	1:46	0:54	1:125
New York	16	5	1:23	1:15	1:74	1:28	1:743	1:96	1:495	1:166
New Jersey State Police	9	—	0:5	1:7	0:5	1:28	0:5	1:72	0:5	1:305
Newark	40	10	1:37	1:17	1:61	1:18	1:184	1:77	None listed	
Oakland	31	4	1:27	1:7	0:27	1:25	1:27	1:63	0:27	1:210
Oklahoma City	15	4	0:16	1:13	1:16	1:22	0:16	1:38	0:16	1:70
Philadelphia	29	20	1:53	1:18	1:172	1:40	1:459	1:120	0:1,377	1:240
Phoenix	8	1	0:7	1:8	1:7	1:32	0:7	1:70	0:7	1:175
Pittsburgh	19	7	1:36	1:11	1:36	1:31	0:109	1:362	1:109	1:242
St. Louis	37	11	1:11	1:9	1:75	1:40	1:56	1:107	0:224	1:165
San Francisco	14	6	0:102	1:8	0:102	1:25	0:102	1:110	0:102	1:165
Tampa	17	3	0:17	1:10	0:17	1:41	0:17	1:38	0:17	1:62
Washington, D.C.	63	21	1:29	1:10	1:186	1:20	1:186	1:58	0:559	1:70

Note: NW, Nonwhite; W, white. —, Less than 0.5 percent.

Source: National Advisory Commission on Civil Disorders (1968).

(b) In Sworn Police Ranks by Location, Race, and Rank (numbers)

City or State	Total Sworn Personnel	Nonwhite Sworn Personnel	Sergeants NW	Sergeants W	Lieutenants NW	Lieutenants W	Captains NW	Captains W	Above Captain NW	Above Captain W
Atlanta	968	98	2	12	3	56	0	15	0	6
Baltimore	3,046	208	7	389	3	105	1	17	1	21
Boston	2,508	49	1	228	0	80	0	20	0	12
Buffalo	1,375	37	1	60	1	93	1	24	0	32
Chicago	11,091	1,842	87	1,067	2	266	1	73	6	66
Cincinnati	891	54	2	68	2	34	0	13	0	7
Cleveland	2,216	165	6	155	0	78	0	26	0	17
Dayton	417	16	1	58	0	13	0	6	0	4
Detroit	4,326	227	9	339	2	156	0	0	0	62
Hartford	342	38	0	32	1	16	0	9	1	2
Kansas City	927	51	7	158	0	36	0	11	1	14
Louisville	562	35	1	42	1	29	0	10	1	7
Memphis	869	46	0	0	4	192	0	45	0	44
Michigan State Police	1,502	1	0	135	0	24	0	19	0	3
New Haven	446	31	0	20	0	16	0	12	0	6
New Orleans	1,308	54	7	107	1	51	0	27	0	10
New York	27,610	1,485	65	1,785	20	925	2	273	3	157
New Jersey State Police	1,224	5	0	187	0	43	0	17	0	4
Newark	1,869	184	5	97	3	95	1	22	0	0
Oakland	658	27	1	95	0	25	0	10	0	3
Oklahoma City	438	16	0	32	1	19	0	11	0	6
Philadelphia	6,890	1,377	26	314	8	139	3	46	0	23
Phoenix	707	7	0	88	1	22	0	10	0	4
Pittsburgh	1,558	109	3	137	3	47	0	4	1	6
St. Louis	2,042	224	21	201	3	46	4	17	0	11
San Francisco	1,754	102	0	217	0	66	0	15	0	10
Tampa	511	17	0	50	0	12	0	13	0	8
Washington, D.C.	2,721	559	19	216	3	107	3	37	0	31
Totals	80,621	7,046	271	6,289	62	2,791	16	802	14	576

Note: NW, Nonwhite; W, white.

Source: National Advisory Commission on Civil Disorders (1968).

TABLE 9-7 Black Representation and Equal Employment Opportunity Compliance of 46 Municipal Police Departments, 1975–1985

City	Percent Black Sworn Ranks			Percent Black Labor Force			EEO Index			Years of Consent Decree (1972–1985)
	1985	1975	Change	1980	1970	Change	1985	1975	Change	
Atlanta, GA	47.2	29.9	17.3	60.9	47.7	13.2	0.775	0.626	0.149	6
Detroit, MI	41.2	22.3	18.9	60.0	41.2	18.8	0.686	0.541	0.145	11.5
Newark, NJ	26.4	21.9	4.5	54.7	48.9	5.8	0.482	0.447	0.035	0
Columbus, GA	24.4	13.5	10.9	29.6	23.8	5.8	0.824	0.567	0.257	0
Oakland, CA	22.8	12.4	10.4	42.6	29.9	12.7	0.535	0.414	0.121	4
Berkeley, CA	22.5	15.4	7.1	16.3	22.4	-6.1	1.380	0.687	0.693	0
Tallahassee, FL	22.2	13.2	9.0	26.9	23.2	3.7	0.825	0.568	0.257	7.3
Birmingham, AL	22.1	6.8	15.3	49.4	36.4	13.0	0.447	0.186	0.261	4.3
Toledo, OH	18.5	7.3	11.2	15.0	12.5	2.5	1.230	0.584	0.646	11
Mobile, AL	17.4	11.2	6.2	30.7	29.9	0.8	0.566	0.374	0.192	0
Raleigh, NC	17.2	11.5	5.7	24.2	20.0	4.2	0.710	0.575	0.135	0
Miami, FL	16.7	11.2	5.5	22.8	20.3	2.5	0.732	0.551	0.181	8.7
Pasadena, CA	14.1	7.4	6.7	18.3	14.1	4.2	0.7700	0.524	0.246	3
South Bend, IN	13.1	8.2	4.9	15.9	12.3	3.6	0.823	0.666	0.157	0
Louisville, KY	13.0	8.2	4.8	24.7	21.3	3.4	0.526	0.384	0.142	6
New York, NY	12.5	8.1	4.4	23.1	18.6	4.5	0.541	0.435	0.106	3
Akron, OH	12.3	2.8	9.5	20.0	15.5	4.5	0.615	0.180	0.435	11
Cincinnati, OH	11.9	7.6	4.3	29.9	24.9	5.0	0.397	0.305	0.092	4.3
Lexington-Fayette, KY	11.8	6.7	5.1	10.8	14.4	-3.6	1.092	0.465	0.627	0
Omaha, NE	11.5	4.9	6.6	9.5	8.3	1.2	1.210	0.590	0.620	5.2
Orlando, FL	10.3	6.3	4.0	24.7	26.2	-1.5	0.417	0.240	0.177	0

Buffalo, NY	9.4	3.3	6.1	23.2	17.5	5.7	0.405	0.188	0.217	7
Newport News, VA	9.0	9.7	-0.7	27.5	24.2	3.3	0.329	0.400	-0.071	0
Norfolk, VA	8.6	11.4	-2.8	29.0	21.8	7.2	0.296	0.522	-0.226	7.3
Tampa, FL	8.3	2.7	5.6	18.9	17.3	1.6	0.439	0.156	0.283	0
Chesapeake, VA	7.2	5.2	2.0	24.8	20.0	4.8	0.290	0.260	0.030	0
Jersey City, NJ	7.2	6.2	1.0	25.0	17.9	7.1	0.290	0.346	-0.056	0
Ft. Lauderdale, FL	6.2	1.8	4.4	18.5	14.8	3.7	0.335	0.121	0.214	5
Madison, WI	5.8	0.6	5.2	2.0	1.1	0.9	2.900	0.545	2.355	0
Columbus, OH	5.7	4.1	1.6	19.3	16.9	2.4	0.295	0.242	0.053	11
Seattle, WA	4.9	2.4	2.5	7.9	6.2	1.7	0.620	0.387	0.233	0
Corpus Christi, TX	4.8	3.4	1.4	4.9	5.4	-0.5	0.979	0.629	0.350	0
Providence, RI	3.9	3.5	0.4	10.3	7.0	3.3	0.378	0.500	-0.122	0
Las Vegas, NV	3.8	2.2	1.6	10.6	9.8	1.0	0.351	0.224	0.127	0
Oxnard, CA	3.3	3.8	-0.5	6.0	5.4	0.6	0.550	0.703	-0.153	0
Rockford, IL	3.2	6.9	-3.7	11.0	7.0	4.0	0.290	0.985	-0.695	0
Allentown, PA	3.0	0.5	2.5	2.3	2.2	0.1	1.304	0.227	1.077	5
Minneapolis, MN	2.9	0.8	2.1	5.7	3.5	2.2	0.508	0.220	0.280	0
Portland, OR	2.8	1.5	1.3	6.4	4.7	1.7	0.437	0.319	0.118	0
Modesto, CA	2.1	1.7	0.4	1.9	1.3	0.6	1.105	1.307	-0.202	0
El Paso, TX	2.1	1.9	0.2	3.7	3.2	0.5	0.567	0.593	-0.026	0
Reno, NV	2.1	2.7	-0.6	2.4	2.3	0.1	0.875	1.173	-0.298	0
Eugene, OR	1.9	1.6	0.3	0.7	0.7	0	2.714	2.285	0.429	0
Mesa, AZ	1.8	0	1.8	1.2	1.0	0.2	1.500	0	1.500	0
Lincoln, NE	1.7	4.4	2.7	1.4	0.3	1.1	1.214	4.000	-2.786	0
Lubbock, TX	1.1	1.3	-0.2	6.9	6.5	0.4	0.159	0.20	-0.041	0

Source: Lewis (1987).

between police and citizens in three cities—Rochester, New York; Tampa–St. Petersburg, Florida; and St. Louis, Missouri. They found that black and white police officers exhibited similar arrest patterns, with black officers in some departments more likely to make arrests than white officers. From another observational study of police and their interaction with the public, Reiss (1971) concluded that both black and white officers were more likely to use excessive force against members of their own race (see also Fyfe, 1981).

Black judges were reviewed by D. Bartlett and J. Steele (cited in Owens, 1987), who analyzed more than 10,000 court documents and more than 20,000 pages of court testimony in a study of the sentencing patterns of 19 judges in Philadelphia. From the arrests for commission of crime through trial and sentencing, they tracked 1,034 individuals indicted for violent crimes during 1971. They reported a complex pattern. A white judge was more likely than a black judge to find both black and white defendants guilty of the major charge against them. In addition, white judges were more likely to convict if the victim was white. However, black judges sentenced defendants convicted of violent crime to longer terms than did white judges.

A later study (Uhlman, 1979) compared 16 black judges and 79 white judges in a large northeastern city. The records of more than 24,000 defendants were reviewed and analyzed, and interviews were conducted with a sample of black judges. The study found that both black and white judges convicted black defendants more frequently and more harshly than white defendants. Uhlman (1979:73) concluded that ". . . black decision-making is difficult if not impossible to differentiate from white behavior."

A subsequent work (Welch et al., 1988) argued that previous examinations of the sentencing behavior of black and white trial judges are flawed to the extent that the prior record of the defendant, examination of the decision to incarcerate, and salient characteristics of the judge were not taken into account. This study analyzed decisions to incarcerate made by black and white trial judges in a large northeastern community, controlling for the variables noted above. The study concluded that in decisions to incarcerate, black judges were more evenhanded in their treatment of black and white defendants than were white judges, who tended to treat white defendants somewhat more leniently. However, in overall sentence severity, white judges treated black and white defendants equally severely, while black judges treated black defendants somewhat more leniently than white defendants. The authors suggest that having more black judges increases equality of treatment by balancing the sentencing patterns of white judges (Welch et al., 1988:126,134–135).

Studies of correctional officers have been rare. One of the few studies investigating the differences in treatment by black and white guards (Jacobs and Kraft, 1978) reported that black guards wrote more tickets for rule infractions and were therefore "more active disciplinarians." The study did not report whether or not white inmates were reported at different rates by black guards. There are no published studies that examine this question.

The decision to parole has been a traditional part of the role of correctional officials. Such decisions partly depend on the actions of guards and other supervisory personnel. Few studies have examined the possible existence of bias in the decision to grant parole or the role of black correctional officials in affecting such bias. A study by Carroll and Mondrick (1976) reported that black potential parolees were less likely than whites to receive parole, but they did not consider the race of the decision makers.

The studies reported above are informative, but they leave many questions unanswered regarding the impact of black personnel on the criminal justice system. They offer very few explanations for the observed patterns of behavior. Yet, despite the scarcity of studies and their incompleteness, they do challenge many of the widely held presumptions about the role of black criminal justice officials. Owens (1987:35) suggests that black policemen and correctional officers who are described in the literature as "more active disciplinarians" (Jacobs and Kraft, 1978) or "more likely to make arrests" (Smith and Klein, 1983) see themselves as doing what they were hired to do—enforcing rules and laws. Also, they may not be out of line with general public opinion in the black community.

Owens (1987:35) also suggests that many officials may see their role as "insuring the equal treatment of all offenders and making the system more responsive to the needs of all citizens." Black judges may administer harsh punishment to blacks who victimize other blacks in response to the high rate of crime in black communities. Indeed, many black judges have made public statements to this effect (e.g., see Wright, 1987). It may be that such black judges are sending a new message to black offenders—the life of a black person is indeed important and the full weight of the law will be used in order to protect black victims.

There is suggestive evidence that black professionals have had an impact in other ways. Historically, a major belief in black communities has been that both black defendants and "innocent" law-abiding citizens are subjected to mistreatment by agents of the criminal justice system. Blacks generally have viewed the system as an arena in which they are likely to endure verbal abuse, racial insults, and other forms of harassment. Bartlett and Steele (cited in Owens, 1987) reported that the district attorney's office was affected by the presence of black judges. In cases coming before black judges, violent crime charges were dropped against 28 percent of black defendants and 20 percent of white defendants. The opposite pattern was noted in cases where the judge was white: charges were dropped for 32 percent of white defendants and 20 percent of black defendants. Similar outcomes may also result when the prosecuting attorney is black (Georges-Abeyie, 1984).

SUMMARY

Historically, discrimination against blacks in arrests and sentencing was ubiquitous. And as late as the early 1970s, very few blacks were employed as law enforcement officials; only in the 1980s did the percentage of blacks in police forces increase considerably more than black representation among attorneys and judges.

Although the evidence is scanty, the behavior of black and white judges appears to be similar. There are some suggestions that black law enforcement officials may be somewhat more active disciplinarians. The extent to which the relatively recent changes in personnel may have affected distrust of criminal justice is not now known.

Blacks have much higher arrest rates, convictions, and imprisonment rates than whites for criminal offenses. Some part of the differences may be due to bias and the resulting differential treatment, but systematic evidence of discrimination against blacks is not evident. Apparently there is substantial variation in discrimination from place to place and over time. When type and severity of offense are controlled, racial differences in sentencing are less clearly due to overt racial bias than to socioeconomic differences between blacks and whites.

Compared with the total population, black Americans are disproportionately victims of crime: twice as likely to be victims of robbery, vehicle theft, and aggravated assault, and 6 to 7 times as likely to be victims of homicide, the leading cause of death among young black males. Blacks also suffer disproportionately from injuries and economic losses due to criminal actions.

Most black offenders victimize other blacks. But offenders and victims are primarily in different socioeconomic strata. The middle-class and near-poor blacks have greater economic losses due to criminal acts than the black poor or than whites at any income level.

Two conclusions seem unavoidable. First, as long as great disparities in the socioeconomic status of blacks and whites remain, blacks' relative deprivation will continue to involve them disproportionately in the criminal justice system as victims and offenders. Second, because of this status difference, the degree to which this overrepresentation can be associated with differential treatment by race cannot be precisely determined.

These inequalities are rooted in a long history of American black-white relations, but they continue to have major effects on black neighborhoods. High black crime rates perpetuate negative stereotypes and fears of blacks, especially of young males. Criminal behavior and its punishment pose significant barriers to educational excellence and to employment for black youth (Chapters 6 and 7). Crime also drains the limited economic resources of black communities and deters the expansion of business enterprises within black neighborhoods.

REFERENCES

Adamson, Christopher R.
  1983 Punishment after slavery: southern state penal systems, 1865–1890. *Social Problems* 30(June):555–569.

Albonetti, Celesta A.
  1986 Criminality, prosecutorial screening, and uncertainty: toward a theory of discretionary decision making in felony case processings. *Criminology* 24:623–644.
Alschuler, Albert
  1968 The prosecutor's role in plea bargaining. *University of Chicago Law Review* 36:50–112.
  1979 Plea bargaining and its history. *Law and Society Review* 13:211–245.
Austin, Roy L.
  1984 The court and sentencing of black offenders. Pp. 167–193 in Daniel Georges-Abeyie, ed., *The Criminal Justice System and Blacks*. New York: Clark Boardman.
Baldus, David C., Charles Pulaski, and George Woodworth
  1983 Comparative review of death sentences. *Journal of Criminal Law and Criminology* 4:661–753.
Banton, Michael
  1964 *The Policeman in the Community*. London: Tavistock.
Bayley, David H., and Harold Mendelsohn
  1969 *Minorities and the Police*. New York: Free Press.
Bedau, Hugo
  1964 *The Death Penalty in America*. Garden City, N.Y.: Anchor Books.
Bell, Derrick A.
  1980 *Race, Racism and American Law*. Boston: Little, Brown.
Berk, Sarah Fenstermaker, and Donileen R. Loseke
  1980– Handling family violence: situational determinants of
  1981 police arrest in domestic disturbances. *Law and Society Review* 15:317–346.
Bernstein, Ilene Nagel, William R. Kelly, and Patricia A. Doyle
  1977 Societal reaction to deviants: the case of criminal defendants. *American Sociological Review* 42:743–755.
Black, Donald
  1970 Production of crime rates. *American Sociological Review* 35:733–748.
  1971 The social organization of arrest. *Stanford Law Review* 23:1087–1111.
  1973 The mobilization of law. *Journal of Legal Studies* 2:125–149.
  1976 *The Behavior of Law*. New York: Academic Press.
Black, Donald, and Albert J. Reiss, Jr.
  1967 Patterns of behavior in police and citizen transactions. Pp. 1–139 in U.S. President's Commission on Law Enforcement and Administration of Justice, *Studies in Crime and Law Enforcement in Major Metropolitan Areas*, Field Surveys 111. Vol. 2. Washington, D.C.: U.S. Government Printing Office.
  1970 Police control of juveniles. *American Sociological Review* 35:63–77.
Blassingame, John
  1977 *The Slave Community*. New York: Oxford University Press.
Blumberg, Abraham S.
  1967 The practice of law as a confidence game: organizational cooptation of a profession. *Law and Society Review* 1:15–39.
Blumstein, Alfred
  1982 On the racial disproportionality of United States' prison populations. *Journal of Criminal Law and Criminology* 73:1259–1281.
Blumstein, Alfred, Jacqueline Cohen, Susan E. Martin, and Michael H. Toury, eds.
  1983 *Research on Sentencing: The Search for Reform*. Vols. I and II. Panel on Research on Sentencing, Committee on Research on Law Enforcement and the Administration of Justice, National Research Council. Washington, D.C.: National Academy Press.
Blumstein, Alfred, Jacqueline Cohen, Jeffrey A. Roth, and Christy A. Visher, eds.
  1986 *Criminal Careers and Career Criminals*. Vol. 1. Panel on Research on Criminal

Careers, Committee on Research on Law Enforcement and the Administration of Justice, National Research Council. Washington, D.C.: National Academy Press.

Bowers, William J., and Glenn L. Pierce
1980 Arbitrariness and discrimination under post-*Furman* capital statutes. *Crime and Delinquency* 26:563–635.

Brearley, Harrington Cooper
1932 *Homicide in the United States.* Chapel Hill: The University of North Carolina Press.

Brimmer, Andrew
1975 The outlook for black business. *Black Enterprise* 5(June):24–27.

Brown, Lee P.
1988 Crime in the black community. Pp. 95–113 in Janet Dewart, ed., *The State of Black America.* New York: National Urban League.

Caplovitz, David
1968 *The Poor Pay More.* New York: Free Press.

Carlin, Jerome E.
1966 *Civil Justice and the Poor: Issues for Sociological Research.* New York: Russell Sage Foundation.

Carroll, Leo, and Margaret E. Mondrick
1976 Racial bias in the decision to grant parole. *Law and Society Review* 11(Fall):93–107.

Christianson, Scott
1981 Our black prisons. *Crime and Delinquency* 27:364–375.
1982 Disproportionate Imprisonment of Blacks in the United States: Policy, Practice, Impact and Change. Paper prepared for the National Association of Blacks in Criminal Justice, Washington, D.C.

Church, Thomas W., Jr.
1976 Plea bargains, concessions and the court: analysis of a quasi-experiment. *Law and Society Review* 10:377–401.
1978 *Justice Delayed.* Williamsburg, Va.: National Center for State Courts.

Collins, James J., Jr., ed.
1981 *Drinking and Crime: Perspectives on the Relationships Between Alcohol Consumption and Criminal Behavior.* New York: Guilford Press.

Cooney, Mark
1987 Racial Discrimination in Police-Citizen Encounters: A Review of the Empirical Literature. Paper prepared for the Committee on the Status of Black Americans, National Research Council, Washington, D.C.

Daniel, Pete
1972 *The Shadow of Slavery: Peonage in the South 1901–1969.* Urbana: University of Illinois Press.

Davis, Kenneth C.
1971 *Discretionary Justice.* Urbana: University of Illinois Press.

DuBois, W. E. B., ed.
1904 Some notes on Negro crime, particularly in Georgia. *Proceedings of the Ninth Atlanta Conference for the Study of the Negro Problems.* Atlanta, Ga.: Atlanta University Press.

Dunbaugh, Frank M.
1979 Racially disproportionate rates of incarceration in the United States. *Prison Law Monitor* 1(March):205, 219–222.

Eisenstein, James, and Herbert Jacob
1977 *Felony Justice: An Organizational Analysis of Criminal Courts.* Boston: Little, Brown.

Farley, John E.
1988 *Majority-Minority Relations.* Englewood Cliffs, N.J.: Prentice-Hall.

Ferdinand, Theodore N.
1967 The criminal patterns of Boston since 1849. *American Journal of Sociology* 73:84–99.

Franklin, John Hope
1980 *From Slavery to Freedom: A History of Negro Americans.* New York: Alfred A. Knopf.

Friedrich, Robert James
1977 The Impact of Organizational, Individual and Situational Factors on Police Behavior. Unpublished Ph.D. dissertation. Department of Political Science, University of Michigan.

Fusfield, Daniel R., and Timothy Bates
1984 *The Political Economy of the Urban Ghetto.* Carbondale: Southern Illinois University Press.

Fyfe, James J.
1981 Race and extreme police-citizen violence. Pp. 89–108 in R. L. McNeeley and Carl E. Pope, eds., *Race, Crime, and Criminal Justice.* Beverly Hills, Calif.: Sage Publications Inc.
1982 Blind justice: police shootings in Memphis. *Journal of Criminal Law and Criminology* 73:707–722.

Garfinkel, Harold
1949 Research note on inter- and intra-racial homicides. *Social Forces* 27:369.

Georges-Abeyie, Daniel
1984 A black district attorney's view of criminal court: an interview with Mr. Howard Stewart, assistant district attorney, Dauphin County, Pennsylvania. Pp. 219–223 in Daniel Georges-Abeyie, ed., *The Criminal Justice System and Blacks.* New York: Clark Boardman.

Goldkamp, John S.
1976 Minorities as victims of police shootings: interpretations of racial disproportionality and police use of deadly force. *Justice System Journal* 2:169–183.

Goode, Erich
1984 *Drugs in American Society.* New York: Alfred A. Knopf.

Green, Edward
1964 Inter- and intra-racial crime relative to sentencing. *Journal of Criminal Law, Criminology and Police Science.* 55(3)[September]:348–358.

Gross, Samuel R., and Robert Mauro
1984 Patterns of death: an analysis of racial disparities in capital sentencing and homicide victimization. *Stanford Law Review* 37:27–153.

Hagan, John
1974 Extra-legal attributes and criminal sentencing. *Law and Society Review* 8:357–383.

Hagan, John, and Kristin Bumiller
1983 Making sense of sentencing: a review and critique of sentencing research. Pp. 1–54 in A. Blumstein, J. Cohen, S. E. Martin, and M. H. Tonry, eds., *Research on Sentencing: The Search for Reform.* Vol. II. Panel on Research on Sentencing, Committee on Research on Law Enforcement and the Administration of Justice, National Research Council. Washington, D.C.: National Academy Press.

Harding, Richard W., and Richard P. Fahey
1973 Killings by Chicago police, 1969–1970: an empirical study. *Southern California Law Review* 46:284–315.

Hardy, Kenneth A.
1983 Equity in court dispositions. Pp. 183–207 in Gordon P. Whitaker and Charles D. Phillips, eds., *Evaluating Performance of Criminal Justice Agencies.* Beverly Hills, Calif.: Sage Publications Inc.

Hawkins, Darnell F.
   1983 Black-white homicide differentials: alternatives to an inadequate theory. *Criminal Justice and Behavior* 10:407–440.
   1985 Black homicide: the adequacy of existing research for devising prevention strategies. *Crime and Delinquency* 31(January):83–103.
Hawkins, Darnell F., ed.
   1986 *Homicide Among Black Americans.* Lanham, Md.: University Press of America.
   1987 Paper prepared for the Committee on the Status of Black Americans, National Research Council, Washington, D.C.
Hepburn, John R.
   1978 Race and the decision to arrest: an analysis of warrants issued. *Journal of Research in Crime and Delinquency* 15:54–73.
Higginbotham, A. Leon, Jr.
   1978 *In the Matter of Color.* New York: Oxford University Press.
Illinois Criminal Justice Information Authority
   1987 Spatial and temporal analysis of crime. Research Bulletin No. 87–89, April. Chicago.
Inciardi, James A.
   1986 *The War on Drugs: Heroin, Cocaine, and Public Policy.* Palo Alto, Calif.: Mayfield.
Jackson, Pamela I., and Leo Carroll
   1981 Race and the war on crime: the non-southern U.S. cities. *American Sociological Review* 46(June):290–305.
Jacobs, David
   1979 Inequality and police strength: conflict and coercive control in metropolitan areas. *American Sociological Review* 44(December):913–925.
Jacobs, J., and L. Kraft
   1978 Integrating the keepers: a comparison of black and white prison guards in Illinois. *Social Problems* 25:304–318.
Jaynes, Gerald David
   1986 *Branches Without Roots: Genesis of the Black Working Class in the American South, 1862–1882.* New York: Oxford University Press.
Johnson, Elmer H.
   1957 Selective factors in capital punishment. *Social Forces* 36:165–169.
Johnson, Guy B.
   1941 The Negro and crime. *Annals of the American Academy of Political and Social Science* 217(September):93–104.
Kania, Richard R. E., and Wade C. Mackey
   1977 Police violence as a function of community characteristics. *Criminology* 15:27–48.
Kephart, William M.
   1957 *Racial Factors and Urban Law Enforcement.* Philadelphia: University of Pennsylvania Press.
Kleck, Gary
   1981 Racial discrimination in criminal sentencing: a critical evaluation of the evidence with additional evidence on the death penalty. *American Sociological Review* 46:783–805.
Klepper, Steven, Daniel Nagin, and Luke-Jon Tierney
   1983 Discrimination in the criminal justice system: a critical appraisal of the literature and suggestions for future research. Pp. 55–128 in A. Blumstein, J. Cohen, S. E. Martin, and M. H. Tonry, eds., *Research in Sentencing: The Search for Reform.* Vol. II. Panel on Research on Sentencing, Committee on Research on Law Enforcement and the Administration of Justice, National Research Council. Washington, D.C.: National Academy Press.

Knoohuizen, Ralph, Richard P. Fahey, and Deborah J. Palmer
1972 *Police and Their Use of Deadly Force in Chicago.* Evanston, Ill.: Chicago Law Enforcement Study Group.

Knowles, Louis L., and Kenneth Prewitt
1972 Racism in the administration of justice. Pp. 13–27 in C. E. Rasons and J. L. Kuykendall, eds., *Race, Crime, and Justice.* Pacific Palisades, Calif.: Goodyear.

LaFree, Gary D.
1980 The effect of sexual stratification by race on official reactions to rape. *American Sociological Review* 45:842–854.

Langan, Patrick A.
1985 Racism on trial: new evidence to explain the racial composition of prisons in the United States. *Journal of Criminal Law and Criminology* 76:666–683.

Lemert, Edwin M., and Judy Roseberg
1948 The administration of justice to minority groups in Los Angeles County. *University of California Publications in Culture and Society I.*

Lewis, William G.
1987 Toward Representative Bureaucracy: An Assessment of Black Representation in Police Bureaucracies. Preliminary results of Ph.D. dissertation research. Published in *Public Administration Review* 49:257–268.

Liska, Allen E., Joseph J. Lawrence, and Michael Benson
1981 Perspectives on the legal order: the capacity for social control. *American Journal of Sociology* 87(September):413–426.

Liska, Allen E., Mitchell B. Chamlin, and Mark D. Reed
1985 Testing the economic production and conflict models of crime control. *Social Forces* 64:119–138.

Lundman, Richard J.
1974 Routine police arrest practices: a commonwealth perspective. *Social Problems* 22:127–141.
1979 Organizational norms and police discretion: an observational study of police work with traffic law violators. *Criminology* 17:159–171.

Mangum, Charles S.
1940 *The Legal Status of the Negro.* Chapel Hill: University of North Carolina Press.

Mather, Lynn M.
1979 *Plea Bargaining or Trial? The Process of Criminal Case Disposition.* Lexington, Mass.: Lexington Books.

Matsueda, Ross L., and Karen Heimer
1987 Race, family structure and delinquency: a test of differential association and social control theories. *American Sociological Review* 52:826–840.

Maynard, Douglas W.
1984 *Inside Plea Bargaining: The Language of Negotiation.* New York: Plenum Press.

McCoy, Candace
1984 Determinate sentencing, plea bargaining bans, and hydraulic direction in California. *Justice System Journal* 9:256–275.

McGarrell, Edmund F., and Timothy J. Flanagan, eds.
1985 *Sourcebook of Criminal Justice Statistics-1984.* Washington, D.C.: U.S. Government Printing Office.

Mendelsohn, Robert A.
1971 Police-community relations: a need in search of police support. Pp. 159–174 in Harlan Hahn, ed., *Police in Urban Society.* Beverly Hills, Calif.: Sage Publications Inc.

Meyer, Marshall W.
1980 Police shootings at minorities: the case of Los Angeles. *Annals of the American Academy of Political and Social Science* 452:98–110.

Michalowski, Raymond J.
1985 *Order, Law and Crime: An Introduction to Criminology*. New York: Random House.
Miethe, Terance D.
1987 Prosecutorial charging and plea bargaining practices under determinate sentencing: an investigation of the hydraulic displacement of discretion. *Journal of Criminal Law and Criminology* 78(1):155–176.
Milton, Catherine H., Jeanne Wahl Halleck, James Lardner, and Gary L. Abrecht
1977 *Police Use of Deadly Force*. Washington, D.C.: Police Foundation.
Moore, Mark
1988 *Drug Trafficking*. Crime File Study Guide, National Institute of Justice, U.S. Department of Justice. Washington, D.C.: U.S. Government Printing Office.
Myers, Martha A.
1979 Offended parties and official reactions: victims and the sentencing of criminal defendants. *Sociological Quarterly* 20:529–540.
Myers, Samuel L., Jr., and William J. Sabol
1987 Crime and the Black Community: Issues in the Understanding of Race and Crime in America. Paper prepared for the Committee on the Status of Black Americans, National Research Council, Washington, D.C.
Myrdal, Gunnar
1944 *An American Dilemma: The Negro Problem and Modern Democracy*. New York: Harper and Brothers.
Nardulli, Peter F.
1978 *The Courtroom Elite: An Organizational Approach*. Cambridge, Mass.: Ballinger.
National Advisory Commission on Civil Disorders
1968 *Report of the National Advisory Commission on Civil Disorders*. New York: Bantam.
National Minority Advisory Council on Criminal Justice
1980 *The Inequality of Justice: A Report on Crime and the Administration of Justice in the Minority Community*. Office of Justice Assistance, Research, and Statistics. Washington, D.C.: U.S. Department of Justice.
Neubauer, David W.
1974 *Criminal Justice in Middle America*. Morristown, N.J.: General Learning Press.
O'Brien, Robert M.
1987 The interracial nature of violent crimes: a reexamination. *American Journal of Sociology* 92(January):817–835.
O'Carroll, Patrick W., and James A. Mercy
1986 Patterns and recent trends in black homicide. Pp. 29–42 in Darnell F. Hawkins, ed., *Homicide Among Black Americans*. Lanham, Md.: University Press of America.
Owens, Charles E.
1987 Blacks and the Criminal Justice System. Paper prepared for the Committee on the Status of Black Americans, National Research Council, Washington, D.C.
Pastor, Paul A., Jr.
1978 Mobilization in public drunkenness control: a comparison of legal and medical approaches. *Social Problems* 25:373–384.
Paternoster, Raymond
1983 Race of victim and location of crime: the decision to seek the death penalty in South Carolina. *Journal of Criminal Law and Criminology* 74:754–785.
1984 Prosecutorial discretion in requesting the death penalty: a case of victim-based racial discrimination. *Law and Society Review* 18:437–478.
Petersilia, Joan
1983 *Racial Disparities in the Criminal Justice System*. R-2947–NIC. Santa Monica, Calif.: Rand Corporation.

Petersilia, Joan, and Susan Turner
1985 *Guideline-Based Justice: The Implications for Racial Minorities*. R-3306–NIC. Santa Monica, Calif.: Rand Corporation.

Piliavin, Irving, and Scott Briar
1964 Police encounters with juveniles. *American Sociological Review* 70:206–214.

Pope, Carl E.
1979 Race and crime revisited. *Crime and Delinquency* (July):347–357.

Powell, Elwin H.
1966 Crime as a function of anomie. *Journal of Criminal Law, Criminology, and Police Science* 57:161–171.

Quinney, Richard
1970 *The Social Reality of Crime*. Boston: Little, Brown.

Radelet, Michael L.
1981 Racial characteristics and the composition of the death penalty. *American Sociological Review* 46:918–927.

Radelet, Michael L., and Glenn L. Pierce
1985 Race and prosecutorial discretion in homicide cases. *Law and Society Review* 19:587–621.

Reid, Sue Titus
1979 *Crime and Criminology*. New York: Holt, Rinehart & Winston.

Reiss, Albert J., Jr.
1972 *The Police and the Public*. New Haven: Yale University Press.

Reiss, Albert J., Jr., and David J. Bordua
1967 Environment and organization: a perspective on the police. Pp. 25–55 in David Bordua, ed., *The Police: Six Sociological Essays*. New York: John Wiley & Sons.

Roizen, Judy
1981 Alcohol and criminal behavior among blacks: the case for research on special populations. Pp. 207–252 in James J. Collins, Jr., ed., *Drinking and Crime: Perspectives on the Relationships Between Alcohol Consumption and Criminal Behavior*. New York: Guilford Press.

Rose, Harold M., and Donald R. Deskins, Jr.
1986 Handguns and homicide in urban black communities: a spatial-temporal assessment of environmental scale differences. Pp. 69–100 in Darnell F. Hawkins, ed., *Homicide Among Black Americans*. Lanham, Md.: University Press of America.

Sellin, Thorsten
1928 The Negro criminal: a statistical note. *Annals of the Academy of Political and Social Science* 140:52–64.
1935 Race prejudice in the administration of justice. *American Journal of Sociology* 41:312–317.
1976 *Slavery and the Penal System*. New York: Elsevier.

Sherman, Lawrence W.
1980 Execution without trial: police homicide and the Constitution. *Vanderbilt Law Review* 33:71–100.

Sherman, Lawrence W., and Robert H. Langworthy
1979 Measuring homicide by police officers. *Journal of Criminal Law and Criminology* 70:546–560.

Shin, Yongsock, D. Jedlicka, and Everett S. Lee
1977 Homicide among blacks. *Phylon* (December):399–406.

Skolnick, Jerome H.
1966 *Justice Without Trial: Law Enforcement in Democratic Society*. New York: John Wiley & Sons.
1968 *The Police and the Urban Ghetto*. Chicago: American Bar Foundation.

Smith, Douglas
  1987 Police response to interpersonal violence: defining the parameters of legal control. *Social Forces* 31:468–481.
Smith, Douglas, and Jody R. Klein
  1983 Police agency characteristics and arrest decisions. Pp. 63–95 in G. P. Whitaker and C. D. Phillips, eds., *Evaluating Performance in Criminal Justice Agencies.* Beverly Hills, Calif.: Sage Publications Inc.
  1984 Police control of interpersonal disputes. *Social Problems* 31:468–481.
Smith, Douglas, Christy A. Visher, and Laura A. Davidson
  1984 Equity and discretionary justice: the influence of race on police arrest decisions. *Journal of Criminal Law and Criminology* 75:234–249.
Spohn, Cassia, John Gruhl, and Susan Welch
  1981– The effect of race on sentencing: a re-examination of an unsettled question. *Law*
  1982 and Society Review 16:71–80.
Thomson, Randall J., and Matthew T. Zingraff
  1981 Detecting sentence disparity: some problems and evidence. *American Journal of Sociology* 86:869–880.
Uhlman, Thomas M.
  1979 *Racial Justice: Black Judges and Defendants in an Urban Trial Court.* Lexington, Mass.: Lexington Books.
U.S. Bureau of Justice Statistics
  1984 *Criminal Victimization in the U.S., 1983.* Washington, D.C.: U.S. Government Printing Office.
U.S. Department of Justice
  1978 *Determinate Sentencing: Reform or Regression?* Summary Report of a Special Conference held June 2–3, 1977, at the School of Law, University of California, Berkeley. National Institute of Law Enforcement and Criminal Justice, Law Enforcement Assistance Administration. Washington, D.C.: U.S. Government Printing Office.
  1983 *Report to the Nation on Crime and Justice.* Washington, D.C.: U.S. Government Printing Office.
Warner, Sam B.
  1934 *Crime and Criminal Statistics in Boston.* Cambridge, Mass.: Harvard University Press.
Welch, Susan, John Gruhl, and Cassia Spohn
  1984 Dismissal, conviction, and incarceration of Hispanic defendants: a comparison with Anglos and blacks. *Social Science Quarterly* 65:257–264.
  1985 Convicting and sentencing differences among black, Hispanic, and white males in six localities. *Justice Quarterly* 2:67–80.
Welch, Susan, Michael Combes, and John Gruhl
  1988 Do black judges make a difference? *American Journal of Political Science* 32(February):126–136.
Wharton, Vernon Lane
  1965 *The Negro in Mississippi 1865–1890.* New York: Harper & Son.
Wilbanks, William
  1987 *The Myth of a Racist Criminal Justice System.* Monterey, Calif.: Brooks/Cole Publishing Company.
Willbach, Harry
  1938 The trend of crime in New York City. *Journal of Criminal Law, Criminology, and Police Science* 29(1):62–75.
  1940– The trend of crime in Chicago. *Journal of Criminal Law, Criminology, and Police*
  1941 Science 31(6):720–727.

Wish, Eric D.
1987 Drug Use Forecasting: New York, 1984 to 1986. Research in Action, National Institute of Justice, U.S. Department of Justice, Washington, D.C.
1988 Drug Testing Crime File Study Guide. National Institute of Justice, U.S. Department of Justice, Washington, D.C.

Wish, Eric D., and Bruce D. Johnson
1986 The impact of substance abuse on criminal careers. Pp. 52–88 in A. Blumstein, J. Cohen, J. A. Roth, and C. A. Visher, eds., *Criminal Careers and Career Criminals.* Vol. 2. Panel on Research on Criminal Careers, Committee on Research on Law Enforcement and the Administration of Justice, National Research Council. Washington, D.C.: National Academy Press.

Wolfgang, Marvin, and Bernard Cohen
1970 *Crime and Race: Conceptions and Misconceptions.* New York: Institute of Human Relations Press.

Wolfgang, Marvin E., and Marc Riedel
1973 Race, judicial discretion, and the death penalty. *Annals of the American Academy of Political and Social Science* 407:119–133.

Wright, Bruce
1987 *Black Robes, White Justice.* Secaucus, N.J.: Lyle Stuart, Inc.

Wright, James D., and Linda Marston
1975 The ownership of means of destruction: weapons in the United States. *Social Problems* 23(October):93–107.

Wright, James D., Peter H. Rossi, and Kathleen Daly
1983 *Under the Gun: Weapons, Crime and Violence in America.* New York: Aldine.

Yale Law Journal, eds.
1967 Interrogations in New Haven: the impact of *Miranda. Yale Law Journal* 76:1519–1648.

Zatz, Marjorie S.
1985 Pleas, priors and prison: racial/ethnic differences in sentencing. *Social Science Research* 14:169–193.
1987 The changing forms of racial/ethnic biases in sentencing. *Journal of Research in Crime and Delinquency* 24:69–92.

Zatz, Marjorie S., and Kathleen A. Cameron
1987 Racial Disparities in Prosecutorial Decisions and Plea Bargaining. Paper prepared for the Committee on the Status of Black Americans, National Research Council, Washington, D.C.

Zatz, Marjorie S., and Alan J. Lizotte
1985 The timing of court processing: toward linking theory and method. *Criminology* 23:313–335.

Zeisel, Hans
1981 Race bias in the administration of the death penalty: the Florida experience. *Harvard Law Review* 95:456–468.

Zimmerman, Hilda J.
1947 Penal Systems and Penal Reforms in the South Since the Civil War. Unpublished Ph.D. dissertation. Department of History, University of North Carolina, Chapel Hill.

Zimring, Franklin E., Joel Eigen, and Sheila O'Mailley
1976 Punishing homicide in Philadelphia: perspectives on the death penalty. *University of Chicago Law Review* 43:227–252.

10

CHILDREN AND FAMILIES

William H. Johnson
Playground Scene (ca. 1939–1942)
Pen and ink with pencil on paper
National Museum of American Art, Smithsonian Institution,
Gift of the Harmon Foundation

The major changes in American society during the past five decades have been accompanied by significant alterations in the family lives of men, women, and, most importantly, children. Trends in fertility, marital status, and in patterns of child rearing have had important effects on both social and economic life. In this chapter, our primary objectives are to describe those trends, discuss various explanations for them, and to consider the implications of them for the current well-being of children and the status of future generations of adults.

CHANGING FAMILY PATTERNS

OVERVIEW

Since 1960 the trends in marital status, fertility, marital stability, and child rearing for both blacks and whites have been similar. Those trends include:

- lower marriage rates and a delayed age at first marriage;
- higher divorce rates;
- lower birth rates;
- earlier and increased sexual activity among adolescents;
- a higher proportion of births to unmarried mothers;
- higher percentages of children living in female-headed families;
- a higher proportion of women working outside the home; and
- a higher percentage of children living in poverty.

The changes, however, have been much more pronounced for blacks than for whites. The result is increasingly different marital and family experiences for the two groups. Indeed, in terms of major statistical indicators of marital status, there were far larger differences in the profiles of black and white Americans in 1980 than there were in 1890 (Walker, 1986:25). While we examine these diverging trends and their possible causes, we stress that both populations have experienced similar changes.

A summary of a few important trends in marriage and family patterns for black and white families highlights changes in black-white differences over the past 40 years (see Glick, 1981).

- While blacks have traditionally married at younger ages than whites, whites now marry at much younger ages than blacks. In 1986, 39 percent of white women aged 20–24 were married, compared with 17 percent of black women.

- On average, black women spend 16 of their expected 73 years of life with a husband; white women spend 34 of an expected 77 years of life married.

- It is estimated that 86 percent of black children and 42 percent of white children will spend some time in a mother-only or other single-parent household (Bumpass, 1984:Table 2).

- The rate at which unmarried black women bear children has declined in recent years; this rate has continued to increase among white women.

These divergencies, in the context of similar overall trends, suggest possible differences in causal circumstances. And such differences exist. For example, the growth in the number of white and black poor families headed by women results from different behaviors: among whites, disrupted marriages; among blacks, a decrease in marriage rates. Other evidence is consistent with the hypothesis that white female-headed households are likely to become poor as a consequence of marital breakup, while black female-headed households are likely to be formed by women who were poor to begin with (Garfinkel and McLanahan, 1986).

Historical and comparative studies suggest that nuclear families are most stable when marriage partners have common and overlapping group affiliations and when the family unit is supported by social circles of other families committed to norms and values of solidarity and permanence. For many people, particularly the minority urban poor, these conditions have become less common during the past few decades. For some groups, extended kinship ties have weakened, and a husband-wife family often is not strongly supported and constrained by the surrounding social structure. External stresses, such as unemployment, may now have greater effects then formerly on family formation and stability because marriage and family stability are only weakly supported by political and social institutions. The deleterious effects on black families are most apparent in the high percentages of black children being raised under conditions of poverty and environmental deprivation.

FERTILITY TRENDS

During the decades after 1939, several changes encouraged lower rates of childbearing among Americans. First, there was the urbanization of the population and a very sharp rise in levels of educational attainment, both of which are associated with family size. Second, there has been an increase in the acceptability and use of contraception, in part because of major developments in technology such as oral contraceptives and more effective intrauterine devices. Third, there has been an increase in the rate of abortions. Although it is difficult to measure trends over time, abortion is now frequently used to terminate pregnancies. In the mid-1980s, there were about 64 abortions per 100 live black births and 30 abortions per 100 white births in a 13-state reporting area (Powell-Griner, 1986:Table A). Fourth, the federal government—as a component of the 1960s War on Poverty—assumed responsibility for providing family planning services to many low-income couples, which was a major change from earlier federal policies. By the mid-1980s, state and federal governments were spending $340 million annually to provide family planning services, an average of about $8 per year for every woman aged 15–39 (Gold and Nestor, 1985:25–30). Finally, there have been changes in the social roles of women, most of them probably leading to lower birthrates. These changes include a rise in the age at first marriage as educational attainment has risen; a growing proportion of both black and white women in the labor force; and an increasing proportion of divorce among married women.

Fertility rates have not declined monotonically throughout the years since 1939, however. At the end of the Great Depression, birthrates were low and the population grew slowly during the war and immediate postwar years. Birthrates then rose, reaching a high level in the late 1950s, and have fallen sharply since then. These patterns can be illustrated by examining changes in the total fertility rate—an estimate of the number of children a woman will bear in her lifetime if she experiences the birthrates of a given calendar year and survives to age 45. Total fertility rates for blacks and whites are shown in Figure 10-1.

In 1939, white women averaged just over 2 births in their lifetimes and black women just under 3. At the peak of the baby boom, white women were bearing about 3.5 children in their lifetimes and black women, 4.5. By 1984, the fertility rate for white women was about 1.7 children; for black women, 2.1. In the decades following 1960, both the black and white populations shifted from high fertility and rapid population growth to low fertility and near zero or negative population growth. The childbearing rates of black women remain above those of whites, although there is evidence of convergence. In 1960, black women averaged about one more child in their lifetime than white women; in 1984, the difference was less than one-half a child. According to the fertility and mortality rates of the early 1980s, the black population—in the absence of international migration—will grow by

FIGURE 10-1 Total fertility rates of black and white women, 1940–1984.

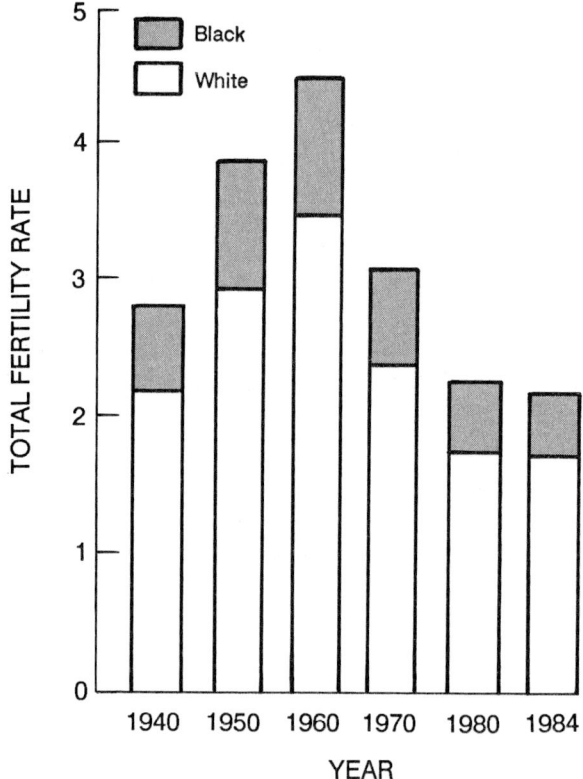

about 3 percent from one generation to the next, while the white population will decline by about 17 percent.

Despite numerous studies, it is still not fully understood why fertility rates rose to post–Civil War peaks in the late 1950s and then fell to extremely low levels (Easterlin, 1962, 1980; Westoff, 1978). Among whites, the change to much earlier marriage during and after World War II and economic prosperity helped to account for the shift from the 2-child family of the Depression era to the 3.5-child family of the Eisenhower period. Among blacks, there is agreement that the spread of diseases played a significant role in reducing fertility throughout the period from the 1870s to the 1930s (McFalls and Harvey, 1984; Wright and Pirie, 1984). The impoverished conditions of blacks and their limited access to health care meant that fertility problems were common. Approximately 30 percent of the married black women who reached menopause in the 1940s had borne no children, a rate that cannot entirely be explained by voluntary childlessness (Farley, 1987). Increases in living standards, the drug treatment of tuberculosis, and the government's fight against venereal disease during World War II minimized fertility problems for blacks, leading to increases in fertility and dramatic declines in childlessness.

After the 1950s, married American couples increasingly used contraception, and presumably abortion, to prevent unwanted births. In this era, planned births became the norm among married couples of both races. The development of better birth control techniques, federal and state support for family planning clinics, and the Supreme Court's *Roe* decision (1973) legalizing abortion help to explain the declines in fertility.

Additional information about these fertility trends is presented in Figure 10-2, which shows birthrates at different ages for 1939, 1959, and 1984. The dramatic rise in fertility at all ages, except the oldest, is clearly seen when the 1939 and 1959 curves are compared. This period was followed by a "birth dearth" so pronounced that the 1984 birthrates for both races and for most ages were at or near their all-time lows.

Childbearing by married women represents the clearest case of the disappearance of black-white fertility differences. Figure 10-3 shows marital fertility, which is how many children a woman would bear if she married at age 20, remained married through age 45, and had children at the rates observed in the years between 1950 and 1985. At the end of the baby boom in 1960, a black woman would have borne 1.5 more children than a white woman—5.6 births for a black woman compared with 4.1 for a white woman. By 1980, this racial difference had virtually disappeared. Among married women—indeed, among all women aged 25 and over—there was no longer a black-white difference in fertility rates.

Childbearing among younger and unmarried women gives a different picture. The fertility rates of black teenagers have declined sharply in recent years, but they remain more than double the rates of white teenagers. In 1960 there were 156 births per 1,000 black women aged 15–19; in 1985 there were 97, a decline of 59 births per 1,000 women. Among whites, the comparable change was from 70 births per 1,000 teenage women in 1957 to 43 in 1985 (National Center for Health Statistics, 1987:Table 4; Public Health Service, 1980:Table 1, cited in Farley, 1987). In the mid-1980s, black women by the age of 20 had borne an average of 510 children per 1,000 black women; white women had borne an average of 216 children. In northern European countries, these rates are below 100 children per 1,000 20-year-old women (Hayes, 1987; Westoff et al., 1983). It is generally accepted that the differences in teenage fertility between the United States and European countries is due to the wide availability of sex education and access to health and contraceptive services in Europe (Hayes, 1987).

One other major aspect of black-white differences in family formation has become much more pronounced since the end of the baby boom: the marital status of women who give birth (see Figure 10-4). Between 1939 and 1959, about 18 percent of black infants and 2 percent of white infants

FIGURE 10-2 Age-specific birthrates for (a) white and (b) black women, 1939, 1959, and 1984.

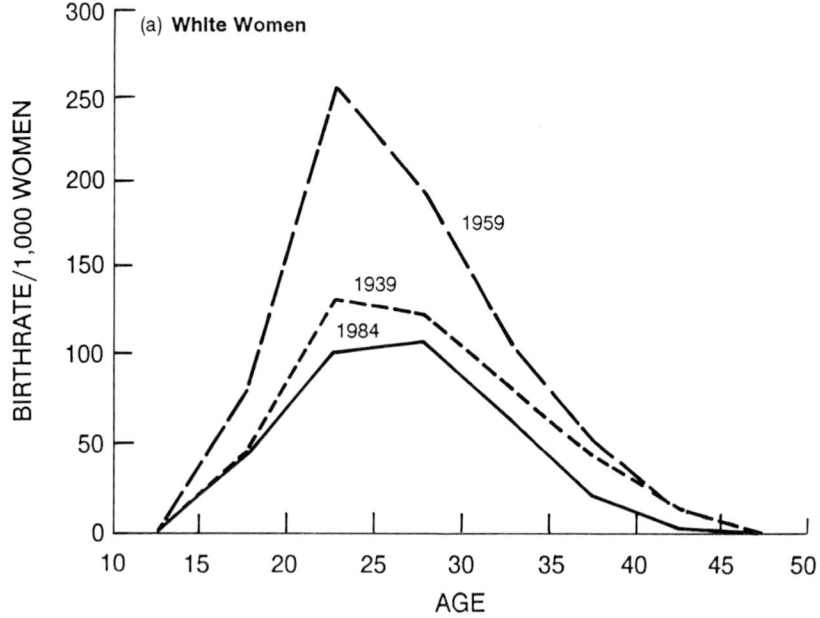

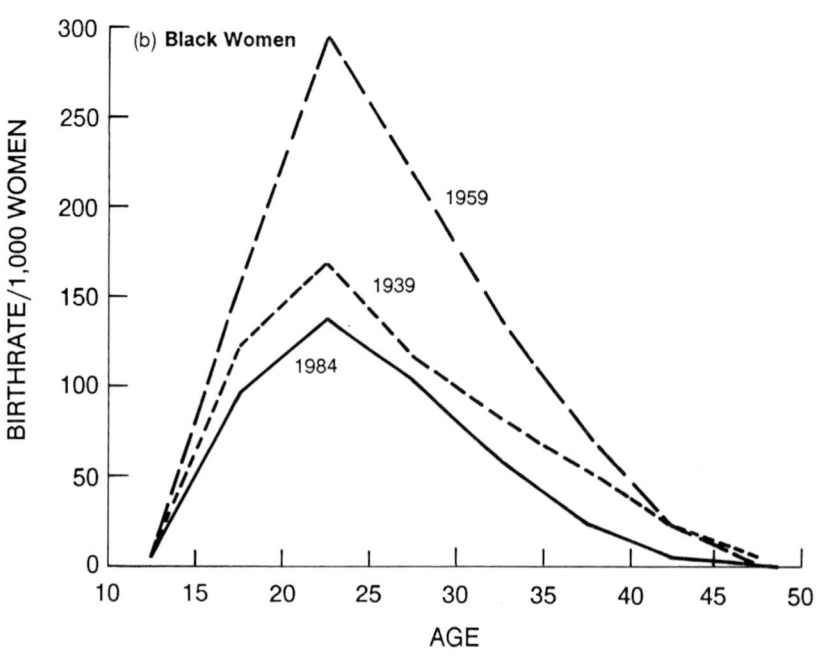

FIGURE 10-3 Marital fertility for black and white women, 1960–1985.

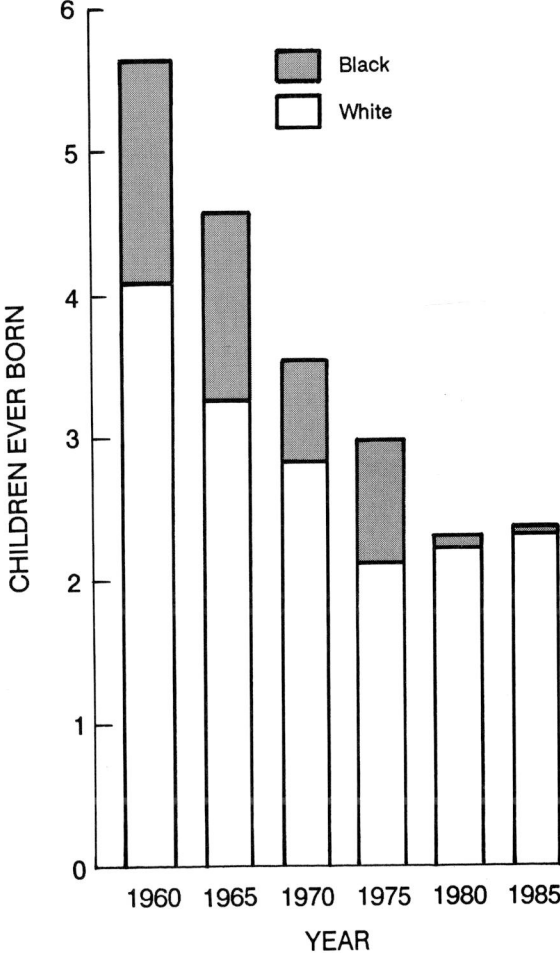

Note: Marital fertility is the estimated number of children ever born to women who marry at age 20, remain married to age 45, and bear children according to the marital fertility rates of 1960 to 1985.

Sources: Data from decennial censuses and Current Population Surveys.

FIGURE 10-4 Births to unmarried women, by race, 1940–1981.

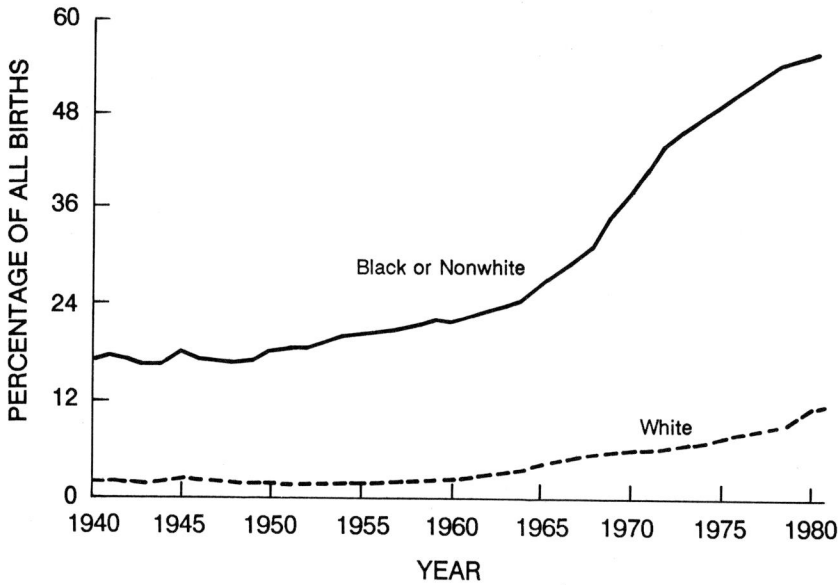

Note: Data for years prior to 1969 refer to whites and nonwhites.

Sources: National Center for Health Statistics (1978, 1983).

were born to unmarried women. These percentages subsequently changed rapidly; by the mid-1980s, 6 black births in 10 and 1 white birth in 8 were to unmarried women.

This change in the marital status of mothers is not due to increases in the rate at which unmarried women bear children. Rather, it is the result of two fundamental demographic changes. First, the age of women at marriage has risen. As a consequence, women are exposed to the possibility of nonmarital pregnancy for a much longer time and to marital childbearing for a shorter time. In the 1960 census, 64 percent of the black women aged 20–24 had married; in the 1986 population survey, 25 percent of the same age group reported they had married. Among white women, the corresponding change was from 72 percent married in 1960 to 45 percent in 1986 (Farley, 1987).

Second, there has been a much greater decline in the fertility rates of married women than in those of unmarried women, a change that produces an increase in the percentage of total births to unmarried women. In sum, the rapidly rising proportion of babies—both black and white—born to unmarried women has resulted from a major shift in the marital status of mothers, not from a higher birthrate among unmarried women.

MARITAL STATUS AND LIVING ARRANGEMENTS OF CHILDREN

According to the Census Bureau's definitions (in use since 1947), a family consists of two or more people who live in the same household and are related by blood, marriage, or adoption. Families are categorized into three types: those that include a married couple are termed husband-wife families; female-headed families typically include a mother and her children but might also consist of sisters or other relatives who live together; male-headed families are headed by a man who lives with one or more relatives but not with his wife.

At all dates, the distribution of kinds of white families differed substantially from that of blacks. While similar trends are evident for both whites and blacks, the timing and magnitude of change differ. In 1940, husband-wife families made up about 76 percent of all black families and 85 percent of all white families. From 1940 to the late 1950s, the proportion of black families headed by a woman remained roughly constant at 19 percent; by 1960 that proportion had risen only slightly to 22 percent. But during the next 25 years the percentage of black families headed by women doubled, to 44 percent. In 1940, the proportion of white families headed by women was 10 percent; by the mid-1980s, it had increased only slightly, to 13 percent.

Two demographic components help to account for the shifting distribution of families by type. First, a decreasing proportion of adults live with a spouse, so a smaller fraction of adults, especially black adults, can be heads or coheads of husband-wife families. Second, the rate at which women head their own families has increased. Since 1960, the proportion of adult women who head their own families rose for both whites and blacks, but the increase was much greater for black women. Among separated and divorced women in 1984, two-thirds of blacks were household heads, compared with one-half of whites. In the past, if a woman experienced divorce, became a widow, or had a child prior to marriage, she was likely to move into the household of relatives. Since 1960, it has become common for such women to head their own families (Ross and Sawhill, 1975). The proportion of separated or divorced black women who headed families increased from 40 to 66 percent between 1960 and 1984. Similar trends are found among white women: in 1960 35 percent of separated or divorced white women headed families; by 1984 this proportion had increased to 49 percent—higher than the 40 percent recorded for black women in 1960. Never-married white women rarely head families; only 5 percent did so in 1984. This was true also of black never-married women in 1960, when 6 percent did so; but by 1984, almost 25 percent of such black women headed families.

These changes can be seen in Figure 10-5a and b. This figure is based on the rates of marriage, divorce, remarriage, and death observed in 5-year intervals between 1940 and 1980. It shows the percentage of the total life span that would be spent in each of five different marital statuses by the average woman if the rates of that period continued indefinitely. For comparative data for men, see Figure 10-5c and d. Of course, not every person

FIGURE 10-5 Percentage of life span spent in five marital statuses for (a) black and (b) white women and (c) black and (d) white men, 1940–1980.

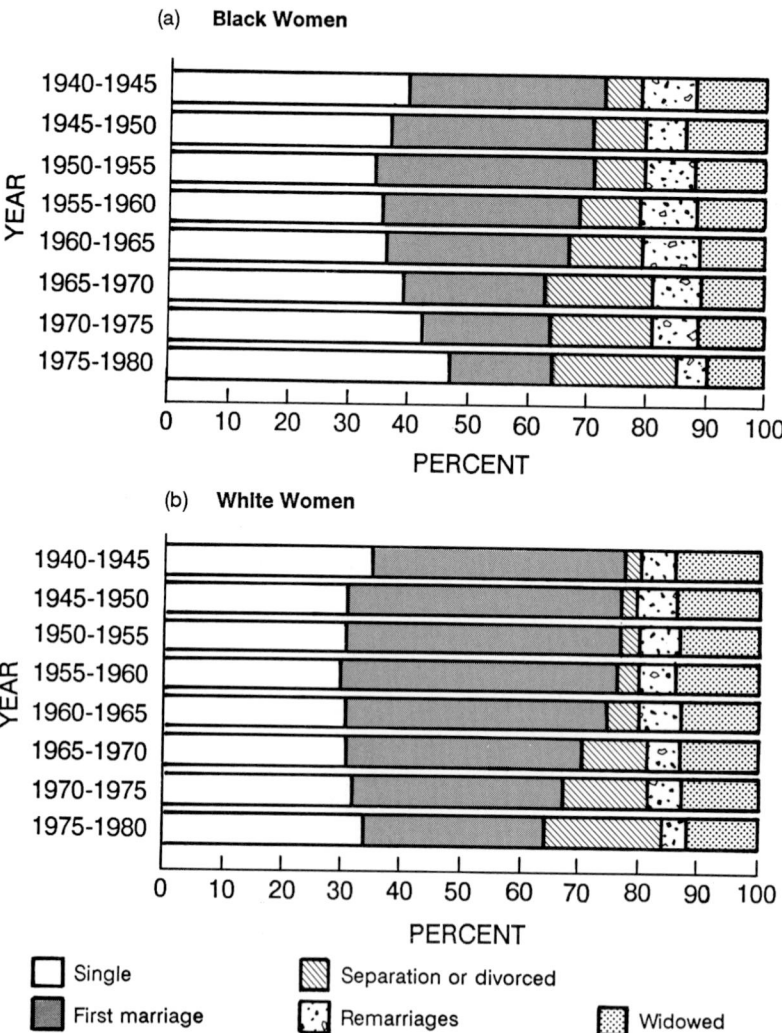

(a)   **Black Women**

(b)   **White Women**

Single
First marriage
Separation or divorced
Remarriages
Widowed

Note: Percentages calculated on the basis of rates observed for each 5-year period.

Source: Espenshade (1985:Tables 2 and 3). Reprinted with permission.

goes through the five marital statuses since some people never marry or, if married, never divorce or separate.

The shift toward much earlier marriage among blacks and whites can be seen in the decline, between 1940 and 1960, in the percentage of time that

FIGURE 10-5 (*Continued*)

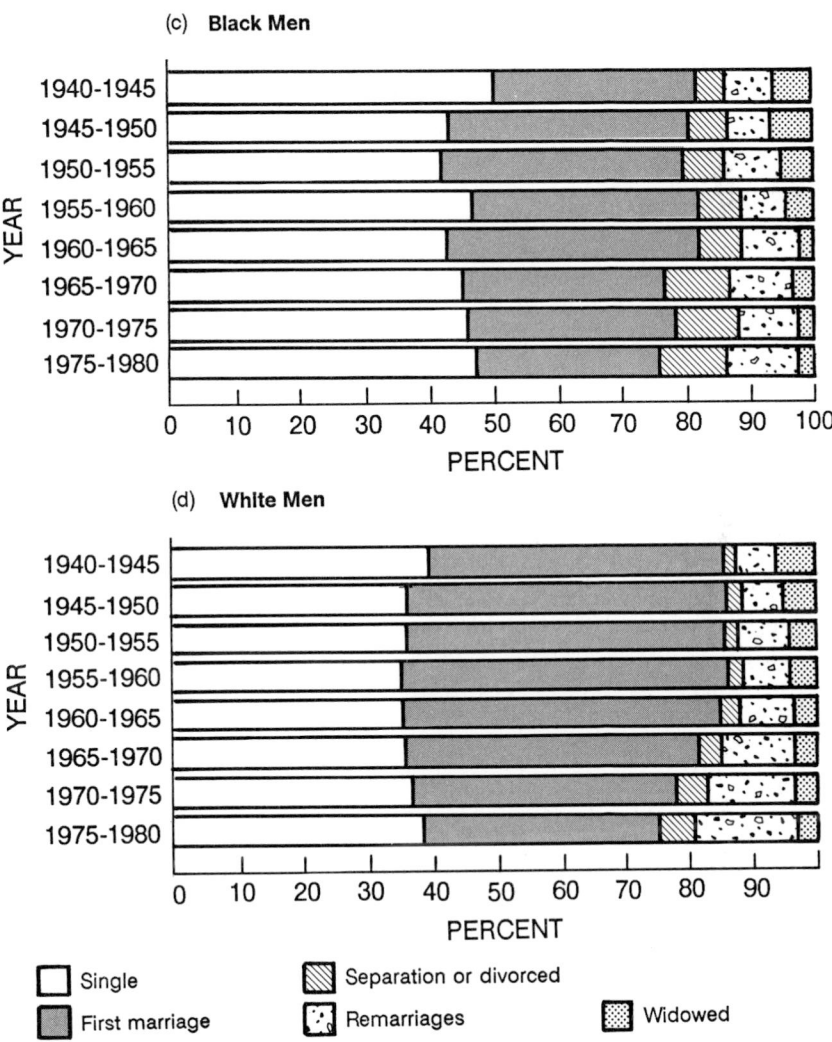

(c) **Black Men**

(d) **White Men**

Single
First marriage
Separation or divorced
Remarriages
Widowed

women spent before their first marriage, that is, as single women. Since 1960, there has been a shift toward later marriage, a reduction in the years women typically spend with their first husbands, and a corresponding lengthening of the interval of separation and divorce between the first and

TABLE 10-1 Indicators of Marital and Family Status (in percent), by Race, 1960–1985

Indicator and Year	White	Black	Black-White Difference
Women aged 15–44 living with husbands			
1960	69	52	17
1970	61	42	19
1980	55	30	25
1985	55	28	27
Births to unmarried women			
1960	2	22	20
1970	6	35	29
1980	11	55	44
1985	14	60	46
Families with children under 18 headed by a woman			
1960	6	24	18
1970	9	33	24
1980	14	48	34
1985	15	50	35
Children under age 18 in mother-only families			
1960	6	20	14
1970	8	29	21
1980	14	44	30
1985	16	51	35

Note: Data for 1960 refer to whites and nonwhites.

Sources: Data from decennial censuses and Current Population Surveys.

second husband. According to the rates of the 1975–1980 period, white women could expect to spend 33 of their 77-year life span as a wife while black women would spend 16 of their 73-year life span with a husband—a black-white difference of 17 years. In 1955–1960, the difference was 11 years, 40 years with a husband for a white woman and 29 years for a black woman. The first panel of Table 10-1 shows the proportion of black and white women of childbearing age (15–44) living with husbands and black-white differences since 1960. Given the delay in first marriage and the decreasing length of the typical marriage, it is not surprising that a sharply rising proportion of births are delivered to unmarried women, a trend that is illustrated in the second panel of Table 10-1.

The fact that young women are delaying their marriages much more than their childbearing and that women are separating but not remarrying so rapidly is reflected in two other important indicators shown in the bottom two panels of Table 10-1: the percentage of families with children headed by a woman and the percentage of all children living in female-headed families.

A smaller proportion of children (persons under age 18) are living with both their parents: in 1985, 51 percent of all black children lived with their mothers but not with their fathers; 16 percent of the white children are in mother-only families. Furthermore, these percentages, based on cross-sectional data, underestimate the proportion of children who spend some time in a single-parent family. Combining estimates of the proportion of children born to unmarried women (such children usually begin life in a mother-only family) with estimates of children who will experience the separation or divorce of their parents before they reach age 18, Bumpass (1984) projects that 42 percent of white children and 86 percent of black children are likely to spend some time in a single-parent household, usually a mother-only family.

An important implication of these trends is the apparent changing sexual division of labor with regard to child rearing. That is, women without a husband increasingly find themselves responsible for this activity. Between 1960 and 1985, the percentage of families that were headed by a woman increased from 22 to 44 percent among blacks; the proportion of white families headed by a woman increased from 8 to 13 percent.

Trends in each of the indicators shown in Table 10-1 and Figure 10-6 are parallel for blacks and whites, but the magnitude of change has been much more accentuated for blacks. These demographic data unambiguously describe an increasing black-white difference with regard to the family living arrangements of adults and their children. The large prevalence of single-parent families has important implications for the resources available to children and the comparative future well-being of blacks and whites.

Poverty among families headed by women is much higher than poverty among husband-wife families. For blacks, 67 percent of all children living in female-headed families were in poverty in 1986. Because of the underlying unequal distribution of income and wealth between single- and two-parent families with children and the higher proportion of black children in single-parent families, 43 percent of all black children under age 18 lived in families below the poverty level in 1986. Among white children, 16 percent lived in poor families. Family background conditions of poverty income levels and very low wealth place many black children at considerable risk of having health problems, a poor education, and poor future employment prospects (see Chapters 6–8).

CHILDREN AND POVERTY: CONSEQUENCES OF FAMILY CHANGE

Because many of the women who head "poverty" households were poor before they became mothers and household heads, the often cited "feminization of poverty" may be partly illusory. The phrase implies that these households are poor because of their female heads, but as Bane (1986) suggested, family breakups may merely reshuffle the female poor from one classification to another. Nevertheless, the combination of increased female, single-parent households with child care responsibilities and low earning

FIGURE 10-6 Living arrangements of (a) black and (b) white children under age 18, 1960–1985.

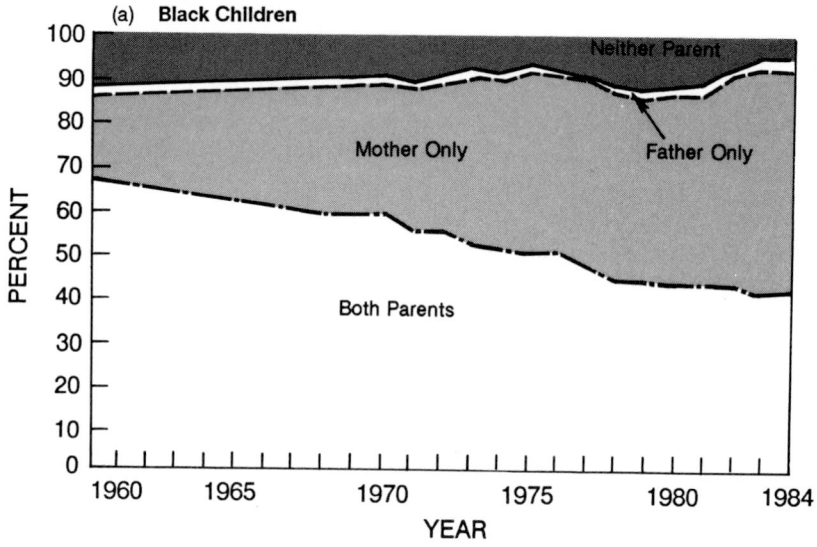

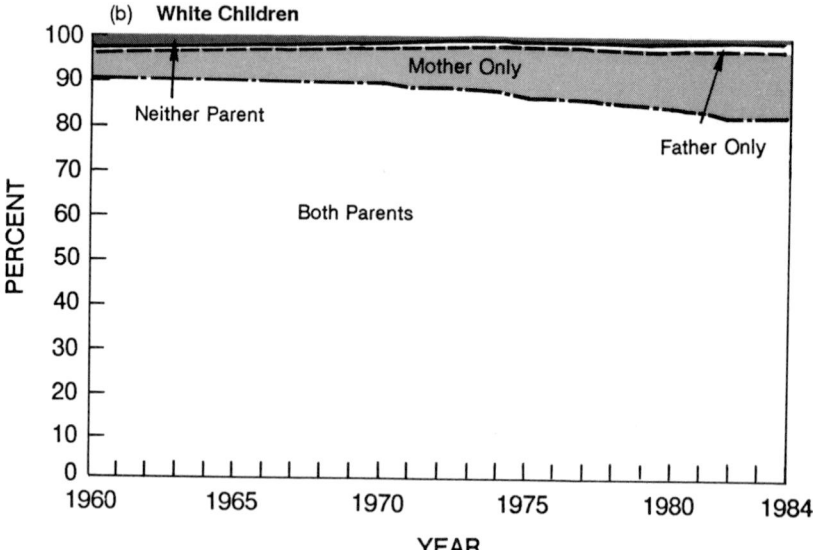

Notes: Data are standardized for age of children. Data for 1960 refer to nonwhites.

Source: Data from Current Population Surveys.

opportunities exacerbates the problem of continued high rates of poverty among black families.

Clearly, the mere fact that a household is headed by a woman does not mean that it will be poor. But several mechanisms by which poverty comes to be strongly associated with female-headed families have been identified. First, many families are kept above the poverty line only because of two employed adults. A single-parent family is more likely to be poor simply because there is usually only one earner. Second, women on the average earn much less than men; so even among single-parent families, those with a female head are much more likely to be poor than those with a male head. Third, young black women who form single-parent households predominantly come from poor households and often lack the requisite skills for high earnings. Fourth, in the absence of relatively inexpensive day care, many single mothers of young children cannot earn enough from outside employment to justify working (see Chapter 6). Fifth, the birth of a child may disrupt the education or job experience of the mother, thus further reducing her opportunities for earnings.

Perhaps the most striking manifestation of these mechanisms is the growing division between the economic status of two-parent and female-headed families. Black husband-wife families have nearly 3 times the median income of black female-headed families. This inequality between family types among blacks has important consequences for the welfare of future generations. Black husband-wife families in 1985 were 51 percent of all black families but had 70 percent of total black family income; female-headed black families were 44 percent of black families but had 25 percent of black family income. For white families, these differentials were far less: overall, 52 percent of black families headed by a woman were in poverty compared with 27 percent of the white female-headed families.

The effects of mother-only families on the subsequent education, occupation, income, and marital status of children as they grow up have been extensively studied. The sheer absence of a father may not be a crucial factor, and some fathers of children in female-headed households are actively involved with the children (Furstenberg, 1976). Unfortunately, much of the available research has not adequately controlled for the confounding effects of low income, low education, the timing of marital disruption, and possibly other factors disproportionately present in female-headed families (see McLanahan, 1985). Although the findings are not definitive, they strongly suggest that as compared with children of two-parent families, children from one-parent families have lower scores on standardized tests of IQ and educational achievement, lower educational attainment, lower occupational status and income, and higher rates of early marriage, births to unmarried women, and marital dissolution.

After controlling the educational attainment and occupational status of the household head and number of siblings, Duncan (1967:366) found that the presence of two parents in a nonwhite man's household at age 16 was associated with an additional 0.43 to 0.77 year of schooling among cohorts born between 1916 and 1950. Controlling these same variables, plus farm and southern origin, Featherman and Hauser (1976:114) found that the educational attainments of black men born as recently as 1937–1951 were about 0.4 year lower when both parents were not present at age 16. The mean difference in schooling between black and white men was 1.4 years in the cohorts born from 1937 to 1946 and 1.1 years in the cohorts born from 1947 to 1951. Thus, elimination of single-parent families—without altering other socioeconomic background factors—would have reduced the difference in educational attainments between black and white men by 27.2 percent in the birth cohort of 1937–1946 and by 39.4 percent in the birth cohort of 1947–1951.

There is some evidence that the effects of living in a single-parent family declined between cohorts born just after World War I and those born just after World War II (Featherman and Hauser, 1976, 1978:330–331). Yet, family instability does not lead directly to an additional deficit in occupational success among black men beyond its effect through years of completed schooling (Duncan and Duncan, 1969; Featherman and Hauser, 1976, 1978). Duncan and Duncan reported that the effects of schooling on occupational success are greater among (black or white) men raised in two-parent families than those raised in single-parent families. This effect is very likely a result of more schooling of men from two-parent families combined with the strong effect of high levels of schooling on occupational standing.

The differences in educational performance and attainment of children in female-headed and two-parent families are reduced when the socioeconomic status of the family is controlled, but daughters of single mothers are themselves especially likely to become unmarried mothers. Whether or not a mother in a single-parent family works outside the home seems to have few clear measured effects on young children; the sheer fact of employment status, if any, is overshadowed by the economic and marital status of the mother (see Garfinkel and McLanahan, 1986:26–37; Hayes, 1987).

The consequences of single parenthood are especially marked when teenagers in low-income families bear children. Teenage mothers are now much more likely than previously to be unmarried and to keep their children. Infants born to such mothers are disproportionately of low birthweight—a condition that often forecasts serious health problems and infant mortality (see Chapter 8). Furthermore, they are likely to receive poor nutrition and inadequate medical care and to live in poverty. These conditions increase the likelihood of a high incidence of single motherhood as these children in turn become teenagers (see Danziger, 1986).

CAUSES OF CHANGING FAMILY PATTERNS

There is no single family structure that fully represents the diversity of familial arrangements among black Americans of the past or present. The Africans who were brought to the New World as slaves came from many different cultures and experienced highly varying conditions after their arrival. It is not possible to say how much of the African-American family tradition is African and how much was developed in the New World (DuBois, 1903; Frazier, 1939; Gutman, 1976; Herskovits, 1941). Doubtless both sources were important.

There were different modes of introduction to the American continent (McAdoo and Terborg-Penn, 1985; Sudarkasa, 1981). Not all Africans came as slaves. A few came as explorers and adventurers, some as freemen before the beginning of slavery, and some who came as indentured servants eventually earned their freedom. Thus, black families varied greatly in legal, economic, and social status. Many of the free and freed black families were headed by entrepreneurs, professionals, artisans, landowners, and businessmen. This small but important black elite contrasted with the majority of blacks who had to struggle to maintain themselves under conditions of economic deprivation and social disruption.

Blacks evinced a remarkable loyalty to the family unit in the face of the disruptive treatment of their families by many slaveowners. When families were not broken apart by the slavery system, nuclear family units of two parents and their children were common. Some families were headed by females and many kinship units were extended, often including grandparents and grandchildren. Other relatives and their young children could be part of a single household. Near-dwelling relatives formed networks of mutual aid and social support (Gutman, 1976; McAdoo, 1987:6–7).

For enslaved blacks, the family was important since it was the primary black institution to which they could openly be committed. Individuals married early and, if necessary, frequently. An important illustration of the extent to which the family was part of the fabric of the Afro-American community was given by the frantic searches carried out after the Civil War by freed people looking for family members from whom they had been separated during slavery. Similarly, thousands of former slaves immediately legitimized marriages that had not been legally recognized by the slave codes. It is important to remember that the institution of slavery did not destroy the black family (Franklin, 1980; Gutman, 1976; Litwack, 1979).

An inventory of possible explanations for the recent decreasing prevalences and the greater instability of marriage among blacks (compared with whites) is long. The most salient proposed explanations include differences in social class and economic position; family assistance benefits; changes in men's and women's economic status; scarcity of men; and a culture of poverty. In this section we comment on each of these hypotheses. First, however, we discuss some important background information as a context.

THE RESILIENCE OF BLACK FAMILIES

A striking finding of modern historical research on black families is that stable two-parent families were maintained during slavery and survived the vicissitudes of poverty, migration, and urbanization (Billingsley, 1968; Gutman, 1976; Pleck, 1979). As Herbert Gutman (1976) concluded:

> At all moments in time between 1880 and 1925—that is, from an adult generation born in slavery to an adult generation about to be devastated by the Great Depression of the 1930s and the modernization of southern agriculture afterward—the typical Afro-American family was lowerclass in status and headed by two parents. . . . This was so in the urban and rural south in 1880 and 1900 and in New York City in 1905 and 1925.

The two-parent black family continued to be common among farm laborers, sharecroppers, tenants, and northern and southern blacks in the great migration to the North that so reshaped the United States in the twentieth century. Poverty and high mortality among black men did indeed result in a greater proportion of female-headed families among blacks than among whites, but even after the Great Depression, in 1940, nearly three-fourths of black families with children under 18 were headed by two parents (see Engerman, 1977).

There was no significant increase in male-absent households even after the massive migrations to the urban North. Until the 1960s, 75 percent of black households with a child under age 18 included both husband and wife (see Table 10-1). The dramatic changes came only later, and in 1986, 49 percent of black families with children under age 18 were headed by women. Since black nuclear families and kin-related households remained intact through slavery, the Great Depression, migration, urban life, ghettoization, and poverty, it appears unlikely that any one of these conditions or their combinations can fully explain the large changes in marriage and family since 1960. More weight must be given to other factors.

Furthermore, since no one family type is representative of all black families, economic and social status differences must be taken into account in any analysis of present-day black families. Especially in black-white comparisons, it is essential when possible to control for differences in income, employment, education, and status of family of origin (Billingsley, 1968). The likelihood of interaction effects between class (especially as it relates to economic status) and race makes this procedure an important precaution against misleading inferences.

SOCIAL CLASS AND ECONOMIC POSITION

Cross-cultural comparisons based on statistical and ethnographic data show substantial regularities in the relations between familial behaviors and basic demographic and socioeconomic conditions. A case in point is the much-discussed matter of births to unmarried women. High rates of such births are regularly associated with the following conditions (Goode et al., 1971: 301–305): low socioeconomic status, urban residence, little education, times of economic depression, prior prevalence of divorce and separation, home background of unwed parenthood, weak parental controls over children, and lack of severe censure or social sanctions for premarital sexual relations and pregnancy. These background conditions are often found in clusters, so that families with few economic and social resources will be least able to control youths or to reward them for confining childbearing within marriages.

But general sociocultural changes are also at work. Thus, the post-1960 movement toward less rigid sexual norms may have increased the incidence of single motherhood, as suggested by the recent rise among whites. General economic changes also have significant effects. And there is other evidence that family stability in general is higher in social strata of higher prestige, income, and wealth, and in stable communities of close social interdependence (Williams, 1970:Ch. IV).

Blacks continue to lag far behind whites on most indicators of economic and educational status. And it is known that desertion, births to unmarried women, and female-headed families are more common among the poor than the well-to-do. Thus, a prominent hypothesis is that black-white differences in family structure can be explained by black-white differences in social class or economic status. This is a difficult issue to disentangle since family status and economic condition are reciprocally related. Nevertheless, the available data suggest that black-white differences in family status are indeed affected by differences in social and economic status.

One example of such an effect concerns marital dissolution. Studies conducted in the 1970s reported that black marriages are about twice as likely as those of whites to be ended by disruption. Table 10-2 shows a comparison of the marital status distributions of blacks and whites, both actual and controlling for differences in educational attainment for men and women and for income distribution for men. Rows (1) and (2) for both men and women show the actual marital status distribution of whites and blacks. Rows (3) show what the marital status distribution of blacks would be if they had the educational distribution of whites but their own education-specific marital status distributions. If black-white differences in marital status were entirely due to differences in educational attainment, then the marital statuses of blacks and whites would be the same once the differences in education (if perfectly measured) were controlled, that is, the figures on rows (1) and (3) would be identical. It is clear they are not similar, and thus, differences in mean years of schooling account for little of the black-white difference in marital status. Data for women lead to a similar conclusion. When educational attainment differences are taken into account, it is still found that black women are more likely to be single or formerly married than white women and much less likely to be living with a husband.

Data in row (4) of Table 10-2 take black-white differences in the income of men into account. A comparison of items in rows (1) and (4) shows that controlling for income reduces the black-white disparities substantially. Hence, one can infer that income plays an important role in explaining black-white differences in the marital status of men. If, instead of their own income distribution, black men had the income distribution of white men,

TABLE 10-2 Marital Status of Men and Women Aged 35–44 (in percent), by Race, 1980

Sex and Race	Never Married	Married Once, Spouse Present	Married More Than Once, Spouse Present	Separated, Widowed, or Divorced	First Marriages Ended by Divorce (estimated)
Men					
White					
(1) Actual marital status	7	66	16	11	29
Black					
(2) Actual marital status	14	49	12	25	42
(3) Assuming white educational attainment	13	51	13	23	40
(4) Assuming white income distribution	9	56	15	20	37
Women					
White					
(1) Actual marital status	5	65	15	15	30
Black					
(2) Actual marital status	13	40	9	38	48
(3) Assuming white educational attainment	12	42	9	37	47

Source: Data from Bureau of the Census (1980:Tables 3, 6).

their marital status distribution would (assuming a direct causal influence) be more like that of white men. However, this analysis does not fully test the hypothesis that differences in family and marital status are due to class or economic differences because it does not compare marital status between blacks and whites of identical socioeconomic status. The data here—and in every other study of which we are aware—do not allow such comparisons.[1] In addition, many correlates of income are uncontrolled in the available data. Nevertheless, we infer that socioeconomic differences explain a significant amount of black-white marital status differences and very likely would explain more, given better data to test the hypothesis.

---

1. There are two primary reasons that such comparisons are difficult. Consider a random sample of blacks and whites of a population taken from a census; within any income interval—say $20,000–$25,000—the sample of blacks will be more concentrated toward the low end than will the sample of whites. In addition, blacks in the interval will have been earning that income for a shorter period of time and will have a lower expectation of having a larger income in the future and lower wealth (see Chapter 6). Thus, cross-sectional comparisons of this type usually leave substantial variation in socioeconomic class between blacks and whites.

FAMILY ASSISTANCE BENEFITS

Because family assistance benefits are available to low-income, single-parent families, they have been seen as rewarding such families and thus encouraging their formation. It has been said to allow pregnant unmarried women to decide to bear and then keep their children. It has also been claimed that assistance payments allow unhappily married parents to split up. In the absence of assistance payments, according to this hypothesis, women and men would have to find other options, and they might be more careful to avoid forming single-parent households. In addition, benefit payments may allow a young woman to live in her own household rather than sharing a residence with her parent(s).

This hypothesis implies that (all other factors being constant) where benefit levels are higher, births to unmarried women, divorce rates, and the number of single-parent families living independently would also be higher. A large number of studies have tried to exploit the large variation in benefits across states in order to assess the impact of public assistance (U.S. House of Representatives 1987:371–372, 578). In 1986, for example, Tennessee and Mississippi paid less than $150 monthly for a family of three, while places in New York and California paid close to $700. Adding the value of food stamps reduces the variation somewhat, but the combined benefits still vary from $400 to close to $800 per month (see Chapter 6). In spite of these large variations, recent studies have found only modest associations between changes in family structure and family assistance benefit levels. The association of benefit levels with the overall number of female-headed families is usually reported to be statistically detectable but quite small (Ellwood and Bane, 1985; Garfinkel and McLanahan, 1986; Ross and Sawhill, 1975). Ellwood and Summers (1986) found that there is no correlation between the percentage of black children in single-parent households and the level of Aid to Families with Dependent Children (AFDC) benefits in different states. And the number of black children living in female-headed households rose sharply during the 1970s while the number of such households receiving AFDC declined.

Other studies have tried to measure the impact of family assistance benefits on specific family structure events, such as divorce or unmarried childbearing. A few studies have reported some effects of assistance on divorce, but these effects are generally small. Using the same longitudinal data, a number of investigators have differed in their conclusions as to whether benefits have an impact on divorce. Moore and Waite (1976) found a small impact in one data set and none in another. Groeneveld and colleagues (1980) inferred significant effects from the negative income tax (NIT) experiments in Seattle and Denver, but these findings have been questioned by Cain and Wissoker (1987–1988). Other NIT sites seem to have shown no impact. Ellwood and Bane (1985) report small effects overall, but a larger effect for marriages that were formed when the wife was very young. Collectively, the evidence is that family assistance benefits play a small part in divorce decisions.

Much attention has been given to the Seattle-Denver experiments with a negative income tax. Early reports claimed that NIT resulted in increased rates of marriage dissolution; however, an elaborate reanalysis of the data has rejected that conclusion. Using the full sample and all years of the experiment for which data are available, the reanalysis concluded that the pure NIT program (without training provisions) had no effect on marital stability of any statistical or practical significance (Cain and Wissoker, 1987–1988:14).

Research has shown even less association between family assistance benefits and births to unmarried women. There is little or no relationship between aggregate benefit levels and rates of illegitimacy (Cutright, 1970; Ellwood and Bane, 1985; Moore and Caldwell, 1976). A major review of research concluded that family assistance has little systematic impact on family structure (Duncan et al., 1988:468); for example, AFDC payments have no measurable effects on births to unmarried women, although they may affect household living arrangements. Most of those who have reviewed the literature have come to a conclusion similar to that reported in a recent National Research Council study (Hayes, 1987:119) on teenage pregnancy:

> Concern over the high rates of welfare dependency in the United States have led many critics to question whether the availability of Aid to Families with Dependent Children (AFDC) and other, non-cash benefits is an unfortunate incentive for young women to give birth outside of marriage. The existing body of research suggests there is no evidence to support this assumption.

While the availability of cash benefits apparently does not lead women to bear additional children, it may reduce the likelihood that an unmarried pregnant woman marries in haste (Moore and Burt, 1982:108–113). It may also lessen the likelihood that she obtains an abortion, and so increase the proportion of unmarried women who keep their children rather than placing them for adoption. The availability of higher family assistance payments is also associated with a lesser likelihood that a mother remarries rapidly after termination of her previous marriage (Hutchens, 1979).

Perhaps the strongest effect identified in the literature is on living arrangements of single mothers—whether they live with a parent or live separately. The increasing proportion of female-headed households reported by Census Bureau surveys partly reflects a change in living arrangements rather than only the prevalence of single parenthood. If an unmarried mother lives in the household of her parents or other relatives, she and her children constitute a subfamily. If she moves into a separate residence, the mother-children unit will be recorded as a female-headed family. The availability of AFDC appears to encourage single mothers to form their own households (Ellwood and Bane, 1985).

Some social commentators question the research results that show few significant effects of family assistance benefits. But the pattern of such benefits over time adds to the credibility of the conclusion of small or nonexistent effects. There were large increases in benefits during the 1960s and early

1970s. In 1984 constant dollars, national average benefits for AFDC were roughly $560 per month in 1960; by 1972, the value of the combination of AFDC increases and food stamps was almost $750, and in-kind benefits such as medical protection (Medicaid) had also increased. In addition, various rules—such as unannounced searches of beneficiaries' homes and against a man in the house—had been relaxed or eliminated. As might be expected, the number of people receiving benefits grew rapidly during the period. But since the early 1970s, benefits have not come close to keeping pace with inflation; the national average real value of AFDC and food stamp benefits in the mid-1980s was about $580—only slightly above the 1960 level (although Medicaid is now also available). And administrative rules have been further relaxed since then. Yet, even though the proportion of children in female-headed families has grown, the fraction of children on AFDC has remained roughly steady since 1973. According to Ellwood and Summers (1986):

> The figures are even more dramatic for blacks: Between 1972 and 1980 [prior to the Reagan era] the number of black children in female headed families rose nearly 10 percent; the number of black children on AFDC actually fell by 5 percent. If AFDC were pulling families apart and enabling the formation of single-parent families, it is hard to understand why the number of children on the program would remain constant throughout the period in our history when family structures changed the most.

If increased family assistance benefits caused more single-parent families to form, it is hard to explain why the trend continued when benefits were effectively cut back sharply (see also Garfinkel and McLanahan, 1986:55–56).

Some critics, notably Murray (1984), have questioned these conclusions, arguing that the early increase in family assistance benefits may have permanently changed attitudes. Murray also believes that the mere availability of benefits may influence family formation decisions, but that variations above some threshold make little difference. This latter argument would be plausible only if nearly all people had an identical and very low threshold; otherwise, more people should be across the threshold in high-benefit states than in low-benefit ones. If there is a threshold so low that it had no impact in Mississippi in 1985, then there really is no way to determine whether benefits had any effects, and many states presumably would have crossed the threshold even by 1960. Perhaps more important, Murray's argument suggests that even large increases or declines in benefits would have little impact on family structure. In any case, the availability of some family assistance has not abolished poverty for children. Indeed, the percentage of children living in poverty in the United States (in 1979 or 1981) was higher by at least 60 percent than the equivalent proportion in any of five other countries studied: United Kingdom, Sweden, Norway, Canada, and West Germany (Smeeding and Smeeding, 1985:13).

CHANGES IN MEN'S AND WOMEN'S ECONOMIC STATUS

The Declining Economic Fortunes of Men

Recently, several researchers have emphasized male joblessness as a factor in the decline of marriage and the increasing proportion of children being born to unmarried women. Wilson (1987) hypothesized that falling employment among black men—described in this report (Chapter 6)—may make marriage less attractive to both men and women. Wilson and Neckerman (1986) noted that the ratio of employed black men to women in the younger age groups has fallen precipitously in recent years and largely mimics the changes in marriage rates. Beginning in 1965, the relative odds of black males aged 16–24 being employed in comparison with white males dropped sharply until about 1977 and then leveled off. As of 1985, a black male was about 2.5 times as likely as a white male to be unemployed or out of the labor force (see Chapter 6). In other work, Wilson and his colleagues have reported that marriage rates generally declined most in those regions of the country where the ratio of employed black men to employed white men has declined most.

Wilson emphasized joblessness, but even the earnings of fully employed men generally (both whites and blacks) have been hit hard. As described in Chapters 1 and 6, for the first time since World War II, the real earnings of full-year, full-time male workers—both black and white—have not risen in more than a decade. Earnings for fully employed workers peaked in 1973 and have yet to regain that level.

Only a few researchers have so far studied the potential significance of this period of no growth in real earnings. Levy (1987) showed just how dramatic the changes have been. The earnings of the cohort of men aged 25–34 in 1949 grew an average of 57 percent in the next decade (adjusting for inflation). Similarly, the earnings of men aged 25–34 in 1959 had grown an average of 52 percent by 1969. By contrast, the earnings of men aged 25–34 in 1973 actually fell slightly over the next decade. For men aged 35–44 in 1949 and 1959, the increases were roughly 30 percent in the subsequent decade, but during the decade since 1973, their earnings fell 15 percent.

Faltering male earnings alone cannot be the whole story, however, for changes in family structure were significant even during the 1960s when the economy was booming. Still, if many young men are unemployed and if young male workers can no longer count on a growing level of earnings, then both marriage and divorce decisions may be seriously affected. There is significant research documenting at least some association between male joblessness and family stress (Garfinkel and McLanahan, 1986). Careful empirical work examining the links between the economic fortunes of black men and the family structure in the black community is only recently re-emerging after a long period of dormancy. The connections of family and economic status define a fruitful area for focused research (see Easterlin, 1980, 1982).

Labor Force Participation and Economic Status of Women

A different explanation for the change in family structure argues that with increased labor force participation, women are no longer so dependent on men for support, and thus there is less pressure to marry and less need for either partner to remain in a marriage that is unsatisfactory. Conversely, increased labor market opportunities for women might be seen as increasing the financial security of married couples and thus making marriage look even more attractive.

Particularly since the early 1970s, the educational attainments of women have increased, their labor force participation rates have risen sharply, and there is evidence suggesting a significant upgrading of the occupational distribution of employed women (Bianchi and Rytina, 1986; Bianchi and Spain, 1986:Ch. 4, 5; Blau and Ferber, 1985; Reskin and Hartmann, 1986:Ch. 2). As the employment of black men decreased, black women have experienced rising employment and relative earnings. Thus, the high rates of joblessness among black men may reduce the incentives of unmarried women to marry or of formerly married women to remarry.

Have black women, in some sense, become economically independent at a faster rate than white women? Does this change explain the growing black-white gap in marital status and family living arrangements? It is extremely difficult to test the hypothesis that marriage is declining in usefulness to women since it is not easy to determine whether the increase in the economic independence of women is a cause or a consequence of changes in marital and family status. However, some evidence implies that, relative to men, women have become more independent in an economic sense and that this change has occurred more rapidly for blacks than for whites.

For every decade from 1940 to 1980 and at every educational level, a higher proportion of black than of white women were in the labor force. The differences were larger for women with more educational attainment: for example, for women with 16 or more years of schooling, the percentage differences between black and white labor force participation were significant:

1940:	+16
1950:	+23
1960:	+28
1970:	+24
1980:	+13

It has long been the case that black women worked for pay outside the home and contributed to family income. Between 1950 and 1980, the income of black women relative to that of black men rose rapidly—from about 29 percent in 1950 to about 70 percent in 1970, with a drop to 63 percent in 1985 (Farley and Neidert, 1986:Tables D,E).

Table 10-3 presents data on median earnings of women as a percentage of that of men of the same race for the post–World War II era. The top panel

TABLE 10-3 Median Earnings or Income of Women as a Percentage of That of Men, by Race, 1947–1983

Earnings Indicator and Year	Black (or Nonwhite)	White
Median wage and salary earnings for all adults[a] reporting earnings		
1947[b]	34	54
1954[b]	43	55
1959[b]	45	49
1964[b]	48	49
1969	46	46
1974	55	45
1979	65	45
1983	78	51
Median wage and salary earnings for full-time, year-round employees		
1954[b]	58	64
1959[b]	66	61
1964[b]	62	59
1969[b]	69	58
1974[b]	73	57
1979[c]	74	59
1983[c]	78	61
Median income for total persons receiving income		
1948[b]	36	45
1954[b]	42	38
1959[b]	41	31
1964[b]	38	31
1969	47	32
1974	52	35
1979	52	36
1983	62	42

[a]Adults were defined as persons aged 14 and over from 1947 to 1974 and aged 15 and over at later dates.
[b]Data for these years refer to nonwhites.
[c]These data refer to total earnings, not just wage and salary earnings.

Source: Data from Current Population Surveys.

shows that the median earnings of black women rose faster than those of black men. In 1947, the wage and salary earnings of black women were 34 percent of those of black men; by 1983 women's earnings were 78 percent of those of men's. The pattern of change was different among whites: the median earnings of women fell as a percentage of men's from 54 percent in 1947 to 51 percent in 1983. The patterns are the same for full-time, year-round employees.

The bottom panel presents data on the median income of those persons who received any income during the year. Income differs from earnings since it includes money received from dividends, interest, or investments, as well as transfer payments such as Social Security, AFDC, or veterans' benefits. For the past two decades, the income of women has risen faster than that of men. Again, a substantial black-white difference is evident: the male-female disparity in income is much smaller now among blacks than among whites.

The hypothesis that increased economic independence of women leads to increased divorce and separation is generally consistent with the research findings (Garfinkel and McLanahan, 1986:63–68). Although a more complex picture emerges from the studies of the effects of male joblessness, the results point to loss of jobs and the stagnation of male earnings as factors in the increase of black female-headed families. A crucial mechanism may be a scarcity of black men who are able to support families. There are substantial shortages of such men for the women most likely to become unmarried mothers—central-city residents with little education and from low-income backgrounds (Wilson and Aponte, 1985; see Chapter 6).

Even though women's incomes have increased and they are able to enjoy more choice and economic independence, it remains true that if women were to combine their incomes with those of a husband, their economic choices and well-being would be even greater. It could be argued, then, that women retain an economic incentive to marry and use their incomes to support families.

SCARCITY OF "MARRIAGEABLE" MEN

A hypothesis that is complementary to the two previous explanations is that changes in the family structure of blacks may result from a shortage of black men for women to marry (see Cox, 1940). Guttentag and Secord (1983:Ch. 8) examined the ratio of men to women and observed that it is uniquely low among blacks (see also Spanier and Glick, 1986; Wilson, 1978:72–92).

If women frequently marry men who are 2–3 years older than themselves, a sex ratio disparity is inevitable in a growing population. In a population increasing by 2 percent per year—about the growth rate for the black population for a decade or so after World War II—the number of women born in any year will be about 6 percent greater than the number of men born 3 years earlier. Given this fact, is the ratio of marriageable black men to black women significantly less than that of whites, as Guttentag and Secord suggested?

The ratios of unmarried men aged 20–26 to unmarried women aged 18–24 between 1940 and 1985 are shown in Figure 10-7. The unmarried category includes all single, widowed, divorced, and currently separated persons (including married people whose spouse is absent). Figure 10-7a presents data from the decennial censuses and the March 1985 Current Population Survey. The trend lines show the demographic effects of the post–World War II baby boom. Women who reached marriageable ages in the 1960s or early 1970s found themselves competing for relatively few men. The population growth rate has slowed since that time, and the situation has improved for women of both races seeking marriage. However, at all dates, there apparently were fewer men per 100 women among blacks than

FIGURE 10-7 Unmarried men aged 20–26 per 100 unmarried women aged 18–24, (a) actual and (b) adjusted, by race, 1940–1985.

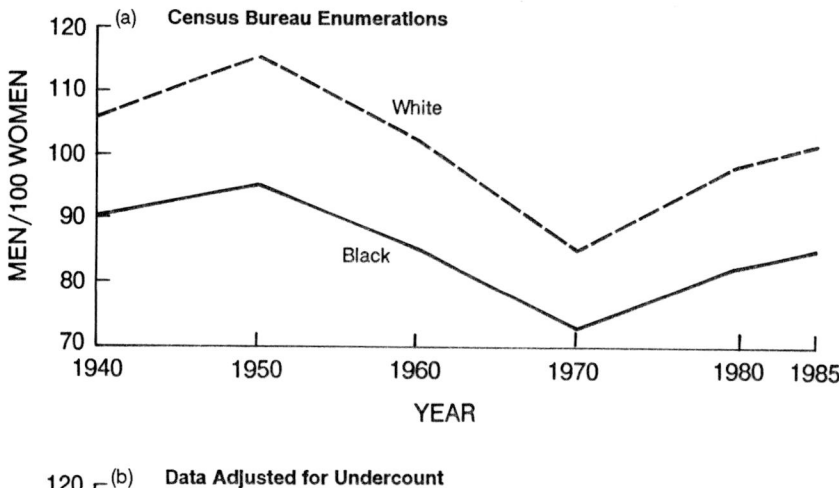

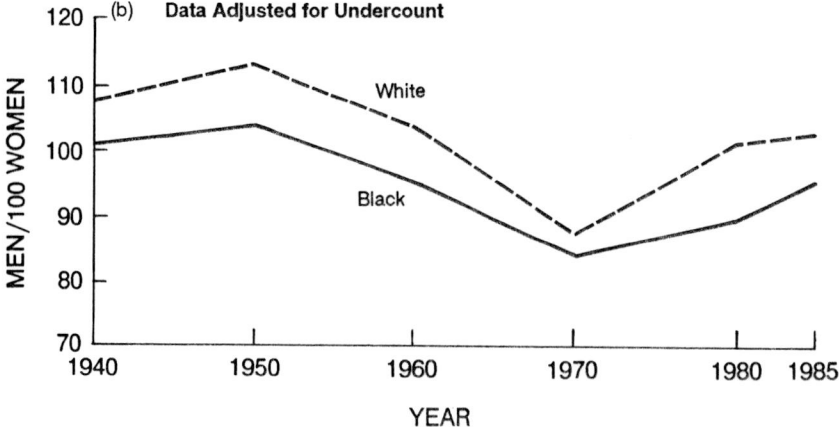

Sources: Data from decennial censuses, Coale (1955), Passel and Robinson (1984), and Siegel (1974).

among whites. According to these data, the sex ratio for these young un-married persons in 1985 was 102 men per 100 women for whites but only 85 men per 100 women for blacks.

But it is known that the census enumeration misses many black men. Figure 10-7b presents data adjusted for net census undercount. The correction produces a modest effect on the sex ratio of whites but makes a dramatic change for blacks, which reduces the black-white discrepancy. On the basis of these corrected data, it may be concluded that black women face a somewhat tighter marriage market than white women. For both races, however, the problem of a shortage of "appropriately" aged men was most acute in the 1960s and has diminished since then. Hence, this factor alone cannot account for the post-1960 decline in marriage rates.

Ratios of unmarried men to unmarried women are very crude indicators of the composition of a marriage market, however. Women may exclude from their marriage considerations not only unmarried men they consider too old or too young, but also those who are incarcerated, who have educational attainment deemed too little or too much, and who have low income. Marital "availability ratios," which take all of these factors into account, have been developed by Goldman and colleagues (1984:7–8). Using their procedure, we calculated marital availability ratios for age ranges using data about actual marriage patterns in 1980.

The data for blacks show that unmarried women above age 22 are in marriage pools that contain relatively few men. For unmarried women at age 25, for example, there were 931 men per 1,000 women. After age 28, the availability ratios for black women fall sharply, and at these ages, there is a substantial shortage of men; for example, for unmarried black women at age 34, the ratio is 642 men per 1,000 women.

Black men can select from a large pool of unmarried women. At ages 25 and over, black men are in a marriage market in which there are 1,100–1,200 unmarried women per 1,000 unmarried men. Similar availability ratios existed for whites in 1985. The same pattern of changes over the age range is evident for both races, but there is a very large black-white difference. The availability ratios for white women, compared with those for black women, are quite high, and until their late 20s, white women (except the least educated) are competing in marriage pools where there is sex parity. At older ages, the sex disparity is much smaller among whites.

Figure 10-8 presents marital availability ratios for three educational levels for each race. Since it was assumed that people with 12 years of education could marry anyone, the availability ratios are highest for this group. In fact, the only black women who are in marriage markets where they are outnumbered by black men are at this attainment level. Black women with other attainments face much more competitive marriage markets. At age 26, those black women with less than a high school education are in a marriage pool that has 651 men per 1,000 women. For black women at this age with some college education, the ratio is 772 per 1,000 women.

While black-white differences in available marriage partners for women may partially explain the large differences in marital and family patterns of black and white women, it is not clear how this condition can explain the growing racial divergence. An additional factor is the growing black-white difference in the proportion of working-age males who are employed. For both the 16–24 and 25–54 age groups, the proportion of black men with jobs has declined more rapidly than the proportion of white men with jobs (see Chapter 6). This trend suggests that the pool of "desirable" (e.g., employed) marriage partners may have grown more slowly for black than white women in recent years, especially if factors beyond educational attainment and age are considered. Overall, when age, education, employment, and other spou-

FIGURE 10-8 Marital availability ratios for black and white men and women (aged 26), by educational attainment, 1985.

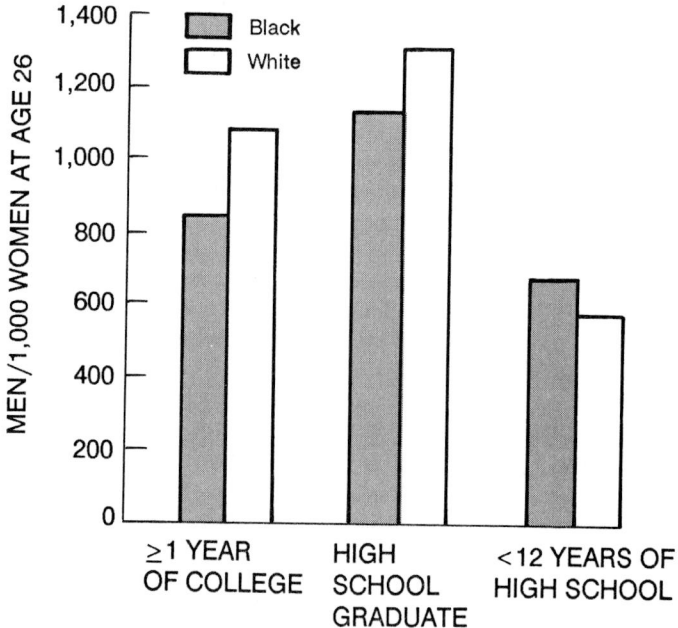

Note: Data adjusted for census undercount.

sal characteristics are added to the definition of available marriage partners, we conclude that male availability, as defined here, helps to explain the growing black-white differences in marital and family status.

We note that the availability ratios have increased since 1970, indicating that the "marriage squeeze" associated with the baby-boom cohorts has diminished. Accordingly, women reaching the ages of highest marriage rates in the late 1980s can select from a larger pool of men than those who reached marriageable ages 15 or 20 years ago.

THE CULTURE-OF-POVERTY HYPOTHESIS

An old and recurrently popular argument holds that poor and segregated populations develop a distinctive set of beliefs, values, and behavior patterns that tend to perpetuate their condition (Lewis, 1955; Rainwater, 1970). Once established, such a subculture—which may be initially adaptive to the given circumstances—is thought to acquire partial independence that works against its people's breaking out of the "poverty trap" through negative feedback effects.

The strong version of the culture-of-poverty hypothesis (Lewis, 1966:xiv) contends that poverty is perpetuated from generation to generation by reason of distinctive norms and values that children learn at an early age and that interfere with educational and occupational advancement. Among these alleged values are self-indulgence, low aspirations for education, and unwillingness to sacrifice for future attainment. Clearly, however, all these imputed values could be inferred from behavior that is based solely on poverty itself: people living on the margin of subsistence simply will be unable to save money, to defer eating, or to realistically plan for higher education.

As Schiller has pointed out (1984:101):

> The culture of poverty hypothesis requires rather stringent evidence. It must be shown that the norms and aspirations—not just the behavior—of the poor are different and that these differences impede escape from poverty. It should also be shown whether and to what degree such differences would disappear under changing socioeconomic circumstances.

To be productive, discussions of the culture-of-poverty concept require clarity in the drawing of several important distinctions. First, "culture" cannot be equated with typical or average patterns of behavior; if the concept is purely descriptive of behavior, it is not needed. Second, if culture refers to the sum of learned behavior transmitted from the past, it is not sufficiently specific to serve as an explanatory variable to account for current behavior. Third, if culture consists of normative patterns (e.g., values, beliefs, knowledge), there are two relevant empirical questions: How closely do cultural patterns predict behavior? Does a close fit between cultural patterns and specific behaviors signify that culture causes behavior, or the reverse, or that both are produced by a third set of influences? Fourth, the culture would have to represent positive preferences, not situational exigencies: a positively valued culture (e.g., religious beliefs, language) is radically different from a set of adjustments to extreme poverty. A crucial needed observation is the speed of change when constraints and opportunities change: If jobs become available, do people who have been out of work take them? Fifth, the conventional notion of culture of poverty implies that given characteristics (values, beliefs, behaviors) are transmitted from one generation to another as self-perpetuating patterns (Lewis, 1966:19): How frequently does this occur? Sixth, "culture of poverty" cannot be equated with all social influences arising among persons who are poor. For example, disruptive classroom behavior in some schools serving low-income populations is not in itself evidence that "culture" accounts for the behavior.

Thus, an essential distinction exists between structural conditions of constraint and opportunity and a subculture of poverty. The former points to employment possibilities, human capital characteristics, social networks, and other objective situational factors. The latter, analytically considered, refers to shared norms and values—to positive preferences as to how one should behave (see Simpson and Yinger, 1985:117). Cultural patterns emerge over time from the shared experiences of people. If these experiences change, the expectable result over time will be a change in culture. Responsiveness to changes in opportunities is likely to be greatest when a culture is a "shadow subculture" that is not strongly valued but rather represents only adaptations to repeated constraints and failures (Patterson, 1981:115–125; Rodman, 1963).

The available evidence, although scattered, is voluminous. Taken as a whole, the data and analyses we have examined throw serious doubt on the validity of the strong thesis that culture of poverty is a major cause of self-perpetuating poverty. First, many families move in and out of poverty several times over a lifetime. The chronically poor are an important minority, but they are a minority of all poor people. Spells of poverty are not closely related to attitudes toward work (Duncan et al., 1988). Primary correlates of poverty are, first, macroeconomic conditions of prosperity or depression and, second, changes in family composition (Morgan et al., 1968–1980; see Chapter 6).

Second, many poor people do not exhibit the stereotypic set of characteristics supposedly constituting the culture of poverty, such as apathy and unwillingness to defer gratification. Many are hard-working people who save when they can, endure numerous deprivations, worry about the future, and urge their children to do well in school and on the job. Third, studies that have compared attitudes toward work, education, government family assistance benefits, and aspirations for family life have found that poor and nonpoor people do not differ significantly in stated values and goals. For example, a study of people in the Work Incentive (WIN) program—who were receiving AFDC and required by law to participate in the program—concluded that there is virtually no evidence that a preference for assistance payments induces mothers to continue receiving them (Goodwin, 1983:45–46). What does happen is that receiving such assistance tends to isolate recipients and to create expectations of continuing to do so. Some recent studies using longitudinal data found little evidence that attitudes cause poverty or dependency on assistance (Hill et al., 1985; O'Neill et al., 1984).

Ethnographic research has consistently found that work for pay that will support a decent living standard—as opposed to some idealized ethic of work for work's sake—is a central value among low-income black men and women (Anderson, 1978, 1985; Liebow, 1967). Reviewing several studies, Macaulay (1977) concluded that children raised in families receiving family assistance are not fated to an adulthood of poverty because of deficient values. Research of the past decade or so has noted that highly motivated youths are a frequent output of black family socialization processes (Allen, 1978; Rosenberg and Simmons, 1971; Scanzoni, 1971). One school of research argues that the great emphasis placed on children's achievement is a major strength of the black family as an institution (see Featherman and Hauser, 1978). In a survey of empirical studies of family assistance dependency, Schiller (1973) concluded that mothers receiving benefits but having little opportunity to achieve upward mobility for themselves placed great emphasis on their children's future success (see also Hill, 1971).

How can such high aspirations be reconciled with low achievement in education and labor force participation? Over 30 years ago in an experimental study of male college student aspiration levels, Hyman (1953) noted that the subjects whose aspirations "far exceeded their achievement were of predominantly *lower* class backgrounds and from minority ethnic groups" (see also Merton, 1968; Miller, 1964). Many studies have shown that the child-rearing and educational goals of black and white mothers, regardless of class, are much the same, but the lower class mothers often lack the skills, knowledge, or financial or social resources needed to interact with their children and with the relevant social institutions in ways that produce the outcomes they desire (Bronfenbrenner, 1958; Davis and Havighurst, 1946; Kamili and Radin, 1968; Lewis, 1955:157; Lightfoot, 1978). Undoubtedly, the insecure and deprived conditions of life of poor families, when long continued, do result in "cultural" differences from well-to-do and secure families. Yet such differences appear to be highly responsive to changes in economic opportunities and social incentives (Jaynes, 1985:32–35; Lieberson, 1980; Steinberg, 1981).

Each of the proposed explanations of changing black family structure we are reviewing is one among several that may have causal weight. It appears likely, for example, that the effects of differences in family structures depend heavily on the social settings in which families function. The bulk of previous research shows that total effects of single-parent homes on youth delinquency appear to be much stronger for blacks than for whites. But when mediating factors, such as social definitions of delinquency and attachments to parents and peers, are taken into account, those effects become trivial. A plausible interpretation is that single-parent families are less able than husband-wife families to provide supervision and to inculcate antidelinquency norms; absent this support, youths are more likely to associate with delinquent peers and to learn prodelinquent social definitions of appropriate behavior. Thus, for example, female-headed families are not per se conducive to delinquency, but they are less likely, on average, to be able to protect children against peer-group and neighborhood influences that are conducive to delinquency (see Matsueda and Heimer, 1987).

In considering cultural characteristics, it is especially difficult to assess their independent causal significance. In any case the culture-of-poverty thesis by itself is inadequate to account for the most recent changes we are seeking to understand. As Walker (1986:22–23) concluded on the basis of an extensive review of research:

> While there are differences in the patterns of beliefs and values of blacks and whites which might be construed as cultural in a broad sense of the term, the available evidence suggests that those differences are diminishing rather than increasing. This is true even among the poorest segment of the population—those who were believed to have been susceptible to the "culture of poverty" (Lewis, 1965)—as well as among blacks and whites who are better off economically (Irelan, Moles, and O'Shea, 1969; Wilson, 1978). But the differences in family patterns of the two groups are diverging rather than converging.

In short, if cultural differences have diminished over the years when family differences have increased most rapidly, there is at the least some doubt that culture of poverty is a sufficient explanation.

OTHER FACTORS

Many other possible factors that may affect marriages and families have been suggested—both in the professional literature and in popular commentaries—including such diverse items as increased sexual freedom (DeLameter, 1981), changed attitudes about marriage and divorce, changes in the amount and type of television viewing, altered drug use, and peer-group cultures. For most of these, little conclusive evidence exists.

The available empirical studies do show marked changes during the 1960s and 1970s among both blacks and whites regarding greater sexual permissiveness in both attitudes and behavior (DeLameter, 1986). But the effects of these changes on births to unmarried women were not large (see Garfinkel and McLanahan, 1986:78–84), partly because such births continue to be disapproved. Somewhat more important may be the high value placed on children among young women in low-income families, in combination with limited educational and employment opportunities. Under these conditions, single motherhood may not be regarded as highly undesirable in comparison with other life options (Hogan and Kitagawa, 1985).

Some of the available findings point to a need for multifactorial research. For example, it is known that variations in age of initiation of sexual activity account for most of the variation in rates of teenage pregnancies (Furstenberg et al., 1987), but also that contraceptive use is associated with substantially reduced rates of pregnancy among those teenagers who are sexually active. Adolescents are often surprisingly ignorant of reproductive processes and of effective contraceptive practices. Also, it has been found that several characteristics increase the probability of pregnancy for black teenage females: lower socioeconomic status; ghetto neighborhood; single-parent family; five or more siblings; a sister who became a teenage mother; and nonstrict parental control of dating. When all these conditions are present, in contrast to when none are present, the rate of pregnancy is 8.3 times higher (Hogan and Kitagawa, 1985:852; see also Udry and Billy, 1987); for a comprehensive review of issues concerning adolescent pregnancy, see Hayes (1987).

CONCLUSIONS

Trends in the marital status of adults, the types of families, and the living arrangements of children are parallel for whites and blacks. However, they have been so much more accentuated for blacks that the marital and family experiences of the two populations have become very dissimilar.

Black and white children are increasingly different with regard to their living arrangements. A majority of black children live in families that include their mothers but not their fathers; in contrast, about four of five white children under age 18 live with both parents. Furthermore, 86 percent of black children, and 42 percent of white children, are likely to spend some time in a single-parent household, usually a mother-only family (Bumpass, 1984).

It is possible that census data understate the extent to which stable two-parent arrangements exist among unmarried couples. One cannot estimate how many fathers not counted as household members may actually aid in child rearing; there are indications that fathers of children born to unmarried women in some instances maintain continuing relationships with the mother and children. Lack of systematic data, however, makes it difficult to estimate the frequency of these relationships. The data do show, however, that only about one in five AFDC recipients receives some child support from an absent father (Duncan et al., 1988:70). Ethnographic accounts also suggest that absent fathers contribute little to the economic support of these children (Liebow, 1967; Robinson, 1987; Stack, 1974). We conclude that the prevalence is not great enough to distort seriously the description based on census and national survey data.

More generally, the significance of changes in family and household characteristics depends greatly on features of the kinship and community context. What counts is how families function and how family members behave (Scott-Jones, 1987:70). The small nuclear unit of husband-wife-children can be weak while the total kinship system is strong (Aschenbrenner, 1975; Bradbury and Brown, 1986; Gwaltney, 1981; Ladner, 1971; McAdoo, 1986, 1987; Stack, 1974:102–103; Willie, 1970). Networks of relatives often sustain what otherwise might be fragmented families. Detailed ethnographic studies show that kinship networks often offer mutual aid, essential for minimal security for many of the urban poor. Obligations to kin, however, often compete with marriage and other stable relationships. Unemployment and low-paying, insecure jobs discourage men from marriage and sometimes render women unwilling to risk possible loss of kin support for an uncertain future with the children's father (Ladner, 1971; Stack, 1974:112–113). Given these precarious conditions, the kin group may regard a marriage as a risk for a woman and her children and as a threat of additional responsibility for them (Ladner, 1971; Stack, 1974:117).

Some once popular explanations of black-white differences in family structure are of little contemporary relevance. Both African cultural heritage and slavery are far removed from the recent changes. Although research on the causes of changes in family structure is still limited and many crucial data have not been collected, other factors emerge from our review as being of greater potential importance for understanding recent developments.

The most powerful hypothesis is that the economic situation in the black community together with residential segregation not only affect the immediate living conditions of blacks, but also strongly influence family structures and thereby alter the social and economic prospects for the next generation. The influence of family assistance benefits seems to have been seriously overstated in popular accounts. In contrast, the role of other factors such as male joblessness appears to be quite large.

Black women face a more limited array of choices in the marriage market than do white women—a factor that may help account for black-white differences in the timing of marriage and the frequency of marital dissolutions. Yet the increasing ratio for both races of men to women since 1970 is inconsistent with the observed pattern of declining probabilities of marriage. It is difficult to determine the attributes of potential spouses for an appropriate model of marriage pools, but both marriage rates and marital stability may be lowered by the low availability of young black males of "appropriate" age, education, and economic status in specific areas. The growing economic independence of women is a factor to take into account. Black women are closer to economic parity with black men than white women are to white men. This may be one reason for the patterns of change, but there still remain economic incentives for women to marry, due to higher per capita income levels attainable in husband-wife families. An increased likelihood of dependable family support from a prospective husband might well, over time, help to reduce the incidence of unmarried mothers and female-headed households.

After these factors have been appraised, much remains to be explained, and the need for more comprehensive and rigorous research is evident. At the same time, the cumulative effects of the conditions we have reviewed are unquestionably very great. It is precisely the interaction of a complex set of mutually reinforcing factors that has so rapidly altered marriage and family patterns in less than three decades.

Our primary interest in studying conditions among families is to consider the welfare of children. That welfare and the lifetime prospects of many children are in jeopardy. High rates of poverty, low educational performance, and health problems are serious obstacles to the future well-being of millions of children. These problems are much more acute among black children. The disadvantage of black children is partly due to location (region and metropolitan residence) and family size. But when these factors are controlled in a multivariate analysis, the disadvantage of black children relative to that of white children is due almost entirely to the low income of black family heads (Kraly and Hirschman, 1987:19).

Approximately one-half of black children have the additional burden of living in mother-only families. Many begin life with an undereducated teenage mother, which increases the likelihood that they will live in poverty and raises additional impediments to their life prospects. The employment and earnings and conditions of education, health, and high rates of black involvement in criminal activity reviewed in this report make it apparent that these conditions are closely interrelated. Indeed, the current status of black Americans in each of these areas is a crucial factor in one or more of the plausible explanations for changes in family structure and children's living arrangements detailed in this chapter.

Further evidence of these interconnections is given by recent research into the motivations leading to teenage pregnancy. A teenage girl's aspirations and perceived opportunities—in terms of her perception of what she would stand to lose if she became a parent—strongly affect her views of unmarried motherhood, especially among blacks (Abrahamse et al., 1988; Hogan and Kitagawa, 1985; see also Clark, 1965). If her aspirations are high and perceived opportunities are wide, she is strongly inhibited against early pregnancy. The policy implications are clear: black youth must be given opportunities in education and employment that are unquestionably superior to alternatives, and they must be made unambiguously aware that such opportunities exist and are attainable. Conditions in the schools will be an important factor in the determination of such opportunities, as will the state of the labor market.

A number of major reports have decried the condition of education in the United States and called for sweeping reforms. The opening paragraph of one recent effort indicates the tone of urgency and near crisis these reports have set (Goodlad, 1984:1):

> American schools are in trouble. In fact, the problems of schooling are of such crippling proportions that many schools may not survive. It is possible that our entire public education system is nearing collapse. We will continue to have schools, no doubt, but the basis of their support and their relationships to families, communities, and state could be quite different from what we have known.

Increasing standards of performance, the introduction of minimum competency tests, more rigorous testing of teachers, and increasing parental choice in the schools their children will attend are among the proposed policy changes (see Chapter 7). Many of these changes, already under way in a number of states, may differentially affect black Americans as students and as teachers. Blacks are a growing proportion of the school-age population. It is predicted that by the year 2000, 35 percent of the nation's population under the age of 15 will comprise minorities; a substantial portion of those in this age range will be blacks. Yet the special needs of black children—large proportions of whom arguably receive the worst quality educations in the nation, in both urban and rural settings—have been largely neglected by this reform movement. Calls for reform have frequently been for higher standards, rather than for higher standards with increased compensatory education programs for disadvantaged students.

Black representation in the overall U.S. population is also growing; see Table 10-4. The Bureau of the Census predicts that the black proportion will rise from about one in eight in the 1980s to one in six by the middle of the next century, a change that will occur most rapidly at the younger ages. The decline in fertility following the baby boom cohorts reveals itself in the falling ratio of children to adults in the population. In 1960 there was a very high ratio of children to adults. In the future, there will be a higher ratio of elderly to adults; see Table 10-5.

The large numbers of young people entering the labor force during the 1960s and 1970s (the baby-boom cohorts) put considerable pressure on the

TABLE 10-4 Blacks as a Percentage of Total U.S. Population, by Age Group, 1940–2020

Year	All	Under 15	25–54	65 and Over
1940	9.7	11.5	9.4	6.8
1960	10.5	12.7	8.7	7.0
1980	11.7	14.8	10.7	8.2
2000	13.3	17.0	13.0	8.5
2020	14.9	18.4	15.3	9.9

Sources: Data from decennial censuses (for 1940–1980) and from Census Bureau projections (for 2000 and 2020).

TABLE 10-5 Persons Aged 0–14 or 65 and Over per 100 Persons Aged 25–54

	Blacks			Whites		
Year	Aged 0–14	Aged 25–54	Aged 65 and Over	Aged 0–14	Aged 25–54	Aged 65 and Over
1940	75	100	12	58	100	17
1960	108	100	18	80	100	25
1980	83	100	23	56	100	32
2000	62	100	20	45	100	32
2020	58	100	29	47	100	49

Sources: Data from decennial censuses (for 1940–1980) and from Census Bureau projections (for 2000 and 2020).

nation's labor market. Other demographic changes, increased immigration and the entry of considerable numbers of women into the labor force, greatly increased the competition for jobs. The 1970s, even without structural shifts in industry and greater international competition against American businesses, might have still been a period of difficult labor market adjustment, particularly for less educated black women and men with little work experience. In the late 1980s, the baby-boom cohorts of labor market entrants have subsided and much of the huge increase in labor supply has been absorbed. This suggests that a much tighter job market can be expected in the near future. If so, more employers will have incentives to train and retrain workers. Such an environment will provide great opportunities for public policy to complement and stimulate employers' policies.

Many such public policies, in the areas of compensatory education and aid to college students, health care, and employment programs, have been shown to improve the position of blacks. The opportunity for launching a concerted nationwide effort to ameliorate the problems of poverty and underachievement may be greater now than they have been in a long time.

REFERENCES

Abrahamse, A. F., P. A. Morrison, and L. J. Waite
  1988 Beyond Stereotypes: Who Becomes a Single Teenage Mother? Rand Corporation, Santa Monica, California.

Allen, Walter
  1978 The search for applicable theories of black family life. *Journal of Marriage and the Family* 40:111–129.

Anderson, Elijah
  1978 Some observations on youth employment. In Bernard E. Anderson and Isabel V. Sawhill, eds., *Youth Employment and Public Policy.* Englewood Cliffs, N.J.: Prentice-Hall.
  1985 The social context of youth employment programs. In Charles L. Betsey, Robinson G. Hollister, Jr., and Mary R. Papageorgiou, eds., *Youth Employment and Training Programs: The YEDPA Years.* Washington, D.C.: National Academy Press.

Aschenbrenner, Joyce.
  1975 *Lifelines: Black Families in Chicago.* New York: Holt, Rinehart and Winston.

Bane, Mary Jo
  1986 Household composition and poverty. Pp 209–231 in Sheldon Danziger and Daniel Weinberg, eds., *Fighting Poverty: What Works and What Doesn't.* Cambridge, Mass.: Harvard University Press.

Bianchi, Suzanne M., and Nancy Rytina
  1986 The decline in occupational sex segregation during the 1970s: census and CPS comparisons. *Demography* 23(1):79–88.

Bianchi, Suzanne M., and Daphne Spain
  1986 *American Women.* New York: Russell Sage Foundation.

Billingsley, Andrew
  1968 *Black Families in White America.* Englewood Cliffs, N.J.: Prentice-Hall.

Blau, Francine D., and Marianne A. Ferber
  1985 Women in the labor market: the last twenty years. Pp. 19–49 in Laurie Larwood, Ann H. Stromberg, and Barbara A. Gutele, eds., *Women and Work, An Annual Review.* Vol. 1. Beverly Hills, Calif.: Sage Publications Inc.

Bradbury, Katharine, and Lynne Brown
  1986 Black men in the labor market. *New England Economic Review* March/April:32–42.

Bronfenbrenner, Urie
  1958 Socialization and social class through time and space. Pp. 400–425 in E. E. Maccoby, T. M. Newcomb, and E. L. Hartley, eds., *Readings in Social Psychology.* 3rd ed. New York: Holt, Rinehart & Winston.

Bumpass, Larry L.
  1984 Children and marital disruption: a replication and update. *Demography* 21(1)[February]: 71–81.

Bumpass, Larry, and Ronald R. Rindfuss
  1979 Children's experience of marital disruption. *American Journal of Sociology* 85(1)[July]:49–65.

Bureau of the Census
  1980 *Census of Population: 1980.* PC80-2-4C. Washington, D.C.: U.S. Government Printing Office.

Cain, Glenn G., and Douglas A. Wissoker
  1987– Do income maintenance programs break up marriages? A reevaluation of SIME-
  1988   DIME. *Focus* 10(4)[Winter]:1–15.

Clark, Kenneth
  1965 *Dark Ghetto.* New York: Harper and Day.

Coale, Ansley
  1955 The population of the United States in 1950 classified by age, sex, and color—a revision of census figures. *Journal of the American Statistical Association* 50 (269):16–54.
Cox, Oliver
  1940 Sex ratio and marital status among Negroes. *American Sociological Review* 5(6)[December]:937–947.
Cutright, Phillips
  1970 AFDC, family allowances and illegitimacy. *Family Planning Perspectives* 2(4)[October]:4–9.
Danziger, Sandra
  1986 Breaking the chains: from teenage girls to welfare mothers, or can social policy increase options? Chapter 5 in Jack A. Meyer, ed., *Ladders out of Poverty*. Washington, D.C.: American Horizons Foundation.
Davis, Allison, and Robert Havighurst
  1946 Social class and color differences in child rearing. *American Sociological Review* 11(6)[December]:698–710.
DeLameter, John
  1981 The social control of sexuality. Pp. 263–290 in Ralph H. Turner and James F. Short, Jr., eds., *Annual Review of Sociology*, Vol. 7. Palo Alto, Calif.: Annual Reviews Inc.
DuBois, William E. B.
  1903 *The Souls of Black Folk*. Reprinted (1965) in *Three Negro Classics*. New York: Avon Books.
Duncan, Beverly
  1967 Education and social background. *American Journal of Sociology* 72(January):363–372.
Duncan, Beverly, and Otis Dudley Duncan
  1969 Family stability and occupational success. *Social Problems* 16:286–301.
Duncan, Greg J., Martha S. Hill, and Saul D. Hoffman
  1988 Welfare dependence within and across generations. *Science* 239[January 29]:467–471.
Duncan, Otis Dudley, David L. Featherman, and Beverly Duncan
  1972 *Socioeconomic Background and Achievement*. New York: Seminar Press.
Easterlin, Richard A.
  1962 *The American Baby Boom in Historical Perspective*. New York: National Bureau of Economic Research.
  1980 *Birth and Fortune: The Impact of Numbers on Personal Welfare*. New York: Basic Books.
  1982 The impact of demographic factors on the family environment of children, 1940–1995. Draft paper prepared for the Conference on Families and the Economy, January 1982, sponsored by the Committee on Child Development Research and Public Policy, National Research Council, Washington, D.C.
Ellwood, David T., and Mary Jo Bane
  1985 The impact of AFDC on family structure and living arrangements. In Ronald Ehrenberg, ed. *Research in Labor Economics* 7.
Ellwood, David, and Lawrence H. Summers
  1986 Poverty in America: is welfare the answer or the problem? In Sheldon H. Danziger and Daniel H. Weinberg, eds., *Fighting Poverty: What Works and What Doesn't*. Cambridge, Mass.: Harvard University Press.

Engerman, Stanley
1977 Black fertility and family structure in the U.S., 1880–1940. *Journal of Family History* 2(2)[Summer]:117–138.

Espenshade, Thomas J.
1985 Marriage trends in America: estimates, implications, and underlying causes. *Population and Development Review* 11(2)[June]:193–245.

Farley, Reynolds
1987 Changes in the Status and Characteristics of Blacks: 1940 to Mid-1980s. Paper prepared for the Committee on the Status of Black Americans, National Research Council, Washington, D.C.

Farley, Reynolds, and Walter Allen
1987 *The Color Line and the Quality of American Life*. New York: Russel Sage Foundation.

Farley, Reynolds, and Suzanne Bianchi
1986 The growing racial difference in marriage and family patterns. Paper presented at the 1986 meeting of the American Statistical Association, Social Statistics Section, Chicago, Illinois.

Farley, Reynolds, and Lisa J. Neidert
1986 A Comparison of Racial Differences in Labor Force Participation, Unemployment, Earnings, and Income: 1940 to 1985. Paper prepared for the Committee on the Status of Black Americans, National Research Council, Washington, D.C.

Featherman, David L., and Robert M. Hauser
1976 Sexual inequalities and socioeconomic achievement in the United States, 1962–1973. *American Sociological Review* 41:462–483.
1978 *Opportunity and Change*. New York: Academic Press.

Franklin, John Hope
1980 *From Slavery to Freedom*. New York: Alfred A. Knopf.

Frazier, E. Franklin
1939 *The Negro Family in the United States*. Chicago: University of Chicago Press.

Furstenberg, Frank F., Jr.
1976 *Unplanned Parenthood: The Social Consequences of Teenage Childbearing*. New York: Free Press.

Furstenberg, Frank F., Jr., Philip Morgan, Dristin A. Moore, and James L. Peterson
1987 Race differences in the timing of adolescent sexual intercourse. *American Sociological Review* 52(4)[August]:511–518.

Garfinkel, Irwin, and Sara S. McLanahan
1986 *Single Mothers and Their Children: A New American Dilemma*. Washington, D.C.: Urban Institute.

Glick, Paul C.
1981 A demographic picture of black families. Pp. 106–126 in Harriette Pipes McAdoo, ed., *Black Families*. Beverly Hills, Calif.: Sage Publications Inc.

Gold, Rachel Benson, and Barry Nestor
1985 Public funding of contraceptive, sterilization and abortion services, 1983. *Family Planning Perspectives* 17(1)(Jan./Feb.):25–30.

Goldman, Noreen, Charles F. Westoff, and Charles Hammerslough
1984 Demography of the marriage market in the United States. *Population Index* 50(1)[Spring]:5–25.

Goode, William J., Elizabeth Hopkins, and Helen M. McClure
1971 *Social Systems and Family Patterns: A Propositional Inventory*. Indianapolis, Ind.: Bobbs-Merrill Company, Inc.

Goodlad, John I.
  1984 *A Place Called School: Prospects for the Future*. New York: McGraw-Hill Book Company.
Goodwin, Leonard
  1983 *Causes and Cures of Welfare: New Evidence on the Social Psychology of the Poor*. Lexington, Mass.: Lexington Books/D. C. Heath and Company.
Groeneveld, Lyle P., Nancy Brandon Tuma, and Michael T. Hannan
  1980 Marital dissolution and remarriage. In Philip K. Robins, Robert G. Spiegelman, Samuel Weinere, and Joseph G. Bell, eds., *A Guaranteed Annual Income: Evidence from a Social Experiment*. New York: Academic Press.
Grove, Robert D., and Alice M. Hetzel
  1968 *Vital Statistics Rates in the United States: 1940–1960*. U.S. Center for Health Statistics. Washington, D.C.: U.S. Government Printing Office.
Gutman, Herbert G.
  1976 *The Black Family in Slavery and Freedom, 1750–1925*. New York: Vintage/Random House.
Guttentag, M., and P. F. Secord
  1983 *Too Many Women*. Beverly Hills, Calif.: Sage Publications Inc.
Gwaltney, John Langston
  1981 *Drylongso: A Self-Portrait of Black America*. New York: Vintage Books.
Hannan, M. T., N. B. Tuma, and L. P. Groeneveld
  1977 Income and marital events: evidence from an income-maintenance experiment. *American Journal of Sociology* 82(6)[May]:1186–1211.
Hayes, Cheryl D.
  1987 *Risking the Future: Adolescent Sexuality, Pregnancy, and Childbearing*. Vol. 1. Panel on Adolescent Pregnancy and Childbearing, Committee on Child Development Research and Public Policy, Commission on Behavioral and Social Sciences and Education, National Research Council. Washington, D.C.: National Academy Press.
Herskovits, Melville J.
  1941 *The Myth of the Negro Past*. Boston: Beacon Press.
Hill, Martha S., et al.
  1985 *Motivation and Economic Mobility*. Institute for Social Research, Research Report Series. Ann Arbor, Mich.: Survey Research Center.
Hill, Robert B.
  1971 *The Strength of Black Families*. New York: National Urban League.
Hogan, Dennis, and Evelyn Kitagawa
  1985 The impact of social status, family structure, and neighborhood on the fertility of black adolescents. *American Journal of Sociology* 90(4)[January]:825–855.
Hutchens, Robert M.
  1979 Welfare, remarriage, and the marital search. *American Economic Review* 69(3)(June):369–379.
Hyman, Herbert
  1953 The value systems of different classes. Pp. 426–442 in Reinhard Bendix and Seymour Martin Lipset, eds., *Class, Status, and Power: A Reader in Social Stratification*. Glencoe, Ill.: Free Press.
Irelan, L. M., O. C. Moles, and R. M. O'Shea
  1969 Ethnicity, poverty, and selected attitudes: a test of the culture of poverty hypothesis. *Social Forces* 47:405–413.

Jaynes, Gerald David
  1985 The Black Family. Memorandum to the Committee on the Status of Black Americans (September), National Research Council, Washington, D.C.
Kamili, Constance, and Norma L. Radin
  1967 Class differences in the socialization practices of Negro mothers. *Journal of Marriage and the Family* 29(2):302–310.
Kraly, Ellen P., and Charles Hirschman
  1987 Racial and ethnic inequality among children in the United States: 1940 and 1950. Paper presented at the annual meeting of the American Sociological Association, August 17–21, 1987, Chicago, Illinois.
Ladner, Joyce
  1971 *Tomorrow's Tomorrow: The Black Women*. New York: Doubleday.
Levy, Frank
  1987 *Dollars and Dreams: The Changing American Income Distribution*. New York: Russell Sage Foundation/Basic Books.
Lewis, Hylan
  1955 *Blackways of Kent*. Chapel Hill: University of North Carolina Press.
Lewis, Oscar
  1966 *La Vida: A Puerto Rican Family in the Culture of Poverty*. New York: Random House.
Lieberson, Stanley
  1980 *A Piece of the Pie: Blacks and White Immigrants Since 1880*. Berkeley: University of California Press.
Liebow, Elliott
  1967 *Tally's Corner*. Boston: Little, Brown.
Lightfoot, Sara
  1978 *Worlds Apart: Relationships Between Family and Schools*. New York: Basic Books.
Litwack, Leon F.
  1979 *Been in the Storm So Long: The Aftermath of Slavery*. New York: Alfred A. Knopf.
Macaulay, Jacqueline
  1977 Stereotyping child welfare. *Society* (January/February):47–51.
Matsueda, Ross, and Karen Heimer
  1987 Race, family structure, and delinquency: a test of differential association and social control theories. *American Sociological Review* 52(6)[December]:826–840.
McAdoo, Harriette Pipes
  1986 Strategies used by black single mothers against stress. *Review of Black Political Economy* 14(2–3):155–166.
  1987 Parenting Within Single Parent African-American Families. Paper presented at the American Association for the Advancement of Science, Chicago, Illinois.
McAdoo, Harriette Pipes, and Rosalyn Terborg-Penn
  1985 Historical trends in perspectives of Afro-American families. *Trends in History* 3(3/4):97–111.
McFalls, Joseph A., Jr., and Marguerite Harvey
  1984 *Disease and Fertility*. Orlando, Fla.: Academic Press.
McLanahan, Sara S.
  1985 Family structure and the reproduction of poverty. *American Journal of Sociology* 90(4)[January]:873–901.
Merton, Robert K.
  1968 *Social Theory and Social Structure*. New York: Free Press.
Miller, S. M.
  1964 The new working class. In Arthur Shostak and WIlliam Gomberg, eds., *Blue-Collar World*. Englewood Cliffs, N.J.: Prentice-Hall.

Moore, Kristin, and Martha R. Burt
  1982 *Private Crisis, Public Cost: Policy Perspectives on Teenage Childbearing.* Washington, D.C.: Urban Institute.
Morgan, James N., Greg J. Duncan, and staff
  1968– *Five Thousand American Families—Patterns of Economic Progress: Analyses and Special*
  1980 *Studies of the Panel Study of Income Dynamics.* Vols. 1–10. Ann Arbor: Institute of Social Research, University of Michigan.
Murray, Charles
  1984 *Losing Ground: American Social Policy: 1950–1980.* New York: Basic Books.
National Center for Health Statistics
  1978 *Vital Statistics of the United States, 1978. Vol. 1: Natality.* Washington, D.C.: U.S. Department of Health and Human Services
  1983 *Monthly Vital Statistics Reports,* Vol. 32, no. 9, supplement. Washington, D.C.: U.S. Department of Health and Human Services
O'Neill, J., D. Wolf, L. Bassi, and M. Hannan
  1984 An Analysis of Time on Welfare. Report prepared for the U.S. Department of Health and Human Services. The Urban Institute, Washington, D.C.
Passel, Jeffery, and J. Gregory Robinson
  1984 Revised estimates of the coverage of the population in the 1980 census, based on demographic analysis: a report on work in progress. Pp. 160–165 in *1984 Proceedings of the Social Statistics Section.* Washington, D.C.: American Statistical Association.
Patterson, James T.
  1981 *America's Struggle Against Poverty, 1900–1980.* Cambridge, Mass.: Harvard University Press.
Plateris, Alexander A.
  1978 *Divorces and Divorce Rates: United States.* U.S. National Center for Health Statistics. Data from the National Vital Statistics System, Series 21, No. 29 (March). Washington, D.C.: U.S. Department of Health and Human Services.
Pleck, Elizabeth Hafkin
  1979 *Divorces and Divorce Rates: United States.* U.S. National Center for Health Statistics. Data from the National Vital Statistics System, Series 21, No. 29 (March). Washington, D.C.: U.S. Department of Health and Human Services.
Powell-Griner, Eve
  1986 Induced terminations of pregnancy: reporting states, 1982 and 1983. U.S. National Center for Health Statistics. *Monthly Vital Statistics Report* 35(3)(July).
Preston, Samuel H., and James McDonald
  1979 The incidence of divorce within cohorts of American marriage contracted since the Civil War. *Demography* 16(1)[February]:1–25.
Rainwater, Lee
  1970 *Behind Ghetto Walls: Black Life in a Federal Slum.* Chicago: Aldine.
Reskin, Barbara F., and Heidi I. Hartmann, eds.
  1986 *Women's Work, Men's Work.* Committee on Women's Employment and Related Social Issues. Washington, D.C.: National Academy Press.
Robinson, Brian E
  1987 *Teenage Fathers.* Lexington, Mass.: Lexington Books/D. C. Heath and Company.
Rodman, Hyman
  1963 The lower-class value stretch. *Social Forces* 42(2)(December):205–215.
Rosenberg, Morris, and Roberta Simmons
  1971 *Black and White Self-Esteem: The Urban School Childs.* Washington, D.C.: American Sociological Association.

Ross, H. L., and I. Sawhill
1975 *Time of Transition: The Growth of Families Headed by Women*. Washington, D.C.: Urban Institute.

Scanzoni, John H.
1971 *The Black Family in Modern Society*. Chicago: University of Chicago Press.

Schiller, Bradley R.
1984 *The Economics of Poverty and Discrimination*. Englewood Cliffs, N.J.: Prentice-Hall.

Scott-Jones, Diane
1987 Black Families and the Education of Black Children: Current Issues. Paper commissioned by the Committee on the Status of Black Americans, National Research Council, Washington, D.C.

Siegel, Jacob S.
1974 Estimates of coverage of the population by sex, race, and age in 1970 census. *Demography* 11(1)[February]:1–23.

Simpson, George E., and J. Milton Yinger
1985 *Racial and Cultural Minorities*. 5th ed. New York: Plenum.

Smeeding, M. David, and T. Smeeding
1985 *Horizontal Equity, Uncertainty and Well-Being*. Chicago: University of Chicago Press.

Spanier, Graham B., and Paul C. Glick
1986 Mate selection differentials between whites and blacks in the United States. *Social Forces* 58(3)[March]:707–725.

Stack, Carol
1974 *All Our Kin: Strategies for Survival in a Black Community*. New York: Harper & Row.

Steinberg, Stephen
1981 *The Ethnic Myth: Race, Ethnicity, and Class in America*. New York: Atheneum Publishers.

Sudarkasa, Niara
1981 Interpreting the African heritage in Afro-American family organization. In Harriette Pipes McAdoo, ed., *Black Families*. Beverly Hills, Calif.: Sage Publications Inc.

Sweet, James A., and Larry L. Bumpass
1974 Differentials in marital instability of the black population: 1970. *Phylon* 35 (3):323–331.

Thornton, Arland
1978 Marital instability differentials and interaction insights from multivariate contingency table analysis. *Sociology and Social Research* 62(July):572–595.

Udry, J. Richard, and John O. G. Billy
1987 Initiation of coitus in early adolescence. *American Sociological Review* 52(6)[December]841–855.

U.S. House of Representatives, Committee on Ways and Means
1987 *Background Material on Programs Within the Jurisdiction of the Committee on Ways and Means*. Washington, D.C.: U.S. Government Printing Office.

Walker, Henry A.
1986 Racial differences in patterns of marriage and family maintenance: 1890–1980. In Sanford M. Dornbusch and Myra H. Strober, eds., *Feminism, Children and the New Families*. New York: Guilford Press.

Westoff, Charles F.
1978 Marriage and fertility in developed countries. *Scientific American* 239(6) (December):51–57.

Westoff, Charles F., Gerard Calot, and Andrew D. Foster
  1983 Teenage fertility in developed nations: 1971–1980. *Family Planning Perspectives* 15(3):105.
Williams, Robin M., Jr.
  1970 *American Society*. New York: Alfred A. Knopf.
Willie, Charles V.
  1970 *The Family Life of Black People*. Columbus, Ohio: Charles E. Merrill.
Wilson, William Julius
  1978 *The Declining Significance of Race: Blacks and Changing American Institutions*. Chicago: University of Chicago Press.
  1987 *The Truly Disadvantaged: The Inner City, the Underclass, and Public Policy.* Chicago: University of Chicago Press.
Wilson, William Julius, and Robert Aponte
  1985 Urban poverty. Pp. 231–258 in Ralph H. Turner and James F. Short, Jr., eds., *Annual Review of Sociology*, Vol. 11. Palo Alto, Calif.: Annual Reviews.
Wilson, William Julius, and Kathryn M. Neckerman
  1986 Poverty and family structure: the widening gap between evidence and public policy issues. Pp. 232–259 in Sheldon H. Danziger and Daniel H. Weinberg, eds., *Fighting Poverty: What Works and What Doesn't*. Cambridge, Mass.: Harvard University Press.
Wright, Paul, and Peter Pirie
  1984 *A False Fertility Transition: The Case of American Blacks*. Papers of the East-West Population Institute, No. 90. Honolulu: East-West Population Institute.

APPENDICES

Appendix A

Notes on Methodology, Definitions, and Needed Data and Research

A CLARIFICATION OF SOME PROBLEMS AND CONCEPTS

MEASUREMENT

In the task of sorting out and evaluating a large set of diverse measures and indicators of conditions and their changes, many of the most interesting questions involve difficult problems of scientific inference. How does one estimate the outcomes of political participation? What definitions and measures should be used to evaluate changes in the economic status of blacks? What factors should be considered in an evaluation of the fairness of the nation's criminal justice system? Hundreds of such choices underlie the text of this volume.

As we noted in Chapter 1, the committee's work involved four tasks:

1. *verification:* critical checking of facts and analyses;
2. *extension:* widening of scope and elaboration of analyses;
3. *discovery:* funding new knowledge; and
4. *assessment:* evaluation of significance and implications of data and analyses.

Verification involves not only ascertaining the validity of evidence, but also *updating:* that is, bringing forward historical series of data into the present to determine their continuing validity.

Our extension involves bringing into a single report a wide range of complex evidence, linking together economic and political changes with changes in family structure, residence, health, and organizational and community life. We found that many widely accepted generalizations are misleading, and we often had to *disaggregate* national data to see important differences among regions of the country, among individuals and families, and among other demographic groups, such as those based on age, sex, or education.

Discovery of new knowledge has been sought primarily by reanalysis of data, as in our study of the changing income distributions of black men and women compared with white men and women (Chapter 6). Occasionally, we found no adequate data available and had to collect new information, as in the work that led to our discovery of the many organized self-help activities in black communities (Chapter 4).

Assessments of significance and of implications cannot be simple extensions of analysis; they must integrate empirical findings with knowledge of the broader sociocultural setting and with interpretations of values and potential policy options.

As these comments suggest, the study confronted challenging technical problems in measuring or indexing changes in the status of black Americans; not the least has been the problem of defining what we mean by "status."

MEANING OF STATUS

In common parlance, status most often refers to a person's or group's relative social position within a hierarchical ranking. The rules governing rank order, formal or not, will usually be greatly determined by the specific contextual situation reflecting the values, norms, and institutions of a society. Intuitively, status means nothing more or less than this.

We might initially pose the question: Whose conception of status? Unfortunately, there exists no universal and unchanging conception of status suspended in the human imagination like a platonic form. The idea of status in this report must be more flexible and amenable to alternative values and beliefs.

Five conceptual dimensions of social status are of interest to this report: (1) social science indices of status variables; (2) white perceptions of black status; (3) black perceptions of black status; (4) black perceptions of white status; and (5) white perceptions of white status. Studies of black status too frequently discuss (1) and (2) exclusively. Omission of the last three aspects of status is a serious error: (3) and (4) are especially important because they represent a crucial and frequently cited criticism of Myrdal's (1944) monumental study. Myrdal's analysis of black status basically discussed external factors and circumstances as if they affected the black community in a vacuum. Virtually no important role was given to the crucial part played by black input and autonomy in spurring black progress and the formation of independent black institutions.

Black status is the creation of American social institutions and the race relations that have developed within that institutional structure. Social indices of black status are concrete representations of that status. As such, measurable status indices are the primary objects of our analysis, and their study encompasses most of the material presented throughout the report. However, beliefs and attitudes—perceptions—are also important in a study of group status. People's attitudes and beliefs about one another are important consequences of the structure of society and its race relations, as well as major determinants of race relations.

One approach to defining status is to simply describe an array or composite of the kinds of statistical indices of status commonly used by social scientists. Average income, education, and deaths per 1,000 population are measures of various aspects of status. But in addition to obvious technical problems—What do we mean by the average? Should we measure educational status by mean or median attainment levels? Should some other statistic be used altogether?—there is a general index problem. Educational status should refer to scholastic achievement and enrollment rates as well as to years of attainment. Other areas have similar problems. There exists a plethora of dimensions of status indices about each general area discussed in the report.

When we say that status has improved or deteriorated what exactly do we mean? It is fine in the detailed presentation of facts offered throughout this report to give a descriptive analysis of a long list of status measures, some of which will have improved and some of which will have shown no improvement. But in our final assessment this will not do. Readers—and we—still want to know: What has happened to black status?

There is no complete answer to this question. No composite measure of status serves as an index that will allow a single statement of this sort to be made. Our resolution of the problem is our major findings (see Summary and Conclusions). A major finding is a statement that is true for a wide variety of different measures and dimensions of status. Their usefulness, of course, depends on their generality—the more status measures included under a statement the more useful it becomes. The use of this concept does not allow us to make a single statement assessing black status, but it does classify questions concerning black status into two categories: those that are consistent with our major findings and those that are not. A discussion of these categories and the major findings then allow an intelligent and not too oversimplified assessment of the status of black Americans.

RACIAL ATTITUDES

In the broadest sense, racial attitudes involve any thoughts, beliefs, and feelings concerning blacks and whites as groups, as well as orientations toward appropriate relations between the two groups. Less globally, racial attitudes refer to consistent tendencies toward positive or negative evaluations of racial groups, their characteristics, and such aspects of intergroup relations as integration, equal treatment, and nondiscriminatory behavior.

By and large we must infer the existence of these attitudes on the basis of replies to questions asked of sample survey respondents or of subjects in laboratory experiments. In some instances, we discuss studies that infer attitudes on the basis of systematic behavioral observations. And, we infer attitudes on the basis of opinions expressed in sources such as newspapers, books, other documents, and lectures. For all of these cases, it is important to note that we are working with indicators of the attitudes, rather than directly measuring the underlying attitudes themselves.

There are several specific reasons for our concern with racial attitudes and beliefs. On the most general plane, Americans' attitudes about the "color line" can be understood as a test of their commitment to democratic values. Tolerance, equality, and respect for minority rights are all core democratic values. Indeed, Myrdal premised his basic analysis of—and his optimism regarding—American race relations on the sharp contradiction between these enduring values and the discriminatory treatment accorded blacks. Although there are reasons to question the extent to which most Americans experienced psychological anguish over the "American dilemma," there is no doubt that the character of racial attitudes and related behaviors reflects on the success of American democracy.

Racial attitudes and beliefs are also important elements of the general social and political climate. Prevailing norms on race can either strongly discourage prejudice and discriminatory behavior or they can encourage such patterns of thought and action. Those who lack strong prejudices may behave in a discriminatory manner if most of their peers expect or demand such behavior. Similarly, those who harbor animosities may refrain from acting on their inclinations if society condemns them for doing so. The prevailing norms on black-white relations are thus aspects of the broader social fabric to which people all must adapt in some way. Studies of attitudes and beliefs provide a key source of information on such norms.

More concretely, however, the underlying preferences of the public are not without consequences for policy making. The will of the people is supposed to rule in a democratic society. However, public opinion on many issues is often unfocused, contradictory, and therefore not readily mobilized. Public opinion must also be mediated through the actions of elected and appointed officials at various levels of government. Yet, when public opinion on an issue is well crystallized, and when there is an overwhelming or growing majority for some issue position, it is likely that policy will in some form come to reflect those mass preferences. This process appears to operate for all policy issues, not just black-white issues. At minimum, it is difficult and costly, in practical terms and in terms of maintaining political legitimacy, for government to implement policies that large segments of the population oppose. Thus, it is important to assess the preferences of blacks and whites on race issues because such preferences play a role, even if indirect, in policy making.

Although attitudes, underlying feelings, and beliefs influence individual behavior, the relationship between attitudes and behavior is seldom one-to-one. Social norms, as noted above, as well as other situational constraints such as laws, expected costs and benefits, and psychological considerations— the intensity of feelings associated with an attitude—affect whether or not an attitude influences a person's behavior. One cannot argue, however, that underlying attitudes bear no relationship to individual behavior. The relationship between attitudes and behavior is complex, yet attitudes are one important guide to a person's likely behavior.

Prior efforts to assess the status of black Americans, whether focused on particular cities (Clark, 1965; Drake and Cayton, 1945; DuBois, 1899) or the nation as a whole (Cox, 1948; Johnson, 1930; Myrdal, 1944; National Advisory Commission on Civil Disorders, 1968), have attempted to understand the sources, character, and consequences of racial attitudes. DuBois recounted a number of incidents in which individual whites, either in response to social expectations or, more often, their own underlying attitudes, discriminated against blacks (1899:322–355). He argued that "color prejudice" contributed to the difficulties blacks faced in getting and keeping jobs; in raising their children in a hostile social environment; and in the ever-present potential for social rebuffs and ostracism.

Johnson, recognizing race as one of many possible bases for group differentiation, traced "race prejudice" to the recognition of group boundaries, especially as such boundaries had been linked to economic and status competition (1930:355–362). In a similar vein, Drake and Cayton's analysis of the "color line" emphasized the consequential, yet complex interweaving of folk prejudices, economic interests, and social status concerns (1945:266–276). Myrdal placed a number of subjective variables, such as valuations and beliefs, at the center of his work. All of these scholars thus recognized the importance of formulating an understanding of the meaning people attach to a phenomenon like race. They suggested, moreover, that the potential for progress of blacks as a group is in part a function of society's prevailing racial attitudes and beliefs.

Our concern with racial attitudes should not be interpreted to mean that attitudes are a fundamental basis of the status of black Americans. Individual attitudes and beliefs are more likely to reflect the current and enduring features of an organized social environment than they are to independently shape or determine such social structures. Furthermore, the status of black Americans is powerfully determined by demographic and economic factors that have little or no dependence on racial attitudes. Yet the types of relations desired by white and black Americans, and Americans' interpretations of the nature of racial inequality, are of unavoidable concern if we are to understand the character of popular discourse on these issues. In sum, prevailing attitudes and beliefs can be viewed as a set of demands on political leaders; as a set of broad constraints on viable reform agendas; as clues to likely individual behavior; and as a measure of success at fulfilling certain democratic values. Racial attitudes are thus a necessary concern of a comprehensive attempt to understand the status of black Americans.

Our understanding of the causes of change in racial attitudes is, however, far less certain than our understanding of the basic patterns of change themselves. The processes that lead from behavioral change to attitude change, or from changing social norms to changes in individual attitudes, are not well understood. In particular, few systematic and longitudinal efforts to link empirical measures of attitudes to measures of contextual factors, such as the integration of a school or workplace, have been conducted.

Furthermore, attitudes and public opinion are part of a dynamic and somewhat labile social process (Myrdal, 1944:1032–1034). Although we expect individuals' racial attitudes to be stable over any short span of time, individuals' attitudes are not entirely static. The direction and magnitude of changes in attitudes can be both large and unexpected. In addition, even though one might like to propose the operation of a process of gradual and continuous positive improvement in racial attitudes, this claim is not consistent with historical experience or with much of the data we present. Change is possible but it occurs in complex ways and for only dimly understood reasons.

Although only a beginning has been made in the needed empirical analysis of these complex effects, we suggest that the generic problem can be seen more clearly than previously. Many of the data we review in this report refer to attitudes as indicated by specific opinions, usually expressed in interview situations. Such opinions are often short-run, volatile phenomena that can shift drastically in response both to microcontexts—situations—and to macroevents, such as an economic depression, national election, and war or other international crises. The constant interaction of transformative social movements, established social institutions and actors, everyday human adaptation and activity, and common-sense understanding affects patterns of racial attitudes and beliefs.

MEANING OF RACE

Throughout this report we use the terms "black" and "white." These are social categories that have long been viewed as meaningful in the United States. The meaning of race is a matter of social interpretation, however, not a fact of biology or genetics.

Since the beginning of European settlement in North America, the cultural models that have defined the status of blacks have gone through several great transformations. Originally the distinction was between Christians and heathens, then between slave and free. As these two definitions failed to distinguish between dominant and subordinate social groups, race was invoked as a quasi-biological concept that was used to explain and justify white supremacy. When doctrines of racial inferiority had to be abandoned and when equal rights became a persuasive political doctrine, "race" came to be largely subsumed under "ethnicity" or "class" or both. At the extreme, it could be argued that a racial category served only as an identification or marker and that the primary dynamics of race relations really were those of class relations. However, since the mid-1960s, a substantial body of thought has developed that supports earlier rejections of the concept that blacks constitute an ethnic group analogous to European-origin ethnic groups.

The rejection is based on objective evidence of the unique extent and harshness of discrimination against and segregation of blacks, as well as on the intensity and prevalence of negative racial beliefs and ideologies. Similarly, it is argued that racial status cannot be reduced to a matter of class position in the marketplace or of the relations to the means of economic production. Thus, an emphasis on the uniqueness of race as an "irreducible" category has emerged from the critical debates over the standard paradigms of prior interpretations. Another ingredient in the reformations of recent decades has been the reworking of "black nationalism" to include modern experiences. All these lines of conceptual analysis converge in formulations that treat the racial category "black" as a social reality that combines class, ethnicity, cultural heritage, political interests, and self-definition (see Omni and Winant, 1986).

Nevertheless, the notion of race often turns out to be vague and to have multiple meanings, and it has varied greatly over time. As Omi and Winant wrote (1986:60):

> Race is indeed a pre-eminently *sociohistorical* concept. Racial categories and the meaning of race are given concrete expression by the specific social relations and historical context in which they are embedded. Racial meanings have varied tremendously over time and between different societies.

In spite of its changing and uncertain meanings, the idea of race as a rigid and unchanging category has been pervasive in the United States and has received detailed legal definitions. As recently as 1970, a Louisiana statute specified that a person with at least 1/32 "Negro blood" was considered black. The definition of racial category in this instance, as in many others, is a political act. American history provides numerous examples of variation and changes in racial categories and the eventual separation of race from nationality or ethnicity and from religious categories.

The concept of "race" has a long and tortuous history and its baggage of meanings is enormous and diverse. Looked at in sociocultural terms, "race" is one among many forms of categorization, a subprocess of the distribution of social identities and roles within populations. People are categorized by other people in many different ways: by age, sex or gender, occupation, intelligence quotient, conformity or nonconformity to social norms, left- or right-handedness, athletic prowess, religious piety, and so on. But some categorizations are more consequential than others. Differences in skin color, type of hair, and facial features that are biologically trivial have been used as markers for ascribing great differences in power and privilege. As Banton noted (1983:77):

> "Race" relations are distinguished not by the biological significance of phenotypical features but by the social use of these features as signs identifying group membership and the roles people are expected to play.

In the United States, race (or color) historically was linked with slavery and subsequently with a harsh and rigid system of stratification. For this reason, many observers have had the opinion that race is a peculiarly rigid basis for ethnic relationships. Comparative analysis of the world's societies shows, however, that race is the *indicator*, not the *substance*, of superordinate-subordinate relationships of distinguishable social groups (see Horowitz, 1985:42–51). Any one of many traits may be used to identify group membership: color, religion, language, dress, speech patterns, food preferences and taboos, postures, and bodily markers, among others. What is used to establish group boundaries may vary greatly from situation to situation and time to time: "It is not the attribute that makes the group, but the group and group differences that make the attribute important" (Horowitz, 1985:50).

When we use the terms "race" or "racial" in this report, we are accepting for convenience a conventional usage that has little precision. "Race" in the United States is a social construct that relies on common understandings and self-definitions rather than scientific criteria.

In general, we avoid treating blacks and whites as internally homogenous groups. Much of our analysis, in fact, seeks to identify sources of variation within each group, and similarities in the attitudes of blacks and whites are also noted. Yet there are frequent and important differences in the attitudes of blacks and whites on race—as well as on many nonracial issues. It is necessary, as a result, to speak of differing tendencies between these social groups.

MEANING OF RACISM

Studies of racial attitudes are often equated with studies of racism. We think it important to be precise in the use of this term. For some people, racism means any form of race recognition, especially instances in which members of privileged groups act in a manner injurious to a disadvantaged group. Others, however, reserve the term for patterns of belief and related actions that overtly embrace the notion of genetic or biological differences between human groups. Still others use the term to designate feelings of cultural superiority. And of course, some definitions include all of these possibilities as manifestations of racism. Each of these uses of the racism concept has some validity, but it is surely unfortunate that a single analytic concept has so many different meanings.

We use the term racism to denote biological racism, as in the second interpretation above. Societal racism, borrowing from Fredrickson (1971), is used to denote negative racial attitudes or outcomes that lack a clear basis in a belief in inherent racial inferiority. Mere recognition of social groups based on "racial" characteristics is not treated here as a form of racism, but as being "race conscious." Cultural preferences that do not include the systematic ranking of social groups and clear hostility toward out-groups is termed ethnocentrism.

The concept of racism, however qualified and defined, involves a value judgment. Racism of whatever variety is undesirable; racist outcomes are wrong; and people who advocate racist ideas are typically viewed as being morally deficient, if not dangerous. Some people question any scholarly use of this concept because it is so manifestly value laden. Others respond, with justification, that no complete and honest treatment of American racial attitudes and beliefs could entirely eschew use of the concept of racism. Both concerns have legitimacy.

NEEDED DATA AND RESEARCH

The committee had to cope with gaps and other inadequacies in the data, even for basic descriptive tasks. Recent changes in the collection and reporting of statistical data by federal agencies, and proposed changes in the national census, may seriously limit the information needed for analyzing demographic, social, and economic changes over time. The scientific importance of maintaining comparable and detailed time series must be strongly emphasized.

For understanding the "why" of changes such as those we discuss in this report it is crucial to have longitudinal information—measurements on the same units over periods of time long enough to detect significant changes. Correlations based on cross-sectional data are difficult to interpret and may often be misleading.

Many needed analyses of the phenomena treated in this report have been limited by reason of the absence of adequate data. Current data on causes of death, for example, do not contain information that sufficiently allows research to pinpoint relationships between socioeconomic status and individuals' health practices. Analysis of the effects of geographic concentrations of poor people in cities is severely impeded by lack of information on mobility and migration patterns. Studies of unemployment and the out-of-labor-force population face an almost total absence of longitudinal data on job search behavior in relation to an individual's educational status, military service, and so on. We have very little information about the life-history transitions from school to work, or to nonwork, for young people.

The data that are available for describing large-scale economic, political, and social conditions typically have been generated for reasons other than scientific relevance. The national census is mandated for legislative, administrative, and other purposes, such as representation in legislatures or monitoring the health of the economy. Valuable as they are, such data only rarely accurately represent variables as conceptualized in basic scientific hypotheses and theories. Thus, great effort and ingenuity often are evident in "making do" with proxy and surrogate variables—indicators that imperfectly correspond to underlying concepts.

As we have examined one substantive area after another, it is instructive to observe how often apparently contradictory or anomalous findings reflect differences in indices, definitions, data samples, or statistical models. Data sources that explicate such differences aid the vigilance of research workers in identifying information that can greatly aid appraisals of factual basis for public policies. Thus figures on "unemployment" need to be interpreted along with information on persons who are not in the labor force. Failure to distinguish between "income" and "earnings" similarly may lead to misleading conclusions.

Our committee noted that discussions found in popular works concerning alleged effects of public assistance on work and family life lacked a definitive factual base. There is much speculation and many anecdotal references, but systematic evidence from well-controlled analyses is rare (see Chapter 10). Specifically needed is comprehensive research on what happens to so-called "cultural patterns" when new economic and educational opportunities are opened to segregated, low-income populations.

Much of the available research on the effects of social contexts is at the levels of aggregation represented by school districts, zip-code areas, and other geographical units. Using such aggregate data, most of the recent research that has used post-1970 statistical methods has found few large effects clearly attributable to collective settings (e.g., mean socioeconomic status, mean proportion black, mean education of parents). This surprising result may be partly due to limitations of data and study designs that made it impossible to adequately specify relevant independent variables and outcomes for suitable populations. For example, many studies have only cross-sectional correlations; many longitudinal studies cover only short periods of time; populations often are not appropriately differentiated by age, sex, race, ethnicity, income, area of residence, and so forth.

There are few studies concerning the actual social structure of high-poverty neighborhoods or the attitudes and behavior patterns of residents. The few ethnographic studies that exist are very useful, but their findings cannot be safely generalized to all other settings. Needed is systematic research, over time, that collects comparable information from strategic sampling locations on changes in job search, employment, family patterns, social services, crime, informal social structures, schools, and residents' views of their situations. Similarly, there is a paucity of observational studies of behavior in different kinds of schools with varying proportions of black and white students.

Evidence received by the committee shows important geographic variations, both local and regional, in basic socioeconomic conditions. In this report, the need for conciseness, as well as a focus on national conditions, led to extensive reliance on aggregated data; it would be valuable if future work drew on more detailed tabulations. Some systematic accumulations of detailed longitudinal information do exist—for example, the national longitudinal surveys of labor market experience. The original cohorts comprised 22,157 individuals (from 13,582 households), to which was added a youth cohort of persons aged 14–21 as of January 1979, an additional 12,686 persons. The scope of potential analyses is suggested by the fact that main data files for the youth cohort contain over 20,000 variables.

This appendix has covered only a few of the more important issues related to methodology and data sources relevant to this report. It is our hope that future research can discover new techniques to deal with the problems noted here and that, indeed, this report will stimulate such research as well as improved data collection.

REFERENCES

Banton, Michael
1983 *Racial and Ethnic Competition.* Cambridge, England: Cambridge University Press.
Clark, Kenneth
1965 *Dark Ghetto.* New York: Harper and Row.
Cox, Oliver C.
1948 *Caste, Class and Race: A Study in Social Dynamics.* New York: Doubleday.
Drake, St. Clair, and Horace Cayton
1945 *Black Metropolis: A Study of Negro Life in a Northern City.* New York: Harcourt Brace.
DuBois, William E. B.
1899 *The Philadelphia Negro: A Social Study.* Reissued (1973), Millwood, N.Y.: Kraus-Thomson Organization Limited.
Fredrickson, George
1971 *The Black Image in the White Mind: The Debate on Afro-American Character and Destiny, 1817–1914.* New York: Harper and Row.
Horowitz, Donald L.
1985 *Ethnic Groups in Conflict.* Berkeley: University of California Press.
Johnson, Charles S.
1930 *The Negro in American Civilization: A Study of Negro Life and Race Relations in the Light of Social Research.* New York: H. Holt and Company.
Myrdal, Gunnar
1944 *An American Dilemma: The Negro Problem and Modern Democracy.* New York: Harper and Brothers.
National Advisory Commission on Civil Disorders
1968 *Report of the National Advisory Commission on Civil Disorders.* New York: Bantam Books.
Omi, Michael, and Howard Winant
1986 *Racial Formation in the United States: From the 1960s to the 1980s.* New York: Routledge and Kegan Paul.

Appendix B

Biographical Sketches of Committee
and Panel Members and Staff

HUBERT M. BLALOCK, JR., is professor of sociology and adjunct professor of political science at the University of Washington. He taught previously at the University of Michigan, Yale University, and the University of North Carolina. He has an A.B. degree from Dartmouth College, an M.A. degree from Brown University, and a Ph.D. degree from the University of North Carolina. His research interests include race relations theory, sociological theory, applied statistics, and research methodology. He is a member of the National Academy of Sciences, a fellow of the American Academy of Arts and Sciences, a fellow of the American Statistical Association, and a past president of the American Sociological Association. He is the author of *Toward a Theory of Minority Group Relations; Black-White Relations in the 1980's: Toward a Long-Term Policy; Race and Ethnic Relations;* and numerous statistical and methodological books and articles.

LAWRENCE BOBO is associate professor of sociology at the University of Wisconsin, Madison. He received a B.A. degree from Loyola Marymount University and M.A. and Ph.D. degrees from the University of Michigan. His research interests include racial attitudes and relations in the United States, social psychology, public opinion, and political behavior. He has been a fellow at the Center for Advanced Study in the Behavioral Sciences. He serves on the editorial board of *Public Opinion Quarterly* and as a member of the National Science Foundation Board of Overseers for the National Opinion Research Center's General Social Survey. He is coauthor of the award-winning book *Racial Attitudes in America* and author of articles on many topics in sociology and public opinion.

LEE P. BROWN is chief of police of the city of Houston. He has a B.A. degree in criminology from Fresno State University, an M.A. degree in sociology from San Jose State University, and M.A. and Ph.D. degrees in criminology from the University of California, Berkeley. He has held positions in the criminal justice system in San Jose; Multnomah County, Oregon; and Atlanta as well as academic positions at Portland State University and Howard University. He is vice president of the International Association of Chiefs of Police and has been a member of the National Research Council's Committee on Research on Law Enforcement and the Administration of Justice. He received an honorary doctorate of laws from the John Jay College of Criminal Justice in 1984; the national law enforcement award from the National Black Police Officers Association in 1982; and the Robert Lamb, Jr., humanitarian award from the National Organization of Black Law Enforcement Executives in 1987. He is coauthor of *The Police and Society: An Environment for Collaboration and Confrontation* and author of numerous articles.

THOMAS E. CAVANAGH is director of the Johns Hopkins University Center for the Study of American Government. He has B.A. and M.A. degrees in political science from Yale University. Previously he was on the faculty of Wesleyan University and Trinity College, served on the staff of the U.S. House of Representatives and the Joint Center for Political Studies in Washington, D.C., and was a guest scholar at the Brookings Institution. He has written widely on the subjects of black politics, voter turnout, Congress, and the U.S. party system.

JOHN BROWN CHILDS is associate professor of sociology at the University of California, Santa Cruz. He has a Ph.D. degree in cultural and urban anthropology from the State University of New York, Buffalo. Previously he taught at Yale University and Amherst College. He has been a Ford Foundation Fellow and an Andrew W. Mellon Faculty Fellow at Harvard University. His research involves populist and elitist social movements and the relationship between religion and political action. He is the author of *Leadership, Conflict, and Cooperation in Afro-American Social Thought* and *The Political Black Minister: A Study in Afro-American Politics and Religion* as well as numerous articles.

SHELDON H. DANZIGER is professor of social work and public policy and also faculty associate at the Population Studies Center, University of Michigan. Previously he was director of the Institute for Research on Poverty, professor of social work, and Romnes Faculty Fellow at the University of Wisconsin, Madison. Danziger received a B.A. degree from Columbia University and a Ph.D. degree in economics from the Massachusetts Institute of Technology. He is the coeditor of *Fighting Poverty: What Works and What Doesn't: The Distribution Impacts of Public Policies;* and *State Policy Choices: The Wisconsin Experience.* He is the author of numerous scholarly articles on poverty, income inequality, and social welfare programs and policies.

KAREN P. DAVIS is chair of the Department of Health Policy and Management in the School of Hygiene and Public Health and professor of economics at Johns Hopkins University. She has a Ph.D. degree in economics from Rice University. Previous positions she has held include deputy assistant secretary for planning and evaluation for health at the U.S. Department of Health and Human Services and visiting lecturer at Harvard University. She is a member of the Physician Review Commission and the Institute of Medicine council and director of the Commonwealth Fund Commission on Elderly People Living Alone. She serves as regional editor for the journal *Health Policy* and is the author of numerous books and articles on health economics and policy analysis, including *Medicare Policy: New Directions for Health and Long-Term Care; Health and the War on Poverty: A Ten-Year Appraisal;* and *National Health Insurance: Benefits, Costs and Consequences.*

DAVID T. ELLWOOD is professor of public policy at the John F. Kennedy School of Government at Harvard University and a faculty research fellow at the National Bureau of Economic Research. He has A.B. and Ph.D. degrees from Harvard University, both in economics. His recent work has focused on problems of the poor and disadvantaged and policies designed to help them, particularly among minorities and women and children in single-parent families. He has also done extensive work examining the causes and consequences of youth unemployment, particularly among ghetto youth. He has served on gubernatorial committees in New York and Arizona and has frequently testified before Congress on reform measures. He is the author of *Poor Support.*

REYNOLDS FARLEY, a demographer, is research scientist at the Population Studies Center and professor of sociology at the University of Michigan. Previously he taught at Duke University. He has a Ph.D. degree from the University of Chicago. His work focuses on the social, economic, and demographic characteristics of racial and ethnic groups in the United States, particularly changes in the status of blacks since the civil rights revolution of the 1960s. He is the author of *Blacks and Whites: Narrowing the Gap?* and, with Walter R. Allen, *The Color Line and the Quality of Life in America.* He has served as president of the Population Association of America.

JOHN HOPE FRANKLIN is the James B. Duke Professor Emeritus of History and professor of legal history in the Law School at Duke University. He is a graduate of Fisk University and has A.M. and Ph.D. degrees in history from Harvard University. He has taught at a number of institutions, including Fisk University, North Carolina Central University, and Howard University, and served as the chair of the Department of History at both Brooklyn College and the University of Chicago. He has served on the National Council on the Humanities, the Advisory Commission on Public Diplomacy, the President's Advisory Commission on Ambassadorial Appointments, and the twenty-first general conference of the United Nations Educational, Scientific, and Cultural Organization (UNESCO). He has been president of the American Studies Association, the Southern Historical Association, the United Chapters of Phi Beta Kappa, the Organization of American Historians, and the American Historical Association. He serves on the editorial board of the *Journal of Negro History* and has written many books on blacks in American history, including *From Slavery to Freedom: A History of Negro Americans* and a biography of George Washington Williams that won the Clarence L. Holte Literary Prize.

JAMES LOWELL GIBBS, JR., is Martin Luther King, Jr., Centennial Professor and chair of the Department of Anthropology at Stanford University, where he has been a member of the faculty since 1965. He has a B.A. from Cornell University and a Ph.D. in social anthropology from Harvard University. He is a fellow of the American Anthropological Association, the African Studies Association, and the International African Institution. His research involves social organization, African ethnology, and culture and personality. He is editor of *Peoples of Africa* and the author of numerous journal articles.

BERNARD R. GIFFORD is vice president of education at Apple Computer, Inc. He has a Ph.D. degree in radiation biology and biophysics from the University of Rochester. Previously he served as chancellor's professor and dean of the Graduate School of Education at the University of California, Berkeley; as vice president and professor of political science and public policy at the University of Rochester; as a resident scholar at the Russell Sage Foundation; and as deputy chancellor of the New York City Public Schools. He was awarded an honorary doctorate of humane letters from Long Island University in 1988. The range of his publications covers applied physics as well as public policy; in recent years he has focused on the process of educational change and reform. His latest books are *History in the Schools: What Shall We Teach?*, *Test Policy and the Politics of Opportunity Allocation: The Workplace and the Law*, and *Testing Policy and Test Performance: Education, Language, and Culture*.

NATHAN GLAZER is professor of education and sociology at Harvard University. He has a B.A. degree from the City College of New York, an M.A. degree from the University of Pennsylvania, and a Ph.D. degree in sociology from Columbia University. He taught previously at the University of California, Berkeley, and has served on presidential task forces and other national committees on urban affairs and education. His published books include *Beyond the Melting Pot* (with Daniel P. Moynihan), *Affirmative Discrimination*, and *The Limits of Social Policy*; he has edited, alone or in collaboration with others, numerous volumes, including *Studies in Housing and Minority Groups, Ethnic Pluralism and Public Policy*, and *Clamor at the Gates: The New American Immigration*.

BEATRIX A. HAMBURG is professor of psychiatry and pediatrics as well as director of the Division of Child and Adolescent Psychiatry at the Mount

Sinai School of Medicine. She has a B.A. degree from Vassar College and an M.D. degree from Yale Medical School. She has held positions at Stanford University; the National Institute of Mental Health, where she organized a national program for research in child psychiatry; and Harvard Medical School, dividing her time between the Children's Hospital and the Division of Health Policy Research and Education. Her major research interests are developmental psychology and neurobiology of normal adolescence and adolescent psychiatric disorders, and she has maintained a strong involvement in health policy research. She is a member of the Institute of Medicine, of the National Research Council's Commission on Behavioral and Social Sciences and Education, and of the board of directors of the American Association for the Advancement of Science. She has received the Alcohol, Drug Abuse, and Mental Health Administration's award for outstanding achievement. She is the editor of two books and the author of numerous scientific articles.

CHARLES V. HAMILTON is Wallace Sayre Professor of Government at Columbia University, where he has taught since 1969. He taught previously at Lincoln University and Roosevelt University. He has a B.A. degree from Roosevelt University, a J.D. degree from Loyola University, and M.A. and Ph.D. degrees in political science from the University of Chicago. He was vice president of the American Political Science Association in 1973–1974. His research is concerned with race and ethnic politics and public policy analysis. He is the author of *The Black Experience in American Politics* and *The Bench and the Ballot: Southern Federal Judges and the Right to Vote*.

JOEL F. HANDLER is professor of law at the University of California, Los Angeles. He received an A.B. degree from Princeton University and a J.D. degree from Harvard Law School. Previously he was the Vilas Research Professor and the George A. Wiley Professor at the University of Wisconsin Law School and served on the senior research staff at the university's Institute for Research on Poverty. He has served on several committees of the National Research Council and as chair of the Panel on Public Policies Contributing to the Deinstitutionalization of Children and Youth. He has been a Guggenheim Fellow and a member of the board of trustees, executive committee, of the Law and Society Association. His primary research interests are in the areas of poverty law and administration, social welfare programs, race, social movements, public interest law, legal services, and law reform activities. He has published a dozen books and numerous articles on these subjects.

ROBERT M. HAUSER is Vilas Research Professor of Sociology and director of the Center for Demography and Ecology at the University of Wisconsin, where he has been on the faculty since 1969. He has also held a faculty appointment at Brown University and visiting appointments at the Institute for Advanced Study in Vienna and at the University of Bergen. He received an A.B. degree from the University of Chicago and a Ph.D. degree from the University of Michigan. His doctoral thesis was chosen for publication in the Rose Monograph Series of the American Sociological Association, and he has won the Paul F. Lazarsfeld award in research methods from the American Sociological Association. He is a member of the National Academy of Sciences and a fellow of the American Association for the Advancement of Science, the American Statistical Association, and the American Academy of Arts and Sciences. His publications related to education and social inequality include five books and numerous articles. His current research interests include trends in educational attainment and social mobility in the United States, cross-national comparisons of social mobility, and the effects on families of social and economic inequality.

DARNELL F. HAWKINS is professor of black studies and sociology at the University of Illinois at Chicago. Previously he taught at the University of North Carolina. He has A.M. and Ph.D. degrees in sociology from the University of Michigan and a J.D. degree from the University of North Carolina, Chapel Hill. His research and publications concern the sociology of law, criminology, and deviance as well as race and ethnic relations. He received a graduate fellowship in 1974 from the National Fellowships Fund, a residency in law and social science fellowship from the Russell Sage Foundation, and a postdoctoral fellowship from the Ford Foundation and the National Research Council. He is a member of the American Society of Criminology, the American Sociological Association, and the National Criminal Justice Association and is a member of the board of trustees of the Law and Society Association. He is the editor of *Homicide Among Black Americans* and author of "Beyond Anomalies: Rethinking the Conflict Perspective on Race and Criminal Punishment" and other journal articles.

M. ALFRED HAYNES is director of the Drew-Meharry-Moorehouse Consortium Cancer Center in Los Angeles. Previously he was president and dean of the Charles R. Drew Postgraduate Medical School. He has a B.S. degree from Columbia University, an M.P.H. degree in epidemiology from Harvard University, and an M.D. degree from the Downstate Medical Center of the State University of New York. He is a past president of the American College of Preventive Medicine; a fellow of the American Association for the Advancement of Science; a member of Alpha Omega Alpha and the council of the Institute of Medicine; and an overseas fellow of the Royal Society of Medicine. His professional work has focused on preventive medicine and community health, particularly of black Americans. He is the author of many journal articles and other publications on the topics of community medicine, black professionals in medicine, health problems of black Americans and residents of the inner city, and doctor-patient relationships.

JAMES J. HECKMAN is professor of economics at Yale University (on leave from the University of Chicago). He has a B.A. degree from Colorado

College and M.A. and Ph.D. degrees from Princeton University. He has taught at Yale University, Columbia University, and New York University and held positions at the National Bureau of Economic Research, the National Opinion Research Center, and the Rand Corporation. He is a fellow of the Econometric Society and the American Academy of Arts and Sciences. He has been a member of committees of the Social Science Research Council and the National Research Council. He has been editor of numerous professional journals, including the *Journal of Econometrics,* the *Journal of Political Economy,* and *Econometric Reviews.* He was awarded the John Bates Clark Medal by the American Economics Association in 1983. He has published two books and numerous journal articles on topics in econometrics.

NORMAN HILL is president of the A. Philip Randolph Institute. He has a B.A. degree in sociology from Haverford College. Previously he was national program director of the Congress of Racial Equality and legislative representative and civil rights liaison of the industrial union department of the AFL-CIO. Since joining the A. Philip Randolph Institute in 1967, he has organized more than 180 affiliates, largely made up of rank-and-file union members engaged in voter registration, voter education, and get-out-the-vote campaigns. He serves on the board of trustees of Freedom House; on the National Committee of Social Democrats, USA; on the board of directors of the League for Industrial Democracy; and on the executive committee of the Coalition for a Democratic Majority. He is a member of Local 3, the Newspaper Guild, AFL-CIO; has published articles in such journals as the *AFL-CIO News, The New Leader,* and numerous black publications; and writes a monthly column for the black and labor press.

JENNIFER L. HOCHSCHILD is professor of politics and public affairs at Princeton University, with a joint appointment in the Department of Politics and the Woodrow Wilson School of Public and International Affairs. She has a B.A. degree from Oberlin College and a Ph.D. degree from Yale University. She has taught at Duke University and Columbia University. Her research interests focus on American social welfare and race policies, with a particular interest in the philosophical and political implications of the changing relationships among race, class, and political power. She has been a fellow of the Center for Advanced Study in the Behavioral Sciences and has received awards or research support from the American Philosophical Society, the Spencer Foundation, and the American Political Science Association, and she has also served as a consultant or expert witness in several school desegregation cases. She is the author of *What's Fair: American Beliefs About Distributive Justice* and *The New American Dilemma: Liberal Democracy and School Desegregation* and a coauthor of *Equalities* as well as a variety of articles in the fields of political philosophy, American political thought, public opinion, and race in America.

JAMES S. JACKSON is professor of psychology, research scientist at the Institute for Social Research, faculty associate at the Center for Afro-American and African Studies and the Institute of Gerontology, and an associate dean of the Rackham School of Graduate Studies at the University of Michigan. He received a B.A. degree in psychology from Michigan State University, an M.A. degree in psychology from the University of Toledo, and a Ph.D. in social psychology from Wayne State University. He has conducted research in several areas, including race and ethnic relations, adult development and aging, social and psychological concomitants of health status, and black political behavior. He is a member of several editorial boards including the *Psychological Bulletin,* the *Journal of Gerontology, Psychological Sciences,* and *Race and Ethnic Relations.* In addition to numerous scientific articles and chapters, he is editor or coeditor of several books, including *The Black American Elderly: Research on Physical and Psychsocial Health*; *Black American Life: A National Survey of Black Adults;* and *Psychiatric Epidemiology and Help-Seeking Among Black America,* and he is the author of the forthcoming book *Three Generations of Black American Families.*

GERALD DAVID JAYNES is professor in the Department of Economics and in the Program in African and African-American Studies at Yale University. He has a B.A. degree in philosophy and a Ph.D. degree in economics from the University of Illinois, Urbana. He is a fellow of the Joint Center for Political Studies and has served as a member of the board of economists for *Black Enterprise* magazine. His published research involves the areas of economic theory, public policy, and American history. He is the author of *Branches Without Roots: Genesis of the Black Working Class in the American South, 1862–1882.*

JAMES JENNINGS is associate professor of political science, senior fellow of the William Monroe Trotter Institute, and former dean of the College of Public and Community Service at the University of Massachusetts, Boston. He received a Ph.D. degree from Columbia University. Previously he taught at Harvard University; Columbia University; Long Island University; the State University of New York, Albany; Cornell University; Boston College; and Northeastern University. He is senior editor of two books, *From Access to Power: Black Politics in Boston* and *Puerto Rican Politics in Urban America.* He has published articles in various professional journals and books; lectured widely on politics and urban education, particularly on black and Latino political experiences; and provided consulting services to numerous governmental bodies and civic organizations.

LYLE V. JONES is professor of psychology and director of the L. L. Thurstone Psychometric Laboratory at the University of North Carolina, Chapel Hill, where he has served as vice chancellor and dean of the graduate school. He attended Reed College and received B.S. and M.S. degrees from the University of Washington and a Ph.D. degree from Stanford University. He was a faculty member at the University of Chicago and has held visiting faculty appointments at the universities of Illinois, Texas, and Washington. He is a member of the Institute of Medicine, a fellow of the American Academy of Arts and Sciences, and a former president of the Association of Graduate Schools, the Psychometric Society, and the Division of Evaluation and Measurement of the American Psychological Association. He is and has been a member of several boards, commissions, and committees of the National Research Council. Among his recent publications are several that focus on differential trends in U.S. school achievement for black and white students.

FRANK LEVY is professor of public affairs in the School of Public Affairs at the University of Maryland. He has an S.B. degree from the Massachusetts Institute of Technology and M.A. and Ph.D. degrees in economics from Yale University. He has taught at the University of California, Berkeley, and was a senior research associate at the Urban Institute. He is a member of the nominating committee of the American Economic Association, the advisory board of the Center for National Policy, and the policy council of the Association of Public Policy and Management. He has been a member of several committees of the National Research Council. His research concerns different aspects of U.S. living standards; his publications include "How Big is the American Underclass?," one of the first systematic attempts to look at permanent poverty in the United States, and *Dollars and Dreams: The Changing American Income Distribution*.

STANLEY LIEBERSON is professor of sociology at Harvard University (on leave from the University of California, Berkeley). He has M.A. and Ph.D. degrees in sociology from the University of Chicago. He was awarded the university's Colver-Rosenberger Prize for the best dissertation in sociology in the preceding 3 years. His research concerns race and ethnic relations in contemporary American society. He is a former president of the Sociological Research Association and the Pacific Sociological Association and is a fellow of the American Academy of Arts and Sciences. He is the author of nine books, including four on race and ethnic relations: *Ethnic Patterns in American Cities; Language and Ethnic Relations in Canada; Piece of the Pie: Blacks and White Immigrants Since 1880* (winner of the Sorokin Award); and (with Mary C. Waters) *From Many Strands: Ethnic and Racial Groups in Contemporary America*; plus many articles on this topic.

MICHAEL LIPSKY is professor of political science at the Massachusetts Institute of Technology. He has a B.A. degree from Oberlin College, an M.P.A. degree from the Woodrow Wilson School, and a Ph.D. degree from Princeton University. His more recent research has focused on social welfare policy, issues of hunger and homelessness, and problems associated with government contracting for social services with nonprofit agencies. He has published books on the politics of relatively powerless groups, *Protest in City*

Politics; societal responses to racial violence, *Commission Politics: The Processing of Racial Crisis in America,* with David J. Olson; and service delivery to needy and dependent populations, *Street-Level Bureaucracy: Dilemmas of the Individual in Public Services.* For the last book, he was awarded prizes by the American Political Science Association and the Society for the Study of Social Problems.

GLENN C. LOURY is professor of political economy at the John F. Kennedy School of Government, Harvard University. Previously, he taught economics at Northwestern University and the University of Michigan and has been a visiting scholar at Oxford University, Tel Aviv University, and the University of Stockholm. He has a B.A. degree in mathematics from Northwestern University and a Ph.D. degree in economics from the Massachusetts Institute of Technology. He was awarded a Guggenheim Fellowship for the academic year 1985–1986. He has served on the National Research Council's Commission on Behavioral and Social Sciences and Education. Loury has published extensively on a variety of topics in economic theory; his current work focuses on the politics and economics of racial inequality in the United States. He is now completing work on a book *Free At Last?,* which provides an analysis of racial advocacy in the "post–civil rights era."

HARRIETTE PIPES McADOO is professor of research and social work in the School of Social Work at Howard University. She has B.A. and M.A. degrees from Michigan State University and a Ph.D. degree from the University of Michigan in educational psychology and child development. She has been on the faculty of Smith College and has been a visiting professor at George Warren Brown School of Social Work and of Human Ecology at Michigan State University. She received the Marke Peters Award from the National Council of Families and the Outstanding Researcher of the Year award for 2 years from the National Association of Black Psychology. She was the elected program vice president for the National Council of Family Relations. She is coeditor (with John McAdoo) of *Black Families* and (with T. M. Jim Parham) of *Black Children: Social, Educational, and Parental Environments*; editor of *Services to Young Families: Program Review and Policy Recommendations;* and author of numerous journal articles and book chapters.

LESLIE BURL McLEMORE is professor of political science, dean of the graduate school, and director of research administration as well as the founding chair of the Department of Political Science at Jackson State University. He has degrees from Rust College, Atlanta University, and the University of Massachusetts, Amherst. His research involves southern politics and the modern-day civil rights movement. His current research deals with Fannie Lou Hamer, a leader of the Mississippi Freedom Democratic Party and member of the Student Non-Violent Coordinating Committee; he is also conducting research on the campaigns of the Reverend Jesse Jackson. McLemore has served as president of the National Conference of Black Political

Scientists and as vice president and program chair of the Southern Political Science Association. He has written numerous articles on blacks and black politics, including ''Election Laws and Their Manipulation to Exclude Minority Voters: A Response,'' ''Black Politics: The View from the Readers,'' and ''Black Independent Power Politics in Mississippi: Constants and Challenges.''

MARY BETH MOORE is vice president and director of communication for PATH (Program for Appropriate Technology in Health), where she oversees the development of health and family planning information and education and communication materials to be used with disadvantaged populations worldwide. She has an M.P.H. degree from the University of Michigan and an M.S. degree in health from Michigan State University. She has worked with the national headquarters of the Planned Parenthood Federation of America and conducted research for the Population Council's Biomedical Division, the Smithsonian Institution, Michigan State University, and the University of Michigan. She also developed a health curriculum for the Michigan Migrant Education Program and worked on clinic evaluation for the Michigan Department of Public Health.

ELEANOR HOLMES NORTON is professor of law at Georgetown University Law Center. She has a B.A. degree from Antioch College, an M.A. degree in American studies from Yale University, and an LL.B. degree from Yale Law School. From 1977 to 1981 she was chair of the Equal Employment Opportunity Commission. She has worked for the American Civil Liberties Union, the Commission on Human Rights of the City of New York, and the Urban Institute and has taught at the New York University Law School. Her work is focused on employment and labor force matters, including labor-management relations, discrimination law, and affirmative action as well as labor law and negotiations. Other areas of interest include women's rights, comparable worth, and racial discrimination. She is the coauthor of *Sex Discrimination and the Law: Causes and Remedies* and is writing a book about the development and impact of antidiscrimination law and affirmative action remedies. She has received more than 33 honorary degrees and serves on a variety of boards, including those of the Rockefeller Foundation, the Yale Corporation, the Martin Luther King, Jr., Center for Social Change, the Metropolitan Life Insurance Co., Pitney Bowes, and the Stanley Works.

JOHN U. OGBU is a Nigerian-born anthropologist and a professor at the University of California, Berkeley, where he received his degrees. He has been a distinguished visiting professor at the University of Delaware and New Mexico State University and a visiting scholar at Morehouse College and the University of Wisconsin, Madison. He is a fellow of the American Anthropological Association, the American Association for the Advancement of Science, the International African Institute, and the Royal Anthropological Institute. He has served on several national and international advisory boards, including National Research Council committees and panels and is a member of the governing council of the Society for Research in Child Development. He received a distinguished scholar award from the American Educational Research Association in 1985 and is the author of two award-winning books and numerous articles on minority education. His current research is a comparative study of community forces affecting the school adjustment and academic achievement of immigrant and nonimmigrant minority students.

DELORES L. PARRON is associate director for special populations at the National Institute of Mental Health. She has a Ph.D. degree in social policy and research from Catholic University of America. Previously, she was associate director of the Division of Mental Health and Behavioral Medicine of the Institute of Medicine, a staff member of the President's Commission on Mental Health, and assistant professor in the Department of Psychiatry at Howard University College of Medicine. She is coeditor (with David A. Hamburg and Glen R. Elliot) of *Health and Behavior, Frontiers of Research in the Biobehavioral Sciences* and (with Frederic Solomon) of *Mental Health Services in Primary Care Settings*.

THOMAS F. PETTIGREW is professor of social psychology at the University of California, Santa Cruz, and the University of Amsterdam in the Netherlands. He has M.A. and Ph.D. degrees in social psychology from Harvard University, where he taught for 23 years. He has specialized in race relations throughout his career and conducted research in South Africa, the United Kingdom, and the Netherlands as well as the United States. He has been active as a consultant and court witness in school desegregation cases, and in 1967 he was a member of the White House Task Force on Education. He is a past president of the Society for the Psychological Study of Social Issues, a Guggenheim Fellow, and a fellow of the Netherlands Institute for Advanced Study. For his research in race relations, he has received the Sydney Spivack Award, the Kurt Lewin Award, and the Gordon Allport Prize. His books, monographs, and numerous articles have focused on the role of social psychological factors in race relations.

DOROTHY P. RICE is professor in residence in the Department of Social and Behavioral Sciences, with joint appointments in the Institute for Health and Aging and the Institute for Health Policy Studies at the University of California, San Francisco. She has a B.A. degree in economics from the University of Wisconsin and an honorary Sc.D. degree from the College of Medicine and Dentistry of New Jersey. From 1977 to 1982 she served as director of the National Center for Health Statistics in the U.S. Department of Health and Human Services, and she previously served as deputy assistant commissioner for research and statistics of the Social Security Administration. She is a member of the Institute of Medicine and a fellow of the

American Statistical Association and of the American Public Health Association. She is a member of several national advisory councils on aging, statistics, the elderly, and program evaluation and methodology. Her major research interests include health statistics, the impact of an aging population, cost of illness studies, and the economics of medical care, and she is the author of more than 100 published articles and monographs.

LEE NELKENS ROBINS is an epidemiologist and professor of sociology in the Department of Psychiatry at Washington University School of Medicine, St. Louis. She has B.A., M.A., and Ph.D. degrees, all in sociology, from Harvard University. She has studied the development of substance abuse and conduct problems from early school years through young adulthood in young black men; the psychiatric problems of black adolescents in inner-city health clinics; the post-Vietnam drug use and adjustment of black and white enlisted men; and the prevalence of specific types of psychiatric disorders in the general population of blacks and whites through the Epidemiological Catchment Area project of the National Institute of Mental Health. She is a member of the Institute of Medicine (IOM) and of the World Health Organization's Expert Advisory Panel on Mental Health. She has served as a member of committees of the National Research Council and the IOM.

STEVEN J. ROSENSTONE is professor of political science and program director at the Center for Political Studies, Institute for Social Research, University of Michigan. He has an A.B. degree from Washington University, St. Louis, and M.A. and Ph.D. degrees in political science from the University of California, Berkeley. His research interests include elections and voting, political participation and political parties, public opinion, and political rules and norms. He is currently a coprincipal investigator of the National Election Studies. He is a member of the advisory council of the Latino National Political Survey and on the editorial board of several scholarly journals. His published works include *Who Votes?* (as coauthor); *Third Parties in America; Forecasting Presidential Elections;* and *Political Participation of Latino Americans.*

ELSIE L. SCOTT is executive director of the National Organization of Black Law Enforcement Executives. She has a B.A. degree from Southern University, an M.A. degree from the University of Iowa, and a Ph.D. degree from Atlanta University, all in political science. She has held academic positions at Howard University, North Carolina Central University, St. Augustine's College, and Rutgers University. She has been a member of the curriculum advisory committee of the State Department's Diplomatic Security Antiterrorism Program; the advisory committee for state and local training of the Federal Law Enforcement Training Center; and the advisory board of the National Institute Against Prejudice and Violence. She is a past president of the National Conference of Black Political Scientists. She is the author of several books on blacks and violence, including *Violence Against Blacks in the United States, 1979–1981* (1983).

JAMES TOBIN is Sterling Professor of Economics Emeritus at Yale University. He has been on the faculty at Yale since 1950 and retired from his teaching position in 1988. He has an A.B. degree from Harvard College and a Ph.D. degree from Harvard University, both in economics. His major research interests have been macroeconomics, monetary theory and policy, fiscal policy and public finance, consumption and saving, unemployment and inflation, portfolio theory and asset markets, and econometrics. He was a junior fellow of the Society of Fellows for 3 years in 1947–1950, the last of which he spent at the Department of Applied Economics at the University of Cambridge in England. He was a member of the Council of Economic Advisers in 1961–1962 and is a past president of the Econometric Society, the American Economic Association, and the Eastern Economics Association. He received the John Bates Clark Medal of the American Economic Association and is a member of the National Academy of Sciences. In 1981 he received the Nobel Prize in economics. He is author or editor of 13 books and more than 300 articles and has written for both professional and lay audiences.

PHYLLIS A. WALLACE is professor of management, emerita, at the Sloan School of Management of the Massachusetts Institute of Technology. She received a Ph.D. degree in economics from Yale University. Her service on panels for the federal government includes the Minimum Wage Study Commission and the President's Pay Advisory Committee. She is a past president of the Industrial Relations Research Association. During the past two decades she has been a researcher and consultant on equal employment opportunity, employment and training programs, and development and management of human resources. She is author or editor of six books and numerous articles on these topics.

NANCY J. WEISS is professor of history and dean of the College at Princeton University, where she has been on the faculty since 1969. She has a B.A. degree from Smith College and M.A. and P.D. degrees in American history from Harvard University. Her research focuses on black history and twentieth century American history. She is the author of *The National Urban League, 1910–1940; Farewell to the Party of Lincoln: Black Politics in the Age of FDR;* and *Whitney M. Young, Jr., and the Struggle for Civil Rights.*

ROBIN M. WILLIAMS, JR., is Henry Scarborough Professor of Social Science Emeritus at Cornell University. He has a Ph.D. degree from Harvard University. He has served as consultant to many governmental agencies and voluntary associations. He is past president and secretary of the American Sociological Association. He is a member of the National Academy of Sciences, the American Academy of Arts and Sciences, and the American

Philosophical Society. For half a century he has been concerned with intergroup relations in American society, in research and in public service. He has written extensively on intergroup relations, conflict, American institutions, values, and social change. In 1988 he received the Commonwealth Award for a career of distinguished achievement in sociology. He is the author of several books on racial and ethnic relations, including *The Reduction of Intergroup Tensions*, *Strangers Next Door*, and *Mutual Accommodations*.

WILLIAM JULIUS WILSON is the Lucy Flower Distinguished Service Professor of Sociology and Public Policy and former chair of the Department of Sociology at the University of Chicago. He has a Ph.D. degree in sociology from Washington State University. He has also taught at the University of Massachusetts, Amherst. He is a member of the oversight body of several organizations, including the Center for Advanced Study in the Behavioral Sciences, the Russell Sage Foundation, Spellman College, and the Chicago Urban League. He is also a member of several national advisory committees. He is the author of *Power, Racism, and Privilege: Race Relations in Theoretical and Sociohistorical Perspectives; The Declining Significance of Race: Blacks and Changing American Institutions;* and the award-winning *The Truly Disadvantaged: The Inner City, The Underclass, and Public Policy;* and he has authored or coauthored numerous books and articles. He serves and has served on the editorial boards of several professional journals. He received a MacArthur Fellowship in 1987.

RAYMOND E. WOLFINGER is professor of political science and director of the State Data Program at the University of California, Berkeley. He has a B.A. degree from the University of California, Berkeley, an M.A. degree in political science from the University of Illinois, and a Ph.D. degree in political science from Yale University. In the 1960s he served as an aide to several legislators, including Senator Frank Church and Senator Hubert H. Humphrey, focusing primarily on the Civil Rights Act of 1964. He also taught at Stanford University. He is a former chair of the board of overseers of the University of Michigan's National Election Studies, the only continuing national survey of Americans' political views and voting behavior. He is president of the Consortium of Social Science Associations and of the Western Political Science Association and a member of the board of directors of the Southwest Voter Research Institute. He is the author or coauthor of books and articles on various aspects of minority politics and political participation, including *Who Votes?*.

Appendix C

Committee Activities

The committee's work required frequent meetings. The main subtopics were given additional attention by five panels dealing, respectively, with education; employment, income, and occupations; health; political participation and administration of criminal justice; and social and cultural continuity and change. In addition to meetings of committee and panel members as a whole, each panel held separate meetings as needed. Some of these meetings included presentations and discussions with invited participants; we appreciate their contributions to the committee's work.

The work of the committee and panels was also helped enormously by a set of commissioned papers. These papers are cited in the text of the report, but we also note here with thanks their contributions.

MEETINGS

COMMITTEE AND PANELS

February 15–16, 1985	December 5–7, 1986
June 7–8, 1985	March 21–22, 1987
October 5–6, 1985	June 26–28, 1987
February 15–16, 1986	October 17–18, 1987
July 7–11, 1986	February 27–28, 1988

ADDITIONAL MEETINGS OF PANELS

Panel on Education

February 13–14, 1986	October 24–25, 1986

Panel on Employment, Income, and Occupations

February 14, 1986	May 26–27, 1987

Panel on Health

May 28, 1985
July 28, 1985
October 3–4, 1985
December 12, 1985
February 14, 1986

April 4, 1986
May 8, 1986
May 18, 1987
August 31, 1987

Panel on Political Participation and Administration of Criminal Justice

April 21, 1985
January 11, 1986
May 3–4, 1986

November 15, 1986
May 31–June 1, 1987
September 27–28, 1987

Panel on Social and Cultural Continuity and Change

April 26, 1985
August 7–8, 1985

December 14, 1985
May 10, 1986

COMMISSIONED PAPERS

ANDERSON, ELIJAH
Of Old Heads and Young Boys: Notes on the Urban Black Experience
BATES, TIMOTHY
Paper on black entrepreneurship
BELL, DERRICK
The Gyroscopic Effect in American Racial Reform: The Law and Race from 1940 to 1986
Memorandum to the Committee on the Status of Black Americans in response to July 31st comments on commissioned paper
BRADFORD, WILLIAM D.
Wealth, Assets, and Income of Black Households
CARSON, CLAYBORNE
Paper on racial advocacy in Afro-American life
COONEY, MARK
Racial Discrimination in Police-Citizen Encounters: A Review of Empirical Literature
DAVIS, KAREN, and MARSHA LILLIE-BLANTON
Health Care for Black Americans: Trends in Financing and Delivery
EITZEN, STANLEY D.
Black Athletes in American Society Since 1940: Continuity and Change in Racial Barriers to Equal Participation
FEINLIEB, MARSHA
A chartbook on the health of black Americans

GATES, HENRY LOUIS
From Native Sons to Native Daughters: The Afro-American Literary Tradition 1940–1985
GLASER, JAMES M.
The Paradox of Black Participation and Other Observations on Black Activism, 1952–1984
HAGEN, MICHAEL G.
Blacks and Liberalism
Racial Differences in Voter Registration and Turnout
The Salience of Racial and Social Welfare Issues
HANKS, LAWRENCE J.
Black Voter Mobilization Since 1960
JACKSON, HENRY F.
The Role of Black Americans in U.S. Foreign Policy: Search for New Power
JOHNSON, SYLVIA T.
Extra-School Factors in Achievement, Attainment, and Aspirations Among Junior and Senior High School-Aged Black Youth
KARWEIT, NANCY
Elementary Education and Black Americans: Raising the Odds
KENDRICK, ANN
A Comparison of the Core Economic Beliefs of Blacks and Whites
The Dynamics of Black Electoral Participation
KILSON, MARTIN
Report on Black Politics in Comparative Perspective
LANEY, GARRINE
The Evolution of Equal Employment Programs, 1940–1985
MALVEAUX, JULIANNE
The Economic Status of Black Women: An Overview and Note on Interpretation
MOSKOS, JOHN, and JOHN S. BUTLER
Blacks in the Military Since World War II
MOSS, PHILIP I.
Changing Public Sector Employment and the Occupational Advancement of Blacks, Women, and Hispanics
MYERS, SAMUEL L., JR., and WILLIAM J. SABOL
Crime and the Black Community: Issues in the Understanding of Race and Crime in America
NELSON, WILLIAM E.
The Role of the Black Church in Politics
NEWBURGER, HARRIET B.
The Impact of Federal Housing Programs on Black Americans
OWENS, CHARLES E.
The Impact of Black Criminal Justice Practitioners on the Criminal Justice System

PALLAS, AARON M.
Extra-School Factors in the Achievement of Black Adolescents
Black-White Differences in Adolescent Educational Outcomes
POWELL, RICHARD J.
The Visual Arts and Afro-America, 1940–1980
SCOTT-JONES, DIANE
Black Families and the Education of Black Children: Current Issues
SCHOFIELD, JANET WARD
School Desegregation and Black Americans
STROMAN, CAROLYN
The Mass Media and Black Americans
TAEUBER, ALMA
Memorandum on issues of resegregation in public schools to the Committee on the Status of Black Americans
WILKINSON, DORIS Y.
A Profile of the Nation's Resources: The Academic Missions and Cultures of Traditionally Black Colleges and Universities
YINGER, MILTON J.
Black Americans and Predominantly White Churches
ZATZ, MARJORIE S., AND KATHLEEN A. CAMERON
Racial Disparities in Prosecutorial Decisions and Plea Bargaining

Index

attitudes on, 122, 126, 127, 137, 140, 223
bus terminals, 65
congressional support for, 223
effectiveness of, 13, 258
and harassment of blacks, 13, 140
litigation and protest and, 185, 221
for military personnel, 70
Public assistance
benefit levels, 289, 310, 531, 533
and culture of poverty, 10, 540–544
disability payments, 30, 310
effectiveness of, 254, 258, 283, 309–310
eligibility standards, 289, 310
human capital development programs, 29,
253–254, 258, 309
means-tested cash assistance, 16, 30, 253,
254, 258, 531–533
means-tested in-kind benefits, 16, 253,
254, 258, 277 n.2, 402, 406, 531
labor supply effects of, 290, 309–310
and marital instability, 310, 531
negative income tax, 30, 290, 531–533
participation in, 283, 309–310; *see also* Welfare dependence
social insurance, 30, 253
working poor's participation in, 283
see also Job training; *and specific programs*
Public Health Service, national health objectives, 397
Public Works Administration, 227
Pulitzer Prizes, 66, 68, 101

R

Race, meaning of, 564–566
Race relations
and antiamalgamation doctrine, 137
busing and, 84
changes over time in, 40–41, 57, 219,
318–319
contemporary, 138–148, 186
defined, 47
and growth of black businesses, 182
historical legacy for, 5, 42
migration and urbanization and, 48, 60–63
in military services, 66–67
preferences of blacks and white for, 5, 42,
136–138, 194, 196–200, 219; *see also*
Attitudes of blacks and whites
resistance to social change and, 6
school desegregation and, 19, 48, 80–81,
84, 103
socioeconomic status and, 3, 5, 11, 40–41,
47–48
World War II and, 60
Racism
in attitudes of whites, 59–60, 148–149,
155
black attitudes on, 197–199
dulling impact on blacks, 167
meaning of, 566–567
Rainbow Coalition, Inc., 187
A Raisin in the Sun, 101, 167
Randolph, A. Philip, 63, 70

Randolph, Bernard P., 71
Rangel, Charles, 253, 257
Reagan administration
antipoverty program cuts during, 254
appointment of blacks during, 241–244
attitudes of blacks on, 136, 210, 218
minority business policies, 256–257
South African policies, 252, 253
tax reforms, 257
Reconstruction era, 210
Redding, Saunders, 101, 166
Reed, Ishmael, 101
Religion, *see* Churches and religious life
Rendezvous with America, 166
Research needs, 567–569
Residential segregation
attitudes of blacks and whites on, 12, 120,
121–124, 126, 130–131, 133, 137–
138, 140–144, 151, 155–156, 194, 200
changes since 1960, 58
and church/worship segregation, 92, 94
and educational attainment, 11, 144–145,
315
explanations for, 50, 140–141
governmental authority and, 58
and health care, 11
indices of, 13, 27, 85, 89, 144
legal enforcement of, 88
in metropolitan areas, 12–13, 27, 78–79,
89–91, 103, 144
migration of blacks and, 88–89
by municipal ordinances and restrictive covenants, 88
in neighborhoods, 90–91
open housing laws and, 89
and opportunity structure for blacks, 9, 27,
29, 50–51, 91, 319–321
of other minorities compared to blacks, 13,
27, 50, 89–90, 144–146
and racial isolation, 13, 90–91, 164
regional differences in, 89, 90–91
and school desegregation, 11, 76–80, 83,
225, 226–227
and socioeconomic status, 26, 144–146,
164, 283–284, 286–287
suburbanization of blacks and, 89
unwritten rules for, 49–50, 88, 141
Retail establishments, harassment of blacks
in, 140
Reverse discrimination, 151, 182
Richard, Little, 102
Richards, Lloyd, 101
Richie, Lionel, 102
Riots
attitudes of blacks about, 199
by blacks (1960s), 4, 31, 131, 186, 199,
477, 479, 489
distrust and suspicion of whites and, 31,
131
following King's assassination, 229
police shootings of blacks in Miami (1980s)
and, 49, 479
by whites, 99